D1556492

MUNICIPAL MANAGEMENT SERIES

Managing the
Modern City

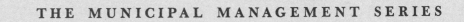

THE MUNICIPAL MANAGEMENT SERIES

James M. Banovetz

EDITOR

Director
Center for Governmental Studies
Northern Illinois University

Managing the Modern City

Published for the
Institute for Training in Municipal Administration
by the
International City Management Association

MUNICIPAL MANAGEMENT SERIES

Managing the Modern City

Principles and Practice of Urban Planning

Municipal Finance Administration

Municipal Personnel Administration

Municipal Police Administration

Municipal Fire Administration

Municipal Public Works Administration

Municipal Recreation Administration

Supervisory Methods in Municipal Administration

Management Practices for Smaller Cities

Community Health Services

Local Public Library Administration

Case Problems in City Management

Effective Supervisory Practices

Municipal Public Relations

Copyright © 1971
by the International City
Management Association
1140 Connecticut Avenue, N.W.
Washington, D.C. 20036

No part of this volume may be
reproduced without the specific
permission of the copyright owner.

First edition, 1971

Library of Congress
Catalog Card No.: 58–9090

Printed in the
United States of America

Foreword

This book is about the management of all kinds of cities. It is built on the premise that management is an integral part of the governmental process and that it is a major factor in the success or failure of government. More specifically, this book approaches urban management from the viewpoint of the chief administrator and the overall perspective needed for effective and responsible government.

MANAGING THE MODERN CITY emphasizes the city as a political, social, and economic institution. It focuses upon the role of the administrator; leadership and decision making; organization theory; computer technology and other management tools; administrative planning and analysis; and personnel, finance, public relations, and other administrative functions. It recognizes that the contemporary administrator spends an increasing amount of time on policy questions that are broader than the professional and technical specialities that used to be his primary concern.

This book, like others in the Municipal Management Series, has drawn on the firsthand experience of governmental administrators. Each incorporates the latest developments in research and teaching. Each has been reviewed by administrators, consultants, teachers, and students.

The 15 titles in the Municipal Management Series have been prepared especially for the Institute for Training in Municipal Administration. The Institute offers in-service training courses designed specifically for local government officials whose jobs are to plan, direct, and coordinate the work of others. The Institute has been sponsored since 1934 by the International City Management Association and is an accredited member of the National Home Study Council.

It is a pleasure to acknowledge the fine work of James M. Banovetz, Director, Center for Governmental Studies, Northern Illinois University, who served as editor and wrote four of the chapters. Professor Banovetz has had extensive experience in teaching, research, and consulting with the League of Minnesota Municipalities, Loyola University (Chicago), and Northern Illinois University.

Recognition should be accorded to THE TECHNIQUE OF MUNICIPAL ADMINISTRATION, the book that pioneered in defining the management job in municipal government. Over the years many distinguished persons worked on successive editions of that book, including the late Louis Brownlow, Jeptha J. Carrell, Herbert Emmerich, the late Lyman S. Moore, Clarence E. Ridley, Charles S. Rhyne, Herbert A. Simon, and Donald C. Stone.

This book, as with others in the Municipal Management Series, has been prepared under the general supervision of David S. Arnold, Assistant Director, Publications, ICMA.

MARK E. KEANE
Executive Director

International City
Management Association

Washington, D.C.
April, 1970

Preface

This is a new book that shows the contemporary role of American cities both old and new. Reflecting the "new look" ICMA—the International City Management Association—it is also a reflection of the new and greatly magnified importance of the American city as it enters upon the last decades of the twentieth century. Even more, it is a reflection of the beginning of a new era in the ever evolving nature of the profession called city management.

Like the retired queen of the seas, the Queen Mary, the old book, THE TECHNIQUE OF MUNICIPAL ADMINISTRATION, has served its function long and well. It has helped several generations of city managers and faithfully served as the flagship of ICMA's familiar fleet of green books, the Municipal Management Series. It provided an effective overview of the challenges confronting the city manager in his moderate-sized community and served as a useful guide in the performance of numerous administrative tasks. But, just as time and changing technologies finally caught up with the Queen Mary, so too did they finally overtake THE TECHNIQUE OF MUNICIPAL ADMINISTRATION. This new book, MANAGING THE MODERN CITY, is to the Municipal Management Series what the Queen Elizabeth II is to the high seas: a new product designed to respond more directly to the needs and demands of the contemporary world.

First and foremost, this book is designed to speak directly to the urban administrator regardless of the nature of his community. It recognizes that the professional administrator or manager now plies his trade in an increasingly diverse number of contexts: he works as a city manager in moderate-sized communities as before, but increasingly he finds himself serving in urban counties; in large, heterogeneous, and complex cities adjacent to the core cities of major metropolitan areas; in administrative and staff positions within the executive branch of these core cities; in administrative departments of cities of all sizes; in regional organizations and associations such as councils of governments; in a growing number of state agencies concerned with community problems; in an expanding lexicon of federal agencies focusing their concern on urban area problems; and in the urban affairs departments of a growing number of private and quasi-public agencies.

In short, this book was not written just for the city manager but for all of the allied professions that have grown with, and in some cases from, city management. In part this broader emphasis is reflected in the book's focus: the previous concern with the administrative mechanics of city government has been replaced with more extensive treatment of the program planning and policy development responsibilities attendant upon public service leadership in today's urban community. In part, too, this emphasis is reflected in the absence of textual references to "city managers." "Urban administrators" have instead been the basic point of reference in all except Chapter 4.

This chapter, dealing with the policy-making roles of urban administrators, makes frequent reference to "city managers" because managers have been the exclusive focus for research on the policy-making function of the urban administrator. This exception, though made in deference to the terminology used in the extant literature on the subject, should in no way be taken to mean that city managers and urban administrators are fundamentally different in nature or in kind. It is in fact a basic premise of this book that they are not different; that city managers, taken together with urban administrators of all kinds and descriptions, form a common profession meeting unique challenges and problems.

Second, then, this book is designed to reflect the new job description which has steadily emerged for practitioners of the urban management profession. During the embryonic years of the city management profession, managerial job descriptions emphasized technical competence: city managers were to bring organization and efficiency out of the chaos and corruption immersing American cities early in the twentieth century. THE TECHNIQUE OF MUNICIPAL ADMINISTRATION, originally designed for this job description, responded admirably with heavy emphasis upon the administrative methods and techniques employed in conducting the daily business of the city.

Since the second world war, this initial job description has been undergoing continuous change, partly because city managers succeeded in bringing organization and efficiency out of chaos and corruption and partly because the urbanization of society was producing new stresses upon city government and raising new problems for city administrators. The job description has thus been altered to acknowledge, first, the political role of managers as consultants and advisors to policymakers, then the political role of managers as leaders in the development of alternative proposals for resolving community problems, and finally the more recent diplomatic role of managers and administrators as spokesmen for their communities in dealings with the national government, state governments, and other local governments on matters of regional concern.

The new job description for the manager or urban administrator also demands of course a new set of qualifications. No longer is technical competence, rooted in civil engineering, the first requisite for the job; in fact, engineering may well be an irrelevant background for most positions in the field today. Similarly, skill in administrative techniques, valuable to be sure, is of less relative importance. Now leading the list of qualifications are sophistication in the management of large, complex organizations; adroitness in the resolution of controversial, seemingly insoluble problems; skill in handling and analyzing vast quantities of data pertinent to key decisions; and proficiency in the art of human relations.

Responding to this new set of job qualifications, this book places its emphasis upon community responsibilities, leadership roles and strategies, organization theory, decision making, planning, communication, data handling, and administrative analysis rather than upon such administrative functions as finance and personnel. Less time, proportionately, is spent replicating the material in other volumes of the Municipal Management Series and more is devoted to new, more theoretical treatment of traditional subjects. Thus, for instance, the chapter on finance avoids a description of the mechanics of budgeting and focuses, instead, upon the policy and procedural implications of budgetary strategies. The chapter on public relations is less concerned with techniques and more concerned with the basic theory upon which effective methods must be predicated.

The book, then, thirdly, makes an effort to reflect the deeper levels of penetration into which recent research has taken extant knowledge about the science of administration. In this respect, hopefully, it will provide a more "relevant" challenge to the graduate students who will use it as a text. Yet, to keep the book simultaneously intelligible to correspondence students well removed from their formal education, the authors have sought to stress fundamental principles and concepts in a readable and readily coherent fashion. The expected result of writing aimed at a double audience is a book in which different people will find different sections most meaningful and useful

Hopefully this will expand, not contract, the book's audience and impact.

Any success this book may achieve is due wholly to the efforts of the individual authors, each of whom selected his own style and approach to his subject. Each man prepared a completely new and original chapter for this book; each has effectively brought his own intellectual vitality to these pages. Together, they deserve much credit.

Besides the authors, many others have added to the quality of this book. Chief among these is David S. Arnold of the International City Management Association staff who achieved a masterful blend of stimulation, encouragement, prodding, patience, and wisdom in his handling of both editorial and production details. This book, hopefully, will be an appropriate monument to his exceptional talent as director of ICMA's publications.

Acknowledgment must also be given to the contributions of David S. Brown and John Pfiffner whose detailed reviews of THE TECHNIQUE OF MUNICIPAL ADMINISTRATION provided the intellectual stimulation for the concept of this book.

Others, too, added their insights in the development of various chapters. In addition to David S. Arnold, this list includes David R. Beam, Wallace H. Best, William E. Besuden, Jerome L. Kaufman, Catherine Papastathopoulos, and Charles Zuzak. Students in several municipal administration classes at Northern Illinois University also reviewed and reacted to most of the chapters in draft form.

Yeoman service was rendered by the secretarial staffs of the Center for Governmental Studies at Northern Illinois University and the Center for Research in Urban Government, Loyola University, Chicago, for preparation of the manuscript in its various drafts. In particular, the contributions of David R. Beam and Linda Dong, who helped tie up the myriad loose ends at the conclusion of the project have been most valuable. Special recognition is owed to Eileen Dubin for preparing the index. Finally, appreciation is extended to Betty Lawton and Elizabeth M. Lee of the ICMA staff for their help on production and copy editing.

The International City Management Association was directed by two men, Orin F. Nolting and Mark E. Keane, during the time this book was in preparation, and both lent much support and encouragement to the undertaking. Most of all, however, I am indebted to my wife, Audrey, and children who suffered stoically through my long hours at the typewriter.

Inevitably any book that has so many authors and that has profited from the inputs of so many people is susceptible to error, inconsistency, and omission. Blame for these faults can be appropriately placed only at the feet of the editor, and I accept this fate.

JAMES M. BANOVETZ

DeKalb, Illinois
April, 1970

Table of Contents

Tables

Managing the
Modern City

Part One

The City

1

The Developing City

This is a book about cities. It is about those places where people live in close proximity with each other; work at related, nonagricultural tasks; and find their stimulations, satisfactions, and solace in frequent and meaningful contacts with each other.

Specifically, this book is for and about the American city, regardless of whether that city is the core of a tumultuous metropolis, a sprawling and bustling suburb, a quiet and peaceful village, a large nonmetropolitan center, or a small hamlet.

More specifically yet, this book is about the management of all of these kinds of city; its purpose is to make more effective the efforts of those people who work to make the city an even better place for the happy pursuit of human life. It is written with a strong conviction about the positive role which the city can and must play in the destiny of mankind.

As never before in history, today's city is being called upon to shape man's destiny. As Henry S. Churchill so succinctly stated, "The City Is the People." He might also have added that "the people are the city," for increasingly the city in modern times has become inextricably interwoven into the very warp and woof of human life. This first chapter will describe the interrelationship of man in his city, discuss some of the forces that pummel it, and review the mechanisms that have been developed to govern it.

The obvious first question which must be answered in any analysis of the city is, simply put, "What is the city?" Like so many other simple questions, this one has no easy answer.

No single definition does justice to the city, for in fact a city is a very complex entity, performing concurrently a variety of distinct, equally important functions. Even in the most rudimentary terms, the city must be described as both a social institution and a legal entity. Implicit, too, in any definition is the need to differentiate between the concept of the "city" and the closely related concepts of "community" and "urban area." Such definitions and distinctions will be the task of this section of the chapter.

Nature of the City

The city has been described as a place of relatively dense population characterized by frequent and meaningful human interactions. This is a simple, largely static definition, however, and one that is based on cursory visual perceptions. In its true, dynamic sense, the city is a much more complex and vibrant integer.

THE CITY DEFINED

Cities are, for example, distinct legal entities individually incorporated under the laws of their respective states and expected to perform certain basic governmental and nongovernmental functions. Cities are thus units of government with established boundaries, with elected leaders, with defined and limited authority, and with taxing and regulatory powers. Unlike most other units of government, however, cities also possess certain characteristics of legal corporations. They exist separately and independently from the individuals who head them at any given time, they can sue and be sued, and they can undertake certain actions, such as the sale of water, which are of an essentially proprietary nature.

Cities can also be defined as economic production units, supplying certain goods and services for public consumption. Included among the commodities marketed by cities, for example, are police and fire protection, water and other utility services, parks, recreation programs, streets and other public works improvements, and sometimes education, welfare, and human development programs. Payment for these goods and services takes the form of taxes, service charges, special assessments, fees, and other sources of municipal revenues.

Third, cities are catalysts for human interaction. Traditionally, they are collection points for people, ideas, goods, and commerce. Located geographically in a relatively small space, their key attractions to people have always been two: access and variety. Because they each collect so many people and so many different kinds of activities and goods, cities have, throughout history, maximized the range of choices on which an individual can spend his time, energy, and resources. Simultaneously, by collecting these people, activities, and goods in a relatively small amount of space, cities have also minimized the distance over which an individual must travel when moving between choices or alternatives. Thus, ready access to a wide variety of human experiences has always been the focus of urban life.

Fourth, because they bring so many people together in the same place, cities can also be defined as social communities. Social cohesiveness has been a characteristic of city life ever since the distinction between urban and rural society first emerged. Cities do in fact represent rather complete social systems: each has a common set of values and goals, a hierarchy of leadership, and a variety of social subsystems or groups which provide a wide range of opportunities for human interaction.

Fifth, cities have always served as the font of knowledge and the education of mankind. It is in the cities that the depositories and transmitters of human knowledge—the schools, universities, libraries, museums, theaters, churches, and cultural facilities of all kinds—first developed and then flourished. It is in the cities that the value of education was first recognized and most appreciated. It is, ultimately, in the cities that the task of educating man for the challenge of survival in an era of nuclear technology and population density must ultimately be met. It is particularly in the cities, where the nonmaterial needs of man have always received proportionately more attention, that the increasingly critical challenge of serving man's aesthetic and psychic needs must soon be met if civilization itself is to be preserved.

Finally, cities might also be defined as the cradles of civilization and the cultural laboratories of mankind. Despite the fact that, historically, only a small portion of the human race has resided in cities, the cities have always played the major role in man's cultural development. With their freedom from the drudgery of tilling the soil and with their greater number and variety of people, cities have traditionally served as havens for the dissatisfied and discontented, for those who were searching for something other than the existing social orders. Thus it was in the cities that new ideas were advanced, innovations attempted, and progress achieved. Cities have therefore served as wellsprings of ideas, focal points of change, and depositories of economic and political power. Increasingly, too, cities are where the people are and it is this fact which gives cities their dominance, both in the social order and as the cultural centers of mankind.

The city, then, is a legal entity, a producer of public services, a catalyst for human interaction, a social system, and a cultural laboratory—it is all of these things and more. It is the seat of government; the home of manufacturing and industry; the center of trade; a haven for the arts; the wellspring of knowledge and education; the melting pot of cultures, nationalities, and races; and the confluence point for transportation networks. *In short, the city is where the people are!*

THE CITY, THE COMMUNITY, THE URBAN COUNTY, THE URBAN AREA

The term "city," then, is amorphous; it has many meanings. Adding to the confusion is the tendency of popular jargon to use the term interchangeably at times with both "community" and "urban area." One basic source of confusion is the word "community" which may be used with equal veracity to refer to a neighborhood within a city (Staten Island), the city itself (New York City), or the larger urban area of which the city is only a part (the New York metropolitan area). Another source of confusion is the colloquial use of the word "city" to refer to the downtown section of an urban area (Chicago's Loop), to the city as it is established under law (the government of the city of Chicago), to the city as a geographic entity (the city of Chicago), or to the socio-economic region of which the city is a part (the Chicago metropolitan area).

Accuracy thus frequently requires that several basic distinctions be made. One is the distinction between the city as a legal entity with certain prescribed, fixed boundaries, and the city as a social community whose more vague and amorphous boundaries might be either broader or more restricted than the boundaries of the legal city. This book will generally use the term in its more precise, legal sense.

A second important distinction is between the word "city" and words such as "village," "borough," or "town." Generally, each of these terms refers to an organized community incorporated under the laws of its respective state for the purpose of providing municipal government services. In that sense, these terms are completely interchangeable. Legally, these terms are used in each state to refer to specific kinds of municipal governments under which individual communities might organize. This book will use the term "city" to refer to all forms of municipal government or to all legally incorporated urban communities.

A third important distinction is that between the city and the urban county. Properly defined, an urban county is any county which, because of the extensive urban development within its boundaries, has assumed some or all of the governmental functions normally carried out only by cities or other incorporated forms of municipal government. Because their broader geographic boundaries embrace a larger socio-economic community, urban counties frequently constitute more functional communities than any of the individual cities located wholly or partially within them. In some instances, the transfer of traditional city powers to the county government has been accompanied by reform of the county government so that, in such counties, the county government is barely distinguishable from city government. Unfortunately, however, reform does not usually follow such transfers with the result that most urban counties are not reaching their full potential as effective governing institutions.

Nevertheless, counties are growing in importance as units of urban government. They are increasingly coming to resemble cities both as legal entities and as social communities. With nearly half the metropolitan areas in the United States located within the boundaries of a single county, and with counties playing a vital role in the government of all metropolitan areas, counties promise to continue growing in significance as urban governing units. Thus, *because this book deals with cities as agents of urban government, it applies with equal force to those counties which have become, or are coming to be, urban governing institutions.* Thus the words "urban county" will apply with equal veracity wherever the word "city" is used in this book.

A distinction must also be drawn between the city (or urban county) and the broader urban area of which the city (or urban county) may be a part. This broader urban area may be of two kinds. The first, and most common, is the *metropolitan* area. In such areas, individual cities have become so closely integrated socially and economically with their neighboring cities that they have lost much of their identity as cities and their formal boundaries have lost all but their legal significance. Secondly, the term "urban area" can also be applied to a *nonmetropolitan* region composed of several cities in which (1) each city has retained its individual identity, (2) nonurban land generally separates one municipality from another, (3) none of the cities are wholly dependent, economically or socially, upon the others, and (4) the cities together share economic or social interests and experience high degrees of interaction between their citizenry. Frequently the most viable social community in the area is one encompassing all of the cities thus related. Examples of such urban areas or "regions of cities" are the Chapel Hill–Durham–Raleigh triangle in North Carolina and the cities on the iron mining ranges of Minnesota.

Finally, a distinction might also be made between the social community of the city and the broader, more amorphous social community of the urban system. As used in this context, the term "urban system" refers to a large urban area plus that outlying region (hinterland) which is moderately dependent upon facilities in the central cities for recreation, shopping, banking, and similar services. Because of this dependence, cities in the urban system of a large city tend to be considerably influenced by the social and economic forces and events taking place within the major city. Since all communities located in rural areas are more or less dependent upon some nearby large city, nearly every community in the United States falls within the urban system or hinterland of some large city. Further, by shrinking the impact of distance, technological innovations in transportation and communication are inexorably drawing all communities under the influence of urban life and culture. The impact of urbanism is thus increasingly pervasive upon all segments of contemporary society.

FUNCTIONAL COMPONENTS OF THE CITY

As the impact of urbanism, and thus of cities, becomes more pervasive upon society, it becomes increasingly important that the internal dynamics of city structure and operation be identified, understood, refined, and controlled. Only by making such comprehension and control effective will man be able to dominate his urban environment and thus shape it in accordance with his plans for his own destiny.

Many different analytic systems can be used to identify the component parts of city life. For the purposes of city administration, it will generally suffice to view the city as having three basic types of components: spatial-physical, cultural-social, and governmental-political.

Spatial-physical components are those which deal with the distribution of events, activities, and buildings throughout the city's land area. In part, these components are the form of the city—the patterns which determine the organization of streets, buildings, transportation and communication facilities, parks and open space, and the availability of public utilities. In part, these components are also the structure of the city—the patterns which determine the distribution of human activities, such as residence, commerce, industry, recreation, and education, throughout the land area of the city.[1]

The cultural-social components are those which describe and determine human activities throughout the city. Included under this general heading would be social rules and regulations; cultural values and mores; organizational structures, including both formally organized and informally established social groups; the personalities of city inhabitants, especially the city's formal and informal leaders; and the particular styles pursued by the inhabitants.

The governmental-political components are the composite of laws—national, state, and local—governing the city's life and activity, the structure of the local governing institutions, the personalities of elected and appointed political leaders, the identity and operating methods of interest groups in the community, local customs and mores regarding political activity, relationships between the city and other governments, the organizational structure and rules established for the administration of governmental activities, and the personalities of the men responsible for such administration. This book will focus on the administrative as-

---

[1] This differentiation between form and structure has been made by Catherine Bauer Wurster, "Form and Structure of the Future Urban Complex," in Lowdon Wingo, Jr., CITIES AND SPACE, THE FUTURE USES OF URBAN LAND, (Baltimore: The Johns Hopkins Press, 1963) pp. 73–100 at p. 75.

pects of these governmental-political components.

An entirely different perspective on the components of the city, and one which is equally useful to the urban administrator, has been offered by Melvin M. Webber. He views the city as comprising essentially two different kinds of communities: communities of place and interest communities. Association in the first kind of community, Webber claims, is based upon the geographical fact of people living and working in close proximity. In interest communities, on the other hand, people interact with each other willfully and intentionally because of common interests, whether these interests are based on occupational activities, leisure pastimes, social relationships, or intellectual pursuits. Obviously, no particular spatial relationships are necessary in interest communities.[2]

This differentiation between place and interest communities is particularly useful in analyzing the impact of contemporary social, economic, and demographic forces upon the urban environment generally and upon the administration of urban government specifically. Historically and traditionally, the city—as a formal, governmental, public service institution—has been tied in space to its prescribed boundaries and has devoted the bulk, if not the entirety, of its attention to the spatial-physical components in its makeup. Moreover, communication and transportation barriers have made "place communities" a more dominant consideration in shaping people's lives than "interest communities."

Now, however, under the pressure of social, economic, technological, and demographic changes, "interest communities" are quickly becoming the chief determinants of individual values and life styles, while "place communities" are increasingly being relegated to a simple housekeeping status and stature. As a consequence, students of urban government are increasingly contending that social and cultural matters must replace spatial and

physical considerations as the dominant concerns of urban government officials.[3]

Generally, this contention is based on the following reasoning. (1) The forces of change are now so powerful and are evolving with such rapidity that they must become man's dominant concern and, hence, the dominant concern of his government. (2) Because the city has always been a dominant cultural institution, because the distinction between legal cities and social communities is very recent, because the city can legislate and enforce rules and regulations governing society, and because the city can control and shape the physical environment in which society functions—in short, because the city is such a vital ingredient of contemporary society—it can and should play a leading role in promoting, overseeing, and guiding social change and development toward those goals prescribed by the society's political system.

This chapter, the three following chapters, and, indirectly, this entire book will describe the forces of change and the role and methods which the city can adopt to control them.

The City in a Governmental Setting

Although it is a vital ingredient in society, the city is not by any means the only governmental agency exercising control over society, nor is it even the dominant one. In fact, the city is but one element in a vast and complex system of government in the United States. This section will describe that system and outline the role which the city plays in it.

THE GOVERNMENTAL SYSTEM OF THE UNITED STATES

The system of democratic government established in the United States is characterized by two key elements: federalism and constitution-

---

[2] Melvin M. Webber, "Order in Diversity: Community Without Propiquity," in Wingo, *op. cit.*, pp. 22–54 at pp. 29–30.

[3] See, for example, John M. Pfiffner, "Three Main Problems Will Characterize the Next Fifty Years," PUBLIC MANAGEMENT, September, 1964, pp. 194–95, 218; Wallace G. Lonergan, "The Management Role in Community Development," PUBLIC MANAGEMENT, January, 1966, pp. 14–19; and John Dyckman, "The Changing Uses of the City," DAEDALUS, Winter 1961, pp. 111–31.

alism. By "federalism" is meant the fact that the United States is governed by two distinct and relatively autonomous levels of government—the central or national government[4] and regional or state governments.

The term "constitutionalism" means, first, that all governments in the United States are established under, and are controlled by, written constitutions, and, second, that all governments in the United States are limited in the exercise of power by the terms of their respective constitutions. All governments in the United States are limited by the principles set forth in the federal constitution; all state and local governments are similarly limited by their state's constitutions.

The structure of the governmental system in the United States is outlined in Figure 1–1. This figure shows three separate levels of government: national, state, and local. It also

---

[4] The central government's correct designation is the "national government," but popular jargon frequently refers to it as the "federal government."

indicates that local governments are subordinate parts of state government and therefore are not generally considered to be autonomous units of government within the federal system.

In fact, all units of local government are strictly creatures of the state and are totally subservient to their respective state constitutions and state governments. Legally speaking, the national government has neither authority nor control over the hours, activities, or operation of any unit of local government in the United States. However, when a unit of local government accepts a grant-in-aid from the national government, it does assume a legal obligation to adhere to the minimum standards established for the grant program by the national government. The state, on the other hand, exercises total control over local government and may, at any time and subject only to restrictions contained within the state constitution, modify any of the powers, structures, duties, or responsibilities of its local governments.

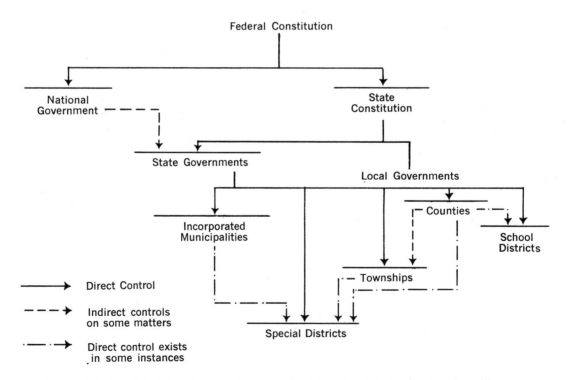

FIGURE 1-1. *The United States federal system ("Incorporated municipalities" refers to cities, villages, boroughs, and, in some states, towns. "Special districts" includes all special districts except school districts.)*

Figure 1–1 also indicates that there are a number of different forms of local government of which the city, or incorporated municipality, is only one. Generally speaking, incorporated municipalities bear responsibility for providing local government services to urban areas while counties and townships share that responsibility in rural areas. Even in urban areas, however, counties continue to provide some functions (e.g., public welfare). As noted earlier, too, the counties now classified as "urban counties" are being authorized to provide an increasing number of urban services. The other units of local government—school and other special districts—provide only one or a very limited number of governmental services. Thus it is the city or municipality in urban areas and the county and township in rural areas that provide a broad range of public services and exercise general public controls. These, then, are the units of general government closest to the people. As such, they exercise an important role in the system of government, especially from the perspective of the individual citizen.

THE CITY AND OTHER GOVERNMENTS

As already noted, cities are the legal offsprings of their respective state governments and are thus subject to their state's constitution and government. Although provision is generally made for cities in state constitutions, it is the state legislature which customarily prescribes their organizational structure, powers, and responsibilities. As a consequence, cities are actually subject to the control of their respective state legislature. The only exceptions to this rule are those cities located in states which have provided for municipal home rule in their constitutions and which have availed themselves of such opportunities. Home rule reduces, but by no means eliminates, city subservience to state legislative control.

Further limiting the powers of cities is the inclination of the courts, prevalent in most states, to apply the concept of "Dillon's Rule" in interpreting statutory or constitutional language authorizing action by cities. In essence, this rule holds that a strict or literal interpretation of the language of the law should be used in defining the municipal powers granted by that law. As a result, cities are generally limited to the exercise of those powers specifically granted to them by the language of state statutes.

Besides serving as a creature of the state from a legal standpoint, cities also frequently serve as the partner of the state in exercising their mutual responsibilities. Thus, for example, cities frequently cooperate with state governments in providing such services as law enforcement, health protection, highway construction, and pollution abatement. Increasingly, too, cities and states are serving as partners in yet anther sense: states now provide a variety of services to aid and facilitate the execution of city business. For example, most states provide a variety of financial aids to their cities. They also provide other services as well, such as financial auditing, police training, and technical assistance in planning and law enforcement. These assistance patterns, of course, vary considerably from state to state.

Interlocal Relations. The intergovernmental problems most frequently confronted by city administrators in their daily work are those involving relations with other units of local government. The proliferation in the number of local units, the increasing obscurity of city boundary lines, the growing tendency to transfer traditional city functions to county or special district governments, the growing competition for financial resources, and the rise in importance of "interest communities" all combine to increase greatly the frequency and complexity of contacts between adjacent and overlapping units of local government.

Generally, interlocal contacts are carried out in an informal manner, chiefly through consultation between elected or appointed officials of the governments involved. On other occasions, however, these contacts are formalized and institutionalized by a variety of legal and extralegal devices.

One such device is the joint law which an increasing number of state legislatures have been passing to authorize their local governments to pool their resources in carrying out all or certain designated functions. These laws have helped to stimulate a larger number of cooperative undertakings between governments, including more sophisticated mutual aid fire pacts, city-school cooperation in recreational programming, regional cooperation among governments in transportation planning, and development of a single public health agency to serve several neighboring municipalities.

Another frequent device used in interlocal relations is the formal contract. Under a contract arrangement, one unit of government will contract with another for the provision of some specified public service. Frequently, for example, cities will contract with their respective counties for the provision of a certain service, such as police protection, health protection, or planning assistance. In other cases, cities will contract among themselves for such services. The contracting device has been most completely developed in Los Angeles County, California, where the county will provide an entire range of municipal services to municipalities under a contracting scheme known as the "Lakewood Plan."

Undoubtedly the most dynamic movement in the field of interlocal relations in recent years has been the development of formal and informal associations of municipal officials in local areas. Sometimes these associations will embrace all units of local governments; others are restricted to cities. Sometimes their membership will include both elected and appointed officials; others are restricted to elected officials; in still others, only chief executive officers—such as mayors, school superintendents, or city managers—are involved. Sometimes these associations are completely informal; others have highly developed organizational structures, elected officers, and dues schedules. Some associations are largely social; others have frequent meetings, heavy agendas, and a large number of major projects or programs. All of them recognize that local government success today is increasingly dependent upon cooperation among local governments.

This trend toward intergovernmental association has culminated in what may well be one of the most significant local government developments in the twentieth century—the council of governments movement. Councils of governments are voluntary associations of local government officials established to promote joint and cooperative action toward the solution of problems common among the participating members. Such councils are currently found in metropolitan areas, but some rural areas have formed similar organizations, usually calling them economic development districts.

The first council of governments was formed in 1954, but the movement toward their establistment gained real steam in 1966 when the federal government made funds available to help underwrite the costs of professional staff help for the councils. Further impetus was added to the movement during that same year when the federal government also began requiring review of applications by regional planning agencies for certain kinds of federal grants to local governments. Since regional planning has been the principal function of the councils, many of them were designated as the regional review agency for these grant applications. The councils thus were given both financial assistance and important functional responsibilities with the result that approximately half of the nation's metropolitan areas established such organizations during the period 1966–68.

Most councils serve an entire metropolitan area, but several serve only defined portions of a metropolitan area. Membership, which is completely voluntary, is usually open to the principal elected officials of municipal and county governments, but sometimes school and other special districts may also join and participate. Generally viewed as forums for the discussion of metropolitan issues and problems, such councils do, in fact, undertake a much broader range of activities. Figure 1–2 summarizes some of the programs of such organizations. Although still in their infancy, these councils have begun to promote more frequent, meaningful, and profitable cooperation among units of local government in their respective areas.

GOVERNMENTAL ROLE OF THE CITY

Despite the increasing complexity of government at local levels, a complexity demonstrated, for example, by the growing magnitude and scale of intergovernmental relations just discussed, the city remains, in urban areas, as the principal instrument of local government. In fact, a good argument can be made for the operational primacy of the city as a unit of government even when the city is contrasted with the national and state government, This case is built upon four propositions:

1. Like the state and national governments, the city is a "general-purpose" government. It is responsible for providing many public services and exercising a wide range of regulatory authority, all for the general purpose of protecting and promoting the health, welfare, and safety of its residents.

2. As a unit of local government, the city is close to the people and their problems. Since it can be especially aware of popular needs and desires, the city is peculiarly able to tailor governmental programs to local needs and conditions. Further, it is in the best position to respond quickly and effectively to new problems and changing conditions.

3. Potentially, at least, cities are more responsive to popular demands. Since they are

Air and Water Pollution
Abatement

Solid Waste Disposal Planning
and Implementation

Sewerage Control

Water Supply

Drainage and Sediment
Control

Noise Abatement

Flood Control

Cooperative Sharing of Health
and Vocational Rehabilitation
Facilities

Regional Community Education
Facilities

Regional Recreation and
Library Development

Computer Time Sharing among
Individual School Districts

Region-wide Teacher Training

Economic Opportunity Programs

Airport and Interregional
Transportation Facilities
Planning

Regional Police and Fire
Mutual Aid

Emergency Snow Removal
Planning

Emergency Civil Defense
Procedures

Uniform Codes and Ordinances

Regional Clinics for Judges,
Public Defenders and
Prosecutors

Computerization of Police
Records for Regional
Accessibility

Traffic Safety and Congestion

Joint Contracting for Purchasing

Manpower Exchange

Census Coordination

Comprehensive Regional Land
Use Planning

Regional Transit and Highway
Planning

Regional Capital Improvements
Studies

Economic Base Studies

FIGURE 1-2. *Some potential council of government activities (Source: Proceedings of the First National Conference of Councils of Government, Metropolitan Washington Council of Governments, 1967, p. 15.)*

closer to the people, more people have more opportunities for more contact with local political officials than with officials from any other level of government. Presumably, too, local political officials are just as responsive to popular demands as are officials at other levels of government.

Frequently, however, cities are charged with being nonresponsive to popular pressures and needs. In part, this is true. Their response capability is impaired by the requirement that they adhere rigidly to procedures and practices set forth in state laws—procedures and practices that are frequently obsolete. Further, their responsiveness is often impaired by local political systems that, formally or informally, systematically exclude representation of certain minority groups in the community. Even where these conditions persist, however, the individual can still play a more active and forceful role in local government than he can at any other level of government and more people are active in government at this level than at any other. Still, contemporary social unrest indicates that all levels of government, cities as well as others, must make far greater efforts to achieve true political responsiveness, to represent meaningfully all groups within the political community—if society is to meet successfully the challenges of urban life.

4. Finally, the city derives its claim to primacy from the simple fact that it is local government, and primarily city government, that provides most of the public services enjoyed directly by individual citizens in the course of their daily lives.

Because of its operational importance and because of its access to the people, the city must inevitably assume an obligation to provide governmental leadership in dealing with local problems and in representing local interests before the councils of state and national governments. Thus, in a governmental sense, Henry S. Churchill's axiom becomes even more meaningful—"The City Is the People."

The Nature of Urban Government

Since city, village, county, and other local governments are the creatures of their respective states, the details of their organization, operation, and powers will obviously differ from state to state. Despite these differences, however, city governments display marked similarities in their basic structure and in the problems which they must face. The following paragraphs will outline briefly the more important of such similarities.

ORGANIZATION OF CITY GOVERNMENT

A typical organization chart can readily differentiate between the legislative and executive, the policy-making and administrative branches of city government (local judicial systems are really branches of state court systems), but these distinctions are not nearly as clear in practice as they are on paper—and this is especially true in smaller municipalities.

The Organization Pattern. Figure 1–3 outlines the organization of a typical city. It shows the usual city legislative authority, the mayor and council; other possible elected officers, such as a clerk, treasurer, or assessor; and typical line or operating departments, such as police and fire departments. The executive officer position noted in Figure 1–3 is subject to wide variation. When the municipality utilizes the council-manager form of government, the city manager serves as the chief executive officer. Under other forms of government, however, the function of this office may be exercised by the mayor, by either an elected or appointed clerk, or by the mayor and council collectively.

Responsibility for Policy-Making and Administration. The legislative authority of the city resides in the mayor and council and, traditionally, it has been assumed that this grant of power included all policy-making responsibility for the municipality. While the authority of the council to make basic policy remains unquestioned, increasing recognition has been given to the need for, and the fact of, executive participation in the policy-making process. Administrative officers have always been accorded some policy responsibility: traditionally they have been charged with the duty of executing the policy decisions of the council under the direct and close supervision of the council.

This traditional conception of the administrative officer's role has been gradually changing as municipal governments have adjusted themselves to the stresses of growing populations and increasingly complex governmental operations. Now it is generally recognized that the administrative officer's training and experience, plus the full-time effort which he devotes to his work, give him a perspective on municipal problems, both current and future, which is both professionally sound and invaluable to the elected councilman, who in turn is able to devote only a small portion of his time to governmental problems. The International City Managers' Association recognized this changing role of the urban administrator when, in 1952, it amended its code of ethics to include a statement describing the city manager's policy-making responsibility.

In essence, municipal administrators are expected to join in policy-making by drawing on their professional background and expertise to recommend new policies or changes in existing policies, to suggest alternative courses of action on existing policy proposals, to supply elected officials with all relevant data and information regarding such proposals, and to advise those officials on the possible consequences of all al-ternative courses of action. Furthermore, once a policy is adopted, it is the administrator's responsibility to make whatever decisions are necessary to execute that policy in a manner fully consistent with the intention of the council, regardless of his own attitude toward the policy.

The administrator's responsibilities do not, however, include participation in any public campaign seeking the adoption of a particular policy proposal by the council or any other local legislative body. Administrators can participate openly in policy proposal campaigns only when the policy proposed has been officially adopted by the governing body. Thus, for example, administrators can openly campaign for public approval of a bond issue that has been approved by the council, but not for an issue which has not been considered, or is currently being considered, by the council. As the City Manager's Code of Ethics says, "The city manager defends municipal policies publicly *only after* consideration and adoption of such policies by the council."[5] (Emphasis added.) Need-

---

[5] On July 1, 1969 the International City Managers' Association amended its constitution to change its

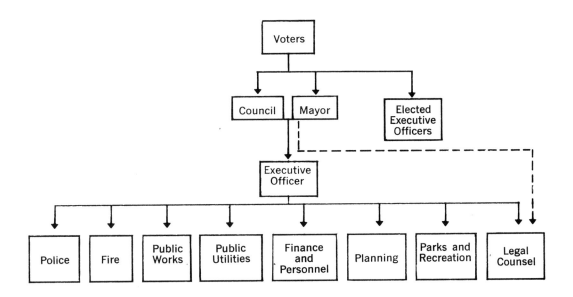

FIGURE 1-3. *The organization of a typical municipality (The mayor may or may not sit as a member of the council. Elected executive officers might include, among others, clerk, treasurer, and assessor—although many municipalities no longer elect such officials.)*

less to say, participation in campaigns for elective public office is not considered a proper function of the administrator.

Not only must the administrator be involved in policy development, but just as important, so too must the council be involved in administration. In any city, the council is ultimately responsible for judging the effectiveness of administration and for supervising the execution of its policies. Trouble, of course, occurs when the council concerns itself with administrative details properly within the purview of the administrator, but any council must concern itself with the over-all administrative policies of its city.

In essence, then, the administrator cannot function unless he is part of the policy development process, and the policy group, the council, cannot function unless it is familiar with, exercises supervision over, and renders a final evaluation of administrative processes.

Professionals in City Government. With the increasing complexity of urban government has come an increasing need for the services of professional specialists in a wide variety of fields. Local governments have traditionally relied upon professional specialists in some fields: all communities, for example, have needed the help of attorneys, accountants, and civil engineers; larger communities frequently employ such specialists as sanitary engineers, traffic engineers, architects, tree surgeons, surveyors, public health doctors and nurses, laboratory technicians, investment bankers, bond attorneys, and juvenile officers.

The expansion in the quantity and complexity of local government responsibilities is now giving rise to demands for new kinds of professional help. Some of these demands are for a broader range of professional talents: human relations consultants, statisticians, and programmers for electronic data processing equipment are now being employed. Other demands

are for the development of entirely new professional specializations in fields peculiar to urban government: urban renewal specialists, advocate planners, and neighborhood development officers are typical examples.

Finally, there is a rapidly growing demand for the development of new kinds of career specializations—paraprofessional specialists—in the public service. Paraprofessionals are persons who are given some basic training in a specific professional specialization so that they can expedite the work of the professionals by assisting them with some of their more mundane tasks. Paraprofessionals are now employed widely in the field of education under the title of "teaching aide." Other fields for which paraprofessionals are being trained include social work, planning, community development, public health, engineering, and recreation.

Further, some urban scholars are even now predicting that urban executives will soon need a staff of social science specialists to aid them in designing and implementing human development and improvement programs.[6] Increased reliance upon professional specialists, regardless of the nature of their speciality, obviously implies the growth of greater expertise in urban governing processes, but it also implies the need for more sophisticated administrative systems: needed are systems which insure desirable patterns of career opportunity for the professional, extract the fullest measure of benefit from his competence, and maintain good working relationships between the professional and his administrative and political superiors.

CHALLENGES OF URBAN GOVERNMENT

The definition of cities indicates that they are both political and social entities. These two aspects of the city both impose certain demands upon the structure of urban government.

As a politico-governmental entity, for example, the city must, to the best of its abilities and to the maximum allowed by its financial resources, satisfy public demands for: (1) public facilities, such as streets, sidewalks, sewers, parks, and boulevard trees; (2) environmental improvements, including such services as neigh-

---

name to the International City Management Association, and to broaden the qualifications for membership to include in the association all persons working as professionals in overall management positions in urban areas. At that time the City Manager's Code of Ethics was revised to conform to the constitutional amendments and its title was changed to City Management Code of Ethics.

[6] See, for example, Pfiffner, *op. cit.,* p. 195.

borhood rehabilitation, subdivision and zoning code enforcement, landscape beautification, and even such mundane activities as street cleaning and weed control; (3) human development opportunities, including recreation programs, library services, cultural facilities, educational programs, and even community social activities; (4) public safety services, including police, fire, and civil defense protection; and (5) public utility services.

As a social and cultural entity, the city must strive constantly to expedite human interaction. In part, this means maximizing the efficiency of the city's transportation and communication systems. In an increasingly larger part, however, this also means that the city must develop, maintain, and improve an environment which is conducive to constructive social interaction and cultural development. Thus it is incumbent upon the city to harmonize relationships among racial, religious, economic, and ethnic groups; to promote educational opportunities; to generate a healthy economic climate; and, in general, to promote the enrichment of human life.

In the past, the primary concern of city government has been focused on its responsibilities as a politico-governmental entity. In the future, however, as society reaches higher and higher levels of material affluence, people will increasingly become concerned with the non-material aspects of life; their demands for cultural fulfillment, cultural variety, education, social enrichment, equal opportunity, and social stability will increase. To retain their status as viable political bodies, city governments must be willing and prepared to meet this changing pattern of popular demand. It is in part the cities' failure to respond to such demands—demands which are already manifesting themselves—that accounts for the unrest and uncertainty plaguing much of urban life.

RESPONSIBILITIES OF URBAN POLITICAL SYSTEMS

Urban political systems, whether they be partisan or nonpartisan, are ultimately responsible for seeing that the tasks of urban government outlined above are accomplished. This means that these political or governing systems must make certain basic decisions and then see to it that the actions required by these decisions are satisfactorily carried out. Implicit in this, of course, is the assumption that these systems will execute their responsibilities in a manner consistent with the principles of American democracy.

Democratic Base of Urban Politics. The principles of American democracy demand, first, that *all* governments, urban as well as other governments, be responsive to the needs and desires of their constituencies, and second, that they be responsive to the needs and desires of *all* of their constituencies. Laudable in theory, neither of these demands is easily satisfied in actual practice; they must be worked at consciously and constantly both by elected officials and appointed administrators.

Although these principles have been a fundamental part of the framework of American urban government for nearly two centuries, the unrest in the nation's urban centers clearly demonstrates that they have not yet been realized. Although riots, disorders, demonstrations, strikes, and boycotts have been, with some justification, charged to growing lawlessness, both their existence and their prevalence are also clear indications that the American political system is failing to respond to the needs and desires of a significant percentage of the electorate. *In short, present urban political systems are not doing an adequate job of responding to all of their constituencies.* As long as minority groups, be they black or white, rich or poor, Irish or Scandinavian, men or women, white or blue collar workers, young or old—or whatever—feel that they can not receive a satisfactory resolution of their grievances from the political system, then that system is failing to meet the standards of American democracy.

The present difficulties confronting urban political systems come at a very inopportune time. Rapid urbanization has generated vast new demands upon these same beleaguered political systems; the need for responsive government has never been more critical. Administrative capability, by itself, can accomplish little unless it is directed by responsive political leadership. Thus the contemporary urban challenge is, first and foremost, a political challenge—a challenge that must be accepted and met by the elected council of every city and village government.

Every elected councilman and every executive officer must, if these democratic precepts are to be met, make a conscious effort to discover and evaluate, in advance, the reaction of every segment of the community to programmatic decisions awaiting final action. These efforts must be made in every community regardless of whether or not that community has experienced, or has been threatened with, outward manifestations of minority group discontent. Fundamental democratic principles demand no less; they can be satisfied with no less.

Basic Decisions Confronting Urban Governments. In fulfilling their responsibilities, urban political systems, operating through urban governments, must make four key kinds of decisions:

1. Each political system must decide what values its urban government must attain and uphold. Of concern are values relating to both the internal operation of governing machinery and the patterns of life extant in the community.

2. It must, in turn, design action programs which will promote and maintain these values.

3. It must decide how much of the community's resources should be diverted from the private to the public sector. In other words, it must ascertain what percentage of the privately owned wealth in the community will be taken through taxation to finance public services.

4. It must seek to achieve an optimum allocation of public resources among the various public services that are provided. In economic terms, this optimum allocation is achieved when the benefits from the last dollar allocated to each public service are equal. In political terms, the best allocation is that which maximizes community satisfaction.

Urban scholars have long been trying to determine the nature of the processes used to make these decisions. Specifically, they have sought to ascertain what persons or groups influence or control the decisions that are made. Their findings indicate that a wide variety of political systems actually exist. In some communities, researchers have found monolithic power structures in which one man or a small group of men exercise control over the decision-making process.[7] Studies in other communities have found that individual decisions are primarily influenced by the actions and reactions of those few groups most directly affected.[8] Still other studies have found that influence over public decisions is widely spread among many formal and informal interest groups.[9]

Developing opinion now favors the validity of a "pluralistic theory" which holds that political decisions in urban communities are the product of the influence of many groups, but with different degrees of influence on different decisions. According to this theory, political decisions are not made until some consensus begins to emerge from the views of the different interested groups. Elected officials presumably play a catalytic role by sparking the emergence of the consensus.

Undoubtedly the validity of this pluralistic theory varies from community to community. There is evidence, for example, of a relationship between pluralistic tendencies and community size with larger communities being more prone to operate in a pluralistic political milieu.[10] What is most important is recognition of the fact that each community has its own unique political system, and that urban administrators must be thoroughly familiar with the operations of the system in their own communities if they are to play an effective role in shaping the decisions that are made.

---

[7] See, for example, Floyd Hunter, COMMUNITY POWER STRUCTURE—A STUDY OF DECISION MAKERS, (Chapel Hill: University of North Carolina Press, 1953).

[8] See, for example, Robert Dahl, WHO GOVERNS? (New Haven: Yale University Press, 1961), which argues that the group or groups most affected by a decision exercise controlling influence over the decision, and Robert Presthus, MEN AT THE TOP, (New York: Oxford University Press, 1964), which describes communities in which two specific groups, economic and political dominants, compete for ultimate control over community decisions.

[9] Edward Banfield, POLITICAL INFLUENCE, (New York: The Free Press, 1961).

[10] Contrast, for example, Banfield, *op. cit.*, with Robert E. Aggar and Vincent Ostrom, "The Political Structure of a Small Community," PUBLIC OPINION QUARTERLY, Spring, 1945, pp. 81–89.

Conclusion

The city is a key element in society. It plays a major role in shaping the physical environment in which city life takes place and, in turn, this environment helps shape the social, economic, and cultural activities that take place within it. The city further shapes these activities through its power to regulate human conduct. As a consequence, the city shapes society.

The city's impact upon society, in turn, places major responsibilities upon the city's government, responsibilities which increasingly must go beyond the caretaker, housekeeping role which city government has played in the past. Now the city's government must also be concerned about the relationship between the city and society, about the life styles of people within the city, and about opportunities for improving the health, vitality, and happiness of those people. These, then, are the ultimate challenges confronting the developing city.

2

The City:
Forces of Change

It is harder and harder to live a good life in American cities today.

Our society will never be great until our cities are great.

Lyndon Baines Johnson

There is a whole generation of Americans who have known the city only at its worst and who have not experienced the pleasures and advantages of true urban life.

Victor Gruen

As these statements so obviously imply, all is not well with the American city. It is assailed on every side by forces for which it is not responsible and over which it has little control. On the one hand, it is experiencing vast increases in the number of people it must serve while simultaneously its people have been cast adrift from their customary life styles by technological change. Moreover, a rising level of affluence leads the populous to demand a wider range of public services, many of which are vastly more complex than the services traditionally expected of government. Meanwhile, on the other hand, the backwash of technological change—the impoverished, the poorly educated, the unskilled—find themselves sinking into relatively lower states of abject poverty despite increasingly expensive welfare programs. Complicating the entire picture is the resilient cancer of prejudice and racism—the distrust of those who appear to be different—which has generated severe problems and critical challenges for both the society at large and the cities which serve it.

All of these forces create demands for more and better city services, yet public attention and governmental taxing capacity are increasingly diverted to the national scene. The capstone to this milieu is the increasingly obsolete structure of law and organization within which cities are forced to conduct their business and solve the public's problems. All of these forces and more have led many urban observers to agree with Max Weber's prophecy of years ago, "The age of the city seems to be at an end."

The city thus is bound up in the vortex of clashing forces and complex changes. Such forces and changes obviously result in problems for the city—and for the men who administer the city. The purpose of this chapter will be to examine these forces in greater detail, survey the problems they cause, and comment on some of their implications for urban administration.

Socioeconomic Trends

Many of the forces of change currently buffeting urban areas are leaving their mark directly on the form and shape of the American city. These forces, which can be collectively labeled "the forces or urbanism," can be distinguished from a variety of other forces that are of major consequence for urban government and with which such governments must cope. These include resource scarcities, technological developments, and the growing affluence of society. Each of these forces will be described below.

THE FORCES OF URBANISM

The forces of urbanism are a composite of tremendous population growth, an increasing concentration of population in urban areas, the geographic expansion of metropolitan areas bringing the rising spector of megalopolises,[1] the dispersion of cities as population density spreads outward from the central core, and the proliferation of local governing units created to service the growing number of urbanites. The quandary of contemporary urbanism might thus be termed the product of growing governmental proliferation and confusion in the midst of demands for services by an incessantly increasing number of people.

Urban Population Trends. In part, the problem of urban population growth is simply an adjunct of national population growth in the United States: the nation's population doubled between 1910 and 1960, and this population growth is expected to continue. The 1960 census count of 180 million increased to 200 million by the mid-1960's and is expected to reach over 235 million by 1976. Population experts expect a national population of over 400 million people within the next 50 years and they are already visualizing a national population of over 900 million people. In other words, population growth is expected to continue at a very rapid pace.

Not only is the nation's population increasing, but so too is the percentage of the population living in urban areas.[2] Not until 1920 did a majority of people in the United States live in urban places, but by 1960 the figure had reached 70 percent. In the decade between 1950–1960, the population of rural areas in the nation actually declined by .8 percent.

Estimates for the years 1960–65 indicated that 79.8 percent of U.S. population growth occurred in urban areas of one million persons or more. Thus it would appear that people are not only moving to cities, but they are moving to the larger cities. Even the nonmetropolitan cities, however, showed a population growth rate (9.1 percent) greater than the national average (2.3 percent) in the same five-year period.

Looked at otherwise, in 1960 there were 150 million persons living in areas that were either urban or were expected to be classified as urban in the next three decades. At least twice as many people are expected to be living in those same areas by the year 2000. These statistics have led experts to suggest:

Assuming that the rural areas and the small towns of the nation will continue to empty out and that the largest metropolitan areas will continue to host the majority of the migrants, an urban pattern is foreseen in which roughly two-thirds of the population of the United States will reside in a couple dozen huge metropolitan areas of over a million population within a decade or two.[3]

One major urban force, then, is the enormous increase in the population of urban centers. A second is the growing dispersion of people within urban areas. Such dispersion, usually known as the flight to the suburbs, has given suburbia an estimated rate of population growth several times that of the core cities, even including the core city population growth stemming from annexation. Figure 2–1 shows the impact over time of these internal population shifts upon the Chicago metropolitan area.

There is every reason to believe that this pattern of change within urban areas is typical.[4] By 1965 it was estimated that, for the first time, less than half the residents of metropolitan areas lived in the central cities. Further, the total as well as the relative population of most central cities has been falling in recent years. Except for those core cities which grew through annexation, the decline in total

---

[1] The term "megalopolis" refers to concentrations of metropolitan areas whose boundaries have coalesced.

[2] As used here, the definition "urban area" is that given to the term by the U.S. Census Bureau. Essentially that term refers to any community of 2,500 people or more.

[3] Wilbur R. Thompson, "Urban Economic Growth and Development in a National System of Cities," in Philip M. Hauser and Leo F. Schnore, THE STUDY OF URBANIZATION (New York: John Wiley & Sons, 1965), p. 478.

[4] Leo F. Schnore, "Municipal Annexations and the Growth of Metropolitan Suburbs, 1950–1960," AMERICAN JOURNAL OF SOCIOLOGY, January, 1962, Tables 5–7 and p. 411.

population for core cities was almost universal between 1950 and 1960. Thus the typical population pattern in metropolitan areas has been one of population increase in suburbia and population decline in core cities.

Urban observers, and especially the friends of the large cities, have looked hard for indications that this flow of people from the core city to suburbia will be reversed, but to date they have looked in vain. Others have argued that the core cities can undertake programs which will stop or even reverse their population exodus, but, as York Willbern has noted, "The overwhelming bulk of the evidence

makes the outward movement seem 'inexorable.' "[5]

Other Demographic Changes. Not only is the sheer magnitude of population change important to urban life, but so too is the composition of such changes. Several qualitative demographic trends are presently bringing changes of major significance to urban America.

First, while the migration into the cities is composed of all kinds of rural people, it is

[5] York Willbern, THE WITHERING AWAY OF THE CITY (University of Alabama Press, 1964), p. 24.

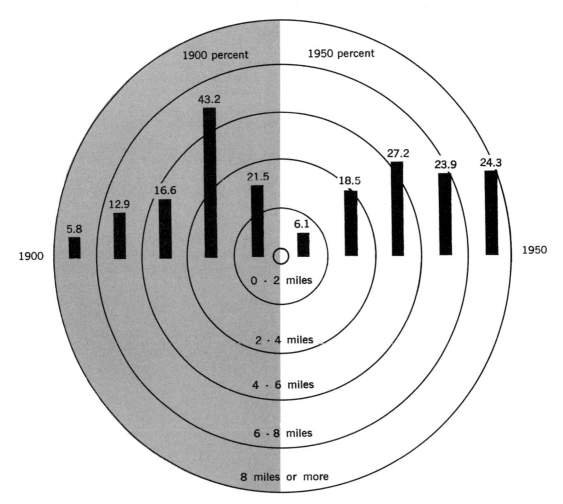

FIGURE 2-1. *Distribution of metropolitan population based on the city of Chicago (Distance shown is measured from the center of the core city. Source: Wilfred Owen,* THE METROPOLITAN TRANSPORTATION PROBLEM, *The Brookings Institution, 2nd ed., 1966, p. 14.)*

made up principally of young adults and marginal farmers who have abandoned farming for urban life. This last group is of particular importance. Many come from poor areas of the nation, such as the Appalachian Mountain region and the rural South, and they arrive in the city with no money, no employment skills, and no knowledge of urban living patterns. They are frequently unfamiliar, for example, with such everyday amenities of life as plumbing fixtures, modern appliances, and rudimentary sanitation procedures. Unaccustomed to municipal garbage pickup, they often dispose of trash by simply throwing it in the backyards or courtyards of residential buildings. The adjustment of such people to urban life is too frequently a slow process which is costly both to the people themselves and to the city around them.

These rural migrants usually settle in the older areas of core cities where buildings are dilapidated and rents are cheap. In such environments, surrounded by their fellow migrants, there are too few neighbors accustomed to urban life whose behavior they can emulate, and consequently their unfamiliarity compounds and accelerates their neighborhood's deterioration.

Accompanying this shift of rural migrants to the city is the movement of middle-class urban residents to the suburbs. This movement, which has been proceeding in a pell-mell fashion since the end of World War II, is a product of many forces, but primarily of pressures for upward social mobility, of the search for better school systems, and of the simple desire for private yards and single-family homes. This latter desire has been held by people everywhere for centuries, but only recently have increasing personal wealth, available long-term monthly payment mortgages, and the automobile made it a practical possibility for the majority of middle-class citizens.

The flight to the suburbs has long been criticized and condemned because of its effect on urban life. It accentuates the demand for suburban land, governmental proliferation, and suburban sprawl. It empties older neighborhoods in the core city of their traditional residents, leaving these areas to lower income residents and, frequently, to more rapid deterioration. Finally, with the middle-class goes the cream of the core city's local leadership talent, thereby depriving the city of its most important asset as it faces the challenges of renovation and modernization.

Another demographic change with serious consequences for urban areas is the change in age structure of the nation's population. The number of people in the unproductive age groups—those under 21 and over 65—is steadily increasing. Since people in these particular age groups place the greatest strain on educational, medical, recreational, welfare, and similar facilities, their percentage growth means increasing demands for basic government services. Further, since it is the people between 21 and 65 years of age who pay the bulk of the nation's taxes, the emerging situation is one in which a smaller percentage of people will be called upon to underwrite more and more public services for more and more people.

Changes in Population Mobility. Finally, population mobility is also a factor of consequence for urban government. The age of the automobile and rapid transportation has brought vast changes to the structure of the city, as well it might since it modifies and facilitates the conditions of human interaction upon which the city depends. Also, by reducing time-space ratios, the improvements in transportation have altered the relationship of the city to its hinterland and to the greater society of the nation at large.

Most important, however, is the changing relationship between the individual and the city brought by this increasing human mobility. Improved mobility has encouraged people to change their residence with increasing frequency. Approximately 3 percent of the nation's population moves across state lines every year and approximately 6.5 percent moves from county to county. As more people move more often, the attachment of the individual to his city weakens: his loyalties to the city are reduced, his concern for its problems is lessened, and his willingness to support changes aimed at upgrading the city is impaired.

Growing Popular Alienation and Anomie. Perhaps the most adverse consequence of population mobility is the rootlessness—the alienation of the individual from concern with his environment and his neighbors—which it engenders and promotes. As residential location becomes more transitory and less stable, traditional relations between individuals and their families, neighbors, and friends are weakened; friendships are increasingly viewed as temporary rather than permanent alliances; neighborhoods lose any meaning other than as places of temporary residence; the sense of community is dissipated; social pressures and values become less consequential; and the individual tends to become increasingly isolated from the larger society and more withdrawn into a concern for self. As Scott Greer and others have noted, many urban observers have "speculated that the sheer complexity and impersonality of urban life must result in a deterioration of customary morality, resulting in collective loss of morale."[6]

Others have been more specific: they charge that such social conditions as familial disorganization, rapid economic change, and population density generate anomie—an absence of social values. The contention is that the twin forces of increasing population density and growing population mobility produce alienation and anomie which, in turn, result in social and cultural disintegration. To the extent that this is true, and there are weighty arguments supporting it, the city not only functions as the cradle of civilization, as noted in the preceding chapter, but also as the coffin of that same civilization, fostering conditions that lead to its demise.

Changes in Governmental Structure. The growth of urban population has been accompanied by a slower but equally burdensome increase in the number of local governments. As urban areas grow, they unfortunately tend to spawn an increase of jurisdictions organized

to govern their populations. These new governments are created both to service land just transformed from rural to urban use and to provide particular services to land already urbanized. In fact, the creation of new special purpose districts far surpasses in number the organization of new municipal governments.

Between 1952 and 1962, for example, 1,190 new municipal governments were formed as compared to 4,283 new special districts. This represents an increase of 7 percent in the number of municipalities and 36 percent in the number of new special districts. To be sure, these increases have been partially offset by a reduction in the number of school districts, but the total number of governmental units in metropolitan areas continues to climb despite school consolidations.

This increase, accompanied as it is by an expanding urban population, would not in itself be necessarily bad were it not for the problems of governmental coordination that accompany it. Just as an arithmetic increase in an administrator's span of control is accompanied by a geometric increase in his problems of staff coordination, so too is an arithmetic increase in the problems of intergovernmental coordination. Such coordination is even more difficult to achieve in metropolitan areas, furthermore, because, with few exceptions, such areas have no central authority responsible for promoting constructive interaction among the myriad, overlapping units of government. Many areas even lack a central agency designated to do so.

Many people look to the newly formed councils of governments to perform this function, but they are not yet in a position to do so. As a consequence, the ongoing proliferation of local governments continues to compound the problems of urban life.

Worse yet, this proliferation impairs urban governments in still another manner: as the number of local governments in any particular geographic area increases, the significance of any given unit of local government decreases. This has two ramifications: (1) as the structure of local government becomes increasingly complex, residents served by that structure become less and less concerned with, and knowledgeable about, their local governing system

---

[6] Scott Greer, et al., THE NEW URBANIZATION (New York: St. Martin's Press, 1968) , p. 189.

and are thus less inclined and competent to exercise adequate democratic controls over it, and (2) popular identification with, and loyalty to, individual units of local government is weakened if not destroyed.

That this is happening is generally unquestioned. As one observer has noted,

The unitary conceptions of urban places are fast becoming anachronistic, for their physical boundaries are rapidly collapsing and, even where (such boundaries) are imposed by legal restraints, social intercourse, which has never respected physical boundaries anyway, is increasingly able to ignore them.[7]

In short, the bonds between individuals and their local governments—the bonds between individuals and the traditional bastions of grass roots democracy—are being steadily eroded in today's urban society.

Conclusion. "The most impressive thing about contemporary urbanization is the fantastic proliferation and multiplication of human and social organizations."[8]

RESOURCE SCARCITIES

As urban populations grow and as the density of urban settlements increases, it is only natural to expect severe problems in the allocation of material resources. Resource allocation problems are not new to mankind—they are as old as human economics. If anything, growing material prosperity should ease these traditional economic problems insofar as most human needs are concerned.

Growing prosperity will not, however, ease the resource allocation problems for four of mankind's most essential commodities: land, space, air, and water. With a predicted national population of 400 million or more, of whom over 325 million will live in cities, problems governing the use of these four commodities threaten to reach proportions of overwhelming complexity.

Two different kinds of problems actually exist. With land and space, it is a problem of physical scarcity as more and more people try to live in narrowly constricted geographical areas. Regardless of city size, land and space must be available for residential, commercial, industrial, cultural, recreational, and circulatory purposes. The future promises intensive competition between these uses for both horizontal land and vertical air space. All such demands must be adequately met if urban life, indeed if society, is to survive. As of yet, however, adequate allocation formulas appear not to be available.

The scarcity of space poses yet another problem. Physiologists have found that population density among lower forms of animal life leads to anxiety, frustration, and possible mental breakdowns in the animals. Biologically, humans are susceptible to the same consequences under conditions of inadequate living space. Thus the problem of population density must be solved from a psychological as well as an economic perspective if human life is to continue unimpaired.

With water and air, however, the allocation problems are somewhat different. These commodities exist in copious quantities, but the supply of either or both in any given place can be rendered unfit for human consumption through contamination or pollution. Furthermore, with water there are ultimate limits to the amount available in any particular vicinity. Theoretically, these allocation problems are manageable: modern technology presumably can find ways to maintain both resources in conditions of acceptable purity while properly designed conservation programs can assure the availability of water.

Neither technology nor conservation will work, however, unless the political system first produces agreement on the methods to be employed and the means to finance them. Many metropolitan areas, for example, suffer from acute water pollution problems because the local political system has not been able to develop a consensus on the kinds of solutions to be employed. Thus the political difficulties are at least as severe as the technological barriers in resolving allocation problems.

---

[7] Melvin M. Webber, "Order in Diversity: Community without Propinquity," in CITIES AND SPACE (Baltimore: The Johns Hopkins Press, 1963), pp. 34–35.

[8] Leo F. Schnore, "The City as a Social Organization," URBAN AFFAIRS QUARTERLY, March, 1966, p. 69.

THE CRISIS OF TECHNOLOGY

It has become almost trite in the space age to note the impact of technology on modern life or to suggest that technological progress is advancing at an increasing rate of speed. Yet such is surely the case, and urban government is no more immune to technology's impact than is any other facet of modern life. In fact, technology affects urban government through its impact upon society, upon organization structure, on management processes, on demands for municipal services, on the future outlook for small urban communities, and upon citizen involvement in local government.

Societal Impact. Technology's impacts on society are obviously legion; their number and complexity defy description here. Some of these effects, however, have special significance for urban governments. One, for example, is the increasing specialization which modern technology demands both of economic units in society and of individual workers.

Intensive specialization renders economic interdependence inevitable; without a high rate of human interaction, technological specialization would strangle itself. The principal, traditional function of the city has been to facilitate such interaction. Thus, as the intensity of required interaction increases, so too must the intensity, efficiency, and effectiveness of the city's efforts to facilitate it. In short, the city must match increases in technological specialization and sophistication with ever increasing facility for the internal circulation of ideas, people, and goods.

Another by-product of technology important to the city is worker obsolescence. Technological change has so increased in tempo that the demand for a given set of worker skills no longer lasts as long as a worker's expected productive life. It is currently estimated that the skills of the average worker will be rendered obsolete at least three times during his working career. The adjustments required by such obsolescence, both for the worker and for the society surrounding him, obviously have serious ramifications for both the economic and political systems.

Economists also assert that technology is reducing the demand for labor itself. Claims are made, for example, that the time can be foreseen when only 4 percent of the population will be able to produce all of the goods and services needed by the entire population. While this figure certainly can be disputed, there can be no doubt that technology will reduce the amount of time an average person must spend in gainful employment during his lifetime. This, in turn, means more city programs and facilities catering to leisure time activities.

Perhaps some of the most significant technological advances, however, are those occurring in the field of communication. The easy and rapid transmission of ideas has always been a specialty of the city, but modern technology has rendered the city unnecessary for this purpose. Thus a fundamental justification for the city's very existence has been removed.

Communication technology has other major ramifications for the city as well. New technology offers potential new methods of communication between city officials and residents. It also greatly amplifies the spread of rumors and false reports, adding to the city's responsibilities for rapid and accurate reporting of factual situations to the public. Modern communications, in fact, make more pressing and potentially more important the public relations programs discussed extensively in Chapter 15.

Modern technology is a two-edged sword: it not only facilitates and accentuates the communication function of such institutions as urban governments, but it also adds immeasurably to the communication skills which individuals must possess. The nonverbal worker—one who has difficulty communicating with words—increasingly finds himself handicapped in his ability to be trained, to follow instructions and directions, to respond effectively to supervision, to avail himself of grievance procedures and other job protections, to qualify for career advancement, to survive economically.

Finally, technological change and specialization are causing still other changes in basic patterns of human life. Commenting on the current "era of radical change," Max Ways has noted:

Within a decade or two it will be generally understood that the main challenge to U.S. society will not turn around the production of goods but around the difficulties and opportunities involved in a world of accelerating change and ever widening choices. Change has always been part of the human condition. What is different now is the pace of change, and the prospect that it will come faster and faster, affecting every part of life, including personal values, morality, and religion, which seem most remote from technology. . . .

So swift is the acceleration that trying to "make sense" of change will come to be our basic industry. Aesthetic and ethical values will be evolving along with the choices to which they will be applied. The question about progress will be how good rather than how much. Already the shift away from purely materialistic and quantitative criteria is well advanced. Change is called "excessive" when it appears to outrun ethical or aesthetic patterns. In the conflicts that arise on this point there are dangers not only for the business system but also for the democratic constitutional state and for the hope that the spirit of individual man can enlarge its freedom.[9]

Ways also noted that accelerating change, fostered and accompanied by the unprecedented mobility of society, has been blamed for juvenile delinquency, the dissolution of communities, a "barrenness in individual life," and the "dehumanization" of man.[10] Regardless of the validity of such claims, it is obvious that technological innovation and its companion, social change, are seriously affecting society and, as a consequence, are posing problems for those who govern society's cities.

Organizational Impact. Technology, by reducing the impact of time, space, and communication barriers, has made possible and practical, in fact has made inevitable, the rise of the large organization. Furthermore, as technology increases the specialization of modern life, the accompanying costs of supporting that specialization simultaneously reduce the efficiency and efficacy of the small organization.

Thus technology has brought a trend to bigness. This, in turn, has added still further impetus to the needs for specialization. Large organizations place increasing emphasis on management rationality and spawn new special-

ties, such as management science and computer science, to provide more sophisticated techniques for directing and controlling their operations. In the process, technology and bigness tend to substitute an organizational society for a society of individuals. Individual effort thus tends to become less significant in and of itself and to gain its importance only as part of a larger team or organizational effort.

As the role of the individual is thus diminished, the individual's relations to his society are suddenly altered and the ominous threat of diminishing personal importance arises. Opposing this threat has been an increasing emphasis by management science on the importance of the individual in the organization, but the struggle between individualizing and dehumanizing forces continues to plague all organizations, including agencies of local government.

Management Impact. By leading to improvements in organizational science, by promoting specialization, and by advancing new management practices, technology has thus had a major impact on management. But its impact does not end there. Not only has it provided the tools to manage larger organizations successfully, but it has also provided the means to increase the quality of management regardless of organization size.

Of major significance, for example, have been technical improvements in the communications field which have greatly accelerated the speed and efficiency of communication over the distance. The result has been improved potential for collecting and pooling information relative to organizational goals and improved capacity for organizational response to changing needs and conditions.

A second major innovation has been the development of electronic data processing equipment and techniques. By making possible faster and more sophisticated analyses of a greater range of relevant data, such equipment has greatly increased management's ability to analyze problems, compare alternative courses of action, and make sounder judgements about them. Furthermore, such equipment has greatly increased management's capacity for internal organizational analysis and for coor-

---

[9] Max Ways, "The Era of Radical Change," FORTUNE, May, 1964, p. 113.

[10] *Ibid.*

dinating and controlling ongoing operations. These capabilities are described further in Chapters 10 and 11.

Government Service Impact. Technology's most obvious impacts upon demands for government services are those stemming from improvements in the transportation field. Both automobile and air transportation have demanded major public facilities from urban governments. The automobile and its roads have radically altered the face of the city and certainly promise to continue doing so. Air transit has made less of an impact to date, but in the future its effects could be as brutal and as decisive as those of the auto.

A second major and direct impact of technology upon government services is the growing demand for worker retraining. Note has already been taken of the rapid and continuing obsolescense of worker skills. While private industry has assumed some of the burden of retraining, the high rate of unemployment among unskilled workers indicates that industrial efforts have not been sufficient. Thus, to avert the undesirable consequences of unemployment, government, including local government, is being forced into the breach with a whole new set of educational programs.

Indirectly, too, technology has generated numerous demands for government services. The social instability noted above, for example, creates demands for more and better public safety, health, and welfare services. Increasing material prosperity and the growing availability of leisure time stimulate demands for parks, recreational facilities, museums, and other kinds of cultural institutions. Finally, technology has increased the speed of obsolescence for capital as well as human resources. Local governments find themselves confronted with more frequent demands for changes in land-use patterns, for the removal of obsolete buildings whether publicly or privately owned, and for the replacement and updating of all kinds of municipal equipment.

Small City Impact. The technological advances have cast some ominously dark clouds over the future of the small urban area. With the reduced labor forces demanded by highly automated factory and office operations, with increasing industrial dependence upon a vast array of professional specialists, and with such public facilities as good museums, technical libraries, and community colleges becoming "necessities," more and more firms are finding it desirable to operate only in communities with relatively large populations. As one urban economist states the consequences:

All in all, when we add together (a) the precariousness of specialization in discretionary goods in the affluent society to (b) the difficulty of supporting a community on the base of a "worker-less" plant to (c) the trend toward more integrated industrial complexes, it is difficult to be sanguine about the economic prospects of small towns or even small cities.[11]

While destroying their industrial base, technology is also eroding the commercial function of small towns. As transportation makes the large shopping centers in the big cities more and more accessible, and as modern merchandising competition increasingly favors the large supermarket and department stores, the commercial centers in small towns find themselves fighting a losing battle in the struggle for survival. As a community's industrial and commercial bases expire, so too does the need for its very existence.

Thus, rural America is witnessing a veritable war of survival by the small community and, unfortunately, the prospects of victory appear dim in the face of present and continuing economic trends.

Local Government Impact. Developments in the communication field, and especially in television, have also had an adverse affect on local government, whether that government is a large metropolis or a rural hamlet. By focusing attention on the glamor of national and international events, the communications industry has given a pale, unattractive cast to local politics and activities. As a consequence, local affairs receive less attention, evoke less concern, and receive less citizen participation than has been or should be the case. In fact, the situation has gotten so bad that one of the advantages sometimes listed for federal involvement in urban problems is the atten-

---

[11] Thompson, *op. cit.*, p. 449.

tion which can be focused on such problems from Washington but not from local city halls.

Summary. Modern technology, then, has wrought changes in industrial and commercial activities, in organizational structure and management, in the demands for city services, and in the functioning of community life. Changes in transportation and communications have been of particular importance, for these, like the city, are the tools of human interaction and interchange, and as "the means of interchange are drastically altered, the nature of the city must also be drastically altered."[12]

THE FORCES OF AFFLUENCE

Modern technology has made possible growing material abundance and prosperity. This is nowhere better reflected than in individual income statistics. For example, in the last 60 years the average American manufacturing worker has had his work week reduced by 30 percent while his wages have increased over 300 percent in constant dollar terms. Furthermore, the outlook is for more of the same. By the year 2000, it is estimated that the average family income will be over $18,000—in terms of present dollar values!

Changes in Consumption Patterns. Such growing wealth is important to cities, for as people gain in affluence, their tastes and consumptive desires change. The poorest man, for example, wants only the necessities for survival; those more wealthy seek some physical luxuries; those still more wealthy seek cultural or aesthetic as well as physical satisfactions. As a main provider of public services, the city is therefore increasingly being asked to provide cultural amenities demanded by an increasing wealthy people.

For example, the demand for more cultural facilities has reached such proportions that new museums, including zoos and aquariums, are currently being opened at the national rate of one every three days. Half of all existing museums in the United States have been established since 1950. And, since 1920, the number

of symphony orchestras in the United States has risen from 100 to more than 1,400.

Furthermore, museums, zoos, aquariums, and symphony orchestras are not the only kinds of cultural facilities which urban people are demanding. Also being sought are libraries, theaters, dramatic performances, art shows, band concerts, community festivals, historical commemorations, and numerous other kinds of artistic, aesthetic, intellectual, and cultural pursuits. Undoubtedly, as material prosperity and personal affluence grow, and as individual leisure time increases, pressures for these and similar kinds of cultural pursuits and facilities will magnify.

The meaning of such changes for cities is quite simple: urban governments are being asked to provide more services aimed at satisfying the cultural and aesthetic needs of the population, while continuing to provide, at a high level, those public services which satisfy the physical needs of the community.

Social Cleavages. A problem of major dimensions for contemporary society is posed by the cleavages that exist between social classes, cleavages based principally on distinctions between race and income, but also on distinctions between such factors as education, ethnic heritage, religion, and neighborhood. To be sure, such cleavages are not new, but a number of factors, including improved communications, growing personal mobility, increasing affluence, and a growing national concern for the plight of the socially and economically dispossessed, are making them increasingly apparent and intolerable on the one hand, increasingly controversial on the other. Their continued presence adds considerable fuel to the flux and instability afflicting society.

Income Segregation. Unfortunately, growing affluence is not evenly divided; there remain pockets of abject poverty, both in the city and in the countryside. These pockets, products of contemporary housing practices, serve only to aggravate established patterns of social class segregation.

In the cities, the poorer classes are increasingly confined in the deteriorating buildings of the core city while persons of middle and upper income status, driven by the human urge to

[12] Willbern, *op. cit.,* p. 14.

seek neighborhood homogeneity and supported by subdivision practices, find themselves segregated in the suburbs. As society grows in size, homogeneous neighborhoods span into whole communities and then into whole clusters of communities. The resulting income segregation quickly becomes a form of class isolation and this, in turn, leads to a whole bevy of social differences. As Wilbur Thompson has noted:

The long standing practice of residential segregation by income class is transformed by sheer size from the relatively innocent act of pursuing personal living amenities into a major impediment to social interaction among classes and to the development of human resources. In an age of rapid and even forced technological change . . . . it could prove to be disastrous to lose contact between classes, from both an economic and ideological point of view.[13]

Racial Segregation. Further complicating the social divisions emanating from income segregation is racial segregation. Increasingly, as lawmakers rule out legal segregation, racial segregation becomes based on informal practices rather than formal rules, but this does little to alleviate its harmful effects.

Regardless of their financial capacity, Negroes tend to be relegated to the least desirable housing facilities by a combination of racial and economic prejudices. As a consequence, they too end up in deteriorating core city

[13] Thompson, *op. cit.,* p. 479.

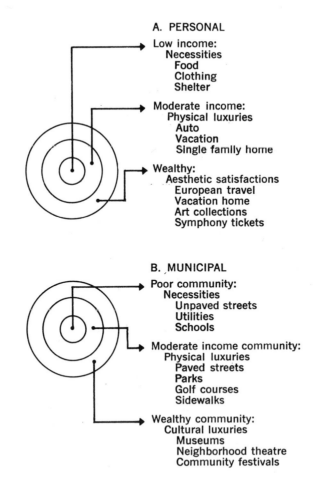

A. PERSONAL

Low income:
  Necessities
    Food
    Clothing
    Shelter

Moderate income:
  Physical luxuries
    Auto
    Vacation
    Single family home

Wealthy:
  Aesthetic satisfactions
    European travel
    Vacation home
    Art collections
    Symphony tickets

B. MUNICIPAL

Poor community:
  Necessities
    Unpaved streets
    Utilities
    Schools

Moderate income community:
  Physical luxuries
    Paved streets
    Parks
    Golf courses
    Sidewalks

Wealthy community:
  Cultural luxuries
    Museums
    Neighborhood theatre
    Community festivals

FIGURE 2-2. *Changes in consumption patterns*

neighborhoods. Because of the racial factor, however, their potential for moving out of these neighborhoods or for merging into middle class society is severely limited. Negroes thus become the victims of both racial and economic degradation.

Isolated as they are from the mainstream of society, the Negroes' plight steadily worsens. Confined to ghetto life, restrained from upward social mobility, exposed constantly to an atmosphere of frustration and despair, and insulated from the attitudes, values, and mores of the rest of society, the cultural gap between the Negro and his suburban neighbor grows steadily greater.

The Consequences. Homogeneous neighborhood groupings, then, are creating a class society in a nation that has always prided itself on being classless. Housing practices create the pattern by segregating income and racial groups. Such segregation, in turn, decreases interclass communication and understanding. The results manifest themselves in the form of racial tension and violence.

While suburbia still stands as a dike protecting the comfortable middle class from the slew of social problems caused by segregating the economically and socially dispossessed in older core cities, it is probable that, unless the impact of such segregation is lessened, the unrest and upheaval will soon overrun city-suburban boundaries. The threats posed by this situation are not theoretical, they are already apparent.

SUMMARY: THE IMPACT OF URBANISM

The forces of urbanism, then, are largely the forces of population growth accompanied by technological innovation, social change, social segregation, and resource allocation problems. Their principal social manifestations are two: (1) people are living under conditions of increasing population density, and (2) virtually all of American society is coming under the web of urban influence. As one writer has noted, "the idea of the city is becoming indistinguishable from the idea of society."[14]

The new urbanism is thus all pervasive: all

[14] Webber, *op. cit.*, p. 23.

of society is being drawn into the web of cultural forces emanating from the large population clusters. Further, the bigger the cluster, the more dominant are the forces. Just as American society has been transformed from a rural to an urban society, so too its orientation toward life is changing from rural to urban. Because it requires whole new life styles, this new urban orientation demands new attitudes, new values, new mores—a whole new culture. Obviously such a vast, total transformation has a transcending impact on the work of those who must shape and manage the environment in this evolving milieu: the urban administrators.

The Problems of the City

The new social milieu and the changing role it demands of urban governments has not eased the problems of urban areas; it has merely added new problems to an already overloaded portfolio of difficulties. This section will describe the problems of the urban milieu, including the old problems, the new problems, and the problems of the future.

THE CONTINUING PROBLEMS

These are problems which have plagued cities in the past, plague them today, and will continue to plague them in the future.

Economic Development. All communities are caught up in a Darwinian struggle for survival: they either must grow and prosper economically or face stagnation and decline. Since the latter is never a palatable alternative, incessant pressure is directed at urban leaders to "attract industry to our town." Yet, as noted earlier, problems of industrial development are becoming increasingly severe for the small, non-metropolitan community. They are also leading to fierce competition between metropolitan municipalities, despite the affluence of today's society.

Transportation. The advent of the automobile loosened a whole host of transportation problems for urban America. Quickly establishing itself as the primary means of human mobility, the automobile has begotten a number of serious dilemmas. For example, it requires broad streets and copious parking facilities; yet as more land is devoted to these purposes, less is available for the residential, commercial, and industrial developments that attract the automobile drivers initially. Furthermore, every attempt that has been made to satisfy the automobile's demand for land has been met with an increase in the number of automobiles demanding space. Meanwhile, the congestion of urban streets increases and even improvements in public transportation appear to have had little effect on the problem. Wilfred Owen, in his book *The Metropolitan Transportation Problem*, sums up the problem in these words:

We have the assurance that the problem of congestion in urban areas has been precipitated by the automobile; that the automobile, on the contrary, has been our escape from congestion; that the automobile and mass transportation are both guilty of promoting congestion; and finally that neither is the primary culprit, but rather a host of other factors that have resulted, thanks to modern technology, in the successful attempt to crowd too many people and too much economic activity into too little space.[15]

Thus the transportation problem is so far from being solved that it is not even clear whether the automobile causes congestion, by making it possible for more people to move about more easily, or whether it alleviates congestion by facilitating the spread of activities over a greater area. Given the critical importance of transportation to human interaction, and thus to urbanism, few problems are so vexing or so impervious to solution as is the transportation dilemma.

Housing. The housing problem in urban America takes three different forms. The first, found largely in the big cities, is the renovation or elimination of blighted, deteriorated, and otherwise obsolete housing stock and the simultaneous provision of suitable replacement housing for the residents of those structures being eliminated. Besides the physical problems of renewal and relocation, a major concern,

and one usually overlooked, is the sociological impact upon the affected residents.

The second form of the problem occurs primarily in the older suburbs of large cities. It consists of preventing neighborhood blight and deterioration by the enforcement of housing codes and land use restrictions. A major problem here is to secure the compliance of property owners, hopefully through voluntary methods.

The third form of the housing problem is the control of new housing development, including the adoption and enforcement of adequate subdivision control ordinances, building codes, and zoning measures. The purpose obviously is to secure the most desirable form of land development.

Land Utilization and Regulation. Among urban problems, those related to land utilization are of relatively recent origin, but their severity increases in direct proportion to the increases in urban population. Today's cities are filled with examples of haphazard land development, more frequently known as "urban sprawl." Proper land utilization is aimed at achieving a harmonious blending of different land uses in a manner designed to protect the public health and safety by promoting the economic, aesthetic, and social goals of the community.

The urgency of sound land utilization policies is being increased by two factors: increasing population density, which intensifies the use of land, and technological advancements, which tend to render land improvements obsolete long before those improvements have served their potential useful life. The product of the latter of course are such things as abandoned factories, vacant stores, and unused railroad rights-of-way, all of which constitute an unhealthy, unsafe, unseemly, and unproductive use of urban land.

Water Supply and Conservation. The problem of protecting and conserving water supplies has long bothered the big city, but now it plagues even the small, rural community. The problem is manifold. It involves the protection of water for drinking, recreational, and other uses; it includes both surface and underground water resources. Only recently has it been real-

---

[15] Wilfred Owen, THE METROPOLITAN TRANSPORTATION PROBLEM (Washington, D.C.: The Brookings Institution, rev. ed., 1966), p. 24–25.

ized that water, like other natural resources, can be exhausted by indiscriminate use. Hence it is necessary not only to maintain the purity of existing water resources, but to conserve the supply of such resources as well. The solution of water supply problems, critical for every community, is rendered even more complex by the fact that water resources in any one geographic location are of major concern to an entire region and to all of the local, state, national, and even foreign governments serving that region.

Law Enforcement. Like other urban services, law enforcement is becoming increasingly complex. Social change and its accompanying instability; economic and racial segregation; the growing cleavage and lack of rapport between rich and poor; the lack of understanding and communication between age groups; and the simple fact of population density all tend to increase social friction and thus generate problems for law enforcement personnel. The result of such trends is currently manifested in the rapidly escalating crime rates and in the rising incidence of public demonstrations. As population density increases, and certainly if the stress of urban living continues to increase, the challenges and problems of urban law enforcement will continue to multiply.

It is now becoming increasingly apparent that the very nature of the law enforcement officer's job is radically changing. In the past, his function has been largely, if not exclusively, the prevention of crime and the apprehension of criminals. Increasingly, however, he finds himself called upon to serve as a community relations officer responsible for maintaining harmony between groups and promoting community welfare.

Public Health. The urban health plagues of past decades have well demonstrated the need for public health services, and the relative absence of such plagues in contemporary times demonstrates the efficiency with which those services are now being provided. Growing urban population density, however, is adding yet another dimension to the problems of public health: statistics indicate that the incidence of mental health problems is apt to increase significantly as population density increases. The

protection of the public's mental health now offers challenging new horizons to the urban health specialist.

Other kinds of challenges are also being raised by contemporary trends in the public health field. Many health professionals are now calling for "comprehensive health planning," with all that the term implies. Being sought, for example, are the establishment of "problem sheds" (effective large-scale service areas) for the organization of health services, the coordination of efforts to increase the interrelationship between the concepts of "public health" and "private health," and the formulation of comprehensive health centers to supplement and replace existing fractionated health facilities and services. Such new dimensions in the public health field are a main point of emphasis in the volume *Community Health Services* published by the International City Managers' Association[16] (now the International City Management Association).

Finance. Urban governments have traditionally been strained by a myriad of financial difficulties, including inadequate taxing powers, unrealistic tax levy limitations, and overly complicated and restricted bonding powers. More recent years have seen: (1) the proliferation of governments dependent upon the property tax, (2) the transfer of most taxable wealth from real to intangible forms of property, and (3) a steadily growing demand for urban government services. These have simply magnified long-standing financial problems.

Staffing. City employees have traditionally been home-grown products. Even those holding administrative positions have frequently started in their department in an unskilled capacity and gradually worked their way into top positions. Such a method of personnel development, however, is no longer adequate given the technical nature of governmental operations and the professional expertise they require.

Tomorrow's city administrator, whether he be an administrator, a department head, or a technical specialist, must be a highly trained and skilled professional, one who bears his pri-

---

[16] International City Managers' Association, COMMUNITY HEALTH SERVICES (Washington, D.C.: The Association, 1968).

mary allegiance to his profession and who views his employing city as the environment in which he can obtain the ultimate proficiency in his particular competence. A primary personnel challenge facing the contemporary urban government, then, is that of recruiting professionally and technically competent employees, fostering their sense of professionalism, and guaranteeing them maximum satisfaction in the exercise of their specialization.

Undoubtedly the most critical personnel problem, however, is that of staffing: the recruitment, training, and promotion of employees. Present trends and comprehensive studies, especially those of the Municipal Manpower Commission,[17] indicate that a severe shortage of professional, administrative, and technical manpower is developing for urban governments. Pressure for increased educational prerequisites for certain key positions such as policemen are further exacerbating the problem. The indicated and apparent shortage is so severe that the situation now appears to be desperate at best, hopeless at worst.

Intergovernmental Relations. The byproduct of federalism and local government proliferation is an urban governing system characterized by: (1) several quasi-autonomous governments (county, city or village, school district, special districts) exercising jurisdiction over the same land area, while (2) numerous governments provide the same governmental services to different portions of a single socioeconomic area (nearly 300 cities and villages serve the Chicago metropolitan area). The consequence, of course, is a tangled web of jurisdictional responsibilities in urban government, a web which is capable of providing effective government only when nurtured by a high degree of cooperation among the individual governing units.

As urban areas grow, the web of jurisdictional relationships becomes more and more tangled, the potentialities for friction among governmental units escalates geometrically, the need for cooperation becomes increasingly urgent, and the difficulty of achieving cooperation

is magnified. The management of intergovernmental relations thus becomes a task requiring increasing time and skill on the part of the urban administrator.

This proliferation of urban governments, accompanied as it is by the fragmentation of the local tax base, magnifies the need for both cooperation among units of local government and more harmonious relationships between governments at the national, state, and local levels. The growing severity of social problems, the increasing financial dependence of local governments upon grants-in-aid, and the dawning recognition of the absurdity of jurisdictional conflicts between units or levels of government have combined to produce a new concept of intergovernmental relationships called *cooperative federalism.* Under this concept, public problems are attacked, neither by the assignment of responsibility for each problem to a particular level (national, state, local) of government nor by the independently conceived and executed action of one or more governments, but rather by the cooperative action of several levels of government, each contributing its special expertise to the effort.

Thus, cooperative federalism is an operational strategy for American governance involving the utilization of inputs from several governments in a coordinated effort at problem resolution or program administration. It has perhaps been most effectively implemented in the welfare field: the national government provides most of the financial resources and general welfare program guidelines; state governments develop, supervise, and enforce basic policies and regulations governing the administration of welfare programs; and local governments provide the manpower, administrative expertise, and local problem familiarity needed to execute the day-to-day work of aiding society's less fortunate members.

While the concept of cooperative federalism offers a much more practical approach to the solution of large scale public problems than the division of responsibility characteristic of traditional federalism, it is neither an unmixed blessing nor a sure cure for all such problems. It too adds to the complexity of intergovernmental relations, complicates program admin-

---

[17] Municipal Manpower Commission, GOVERNMENT MANPOWER FOR TOMORROW'S CITIES (New York: McGraw-Hill, 1962).

istration, and adds new dimensions to the challenges confronting urban administrators.

THE NEW PROBLEMS: "PEOPLE PROBLEMS"

The urban problems already discussed are of two general kinds: structural problems involving the physical form and operation of the urban area and administrative problems concerning the management of the city. In addition, urban areas now find themselves confronted with a new breed of problems: people problems. These fall into three categories: those involving services to individuals, those concerned with the cultural habitat of the city, and those related to the political responsiveness of the community's decision-making processes. Each will be discussed in turn.

Service Problems. Many of the services provided to individuals by urban governments are not new. Education, welfare, medical care, recreational programming, these and related services have long been part of the urban portfolio. The problems of the sixties—the unemployment of unskilled family heads and youth, educational deficiencies, social isolation, hereditary poverty, and subcultural barriers to communication and their accompanying symptoms, crime, juvenile delinquency, economic dependency, and racial tensions—are posing vast new demands for municipal services.[18]

Because these problems are just now being fully recognized, too little programming has yet been scheduled to resolve them in most municipalities. Further, many of the programs thus far designed—the so-called "war on poverty" programs—have been hampered by extensive, often excessive controversy. Sometimes they have even bypassed city hall in their execution. Thus the record of urban governments in this area remains largely unmade. Yet, it is in precisely this area that the success or failure of urban government will ultimately be measured, for as one urban expert acknowledged:

The primary function of the municipality is to foster the enhancement and development of its citizens rather than to engage in the scramble for new industries, subdivisions, and sources of revenue.[19]

Environmental Problems. While it is true that the city should foster and accentuate cultural variety, a cohesive society must inevitably place some limits upon the scope of allowable individual behavior and demand certain other kinds of behavior from its residents. For example, urban society in the United States does not condone garbage dumping on streets or keeping chickens in residential areas. It demands some knowledge of the English language and compliance with civil laws. At present, urban society is also taking a firmer attitude against all forms of racial, religious, and ethnic discrimination.

Traditionally, the American city has played a massive role in integrating the hordes of immigrants from foreign lands. Although the flow of foreign-born is declining, problems of cultural assimilation remain great, particularly because of the urban in-migration of poor rural residents, but also because assimilation problems are now stemming from at least four different sources: (1) racial minorities, especially where social barriers have erected notable differences in life styles;[20] (2) cultural minorities, including both new immigrants and the descendents of former immigrants who have stayed in their ethnic ghettos; (3) persons of rural background who have emigrated to urban areas; and (4) urbanites who have moved from one urban environment to a different urban environment, such as migrants from the core city to the suburbs or migrants from a midwestern region to an east coast community.

As population density and human mobility increase, as more people interact with more other people, the friction that can emanate from interaction between different cultural patterns, practices, and values will have much more explosive potential for society. Further, problems of individual adjustment to changing

---

[18] Norvel Smith, "Human Development in Urban Communities," lecture delivered at the 50th Annual Conference of the International City Managers' Association, September 28, 1964.

[19] Desmond L. Anderson. "Achieving Community Consensus," PUBLIC MANAGEMENT, March, 1961, p. 62.

[20] Reference to racial minorities here includes Mexican, Spanish American, Asiatic, and American Indian minorities as well as Negroes. In fact, some of the most severe problems of cultural assimilation are those involving the American Indian.

social conditions are apt to be further inflamed by cultural variations.

To minimize these problems, government, and especially urban government, must concern itself with the tasks of human integration and cultural assimilation in a much more intensive manner. Governmental programs directed at these problems must not seek a homogeneous society for that in itself would be inconsistent with the city's goal of maximizing varieties in life style opportunities. Rather it must achieve a degree of social conformity consistent with the requisites of a national culture while fostering greater popular understanding and acceptance of the cultural traits of others. In short, it is becoming increasingly important that government actively promote the evolution of a more tolerant society.

Political Problems. As they grow, urban areas must also adjust to changing political conditions. Popular participation in government and the political responsiveness of public leaders are very different commodities in large cities, teeming suburbs, and small villages. Each type of community has its own form of grass-roots democracy, but the form can be very different in each case. No one form is necessarily superior to any other form; each is constructed to meet the demands of a different kind of environment. It must be recognized, however, that changes in the political process frequently accompany changes in the size, structure, or demographic characteristics of a community, and that care must be taken to maintain a proper synthesizing of city programs with the dominant attitudes and values of a city's changing population.

Sometimes changes in size, structure, and demographic characteristics require modifications in the form of urban government, such as a switch from a ward to an at-large system of electing councilmen; at other times changes in city personnel might be necessary, such as modifications which assure minority group representation on elected bodies or the employment of more minority group members in such sensitive administrative agencies as the police department; and, finally, in still other instances simple responsiveness to the needs and demands of new groups in the community will suffice. In any event, urban leaders, both elected and appointed, must recognize that political responsiveness becomes a harder and more complex task as the size and diversity of the population served increases.

Problems of political responsiveness are most likely to be found in either of two different kinds of settings. The first, and most widely recognized, is that in which a new group either moves into a community or rapidly increases its percentage of the community's total population. Difficulties are frequently encountered in reflecting the views and attitudes of the new group in policy-making processes. This situation today is most frequently encountered in communities experiencing a heavy in-migration of Negroes, but it is not restricted to racial situations. Another common setting is the rural community which has experienced a heavy in-migration of employees for a new industry, with a resulting political cleavage between the "newcomers" and the "oldtimers."

A second setting particularly sensitive to problems of political responsiveness is found in the community experiencing rapid population growth. One of the major challenges confronting such a government is that of bridging the gap between large populations on the one hand and the traditional intimacy of personal participation in small local government on the other hand.

Problems of political responsiveness may seem highly academic to many participants in urban government, yet the failure to perceive such problems as real is a fundamental failing behind many of the political difficulties extant in contemporary urban societies. Unfortunately, those possessing political power or influence are rarely cognizant of their own shortcomings, including their own failure to respond adequately to all segments of the community. Yet such response is essential both to the maintenance of traditional political values and to the continued viability of the system of local government itself.

The problem of assuring political responsiveness is one of the major challenges confronting urban government.

A. The Problems

B. The Administrator

The Continuing Problems

Economic development
Transportation
Housing
Land utilization and regulation
Water supply and conservation
Law enforcement
Public health
Finance
Staffing
Intergovernmental relations

The New Problems—"People Problems"

Unemployment
Educational deficiencies
Social isolation
Communication barriers
Emigrant assimilation
Sub-cultural frictions
Political responsiveness

The Urban-Suburban Problems

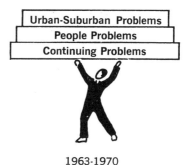

Poverty
Prejudice
Crime

Problems of the Future

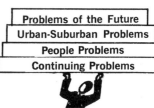

Disappearance of economic incentives
  as a guide to human behavior
Accelerating pace of technological
  and social change
The "cultural lag" of government
  policy
Population density

FIGURE 2-3.   *The problems of the city*

URBAN-SUBURBAN PROBLEMS:
POVERTY, PREJUDICE, CRIME

For most Americans, the problems of big city living have become deeply depressing. The most worrisome of these problems are not the noise, dirt, and congestion traditionally associated with the big city—these are manageable problems—they are the problems of poverty, prejudice, and crime which sorely beset the cities and, as a consequence, all of society.

Poverty, prejudice, and crime are the hard problems. They are not manageable problems: they have no apparent cure. They are not chronic problems that can be ignored: the poor and the disadvantaged have learned to give powerful expression to their plight and deprivation. They are not problems that can be solved by those personally afflicted with them: too often these people are being victimized by economic forces beyond their control. They are not problems that can be suppressed: the Judeo-Christian tradition that dominates the nation's culture frowns on the suppression of human misery. They are not even problems that can be contained within the core city: today the poor have too much mobility, the segregated have too much affluence, and the deprived have too much pride to accept containment as second-class citizens.

What the complacent white suburbanite of the 1960's has failed to realize is that the problems of the big city ghetto—the problems of poverty, prejudice, and crime—can no more be contained within the central city than the armies of Hitler's Third Reich could have been contained within Germany by policies of appeasement. Suburban complacency today tends to write off poverty, prejudice, and crime as big city problems, not realizing that they are regional in scope, that they are suburban as well as urban problems, and that they can be solved only by the enlightened involvement of the entire urban and suburban area.

There are many reasons why suburbanites must join with their big city neighbors in seeking to understand and resolve these problems, but three are of special impact.

First, it is simply in the suburbanites' own best long-range interest to do so. The problems plaguing the big city will, if left unresolved, plague the suburbs tomorrow. Three forces are already at work which dictate that these problems will inevitably become suburban problems. The first is urban renewal which is steadily clearing out the old neighborhoods of the big cities, sending the poor in search of new homes. Each such project tends to move more and more residents farther from the core of the big city and closer to suburban environs. The second is the inevitable aging of suburban residences. As these homes continue to grow older, they will be less attractive to middle class residents and more attractive and available to lower class persons. Finally, the suburban quest for industrial development also acts as a magnet, attracting society's less fortunate members to suburbia. Such industries need workers, not only of the white-collar, professional variety, but also of the blue-collar, skilled and unskilled variety. Since most people prefer to live as close to work as possible, the development of skilled and unskilled jobs in suburban industries inevitably leads to housing demands by and for such workers.

The second principal reason why suburbanites must join with their neighbors in seeking to resolve the problems of poverty, prejudice, and crime is that survival, not just of suburbia, but of all society depends upon it. As the *Report of the National Commission on Civil Disorders,* the so-called Kerner Commission Report, has pointed out:

Segregation and poverty have created in the racial ghetto a destructive environment totally unknown to most white Americans.

What white Americans have never fully understood—but what the Negro can never forget—is that white society is deeply implicated in the ghetto. White institutions created it, white institutions maintain it, and white society condones it.[21]

Worse yet, the Commission also warned:

Discrimination and segregation have long permeated much of American life; they now threaten the future of every American. . . .

To pursue our present course will involve the continuing polarization of the American com-

---

[21] REPORT OF THE NATIONAL ADVISORY COMMISSION ON CIVIL DISORDERS (New York: Bantam Books, 1968), p. 2.

munity and, ultimately, *the destruction of basic democratic values.*[22]

Finally, suburbia must join in the fight against poverty, prejudice, and crime simply because it is the right thing to do: it is the action dictated by the philosophical foundations of the nation's cultural heritage. In a nation committed to the political premise of equality before the law for all men, and in a society guided by the Judeo-Christian precept of love for fellow men, there is simply no other path that can be followed in right conscience.

Poverty, prejudice, and crime, then, are the hard problems facing today's urban and suburban governments alike. Whether the nation's governing system—the tiers of national, state, and local government and the web of local governments—can work together to resolve these basic problems may well provide the ultimate test of the efficacy of democratic federalism in the decades to come. Whether suburban governments can address themselves meaningfully and constructively to the hard core urban problems now centered in the core cities might well be the key question that determines their ability to survive as autonomous units of government.

That these questions pose a threat to the survival of present forms of local government is a question about which there can be little doubt. Too many observers of local government have issued warnings about the system's survival:

The threat of the eroded central city and the crazy-quilt triviality of suburbia is the threat to destroy the potential of our maintaining and reconstructing meaningful political communities at the local level. What has been treated as a threat to our physical well-being is in reality a threat to our capacity to sustain an active local civic life.[23]

The dire danger of a continuing trend toward the accumulation of low-income, minority families in the core city and wealthier whites in the suburb must be recognized for what it threatens, politically, socially, and humanely.[24]

There is still a distinct possibility that present systems of government in metropolitan areas will be abruptly changed. Such changes . . . may be internally caused by the accumulated weight of problems that were only partially or temporarily alleviated by satisfying expedients. Race riots are a product of this latter category.[25]

Local governments currently have what may be their last chance to show that they can largely work out the problems of the area which they commonly occupy.[26]

These warnings have been officially sanctioned by governmental agencies. The Advisory Commission on Intergovernmental Relations, for example, has pointed out that:

The aggravation of fiscal disparities among local governmental jurisdictions in metropolitan areas has ominous implications for the future economic and social base of American society and its cities. . . . The gap between the have and the have not jurisdictions in metropolitan areas is great and widening rapidly. . . . *The United States simply can no longer afford the economic and social erosion now destroying the very foundations of our urban society.*[27]

Further expression of concern for this situation has come from numerous other governmental agencies. Typical, for example, is the following statement by the U.S. Department of Health, Education, and Welfare:

Almost 20 percent of all Americans—more than the entire population of Canada—live in abject poverty and despair. They are deprived of the basic advantages which should be the rightful heritage of Americans.

Millions are crowded into the slum areas of America's cities, living without comfort, and without hope, and serving as an ever present bad conscience for the affluent majority. The poor know only too well the extent of the gap between the opportunities enjoyed by this majority and their

---

[22] *Ibid.*, p. 1, italics added.

[23] Norton E. Long, "Citizenship or Consumership in Metropolitan Areas," JOURNAL OF THE AMERICAN INSTITUTE OF PLANNERS, February, 1965, pp. 4–5.

[24] Mitchell Gordon, SICK CITIES (New York: The Macmillan Co., 1963), p. 345.

[25] James M. Banovetz, PERSPECTIVES ON THE FUTURE OF GOVERNMENT IN METROPOLITAN AREAS (Chicago: Center for Research in Urban Government, Loyola University, 1968), pp. 16–17.

[26] John C. Bollens, "Approaches to Metropolitan Problems: Revolution and Evolution," ARIZONA STATE UNIVERSITY PUBLIC AFFAIRS BULLETIN, Vol. 6, No. 1, 1967, p. 4.

[27] Advisory Commission on Intergovernmental Relations, FISCAL BALANCE IN THE AMERICAN FEDERAL SYSTEM, VOLUME 2, METROPOLITAN FISCAL DISPARITIES (Washington, D.C.: The Commission, 1967), pp. 4–5, 7–8, italics in the original.

own—they can't seem to bridge that gap. Some riot in the streets—violent, alienated men with nothing to lose. *It is increasingly clear that Americans will either have to abolish the slums or the slums will destroy the very fabric of our society.*[28]

It has by now become abundantly clear that the central cities of metropolitan areas cannot, by themselves, resolve the hard core problems. Thus the sole remaining hope for a local resolution of such issues lies in core city–suburban cooperation. One of the other challenges for local government then lies in the suburbs' ability to find methods of cooperating with the core cities in a constructive, reasoned approach to the solution of problems emanating from poverty, prejudice, and crime. This in turn may well require that the suburbs provide more than moral, financial, and personal leadership: it may dictate that the suburbs shoulder some of the burdens of housing those who now are confined to the impoverished, segregated, crime-prone neighborhoods of the central city.

Solving this vital problem is thus a dominant challenge facing today's urban government. As Robert F. Kennedy noted:

What is at stake is not just the fate of the (disadvantaged) in America; at stake is the fate of all America, of the legacy of our past and the promise of our future.[29]

PROBLEMS OF THE FUTURE

Social scientists take great pleasure in speculating about the future of society. They are now, for example, projecting three important changes in the style of life in the future. These are: (1) a wider living space—individuals will range over a greater geographic area during their lifetime; (2) a wider choice of living environment—increasing mobility and affluence will enable people to select between a much wider range of habitats for their residential location, and more families will have

homes in two or more habitats; and (3) a wider community of interest—individuals will continue to be less interested in local events and more interested in the broader society and its affairs, leaving local government increasingly in the hands of professionals.[30]

Despite the difficulties of prognostication, it is also possible to enumerate several other changes that will affect the urban area of the future and the demand for the services of urban governments.

One major change in the future will be the gradual disappearance of economic incentives as the dominant basis for human action. Other forms of motivation must be developed to keep people constructively occupied and to replace the cultural values and norms that presently emanate from conditions of economic scarcity. While many have predicted the disappearance of such incentives, few have speculated about the resulting social consequences. For urban governments, it can readily be suggested that they will have to cope with more people spending more time in residential neighborhoods and making more demands for facilities and activities that will make constructive use of their leisure time.

Note has already been taken of the accelerating pace of technological and social change and the effect of that change upon human life. Change, for example, tends to produce conditions of instability and uncertainty which, in turn, generate personal anxieties and tension. Since change produces problems of social adjustment and mental health, and since the pace of change can only be expected to increase, it is obviously important that ways be found to ameliorate its affects. In other words, ways must be found to improve human adaptability to change.

Human needs and expectations change as rapidly as do the conditions of life within society. Cultural institutions, including government, tend to respond to changing needs and expectations slowly, thereby creating a "cultural lag." Such cultural lag obviously must be

---

[28] U.S. Department of Health, Education, and Welfare, A CITY FOR MAN (Washington, D.C.: The Department's Center for Community Planning, 1968), p. 5, italics added.

[29] Robert F. Kennedy, "Policies to Combat Negro Poverty," in Brian J. L. Berry and Jack Meltzer, eds., GOALS FOR URBAN AMERICA (Englewood Cliffs, N.J.: Prentice-Hall, 1967), p. 132.

[30] John Friedman and John Miller, "The Urban Field," JOURNAL OF THE AMERICAN INSTITUTE OF PLANNERS, November, 1965, pp. 316–17.

minimized if human institutions are to continue satisfying the needs which gave rise to their creation. Thus, government must be prepared to modify more rapidly its structures, procedures, and even its values if it is to stay attuned to the expectations of the people it serves.

Needless to say, the future also holds all of the problems emanating from population growth and density, technological change, economic affluence, social cleavage, and the other forces that were outlined and described earlier.

In a very real sense, then, the problems of the future will not be quantitative problems of providing public services nearly as much as they will be problems of improving the quality of urban life. As already noted, "The primary function of the municipality is to foster the enhancement and development of its citizens."[31] As still another urban observer has noted:

A great deficiency of American cities, and of legal regulations which have been devised to meet quantitative needs, is that they have developed with only the most primitive concept of the values to be achieved in urban life. . . . Only now, with technology solving our quantitative problems, have we an excess of energy which we can devote to achieving quality. And high time it is, for quite the most important land planning problem facing this generation is how to make urban life humane and worthwhile. In a world which has become almost too travelable, we must create a feeling of attachment and commitment, of zest and well-being. To realize our dreams, we must build urban organisms which, in Antigone's words, "live not for today and yesterday, but forever."[32]

The Policy Issues

The forces of change and the problems emanating therefrom obviously present urban administrators, and their superiors, elected urban officials, with the task of resolving numerous and very critical policy issues. While the specific nature of these issues varies from community to community and from metropolitan area to metropolitan area, it is possible to sketch, in very general terms, the basic designs which those policies must seek to achieve. The following paragraphs will undertake such a sketch.

COMMUNITY DESIGN

Urban officials in the future must continue and intensify their concern with the design of urban areas. Community design problems, for example, will involve planning and control over land use for the purpose of:

1. Improving the spatial relationships between various land functions. The irrational and uncoordinated jungle of land uses characteristic of so many urban areas, and particularly of the older portions of such areas, must be replaced with planned land use designs which will facilitate higher density living, improvements in transportation systems, and generally upgrade the aesthetic quality of life.

2. Land reclamation programs must be instituted to insure that all land within the urban area is being utilized, in the first place, and utilized most effectively, in the second place. Some planners, for example, anticipate the initiation of urban land rotation schemes under which all urban land uses will be re-evaluated at periodic intervals, such as 30 to 50 years, with inefficient land uses being converted to more productive purposes.

3. Realistic transportation policies must be formulated which will give due recognition to demands and preferences for private transportation, yet which will also optimize the benefits that can be received from public means of transport. Transportation planning must go hand in hand with land use planning to optimize the contribution which each can make to the success of the other.

4. The role and function of central business districts must also be made a point of central concern. It is around the central business district that community life has traditionally been oriented, and the survival of a community's individual identity might well depend upon the future strength of this district as a focal point for community activities, whether those activities be commercial, recreational, educational, or cultural.

---

[31] Anderson, *op. cit.*
[32] Jesse Dukeminier, Jr., "Forward: The Coming Search for Quality," UCLA LAW REVIEW, March, 1965, pp. 708–9.

5. Most important of all, urban design policies must deal with the problem of space. With growing population densities, space becomes a very scarce and precious resource. It is of critical importance on two counts: adequate space must be provided for a vast array of different activities and each individual must have sufficient space to minimize the psychological difficulties caused by population density. It is entirely possible, for example, that urban officials might be called upon to construct and enforce space allocation designs or formulas as a means of accomplishing those two goals.

HUMAN DEVELOPMENT NEEDS

The most critical policy issues of the future will be those concerned with human development. As already noted, the importance of such development will become increasingly critical as a consequence of population density, technological development, personal affluence, and the increased availability of leisure time. Urban officials of the future will have to formulate policies dealing with several different aspects of human development needs.

In the first place, officials should seek to maximize the unique benefits afforded by urbanism: the ability to satisfy simultaneously human demands for neighborhood homogeneity in an atmosphere of maximum cultural variety. As one observer views the future:

Rather than a "mass culture" in a "mass society," the long-term prospect is for a maze of subcultures within an amazingly diverse society organized upon a broadly shared cultural base. This is the important meaning that the American brand of urbanization holds for human welfare.[33]

Current events make a second human development need confronting urban officials painfully obvious: policies must be developed and implemented which will insure racial, ethnic, and cultural integration while continuing to permit and promote diversity in life styles.

A third major human development need confronting urban officials is education. The technological society of the future will require higher levels of basic or initial education, vastly expanded facilities for vocational training and retraining, and multitudinous opportunities for avocational development.

THE PROBLEM OF POLITICS

In a technological society of increasing size and complexity, responsibility for urban policy development and implementation will necessarily and increasingly fall into the hands of professionals, highly trained administrative, professional, and technical persons who devote their full time and skill to problems of urban living. As elected urban officials find themselves obliged to rely more and more upon the advice and competence of such persons, and as the staffs of urban governments increase in size, the potential incompatibility of democracy, bureaucracy, and technocracy will compel the development of new, more effective policies and procedures aimed at ensuring the political responsiveness of urban governments and their employees.

Management in the New Milieu

It is inevitable that the forces of change in urban areas, and the problems and policy issues emanating therefrom, should have a substantial impact on the management of urban government. Clearly the large urban areas of the future will require municipal management on a much more complex and sophisticated scale as the growth of cities and counties and the forces of change bring alterations in the basic nature as well as the scale of urban government. At least six changes of a far reaching nature can already be anticipated, two of a policy nature and four of an administrative nature, and the list will undoubtedly grow as the forces of change make their impact increasingly felt.

THE POLICY CHANGES

Most fundamental of all, the primary concern of urban administrators will shift from a traditional concentration on the management of such line or functional agencies as the police, fire, and public works departments to an intense preoccupation with problems of a policy nature. To be sure, the work of the traditional

---

[33] Webber, *op. cit.*, p. 29.

line departments will grow in importance as urban areas expand, but these concerns will inevitably receive less attention from top level administrative officers as those administrators grapple with the social, economic, spatial, and aesthetic problems of the urban community.

As concern for such problems increases, furthermore, it will become apparent that urban governments will find themselves demanding an accumulation of much more extensive social, economic, and demographic data and relying upon increasingly sophisticated analyses of such data. This, in turn, will lead to the employment of professional social science staffs by urban governments. Social scientists, in fact, will be as important to the city of the future as the civil engineer has been to the city of the past. Several cities have already recognized this

trend with the establishment of new departments concerned with human resource development[34] and students of urban management have regularly been noting that "the municipal official [is becoming] increasingly a new kind of social engineer."[35]

Since the future will demand a more policy-oriented approach to urban management, it will also alter the nature of such management by requiring professional administrators to as-

[34] Oakland, California, pioneered in this field. Its department is discussed further in Chapter 3. Other cities have slowly been following Oakland's lead, particularly as they seek to improve the organizational pattern set up to handle poverty war programs. Chicago's Department of Human Resources is an example of this effort.

[35] Arthur W. Bromage, "Managers Become More Oriented to Human Values," PUBLIC MANAGEMENT, October, 1965, p. 216.

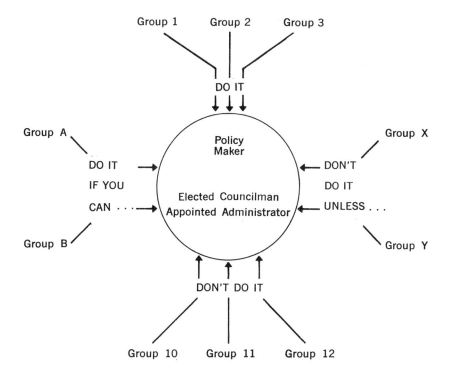

FIGURE 2-4. *The dilemma of the policy maker (As illustrated above, the dilemma is posed by the multitude of different interest groups making a wide variety of demands regarding the resolution of a particular issue or proposal. The policy maker's challenge is therefore to find a solution to the issue or proposal which will be acceptable to all of the interest groups, or, at a minimum, which will not unduly aggravate any of these groups. Since the demands of the groups are often directly contradictory, this challenge poses a major test of the policy maker's creativity and ingenuity.)*

sume the mantle of policy leadership. Whether he is a city or county manager, a chief administrative officer, a department head, or an advisory staff member, the urban administrator will increasingly find himself playing the role traditionally ascribed to the politician: a catalyst in the formulation of urban policy, "brokering" or compromising and satisfying the multitudinous and conflicting demands made by special interest groups. Obviously this function, when added to the administrator's traditional role as advisor and expert witness in the policy formulation process, will make his task far more sensitive and complex.

In his role as "broker" of special interest demands, the urban administrator will find himself responsible for: (1) promoting interaction among interest groups on matters of urban concern; (2) finding solutions to policy problems that will satisfy, in at least a minimal manner, all of the various interests concerned with the problems, (3) providing staff work for formal and informal committees and associations that concern themselves with urban problems, and (4) serving as a complaint department to which those dissatisfied with existing conditions can take their problems, criticisms, and suggestions. All of these brokerage tasks will become increasingly important, but the second will be especially crucial: the success with which it is executed will largely determine the economic and social well-being of the community.

THE ADMINISTRATIVE CHANGES

Management in the new milieu will also be characterized by four administrative alterations. It now appears inevitable that the future will require greater professionalization of employees, more delegation of responsibility by top administrative officials, better internal and external communications systems, and more sophistication in the art of intergovernmental relations by urban units of government.

The complexity of the problems with which urban administration must cope will necessarily require increased emphasis upon the professionalization of governmental employees, especially those below the top executive level, and upon task specialization by employ-

ees at all levels. This has numerous ramifications, including the fact that employee participation in professional organizations should be encouraged if not required, but most importantly it means that there will be an urgent need for more intensive and effective employee training programs both at the career entry level and at midcareer levels. This training must not only seek to upgrade the technical competence of employees, but also to inculcate in them a deeper understanding of the complexities of the problems with which they deal and a greater proficiency in the application of fundamental human relations skills.

Another modification in municipal management, made necessary by the growing complexity of the urban administrator's job, will be the delegation of more and more authority by the administrator to his subordinates. Responsibility for the supervision of routine governmental functions will be delegated with increasing frequency. This, in turn, will require:

1. More dynamic leadership on the part of the urban administrator as he finds it necessary to motivate, stimulate, and control more subordinates who, in turn, are vested with more responsibility and authority;

2. More effective supervisory techniques to achieve better coordination and control of subordinates' work;

3. Improved systems, both formal and informal, for internal reporting, auditing, and control; and

4. Generally more effective systems of internal communication between administrators and their subordinates and between the subordinates themselves.

Just as these dynamics of internal administrative control will be rendered more complex in the future, so too will the urban administrator's systems of external reporting and public relations. If the administrator is going to participate in the process of policy formulation and execution, and if he is to do so in a manner fully compatible with the tenets of democratic theory, then both the quantity and the quality of communication between the administrator and the public which he serves must be maximized.

In the future, furthermore, this will have to

be accomplished despite growing public apathy regarding the affairs of local government and a diminishing identification by the individual citizen with his city and county. Thus municipal management must also be modified to permit administrators to increase both the time which they devote to public relations and the skills with which they handle this task.

Finally, municipal management in the future must be geared to the practice of more intensive intergovernmental relations. As noted earlier, the number of governments in urban areas can be expected to increase steadily, national and state governments can be expected to magnify their concern for urban problems and expand the number of programs through which they manifest this concern, and suburban governments will find themselves drawn increasingly into the web of hard core socioeconomic problems which plague the inner cities. Urban administrators can thus expect to devote both more time and more skill to coordinating the work of their respective governments with the activities of a wide array of other governmental units. They will, in a very real sense, be required to become "diplomats" trained in the science of relations among governments and skilled at working with a multiplicity of governments toward the solution of major problems.

Conclusion

Change is a constant, all-encompassing force that is incessantly and indelibly affecting both the urban place and the job of the urban administrator. Besides elevating it to a position of more critical importance, the forces of change are rendering the administrator's job more difficult, more complex, more challenging, and certainly more exciting.

3

The City and Change:
Programming for Control

THE FIRST TWO CHAPTERS of this book have made two propositions abundantly clear. The first is that urban areas in the United States are caught up in a massive period of growth, expansion, technological change, and veritable cultural revolution—a period that will leave urban areas and, in fact, national life very different from the conditions that existed prior to the beginning of this era. Whether these changes will be constructive or destructive is yet to be decided: the fate of urban society literally hangs in the balance, awaiting a positive response to the challenges being raised by the forces of change.

The second proposition is that the nation's urban governments can no longer confine their activities and concerns to their traditional caretaker functions: public safety, utilities, public works, parks, libraries, regulation of land use, and protection of public health and morals. Environmental conditions and public demands are combining to turn government's focus from the physical needs of people to their social and economic needs. This revised emphasis is typified by such national campaigns as the war on poverty, the civil rights movement, the model cities program, and a national assault on educational problems.

By directing its attention to such programs, the national government has registered a total concern for human social and economic needs as well as the more basic physical requisites of life. State governments also can be expected to

move in the same direction, especially in response to new federal grant programs and legislative reapportionment. If urban governments want to remain viable units in American federalism, if they want to be something more than custodians for American society, then they too must begin to play a leadership role in correcting the social and economic ills of their citizenry and in moving to prevent new problems from arising or old problems from worsening.

To be sure, any discussion of urban government must recognize the monumental achievements produced by the American way of life, its existing governmental system, and its traditional approaches to urban government. American cities today are the largest and wealthiest the world has ever known. They provide, on the average, higher standards of living, greater freedom of personal choice, more cultural variety, and more educational opportunity than have ever been offered by any cities at any time. Further, despite their multitude of problems, their transportation systems move more people to more places more often; they have achieved the world's highest standards of public health; and they make more public utilities available to more people. In short, from a physical sense and when compared with cities of the past, American cities most nearly approximate utopian ideals.

Yet, these same cities are plagued by social turmoil, by rising crime rates, by increased rioting, by growing welfare burdens, and by increasing social stratification. These key indicators of social disintegration indicate that those systems of government which achieved so many successes in the past are no longer fully capable of meeting the problems of the future—the human problems emanating from changing value systems, from increasing population density, and from the ever-quickening pace of technological change.

This third chapter will continue this discussion by pointing out what urban governments can do to adjust to changing conditions and thus to retain their viability within the nation's present governing system. Although acknowledging that two basic kinds of adjustment are needed—political and administrative—this discussion, in keeping with the tone and function of the book, will focus most particularly upon administrative adjustments, upon the alterations needed in the organization and methods with which urban governments conduct their daily business.

Political adjustments, alterations in the way in which urban governments respond to their citizenry, will be described only indirectly and briefly at several points in the chapter and directly only in the closing paragraphs. This comparative paucity of treatment in no way reflects on the relative importance of such changes, however, for no amount of excellence in administrative structure and operations can compensate fully for a governmental unit which has become politically "irrelevant" (i.e. out of touch with its citizens).

Three different levels of administrative response are described in this chapter. The first level suggests a strategy of response, recommending the establishment of community development goals and methodologies designed to transform such goals into meaningful guides to action. The second level deals with programmatic considerations, discussing first the challenge of providing traditional municipal services in urban and metropolitan areas and then describing methods of modifying existing governmental structures to provide urgently needed human development services. Finally, the third level views administrative response from the standpoint of required expertise: it

suggests that the new challenges of urbanism impose requirements for new kinds of administrative expertise, and that urban governments must be prepared to acknowledge and meet these requirements.

The final section of the chapter deals directly with political adjustments to the new urban milieu.

It would be presumptuous to claim that this chapter or this book could provide a complete blueprint for urban problem solving. This is simply not presently possible in any book of any size. What is possible, and what this chapter will seek to do, is to describe ideas and concepts currently being advanced as possible solutions and to suggest basic modifications that should be taken as a first step in the search for guidelines to effective urban development and fulfillment.

Developing a Program for Change

The first, essential prerequisite for governmental adjustment to current problems is a basic alteration of the traditional patterns by which local governments have conducted business. Partly, as already noted, this alteration requires a shift in focus from the traditional caretaker functions of local governments to a greater concern for human or "people" problems. More important, however, must be a change in the way urban governments solve their problems.

The traditional pattern of problem solving consists of two basic elements. The first is a strong tendency to postpone making any decision as long as possible. This approach is akin to the reaction of the ostrich which sticks its head in the sand to avoid danger. To avoid making decisions that might later prove unpopular, local officials frequently procrastinate about problems, hoping the problems will either disappear or solve themselves.

When problems become so pressing that they can no longer be ignored, resort is made to the second step: a course of action will be chosen that appears to alleviate the problem, but which really invokes as little risk of opposition as possible. Short-range concerns, such as existing public attitudes and immediate relief from the problem, are the dominant considerations in the calculations of those who must make the decision. Complex, long-range strategies lacking immediate results or requiring substantial changes rarely find favor among local officials.

Typical of this approach is the common response by local officials to a sharp increase in juvenile delinquency. Commonly adopted solutions include the imposition of a curfew, increased emphasis on police surveillance of juvenile activities, and the imposition of harsher penalties by the courts. Such solutions are obviously not aimed at the root of the problem; they do nothing to rectify the causes of juvenile delinquency. Even when a local government's response to delinquency does include some actions presumably aimed at the causes of delinquency, these actions are too likely to be thoughtlessly shortsighted. Thus, to eliminate delinquency, public officials will sometimes provide more recreational facilities and then erect fences around the facilities to restrict their use to certain, authorized daylight hours.

Such solutions do have a salutory short range effect. They often reduce vandalism at least until juveniles find new ways of evading the police and circumventing the curfew, and until less obvious and more undesirable recreational sites and activities are found to replace the parks and playgrounds.

FIGURE 3-1. *Shortsighted city programming*

The shortcomings of this approach should be clear; the solutions too frequently adopted are the easy solutions. They are those directed to the symptoms of the problem, thus appeasing an aroused public by magnanimous displays of concerted governmental action, but without either striking at the fundamental causes of the problems or evaluating the long-range consequences of the solution upon the basic patterns of communiy life. For example, curfews are frequently praised for getting juveniles off the streets, but rarely criticized for driving them into dark alleys where delinquency and vandalism are encouraged. Nor do curfews contribute anything to the positive development of juveniles into well-adjusted, desirable community residents.

Worst of all, however, such short-term responses are deficient because they are not derived from any previously planned, clearly enunciated set of community goals. Little thought is given to coordinating such solutions with other community programs and little effort is made to relate them to a long-range strategy for community development and improvement.

Over time, the accumulation of short-term solutions concocted to deal with specific problems leaves the community with a hodge podge of rules, regulations, and programs, each of which is designed to alleviate some particular community problem rather than to make a positive contribution to community improvement. In brief, such solutions are defensive measures, intended to ward off the evil effects of society, while what communities really need are well-planned, coordinated, long-term offensive programs aimed at making the community a better, happier place for human life.

AN URBAN DEVELOPMENT SCHEME

A more positive kind of response to urban problem solving is thus one which is offensively oriented: one which seeks solutions to community problems that will, by their implementation, alleviate immediate, short-range needs while simultaneously making a positive contribution to the success of an overall plan for the improvement of community facilities and living patterns. It is impossible, of course, to ensure that any system of governance or administration will either find or implement such problem-solving solutions. Nevertheless, the odds on finding them can be improved if the community has enumerated a clear-cut set of objectives or goals, if it is constantly engaged in gathering and interpreting data on trends affecting goal achievement and community development, if it anticipates problems and acts to correct them before they become critical, and if the formulation of all policies and programs is specifically designed both to contribute to the achievement of community goals and to be consistent with other policies and programs having the same goal centered purpose.

These four ingredients, (1) goal formulation, (2) continuous data collection and analysis, (3) anticipation of problems, and (4) goal centered policy development, constitute the basic framework of an urban development scheme through which communities can gain the offensive in combatting their problems, adjusting to changing social and economic conditions, and building the basis for community development. Each is described further below.

Goal Formulation. The field of management science has long been aware of the critical role played by goals and objectives in organizational leadership. It is well known, for example, that clearly enunciated organizational goals serve as guidelines in policy formulation, direct and stimulate employee activities by casting them in a more meaningful framework, and promote internal consistency in organizational activities. Since urban communities are simply a higher level of human organization, clearly enunciated statements of community goals and objectives can make the same contribution to community government. In fact, to the extent that such goals are not enumerated, efforts at both government and development are hampered.

Certainly the commonplace planning activities carried out by most communities through the development and adoption of a general plan do not serve as a clear statement of community objectives nor as a guide to overall community development. The general plan, as defined by T. J. Kent, is simply, "The official statement of a municipal legislative body which sets forth its major policies concerning *desirable future physical development.*"[1] They are relevant as goal statements only to the extent that they identify, restrict, or encourage the attainment of social and economic objectives.

They fail as general statements of community objectives primarily because they fail to state such objectives. Further, they are designed to deal only with specific governmental functions such as the regulation of land use, the provision of parks, and the location of streets. "These methods are well suited to the unitary setting, i.e., the single client with the single site, in which they were refined, but they have not been as applicable to the complex and mercurial city."[2] Finally, although they have frequently served as successful guides to community physical development, such general plans have totally failed to provide solutions to the growing discontent within urban areas.

Suppose we develop more scientific land-use planning, better community analysis, and better urban design. These are necessary, but . . . . community rates of disease, crime, and other forms of social maladjustment do not appear to have been significantly reduced by such projects.[3]

What is needed, rather, is a statement of concise and pertinent municipal goals and objectives upon which all community policies and programs would be based, including but not restricted to physical development considerations. The typical general plan would be derived from such a document of community objectives since the plan would detail ways of achieving goals and objectives through the regulation of land, provision of community facilities, and development of transportation systems for the circulation of people and trade. In addition, however, a community-objectives

document would provide guidelines for decisions concerning municipal service programs and human development activities.

In short, a community-objectives document, containing a clear, explicit statement of community goals, would seek to deal with the total complexity of urban life, with human as well as environmental considerations, with service as well as developmental functions. It would orient the daily activities of government to specified objectives, offer a vehicle for anticipating and adapting to social and economic changes, and provide a guide to decision making when unforseen opportunities and problems arise.

Despite the apparent value of a community-objectives document, however, the International City Managers' Association estimated in 1965 that only some 30 cities had prepared such a guideline.

Anticipation of Problems. As noted above, local government officials have an unfortunate tendency to procrastinate about problems and defer action on them as long as possible, thereby avoiding the adverse political consequences that might stem from an unpopular action. Certainly it is the tendency of local policy-making bodies, city councils, to wait until problems have become pressing and remedial action is no longer deferable before taking corrective action. Legislative attention thus tends to restrict itself only to problems presently existing and of immediate import.

For administrators, too, the easiest course is to restrict oneself to current, pressing problems. These are the problems about which complaints are being made. These are the problems attracting council interest. They are also the ones which, in the short run, will have the greatest effect on the administrator's reputation and standing in the community. Finally, they are also the problems for which it is easiest to marshal resources toward a solution: to gain appropriations of needed money, to stimulate employee enthusiasm and concern, and to solicit public consensus and support.

Yet, despite the relative ease of attacking them, current problems are also the ones on which an administrator can do the least amount of good. In dealing with them, he

[1] T. J. Kent, The General Urban Plan (San Francisco: Chandler Publishing Co., 1964), p. 18, italics added.

[2] International City Managers' Association, Principles and Practice of Urban Planning (Chicago: The Association, 1968), Chapter 12.

[3] Joseph M. Heikoff, "Planning is the Responsibility of the Executive," Public Management, July, 1965, pp. 158–59.

must spread his attention over several tasks: he must seek to resolve the problem, prevent its future recurrence, and rectify the damage already done by the conditions needing correction.

It is this last step, rectifying the damages, on which the administrator can rarely be very effective. No adequate reparation is possible, for example, to victims of physical violence, to persons who lost valuable time snarled in traffic, to mothers forced by snow-blocked roads to bear children outside hospitals, or to youngsters whose formative years have been blighted by inadequate educational or recreational facilities. There is truth to the old adage that an ounce of prevention is worth a pound of cure. Or, to use more legalistic language, preventive justice is surely more effective than remedial justice. The key, of course, to preventive justice is problem anticipation and resulting action to prepare for the conditions that would give rise to problems.

The challenge of problem anticipation is one of priority in the allocation of time and effort. The first step is to allocate significant segments of prime time and energy to the task. In a sense, the rules here are much like rules for saving money: pay yourself first each payday by making a deposit in a savings account. In the case of time allocation, it is necessary to set aside during each work week fixed time periods during which all attention is devoted to the future, to determining what the future holds, to planning strategies for shaping the future in accordance with community objectives, and to offsetting problems before they arise.

The second step is to make problem anticipation itself a prime objective of the government's administrative organization. Elected policy makers must be made aware of the urgency of planning and problem anticipation. Government employees must be apprised of the necessity and urgency of this task. Everyone in urban government must key his thinking to the future, making problem anticipation a concern which is foremost in his mind.

Finally, the third step in problem anticipation is to collect the relevant information needed to gain insights into what the future holds for the community. Not even expert

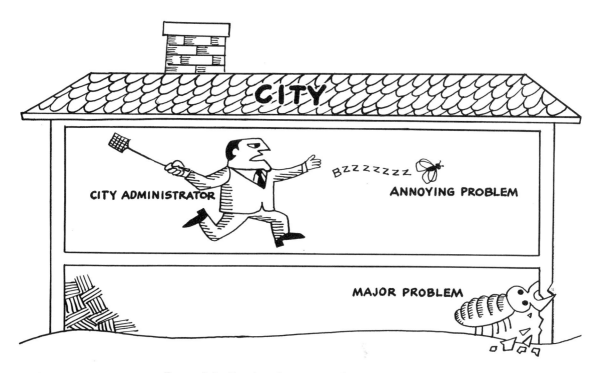

FIGURE 3-2. *Focusing urban concern on important problems*

statisticians or those presumably gifted with extrasensory perception can anticipate the future with a high degree of precision, but nevertheless existing techniques and methodologies are sufficiently accurate to make the effort worthwhile, and, furthermore, advances in data handling techniques are constantly increasing problem anticipation capability.

Even if problem anticipation does not permit advance action to prevent problems from arising, it does at least give local officials an opportunity to plot strategies for coping with problems, limiting their severity, and reducing their adverse impact upon the long-range objectives of community development programs.

Continuous Data Collection and Analysis. A key requisite to both goal formulation and problem anticipation is the constant collection and analysis of data on social, economic, demographic, and political trends within the community and within the larger economic region of which the community is a part. Data collection and analysis are crucial to goal formulation because such formulation is a constant process: once goals are formulated, constant reevaluation of them is necessary to assure their adequacy, desirability, and feasibility. The same data activities are equally important to problem anticipation. In fact, such anticipation is severely hampered, if not rendered virtually impossible, without a constant flow of up-to-date information on trends and developments.

It is because of the pressing need for data for these undertakings—a need daily growing more critical—that urban governments are being urged to add trained social scientists, persons skilled in collecting and analyzing such data, to their top management and planning staffs. Descriptions of what some cities are already doing in this regard are presented later in this chapter.

Goal-Centered Policy Development. Finally, the fourth step in an urban development scheme is goal-centered policy development. This term refers to the practice of deriving all operational policies and programs from the statement of community objectives. It is simply an insistence that all activities be formulated in accordance with the specifications in the

community objectives document. A technique for doing this is described in summary fashion below.

THE TECHNIQUE OF GOAL-CENTERED COMMUNITY PROGRAMMING

Whether coping with present problems or anticipating future problems, the technique of community programming is essentially the same: community objectives should be formulated as a first step and all actual policies and programs should then be derived from the statement of objectives. Suggestions for executing each of these two steps are discussed below.

Formulating Objectives. The task of goal formulation is not one which the professional administrative officer is equipped to perform. Rather, this is a task for the community as a whole, and specifically for the community's elected and appointed policy makers: the members of the city or village council, the planning board, the school board, and similar governmental bodies. Prime responsibility for this task lies with the elected representatives of the community's general government—the city or village council in incorporated areas and the county board in unincorporated areas. They in turn draw upon the expertise and assistance of their own government's professional staff; of the elected and appointed policy makers and administrative staffs of other governmental agencies serving the same area; of the planning commissions, if any, serving the larger socio-economic region of which the community is a part; and finally of the members of any special advisory bodies which the council or board organizes to assist it in the discharge of this responsibility.

What is sought, then, is an expression of attitudes and opinions from all identifiable segments and interest groups in the community, brought together under the aegis of the community's elected policy makers. The goals formulated by any community will only be useful and attainable to the extent that they are based upon and reflect a genuine community consensus. However, since they alone are ultimately responsible for designing the programs needed to achieve the goals that are formulated, the community's policy makers must take final responsibility for deciding what the goals will be, how they will be stated, and what priority will be given to their attainment.

The community-objectives document itself must deal with a wide range of different problems and concerns. It must, in essence, seek to define the particular style of life which the community seeks for its residents. This means that it must concern itself with such basic matters as alternate forms of development, rates of growth, character of the local economy, levels of desired public services, and intensity of urban development. It must seek to define its objectives in terms sufficiently specific to be useful as a guide to decision making, but not so specific that flexibility and discretion in designing programs to achieve the objectives are unduly encumbered. In short, it must seek a level of specificity that constitutes a workable compromise between utopian dreaming and technical blueprints for community action.

The community-objectives document must seek to provide guidelines, not only for the technical elements commonly included in a general plan—guidelines relating private land use, community facilities, and transportation routes—but equally to the more important if less tangible human development concerns: education, welfare, job training and retraining, cultural assimilation of newcomers, medical care, shopping, housing, zoning restrictions, cultural and recreational programming, intergroup activities, and similar considerations which affect the pace and style of life in the community's neighborhoods.

A successfully utilized community-objectives document should ultimately provide the community with a distinctive life style tailormade to resident tastes and preferences. As Leo Molinaro suggested, "No matter how small your community is, there is a difference in living in your community as opposed to somebody else's, or your community shouldn't exist."[4]

Formulating Programs. There is, of course, only one difference between program formulation as a part of an urban development scheme or a goals-centered community program and

traditional methods of program formulation. In goal-centered community programming, *all* programs are derived from the community-objectives document. While being formulated, programs are designed specifically for the purpose of achieving explicitly stated objectives, not simply to alleviate short-range community problems or to patronize political demands. All programs of the community can thus be bound together in an harmonious movement toward a common goal.

Actually, program formulation is the culmination of a three-stage process in goal-centered programming. The first step is the community-objectives document, described above, which sets forth basic principles or precepts of community life as a framework upon which more detailed decisions can be made. A second step is a listing of proposals that will or can be used to achieve the desired objectives. In the early stages of development, this listing would present broad alternative courses of action. As the listing is refined, specific alternatives would be selected as interrelated component parts of overall strategy designed to realize the life style conceptualized in the objectives. Finally, the strategy must be implemented through the design and execution of detailed action programs.

Traditional governmental operating methods embrace the latter two steps, at least insofar as the development of the physical environment is concerned. Comprehensive long-range plans generally outline alternatives and select among the possibilities. They then offer suggestions for implementing the selected policies and programs. The difficulties with this procedure, as already noted, are two: (1) this procedure, as presently executed, is almost universally limited in scope to environmental concerns; and (2) courses of action are selected upon the basis of felt needs rather than upon any overall development scheme. The result is a hodge podge movement toward urban development: zoning regulations are devised to control undesirable urban sprawl and prevent incompatible land uses, street layouts are designed to please merchants and residential property owners, parks are developed and designed in response to the patterns of demand emanating from different neighborhoods and with some vague

---

[4] Leo Molinaro, paraphrasing of remarks made at the International City Managers' Association's first Urban Policy Seminar, 1964.

concern for general rules regarding the proper parkland acreage per 1,000 population. Any coordination between such actions and living patterns is strictly accidental.

Not only does coordinated control over urban development demand that the traditional planning and execution steps be preceded by the formulation of community objectives, but it also demands that care be taken to complete each stage of the process in its proper sequence. The effect of making second or third stage decisions before work on the earlier stages has been completed is simply a reduced range of discretion available to policy makers in formulating the earlier stages of the scheme.

For example, a first level or community-objectives decision might call for transforming the central business district of a given community into a center for cultural as well as commercial activities. At the second level, several possibilities suggest themselves, including increased CBD accessibility, improved landscaping, increased intensity of land use, and the development of multipurpose facilities for community meetings and activities. The third stage of decisions, or the implementation level, would call for such programs as arterial street improvement, tree planting programs, new multi-storied buildings to increase land use intensity, and a community center building.

A decision made prematurely to emphasize the development of mass transportation systems in the community might, however, jeopardize, if not destroy, the desire to make the CBD into a cultural as well as a commercial center if residents of the community feel that cultural facilities should be more accessible to convenient parking facilities rather than to mass transit lines. If this were the case, a premature decision to develop mass transit at the expense of increased parking would impair the community's ability to centralize cultural facilities in its central business district.

In other words, the execution of specific community action programs ultimately reduces the community's range of future discretion in establishing goals and determining life styles. Thus, it is critically important that a community-objectives document be established early and then used as the central ingredient in for-mulating future action programs. Further, it is equally important that these action programs be formulated step-by-step in accordance with the general procedure outlined above.

Since the past inevitably conditions and restricts the formulation and execution of urban development schemes, another valid consideration is the extent to which past commitments should be permitted to influence future decisions above and beyond the influence necessarily ascribed to them. Whether the reference is to values, goals, or forms of life, the past must realistically meet two criteria before it should be allowed to modify goal-centered planning. The first criterion—is the past worth preserving (or regaining)—is strictly a value question which can be answered only by the people of the community itself. The second criterion is one of feasibility: is it possible to preserve the past? If not, can the past be preserved in some modified form or can the same result be achieved through some other device?

These two criteria, supplemented by a third, should be applied when evaluating all policy and program proposals. The third criterion is one of foregone alternatives, or, as Leo Molinaro stated it:

The real question in evaluating policy making, and therefore incorporated in policy planning, is what will one policy (program) produce as opposed to the other policy (program) in creating new sources of material and human energy, in identifying new tasks for the city to tackle, in identifying new opportunities to engage the people, and in creating new values which will be worthy of the values that are wrapped up or displaced by the changing times.[5]

In other words, the question is this: are the particular benefits or advantages to be gained from the adoption of a particular policy or program worth foregoing other benefits or advantages obtainable only through the adoption of a different, alternative policy or program? Again, an affirmative answer is required if the proposal is to fulfill satisfactorily this criterion.

The criteria relating to values and foregone alternatives are matters requiring at least equal measures of judgement and factual information. Questions of program feasibility, how-

---

[5] *Ibid.*

ever, are highly dependent upon hard, factual data on a wide range of considerations. These include the following:

1. Technological capabilities. Modern technology is such that almost any plan or policy can be implemented. In addition to considerations of desirability, however, problems of cost do impose limits on useable technology.

2. Political practicality. Of concern here are questions such as: "Can public support be obtained?" "Can the support of affected private interests be gained or the opposition of such interests overcome?"

3. Social and economic consequences. Insofar as possible, data must be collected and then supplemented by informed judgement regarding a proposal's effect on the community's social and economic life. The probable response of those who would be affected by the proposal should also be anticipated and taken into account.

4. External conditions. External conditions are those social, economic, and political factors which effectively are beyond the control of the community. These include such factors as population migration, technological changes, changes in the national economy, and relevant developments on the international scene. While such factors cannot be controlled, attempts should be made to estimate their occurrence and subsequent impact upon community programs.

5. Internal conditions. These are social, economic, and political factors within the community and over which the community can exercise some influence. Typical internal conditions, for example, would be the characteristics of the local labor force, the local tax structure, the available recreational and leisure time facilities, and the kind of capital formation in the area. Estimates should be made of the effect of these factors upon proposed programs as well as the effect of the programs upon such factors.

In evaluating factors such as these, the difference between short-range and long-range considerations must be taken into account. For example, an administrative agency's ability to adopt new technologies in the execution of its program might be limited in the short run by the skills and capabilities of the agency's staff.

In the long run, however, additional staff with required capabilities could be hired so that staff capabilities would no longer be as meaningful a limitation on technological feasibility.

THE ADMINISTRATOR'S RESPONSIBILITY IN GOAL-CENTERED PROGRAMMING

Neither the chief administrator nor any other administrative officer should have a formal voice in the final decision establishing community goals or objectives. As recognized by the International City Management Association Code of Ethics, however, managers and administrative officers do definitely have a key role to play in the process of goal formulation as well as in the design and execution of community policies and programs.

Specifically, the administrative officer has five separate functions to perform in this process. First, recognizing its importance, the administrator should stimulate and encourage elected policy makers to formulate community goals or objectives and execute those goals in accordance with a scheme similar to that described here. Second, the administrator should assist his policy-making superiors by formulating and articulating the alternatives available to them at each stage in the process of goal-centered programming. Third, the administrator and his staff should assume total responsibility, at the direction of the policy makers, for the collection, analysis, and interpretation of relevant data. Fourth, administrators should serve as expert witnesses and counselors to the policy makers, giving the latter officials the benefit of their professional expertise, insights, and experiences. Finally, once community goals and programs have been approved, the administrator must interpret and explain them to his staff, providing the direction and motivation needed to implement them.

Programming for Urban Services

Urban officials today are confronting a stark dilemma in fulfilling their service responsibilities. On the one hand, the incessant increase in the growth and density of the urban population necessitates constant expansion in urban service levels. As one study reported:

Every increment of 1,000 metropolitan residents in the United States necessitates *additions* of 4.8 elementary school rooms and 3.6 high school rooms, 100,000 gallons of water, 1.8 policemen and 1.5 new firemen, 8.8 acres of land for schools and recreation areas, 1 hospital bed, and a fraction of a jail cell.[6]

Not only must traditional services expand, but the increasing population density also forces the initiation of new services. Air pollution control, for example, is one recently added service at the municipal level, the origin of which is directly traceable to population density.

On the other hand, urban officials are now discovering that they must devote proportionately less of their concern to their traditional service programs while devoting considerably more attention to the social or human needs of the community. As a former president of the International City Management Association has noted, "It has become necessary that we find more effective ways of doing our housekeeping functions so that we can re-direct more of our limited resources to the basic task of developing our human resources."[7]

Further complicating this dilemma are those urban service problems which transcend physical, governmental boundaries. The list of such problems, continually growing, already includes water and air pollution, neighborhood deterioration and substandard housing, transportation, poverty, education, civil rights, housing, worker retraining, water supply, recreational demands, and pathological patterns of deviant human behavior. The problems on this list, including both the traditional housekeeping problems and newer human development concerns, are all particularly acute in metropolitan areas where governmental boundaries create artificial jurisdictional problems in coping with them.

This section of the chapter will discuss difficulties in programming to solve traditional service problems, both from the standpoint of the local community and of the urban region or metropolitan area, while the next section of this chapter will focus on the newer human development concerns.

---

[6] METROPOLITAN AREA PROBLEMS (State University of New York, Graduate School of Public Affairs) , September–October, 1964, p. 7.

[7] Wayne E. Thompson, in a paper delivered at the 70th National Conference on Government sponsored by the National Municipal League in 1964.

DUTY SHEET
1. Set goals
2. Design strategies
3. Take action

Note: Follow
this sequence

DUTY SHEET
1. Encourage goal formulation
2. Outline alternatives
3. Provide data
4. Give advice to council
5. Interpret decisions to staff

Councilman   Urban Administrator

FIGURE 3-3. *Goal-centered programming*

PROGRAMMING IN THE LOCAL COMMUNITY

With the exception of those changes required by human resource development programs and discussed in the next section of this chapter, no radically new or different urban programming techniques seem to be immediately indicated. As already noted, present programming techniques have produced a level and quality of urban services which have raised American cities to a level unmatched in history. Yet adjustments must continually be made if urban governments are to meet the challenges confronting them. The adjustments most frequently recommended include improved administrative planning and analysis, the utilization of systems development techniques, expanded and improved managerial staff activities, more and better personnel training programs, and intensified cooperation with other governmental units in solving problems and providing services.

Administrative Planning. Nearly every action initiated within an organization requires some foresight and deliberation before a decision to proceed can be made. The application of this process, commonly called administrative planning, is an essential element in all governmental activities and is or should be found at all levels in the administrative structure. Only competent administrative planning can provide maximum assurance that service programs are being executed with optimum effectiveness.

Administrative planning should not be confused with those activities that culminate in the formulation of a general plan for community development. The latter is a general guideline for policy formulation and implementation while the former is concerned with the design and execution of the day-by-day administrative operation of the government's agencies.

Administrative planning is still a largely underdeveloped science. Although regularly undertaken by all governmental agencies, administrative planning is too frequently a subconscious rather than a conscious process, especially by smaller organizations. To be of maximum value in governmental operations, and to facilitate better urban service programming, administrative planning needs to be un-dertaken in a much more deliberate, systematic manner.

Chapter 10, "Administrative Planning," discusses this subject further and makes specific recommendations for increasing its contribution to the management process.

Systems Development. One of the most rapidly developing and exciting trends in management today is the development of administrative systems. These are, essentially, tools and techniques designed to enhance the efficiency and effectiveness of daily operations. Some of them, such as work simplification studies, are designed to measure, evaluate, and suggest improvements in existing procedures. Others, such as record management programs, are designed to provide more efficient methods of conducting daily operations. Some of these techniques, such as operations research, are heavily dependent upon the application of mathematics and statistics; others, such as form distribution charts, require no mathematical skill at all; still others, such as performance evaluation review techniques (PERT), are applications of sophisticated common sense that are enhanced by, but do not necessarily require, any particular mathematical or quantitative skill.

Increasingly, as demands for efficient, effective program administration gain momentum, as the sophistication of analytic techniques increases, as programs are developed applying these techniques to municipal management problems, and as the cost and complications of applying them are reduced, urban governments will find that these techniques and systems offer great potential for increasing the capability of existing administrative operations. Urban governments in the future will, in fact, come to place increasing reliance upon such devices.

Chapters 9, 10, and 11 describe these tools of modern management and how they can be utilized to upgrade administrative planning, analysis, and operations.

Employee Training and Development. Problems of employee training and staff development have always been high priority items on the list of the municipal administrator's concerns. As the range and complexity of urban services increases, however, this particular concern gains in urgency. Besides the customary demands to increase the skills of governmental employees, the changing nature of urban government responsibilities also requires that employees, and especially key staff and administrative officials, be increasingly aware of the nature, complexities, and intricacies of the problems confronting the community's government and that they be more alert to possible solutions to these problems.

The development of increasingly effective training programs can be significantly expedited in several ways. First, employee training can frequently be conducted more intensively and with greater quality when several units of local government jointly undertake the sponsorship of employee development programs. Not only are more resources available to support the training program in this way, but also the content of the program benefits from the wider range of experiences and insights brought when representatives from numerous governmental jurisdictions are participating.

Second, universities, colleges, and junior colleges frequently can play a significant role in employee training programs. This is particularly true now that federal funds, under Title I of the Higher Education Act of 1965 and Title VIII of the Housing Act, are available to help finance such programs. Better rapport between local government officials and area colleges and universities, if established, can do much to make the academicians more aware of the training needs of local government personnel and thus encourage the development of needed training programs.

Other sources of federal financial assistance are also available for training purposes. Titles IX and X of the Demonstration Cities Act of 1966 also provide funds that may be used for this purpose. The Department of Housing and Urban Development administers a fellowship program, underwriting the cost of graduate studies in planning, urban affairs, and related fields. High priority in this program is given to midcareer persons seeking further training opportunities. The recently passed Public Service Education Act, when funded, will further enhance training opportunities for municipal employees. Finally, Congress continues to consider still more legislation in this field, so the future outlook is quite hopeful.

Because of the importance employee training has achieved, it is generally recommended that every local government unit designate specific responsibility for initiating and executing training programs to some specific member of the government's top management staff. Further discussion of employee training programs and other facets of personnel administration is contained in Chapter 13 of this book.

Management Staff Development. The growing responsibilities of urban management can be best met only by the most capable administrative leadership and by the efficient utilization of management staff. In all but the smallest urban governments, the chief administrative officer should have at his disposal one or more staff (administrative) assistants capable of helping him bear the burdens of his office. These staff people can perform many functions. They can: (1) conduct studies on administrative problems and collect the data and information needed in decision making; (2) improve executive oversight and general supervision over the government's operating agencies; (3) assume responsibility for certain basic staff functions such as personnel administration; (4) undertake special assignments on a troubleshooting basis; and (5) provide continuing assistance to the chief administrative officer with the routine tasks and paper work that are a basic part of all administration.

In larger communities capable of providing several staff members for their chief administrative officers, these assistants might aid in program formulation and execution by specializing in the performance of certain staff functions. For example, one or more assistants might specialize in the area of administrative planning and analysis, in intergovernmental relations, in training and employee development, or in human development programming.

Regardless of its size or functions, management staff assistance can contribute much to effective urban leadership, not only by allowing the chief administrative officer to expand the scope of his concerns and responsibilities, but also by performing much of the research and data analysis so increasingly critical to good urban government. Further discussion of administrator–staff relationships is presented in Chapters 4 and 5.

Intergovernmental Cooperation. Since urban problems often show no regard for governmental boundaries, frequently the solution to a given problem or the provision of a particular service can best be handled by several governmental units working together in a cooperative effort. For example, most average sized communities can't afford a full-time public health staff, but several communities together can easily underwrite the cost of a very adequate public health program. Such intergovernmental cooperation obviously promises rich dividends to communities in metropolitan areas, but benefits are in no way confined to such communities. The subject of intergovernmental relations is discussed further in the next subsection, later in the chapter, and at length in Chapter 17.

PROGRAMMING IN METROPOLITAN AREAS

In searching for better patterns of urban organization and government, constant attention has been given to the possibility of restructuring the metropolitan area. Such attention generally concludes that some basic renovation is necessary in these large urban complexes. The proposed suggestions generally fall into two basic categories: (1) those dealing with the horizontal–structural form of urban organization, the spatial arrangement of urban life and especially the patterns of land use within the metropolitan area, and (2) those dealing with political organization, the structure of local government in the metropolitan area. Either or both kinds of reorganization are often viewed as a veritable prerequisite to the improvement of living conditions in metropolitan areas.

In fact, such speculation is generally utopian in nature: the new forms proposed are usually ideal types that have no practical chance of adoption. Still, they do have some utility. Martin Meyerson, for one, urges urban planners to engage in such speculation, arguing that it offers a potential source of new ideas and facilitates comparisons involving different sets of planning principles.[8]

On the other hand, it can also be argued that such speculation too frequently confuses the possible and the impossible, the reality with the fantasy, with the result that efforts to achieve structural improvements are impeded. Nevertheless, speculative as well as pragmatic proposals are all a part of the continuing dialogue about the adaptation of urban areas to the changing world environment.

The following paragraphs describe the more common of these suggestions, offer some comments on them, suggest several ways of improving intergovernmental coordination, and reflect upon the probability of change in the structure of urban government.

The Metropolitan Approach: Spatial Reorganization. Spatial reorganization schemes for urban areas are those referring to patterns of land utilization rather than governmental structure. They seek to develop a physical environment more conducive to human life by seeking a more orderly arrangement of residential, commercial, industrial, and open space land uses combined with more logical, functional patterns of intra-area transportation. Generally speaking, such schemes are not explicitly tied to any particular format for urban governance.

Schemes suggested for the spatial or geographic organization of urban areas generally fall into one of five categories. The first, called the "dispersed" form, has been advocated principally by architect Frank Lloyd Wright. It calls for a maximum dispersion or spread of both population and commercial, industrial, and cultural activities over a large geographic area, with substantial allowances for open land within the area. The primary changes required by this form would be the complete breakup of the downtown or loop sections of the core cities and the dispersion of population now clustered densely around those central areas. Such a scheme would require vast amounts of land,

---

[8] Martin Meyerson, "Utopian Traditions and the Planning of Cities," DAEDALUS, Winter, 1961, pp. 180–93.

would be totally dependent upon private forms of transportation, and would generate problems of social integration within the community.

The opposite extreme in spatial organization has been termed the "super city." It calls for high density, three dimensional urban settlement with all residential, industrial, commercial, and cultural activity concentrated in as little space as possible. Many versions of this scheme call for vertical as well as horizontal variations in land use, with structures providing transportation and industrial facilities on lower floors; commercial, office, and cultural activities on the middle floors; residential dwellings on the upper floors; and park land development on the roofs. Such a scheme could obviously be established only by powerful governmental action. In addition, it would create monumental problems of interpersonal and group relations while leaving unsolved the demands for weekend privacy, seclusion, and natural surroundings.

A third proposal is the "constellation of cities" plan. Under this scheme, urban settlement would be confined to relatively small geographic and population units, each separated from the other by open space. This scheme would preserve the central city while permitting each of these separate, galaxy cities to develop in accordance with its own notions of urban life and character. It also promises to maintain maximum variety of urban life forms, adequate amounts of open space, and both public and private forms of transportation. The major problem of this scheme is the cost and degree of governmental control needed to acquire and retain the specified open spaces.

A number of plans might be lumped under the heading "directed development schemes." Variously referred to as "the ring," "the urban star," "the finger plan," and similar terms, these plans all call for a high degree of order in the horizontal distribution of land uses and population densities. In general, they seek to lump similar uses together in compacted units, provide for adequate open spaces, and derive maximum benefit from an orderly transportation network. They, too, are dependent on a high degree of centralized government control over land use and development.

Finally, the last category of proposals is really a projection of present trends, modified by improvements in transportation systems, in core area housing, and in provisions for open space. All too obvious are the basic defects of this scheme as are the strong probabilities that it will continue to dominate future urban development.

Since each of the first four of these alternative forms of spatial development would require certain basic changes in urban development policies, and since such changes could only realistically be invoked by some radically altered structure of urban government, the outlook for these proposals, regardless of their advantages, seems tied to the outlook for governmental reform in metropolitan areas. Further, their future seems most closely tied to those very proposals for governmental reorganization, the "metropolitan area government" proposals, which to date have proved most unpalatable to urban voters.

The Metropolitan Approach: A Super Government. Numerous proposals have been advanced for the reorganization of government in metropolitan areas. The most extreme of these have been the "metropolitan government" schemes. These generally call for the organization of some form of metropolitan area federation operated by elected representatives and responsible for the provision of a variety of area-wide local services. Such governments have been imposed by their respective provinces upon the metropolitan areas embracing Toronto and Winnipeg in Canada, but similar proposals have been rejected by voters in U.S. cities. St. Louis represents perhaps the outstanding example of the futility of proposals for metropolitan governing systems in the states. The closest U.S. corollaries to Canada's metropolitan governments exist in Miami, Florida; Nashville, Tennessee; and Jacksonville, Florida.

In Miami, many of the city's traditional prerogatives have been transferred to the reorganized, administratively modernized county government, Dade County. The county thus

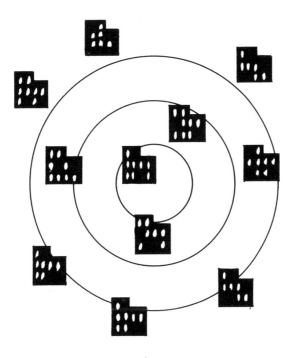

FIGURE 3-4. *The dispersed city*

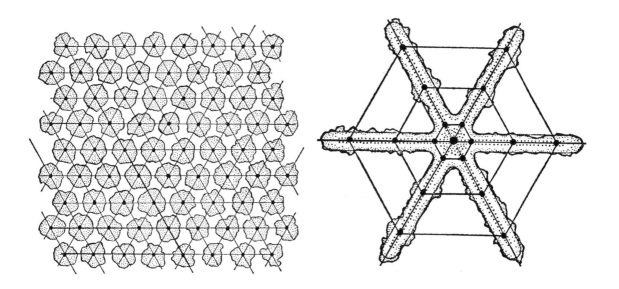

FIGURE 3-5. *The galaxy*   FIGURE 3-6. *The star or finger plan*

operates under a two-tiered, federated form of government with certain functions delegated to the county and other functions remaining in existing municipalities. Functions delegated to the county include arterial highways, parks, water supply, sewerage planning, and police and fire protection. In some cases, the county's authority also extends to housing and education.

The Nashville system, essentially, is one of city-county consolidation. The city of Nashville and the county of Davidson were consolidated into a single governmental jurisdiction with boundaries identical to those of the county. The new government covers two separate service districts—an urban district and a rural district—each with its own service level and tax rate, but with an integrated system of administrative management. The more recently established Jacksonville, Florida, system is similar to the Nashville arrangement.

Neither of these urban governing formats provides a true metropolitan system, however, for both fail to make any provision for expanding the governmental scheme beyond the boundaries of the original county. Dade County's metropolitan area is already spilling beyond the county's borders. County-wide schemes, thus, promise to be only partial and perhaps temporary solutions to metropolitan governing problems.

On the surface, proposals for metropolitan government appear to have much validity. They have a logical ordering of affairs about them. They would eliminate the fragmentation of political control and the allegedly meaningless boundary lines which impede the orderly provision of urban services. They would transfer metropolitan functions to a metropolitan government, leaving local functions to be performed by the remaining, if somewhat less potent, local governments. For advantages, they offer more rational and positive control over area development, with a single political authority exercising jurisdiction over the entire area. Further, they promise better coordination of area-wide services by placing such area services under a single management.

Pointing to past experiences, most observers readily agree that metropolitan government schemes are simply not politically feasible. The obstacles confronting them are both numerous and ponderous. They include the task of settling tax burden reallocations under a changed governmental format, the suburbanite's strong attachment to the sovereignty of his local government, the reluctance of big city minority groups to dilute their growing power in their city's politics, and the universal lack of any agreement on the need for governmental reform, let alone the form which such change should take.

The Metropolitan Approach: Other Political Alternatives. Popular aversion to metropolitan government schemes in no way dispels the hope that some form of governmental reorganization might bring about better urban development and service programming in metropolitan areas. In fact, a number of proposals have been advanced to help ameliorate the urban dilemma. These proposals range from drastic governmental reorganizations to relatively simple expedients calling for greater intergovernmental coordination.

Perhaps the most far reaching proposal calls for the transfer of responsibility for certain area-wide services from local units of government to the state. Air pollution control, water pollution control, land development regulation, and development of expanded park and open space land are the services most frequently suggested for this treatment. While state governments are obviously better able, financially and geographically, to provide such services effectively, it is highly doubtful that most of them have the political competence needed to do so. In short, the practical feasibility of these proposals remains in doubt.

A proposal gaining increasing attention and experiencing growing adoption is that which calls for the establishment of urban counties to supplement the existing system of municipal fragmentation. This plan is essentially similar to metropolitan government schemes. It calls for the transference of certain services from municipal governments to the geographically larger county government. Dade County, Florida, and Davidson County, Tennessee, are the outstanding examples of this plan, but other communities have tried it as well. The plan has certain advantages, notably a high degree of political feasibility and centralization of certain service responsibilities in a geographically larger government, but it also has a major drawback; county boundaries rarely coincide with urbanized areas in the larger metropolitan areas where the problems are most urgent. Thus, as already noted, this scheme is, at best, only a temporary or partial solution.

A long standing, common solution to metropolitan problems has been the creation of special governmental authorities or districts to provide a stipulated public service without regard to municipal boundaries. This solution has come under increasing fire, however, for it adds to the fragmentation of local government responsibility and creates governmental authorities whose political responsiveness is open to question.

An alternative to the special purpose district has been the suggestion of a multiple purpose district created to perform several governmental services within a metropolitan area. Resembling in many respects the metropolitan super government, it has received approximately the same unfavorable public response. To date, only the municipality of metropolitan Seattle uses this scheme, and its responsibilities are presently, though not necessarily, confined to the related functions of water pollution control and sewage disposal.

Two additional proposals are fundamentally related to each other. One suggests that municipal governments be given extraterritorial powers to control land development and provide urban services in unincorporated areas near their borders. The other suggests that annexation laws be modified to permit cities and villages to take by annexation unincorporated urban areas adjacent to their boundaries. Neither of these proposals offers much hope to the larger metropolitan areas which are already filled with incorporated cities and villages. They do, however, offer much hope for more orderly development on the fringes of metropolitan areas, where unincorporated land remains, and in rural communities experiencing rapid population and commercial growth.

Easiest to implement are the many proposals suggesting methods of achieving greater inter-governmental cooperation in the provision of basic urban services. These include schemes calling for voluntary councils of governments, joint exercise of powers, intergovernmental contracting for services, and increased informal communication between officials of neighboring communities.

All of these proposals must be evaluated on the basis of three criteria: (1) to what extent will the proposal result in the design and execution of better urban service and development control programs; (2) will the proposal provide a governmental structure that is responsible to popular desires and control; (3) will it be politically feasible—will it be a plan which is acceptable both to those entrusted with policy-making responsibility and to the people generally. This last criterion has, in fact, been most significant. As one writer stated the case:

The history of these alternative approaches (to metropolitan government) indicates that the American people have been willing to make specific *ad hoc* improvements in the existing political machinery but are quite reluctant to approve a new governmental structure that is believed to threaten the *status quo* of political power or financial interest.[9]

Intergovernmental Cooperation. Among professional observers and practitioners in local government, increased intergovernmental cooperation, sometimes dubbed the "metropolitan cooperation movement," is generally conceded to promise the greatest short range potential for redressing the problems associated with urban growth, governmental fragmentation, and increasing population density. Most recently, the enthusiasm of intergovernmental relations advocates has been directed toward a relatively new phenomenon: the council of governments movement.

These councils, variously organized in a number of different metropolitan areas, are made up of elected or appointed officials from most or all of the governmental jurisdictions serving a particular area. Since they are entirely voluntary in nature, these organizations

[9] Joseph F. Small, GOVERNMENTAL ALTERNATIVES FACING THE CHICAGO METROPOLITAN AREA (Chicago: Center for Research in Urban Government, Loyola University, 1966), p. 25.

seek common approaches to metropolitan problems through research, discussion, and, ultimately, consensus. Although their proposed solutions are dependent upon voluntary collaboration rather than legal sanction for implementation, their efforts have met with some success. Various councils in different parts of the country have undertaken studies of such subjects as air pollution, water pollution, use of open space for recreational facilities, mass transportation, uniform traffic codes, and land use studies.

Because of their dubious ability to handle controversial problems, the utility of these councils may be ultimately limited, but, as the Advisory Commission on Intergovernmental Relations has noted, they do offer a "real prospect of bringing mild chaos out of the utter chaos which afflicts most metropolitan areas in the country."[10]

Another device of intergovernmental cooperation which has been used with notable success to combine central management of urban services with local control over service levels is the contract plan. Under this scheme, one unit of government contracts with another unit for the provision of some stipulated service, such as police protection. The contracting unit, by stating the terms of the contract, can stipulate the level of service which it wishes to provide its citizens while the governmental unit providing the service does so by simply expanding the geographic coverage of its own service facility into the contracting area.

The contracting device has three basic applications. In the first, several units of government contract with each other to provide jointly a quality of service which none of them could individually afford. In the second, a small unit of government will contract with a larger neighbor for the provision of some particular service. In the third application, some unit of local government, such as a city or village, contracts with the county of which it is a part for the provision of one or more urban services.

Los Angeles County, California, has pioneered the utilization of this third application as a means of solving certain of the problems connected with providing urban services in metropolitan areas. Initiated by a contractual agreement between Los Angeles County and the city of Lakewood, California, which contracts with the county for fifteen different urban services, the contract plan, commonly called the Lakewood Plan, is now utilized by numerous other incorporated communities within the county which, in turn, has become the single largest supplier of urban services in the area.

As already noted, county-community service contracts have much to recommend them as effective means of programming for more effective provision of urban services in metropolitan areas. They provide centralized service management, retain local autonomy, reduce the need for special districts, and can reduce the unit cost of providing urban services by realizing economies of scale. The plan does, however, have its weaknesses. It can lead to the unwise incorporation of underdeveloped territory, fail to provide an adequate mechanism for settling conflicts between area-wide and local community interests, and remove urban service agencies further from the control of the voter or his locally elected representative. Despite Los Angeles County's success with the plan, there has been no important movement to transport the device to other metropolitan areas on any significant scale.

A related development offering more encouragement to local government officials has been the sharp increase in the number of "joint powers laws" passed recently by state legislatures. These laws authorize units of local government to exercise, jointly or cooperatively, powers of government which both are authorized to undertake individually. While they do not, by themselves, guarantee intergovernmental cooperation, they are certainly a necessary first step toward making such cooperation legally possible. Many states, furthermore, now have "joint powers laws" which authorize any two or more units of local government to exercise jointly *any* function which all of the participating units are authorized to perform individually. In other words, these states give

---

[10] Advisory Commission on Intergovernmental Relations, METROPOLITAN COUNCILS OF GOVERNMENT, Report M-32, August 1966, p. 29.

their local governments unlimited authority to cooperate with one another in all feasible and desirable ways.

An interesting prospect for the future is the possibility of intermetropolitan area cooperation, in which the governments from several areas join together in efforts to solve common problems. One such cooperative venture is already completed: the Tulsa Metropolitan Data Center Project, started in 1961, was an experiment involving the Tulsa, Denver, Fort Worth, Little Rock, and Wichita metropolitan areas in a collaborative research experiment with the application of automatic data processing techniques in various aspects of the planning process. Another collaborative project, this one concerned with the relationship between housing and regional planning, is now being conducted by Dade County, Florida, Minneapolis–St. Paul, and the state of Connecticut.

Summary. Urban officials today are faced with a double challenge. On the one hand, they are being forced by the changing demands of contemporary society to provide present services more effectively so that more time and attention can be given to the broader social and economic demands of community life. Simultaneously, they find their communities affected by a web of regional forces which they can neither ignore nor effectively control. This double challenge means that urban officials must program their urban service commitments on two levels: in their own community where greater operating effectiveness is constantly demanded, and in their community's economic region where methods must be found to overcome the service limitations imposed by ineffectual, artificial governmental jurisdictions. Needless to say, these challenges are especially severe in metropolitan areas.

Better administrative planning and analysis, more sophisticated staff work, and improved employee training hold the greatest promise of success in dealing with the first challenge. Despite all the elaborate schemes concocted, the intensified application of a familiar tool, intergovernmental cooperation, seems to hold the most promise in coping with the second level of problems. Neither challenge can be postponed awaiting a refinement of better

tools, for it is only in the process of coping with these challenges that the needed tools will emerge.

Programming for Human Needs

To implement the suggestion that urban governments reorient their thinking by adding human needs or "people problems" to their list of concerns, and to give such problems increasing priority by allocating more of the time and energy of top policy and administrative personnel to them, some modifications of traditional organizational patterns are necessary. It has already been suggested that "people problems" be a main concern of one or more members of the chief administrator's staff. This section of the chapter will elaborate on this suggestion and present other organizational alternatives devised to meet the same end.

ORGANIZATIONAL ADJUSTMENTS

To develop effective service programs that will meet the social and economic challenges of modern urban life, and to develop fully the human resources in their communities, urban governments must have social science perspectives and skills in their planning and analysis staffs. These staffs, which should be something quite separate and apart from the traditional community planning department, should supply community leaders with basic information, strategic insights, and policy recommendations dealing with the community's human problems and needs. Where possible, furthermore, these staffs, to deal effectively with the complexity of contemporary social and economic problems, must have inputs from specialists trained in a variety of intellectual disciplines, including economics, demography, political science, psychology, sociology, planning, urban renewal, statistics, recreation, and architecture.

There are several ways of integrating such staff resources into the organizational structure of the urban community. These various alternatives fit roughly into three different categories: the executive staff, the department, and the task force. These categories do not represent mutually exclusive alternatives; there is no reason why elements of all three categories cannot be included within the organizational format of a single community. In fact, Oakland, California, integrates all three approaches into its attack on human problems. Each of the categories is described below.

The Executive Staff. One organizational alternative would place responsibility for human needs and development programming directly in the office of the city manager or chief administrator where it would be assigned directly to one or more staff men or units. Such a scheme has several advantages. It keeps the chief executive officer and other city policy makers closely attuned to social trends, problems, and program suggestions. It gives the social programmers more status in their dealings with other departments and with other units of government. Finally, it gives the chief executive better access to the staff and to its information which is so vital to the successful fulfillment of the executive's community leadership responsibilities.

The executive staff format is used in the city of Berkeley, California, where the city manager's officer contains a division of social planning which is responsible for dealing with social problems in the city. The division functions in a dual capacity. It provides the staff work for the city's human relations and welfare commission and for associated citizens' committees. It also works directly for the city manager as part of the administrative setup, involved in such activities as neighborhood planning with the planning department, redevelopment activities with the redevelopment agency, and social problems of concern to the police department.

The Departmental Approach. The second organizational approach to programming for human needs and problems is the establishment of a separate department within the regular administrative structure of the governmental organization. Such a department, organizationally similar to the public works or police departments and subordinate to the city manager or chief administrative officer, would have several functions. Like the executive staff, it would conduct research on social

trends and problems; advise the chief administrative and policy-making officials of new programs or modifications of existing programs that might be needed; assist other municipal departments in their efforts to solve human problems and further develop human programs; and coordinate the related efforts of other municipal departments on common problems.

In addition, such a department could also assume primary responsibility for the actual administration of ongoing programs falling within the realm of its special competence. In Chicago, for example, the city's department of human resources administers many of the city's poverty programs. Besides Chicago, such departments are found in New York, Oakland, and an increasing number of other cities.

A somewhat related scheme practiced in several cities is the establishment of a department of city development. Such departments seek to centralize in one administrative agency responsibility for such related programs as city planning, public housing, urban redevelopment, and building code enforcement. While such organizations are primarily concerned with the physical development of the community, they can facilitate social or human planning as well since they administratively integrate several basic activities whose work should involve human as well as physical development concerns. The department of city development in Milwaukee is typical of this organizational format.

The Task Force Approach. The final, basic organizational approach to human resource programming is the task force approach. In this method, a group of people, representing different governmental units, different administrative agencies within a governmental unit, different professional specializations, different interest groups within the community, or some combination of these classifications, jointly exercises responsibility for some function, program, or group of functions or programs in the human resource area. Such task forces might be official or unofficial bodies; they might be contained wholly within a governmental unit or they may span several governmental units; they might be composed of professional or volunteer workers; and they may be administrative, advisory, or simply coordinative in function.

Individually, such task forces are more limited in function than either the executive staff or the department form of organization. They are usually better suited to performing a single function or a single range of functions than a range of heterogeneous responsibilities. Most frequently, they will be organized to direct or execute a specific function, such as conducting research and advising the chief administrative and policy-making officials on the social and human resource needs of the community.

The task force concept can be utilized in two different ways: it can serve as the unit of central administrative authority for the execution of a specific program or function or it can be utilized as an administrative tool in program execution. The city of New Haven utilizes the task force concept in this latter way. To preserve six middle-aged areas in the community from inevitable decline and obsolescence, the city has sent a task force composed of a lawyer, planner, recreation and cultural art specialist, social worker, and health worker into each area. These teams, operating out of local school buildings, work with the high school drop-out, the delinquent, the unemployed, the adult illiterate, and the poorly housed family, helping these people function more effectively in the social and economic climate of the community. Their efforts are also complemented by other governmental efforts to improve housing, neighborhood standards, educational opportunities, and health and recreational facilities in these areas.

The Administrative Approach. Another organizational approach, neither incompatible with nor an alternative to those already discussed, is the adaptation of regular administrative processes to the decision-making challenges of the urban present and future. Essentially, this involves the utilization of administrative techniques, such as budgeting or personnel training which have proven successful in their own right, to help the administrator resolve resource allocation and program development

problems posed by the emerging patterns of urban demands.

The city of Philadelphia, for example, has adapted capital budgeting procedures to help it coordinate human and physical development activities. The city annually goes through a procedure similar to capital budgeting, in which it develops a document detailing the expenditure of funds for both capital construction activities—streets, schools, parks—and human resource development programs—adult education activities, juvenile delinquency prevention programs, and employment retraining activities. This undertaking, a part of the city's community renewal program, provides a yearly opportunity to coordinate these activities and further ensure optimal use of scarce financial resources.

Staffing in the Small Community

While financial limitations impose major restrictions upon human development programming in all communities, they impose particularly severe restraints upon the very small communities where the number of full-time governmental employees is small and where the chief administrative officer has little, if any, staff assistance. Yet, while it is frequently not so dramatically evident, the need for human resource development work is just as pressing in these communities as in their larger, older neighbors. There are several ways such communities might compensate for their lack of staff.

First, if at all possible, an assistant manager or administrative assistant should be added to the chief executive's office and assigned specific responsibilities for human resource research and programming. Where staff additions are impossible, these responsibilities should be assigned to some other individual in the administrative structure who can devote time to them.

As a second alternative, communities might contract with a consulting firm or with a university-related bureau of public affairs research for advice and assistance in gathering the needed data and formulating specific human resource development programs. Such services might be retained in connection with a specific program or problem or they might be utilized on an ongoing basis. Very frequently, universities have a good pool of manpower available at a relatively low cost.

Finally, some communities have been able to obtain, at a relatively low cost, student interns from university graduate programs in public administration, city management, or urban studies. These interns are generally capable of doing much of the basic data collection and research so necessary in the formulation of human resource development programs.

Although they may be of special utility or significance to the small community, these sources of programming assistance may be equally valuable to the large community as well.

Finally, both the large and small community alike should be aware of the mushrooming number of national and sometimes state programs of financial aid and assistance to local governments. These aid programs frequently will provide the total additional cost of operating large-scale urban development programs, and their potential impact upon human development activities should not be underestimated, especially by the small communities. In fact, a number of these new programs are specifically restricted to the small communities. The International City Management Association, the National League of Cities, the U.S. Department of Housing and Urban Development, and state municipal leagues can all provide further information about such programs.

New Administrative Challenges

The challenges which urban governments of the future must confront and surpass will quite certainly demand more than the adjustments which can now be envisioned. To be sure, the development of staff to deal with the human development challenges is currently a maximum priority item as are the organizational and administrative improvements described in the first section of this chapter. Other kinds of challenges, however, are also certain to arise.

Some of these will stem from the development of problems not now envisioned; others will be related to new administrative demands quite apart from those involved in providing environmental and human development services.

In short, urban governments can look forward to the task of developing the administrative expertise needed to deal with specific new areas of concern. Some of these areas of concern are already apparent; new skill is already being required in the fields of communication, participatory democratic politics, intergovernmental relations, and employee relations. The future is certain to be accompanied by the demand for other kinds of new expertise.

To demonstrate the nature and implications of these demands, the following paragraphs will review each of the concerns mentioned above and describe the administrative implications they are expected to entail for urban governments.

COMMUNICATIONS

The recent turmoil on the streets of the nation's cities has been blamed on many causes, including U.S. involvement in an immoral war, white racism, unemployment and underemployment, inadequate schools, rat-infested housing, the hopelessness of poverty, lawlessness, and lack of concern for the plight of the impoverished. Regardless of cause, and regardless of the efficacy or morality of the demonstrators' actions, the continuing incidence of threatening and violent confrontations in a democratic society—confrontations which can be sustained by their instigators only with the open or tacit consent of a significant percentage of the population—is a clear indication that the communication between governors and governed so vital to a democratic system is no longer adequate. In short, the turmoil in U.S. society is strong evidence that government—especially local, urban government—is no longer serving its proper function of political representation.

The *prima facie* cause of this functional breakdown is the absence of effective communication between political leadership and disgruntled groups in society. The traditional communication channels between these groups and government leaders have proven inadequate under the strain of contemporary problems; they must be supplemented or replaced if these alienated groups are to be returned to the fabric of society.

This alteration will not be easy and, increasingly, it is becoming apparent that it can not be left to chance. As urban administration becomes increasingly professional—as indeed it must if it is to cope adequately with the magnitude of urban problems—it widens the natural gap between itself and those in the community who lack the education, background, and economic affluence of today's professional groups. Consequently, the professional's ability to understand the problems and plight of the less advantaged, or to empathize with their concerns, is severely diminished. As a result, even direct, verbal communication between the two groups is seriously reduced in effectiveness.

It therefore behooves urban government to develop new channels of communication between itself and the less advantaged groups in society, to acquire new expertise in maintaining a meaningful flow of information and understanding with these groups. This may require, for example, a new unit on the chief administrator's staff, complete with a field staff of community relations experts and skilled information analysts; it may require the addition of such persons at the top levels of key departments, including human resources, planning and development, urban renewal, police, and parks and recreation; it may require some combination of these alternatives; it may require some other form of administrative modification; but certainly it does require some kind of organizational response from urban government.

These new communication channels must serve several purposes:

1. They must provide a constant flow of information regarding the needs and desires of people in less advantaged circumstances for public services.

2. They must provide accurate measures of the intensity of concern manifested by such people for each of the demands being imposed upon government.

3. They must provide a continuing and accurate feedback of information regarding community response to the level, efficiency, and effectiveness with which public services are provided.

4. They must transmit to such people an understanding of the complexity of the problems confronting urban governments, the constraints under which such governments must operate, the totality of the government's efforts to respond to their problems and demands, and the rationale behind governmental decisions affecting their interests.

PARTICIPATORY DEMOCRATIC POLITICS

In their wake, the contemporary turmoil and confrontations in the nation's cities and on the nation's campuses are leaving a number of modifications in American political practices that must be presumed to be relatively permanent additions to the governmental scene. These include a role and technique for popular participation in daily decision making by governmental bodies; a new sense of political efficacy for small groups and less advantaged members of society; a decrease in the sense of political anomie and impotence which has long served as a justification for political inaction by minority groups and the less advantaged; a new tradition for decision making via confrontation; and certainly a new intensity of popular concern for social issues and governmental policies. In short, popular participation in government—including local government—can be expected to reach new levels, quantitatively and qualitatively.

Urban administrators, of course, must be prepared for this modification in governmental practice. At a minimum, they can expect to deal with more people possessing a higher level of emotional involvement and a more sophisticated grasp of political strategy than has previously been the case. At a maximum, they might find the whole process of political decision making substantially modified and, consequently, their administrative roles and programmatic concerns drastically altered. In short, they must be prepared to cope with, adjust to, and operate within a changing socio-political-administrative environment.

Preparations designed to resist or minimize these changes promise to result only in futility and frustration: the gathering forces of change are larger than any one administrator and stronger than any professional group. Change is never to be demurred; it is always inevitable, the more so when its instigator is a changing popular conception of the tenets of social and political equality. Preparations for change, rather, should be directed toward channeling the energy motivating change toward desired and desirable goals. The current impetus for change places at the disposal of the urban administrator rare opportunities to bring about improvements in his administration, his government, and in his society. It gives him a chance to be an organizational architect in his government and a social architect in his community. In short, it gives him a real capability to produce a better world.

There is no single prescription that will enable the urban administrator to accomplish these goals—that will give him proper direction in making his preparations for the changes now occurring. Having grasped the significance of the situation and its potential, the urban administrator must rely upon his own skill and creativity in plotting a strategy that will be successful within the particular political and social context in which he works.

INTERGOVERNMENTAL RELATIONS

The demand for expertise in the fields of communication and participatory democratic politics is relatively subtle and difficult to recognize. This is not true of the demand for expertise in the field of intergovernmental relations. The increasing level of interaction between units and levels of governments has become a chief characteristic of contemporary American government in both the United States and Canada. This reflects a situation brought about by the expanding scope of national concern for domestic social problems; the continuing popular acceptance of the theories of "cooperative federalism" and "creative federalism;" the increased willingness of state and national governments to assume responsibility for sharing the financial burden of local public services; the accelerating tendency for problems to become regional rather than local in scope; and the growing willingness of local officials to work together toward the solution of common problems.

The emergence of high intensity intergovernmental relations has added a new dimension to the job of the urban administrator. Urban management can no longer focus solely, or even primarily, on the direction of operating agencies hierarchically subordinate to a single administrator or council; it must instead coordinate the contributions which can be made by many different agencies, responsible to different governments and to the needs of different constituencies, in fulfilling many of its service responsibilities. Law enforcement, for example, can no longer be provided simply by directing the work of a police department. Increasingly, law enforcement work must be coordinated with the work of neighboring police departments through mutual aid pacts, joint communications systems, cooperative training programs, and coordinated criminal investigation efforts. Even more striking is the degree of coordination required to implement long range planning, rehabilitate blighted neighborhoods, or control air and water pollution.

The importance of intergovernmental coordination in administering urban government can only increase in the future as more local governments are formed, the service responsibilities of all governments multiply, local dependence upon state and federal financial aid increases, and the efficacy of intergovernmental cooperation as an approach to urban problem solving becomes more apparent and more widely recognized. Thus intergovernmental demands upon the urban administrator will be compounded, not reduced, in the years ahead.

In fact, intergovernmental demands are already becoming so intense that an increasing number of administrators are recognizing that effective response to them requires: (a) unique expertise, and (b) specialized personnel devoting most, if not all, of their time to this task. Effective performance in intergovernmental relations requires, for example, a thorough knowledge of state and federal programs and activities affecting local government, good contacts with key state and federal officials, skill in program design and the construction of grant applications, close working relationships with key officials in other local governments in the general area, a good sense of strategy, and negotiating ability. It requires also large blocks of time available for the routine tasks of attending innumerable meetings, maintaining contacts and relationships with officials from other governments, and keeping abreast of developments locally and at the state and federal levels.

So demanding, in fact, has the task of intergovernmental liaison become that, in many governmental units, it is not only a major preoccupation of the chief administrative officer, but the principal or single concern of one or more of his administrative staff aides. Some governments have even gone so far as to retain a resident representative in key governmental centers, such as the nation's capital, to promote and participate in this liaison work.

Such steps are simply the initial stages of what promises to become a major organizational adjustment in urban governments to meet the challenge of intergovernmental relations. In the near future, urban governments can be expected to move toward the development of a specialized staff unit in the chief executive's office, a new line department, or both, to deal with the complexities of intergovernmental relations and to assure the community that it is receiving maximum benefits from the opportunities and advantages available through coordinated work with other governmental agencies.

The whole subject of intergovernmental relations is treated in more depth in Chapter 17 of this book.

EMPLOYEE RELATIONS

Undoubtedly the principal development in public personnel administration during the decade of the sixties was the growth of public employee organizations and the increasing role which such organizations succeeded in playing in the establishment of personnel policies. This development, furthermore, was more keenly felt by governments in urban areas than by their counterparts at the state and federal level. Further, all signs indicated that the trend was just gaining momentum. As a Public Personnel Association publication observed:

Whether municipal officials like it or not, it must be recognized that employee organizations are steadily demanding and winning a bigger role than ever before in influencing the official policies and practices that affect them.

. . . The future will see a continued steady growth in the number of employee organizations, in the number of people holding membership in them, and in the strength and influence that will be brought to bear on local government with respect to all matters affecting public personnel.[11]

This trend poses obvious challenges to urban administration. It means, for example, that the task of setting municipal personnel policies is becoming far more complex for the typical governmental unit. It means that the administrator's freedom and range of flexibility in setting personnel policy is becoming more and more circumscribed. It means that employee strikes, court action, and similar strategies have become much more realistic and likely possibilities. It means, ultimately, that a whole new technique must be devised for the establishment of personnel policy.

No longer, for example, is it adequate simply to prepare a set of recommendations regarding annual changes in pay plans, working conditions, and other matters of employee concern. Now, increasingly, such preparations must be augmented by the preparation of elaborate strategies to guide management behavior during direct negotiations with employee groups, and perhaps to guide management response if the employee groups appeal their cause over the heads of the government and directly to the people.

Further complicating the situation is the probability that the employee organizations

[11] Douglas G. Weiford, "Organizing Management for Employee Relations," in Kenneth O. Warner, ed., DEVELOPMENTS IN PUBLIC EMPLOYEE RELATIONS (Chicago: Public Personnel Association, 1965), pp. 90–103 at p. 91.

will undoubtedly develop their own negotiating strategies and, further, will probably have access to the services of veteran union negotiators, men who make a career of representing employees in labor-management bargaining. Against such seasoned professionals, the urban administrator and his legal and personnel staffs —men who generally have had little experience in the labor relations field—are likely to be badly mismatched in the bargaining sessions.

Thus it becomes increasingly important that urban governments develop their own negotiating expertise, including both sophistication in the development of strategy, and skill in the techniques of effective bargaining. To be sure, such expertise will gradually be acquired by the government's own staff men as a result of repeated encounters with employee organization representatives, but compensatory steps must be taken to acquire such expertise until that experience can be obtained. Once acquired, furthermore, special efforts must regularly be taken to develop negotiating expertise since, increasingly, the effectiveness of governmental personnel policies will depend upon the maintenance of a relative parity in the skills of both management and employee negotiators.

The rise of employee organizations and the advent of collective bargaining on the governmental front, then, have added the necessity for yet another skill in the portfolio of expertise at the disposal of the urban administrator.

SUMMARY

Communications, participatory democratic politics, intergovernmental relations, and employee relations are just four of the new areas in which urban governments are finding themselves required to develop new staff expertise. Certainly the pace of events and the never-ending cycle of change have and will add other areas to this list, each addition complicating further the task of urban administration. From the administrator's standpoint, the continuing evolution of such demands requires that he maintain: (1) sensitivity to such needs as they arise, (2) receptivity to the demands which they impose, (3) the flexibility needed to make the organizational adjustments and program innovations required to meet them, and (4)

the political capability to achieve community consensus about the direction and form which such innovations should take.

Political Adjustments to Change

Thus far this chapter has attempted to define an administrative response to the problems of urban change. Such a response will not, however, in and of itself assure the viability of local governments in the American federal system. As noted at the beginning of the chapter, no amount of excellence in administrative structure and procedure can compensate fully for a governmental unit which fails to respond politically to the demands of its citizenry. Just as the evolving urban milieu generates new problems and new challenges for the municipal administrator, so too does it for the municipal policy maker, be he elected or appointed and regardless of whether his position is executive or legislative in nature.

THE PROBLEM OF REPRESENTATION

The basic consideration in maintaining political responsiveness is the effectiveness of communication channels between public official and constituent. As noted under the discussion of "Participatory Democratic Politics," the political environment of urban government is undergoing considerable alteration and the turmoil in the streets indicates that communications between governor and governed are breaking down. Thus some form of political response seems necessary if urban governments are to continue as viable governing units in American democracy.

Traditionally, the communication channels in American local government have taken one or two forms. The first, the big city form, is a scheme under which precinct and ward committeemen serve as intermediaries or communication channels between the citizen and government officials in city hall. The second form, the small city form, is characterized by intimate, face-to-face relationships between government leaders and their constituents. In small communities, the communication occurred regularly during the government official's daily encounters with his constituents in the stores, churches, clubs, and streets.

Today, however, the role of the political party machinery—the ward and precinct officials—has been downgraded in the big cities and has never been established in the suburbs. Suburban officials, simultaneously, deal with a population that is too big and too mobile for meaningful face-to-face relations with their leaders. Thus some new mechanism, some new form of communication system, is needed to sustain the responsiveness of local government in an urban milieu.

The problem of communication with constituents, and responsiveness to constituent demands, is first and foremost the concern of the community's elected officials: the mayor and councilmen. This fact does not, however, diminish the responsibility incumbent upon appointed administrative leaders to sustain, increase, and maximize the political responsiveness of the governmental unit. The administrator's responsibility is, in fact, twofold. On the one hand, the administrator must assure the maintenance of good relations between all administrative departments and all community groups, seeking to avoid misunderstandings if possible and correct them when it is not possible. In part, this is a public relations challenge and is discussed further in Chapter 15. In part, too, it is a purely political challenge: it requires administrative willingness to respond positively and willingly to constituent demands and expectations.

On the other hand, the administrative official must seek to cultivate good relations between elected officials and the community which they serve. He must aid and encourage the development of good rapport and communications within the community, thereby promoting the responsiveness of the government which he serves. A variety of obligations are involved in the discharge of this responsibility. First and foremost, this responsibility requires that officials make a conscious and concerted effort to: (1) maintain communication with all groups in the community, especially including minority and less advantaged groups; (2) sharpen their sensitivity to the needs of these groups; and (3) increase their own ability to empathize with the viewpoints and motivations of these groups.

These tasks sound easy, but in fact they are not. Minorities and less advantaged groups are generally not a part of the usual sphere of social and professional acquaintances with whom the urban administrator interacts. As a result, special efforts must continually be made to maintain contact and rapport with these groups. This is particularly true when these groups are not directly represented on the governing board or council.

Second, professional administrators must, in their role as representatives of the whole community, seek to compensate for the absence of minority and interest group representation on the council by seeing that the viewpoints of such groups are brought to the council's attention. At times, this may require the administrator to solicit testimony from members of interests not represented on the council; more frequently, however, it requires that he acknowledge the viewpoints of such groups in his reports and advice to the council.

Third, administrative officials can improve rapport between the government and minority groups in the community by broadening the base of governmental employment to include as many minority group members as possible. Public employees serve as excellent intermediaries between the government and the governed: if large numbers of persons from less advantaged and minority neighborhoods are employed by the community, and if their morale is high, then relations between those neighborhoods and the government will usually experience substantial improvement. The higher costs sometimes incurred in recruiting and training workers from such parts of the community are usually good investments in improved public relations.

Finally, the administrative officer should seek to educate his elected leaders on the importance and methods of maintaining good rapport with all community groups. The fact that a council member has proven his political skill by winning election to public office does not assure that official's sensitivity to all segments of the community which he governs. The tendency to give priority attention to the concerns and attitudes of political supporters is strong and tends to assert itself even when it is not intended. As a relative newcomer to official position, and as a part-time official, the elected urban leader is not likely to be aware of such political pitfalls. It is therefore the responsibility of the administrative officer to help his elected superiors avoid such difficulties and broaden the base of their responsiveness.

THE POLITICAL ENVIRONMENT OF URBAN GOVERNMENT

Political responsiveness to citizen preferences and demands, supported by administrative responsiveness to a changing physical and human environment, is the key to effective local government in urban areas. The development of effective political and administrative responses to the evolving city is thus of critical importance, but this alone will not cure all of the ills of the contemporary community. There remain a number of additional handicaps which must be met if the city of the future is to master its environment effectively, and which are a part of the political climate and culture of the modern city.

The first of these handicaps is the extent to which the actions of urban governments are encumbered by state laws—laws which are all too frequently outmoded and obsolete. Modernization of these laws is a challenge over which urban governments can exercise only limited influence, but, with legislative reapportionment supplemented by informed and coordinated action by urban officials, the future prospects for legislative changes are brighter than at any time in recent decades.

This is especially true if urban officials take upon themselves the responsibility of preparing comprehensive urban programs for consideration of their state legislature. It is becoming increasingly clear that without such programs, the reapportioned state legislatures are unlikely to be significantly more responsive to the needs of urban areas. State legislatures will not be more attuned to the needs of urban areas until urban officials produce comprehensive programs for legislative consideration and the urban consensus needed to produce legislative action.[12] Until their officials assume the responsibility for such leadership, however, urban governments must continue working within their present, outmoded legal authority to achieve their purposes.

Two other handicaps are more within the control of urban governments, but might be even more difficult to change. The first of these is an over attachment to a traditional system of values about government and governmental activities. While many long-held notions about government have unquestioned validity, such as the attitude that government should be responsive to popular demands, others, such as the conviction that government spending ought to be held at the lowest possible level or that government should not concern itself with the social or economic problems of the citizenry, are open to serious question. In fact, the preponderance of the American public has readily discarded many of these notions, such as the two stated above, in their approach to national affairs, but they continue to apply restrictions consonant with these ideas to their urban governments. Partly as a result, the initiative in dealing with public problems has passed from the local government scene to the national political arena.

Another locally imposed handicap of urban governments is their dependence upon local political systems which are overly monolithic in nature. Such systems reduce governmental capacity to settle major public issues by restricting the number of positions and ideas on the issue that can be effectively and influentially expressed. This weakness is especially prevalent in suburban governments where, too frequently, informal political caucuses and the demands of social homogeneity so stifle political originality that even contests for elective public office are discouraged, if not eliminated. As a consequence, creative and imaginative approaches to local problem solving are discouraged, governmental activity is contained within the straitjacket of tradition, and the effectiveness and viability of local government are compromised.

---

[12] Samuel K. Gove, REAPPORTIONMENT AND THE CITIES (Chicago: Center for Research in Urban Government, Loyola University, 1968).

Summary

Needless to say, these handicaps must be overcome if the importance of local government—of the city and the county—is not to be diminished in the governmental structure of the future. With virtual unanimity, political scientists predict that the federalism of the future will be a system of cooperative federalism in which all levels of government pool their special resources and talents in a joint effort to provide public services and attack public problems.

In such a system, the role and significance of urban governments as autonomous political bodies providing special protection to the interests of their constituents will be directly proportional to their viability as governing units. In other words, the future of urban governments will depend upon their responsiveness to public demands, upon their ability to work effectively with each other, upon the caliber of their leadership, upon the quality of their administration, and, in short, upon the effectiveness with which they cope with the needs of their citizenry.

Following the theme of the first two chapters, when emphasis was placed on the changes confronting urban governments and on the necessity for such governments to focus their concern on the social and economic as well as the physical needs of their citizens, this chapter has attempted to outline, in rudimentary fashion, the ingredients of a response to these challenges. It is only through such a response that American cities will be able to retain their viability and autonomy in the American system of federation.

Part Two

The City Administrator

4

The Environment and Role
of the Administrator

THE 1960's HAVE BEEN a traumatic period for American cities. Many have been scarred by riots. Others have been beset with fears that they too would suffer the emotional and physical wounds of civil disorder. Life on what Robert Weaver has called the "urban frontier" has been filled with tension, stress, and hazard.

During the summer of 1967, in the wake of several major disruptions, President Lyndon B. Johnson addressed the American people. In that speech he said to public officials, "Yours is the duty to bring about a peaceful change in America. If your response to these tragic events is only business-as-usual, you invite not only disaster but dishonor."[1] His comments did not distinguish between elected and appointed officials. They were directed to all who are involved in policy formulation and implementation. And this, of course, encompasses administrative officials, including city managers, county managers, and other urban executives.

Inevitably, as the imperatives of the time clearly indicate, city managers, county managers, and other urban executives will be central participants in the efforts to improve and enrich life in communities large and small, and in the struggle to cure the festering social ills which generate communal decay. They will be principal actors as the change process described by President Johnson accelerates in intensity and as communities attempt to build, to rebuild, and to accommodate to ever-changing conditions and rising expectations.

To say that the tasks are difficult is simply to state the obvious. The problems, which concern not only the physical features of the city but also the social and psychological conditions of its inhabitants as well, are frustratingly complex, divisive, and challenging. Of all the categories of affected public officials, the city manager may well find himself in the most uncomfortable position of all.

Many managers and those with whom they work define the responsibilities of the city's top executive as incorporating more than neutral, mechanical, and efficient implementation of council decisions. They expect the executive to function as a vital element in the community political system and to play an important role in community policy making. Even so, these expectations have generally been defined imprecisely, meaning that the contours of the manager's role have traditionally been somewhat ambiguous.

This ambiguity has facilitated managerial accommodation to diversity from community to community and to evolutionary role revisions apace with alterations in the pattern of municipal responsibilities. Now the problem of role definition is intensified because situations in many cities have created extraordinary pressures for rapid—even revolutionary—changes in community conditions. Against such pressures the question of the role of the city manager is starkly raised, particularly in regard to his leadership functions.

Suggestions that city managers should be agents of change in the community cannot eas-

---

[1] NEW YORK TIMES, July 28, 1967, p. 11.

ily be squared with the historic tendency to minimize their leadership role. It is this ambivalence, this characteristic of being neither fish nor fowl, neither elected official nor disinterested functionary, that can be the source of acute discomfort.

Because of what is happening in the cities, then, the features of the city manager's role are in a state of flux. Within this context, the profession itself is characterized by a measure of disagreement. Across the country, city councilmen and others in communities have varying expectations. Furthermore, differences in objective conditions, such as population composition, locale, and social, economic, and political circumstances among the approximately 2,000 council-manager cities, naturally cause diversity in perspectives and practices.

Accordingly, it would be foolhardy and self-defeating to attempt to define rigorously a managerial role or detailed specifications for city managers to follow. A wiser course would be to suggest in broad terms the more important factors which color and shape the role of the manager and the general nature of the position which seems to be emerging. Emphasis accordingly will be upon sensitizing the prospective professional manager to the forces he will face in the community so as to enhance his ability to contend with problems, and to survive his more exposed leadership position under conditions of democratic responsibility. This is best done by examining what managers do and the forces which affect their actions within the context of the community political systems.

Although most of the discussion that follows focuses on the city manager, it has a broader applicability. The basic notion of professional administration at the local level has undergone considerable extension. County managers, council- and mayor-appointed generalist administrators with overall management responsibilities, directors of councils of governments, executive heads of special districts, and many others have joined city managers in the genus "professional urban administrator." Needless to say, these positions have a great deal in common and individuals switch increasingly from one to another during the course of their ca-

reers. Therefore, the following discussion, although principally about city management, has considerable relevance for other local administrative positions. To underscore the point, the term "urban administrator" will be used from time to time.

To provide the foundation for a discussion of contemporary circumstances, the first section will concern the genesis and early development of the council-manager system of government and what might be termed a distilled "classical" concept of the city manager's role, as compared with a more contemporary view. The second and third sections will deal with community political systems and the manner in which managers fit into the processes through which communities make important choices. Then a section will focus upon certain critical aspects of the manager's position: his relationships with the mayor and the council, other governments, his subordinates, and the public. A number of brief observations regarding the future will conclude the chapter.

The City Management Profession

One of the characteristic defects of any society is that, when circumstances change, the changes may not be perceived generally with the result that the thoughts and actions of men and institutions are out of joint with reality. Professions are especially prone to such obfuscation. Trained in traditional precepts, and in a sense required to accept them as a condition for admission to the calling, the membership at times resists making alterations in established notions. Even the comparatively youthful city management guild shares some of these characteristics, but they appear not to be dominant. Quite the contrary. As Edwin O. Stene has noted:

Perhaps the most significant feature of the council-manager system of government has been its adaptability to changing technology, to expanding urban needs, and to changing theoretical concepts of public administration and institutional decision-making.[2]

_____
[2] Edwin O. Stene, THE CITY MANAGER: PROFESSIONAL TRAINING AND TENURE (Lawrence: University of Kansas, Governmental Research Center, 1966), p. 78.

Prior to noting changes in the city management profession, however, the profession's origins should be examined.

GENESIS

Not long after the turn of the century, a leaky dam gave way near Staunton, Virginia. The city council was told by a contractor that repairs would cost $4,000. Subsequently, someone thought to seek the opinion of Charles E. Ashburner, a maintenance engineer for the Chesapeake and Ohio Railroad. He estimated that the necessary work could be done for $737 if his recommendations were followed. City councils rarely spend $4,000 if there is a possibility that the same results can be achieved for considerably less, so Ashburner's directions were tried, and they worked.

Shortly thereafter, sentiment grew for altering the structure of Staunton's government. The commission plan, then highly favored by those advocating municipal reform, was precluded by Virginia law. Searching for alternatives, the idea of a general manager for the city was conceived. In part, no doubt, because of his bridge success Ashburner was tapped for the position and thus is generally considered to be the first city manager.

After Sumter, South Carolina, explicitly adopted a council-manager scheme in 1912, based upon a model charter drafted by Richard S. Childs, then secretary of the National Short Ballot Organization, the form became very popular. By 1927, 375 cities had adopted it. Since then, the number has grown to several times that figure.

The Spirit of Reform. The development and spread of council-manager government and

SPECIES OF GENUS URBAN ADMINISTRATION

FIGURE 4-1. *The profession of urban administrator*

the content of the "classical" managerial role concept were shaped by powerful reform impulses which swept the nation during the late nineteenth and early twentieth centuries, seeking to cope with the social, economic, and political dislocations brought by the industrial revolution. No corner of national life was immune from their impact and from the necessity of undergoing painful and often acrimonious adjustment.

Municipal reform, including the council-manager plan, came into being within the climate of ferment suggested by the images of populism, "robber barons," the Pullman strike, the Sherman Antitrust Act, Woodrow Wilson's "New Freedom," and the muckraking of Lincoln Steffens. Although less radical, less proletarian, and less hostile to business than many other specific movements of the period, generic municipal reform could not help gaining impetus and ideas from these developments, particularly ideas about democracy. Even as cities continued to revise their forms of government in the period of "normalcy" which followed World War I, the influence of propositions developed in more unsettled times was felt.

Municipal reform focused its attack on "politician government" and "waste, extravagance, and . . . corruption."[3] Existing systems marked by these characteristics seemed incapable of responding effectively to the growing urban population and demands for increased services. Especially when compared with the administrative sophistication and results achieved by business enterprises, the cities were found wanting. Leonard D. White summarized the indictment:

Low standards of municipal accomplishment, waste and misapplication of public funds, lack of vision with regard to the city's future and lack of energy in pursuing even the most limited objectives, government by political machines for the purpose of maintaining the strength and controlling power of the machine rather than by independent officials for the good of the community, jealousy and ill-will between communities even where cooperation was essential, concealment of the real condition of public business rather than frank recognition of the right of the public to know the facts of public affairs. . . .[4]

Obviously not all cities were *in extremis.* But many which did not manifest the cynical corruption of a New York or Chicago were plagued with incompetency and mild venality.

Guiding Principles. Those who were dissatisfied with the status quo saw two fundamental goals to be achieved: securing effective and efficient administration of municipal programs and realizing meaningful democratic responsibility at the local level. Neither of these elements, it was felt, was provided by the traditional approach to municipal affairs or by the existing pattern of partisan politics.

Despite the fact that there is a degree of fundamental incompatibility between the two goals, in that what the electorate wants may not be efficient and effective administration judged on the basis of the accounting ledger, an orthodoxy of reconciliation was developed and generally accepted. The major elements were sets of interrelated administrative and political arrangements and processes:[5]

1. Administrative arrangements and processes

   a. unification of governmental power, but separation of functions

   b. enhancement of the power of the chief executive through executive integration and provision of stronger managerial tools such as budgetary and personnel controls

   c. removal of partisan politics from administration through the establishment of merit as the basis for personnel decisions

   d. application of modern managerial techniques, drawn principally from business practices

2. Political arrangements and processes

   a. simplification of the task of voters through reducing the number of elected officials and increasing public awareness by improved public reporting and the activities of independent citizen research organizations

---

[3] *Ibid.,* p. ix.
[4] *Ibid.*

[5] For discussion of these points see: Dwight Waldo, THE ADMINISTRATIVE STATE (New York: The Ronald Press, 1948) , p. 37; Edward C. Banfield and James Q. Wilson, CITY POLITICS (Cambridge: Harvard University Press, 1966) , pp. 140–41; Wallace S. Sayre and Nelson W. Polsby, "American Political Science and The Study of Urbanization," in Philip M. Hauser and Leo F. Schnore, THE STUDY OF URBANIZATION (New York: John Wiley and Sons, 1965) , p. 122.

b. enlargement of the capacity of voters to control elected officials through opening the nominating processes and establishment of procedures for initiative, referendum, and recall

c. insulation of local from partisan politics by holding municipal elections on a nonpartisan basis, electing councils at large rather than from wards, separating the timing of municipal from state and national elections, and home rule.

The manner in which the components listed under the administrative and political categories interrelate in the achievement of the basic goals and the degree to which they are mutually supporting is quite clear. To select just one example, not only does the establishment of a merit system theoretically facilitate efficient administration by removing narrow partisan loyalties as significant factors in the execution of programs, it also eradicates an important, continuing basis of partisan political power in the community.

THE EARLY PERIOD OF THE COUNCIL-MANAGER PLAN

There was considerable experimentation during the period; the strong mayor and commission systems each enjoyed a vogue. But much more than these, the council-manager plan satisfied the requirements as defined by those identified with municipal reform, and it quickly became the preferred mode of the reformers. Many agreed with Leonard D. White that it was "the most perfect expression which the American people [had] yet evolved of the need for combining efficient administration with adequate popular control."[6]

Form. The basic characteristics of the plan have not changed a great deal since its early days. The model arrangement calls for a small council to be elected on a nonpartisan, at-large basis. A mayor is selected who sits as a member and the presiding officer of the council.

A manager who is professional in skills and attitudes is chosen by the council to serve as the city's chief executive. He continues in office so long as his performance is satisfactory to the legislative body.

---

[6] White, *op. cit.,* p. 295.

The duties of the manager, as spelled out in the early charters, included such items as program execution, department head selection, general personnel supervision, and budget preparation, all free from specific and detailed interference from the council. Further, the manager was to act as a source of expert advice for the council, make recommendations when appropriate, and inform the general public as to the city's affairs through reporting to the legislative body.

The Manager's Role. Understandably, as the number of cities utilizing the council-manager approach increased, variations in thought and practice appeared as to what managers should be and do. It was not unusual for a local politician to be named the first incumbent of the managerial position or to be placed in office after experimentation with an "outsider," resulting in old ways being perpetuated. Then, as now, some communities were not willing to trust strangers or to pay the price required to secure high-level administrative skills. However, the strongest thrust by far in manager cities was to employ technically qualified people who brought with them a professional identification.

Out of the theoretical foundations of the reform movement, the special characteristics of the council-manager form, and experience, an approved though not unanimous set of expectations of the role of the manager in the community emerged. Sketched broadly, it held that partisan politics was to be avoided absolutely, as was functioning as a visible community leader or independent force in policy matters, at least beyond the point of making factually based recommendations to the council. Neutral competence and the application of sound business practices to municipal affairs were to be emphasized over and above personal values or policy preferences.

The accepted notion compartmentalized city functions. The democratically responsible council would relate to the community in the political sense and develop and enunciate policy. Employing his expertise, the manager would direct its implementation in the most efficient and effective way. His instrumental decisions were considered to be beyond politics and thus uniquely within his own province.

Practice never perfectly corresponds with an "ideal-type" construct such as the preceding. And there were specific exceptions recorded to the validity and propriety of the approach to the manager's job suggested by this description. Although some saw room for more dynamic leadership and innovation in the role of the manager and others foresaw difficulties in attempting to define policy almost solely in terms of elective politics,[7] theoretically and organizationally the narrower view dominated thought on the question of role for many years and retains some significance today. Viewed from the present, the conceptualization may appear somewhat restrictive and conservative, but during the formative period it made considerable sense and deserves more than the wry amusement expressed by some contemporary critics.

The admonitions against political activism owed much to normative views about partisan politics at the local level, but they were also a natural protective device. During the early days for a manager, especially one from outside the community, to play a visible, activistic role or to be drawn overtly into the vortex of policy-making, even on the basis of expertise, would have provided support for claims frequently voiced that the manager system established irresponsible power. In many a community his effectiveness would have been impaired, and perhaps the plan itself might not have survived. Viewed in this way, the early managers may be excused for their caution and a certain rigidity and protectionism in delineating the limits and prerogatives of professionalism.

Substantive Concerns. In this connection, it would be appropriate to note that the dominant action priorities of the time were compatible with an emphasis on the city manager as technician employing neutral competence rather than as leader in policy development.

The problems of people and the conditions necessary for improving the quality of life were not completely overlooked by any means. Realistically though, amenities and the fundamental social, economic, and psychological well-being of all segments of the community did not have the immediacy as public policy problems in the 1920's as they do in the 1960's and 1970's. The more obvious tasks were to develop the physical aspects of the city to meet contemporary needs and to implant modern administrative structures and processes in city hall. Many of the most relevant questions could be put in technical terms, enabling managers to supply technical answers on the basis of their expertise without seeming to be engaged in policy-making in the broad sense.

A CONTEMPORARY VIEW

A candid job description for a city manager now would differ considerably from a comparable document drafted 30 years or so ago, as would the most common expectations regarding his role in the community. Of foremost importance, it would indicate that a city manager, "by the very nature of his job,"[8] has a significant function to fulfill as far as policy is concerned. This is borne out by changes that have been made in the International City Management Association's Code of Ethics, experience, and numerous in-depth studies. An analysis of several council-manager cities in Florida concluded, "We found no managers . . . who were not involved in the making, shaping, or vetoing of policy proposals."[9] A similar investigation in North Carolina found that "in many cities the manager clearly emerges as the person who has the greatest influence over what is happening at every stage of the policy-making process."[10] Aaron

---

[7] For example, William Bennett Munro noted: "A manager who is really a master of his job ought to have little difficulty in wielding a large influence in the commission's deliberations. Knowledge is power." MUNICIPAL GOVERNMENT AND ADMINISTRATION (New York: The Macmillan Co., 1927), p. 423.

[8] Clarence E. Ridley, THE ROLE OF THE CITY MANAGER IN POLICY FORMULATION (Chicago: The International City Managers' Association, 1958), p. 1.

[9] Gladys M. Kammerer, Charles D. Farris, John M. De Grove, and Alfred Clubok, CITY MANAGERS IN POLITICS: AN ANALYSIS OF MANAGER TENURE AND TERMINATION (Gainesville: University of Florida Press, 1962), p. 83.

[10] B. James Kweder, THE ROLES OF THE MANAGER, MAYOR AND COUNCILMEN IN POLICY MAKING: A STUDY OF TWENTY-ONE NORTH CAROLINA CITIES (Chapel Hill: University of North Carolina Institute of Government, 1965), p. 31.

Wildavsky's examination of Oberlin, Ohio, revealed the key role played by the city manager in policy matters.[11] In two of the four Michigan cities studied by Oliver Williams and Charles Adrian, the manager "was a key leadership figure and policy innovator."[12] By and large managers see themselves in these terms also. In a survey undertaken by Clarence E. Ridley some years ago, all the respondent managers believed they had "a definite responsibility to participate in policy," and 77 of 88 indicated that they initiated policy changes "as a matter of course."[13]

A General Characterization. Managers speak to and for their cities. They are involved broadly in the processes through which the community decides what is to be done and the means to be used, at times even concerning matters which lie outside the formal jurisdiction of city hall. In exercising leadership, managers are publicly and privately involved in identifying problems, formulating responses, and stimulating action. However, reflecting a "more inclusive concern for problems that face people in our urban civilization,"[14] they are increasingly impelled to assume the burden for advocating change and by implication stimulating controversy in order to foster community-wide social and economic well-being. The traditional managerial tasks of planning, organizing, directing, and communicating are still important, but more and more they are exercised at a new level of generality and extended deeply into the community.

Managers, especially in larger cities, tend to be less concerned now with housekeeping and the nuts and bolts of day-to-day administration and more involved in general supervision, broad-gauged program planning and development, and establishment of priorities. Finally, they must spend a good bit of time looking outward and representing the interests of their cities on both administrative and substantive

matters within an intricate web composed of numerous other governments.

Change Factors. Explanation of the evolution of the manager's role and the nature of his concerns involves a number of elements. Based upon a variety of changes in society, they relate to both the capacity and inclination of managers to act in different ways as well as to altered expectations within communities.

Not the least of the underlying factors is the maturation of the council-manager system and of the profession itself—developments which support more assertiveness on the part of managers. A measure of security has come with the second half-century in the history of council-manager government. The plan has been widely accepted; it can no longer be considered new, revolutionary, or experimental. A strong element of public confidence is present. And managers themselves draw confidence from their membership in an established profession and the career alternatives provided by a large number of council-manager cities and other opportunities for professional administrators.

Related to the fact of community acceptance is community support for professional administration throughout the municipal organization, rather than just at the very top. Managers in many places have help in the form of professionally trained and oriented administrative assistants, organization and management experts, personnel and budget specialists, engineers, planners, police officials, and community relations staffs. Consequently, much in the way of day-to-day administrative chores has been removed from the manager's shoulders in many places. So freed, he has the time, in addition to the staff support, to give extensive and meaningful attention to broader questions that take him outside city hall and into the community. And the very existence of these resources stimulates additional demands on city hall for broadened managerial interests.

Circumstances tend to channel behavior into certain patterns, but individual preferences and choices are significant determinants also. The background and training of managers have been important in shaping prevalent concepts about their position. There still exist

[11] Aaron Wildavsky, LEADERSHIP IN A SMALL TOWN (Totowa, New Jersey: The Bedminister Press, 1964).

[12] Oliver P. Williams and Charles R. Adrian, FOUR CITIES: A STUDY IN COMPARATIVE POLICY MAKING (Philadelphia: University of Pennsylvania Press, 1963), pp. 307–308.

[13] Ridley, *op. cit.,* pp. 18–19.

[14] Stene, *op. cit.,* p. 79.

wide variations, but engineering, the preferred starting point for a good many years, has given way to other preparations. Increasingly those who enter the profession do so after specific training for a career in the public service which contains a heavy dose of the social sciences. To hazard a very broad generalization, this kind of preparation produces managers who tend to be more perceptive about community politics, more sensitive to community needs in the inchoate social realm, more inclined to an aggressive exercise of their responsibilities, and thus more likely to be involved in community policy making along an extended front.[15]

Collective initiative and leadership do not come easily. Experience has shown that city councils, which after all are ordinarily composed of amateurs devoting only a portion of their time to municipal affairs, have rarely been willing or able to monopolize responsibility for policy formulation. It is quite natural for managers to fill partially such voids when they exist.

No doubt the heightened complexity of municipal government in communities of all sizes has emphasized the importance of the professional vis a vis the amateur. Technological change, among other factors, creates problems cities must cope with. But technological and managerial advancements also supply more sophisticated ways for dealing with old problems and brand-new tools for getting at new items on the agenda. Demands for municipal services have escalated within the context of severe restrictions on revenue raising capacities. Expectations regarding even traditional

_____

[15] Ibid., p. 22.

municipal enterprises such as streets, police and fire protection, and recreation have increased enormously. In addition, a range of new concerns and undertakings have been added to the list of top municipal priorities, such as economic development, poverty eradication, housing and urban renewal, and minority group relations. Many essentially concern the social or economic as compared with the physical dimensions of the city. The intricate, sensitive issues which are now of greatest importance in many cities reach into the vitals of the community. There is no real way for managers to remain completely aloof from deliberations about the responses cities should make.

Intrusions from the outside are also significant factors. Population mobility has created communities in flux. Movement in and out of the city not only spawns difficult substantive problems, it erodes stability and a feeling of community, with important consequences for local politics. These conditions may well function to expand the discretion of city managers.

Their role has also been enlarged because, increasingly, cities must take other governments into consideration in deciding upon courses of action and negotiate agreements on matters of common interest. Thus, officials from various jurisdictions are constantly drawn together on critical and often arcane matters. The states are and have always been significant for cities as a result of constitutional relationships and their direct legislative power in local affairs. Programs in cooperation with the federal government have mushroomed since the end of World War II. The urban explosion has placed incorporated places on one another's

Period 1 1900-1940	Period 2 1940-1965	Period 3 1965—
Clean up corruption and provide business-like efficiency in government	Control the development of rapidly growing communities	Promote the American ideals of equal opportunity, tolerance, understanding, and improve the quality of community life.

FIGURE 4-2. *The evolving focus of managerial responsibility*

doorsteps, making the problems of one the problems of many and requiring cooperation and coordination among neighbors. Special districts make similar demands. For reasons of time and expertise, managers in the main tend to assume the ambassadorial function, which in turn requires them to negotiate decisions of considerable import for the community.

The City Manager and Community Decision Making

Although the city manager will not hold center stage in each major community decision, he will have a leading part to play in many of them. There will be variations from community to community, depending upon a host of factors, but in all probability his impact will be extremely confined only in rare instances, if ever. A more precise notion of his place as decision maker in the community can be suggested by examining a categorization of community decisions, the process through which important community decisions are made, and the bases for participating in and influencing those decisions.

DECISIONS: CATEGORIES AND STAGES

Not all of the important decisions made in a city involve city hall directly, of course, but a good many of the processes which result in choices being made that significantly affect the community flow through its corridors at some point. The conflict and controversy resulting from interests being in contention often ignite around public officials, whether they actually make the decisions themselves in the formal sense or whether their prior decisions or informal reactions influence the decisions of others.

Public and Private. Given the amorphous character of the phrase "community decision making," some categorization will be useful. First, a distinction can be made between decisions that are formally made by appropriately constituted public authorities and those made by individuals and groups acting in a private capacity. The two are often closely related. A developer's decision to open a particular tract

of land quite clearly will have significance for a whole range of public decisions. Conversely, when a city establishes a park in a certain area, this action becomes a factor in numerous subsequent private decisions.

Although the focus here, understandably, is upon those decisions made by public officials, their close connection with other decisions in the community should be kept in mind. Private decisions may in some degree bind and limit the discretion of public officials; and public decisions have a rippling effect in that their impact continues to be felt over time in other choices which seemingly are made exclusively within the private sector. That is to say, government officials in a diffuse way have a potent impact on choices affecting an extensive portion of the community even when they are not immediately or consciously involved.

A Traditional Distinction. For a long time the decisions made by public officials at the local level were generally discussed as concerning either policy or administration, with the former suggesting selection among goals and the latter rather straightforward implementation. Some confusion regarding the role of the city manager was stimulated not so much because of any inherent objective inadequacy in the distinction, but by a tendency to associate a particular type of decision with a particular place in the governmental structure. Policy decisions were seen as properly made by councils, or elected officials, while matters concerning implementation fell within the purview of the principal executive and his staff. Also adding to the problem of understanding was an insensitivity to the dynamic relationship between the two types, such as the potential for seemingly routine matters suddenly to assume larger and more controversial proportions. Another difficulty was a reluctance to consider that those who make decisions formally do not do so in a vacuum, but are subjected to a variety of influences. Realistically, an examination of decision making must not only deal with those who formally decide, but also those who influence. The fact that a council formally ratifies a matter does not mean an absence of other participants, such as managers.

Routine, Program, and Policy Decisions. A

three stage typology of decisions as either routine, program, or policy in nature, though abstract, more accurately suggests what occurs in and around city halls. Policy decisions are those which are comparatively broad and continuing in their effects throughout the community. They involve choices among or, more frequently, compromises of competing goals, aspirations, and interests, and consequently they tend to be controversial at times. They may be made explicitly by voters or by public officials. Examples might be the election of a reform city council, refusal to pass an open housing ordinance, the institution of an urban renewal program, the professionalization of a police force, or embarkation upon a general cost-cutting program in city hall. It should also be recognized that policies do not result only from explicit choice. They may evolve from a number of limited decisions, which together indicate an orientation or a policy.

Policy decisions are rarely self-executing. Derivative choices concerning program implementation must be made within the context of policy. These too may be controversial and lead to reassessments of prior decisions. For an example of a set of program decisions *per se,* consider a city which has decided to allocate a greater share of its resources to capital improvements, with the great bulk of the increased funds going for streets. Construction priorities must be developed, specifications prepared, and contracts let. In all of these decisions, various interests stand to gain or lose. Although often formally made by councils, they tend to require the application of considerable technical expertise, and thus the participation of the city's administrative staff becomes very significant.

The third category, routine decisions, are those which require the exercise of little, if any, discretion and are made and carried out in a programmed matter. Again, although many are made solely by administrative officials, they may formally involve elected officials, as in the authorization of purchases.

DECISION STAGES

The direct and indirect involvement of city managers in routine or program decisions is readily apparent. Their involvement in more fundamental choices made by and for the community is in part submerged and difficult to grasp. If, however, decision making is broken down into a set of interrelated stages and the means for influencing decisions are examined, the manner in which city managers may affect such choices becomes clearer.

Decision making, of course, is extremely complex when one sets out to "understand" it. A simple model, such as the one that follows, is an abstraction intended to facilitate analysis and understanding, not a description of reality in any exact sense. Processes do not necessarily flow in neat, logical sequence. And one could appropriately question whether the rationality implied by the sequence is valid.

Nevertheless, the stages are as follows: (1) recognition by some person or group that a problem exists and that action ought to be considered at some time; (2) development of a judgment that the problem is sufficiently acute, as compared with others that have also been recognized, to warrant allocating scarce resources to dealing with it; (3) definition of the problem in its various parts with some degree of specificity in order to provide a workable basis for further consideration; (4) framing meaningful alternatives for dealing with the problem; (5) evaluation of alternatives and selection from among them, a process often incorporating bargaining and compromise; (6) formalization of choice by constituted authority; and (7) implementation of the decision, a process which itself may involve repeating a sequence such as this several times over.

A number of important points are suggested by the sequence. First, each stage is important in terms of the ultimate outcome. Second, participation in even one of the stages may constitute significant involvement. That is, if one does nothing more than contribute to placing a matter on the agenda, the impact has been notable. Third, in any given community the breadth of potential involvement is startling and the theoretical combinations of participants are practically endless.

The categories of potential participants include city officials of all kinds—councilmen, appointed members of boards and commissions, and administrative personnel. From the community, there are the communications media and citizens acting in an individual capacity, or more commonly as members of organized groups and associations. Participants from outside the city, such as officials of other governments and municipal bond experts, may also be involved.

PARTICIPATION AND INFLUENCE

Realistically, it is clear that participation in making particular community decisions always falls far short of its potential. Who actually is involved in making decisions, or to use Robert Dahl's phrase, "who governs?," and what are the bases for participation and influence?

One set of answers, principally identified with sociology, draws heavily from theories relating to social stratification. Wallace S. Sayre and Nelson W. Polsby have summarized its major propositions in this way:

. . . (1) an upper class power elite rules, (2) politicians and civic leaders are subordinate to this elite, (3) there is only one elite in each community, exerting dominance on substantially all nontrivial community issues, (4) the elite rules in its own interests exclusively, and largely to the detriment of the lower classes, and (5) as a consequence, social conflict takes place primarily between the elite and the nonelite.[16]

Taking this view, the city manager must be described as inevitably responsive to a single elite and its interests, to the exclusion of others. Power is concentrated and will have its way.

An alternative and perhaps more realistic view has been developed by a number of scholars, principally political scientists, who have identified a pluralistic pattern.[17] According to this version, it is true that decisions tend to involve a relatively small number of participants. Characteristically, however, there is no single elite in the community; there are several overlapping elites with limited policy interests. On ordinary matters, participation is usually restricted to the "regular" activists, but from time to time a problem may be magnified

sufficiently to involve people in extraordinary numbers. On the whole, the pluralistic conception, as compared with the elitist, posits a system which is "fragmented, competitive, open, and fluid."[18] If this depiction is accurate, the question, "who governs?," may not necessarily be answered in the same manner from day to day, or from issue to issue.

One of the important elements in this characterization of community political systems is the view that there are many resources for influencing policy other than just socioeconomic standing, though that may be very important. Time, expertise, reputation, persuasive ability, sheer physical stamina, and position (including official position) are examples of other salient factors. A combination of these, used in a knowledgeable and concerted way with political sensitivity, is the foundation for influencing important community decisions.

In cities the attributes will be distributed varyingly, resulting in what Dahl has called a system of "dispersed inequalities."[19] This means that different segments of the population have differing sources of political influence and diverse capacities for exercising influence.

What, then, is the place of the city manager? In the system of "dispersed inequalities" he may find himself to be more equal than many others in the community. His formal position alone confers authority and a certain legitimacy to sweeping participation, much of which comes as a matter of course. Supported by his staff, he can be expected to possess other bases for the exertion of influence, such as time, experience, and technical expertise. Thus, as a "natural" participant in the various decision stages and with formidable resources for affecting outcomes, his policy impact is bound to be powerful because of the inherent characteristics of the position even if he attempts to minimize his involvement. This association with policy matters, of course, means an intimate association with broad community political processes.

[16] Sayre and Polsby, *op. cit.,* p. 128.

[17] For a premier example, see Robert Dahl, WHO GOVERNS? (New Haven: Yale University Press, 1961).

[18] Wildavsky, *op. cit.,* p. 8.

[19] Robert A. Dahl, "Equality and Power in American Society," in William V. D'Antonio and Howard J. Ehrlich (eds.), POWER AND DEMOCRACY IN AMERICA (South Bend: University of Notre Dame Press, 1961), p. 82.

Community Values and Their Manifestation

Community values—or interests and preferences of people—are the prime stuff of community politics. The city manager, as a central participant in the local political system, is deeply entwined in the processes through which they are articulated and conflicts among them are resolved. Not only do they constitute a vital part of his environment, they are in a way the important raw materials with which he works.

Matters pertaining to values also pose problems for him. One, inherent in the position, is that differing claims embroil him in conflict. Another is not quite so obvious, yet increasingly critical. As the city manager, he has a professional obligation to consider the whole range of values in the community to the extent he may know them, and to attempt to serve the best interests of the city as a whole. Yet the criteria of democratic responsibility require also that he function under the direction of, and be responsible to, an elected council which may have narrow perspectives.

Contradictions between the values which exist in the community and derivative feelings about community needs, and those values and views of needs which win out in periodic democratic contests provide the basis for perhaps the most intractable dilemmas which managers face. An illustrative discussion of value patterns as they are manifested and the processes through which this occurs will provide the background for further examination of the problem.

Cities are curious things. Many times on the surface there appears to be pretty general agreement on basics. Those who are responsible for making decisions should realize, however, that surface appearance may be only an illusion masking a much more complex reality. Consequently, the assumption that the obvious provides a reliable basis for assessing the range and intensity of community feelings entails a certain risk. Deeper exploration would probably reveal other values or preferences which are significant for the matter under consideration.

PATTERNS

Perhaps the first and strongest natural association one makes with the word "community" is in terms of ties that bind, or the shared "values, habits, sentiments, myths, and understandings"[20] that function as integrative forces in society. Some have questioned whether it is realistic to discuss cities, especially large ones, in a way that attaches general significance to characterizations implying unity. Even assuming the existence of cohesive factors which pervade the city, beyond chance geographical proximity and the resulting interactions and mutual dependencies, specifying them is difficult in any particular case. To the extent they exist, they are hazy and hard to discern and describe. Their effects are uncertain. The disintegrative ingredients based upon heterogeneity—social, economic, ethnic, racial, areal, generational, and length of residence differences, for example—are much clearer to the eye, if one takes the trouble to look; and they exist in varying combinations and degrees in all cities.

There may have been a time when integrative forces were more pronounced than their opposites in a sizeable number of small cities possessing homogeneous, stable populations and an absence of extremes in social and economic standing, resulting in conditions of consensus overriding those contributing to conflict. Now such places are rapidly disappearing, even among small upper and middle class suburban communities. There are many causes, but large-scale population mobility is certainly one of the most significant. As people flow continually from rural to urban areas and from city to city, traditional associations are broken and entirely new mixes containing a variety of elements develop in short periods of time. Assimilation of in-migrants into a community does occur, but never perfectly or with great ease and rapidity. The greater the apparent cultural and physical differences, the slower the rate will be. As a result of society's dynamics, therefore, there is an increasing tendency for the conditions of divisiveness to be strengthened as opposed to the consensual.

---

[20] Banfield and Wilson, *op. cit.*, p. 4.

Not all of the value differences and contradictions which have a potential for creating public policy conflicts actually result in that. The four-part typology which Oliver Williams and Charles Adrian have suggested as useful for classifying middle-sized cities includes one in which hetereogeneity and value conflicts are such that no single set of preferences gains ascendency. Differences are articulated clearly and the prime task of government becomes arbitration among conflicting interests in an effort to satisfy a varied set of claims.

In the other three types which they develop, public policy patterns suggest the domination of values so compatible as to justify designating a city government's mission as either instrument of community growth, provider of life's amenities, or caretaker.[21] This is not to argue the complete absence of conflict or sources of potential conflict in cities which might be placed under one of these three headings. Quite the contrary. There will always be a measure of disagreement. If the policies followed in a particular community reflect an emphasis on community growth, it does not necessarily mean that all or even most people in that community believe this to be the proper course to follow. It means that those who have the most potent influence over policy think in these terms. Nor is a particular orientation necessarily static, for it may change with shifts in political participation and in the distribution of influence.

ELECTIONS

Political systems provide mechanisms for determining the relative emphasis to be accorded values held in the community. The political process provides means for articulating policy preferences, securing influence, and shaping public policy through the exertion of that influence. And one of the most important of these means is the electoral process. Elections which produce city councils, under whose direction managers serve, are of particular interest since they create some of the most immediate conditions affecting the performance of managers; the value context within which policies

are framed and implemented in large arises from them.

The first point to note about municipal elections is that they almost inevitably produce a distorted or partial picture of community values. There are many reasons for this, but one of the most important may be low voter turnout; many people do not participate in even this elementary way. This is more—but not exclusively—characteristic of those in the lower reaches of socioeconomic scales.

There is a circular effect. Certain groups of people do not place a high premium on participation in electoral politics. As a result their values and specific claims are not asserted forcefully; their influence is limited. Feelings that city hall is unsympathetic are generated, alienation is intensified, and a "what's the use" attitude is reinforced. At the same time discontent may fester, perhaps to be subsequently released by a catalytic force and expressed in very blunt fashion, even in civil disorder. Attempts to alter the form of a city's government often may have their roots in dissatisfactions of this sort.

Nonpartisan and At-Large Features. There are two distinctive electoral system features which require special attention because they are usually found in conjunction with council-manager government and because they have particular significance for the manifestation and assertion of values in the community: nonpartisanship (no party designation on the ballot) and the selection of council members on an at-large rather than ward basis.[22] Both were intended to break the corrupt grip of partisan politics on city halls and to facilitate the conduct of municipal affairs on the basis of broad community interests as compared with parochial ones.

Their purposes are only imperfectly realized at times. In cities that have decreed that elections be nonpartisan, several patterns of political organization are observable. One condition, especially found in smaller cities, is the absence of formal organizations involved in struggles in the public arena. Candidates for

---

[21] Williams and Adrian, *op. cit.,* pp. 23–26.

[22] Various combinations of at-large and ward electoral bases are employed in some cities.

city council enter contests through self-nomination and depend for electoral support upon a loose collection of associates and friends.

In other places, local, independent political groups which focus on city affairs perform some of the functions traditionally associated with political parties. They may crystallize around a particuclar issue or set of issues for the purpose of fighting a certain election, or they may be a continuing factor in community politics. Generally they possess a rather narrow organizational base, drawing members and leaders from a limited segment of the population.

Less frequently, political parties may actually be spasmodic participants. Then there are cities such as Chicago where nonpartisanship is a fiction. There the regular Democratic and Republican party organizations continually vie for power in a charged partisan atmosphere and utilize partisan means.[23]

Implications. The most significant points regarding the nonpartisan and at-large election devices do not concern variations from the theoretical ideal, but the effects they tend to have on interest representation and the distribution of the means for influencing public decisions in a community.[24] Participation in the community's political life as voter and office holder is of fundamental importance. There is cause for suspecting that nonpartisan and at-large elections tend to depress voting turnout below what would be expected under other circumstances, especially among the lower socioeconomic groups. They also tend to produce office holders drawn from the middle

and upper socioeconomic levels: professionals, managers, and businessmen who generally live in the "better" parts of town. The chances of minority groups living in particular residential neighborhoods for securing direct representation are minimized. Additional indications are that recruitment for office may be guided centrally by rather small elite groups under these circumstances.

That a high proportion of those who hold elected municipal office are drawn from the more reputable and affluent is not highly significant alone, because this tends to be true for office-holding generally. The more important questions concern the connections between officials and the rest of the community, and the extent to which the circumstances cause them to serve willingly or unwillingly as conduits for interests and concerns which are not naturally associated with their own immediate environment. On balance it seems that nonpartisan and at-large elections restrict access to the places where decisions are made and blur the lines of responsibility between office holders and electorate. Nonpartisanship often means the absence of continuing, competing, community-wide organizations or factions thereof which aggregate interests, stimulate participation, provide voters with rough indications as to candidate positions, and offer channels of communication between citizens and candidates or officials.

At-large elections mean that the necessity for close association between politicians and particular neighborhoods in the community, and for acute sensitivity to special neighborhood problems, is obviated. Emphasis in campaigns ordinarily is placed on name identification and vague stances designed to appeal to the largest number of voters without offending any sizeable segment. It is not necessary, nor is it really smart politics, to become closely identified with any particular group, especially if it is one whose votes would not be determinative, or whose interests are somewhat apart from those of the larger community.

Thus the conditions of election heighten the chances that men will come into office without having had to develop concrete appeals based upon the real pattern of interests in the

---

[23] Banfield and Wilson, *op. cit.,* pp. 151–52.

[24] Assessing the consequences of nonpartisanship and at large elections is a terribly complex problem. Many unanswered questions remain, despite a voluminous literature. Some examples of empirical studies which are relevant include: Eugene C. Lee, THE POLITICS OF NONPARTISANSHIP: A STUDY OF CALIFORNIA CITY ELECTIONS (Berkeley: University of California Press, 1960); Robert R. Alford and Eugene C. Lee, "Voting Turnout in American Cities," AMERICAN POLITICAL SCIENCE REVIEW, September, 1968, p. 796; Robert L. Lineberry and Edmund P. Fowler, "Reformism and Public Policies in American Cities," AMERICAN POLITICAL SCIENCE REVIEW, September, 1967, p. 701; and Robert H. Salisbury and Gordon Black, "Class and Party in Partisan and Nonpartisan Elections: The Case of Des Moines," AMERICAN POLITICAL SCIENCE REVIEW, September, 1963, p. 584. Detailed summaries of research may be found in various texts.

community, with little in the way of obligations which are unnatural to them or incompatible with their own value preferences, and with few incentives to listen sharply while holding office for rumblings in parts of the community unfamiliar to them. Limited sensitivity to the entire community is supported by the part-time nature of councilmanic positions and the fact that many incumbents do not desire to continue in office over an extended period of time.

OTHER MEANS

Beyond elections and the activities associated with them, there are several other natural avenues for expressing values, making claims, and asserting policy preferences, notably through individual action, interest groups, and communications media.

Individuals. Most cities contain a number of self-propelled individuals who act essentially for themselves, often taking contrary positions and gaining reputations as eccentrics. Other activists constructively operate from a base of "respectability." Perhaps continually and importantly involved in a particular problem area such as recreation or planning, they may exercise considerable influence. Whether speaking as private citizens or serving as members of a board or commission, activists generally can be said to represent the values of certain others in the community. But they tend to come from a restricted segment of the population.

Aaron Wildavksy's Oberlin findings are suggestive. He discovered that activists were generally drawn from the part of the city that was relatively affluent, relatively well-educated, and which saw itself in class terms as at the top of the community pyramid. Further, these delimiting characteristics were accompanied by feelings on the part of the individuals concerned that government was important, that they had an obligation to the city, and that results could be accomplished through use of the resources they possessed,[25] feelings not necessarily found in all population groups.

Interest Groups. Significant, potent influences may emanate from organized groups. The propensity of Americans to organize for collective action has been the subject of comment for decades, and there is no community of any size without a panoply of organizations around which life within it revolves. Many, such as churches and lodges, very rarely, if ever, become interested as organizations in political matters or public conflicts. For some broad-based organizations, such as chambers of commerce, involvement may be continuous and over a broad front. But in most cases, public policy interests are narrow and involvement is selective. An association of downtown businessmen will be concerned with matters which affect them directly, such as parking ordinances and their administration, or downtown renewal. Such an association would probably not pay much attention to the nature of the park and recreation department's summer program. Labor unions might be concerned with policies governing the use of police in strikes but not about the operation of the city's sewage treatment plant.

The level of interest group activity will vary from community to community. In general, groups may not appear as significant at the local level as they are in state and national affairs. For example, the study of North Carolina council-manager communities revealed little in the way of group participation.[26] The nature of the issues ordinarily present in a city may be one factor affecting group involvement levels. Another concerns the structure of community power, or the lack of it. That is, where the distribution of political power is relatively set and narrowly based, the chances of groups not associated with the "ins" successfully influencing policy is diminished, as is their motivation to expend resources for that purpose. Finally, the size of the community may be a factor. In smaller places, the informal and personal nature of relationships may disguise the assertion of group interests in a way that is not possible in large cities, where more formal and impersonal approaches are required.

In any particular community, as in the case of elections and individual activism, the mes-

---

[25] Wildavsky, *op. cit.,* p. 32.

[26] Kweder, *op. cit.,* p. 63.

sages that come through from group actions and expressions will be imbalanced. Not all community problems will draw the attention of groups; not all perspectives on issues will necessarily be reflected by them. Those who see a direct and immediate effect on their interests are most likely to speak, while those who are affected indirectly or in a diffused way tend to be silent. For example, important land use planning decisions will have a general impact on the community's future, yet participation in the battles that are often fought on such matters is usually restricted to the owners of property immediately concerned and realtors, among others, who have a business stake in the matter.

Also, the resources for effective group activity are not distributed evenly through the community. The organizational skills, financial means, articulateness, leisure, status, and other characteristics that are vital in putting groups together, leading them effectively, gaining access to decision-makers, and achieving organi-

zational victories are found more among the middle and upper socioeconomic strata. So the community group dynamic often results in disproportionate representation. Certain parts of the community are in a more advantageous position than others to employ the collective approach to influencing public policy.

The Media. Communications media are also vital influences, more so when community politics is nonpartisan and political power is relatively diffuse. But again, newspapers, radio, and television only partially reflect the community. Coverage is restricted. Many of the communications firms do not choose to spend large sums of money to cover the city and its problems, and the skills necessary to approach contemporary urban affairs meaningfully are in short supply. Heavily dependent upon the local business community for advertising revenue, they are inclined to avoid antagonism and controversy. There may be periodic crusades and limited attention to particular problems, but the tendency is toward a noncritical

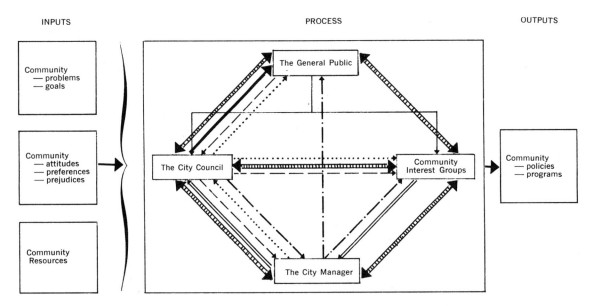

FIGURE 4-3. *Community policy-making dynamics (The dynamic process through which community policies are made and programs formulated involves intensive and extensive communication and interaction between public officials and formal and informal interest groups. As leading public officials, the city managers [urban administrators] can expect [and can be expected] to play a major role in this process. A depiction of communication and interaction channels and purposes is shown here. Throughout, the processes are governed by the general, frequently unarticulated but nonetheless understood, values and attitudes of the general public. Similarly, these same attitudes and values will ultimately sit in judgment upon the results of the decision processes.)*

promotion of the city, as Banfield and Wilson have noted.[27]

THE RESULTS AND THEIR IMPLICATIONS

Community political systems, as they have been described, have an aptitude for reducing conflict and keeping the claims that are made on institutions of government within manageable limits. In some instances, of course, conflict over fundamentals remains at a high, even chaotic level. But not infrequently certain values become dominant and greatly affect performance of the managerial function for a particular time and place. Other values, though shared by a sizeable number of people, may not be raised to a level of even minimal visibility through the natural functioning of the system in a particular community. Consequently, when the manager sits in his office dealing principally with his staff, the council, and other acknowledged community leaders, and making himself accessible to all who wish to communicate with him, though conflicting views may reach him, he is getting only part of the story. He is hearing only *some* versions of what the city's problems are and what the priorities ought to be, not all of them by any means.

This situation is the foundation for a number of vexing problems for the manager. They concern the possibility of reactions in the community and conflict between professional obligations and immediate pressures. Although there is not absolute protection, professionalism is one of the most effective available resources the manager has at his disposal. These problems and the importance of professionalism are the focus of the following paragraphs.

Reactions. Insensitivity on the part of the manager, resulting in his having inadequate information, may cause mistakes of omission or commission which will come back to haunt him. This is not to suggest that information can ever be complete, that managers should survey the community every time they start to do something, or that all concerned can be perfectly satisfied in the choices that are made.

Obviously, if a manager attempted to operate on these assumptions, nothing would ever get done; he would be a prime candidate for dismissal, and probably for a long rest and a bit of treatment by an entirely different type of professional. Rather, the point here is that antennae may be tuned to be relatively sensitive or relatively insensitive to what is going on in the community. There is a basis for asserting that the manager who depends entirely on what happens naturally for assessing feelings and who exercises no initiative in discovering community reality runs the risk of misreadings and consequent missteps which otherwise might be avoided.

Probably one of the greatest causes of managerial insensitivity is a tendency to see problems and their solutions as abstractions, neglecting the human element and failing to realize that others may interpret matters in quite different terms. There may be reactions resulting from dissatisfactions on being "left out" and misunderstandings which may destroy much good work.

For example, in 1953 a reform group gained sufficient strength to adopt council-manager government in Peoria, Illinois. Just about two years later, the reform faction lost its majority on the council. Various "rational" actions had been initiated with little appreciation for the community-at-large and the necessity for broad popular support. Awhile after the election, one member of the city manager's staff said:

At first the election seemed a repudiation of everything we stood for. But maybe it was good for us. We experts have a tendency to take ourselves too seriously, to think that "papa knows best," to just go ahead and do things. In administrative government you forget that politics underlies everything in a democracy.[28]

Although the sensitivity problem has been around for a long time, it is now accentuated. In many places, urban interests which traditionally have not figured largely in the community political system are becoming less compliant, more insistent on recognition and involvement,

[27] Banfield and Wilson, *op. cit.*, p. 321.

[28] John Bartlow Martin, "The Town That Tried 'Good Government,'" in Edward C. Banfield (ed.), URBAN GOVERNMENT (New York: The Free Press of Glencoe, 1961), p. 284.

and more inclined to react strongly to decisions which are objectionable to them.

Ethics. There are also conflicts of professional obligation involved. The manager's professional code of ethics requires him to maintain a "constructive, creative, and practical attitude toward urban problems" as well as "a deep sense of his own social responsibility as a trusted public servant." He is to recognize "that the chief function of the local government at all times is to serve the best interests of all the people." In the immediate sense, however, he is obligated to work in a context and through means acceptable to a majority of that group, no matter how limited its perception or narrow its orientation. Therefore, on the one hand he is required to seek understanding as to the whole range of needs and interests in the community, to be sensitive even to those values which, though very important to some people, rarely find meaningful political expression in the community.

But he may be faced with a council which refuses to recognize certain interests or to consider them legitimate. In the extreme, council preferences may not be in accord with seemingly obvious conditions and needs, such as improvements in fire and police protection. Or a council composed of the more affluent and better educated might be quite willing to spend money for stimulating economic growth and providing amenities important to their own neighborhoods, yet be quite insensitive to pathological social and economic conditions, or the most basic interests found in parts of the community with which they do not come into contact. A common example is the institution of an urban renewal project without real regard for the people whose neighborhood will be destroyed.

What should the manager do under such circumstances? How can he adjust his conflicting obligations to relate to the community as a whole in his work and at the same time function within the constricted framework established by the council?

Professionalism. The snap response is, when the conflict becomes intolerable, resign. Managers may indeed face such a choice. But before that point is reached, managers may employ their own resources in influencing situations and handling problems of the sort that have just been discussed. A good many of his resources are inherent in his professionalism—his substantive and procedural expertise. The skills and knowledge which professionalism suggests he possesses are obviously important for dealing with difficult or touchy problems.

But in addition, his *status* as a professional has its own impact in his dealings with the community and the council. The professional manager can speak to the council as a nonpartisan and as one without a personal stake in community issues. He can speak on the basis of his expertise in governmental matters and his responsibility for considering the best interests of the community as a whole. Working from this perspective, he may expand the range of problems and interests considered by the council members beyond that which would spontaneously occur to them and lead the group to weigh actions which would not be immediately apparent to it. For example, he can point to the existence of dissatisfaction about conditions in a particular part of town as a fact which the council should know, and provide his expert assessment of the reasons, together with specific recommendations for remedial steps that can be taken to solve the problems.

There are a host of specific things the manager may do in order to educate the council and, in a sense, serve as a bridge between members and parts of the community to which they are not naturally oriented. Personal qualities, such as a talent for diplomacy, are important. But in the final analysis, professionalism is the manager's most potent resource in "leading without alienating to the point of losing effectiveness," as Duane Lockard has put it.[29]

Professionalism involves more than just a claim or an educational history; it must be constantly substantiated in order to be a viable resource. This raises the question as to how professional status can be built and maintained over time in the individual case.

George K. Floro has concluded that managers increase their professional status either by rising through a succession of increasingly pres-

[29] Lockard, *op. cit.,* p. 233.

tigious manager cities, or by staying in one place and earning a reputation for that city being well managed. In either case a "potential to move is required."[30] There are two aspects to this potential. In order to repulse pressures for unprofessional actions in the conduct of his job, ideally he must avoid becoming entrenched, remain aloof from local alignments, and have the ability to move easily if he so desires. In order to maintain this ability to move, he must build a reputation within his city for effective and professional managment. This means he must avoid turmoil and antagonistic relations with the council, and he must at the same time handle problems in accordance with professional standards so that his reputation beyond the city is protected. Thus a potential to move, the basis of professional status, requires a regulated, controlled environment in which the manager is involved, but not too deeply, in the community, and performance which meets two sets of standards, standards which at times may vary considerably.

Perhaps when the concerns of cities were more limited and when those who felt alienated from community decision making remained meek and quiet, and when some people, including city managers, were not so sensitive to fundamental problems, the difficulties in maintaining the requisites for professional status as described above were not so acute or crucial to the manager's success.

But present conditions are different. Apathy is being shaken off in the cities. Interests once relatively disorganized and quiet are now more vocal and organized. Circumstances, including new federal programs, have forced cities into very touchy, divisive areas. Yet the dominant elements in the political system and on the council may not be flexible and responsive. A manager may find it increasingly difficult to handle the new order of problems well and at the same time maintain proper relations with the council if these conditions prevail. In either case, his potential to move is diminished, his position as professional manager in his city is concurrently reduced, and his professional status is jeopardized among interest groups and within the community as a whole.

Compatibility. The preceding has been put rather starkly in order to emphasize certain basic problems. There are a number of reconciling factors. One of the most important concerns the recruitment and employment of managers. In one reported situation, the city manager involved commented upon his preliminary conversations with council representatives about assuming the position. "The talks yielded some consistent opinions about the style of administration that Valley's leading citizens felt suitable for their town." It was indicated to the prospective manager that, "Valley had its own quiet ways of community living and that it would not accept as manager anyone who pushed for changes too strongly or too rapidly."[31] Thus, in the process of selection, the participants have an opportunity to judge the proclivities, styles, and preferences of one another. Clues given to the manager regarding standards of acceptable performance may allow him to draw conclusions as to whether he would be comfortable and whether his own personality and concept of the professional manager's role would fit.[32]

Of course, prior understandings of this sort can never be complete. Unforeseen circumstances or problems of a divisive nature may arise. The composition of the council may change, resulting in a different set of value preferences becoming ascendant, as for example when a manager who was hired as a "builder" suddenly finds himself facing a council hostile to this approach and dedicated to keeping services at existing levels. When such changes occur, regardless of his skills or professionalism, the manager is quite likely to find himself to be "one of the most dispensable men . . . [in the] political community."[33]

---

[30] George K. Floro, "Continuity in City-Manager Careers," AMERICAN JOURNAL OF SOCIOLOGY, November, 1955, p. 246.

[31] Frank P. Sherwood, "A City Manager Tries To Fire His Police Chief," in Edwin A. Bock (ed.), STATE AND LOCAL GOVERNMENT: A CASE BOOK (University, Alabama: University of Alabama Press, 1963), p. 342.

[32] For reasons suggested in this section, some cities still look to the amateur, perhaps a local figure, to hold the managerial position—someone safe politically or substantively.

[33] Kammerer, Farris, DeGove, and Clubok, *op. cit.,* p. 81.

Relationships

Within the context of the community political system, the city manager is involved in a network of often delicate relationships with the mayor and council, his subordinates, other governments, and the public. The following discussion focuses on the nuances of these relationships, factors affecting them, and some of the more common problems that arise from them.

RELATIONSHIPS WITH THE
MAYOR AND COUNCIL

Expectations. To begin with, there are sets of generally accepted mutual expectations regarding relationships between the city manager and the council, derived from their formal positions.[34]

The council expects the manager to:

1. Be the chief administrative officer of the city and be responsible to the city council for the proper administration of all affairs of the city.

2. Appoint and, when necessary, suspend or remove officers and employees of the city except as otherwise provided by the city charter or law, and to direct and supervise their work.

3. Prepare the budget annually, and submit it to the council annually, together with a message describing its important features, and be responsible for its administration after adoption.

4. Prepare and submit to the council as of the end of the fiscal year a complete report on the finances and administrative activities of the city for the preceding year.

5. Keep the council advised of the financial condition and future needs of the city and make such recommendations as he may deem desirable.

6. Recommend to the governing body a standard schedule of pay for each appointed office and position in the city service, including minimum, intermediate, and maximum rates.

7. Recommend to the governing body (from time to time) adoption of such policies as he may deem necessary or expedient for the health, safety, or welfare of the community, or for the improvement of the administrative services.

8. Consolidate or combine offices, positions, or departments, or units under his jurisdiction, with the approval of the city council.

9. Attend all meetings of the city council unless excused therefrom and take part in the discussion of all matters coming before the council.

10. Supervise the purchase of materials, supplies, and equipment for which funds are provided in the budget.

11. See that all laws and ordinances are properly enforced.

12. Investigate the activities of the city or of any department or division. Investigate all complaints in regard to matters concerning the administration of the government of the city and in regard to service maintained by the public utilities in the city, and see that all franchises, permits, and privileges granted by the city are faithfully observed.

13. Devote his entire time to the discharge of his official duties.

14. Perform such other duties as may be required by council.

Conversely, the manager expects certain things from the council; optimally, he needs a council which:

1. Gives the manager the tools he needs for the jobs assigned to him.

2. When assignments are given to the manager, makes clear what is to be done and when work is to be completed.

3. Criticizes the work of the city manager when it is deserved, but gives the criticism in private or in an impersonal manner so that the issue can be objectively analyzed in an atmosphere of mutual understanding.

4. Assures the manager of a fair hearing in controversial situations, and does not question the manager's motives until he has had a chance to tell his side of the story.

5. Acts in an understanding and sympathetic manner.

---

[34] What follows on mutual expectations is drawn essentially from the previous edition of this book: International City Managers' Association, THE TECHNIQUE OF MUNICIPAL ADMINISTRATION (Chicago: The Association, 4th ed., 1958), pp. 17–19.

6. Gives the manager a respectable hearing on his recommendations and proposals.

7. Keeps public meetings on a high plane by avoiding ridicule and sarcasm in relations with fellow councilmen, the city manager, or other city employees.

8. Deals with administrative officers or employees who are under the jurisdiction of the city manager solely through the manager in any matters of importance.

9. Issues directives only as a body to the manager.

Bases for Conflict. No sets of general expectations of this sort, even if perfectly understood and accepted intellectually, can provide a guide to behavior in all circumstances. And even within the context they provide, there are sources of tension and potentials for conflict inherent in the relationship between managers and elected officials.

First, there is the very simple matter of differences in backgrounds, orientations, and positions which may become distilled into "personality" considerations, or vague likes and dislikes. In his study of conflict between managers and councils, Jeptha J. Carrell found councilmen quite willing to tag managers with less than complimentary characteristics, such as: "blunt, bullheaded, inflexible, somewhat snobbish, cold and unfeeling, proud and self-satisfied, stubborn, red-tape-happy, too formalistic and business-like, undiplomatic, arrogant, conceited, looks down his nose. . . ." Conversely, managers saw council members as "easily influenced, too lenient, too friendly, touchy, and sometimes skeptical and hard to impress."

Considered in an isolated fashion, such impressions may not be very significant, but in conjunction with other factors they may be quite critical. As Carrell notes, "Personality clashes may interact with conceptual differences to form a high-voltage amalgam of tensions and stresses."[35]

A manager's personal concept of appropriate professional style and his resulting behavior may also be divisive, to the extent that a pro-

pensity to take a long run view, to prevent problems from developing, to emphasize the need to maintain the integrity of a policy, or even to resist making adaptations in policy implementation, for example, may be contrary to the tendencies of councilmen to emphasize the short-run and the expedient.[36] And such differences may occur without the manager being conscious of them or their causes. Carrell's investigation reported that although managers saw themselves as following a "realistic approach," their councils perceived a less compromising, less politically sensitive, more rigid, and "more all-seeing and all-doing" stance and a greater interest in technique than in substance.[37]

There also may be differences in the way proper roles are perceived. A survey of Colorado city managers and councilmen revealed that 67 percent of the managers felt they ought to play a *leading* role in policy making, but only 39 percent of the councilmen felt the same way.[38]

Probably one of the most significant sources of tension and conflict lies in the problem of defining exactly who is to do what from day to day, or determining the precise nature of the amorphous distribution of prime policy responsibilties to the council and administrative responsibilities to the manager in particular situations. Clarence E. Ridley has concluded that "practice in council-manager cities indicates that policy and administration do not come in separate compartments. Objective determinations are almost impossible; therefore it is rare to see rigid functional divisions."[39]

As a result, for matters falling in the vast middle ground between the highly charged political issue and the very routine administrative matter, responsibilities tend to be allocated in a rough, common sense, *ad hoc* manner. Loosely defined spheres of principal concerns

[35] Jeptha J. Carrell, "The City Manager and His Council: Sources of Conflict," PUBLIC ADMINISTRATION REVIEW, December, 1962, pp. 204–206.

[36] *Ibid.,* pp. 205–206.

[37] Jeptha J. Carrell, "The Role of the City Manager: A Survey Report," PUBLIC MANAGEMENT, April, 1962, p. 76.

[38] John C. Buechner, DIFFERENCES IN ROLE PERCEPTIONS IN COLORADO COUNCIL-MANAGER CITIES (Boulder: University of Colorado Bureau of Governmental Research and Service, 1965) , p. 16.

[39] Ridley, *op. cit.,* p. 2.

develop. Ridley describes one aspect of the process as "tentative delegation of power from the city council to the city manager subject to continuous review by the council. The actual administration of policy may suggest necessary changes which again involve council action."[40]

These comments imply a dynamic quality in the relationship, and that the balance of council and managerial concern may shift over time on the same matter or category of municipal activity. Concerning administrative activities, for practical reasons including the time factor, most councils will not regularly interest themselves in narrow problems, although there will be a measure of general oversight. Under certain circumstances, however, members of the council, collectively or singly, may intervene on a point that is important to them, but which is considered by the manager to be within his jurisdiction. This is more likely when representation is based on wards, but it can happen any place because of the general absence of definitional precision. One councilman has been described in this manner: "He does not deem it proper to interfere in administrative matters within the province of the city manager. But he tends to view the area of policy belonging to the council as wide enough to do what he wants."[41]

40 *Ibid.*, p. 11.
41 Wildavsky, *op. cit.*, p. 241.

On the policy side, managers may find themselves operating within an environment of councilmanic uncertainty, both as to what ought to be done and who ought to do it. The following description, concerning a long-time manager of Beloit, Wisconsin, is indicative.

While [Archie D.] Telfer believes it is a manager's duty to carry out the will of his council, he knows from long experience that city councils do not always know their own will. This is most likely to occur with a problem whose political dimension is not clear. In such a case councilmen may either ignore the issue in the hope that it will go away, or offer some informal authorization for action to avoid going officially on record. Telfer knows that a nod of the head from a key councilman, or an oblique remark in informal conversation may (or may not!) be as significant a cue to action as a formal resolution. As manager he is then left with the dilemma whether or not to make a decision on the matter himself, and if he does so, what that decision is to be.[42]

It is not always easy to predict a specific or general reaction. Variations over time are quite likely in a particular community, and differences are apparent from city to city, depending upon the makeup and inclinations of councils. For example, Kweder found that in his North Carolina cities, councilmen were "dis-

42 Warner E. Mills, Jr. and Harry R. Davis, SMALL CITY GOVERNMENT: SEVEN CASES IN DECISION MAKING (New York: Random House, 1962), pp. 31–32.

THEORETICAL RELATIONSHIP

Council   Manager

Council dominates manager

DISTORTED RELATIONSHIP

Manager   Council

Manager dominates council

FUNCTIONAL RELATIONSHIP

Manager   Council

Manager and council work together in atmosphere of trust and cooperation, each with his own sphere of responsibility, but with ultimate responsibility residing with the council.

FIGURE 4-4. *Relationships between council and manager*

tressed" when managers did not offer leadership.[43] But Carrell discovered "a vague sense of malaise about their power" among the councilmen he surveyed.[44]

Certain facts about a community and its politics will have a bearing upon the general pattern that develops in the allocation of responsibilities and the level of tension that exists. A popularly elected mayor who sees himself as the policy leader in city hall may utilize his position to narrow the manager's scope of action.[45]

A stable majority on the council representing a faction in the community may reduce uncertainty in either direction, by sanctioning a wide swath for managerial action or holding the manager tightly on a leash. In either case, what is expected of the manager may be fairly clear. When the community is split into competing factions of more or less equal strength, a skillful manager may find the situation conducive to a broad construction of his functions. One less skillful may discover that the splits in the community produce a stalemate and require him to tread cautiously.

Another conceivable situation is for there to be conflict, but neither a stable majority on the council nor a factional stalemate. A majority must be carefully put together on each issue, making it difficult for a manager to rise above the routine. The manager probably encounters the least difficulty regarding the nature of his role in homogeneous places lacking community conflict and organized politics.[46]

Operational Guidelines. In response to the inherent perplexities in council-manager relationships, several generally accepted norms of professional conduct have emerged. Many of them are manifest in the International City Management Association's Code of Ethics. They suggest that the manager should:

1. Overall, ensure that his actions consistently reflect his status as subordinate to the council. Avoid public criticism of the legislative body, and take care not to embarrass it.

2. Avoid competing with the council for public attention; allow it to receive credit for success.

3. Remain aloof from basic political conflict in the community, such as councilmanic elections.

4. Relate to the council essentially as a collective body rather than as a group of individuals in order to avoid suspicions of favoritism.

5. Stimulate the council to exercise initiative and to fulfill its leadership role. Arthur Bromage has noted that one of the manager's greatest problems is getting "the councilmen out of the trenches of routine decision and into attacks on crucial community problems. . . ."[47] This of course requires that the manager himself understand a wide range of community feelings and know what the problems are. He must funnel ideas and facts into the council in a way that educates, sparks curiosity, and raises challenges.

6. Prepare the council for forthcoming recommendations and put proposals and supplementary material in a form so that the members can work their will in a meaningful way.

7. Base recommendations and positions on factual analyses rather than simple statements of preference. If there is a factual base for what the manager says, the danger of erosion in his position is minimized when he finds a majority of the council taking a contrary view.

8. Once a council decision has been made, defend that choice in the community.

9. Appreciate the limits within which elected public officials work. Do not ask for the impossible.[48]

Obviously these are general guidelines which require adaptation to particular situations. Some of them may be impossible to follow at times. A council may be so bland and retiring that a manager cannot avoid appearing dominant in the relationship. For its own reasons,

---

[43] Kweder, *op. cit.*, p. 68.

[44] Carrell, "The City Manager and His Council: Sources of Conflict," *op. cit.*, p. 204.

[45] Gladys M. Kammerer, "Role Diversity of City Managers," ADMINISTRATIVE SCIENCE QUARTERLY, March, 1964, p. 426. She sees the presence or absence of an elected mayor as the prime determinant of the managerial role. Kweder takes exception, *op. cit.*, p. 78. Williams and Adrian found the mayors in their four cities to be relatively quiescent, *op. cit.*, p. 295.

[46] Banfield and Wilson, *op. cit.*, pp. 177–80.

[47] Arthur W. Bromage, "Managers Become More Oriented to Human Values," PUBLIC MANAGEMENT, October, 1965, p. 259.

[48] Kammerer, *op. cit.*, p. 429.

the council may literally thrust a manager into a very public role of policy leadership. Further, the manager cannot control what other people think about his position, how they interpret events in the community, nor how the communications media will depict the conduct of the city's affairs.

Although the manager may not participate in councilmanic elections, he may influence their outcome, consciously or unconsciously, in a variety of ways. For one, many managers are constantly scouting for potential community leaders to assist in various aspects of city government, such as serving on boards and commissions. Through his recommendations, then, individuals may be placed in the public arena and in a position subsequently to seek elective office.

It is difficult for a manager to relate to the council as just a collective body when there are marked variations in the interest, initiative, and capacity of councilmen, or when there is a faction distinctly antagonistic to him. Also, emphasis on the collective relationship leads to formality which may restrict the free flow of communications. The manager may find it difficult to get evaluations of his performance, and attention to other delicate matters best talked about privately and informally may be forestalled. Finally, there is an obvious potential contradiction in the admonitions to catalyze the council into exercising its leadership role and to avoid pushing too hard and too fast.

These qualifications do not call the essential utility of the norms into question. They simply point to some of the problems that managers must continually face and indicate that a consistent set of hard and fast rules which provide all the answers are no more available for city managers than for any other professional performing important and sensitive tasks. Rather than absolute answers, experience has shown them to be valuable aids to the manager in carrying out his responsibilities for meeting community needs under conditions of democratic responsibility.

RELATIONSHIPS WITH SUBORDINATES

One of the most significant characteristics of the city manager's position is his "in-between-ness," with the mayor and council on one side and his subordinates at city hall on the other. At worst, this places him between two powerful pinchers who press in upon him; at best he must contend with conflicting pressures and represent the two elements to one another.

The major responsibilities of the manager toward his subordinates are to provide the requisite administrative leadership and direction and to secure the conditions and resources for getting jobs done. The exact nature of his executive functions will vary with a number of factors, including size of the city and the degree of professionalism below the managerial level. In some places, the city manager will be deeply involved in the details of day-to-day administration. In others his major concerns will be much broader. But whatever the mix, he will find that his position of formal hierarchical superiority does not mean that his legally established authority over subordinates is limitless or can be exercised in an uncompromising manner.

Administrative Leadership. Nurturing and maintaining the organizational morale and spirit indispensible for effective overall program implementation requires the manager to be sensitive to the varied interests of municipal employees. He is expected to function as a buffer between them and the community and serve as a shield against pressures and reactions stimulated by efforts to perform responsibly. Managers who use subordinates as scapegoats when things go wrong, or place them in jeopardy of public embarrassment by shoving them to the forefront on controversial matters, are considered to violate their professional obligations, and they risk destroying the respect and confidence which contribute to effective administration.

Major problems are created for the manager by the need to be constantly concerned with the viability of the city organization in the large sense. Such problems have their origins in the fact that the "correct" response to a problem often differs, depending upon the context within which it is considered. A specific reorganization or change in procedures viewed narrowly might clearly make a significant contribution to efficiency, but examined in terms of its impact on the people involved, the disruptions might cause negative effects outweighing any potential gains. The existence of professional canons and generally accepted administrative techniques are often of little assistance in perceiving and properly weighing limited problems in their broad implications and cumulative effects. It is at this point that an almost artistic talent for management becomes significant.

Judgments involving comparisons of short-run gains versus long-run effects on performance capacity are not just restricted to questions of how the city's affairs are to be administered. They must often be made on substantive proposals that arise from the staff.

In utilizing a managerial style which will generate the ingredients of viable administrative leadership, such as loyalty and a cooperative spirit, the manager may find his professional obligations and interests in conflict. In order to maintain an appropriate morale level among his staff, he may feel impelled to take matters to the council which he feels will be poorly received, and thereby perhaps weaken his personal position and diminish his standing with his superiors. He may consider it necessary to approve and endorse specific proposals about which he has doubts, because he feels that the adverse consequences for the city— such as losing a valued department head— would outweigh the immediate results of his approval.

Constraints. There are other forces shaping the nature of the relationship between the manager and his subordinates, with origins in the distribution of the real means for influencing decisions. Despite the importance of formal position and delegation, every city manager will find, as does every President of the United States, that no matter how broad and comprehensive the formal executive mandate, its reach is limited. It is limited because the positive grant is not accompanied by interdictions against the power and authority of others. When differences arise between a manager and those beneath him, they will do so not under the conditions implied when the municipal organization is viewed in terms of formalistic superior-subordinate relationships. Rather, various participants will have resources that can

be used in asserting a position, of which hierarchical place is but one.

For example, one of the most important such resources is expertise. How many city managers have sufficient knowledge to challenge technical experts on questions such as the proper processes to use in a new waste treatment plant, or the correct composition of street building materials? The same problems exist in social areas, as in determining the "right" components for a city recreation program. Although he may have nagging doubts and intuitively feel that something is amiss, can he reject the recommendations of experts on grounds that are nebulous? Obviously the manager's discretion is limited by the specialized knowledge of his subordinates; in a sense he is a captive of it.

Viewing the municipal organization in a broader sense, the manager is dependent for performing his own job effectively upon items controlled in the first instance by subordinates. Information which can be withheld or distorted is an obvious example. The position of subordinates relative to information, plus their direct access to the tools used to carry out tasks and to the people whom the organization affects, provide them, potentially, with a certain independence and directive force of their own which may be used to seek goals which are not those of the manager.

Further, individual employees may have ties to the community and perhaps to the council, as a result of having local origins or long tenure in their position. Indeed, despite charter provisions and merit systems, they may actually be in their jobs because of such relationships. Even short-term professionals may have developed sufficient reputation and connections with groups in the community to provide an individual luster and a measure of independence. Under such conditions, there is always a possibility for taking disagreements with the manager into the community as a whole or into the council, and defining them in terms of personalities. Many managers have had to contend with employees, even departmental administrators, who, if not incompetent, were not responsive to managerial leadership and even inclined to oppose it, yet who were secure in their positions because of community ties.

The collective political power of city hall employees in the community may be quite significant. In one of the Florida cities studied by Gladys Kammerer and her associates, city employees, their families and friends accounted for about 3,000 votes, or approximately one-third of those cast in municipal elections. Ordinarily employees as a group are most concerned with the personnel system and conditions of work. This results in an interest in the selection and retention of top-level administrators, including the manager, who are in a position to make decisions about such matters.[49] Thus, dissatisfactions in city hall may cause problems for the manager in the community at-large. But also, satisfaction contributes to dispersed support for a governing group throughout the community, including by implication support for substantive policies and the manager's stewardship.

A basic difficulty lies in what employee groups are likely to seek. Very often they are inclined to reach for autonomy in regulating working conditions and routines. Rigid approaches are likely to be preferred. Managers may well see the results as dysfunctional for accomplishing program objectives with a reasonable degree of efficiency. Change may be difficult to accomplish. A very good example concerns the combination of fire and police departments in smaller cities, which many feel to be a sound notion. The fact that it has been accomplished in only a very few places testifies to the difficulty of altering traditional arrangements when the relevant groups are opposed.

The trend toward public employee unionization, with agreements negotiated periodically about such matters as wages, working conditions, and grievance procedures, means further restraints on managerial discretion. And there are other implications for the relationships in city hall. Briefly, they include: growing depersonalization in hierarchical relationships; the inclusion of "outsiders" in the form of such persons as union officials, mediators, and perhaps arbitrators in making administrative decisions; a confusion in council-manager roles

vis-a-vis subordinates, resulting from the participation of council representatives on bargaining teams, as is the case in some places; heightened conflict resulting from struggles over the right to represent employees; and the ever present possibility of ultimate employee sanctions over management in the form of strikes, whether legal or not.

In summary, the relationship between manager and subordinates (and consequently the role of the manager) is tempered by the requirement that formal authority not be exercised arbitrarily and insensitively and by the fact that a variety of resources for influencing municipal decisions are inherent in subordinates whether they are organized or not. The problem for a manager lies in balancing what he feels is necessary for top administrative performance, what others at city hall feel is required, and what councils want and expect. The three are not necessarily the same.

RELATIONSHIPS WITH OTHER GOVERNMENTS

The entwining web of intergovernmental relationships where the activities of the manager's city constantly intersect with those of other jurisdictions grows larger in importance for him. The federal government is increasingly involved at the local level, particularly through its multitudinous grant-in-aid programs. States have always been significant in a rather negative way, but more positive interests are being manifest in diverse areas, such as urban transportation and the administration of justice. Cooperative patterns at the local level have been long established, because of obvious program overlaps and interconnections. However, innovations represented by such institutions as multipurpose special districts, regional planning agencies, and councils of governments are adding interesting new dimensions to the pattern of relationships. Jurisdictional exclusiveness has become less and less pronounced. Now, most of the important things a city does will likely involve a number of other governments at some stage, with some interesting consequences for the manager.

One result is that increasingly large chunks of the manager's time and that of his staff are allocated to external relations. The nature of

---

[49] Kammerer, Farris, DeGove, and Clubok, *op. cit.*, p. 45.

this involvement may be quite varied, ranging from handling rather routine matters and asserting the parochial interests of the city, such as negotiating with the water district to ensure that lines are laid before a new city street is constructed, to attempting to influence general policy made in state capitals and Washington. Thus the manager is required to become familiar with people, programs, and procedures in many places in order to carry out his duties. Furthermore, adeptness in maneuvering within the intergovernmental complex and the circumstances it creates no doubt will become increasingly important factors in performance evaluation.

In this conjunction, the changes which have been briefly noted present an interesting paradox for the urban executive: they have the potential for both expanding and constricting his options in policy development and implementation. External stimuli may cause officials and people in a community generally to be more perceptive, imaginative, and receptive to new ideas and program innovations. Financial assistance from the outside or a combination of resources, at the local level, may allow governments to undertake tasks which otherwise they would not. Requirements, such as for a more effective water pollution control effort or for conformance with a regional development plan, may assist officials in building community support for new ventures. In city hall, more sophisticated administrative techniques, more professional staff, and staff in entirely new areas may result.

A variety of constraints are conceivable. Even the availability of financial assistance may function as one. For example, there are limited federal funds for neighborhood redevelopment. A city might well be tempted to defer steps which would otherwise be taken until such time as grant money was available. The external stimuli may run counter to the priorities of the community or significant parts of it, and in response, action may be forced into low priority areas according to some local assessments. Community conflict may be exacerbated and the task of governing made more difficult by disagreement over priorities, varying perspectives among jurisdictions, and differ-

ing interests that are revealed starkly by intimate relations among a variety of governments. Fears may be generated about loss of identity and control when larger governmental units are seen as exercising power in the community.

Among the possible administrative constraints are requirements that affect the allocation of administrative resources, specify certain types of administrative structures, as in the case of the model cities program, or necessitate certain administrative practices, as when particular qualifications for program personnel are demanded. Dependence upon decisions made elsewhere produces unsettling effects: red tape, waiting, and the continuing possibility of jolting policy changes over which there is little direct control.

The various problems raised by more intimate relationships among governmental units suggest a final implication for managers and other officials: concern for the workability of the system. More and more attention is being given to developing new and revised organizational and administrative procedures and arrangements to facilitate the increasing interactions among governmental units.

RELATIONSHIPS WITH THE PUBLIC

If queried, most local chief executives would probably put relations with the public near the top of their list of major functions, in terms of both time required and significance for the general operations of the city. In one way or another, a great deal of this chapter has pertained to the matter, especially those segments concerning the manifestation of community values and community policy making. This part will focus more explicitly on the manager's personal involvement as a vital link in the connecting chain between government and citizens.

There are two allied dimensions to relations with the public. One is the maintenance of general conditions of openness, responsiveness, and fairness in the conduct of public affairs. In a more specific sense, relations with the public involve the communication of messages to officials that are the raw materials for decisions and action. Moving in the other direction, there are messages flowing from officials to the

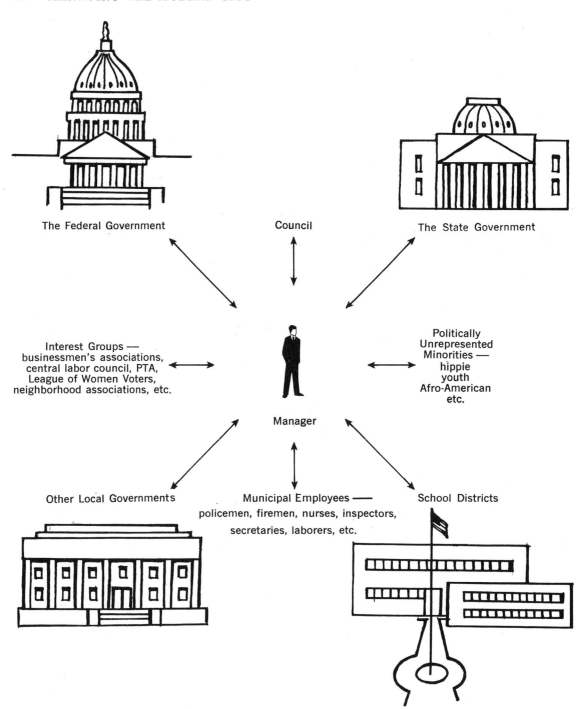

The Federal Government

Council

The State Government

Interest Groups —
businessmen's associations,
central labor council, PTA,
League of Women Voters,
neighborhood associations, etc.

Manager

Politically
Unrepresented
Minorities —
hippie
youth
Afro-American
etc.

Other Local Governments

Municipal Employees —
policemen, firemen, nurses, inspectors,
secretaries, laborers, etc.

School Districts

FIGURE 4-5. *The world of the manager (In performing his everyday duties, the manager is expected to remain sensitive to all groups. He should further seek to balance his sensitivities, slighting none of these groups. Every group slighted by the manager, or every group which feels slighted by the manager, poses a major threat to the community's harmony and stability, to say nothing of the manager's job tenure.)*

public in order to stimulate reactions to situations, explain decisions, or justify them. A plethora of difficulties is inherent in the relationship between officials and their constituents. A good many are those commonly experienced in any communications process, such as blockages, mischanneling of messages, or distortions—each having an infinite number of causes.

Obviously the city manager is only one of many involved in the relationship being discussed. Even a great deal in the way of city hall activities which concern relations with the public may be beyond his knowledge or specific control. When he does participate, he may be constrained by his position as intermediary between various parts of his organization and the outside world and his relationship with the council. And his capacity to influence those factors affecting relationships which are centered beyond city hall, in the media, and among the public in general and interest groups in particular is clearly quite limited.

Nevertheless, his position is certainly one of the most critical in its impact on the nature of the relationship which will be established with the public. What he does or does not do will have considerable significance to the extent that he has a distinctive approach at all, and if so, whether it is essentially reactive, manipulative, or something else. One way is through his role as spokesman, in which he continually makes "in person" representations to the community through various means, ranging from news conferences and formal speeches to responding to the complaints or pleas of individuals. What he says and the conditions under which he says it are important in and of themselves. They will have a direct impact on the community in terms of understanding public policy problems and the city's operations, and on the environment within which decisions are made and operations carried out.

The manager's role as spokesman to the community and as one of the conduits through which messages from the community pass into city hall is highly visible, and there is a common tendency to see his involvement in relations with the public almost exclusively in those terms. In actuality, the matter is a bit more complex. First, the example he sets is also significant; that is, his public conduct may have a disguised effect on other officials. If a manager is insensitive to problems of injustice that may be created by administrative decision or is inclined to be reserved and somewhat secretive, his subordinates may be influenced to follow the same patterns, at least in part. If a manager is preoccupied with interacting with citizens on essentially minor problems, or emphasizes a manipulative approach for the purpose of creating favorable public opinion for his program and his administration, other city employees may well pick up the clues and behave in a comparable manner in their relationships with the public.

Second, as chief administrator and advisor to the council, a manager has a continuing opportunity to make decisions which are not immediately apparent to the public but which in the long run may have a greater impact on the relationship between city government and citizens than any of his visible activities. Through these decisions, an approach may be implemented, assuming the manager has conceived one, in a diffused way. Some, but by no means all, of the factors he may affect include: the general degree of sensitivity to the nuances of relations with the public and communications processes among public officials; the development and employment of expertise regarding the use of various techniques for relating to and communicating with the public; the procedures for the administration of programs as they relate to fairness and equity for citizens; the manner in which citizen complaints and grievances are handled; the pattern of structured interest representation as may be found on various advisory bodies or boards and commissions; and the conduct of council proceedings.

No doubt many other examples could be provided. But the central point should be clear: the manager's involvement in relations between government and the public is central; it pervades and thereby affects practically everything he does, though often in an implicit manner. Consequently, the general state of the relationship that comes to exist will be molded in large part by him.

A Final Note

Council-manager government has come several long steps since those first tenuous beginnings in Staunton, Virginia, and Sumter, South Carolina, more than half a century ago. As York Willbern has put it, "The bits and pieces of change mount up."[50] At times they mount up rapidly. Witness the differences between this book and its predecessor. And no doubt its successor will be an even more striking departure.

What then can be said by way of speculation on the world of the city manager or urban administrator as it will develop in coming years? "Not very much," is probably the sensible answer, given the almost inevitable tendency of social and political predictions to become discredited by events almost as soon as they are uttered. Nevertheless, some soothsaying seems to be a requirement for such enterprises as this.

At the risk of being trite, one thing is certain: the continuing existence of urban problems. Indeed, just about all of the pressing domestic problems, from civil rights to environmental quality, fall into this category. Thus municipalities and other local governments are squarely and permanently in the national spotlight as agents having a vital role to play in dealing with problems of broad concern. Needless to say, those in leadership positions at the local level will continue to bask (or wither) under that focus.

The national preoccupation with problems which may be defined in urban terms unfortunately will not be accompanied by pat or easy solutions. Demands and expectations, over which administrators have little control, will continue to exceed the progress allowed by economic, social, and political conditions. Complicating matters further, the absence of common agreement on what cities ought to be, even though the surface similarity of people may become greater, means that contradictory expectations, or conflict, will be a constant. Progress no doubt will be made on a variety of fronts on the basis of limited agreements, such

as that substandard housing is bad. However, new problems and ever higher expectations will continue to emerge, thus ensuring that jobs will never become routine and dull.

The structural context within which officials will function will be marked by the accelerated involvement of a variety of governments, including the federal, in dealing with urban-centered problems. So far as the structure of local government within urban areas is concerned, the trend increasingly seems to be away from attempts at comprehensive integration to a more varied set of arrangements, including restricted regional organizations such as planning agencies and councils of governments, which may go beyond serving simply as coordinative mechanisms and assume functional responsibilities; an increased number of special districts; expansion in the services provided by urban counties; expanded contractual relationships among municipalities; and the accelerated utilization of joint public-private associations. York Willbern has said,

Viewed in this light, the municipal corporation becomes just one variety of associational arrangement, a sort of multi-purpose special district, with some of its purposes and functions applying to all persons living within a specified limit, and some to only portions of the citizenry within those limits, and some to interested customers or participants in an area overlapping the geographical limits of the unit.[51]

If the projection is accurate, it means that urban administrators will confront a much more varied set of situations and tasks than now is ordinarily the case. Further it means that the correlation between urban administration and employment by cities (as city manager for example) will become less and less.

There is no reason to believe that the rising professionalization of local government personnel will cease. Further, the explosion of managerial technology will enable local administrators to do more and will consequently contribute to raised expectations about what ought to be done. The increased use of electronic marvels and instruments such as planning, programming, and budgeting systems will not only facilitate more effective management,

---

[50] York Willbern, THE WITHERING AWAY OF THE CITY (University, Alabama: University of Alabama Press, 1963), p. 117.

[51] Ibid., pp. 121–22.

but may well open local operations more extensively and precisely to public view.

As concern about urban problems grows and as familiarity with them is distributed more widely, there may well be expanded active involvement at the local level of able and informed citizens who are attracted to places where the action is. Council and mayorality positions, for example, may come to be filled increasingly by people who are more knowledgeable, assertive, and demanding than is generally the case today. Coupled with the prospect of a new breed of official participants is the prospect of changing participation patterns within the community at-large. If current movements aimed at broadening the scope of participation in community decision making are successful, the complexity, diversity, and thus conflict-generating capacities of community decision-making processes will be increased. The implications for appointed executives are obvious.

What then of city managers? First, they probably will come to comprise a genus within the species professional urban administrator, a trend that is now quite apparent. In all cases, problems, expectations, and circumstances will combine to propel the administrator further into the community. Supported by an increasingly professional staff, he will move above day-to-day routine to serve as the connecting link between policy formulation and program development and implementation. He will be deeply involved in the systematic identification of problems and concerned with general questions of resource utilization.

His role will continue to grow in importance in the community, as will his exposure and probably also the range of interests with which he must deal and the difficulty of the substantive problems he must face and the responses he must devise. Indeed, some of the problems may be beyond solution in any final sense, leaving the administrator with no recourse except to cope as best he can. In any case, they will require administrators to develop expertise in new areas constantly. Labor-management relations, recruiting and training the hard-core unemployed, and economic development are three contemporary examples. To add a melancholy note, in some small places managers may have to develop and apply expertise on the demise of nonviable communities. However, other managers may enjoy opportunities to participate in the creation of brand new communities from scratch.

Community leadership, serving as an agency for innovation and change, and politics in the broad sense will become more explicitly associated with the position. Consequently, political skill and social sensitivity will outpace technical administrative knowledge as requisites for filling top positions.

The foregoing characterization is compatible with Duane Lockard's comment on the traditional American inclination to move to strong executives, to a "policy initiating, policy promoting center of power."[52] One might add that this tendency is more marked in times of crisis. The clear implication is that during the era of the urban crisis, it is reasonable to assume that the role of the top urban administrator will continue to evolve in this direction, with the attendant increases in responsibility, challenge, and risk. Obviously a certain amount of pain will be engendered by the alterations. But difficulties and risks must be balanced against opportunities for accomplishment, and pain against rewards.

The urban administrator of the future no doubt will suffer a plenitude of wounds during his career, but for many these will be more than offset by the satisfactions of accomplishment and service.

---

[52] Lockard, *op. cit.,* p. 235.

5

Leadership Styles and Strategies

URGINGS TO "BE A LEADER" represent the single most important set of demands placed upon the urban administrator. Leadership is expected of him in a complex variety of settings and situations.

A community's chief administrative officer is required, for example, to lead his subordinates in the administrative structure. He is also required by the code of his own profession, by the exigencies of his job, by the plight of the urban environment, and usually by the members of his council to offer guidance and direction—hence, leadership—to the council in its deliberations. Interest groups view him as a leader of the community and rightly expect him to play a leading role in the execution of public business. The community's interests require that he exercise leadership in dealings with officials from neighboring and overlapping governmental units. His friends will look to him for leadership in interpreting and understanding municipal affairs. Even his critics increasingly expect him to become the leading apologist for the actions of the community's government.

Given then the centrality and importance of the urban administrator's leadership role, it is unfortunate that the concept of leadership is neither readily defined nor its prerequisites easily determined. The clienteles of leadership—the "followers"—in the setting of local government are so diverse, and the situations in which they are encountered so dissimilar, that the practicing administrator may indeed question whether it is possible to conceptualize or discuss them as a coherent whole.

Nevertheless, this chapter will treat the problems of leadership in a unified fashion. In so doing, it will build upon the descriptions of the administrator's multiple roles and responsibilities contained in the preceding chapter. Portions will review the essential nature of leadership; describe followers and their motivation, leadership styles, and resources; and examine the strategies associated with the selection and execution of various leadership tactics.

The Nature of Leadership

As is common to nearly every topic subjected to intense academic scrutiny, leadership has been defined in many ways by many different people. One example is the definition provided by Ordway Tead in his book, *The Art of Leadership*. Leadership, Tead said, is "the activity of influencing people to cooperate toward some goal which they come to find desirable."[1] In their widely used text on public administration, John Pfiffner and Robert Presthus term leadership the "art that stresses the attainment of mutual ends through the coordination and motivation of both individuals and groups."[2]

---

[1] Ordway Tead, THE ART OF LEADERSHIP (New York: McGraw-Hill, 1935), p. 20.

[2] John M. Pfiffner and Robert Presthus, PUBLIC ADMINISTRATION (New York: The Ronald Press Co., 5th ed., 1967), p. 88.

Such definitions provide insights into the nature of the leadership function, as well as into the various ways in which that function may be interpreted. Still another definition is recommended here; it will serve as the working model for this discussion.

LEADERSHIP DEFINED

Leadership can usefully be viewed as that *interaction between two or more people in which one person (the leader) is able to exert some control over the behavior of the other person or people (the follower or followers) over a period of time.*

There are several aspects of this definition which demand elaboration. First, the function of leadership requires two or more people: a person exerts no leadership if only his own conduct is affected. Second, while leadership is a function of the interaction between people, that interaction need not be based on face-to-face contact, or even necessarily be interaction of which the participants are conscious: it is possible for a leader to affect the behavior of vast numbers of persons whom he has never met. Evangelist Billy Graham, for example, has provided spiritual leadership to thousands of persons with whom he has had no direct contact. United States' presidents provide leadership for the governments which they head, yet they rarely meet more than a tiny fraction of the people who are their "followers."

Third, the definition requires that "control" be exerted: the leader must alter the behavioral patterns of the follower. This control can be direct and overt, as through the orders of a ship's captain to his crew, or it can be vague and intangible, such as the good example provided by the exemplary conduct of a religious leader. Further, the leader-follower relationship implies some willing acceptance by the follower of the "controls" of the leader. This acceptance might be given enthusiastically, as ball players eagerly respond to their coach during a crucial game, or it might be given only reluctantly under threat of punishment, as children behave when threatened with a spanking.

Finally, the definition implies that the leadership must prevail for some "period of time." This distinguishes an act of leadership from isolated stimulus-response situations: the fact that drivers passing through a busy intersection respond willingly to the commands of a traffic policeman hardly makes a leader of the policeman or followers of the drivers. This definition then, suggests that leadership involves three components: the leader, the follower, and the situation. Each of these requires explanation and brief elaboration.

The Leader. In the instance of the leader, it is most important to note what he is *not*. Specifically, he is *not* a certain kind of person, a man of a specific temperament or personality.

The professional literature includes many studies of supposed "traits" possessed by leaders. Taken together, this research can lead only to the conclusion that there is, in fact, no trait or complex of traits generally associated with leadership. These trait analyses themselves point up the inconsistency: Gordon Lippitt has found that, in 106 such studies, no more than 5 percent of the traits identified appeared in more than four of the studies.[3]

Still, there can be little doubt that the leader's own personality and behavioral patterns are instrumental in determining both his leadership potential and his realization of that potential in specific situations. Harry R. Knudson, Jr. identifies the following important internal forces that affect a person's leadership capabilities: (1) his value system, including his attitudes towards such organizational characteristics as decentralization, organizational efficiency, personal growth of subordinates, and the allocation of responsibility; (2) his confidence in his subordinates; (3) his own leadership inclinations; and (4) his feelings of security in an uncertain situation.[4]

This is not to suggest that there is a particular "right" response to these forces, but rather that such forces have a bearing on the effectiveness of leadership attempts in any particular situation with any particular set of followers.

---

[3] Gordon Lippitt, "What Do We Know About Leadership," in LEADERSHIP IN ACTION (Washington: National Training Laboratories, National Educational Association, 1961), p. 7.

[4] Harry R. Knudson, Jr., HUMAN ELEMENTS OF ADMINISTRATION (New York: Holt, Rinehart, and Winston, 1963), p. 124.

Ralph M. Stogdill has summarized both points well:

A person does not become a leader by virtue of the possession of some combination of traits, but the pattern of personal characteristics of the leader must bear some relevant relationship to the characteristics, activities, and goals of the followers.[5]

And, it should be added, some relationship to the goals and structure of the organization.

The Followers. It is, then, the nature of the followers—not some generalized "nature of leaders"—which most nearly defines the leadership situation. Simply put, to lead is to gain acquiescence and support—leadership can be understood only through attention to those who comply.

The category "followers," of course, includes people with as varied personality traits as any other large group. These differing traits, in turn, lead subordinates to respond differently to various kinds of motivation, direction, and control. For example, a person who lacks confidence is more likely to respond satisfactorily to a supervisor who is positive and rewarding than he is to a supervisor who tends to be highly critical of his work.

Furthermore, different classifications of followers may respond differently to alternative leadership methods. It seems fairly obvious, for example, that the basic technology of leadership should be applied differently when the followers are manual laborers working on a street improvement project as opposed to a group of professionally trained social workers involved in the development of community action programs. Some followers are more willing to be led forcefully than others: the military techniques, including rigid discipline, necessary to mold soldiers out of civilian draftees are not at all appropriate in developing esprit de corps among a group of volunteers working for a charitable organization. For this reason, retired military officers who are unable to substitute civilian leadership styles for the habit of command are apt to make poor city managers, even though they possess many of the requisite technical skills.

[5] Ralph M. Stogdill, "Personal Factors Associated with Leadership: A Survey of the Literature," JOURNAL OF PSYCHOLOGY, January, 1948, p. 64.

The psychological needs and personal goals of followers are most important in determining the appropriate leadership style. Persons who have joined a group because of a strong personal commitment to the achievement of that group's goals—people who become active, for example, in political campaign work because of a personal concern for the victory of a particular party or candidate—will more likely respond to very directive leadership patterns than will members whose participation is based principally on a need for enjoyable social experiences. Similarly, people who are dependent upon organizational membership for earning their livelihood will be willing to accept more authoritarian leadership than will persons who are not so financially dependent.

Followers are important not only because they either accept or reject the leadership or the particular leadership style being utilized, but also because they give the leader whatever power he may have. A leader's ability to direct is wholly dependent upon his followers' willingness to respond in the desired manner. Formal or legal authority means little if people will not respect that authority. Thus, while a department head may have the legal authority needed to issue directions to his subordinates, that legal authority is meaningless unless his subordinates are willing to accept and carry out those directives. Ultimately, of course, a legal superior, such as the department head, may be able to compel obedience through the threatened use of such sanctions as dismissal of his subordinates, but obedience which is secured under the threat of sanctions is far less productive than obedience which is voluntarily given. Effective leadership is thus leadership which is designed to maximize the enthusiasm with which directives are accepted by followers.

Leadership Situations. Just as the ingredients necessary to leadership are a function of, or are determined by, the nature of the followers, so too are they also a function of the situation: different kinds of situations demand different kinds of leaders.

It has often been noted that some men emerge as leaders under short-term conditions of severe crisis who, in normal situations, have neither the inclination, interest, nor ability to act with authority. J. M. Barrie's classic tale, *The Admirable Crichton,* in which the household servant replaces the father as a family's chief decision maker while all are shipwrecked, is a useful example. For a more extreme instance, persons filing out of a burning building are very likely to follow any individual who panics and runs for the nearest exit. The panicky person may have no overt leadership abilities, but his actions provide leadership in the crisis situation. Edwin B. Flippo has summarized this aspect of leadership by noting:

Perhaps the most significant result of recent research into leadership is the development of the situation viewpoint, which maintains, in effect, that the situation (the problem and its environment) will structure the type of leadership that is called for. In this sense, a man may well be a leader in one situation and a follower in another. He may be a leader of the group at one time and find that his particular talents are not required at another.[6]

Applications of this principle manifest themselves in many different ways. It is quite clear, for example, that different hierarchical levels of an organization require different leadership patterns: the supervisor of a work crew and the president of a large corporation face very different leadership situations and, consequently, need very different styles. Different organizations, too, require different kinds of leaders. A sales organization may demand a leader who is skilled at the science of human relations, a man who is dynamic and outgoing in his personal relationships. An accounting organization, on the other hand, may require a leader who is adept at handling numbers and who has an analytic mind capable of paying great attention to minute detail. Finally, different kinds of tactical situations demand leaders possessing differing kinds of skills. The quarterback of a professional football team, for example, must make instantaneous decisions based on very sketchy visual information when calling audibles at the line of scrimmage, whereas the leader of an architectural team must deliberate over great volumes of data before giving final approval to an architectural design.

Such considerations have been categorized by Knudson into a four-fold typology. The major factors which affect the nature of the leadership situation, in his terms, are the organization type, the work group, the nature of the problem, and the pressures of time.[7] These items are largely self-explanatory; the examples given above can readily be fitted into the various categories. The important point that an administrator need recognize is that his own success as a leader will be determined in part by his ability to adapt himself to the varying demands rooted in such situational differences.

Summary. Leadership, then, is a product of the interaction between the personality and behavioral patterns of one person—the leader —with the personalities and expectations of other people—the followers—within the context of particular circumstances—the situation. In essence, it might be said that leadership is the end product in an equation blending leader, followers, and situation.

THE LEADERSHIP ENVIRONMENT OF THE ADMINISTRATOR

Leadership in urban management is a particular brand of leadership: it is leadership conducted within the formal organizational structure of the community's government. Thus, it is leadership which is both public and administrative in nature, conducted in an organization setting, and with ultimate responsibility owed to both the organization's membership and the community at large.

The Nature of Administrative Leadership. Administrative leadership is that leadership which is exercised within formal, bureaucratic organizations. But a distinction must be made here, for in most organizations there are clearly two sorts of leadership exercised.

When leadership is exercised by persons to whom the leadership responsibility has been officially delegated by the organization's structure and rules, it is termed *formal leadership.* When leadership is exercised by persons within the organization to whom such responsibilities have *not* been so delegated, it is termed *infor-*

---

[6] Edwin B. Flippo, MANAGEMENT: A BEHAVIORAL APPROACH (Boston: Allyn and Bacon, 1966), p. 229.

[7] Knudson, *op. cit.,* pp. 125–27.

mal leadership. Alternately, the term "formal leadership" refers to the leadership (normally and supposedly) exercised by persons of higher rank within a hierarchy, while "informal leadership" is that exercised by coworkers or others who are unofficially viewed as "leaders" or "opinion makers" by organization members.

Both kinds of leadership exist in every organization. They may, however, exist in entirely different realms. In some instances, the areas of informal leadership may be of minor consequence: the secretary who sets fashion styles for the other girls or the mechanic who decides whether to play poker or baseball at lunch. What is more important, however, is the recognition that informal leadership may well exist in areas of substance: the setting of work rates or the formulation of attitudes toward superiors.

Ideally, formal leadership and informal leadership should be exercised by the same person; formal leaders should behave in such a manner that their subordinates will look to them for leadership on an informal as well as a formal basis. In other words, formal leaders should be persons whom their subordinates would choose to follow if they had the opportunity to make such a choice.

Unfortunately, however, formal leadership and informal leadership are not always exercised by the same person. Such separations stem from several causes. Leadership selection procedures, for one, are not infallible. Furthermore, the leadership expectations of followers and the nature of situations tend to change more rapidly than the identities of persons charged with formal leadership responsibility. Informal leadership can be and tends to be more unstable in the sense that its location within a group may change periodically, as the concerns and situations of the group change, even though the group's membership and its formal leadership remain constant.

Finally, formal and informal leadership may not be exercised by the same person because formal and informal leadership designations are made by different members of the organization: formal leaders are designated by the organizational hierarchy, whereas informal leaders are chosen by the persons being led.

For example, the selection of a person to hold the rank of police sergeant is typically made by the police chief, but the patrolmen themselves decide to whom they will look for advice and counsel.

The desirability of having both formal and informal leadership combined in a single person does not mean that formal leaders should be chosen on the basis of their popularity with the persons whom they are to supervise. It means, rather, that in addition to the considerations of technical skills required by the various administrative positions, supervisors should be chosen for their ability to act as leaders; in other words, for their ability to adjust their behavioral patterns to the varying leadership demands and expectations that will be imposed on them by both superiors and their subordinates.

The Organizational Nature of Administrative Leadership. Administrative leadership functions in an organizational environment; urban administrators are expected to exercise leadership within the organizational structure of their community's government. The fact that leadership is to be exercised within a structural, organizational setting poses certain constraints and bestows certain advantages upon the administrator. It also serves to define rather precisely the nature of the leadership task.

From a formal, organizational perspective, the principal function of the leader is to coordinate the work of his subordinates toward the achievement of certain defined objectives. The objective in a street department may be the maintenance of roadways in a specified state of cleanliness and repair with a minimum expenditure of effort and resources. In a police department, the organizational objective might be broadly defined in terms of reducing the incidence of crime, but the leader, e.g., the police chief, may want to specify goals in an even more operational sense: he may describe goals in terms of the number of man-hours on patrol, the speed with which the department responds to requests for assistance, and similar indices of services rendered to the community. Regardless of the administrative tasks involved, and regardless of the manner in which goals are specified, it remains the principal duty of administrative leaders to promote maximum effort toward the achievement of these organizational ends.

This general function may be analytically divided into four major responsibilities. These are:

1. *Communication of Goals to Subordinates.* A leader's first responsibility is to communicate to his subordinates those goals toward which the subordinates are to direct their efforts. The more fully workers understand the goals toward which their effort is directed, the better they are able to allocate time, make decisions, and interpret orders. Furthermore, worker satisfaction is apt to be increased if the workers perceive themselves as accomplishing well-defined and articulated objectives. (This implies, of course, that the objectives established are realistically achievable given the capabilities of the workers.)

2. *Motivate Workers.* The second principal responsibility of the leader is to motivate the workers under his authority. This means that workers must be stimulated to work willingly and even enthusiastically at the tasks assigned to them. Such a situation is most likely to exist when there is a strong, positive rapport between leader and followers, when the leader has identified the goals of the organization in terms of the goals which motivate the workers themselves, and when there is a working atmosphere which meets the needs and expectations of the workers.

3. *Coordination of Effort.* The most time-consuming of the leader's responsibilities normally involves the coordination of worker efforts toward the achievement of common goals. Such coordination requires: (1) advance planning of the strategies and methods to be employed; (2) training and instruction of workers; (3) direction and supervision of worker effort; (4) the coordination of the activities of the workers themselves; (5) coordination of the work of the leader's agency with the efforts of other agencies seeking the same goal; and (6) the tasks of resolving problems, altering plans, changing directions, and providing the ongoing inspiration needed to maintain the desired level of worker motivation and enthusiasm.

4. *Reporting on Accomplishments.* Finally, the leader must also assess, at periodic intervals, the degree of success achieved in realizing the stipulated organizational objectives. Such assessments are necessary for two reasons: (1) they are generally required by the leader's own superiors in the organizational hierarchy, and (2) such assessments provide an important source of feedback about organizational activities which, in turn, can be used to generate a sense of worker satisfaction with accomplishments, motivate workers to higher levels of output, and adjust organizational activities to remedy problems and increase proficiencies.

THE POLITICAL NATURE OF ADMINISTRATIVE LEADERSHIP

The urban administrator, as all public administrators, has a dual responsibility. He is responsible, on the one hand, for the provision of effective organizational leadership: his is the task of running a "taut ship" in directing the programs and workers under his supervision. He is responsible, on the other hand, to the public which he serves: as a government employee, he is required to act in a manner which meets common expectations regarding responsive and responsible democratic government.

This responsibility to the public involves two components: imbuing the organization with the spirit of service in the public interest and embodying in all actions an interpretation of the public will. Neither, of course, is an easy task. The "public interest" is not clearly definable, objectively measurable, or even generally perceived. The "public will" is commonly composed of many differing, often quite contradictory voices.

But this public component of the urban administrator's role clearly affects his position as a leader. Most clearly, it places a special trust upon him when he acts as an advisor to the council or to the community. His proposals and actions must sustain the general welfare in its broadest sense and, ideally, seek the greatest possible reconciliation of the preferences of every citizen and citizens' group.

These same considerations, in perhaps less obvious a fashion, can have ramifications for the urban administrator vis-a-vis his organizational subordinates. He must, for example, attempt to instill in them an appreciation of their own responsibility as agents of the community. This responsibility demands courtesy and good faith in all dealings with citizens—not, as in a private business, as a matter of retaining customers, but as an ethical obligation.

Beyond that, the urban administrator may be asked to obtain employee compliance with public policies they dislike. Some employees will, out of professional commitment or personal preference, be dedicated to certain ways of conducting business: social workers, engineers, policemen, planners, and health technicians are frequently bound by some formal or informal occupational "code." In some instances, council-formed policies will contradict these preferences; nonetheless, the administrator must seek to gain employee acceptance or, at least, to strike an acceptable bargain between the council and the "professionals." The dedication of such "professionally-oriented" employees is often a mixed blessing; it can complicate the leader's task.

The public environment may at the same time circumscribe the administrator's ability to use administrative tools and resources. He is, for example, normally saddled with civil service requirements which—whatever their merits—do not give him full formal authority over the hiring, promotion, and dismissal of employees. He may have less freedom than a comparable private manager in matters of internal organization and policy.

Moreover, since his actions are more visible than those of a private administrator, they may need to be defended or modified as a result of council or interest-group "pressure." In practice, the line which separates "administration" from "policy" is fine indeed. Council members may, for example, press for the use of merit pay plans—which are clearly administrative instruments—because they feel that their implementation would provide the community with greater employee output. Similarly, various citizen groups may show concern for such essentially administrative matters as police disciplinary procedures, salary levels, hiring practices, methods of dealing with citizen complaints, and the employment of nonresi-

dents by the agency. While such concern may strike the administrator as "political meddling" in organizational affairs, it is natural and certainly proper in a democracy. At any rate, these "public" aspects of the urban administrator's leadership role necessarily affect his own decisions and strategies.

The political responsibility of the administrative leader in an urban setting is discussed at considerable length in Chapter 4.[8]

Developing Leadership Capacities

One finding reported above, that leaders are not people of a specific type, holds out hope for the urban administrator. It suggests that some leadership skills may be learned or developed. To the extent that this is true, an administrator can successfully work to improve both his own leadership abilities and those of key officials around him.

Preceding sections have noted that leadership is a process of human interaction. Its skillful exercise involves an appreciation of several human qualities. These include, first, an awareness of the nature and motivations of subordinates in the organization, those factors which lead them to work—well or poorly—in the way they do. Second, they include self-awareness, an accurate perception of the patterns of leadership habitually employed. Finally, they include an appreciation of the various "leadership resources" which might be brought to bear more fruitfully in future efforts.

Taken together with an understanding of the constraints and requirements imposed by specific situations, knowledge of this sort should permit the planning of more effective leadership strategies and tactics. The following portions of this chapter deal with these topics.

FOLLOWERS AND THEIR MOTIVES

"Followers" are generally people pursuing certain kinds of roles, not certain kinds of people. Just as trait lists cannot be used to distinguish a leader "type," neither can they define the

---

[8] See especially the section on "Community Values and their Manifestations."

characteristics of a typical "subordinate." Moreover, the two sorts of roles are in many ways similar: the ideal "follower" would show the same kind of initiative, purposiveness, and decision-making capacity that normally is thought to characterize the ideal "leader." As any supervisor knows, such subordinates would make organizational life much simpler.

That followers cannot be understood in terms of any simple stereotype or "model" will emerge as a major theme in the succeeding paragraphs. Subordinates, to repeat, are people, and as varied as any other category of mankind. Their actions spring from as broad a range of human motives as those of others; those who motivate followers, then, must look for their "rules" from what is known of human needs generally, and what they know of their own subordinates in particular.

It must also be clearly understood that the problem of interpreting employee motivation is a complex of several interrelated questions about each individual worker. A list of these might include:

1. Why does he work at all?

2. Why does he follow this particular vocation?

3. Why does he work for this particular agency?

4. Why does he work so well (hard, reliable, capably) —or why doesn't he do better?

Each of these questions, of course, requires a somewhat different kind of answer. While all are important, the latter two are of particular relevance to the urban administrator: questions of motivation "on the job" normally arise when it is difficult to hold men in necessary positions, when absentee rates are excessive, or when employee output is "below par." These matters, then, receive special attention in the discussion that follows.

Basic Motivators and Human Needs. Abraham Maslow's concept of the "hierarchy of needs" provides perhaps the best introduction to the complex questions surrounding employee motives. Maslow has argued that man's many needs—all of which may act as behavior motivators—are best viewed as a ladder-like set of definite stages. As the needs related to one stage are satisfied, their effectiveness as motiva-tors ceases, and new, higher order needs take their place.

As summarized by Douglas McGregor, the need hierarchy includes:[9]

1. Physiological needs: e.g., food, rest, shelter.

2. Safety needs: e.g., protection from danger or deprivation.

3. Social needs: e.g., the desire to "belong," for friendship and love.

4. Ego needs: e.g., self-esteem, personal competence and social status, recognition.

5. Self-fulfillment: e.g., creativity, self-development.

The point is that all of these needs may exist in people and thus shape their behavior and that they do not all exist at the same time. As McGregor cogently puts it, "Man lives for bread alone, when there is no bread."[10] When there *is* bread, he turns toward other objects for need fulfillment.

It is worthwhile to consider how each of these needs might relate to on-the-job performance. Physiological needs could, superficially, seem of primary importance: a man, in this view, works to earn food and shelter for himself and his family. In truth, however, needs of this sort seem to have little relevance.

For the supervisor, the most important questions to be answered by motivation research pertain to turnover, absenteeism, and work output. These performance factors have little relationship to the fulfillment of physiological needs—except, perhaps, in time of depression. Most men can easily obtain many positions which will enable body and soul to be kept together. Moreover, in periods of prosperity, the salary raise which might come from superior performance would most likely permit the purchase of a second (or third) car, not the maintenance of life.

The findings of one nationwide survey of employed men embellishes this point. A pleasant hypothesis was posed for the research subjects: "If by some chance you inherited enough money to live comfortably without working, do

---

[9] Douglas M. McGregor, 5th Anniversary Convocation, School of Industrial Management, Massachusetts Institute of Technology, Cambridge, Massachusetts.
[10] *Ibid.*

you think you would work anyway or not?"[11] Fully 80 percent reported that they would. Work, the men commonly noted, keeps one occupied and interested; some thought they would feel "lost," "bored," or "wouldn't know what to do" without it. Work, in other words, serves many needs beyond those of mere survival.

"Safety needs" are of greater on-the-job consequence. For the administrator, these might be seen as including the desire for fairness, for freedom from arbitrary or discriminatory action. The threatened employee is apt to be concerned about few other aspects of his job, and threats—intentional or as a result of poor communication—are found in too many organizations.

Social needs and ego needs are of special consequence, and are often underrated by supervisors. One survey of employee attitudes in this regard is particularly suggestive, as it not only illustrates the importance of these values to workers, but the extent to which these values are misperceived by leaders.

In this study, employees were asked to rank ten job factors in order of importance to them; in addition, their supervisors were asked to rank the same factors as they thought their employees would.[12] "Good wages" were rated first by the "empathizing" supervisors, but fifth by the workers themselves. More interesting still, the three factors deemed most important by the employees were viewed as least important by their supervisors. These (in the order the employees ranked them): "full appreciation of work done," a "feeling of being in on things," and "sympathetic help on personal problems." All of these, obviously, relate to the social and ego realms.

The importance of self-fulfillment needs is a matter of some controversy. Clearly—and perhaps unfortunately for society, if not for its organizations—most jobs offer little opportunity for the free play of creativity. Too, most men are sufficiently preoccupied with the

lower hierarchical stages that "self-fulfillment" is a lesser and occasional concern. But the factor may at times seem significant for those in comparatively unstructured occupational roles, and for some people in jobs of every sort.

Motivation for What? The ways in which human motives shape activity differ for various aspects of organizational endeavor and from individual to individual. To return to a previous point, the question "what motivates men" should always be sharpened: "motivates men to do what?" Illustrations can be obtained by reference to the two major problem areas identified earlier, the problem of labor "input" —relating to job turnover and absenteeism— and "output"—the quality and quantity of production.

Numerous studies have demonstrated the existence of a relationship between employees' "job satisfaction," turnover, and absenteeism.[13] Men who are satisfied with their jobs hold them and report to work regularly. The administrator might, therefore, expect that he can motivate his workers for greater "input" by doing whatever is needed to increase job satisfaction. In general, research would indicate that this calls for raising levels of job security, intrinsic job interest, opportunities for advancement, and appreciation from supervisors.[14]

The complexity of the motivation problem can be made clear by noting that these same tactics will not necessarily improve labor "output" or production. Researchers have generally found that job satisfaction and performance are *not* related. One survey of the literature concluded by noting:

In summary, it appears that there is little evidence . . . that employee attitudes of the type usually measured in morale surveys bear any simple—or, for that matter, appreciable—relationship to performance on the job.[15]

---

[11] Nancy C. Morse and Robert S. Weiss, "The Function and Meaning of Work and the Job," THE AMERICAN SOCIOLOGICAL REVIEW, April, 1955, pp. 191–98.

[12] Reported in Bradford B. Boyd, MANAGEMENT-MINDED SUPERVISION (New York: McGraw-Hill, 1968), p. 122.

[13] For one summary of the relevant literature, see Philip B. Applewhite, ORGANIZATIONAL BEHAVIOR (Englewood Cliffs, New Jersey: Prentice-Hall, 1965), pp. 26–28.

[14] See Milton L. Blum and James C. Naylor, INDUSTRIAL PSYCHOLOGY: ITS THEORETICAL AND SOCIAL FOUNDATIONS (New York: Harper and Row, 1968), p. 371.

[15] Daniel Katz and Robert L. Kahn, THE SOCIAL PSYCHOLOGY OF ORGANIZATIONS (New York: John Wiley & Sons, 1966), p. 374.

In the same fashion, fringe benefits and other rewards which can be obtained by staying with the organization may be expected to reduce turnover problems, but these same motivators will not normally raise productivity.

To shift ground, Katz and Kahn have noted that what once was termed "craftsmanship"—a motivational pattern based in self-expression—is "the most conducive to the achievement of high quantity and quality of role performance."[16] The man who delights in what he creates will prove diligent and careful. But, the writers add, such a man frequently feels but weakly tied to any particular organization, and may have little commitment to organizational goals unrelated to his specific role.[17] The craftsman "type," then, is apt to be more attached to his own work than to his employer and his employer's broader concerns.

Thus, no single motivational factor can consistently be related to high levels of work output. Motivational tools are a "sometime thing": those which are successful in certain situations may backfire in others, and those which have a positive effect upon one aspect of performance may prove detrimental in other areas.

Motivating men, then, demands a selection of instruments which depends in part on the problem at hand. For the administrator, there is no substitute for the ability to perceive the frustrations and satisfactions existent and potential, associated with each particular job.

Administrators and Motivation. The preceding description of the "motivators" of organizational activity is, of course, only suggestive. No comprehensive review of the relevant behavioral science literature was attempted or provided.

One scholar has, however, attempted to summarize the ramifications of research findings as they pertain to supervisors at every level.

Some of his major points are repeated here; they deserve careful thought.

1. The job of a manager is to get things done *through people.*
2. Most employees expect to work, want to work,

and are most satisfied in a department where they are producing.
3. Employees by and large would rather please their boss than displease him.
4. For most people work is one of the most meaningful aspects of their lives. They can find in work both dignity and personal satisfaction depending upon how the supervisor presents it to them.
5. The individual can control how hard he will work—indeed, whether he will work at all. This raises the question of who really is the boss. The challenge facing supervisors is to continue to create a climate in which a man will want to continue to give his best.[18]

But, since the practicing administrator *is* an administrator, not a researcher, he must be more concerned with particular individuals in particular organizations than with the generalities of human action. What the discussion above should have suggested is that the considerations which move men to work as they do—and, hence, might be used as levers to make them work better—are many and varied. They pertain, in general, to the broad social and psychological aspects of situations on the job. Most "rules of thumb" are not tenable; a skillful leader's strategies must be based upon an acute sensitivity to the human needs of those around him.

A follower's goals, it should be stressed, are without doubt the most important link in the leader-follower relationship. Every follower "submits" to a leader because he perceives such followership as an effective means for the achievement of his own, very personal goals—for the satisfaction of his own needs. In consequence, the more a leader helps other group members achieve their personal objectives, the greater will be the group's acceptance of him as a leader; the more effective his leadership is, the greater will be the organization's likely success in achieving its goals.

This does not mean that the leader must subordinate the organization's goals to those of its individual members, but rather that: (1) the leader should recognize the goals of followers and attempt to synchronize these with the organization's goals, permitting both to be achieved simultaneously, and (2) the leader

16 *Ibid.,* pp. 362–63.
17 *Ibid.,* p. 363.

18 Boyd, *op. cit.,* pp. 90–91.

should seek to maximize the extent to which members make the organization's goals their own, adding corporate purposes to their list of personal objectives.

From this discussion, another point should have emerged: there are probably fixed limits to what men can be motivated to do. The problem is not simply one of putting a properly qualified man in a job and then manipulating a sophisticated "carrot and stick" combination, thus extracting high levels of performance. Many motivators are intrinsic to the job itself; lacking these, no external consideration may be sufficient to produce real excellence.

For this reason, motivation may frequently have to take the form of changing the job, not moving the man. If some people "just won't work," some jobs just aren't "workable." In this regard, Argyris perhaps discouragingly reports a situation in which mentally-defective girls made better and more reliable employees than their normal workmates.[19] Some jobs are so menial or unchallenging that the mature person simply may be unable to do them well.

The administrator, of course, has constraints beyond those of human motives. Some unpleasant jobs must be performed, and cannot—though the effort is too infrequently made—be rendered satisfying. In other circumstances, the use of monotonous techniques may be economically advantageous even if lower morale, increased turnover, and "slowdowns" result. But when such choices are made, they should be made consciously, with full knowledge of all probable consequences.

The application of knowledge and perception of human motives in individual cases is not a science, but an aspect of the art of personal relations. A more extensive discussion of the problems of applying such information in particular instances appears in later sections entitled "Leadership Strategies" and "The Tactics of Leadership."

LEADERSHIP STYLES

Those who lead do so in many different ways. Out of habit, preference, or design most leaders adopt a "style" which pervades their every action, and ultimately leaves its mark on the entire organization.

The literature on leadership includes many attempts to classify and categorize such "leadership styles." The process of reducing complex human behaviors into such "models" or "ideal types," of course, results in a substantial loss of individual detail: perhaps no real person exactly fits any of these stereotypes. Yet a description of leadership styles serves two distinct purposes. First, they provide a framework by which a person can analyze and understand his own leadership behavior. Second, these styles may suggest alternative behavioral modes among which a leader can choose in plotting his own leadership methods. This is the case even though the style of leadership exercised by most people is less commonly a matter of conscious choice than an expression of innate characteristics of personality, training, experience, and background. While every leader is in some degree a prisoner of his personal heritage, few are so constrained that no alternatives are open to them.

The Basic Styles. Of the various styles of leadership behavior discussed in the literature, three are most frequently mentioned: the authoritarian, the democratic, and the participative. In a sense, these describe a complete range of behavior, from the dominating autocrat to the retiring nonleader.

The autocratic or authoritarian leader is one who insists upon holding and exercising personally all of the decision-making power placed in the work unit by the formal organization. Often seen as "hardboiled," this type of leader generally insists that every decision be made by him, that he and he alone issue all orders, and that subordinates be unfaltering in their subservience to his commands. Typically, such a leader—a hard driver of others—works hard himself.

Many authoritarian leaders frequently threaten and use negative sanctions to enforce their authority. They may show little concern for the needs and problems of subordinates. The latter, in turn, normally respond to such leadership by being tense, resentful of the "system," and quarrelsome among themselves.

---

[19] Chris Argyris, PERSONALITY AND ORGANIZATION (New York: Harper and Row, 1957), pp. 67–68.

A variant mode of authoritarian leadership is more benevolent in tone. Its practitioners employ more positive techniques in gaining support—use rewards as incentives for followers—and hope that the resulting follower loyalty will produce the desired obedience. Although subordinates may respond more positively to this benevolent authoritarianism, they still do not share in organizational decision making. Typically, such leaders do not feel reluctant to share this prerogative, but are simply incapable of doing so.

Authoritarian leaders in either pattern also tend to insist upon strict compliance with rules and regulations, to establish complex operating procedures designed to reinforce and guarantee their authority, and to place heavy emphasis upon mechanical considerations of operational efficiency. Adherence to rules, in fact, frequently becomes so important to the authoritarian leader that the achievement of organizational goals is subordinated to procedural perfection.

At the other end of the stylistic spectrum is the democratic leader. In this style, the leader refrains from singular decision making either by delegating such responsibilities to his subordinates or by giving the subordinates an equal voice in policy determination. Generally, such a leader's prime concern is with his followers' acceptance of him as a peer. Seeking to be "one of the boys," the leader will typically manifest great concern for the needs and welfare of his followers, but will refrain from either establishing or enforcing rules or otherwise asserting his formal prerogatives.

The work environment in such a situation tends to become largely leaderless, unstructured, and often either chaotic or stagnant. Subordinate tension and unhappiness may be minimized by the absence of rule enforcement, but frequently, too, the absence of a structured work environment and clear leadership directives generates tension. Productivity may or may not be adversely affected. Generally, however, employee resentment against such a system is noticeably less than under authoritarian leadership schemes.

The participative leadership style represents an intermediate position between these extremes. Under it, the leader shares some decision-making authority with his subordinates, but clearly retains ultimate responsibility for the decisions that are made. Commands are issued and adherence to rules is expected under this type of system, but these response expectations are likely to be accompanied by positive rewards as wel as negative sanctions— with the emphasis likely to be on the use of positive incentives. Goal achievement is apt to be stressed as fully as adherence to established rules and procedures.

Other Leadership Patterns. Besides this common trichotomy of styles, a number of other "ideal types" have been suggested in the literature on leadership. Each of these provides added insights into the nature of leadership behavior and, thus, an understanding of the consequences of such behavior. Many of them are not mutually exclusive: a leader might, for example, adhere to an authoritarian style and still exhibit certain characteristics included in some of the styles described below. This is the case because each typology focuses on different aspects of the leader's actions.

Glenn A. Bassett has made a useful distinction between "failure avoidance" and "success seeking" styles.[20] The leader pursuing a failure avoidance strategy places a greater emphasis upon avoiding mistakes than on producing major accomplishments. Accordingly, such leaders equate good administrative performance with rote acquiescence to tradition, rules, regulations, and established procedures. The status symbols connected with formal leadership tend to be emphasized in this system, change tends to be discouraged, and success is measured by the smoothness of operations and the absence of problems.

The success seeking style is just the opposite. Such leaders view innovation and goal accomplishment as their principle task and see the prospects of problem solving, risk taking, and conflict development as sources of energy which contribute to organizational vitality and, hence, to the maximization of programmatic success. Between these polar extremes,

---

[20] Glenn A. Bassett, MANAGEMENT STYLES IN TRANSITION (New York: American Management Association, 1966), pp. 96–110.

finally, Bassett sees a middle position, a "resource allocator," who adapts leadership styles to the situation, sometimes acting in failure-avoidance patterns and sometimes in success-seeking patterns, depending upon particular conditions.

Berelson and Steiner have observed that group functioning demands leadership of two sorts: instrumental-adaptive leadership ((task-oriented) and integrative-expressive leadership ("socially" oriented.) [21] As the parenthetical notations indicate, each type places emphasis upon a different group need. Normally, these different and often conflicting roles are handled by two separate individuals. The authors note that when a single person is forced to choose between the roles of the instrumental-adaptive leader and the integrative-expressive leader, most will opt for the latter. Popularity, it appears, is more widely valued by leaders than authoritativeness.

Still other categorizations have been suggested. Edwin Flippo, for instance, has differentiated "negative leadership strategies," which seek to employ fear and the threat of sanctions in the motivation of employees, and "positive strategies," which exhibit an affinity for incentives and rewards as a means of accomplishing the same end. [22]

Henry Albers added still another distinction in writing of the difference between "lenient" and "strict" supervision. [23] The leader attached to a strategy of leniency is given to permissiveness in superordinate-subordinate relationships. Thus the lenient leader may overlook minor policy infractions within the organization and occasionally wink at major discrepancies. Moreover, subordinates are granted leadership help in lessening the difficulties of the workaday world. In return, the leader expects employee cooperation and help even to the point of maximum productivity. Mutual dependence upon good will is a major characteristic of the lenient leader strategy.

Guidelines for strict leadership are found in the rules and regulations of the organization; such leaders enforce them rigidly. Because of his rigid rule adherence and enforcement policies, the strict leader is able to appear faultless when dysfunctions occur in subordinate output.

Leadership behavior and decision making, as presented by Robert Tannenbaum, appear on a continuum between "boss-centered" and "subordinate-centered." [24] This particular typology minimally evidences a seven-stage continuum. At one extreme the leader is the chief decision maker, and his decisions are voiced without group participation. At the next stage, the leader attempts to sell his decisions, normally because he is aware of resistance possibilities and attempts to circumscribe that resistance. Further inward movement brings one to the point where there is a leader-led presentation of ideas and acceptance of subordinate questions. This type of attitude affords subordinates an opportunity to gain a wide comprehension of leadership intentions through detailed explanations. At the center position, between the two extremes, is the leader who announces tentative choices left subject to change. Choice selection accrues to the leader but subordinate opinions are heard prior to rendering a final decision.

Movement away from the center and toward the extreme right locates a leader who still makes the final decisions, but places heavy reliance on his followers. The decision-making progression at this stage of the continuum features problem presentation by the leader and his solicitation of subordinate suggestions. Group decision-making activity is greatly enhanced at the next stage. A decision is made by the group after the leader indicates the parameters in which a solution must be sought. The only constraints stem from organizational capability and resources that could affect proposed solutions. Finally, at the extreme right, the leader allows the subordinates a high degree of decision making within set limits. The onus of problem identification and the selec-

[21] Bernard Berelson and Gary A. Steiner, HUMAN BEHAVIOR: AN INVENTORY OF SCIENTIFIC FINDINGS (New York: Harcourt, Brace and World, 1964), pp. 344–46.

[22] Flippo, op. cit., pp. 228–32.

[23] Henry H. Albers, PRINCIPLES OF ORGANIZATION AND MANAGEMENT (New York: John Wiley and Sons, 1961), p. 570.

[24] Robert Tannenbaum, ed., LEADERSHIP AND ORGANIZATION (New York: McGraw-Hill, 1961), pp. 69–72.

tion of group-designed solution alternatives now devolves on subordinates. Participation by the leader is as a peer of the group.

The chief import of this leadership continuum is the obvious overlapping that occurs all along the line. Fixed categorical limits are difficult to draw because a leader's behavior is influenced both by the situation and the person or persons with whom he interacts. Astute leaders, cognizant of the variations that occur between the extremes of permissiveness and authoritarianism, realize that hard selections need not be made between styles and that such categorizations serve basically as reference points for the study and analysis of leadership.

Summary. This examination of leadership styles points out the importance of a number of key variables in leader-follower relations. These include: (1) the degree of sharing in decision-making functions that exists between leader and follower; (2) the rigidity with which rules are enforced and adherence to procedures is required; (3) the concern manifested by the leader for the needs, problems, and personal welfare of subordinates; (4) the nature of sanctions, positive or negative, employed to secure subordinate compliance with directives; and (5) the psychological response of the subordinates to the leadership patterns. It is these variables that should be the focal point of individual concern in the selection of a particular tactic for use in any particular situation.

No one of the styles described above is necessarily best, or even necessarily better, than other styles for all situations. Leadership is, after all, a functional relationship between the leader, the followers, and the situation. The nature of both the followers and the situation will dictate the leadership style that will be most effective.

THE RESOURCES OF LEADERSHIP

An organization for some purposes can be analyzed as a kind of exchange economy. Employees give something—time, effort—and in return receive financial rewards, status, satisfaction, or whatever. Leaders are, of course, employees too, but the exchange principle also applies to their role of organizational coordinator. In effect, leaders purchase the subservi-

ence of others by trading leadership resources for it.

Some of these resources are supplied by the organization; for others, the leader must rely upon his own intellectual and personal capabilities. Formal leaders generally have access to both, and exercise the most effective leadership when each is used, in proper balance, with the other. Informal leaders, on the other hand, are totally reliant upon their own devices. Formal leaders who wish to be informal leaders will find that they must duplicate the tactics of such unofficial "administrators."

Authority: The Formal Resource of Leadership. The formal resources of leadership are those resources provided to the formal leaders by the organization itself. They are bestowed upon the leader by a mandate of the organization as a consequence of the leader's position in the organization's hierarchical structure. They are the perquisites which the superordinate is able to exercise over his subordinates as a consequence of the organization's authority structure.

Perhaps chief among these resources is the superordinate's authority to issue commands, directives, or orders, with the reasonable expectation that they will be followed and obeyed. To some, indeed, such authority appears to be the only real resource a leader has.

Authority can be defined as the legal, accepted, or rightful power either to act or to command others to act. The founder of contemporary organization theory, the 19th century German sociologist, Max Weber, suggested that such authority stems from one of three different sources. The first and most common source of authority is the law. Most organizations operate on the basis of laws, rules, and regulations, and when these are impersonally administered, they are generally regarded as a good and sufficient source of legitimacy for the actions undertaken in compliance with them.

Tradition is a second basis of authority: in an organizational setting, such authority is predicated on the basis that the organization and its values are hallowed by age and ought not to be challenged or overturned except in the most serious and compelling circumstances.

Finally, Weber asserted that authority is

sometimes based upon charisma, upon an irrational faith in leadership which is assumed to
have powers that are magical, supernatural, or
certainly super-rational in nature. Unlike the
authority of law and tradition, the authority of
charisma is not impersonal: it is based wholly
upon the personality and popular appeal of
the leader, generally called a "charismatic
leader." Most organizations try to enlist all
three of these authority sources in justifying
the demands for obedience placed upon their
membership.

Another principal contributor to the development of organization theory, Herbert Simon,
has suggested that the acceptance of authority
has four different bases.[25] In the first, termed
authority of confidence, authority is accepted
because of the follower's trust or faith in the
person asserting the authority. Such a trust or
faith might, in turn, be based upon any of the
following traits possessed by the leader: (1)
his status, either in the organization, in the
peer group, or in the society at large; (2) his
technical competence or, in other words, his
competence in performing the task for which
the group is responsible; and (3) his charismatic leadership characteristics.

In the second, called authority of identification, authority is accepted because the follower
accepts and identifies with the attitudes and
proposals of the leader, persons, or groups from
which the exercise of authority stems. Thus,
for example, police chiefs tend to identify professionally with the International Association
of Chiefs of Police and thus accept the Association's attitudes and viewpoints on law enforcement problems as those of the group exercising
authority.

The third basis of authority, categorized the
authority of sanctions, is predicated upon the
follower's fear of reprisals or punishments. It
is a negative form of authority, a form which
is accepted only because the follower fears the
consequences of failure to do so.

Finally, authority may also be accepted because the follower simply feels that it is necessary to do so. Such "authority of legitimacy"
may be based upon religious tenet, a felt need
to conform to social custom, a conditioned response to hierarchical leadership, or some similar compulsion stemming from a person's inner
values and personality characteristics as they
relate to the work situation.

Simon also makes the important point that
all authority has certain "zones of acceptance";
if these are transgressed, disobedience will follow. In other words, subordinates will accept
authority only within certain definable limits: when that authority makes demands which
are viewed as being unreasonable or unacceptable, subordinate disaffection and disobedience
will result. The nature of such zones of acceptance is demonstrated in Figure 5–1.[26]

In the light of such bases upon which authority is predicated, and upon the existence of
such zones of authority, the challenge for organizational leadership would seem to be twofold: (1) maximizing the bases upon which
organizational authority is predicated; and
(2) keeping the exercise of authority well
within the subordinates' zones of acceptance,
either by restricting the use of authority or by
employing external devices (pay increases, promotions, public recognition or similar status,
and goal related rewards) to expand the subordinates' zones of acceptance sufficiently to include the authority that is to be exercised. Simon relates the size of the zones of acceptance
to the nature of the sanctions which the organization might employ; the size of such zones is
also related to the nature of extant employees'
motivations. In other words, as a general rule,
the more the organization motivates the employee to pursue its goals, the broader will be
the employee's zone of acceptance for organizational authority. Thus, in large part, employee
acceptance of authority is directly related to
the key element of motivation.

Rewards and Sanctions. Authority is but
the most easily perceived resource of formal
leadership. A second resource is the formal
leader's access to sanctions through which his
directions can be enforced. Some of these sanctions are formal: the superordinate generally

---

[25] Herbert Simon, Donald W. Smithburg, and Victor A. Thompson, PUBLIC ADMINISTRATION (New York:
Alfred A. Knopf, 1962), pp. 188–200.

[26] Herbert A. Simon, ADMINISTRATION BEHAVIOR (New
York: The Macmillan Company, 2nd ed., 1961), p. 12.

CASE I: POLICE DEPARTMENT COMMANDS

All leaders are limited in their ability to exercise authority by the willingness of their followers to accept their authority. Their orders, that is, must be viewed as reasonable by their followers; if they are not, their followers might not accept their authority.

Line AD represents orders that could be given to a police department during large scale looting of stores in a business district. It is a continuum showing all possible orders from one extreme to the other extreme.

Point A—the order to shoot all looters

    B—the order to make mass arrests

    C—the order to arrest only flagrant looters

    D—the order to ignore all looting

Under normal circumstances, neither point A nor D is apt to meet the acceptance of policemen who are trained not to ignore the law violations and who are reluctant to shoot and kill people unnecessarily. Therefore, authority dictating these extreme actions may not be accepted by individual policemen.

It is likely, however, that they will accept orders represented either by point B or C and consequently all orders falling between those two points.

The area B-C thus represents the policemen's Zone of Acceptance. Orders given which fall in the range B-C are thus apt to be accepted, or in other words, this authority will be accepted. Orders falling in the ranges A-B or C-D, however, fall outside the zones of acceptance and may be met by follower disobedience. Authority in these ranges will be more difficult, if not impossible, to enforce.

CASE II: THE COFFEE BREAK DECISION

Sometimes leaders find themselves caught between the preferences of their followers and the preferences of their superordinates. Again, their decision must fall into a **Zone of Acceptance** to be satisfactory to all concerned and thus to gain compliance or acceptance of authority.

Line MP is a continuum showing all possible decisions regarding policy on coffee breaks.

Point M—no coffee breaks permitted

    N—two 15 minute breaks per day

    O—five minute break per hour

    P—15 minute break per hour

Subordinate **Zone of Acceptance:** in this case, subordinates will accept any decision falling between point N and point P.

Superordinate's **Zone of Acceptance:** the superordinate will accept any decision falling between point M and point O.

The **Zone of Acceptance:** the area between N and O. Any decision in this area will be accepted by superordinates and subordinates alike and the supervisor's authority will be accepted and reinforced. Decisions in the area O-P will be unacceptable to the superordinates and may cause the superordinate to rescind supervisory authority. Decisions in the area M-N will be unacceptable to the subordinates and may cause disobedience or other rejection of authority.

CASE III: SHIFTING ZONES OF ACCEPTANCE

Zones of Acceptance can shift over time. In Case I, policemen may initially accept only orders in the acceptance zone B-C from their supervisor. If, however, several policemen are injured in stopping the looting, the policemen's Zone of Acceptance may shift.

Because of injuries while on duty, then, the policemen's Zone of Acceptance may shift from B-C to A-B. If the supervisor's commands do not simultaneously shift from B-C to A-B, the supervisor may find his authority challenged or eroded.

Subordinates, by their Zones of Acceptance, have an impact upon the nature of the commands given to them.

FIGURE 5-1. *Zones of acceptance in leadership authority*

has the authority to mete out oral and written reprimands; to prepare periodic evaluations of his subordinates' work, which subsequently become a basis for decisions regarding pay and promotion; and either to recommend or to direct the use of such severe sanctions as suspension or dismissal. Informal sanctions are also available: for example, the prerogative of varying work loads, including the quantity and desirability of work assignments; of varying assignments to different work shifts; of determining holiday, vacation, and overtime work schedules; and generally of making life within the organization either pleasant or miserable for subordinates who do or do not cooperate.

In addition to sanctions, superordinates within an organization also exercise some controls over the distribution of rewards associated with organizational membership. These might include, for example, access to such status symbols as a private office, a private secretary, a personal telephone line, newer office equipment, an expense account to attend professional meetings, the location of desks within an office, or perhaps even the right to have one's own telephone, stapler, or desk name plate. Such status symbols may seem, at first glance, relatively unimportant, but to members constantly searching for clues as to how superiors rate their performance, such "unimportant" symbols can assume gigantic proportions.

There are other perquisites of leadership available to the formal leader in an organizational structure. These include, for example, the right to sit in on and help make policy at higher organizational levels, access rights to persons at still higher levels in the organizational structure, and frequently access to greater quantities of information about organizational policies, programs, and activities. Ultimately, of course, the leader's most important organizational prerogative is the influence which he has with higher levels in the organizational structure and which he presumably can use to promote, to hinder, or perhaps even to veto the requests, either personal or programmatic, made by his subordinates.

Intellectual and Personal Resources. Intellectual and personal resources are those leadership capabilities brought to the organizational situation by the individual himself. Included under this heading are such qualities as a person's familiarity with leadership techniques, his ability to communicate ideas, his "social grace," the ease with which he interacts with people, his ability to inspire confidence in his ideas, and, in general, his ability to relate to other persons. Important, too, are technical skills. The person with greater technical skill for the job at hand is frequently regarded as a leader by his peers; certainly technical skill, when combined with a set of relevant personality factors, greatly facilitates the exercise of leadership.

In discussing positive leadership in his book on management, Flippo describes ten specific areas through which persons (leaders or potential leaders) can influence the behavior of others (followers or potential followers). These, it will be noted, relate closely to the factors considered earlier in the section entitled "Followers and their Motives." Indeed, a leader's resources are but the reverse face of such motives; they are the use of these motives to promote organizational ends. These techniques are:

1. Judicious use of praise. "But praise is an art that can be overused or misused crudely and without tact, or it can be skillfully given when deserved."

2. Public recognition of accomplishments. "The need for recognition can also be satisfied . . . through means that tend to raise the subordinate in the eyes of his peers."

3. Delegation of more responsibility.

4. Development of an atmosphere that suggests productivity and creativity.

5. A sincere interest in the people with whom one works.

6. Competition.

7. Information. "People usually like to know why they are told to do things."

8. Money. "Money can be used as a positive leadership tool, but this is not as simple as the traditional manager has always assumed."

9. Security. Both too much and too little security—of both job and income—are equally disastrous.

10. Participation. "Most behaviorists believe that participation in management decisions is

a positive approach to the problems of influencing employees."[27]

The person who, in his relations with his work associates, can utilize and manipulate these considerations is well on the road toward the achievement of positive leadership, regardless of whether or not he holds a position of formal leadership, but especially if he does have such a position.

Summary. There are, thus, two kinds of leadership resources: formal and personal. There is, furthermore, a growing consensus among students of leadership and organization that the personal resources of leadership are of much greater consequence. The chief perquisite of formal authority—the "power of command"—is generally a very empty power. Describing the powers of command possessed by the President of the United States—the formal job generally considered the most powerful in the world—Richard Neustadt has said that "command is but a method of persuasion, not a substitute, and not a method suitable for everyday employment."[28]

In an even more poignant statement on the same matter, former President Dwight Eisenhower complained that, "I sit here all day trying to persuade people to do the things they ought to have sense enough to do without my persuading them . . . that's all the powers of the President amount to."[29] Harry S Truman, comparing the situation of military and civil leaders, anticipated Eisenhower's dilemma: "He'll [Eisenhower] sit here and he'll say, 'Do this! Do that!' and nothing will happen . . ."[30]

Leadership Strategies

Many aspects of organizational activity are susceptible to scientific analysis. Through the techniques of careful observation and thought, it is possible to understand the motives of people within organizations, describe the roles of their leaders, and classify the variety of situations which are encountered.

Preceding sections have dealt with these topics and summarized certain of the fruits of such analysis. The ideas described were those upon which, in broad outline, there is some intellectual consensus.

The discussion which follows deals with a different sort of knowledge, and for this reason has been treated differently. The formulation of leadership strategies is an art, not a science. It does not lend itself to specification; for this reason, no broad principles of "strategy formulation" are possible, or are offered.

Instead, various sections illustrate the problems which arise in formulating leadership strategies; they show, through example, the varied dimensions of organizational activity which must be taken into account. While not prescriptive, such analysis should assist the urban administrator to sensitize himself to the problems of formulating strategies of his own.

THE GOAL OF LEADERSHIP STRATEGIES

The fundamental core of all leadership strategy is the manipulation of the rewards received by followers for following. Leadership, in the contemporary context, is therefore best viewed as motivational analysis *applied,* the "engineering" of acquiescence, support, and, hopefully, enthusiasm.

Historically, strategies have been shaped by the nature of the rewards available to leaders for disbursal; this is equally the case today. In the past, some leaders could grant or withhold life itself for their slave-"followers"; industrial managers but a century ago controlled jobs and wages which were necessary to life.

The use of these rewards has been largely precluded by the conditions of modern life. Developed societies protect their members from threats of starvation or physical coercion. Indeed, few leaders have less potential for influencing the physical needs and desires of followers than American urban administrators. A "seller's" labor market, rigid seniority rights and "merit" systems, and the need to follow established community pay scale norms, enforced by perpetual surveillance by legislatures and taxpayers, have built a tight wall limiting the variation of acceptable financial recompense to slight marginal differences.

---

[27] Flippo, *op. cit.,* pp. 233–35.
[28] Richard E. Neustadt, PRESIDENTIAL POWER (New York: New American Library, 1964) , p. 41.
[29] *Ibid.,* p. 22.
[30] *Ibid.*

Because of the modern leader's minimal control of material satisfactions for followers' physical needs, his strategy must aim toward coupling the satisfaction of "higher" needs and desires with organizational goals. Psychologists identify these higher motivations as "esteem" needs: the need for self-esteem and for the respect of others.

Strategies To Build Self-Esteem

The leader influences the follower, as always, through his potential as an agent in the satisfaction of follower needs. The modern, well fed, physically secure follower needs self-esteem. He obtains this when he believes he is fulfilling the elements of a complex mental picture which represents to him the person he should be. The picture contains shifting and contradicting elements, and it is too complex to be completely understood by the leader, the follower, or anyone else. But the leader must deal with this picture, since it is his job to influence the follower so that attainment of self-esteem needs implies attainment of organizational needs, and vice versa.

To fit the follower's esteem needs with organizational needs, the leader must: (1) show the follower the relevancy and importance of his tasks to the organization as a whole; (2) convince the follower that he is or can become competent to do his assigned tasks; and (3) seek to cause the follower to use his role performance as a factor in his self-evaluation.

All are needed: the follower cannot obtain gratification of esteem needs if he sees his role as irrelevant or trivial; he will abdicate his efforts if he feels that assigned tasks overwhelm his capabilities; if he feels he is right in blaming his shortcomings on others he will be quite content to do so. Motivating employees to fit the organization thus becomes the task of enlarging and shaping that part of the follower's self-evaluation process which involves his organizational activities.

Relevancy and Importance. The leader often attempts to broaden the follower's organizational perspective and to make it more like his own. It is desired that the follower should have a fuller picture of organizational aims so that he may relate his own job to the whole and thus appreciate its importance. Modern corporate leadership commonly attempts to broaden follower understanding of the "whole picture." House organs, employee group meetings, and even much commercial advertising is aimed at this purpose. Governmental organizations also employ similar devices, such as newsletters, staff meetings, or suggested employee attendance at council meetings. Often this task is made easier by the news media's attention to governmental functions.

The leader also tries to increase the follower's assessment of the importance of his part in gaining organizational objectives. To the extent the follower feels his job is important, he will tend to view its successful performance as a positive measure of his own worth. The leader may use the status of his own position, or he may borrow status from higher sources, to give authority to this upgrading process. Higher authority is co-opted, for example, by the platoon sergeant whose company commander accompanies him during inspections of troop quarters. Much of the "social distance" between ranks, the trappings of office, and organizational ritual is aimed at causing the follower to feel the importance of his task and of the people who say that it is important.

Competency as an Esteem Measure. Leaders long ago discovered the salutary effects of praise on follower performance. But the relationship between praise and good worker performance is seldom analyzed since it seems fair to say that it is the "nature" of man to work better for praise than in fear of censure. Praise, however, does not always produce better performance. Some work situations provide such obvious standards for assessing the effectiveness of individual performance that praise is either superfluous or false: "My, but you carry bricks well." The performance of simple, directly measurable tasks, involving little room for the play of imagination or the exercise of special skills, is seldom enhanced by praise.

A great bulk of modern organization work, especially in nonprofit organizations, cannot be easily weighed by objective standards. Some person must make a judgment as to the competency of the individual who performs it. Since his competency is a prime determinant in the follower's assessment of his own esteem, he craves authoritative judgment as to its presence. If the judgment is repeatedly negative he will retreat from this deprivation of esteem needs, either by damning the judge as incompetent or by surrendering that part of his ego picture which had led him to attempt to perform well in the first place.

In either event, the organization is left out in the cold: the authority of the damned organizational agent is rejected or the follower simply shrugs off his responsibility by deciding he couldn't perform properly if he so desired. While his esteem may suffer temporarily, the follower simpy *cannot* allow the psychological disparity to remain since his self-esteem is not just a desire, but the need of a healthy mind. The leader who recognizes the importance of this need, and of the authoritative judgment he must provide, will neither counterfeit and thus debase praise, nor will he neglect to provide it when warranted.

Cultivating Follower-Organization Identification. Most important is the desire on the part of leaders to cause the fusion by the employee, consciously or unconsciously, of individual self-esteem needs with organizational desires and goals. The satisfaction of esteem needs can be provided by the informal organization and through primary group affiliations, not always to the benefit of the formal organization. Ego gratification is received by the compulsive braggart, the office Lothario, and the informal leader who is hostile to the organization; each receives esteem without regard to organizational goals. The leader's best defense against the effects of deviant and usually unalterable motivation is to surround such personalities with unappreciative, well-motivated, primary group constituents. Even the bad actor seldom performs to a hostile audience.

Effective organizational leadership is more concerned with positive means of causing proper follower identification than with preventing dysfunctional informal relationships. Post-entry training is often aimed as much at employee motivation as it is at improving technical expertise. Conventions and "training seminars" are often used primarily for extra-organizational social purposes, as indicated by the familiar opinion of those attending that they "get more from the 'bull sessions' than from the speakers." Viewed in motivational terms this may be quite correct, since the participating individual is invited to such gatherings on the basis of his *organizational* role. During his attendance, his social standing is infused with this fact, and he thereby gains practice in thinking of himself in organizational terms. Further, the mere presence of many other similarly selected individuals lends importance to their common organizational tasks.

Purely technical training contains motivational aspects also. The leader who encourages mid-career training for his followers is often as concerned about their job attitudes as he is about their skills. The more a worker sees himself as a professional, the greater will be his esteem-seeking identification with the organization, and the greater will be his commitment to organizational objectives.

Far more important than training, from a motivational point of view, is the quality of the interpersonal relationship between the leader and the follower. If the leader wishes to engender any degree of independent initiative or creative problem solving in the follower while furthering his organizational identification, his relations with the follower will be carried on in an atmosphere which bespeaks the presumption of mutual good intentions and intelligence: the follower will be listened to, his suggestions will be treated as having the same currency as the leader's, and they will be subject to the same kind of consideration—as *ideas,* not as "employee suggestions." As a valid contributor to the organization, the follower develops the sense of identification which it is the leader's job to promote. As an added bonus, the follower's ultimate potential as a strong, reliable recipient of delegated authority is increased. While this method of motivation has situational aspects which depend on the type of work and the follower's personality, its application is relevant to such a large proportion of urban administration that it deserves strategic classification.

THE "CURRENCY" OF LEADERSHIP

Since the elementary ingredient of the leadership function involves the giving, by the leader, of some sort of reward (or "output" from the leader) in return for followership (or "input" to the leader), some scholars have developed descriptions of the process which take the form of "models" resembling running engines or living organisms. These "systems" models stress the existence of a continuing exchange between the leader and his followers, an element which is lacking in the static picture provided by formal organization theories.

Viewed formally, the leader draws upon an inexhaustible supply of authority. The fact that a leader has issued an order one day ought in no way to prevent him from issuing others on the next. Continuing follower obedience is taken for granted.

Anyone who asks a "favor" of another draws upon good will, a resource which has certain limits. Too many requests will normally result in some denials—unless the "supply" of "good will" is built up at appropriate intervals by favors returned.

The leader as strategist is in the latter position. The leadership resources upon which he draws are a commodity, increased by some actions, decreased by others. Effectiveness demands that the two be kept in an appropriate balance.

"Desired actions" are the currency of the administrative realm. By acting in such fashion as to meet a follower's needs, the leader "purchases" additional influence. This influence in turn may be used at a later time to "purchase" a desired employee response.

The point of these analogies is that they enable the administrator to recognize that what he gets from followers depends upon what he gives to them. Both his strategies and tactics must reflect both of these aspects of his leadership task.

The Tactics of Leadership

Matters of scale distinguish tactics from strategy. Tactics are more variable, the shifting means needed for the furtherance of broad, fixed ends. Ultimate strategies are directed toward the meshing of individual and organizational needs; tactics must take into account the varying situations within which this overall purpose must be accomplished.

The dimensions of situations have both "structural" and "personal" components. They are defined in terms of the time available for the completion of a task and the individuals who will be involved. This multiplicity of dimensions means that the tactical situations which confront the administrator are too varied for the application of any general principle. What works one day, with one person, may not work tomorrow with someone else. A full consideration of the many dimensions outlined above should suggest why two seemingly similar situations in fact differ, and lead to the development of more productive alternatives.

THE USE OF TACTICS

The use of the term "tactics" in describing an administrative method indicates at least some ineffectiveness of formal command: either an outright lack of jurisdiction or the presence of less than absolute controls over the actions of subordinates. Commands are made in the field of recognized *authority;* tactics are employed to create *influence.* Military command, for example, refers to hierarchically authoritative orders; military tactics are employed to influence persons outside the purview of authority: the enemy.

The use of leadership tactics, rather than direct command, is prompted first by the inability to demand certain sorts of follower performance: creativity, innovation, and initiative cannot be instilled in followers by fiat. Moreover, few leaders would wish to author executive orders so detailed and complete as to regulate the totality of followers' performance. Finally, certain aspects of a subordinate's behavior cannot be objectively described, and commands attempting to promulgate rules in these areas would necessarily be overly general or ambiguous.

"Treat customers well" is an example of such a command. Its purpose is better served by certain tactical methods, whose selection depends on the character of the job setting. The leader skilled in public relations may "model" his own customer handling style to serve as an example for followers; if clientele relations are vital, and resources are available, he may establish a formal "courtesy class" for employees; if employee motivation is minimal, he may let it be known that "spotters," posing as customers, are likely to report discourtesy. Extreme variability and close situational relevancy are distinguishing features of tactics: there are many ways to skin a cat, and there are many, many ways to get things done in urban administration.

APPLICATION OF TACTICS

There are a number of factors which influence the choice of tactics. These include the source of problem inputs, time frame variations, the resources of leaders and followers, the character of the job to be done, and the degree to which dysfunctional informal structures are entrenched.

Input Source. Suggestions, complaints, ideas, bits of information—all of which may be termed "inputs"—come to the administrator from a variety of sources. What he does in response will depend not only upon the nature of the input itself, but also upon the nature of its source. Suggestions from the council, for example, will have to be handled differently from suggestions by department heads.

Frequently the leader must decide whether or not to identify the source of a policy in his subsequent dealings with followers. Should he borrow authority by speaking of the "city council's proposal" or assert his own authority by hiding its source? Sometimes identification of a particular source will increase the followers' responsiveness to a problem, while other sources will degrade the importance of an issue.

Hated clients or hostile departments may have provided the impetus for needed actions, and the wise leader frequently veils such sources from his followers' eyes. Conversely, the leader may seek to obtain permission from authoritative or esteemed individuals and organizations to attach their names to his own ideas. Leaders have even been known to promote good ideas by surreptitiously dropping hints to the "right people" in such a way that the leader's authorship will be forgotten when the idea has become publicly known and when follower action is required.

It is well known and accepted that administrative handling of an issue is greatly affected by the character of its input to the organization. For example, folklore now generally accepts the supreme efficacy of the congressional contact and the letter to the corporation president. The relative importance of this input varies inversely, however, with the frequency of its employment, and it may be safely predicted that the widening popularity of the "call-the-top-man-first" doctrine will ultimately deflate its tactical importance to a level equal to that of commonplace inputs. Similarly, when all problems are stamped "special handling," the special becomes routine.

Time Frame. The "time frame"—the length of time available to complete a task—is an important determinant of tactical approaches. Little leadership skill is needed to impress followers of the need for speed and obedience to commands while quenching a flaming building. Accordingly, the tactical approach taken in organizations dealing with recognized emergencies stresses routine and repetitive training toward the development of conditioned reflex in followers. Fortunately, the existence of simple and direct objectives for emergency units often promotes the organizational identification which produces needed "team spirit," cooperation, and follower identification.

Most organizational tasks lack the obvious urgency of a house afire; the objectives of many organizations are remote and sometimes obscure. Some governmental endeavors have no intrinsic time frame, but are simply jobs to be done—sometime. In others, the time requirements are arbitrarily set by legislative deadlines or by budgetary cycles.

The leader, through his place in the formal communication system and his superior knowledge of organizational requirements, can often influence the follower's perception of the urgency of tasks to be done. This tactic is seen in its simplest form in military leadership. The descriptive expression "hurry up and wait" usually springs from the tendency of leaders at lower hierarchical levels to add "lead time" to their superior's requirement. The general wishes to review the troops at noon; the battalion commander tells the company commander to be prepared at half past eleven; the first sergeant is told to have the men ready at eleven, and so on down the chain to the grumbling private who is ready hours too soon.

This tactical ploy has its limitations and dangers in public administration. Followers who struggle to finish work in time for a phony deadline, only to find it unused a month later, will require greater motivational effort in other matters. The boss who "cries wolf" too often is soon found out. He must remember that the informal communication system provides numerous bypasses around the filters he is able to maintain in the formal system.

Effective leadership cannot depend principally on the tactics of withholding or manipulating information. Instead, it requires the establishment of reasonable deadlines coordinated with other organizational activities (as through the PERT or "critical path" method), and attention to the confluence of the other inputs so as not to allow the followers' product to languish unused. While the manufacture of synthetic urgencies and irrational deadlines can sometimes be a useful tactic, its effectiveness, like that of authority-borrowing, dwindles quickly with excessive use. Repeated use of such tactics, furthermore, tends to erode leadership credibility with followers and consequently reduce the overall effectiveness of that leadership.

The Quality and Kind of Human Resources. The situational variations of resource availability play a large part in the selection of tactics. The leader, faced with a problem which suggests new courses of action, strongly considers the character of followership he can expect. His tactical approach may vary from one of direct command, "Do it my way!," to the most subtle persuasion, "Your way is probably better, but why don't we try it my way for awhile just to prove you're right." It is virtually impossible to catalogue all the combinations of leader and follower personality traits which would enter into the selection of these and intermediate tactics, and absolutely impossible to list the permutations arising from historical and situational factors.

There are however, certain rather general findings about specific leader-follower combinations. It is not surprising that studies have indicated that followers with lower than average I.Q. respond better to the "do-it-my-way!" authoritarian approach than to a more democratic treatment, and, conversely, that higher I.Q. followers perform better when their own opinions are used in policy determination. As with many other administrational generalities, however, these findings offer no "first principles" for tactical selection, since neither the ignorant but independent employee, nor the intelligent but dependent employee, is a rare bird. What they do offer is a wise message for a wary leader: no single tactical approach can be counted on to carry the day under all conditions.

Frequently, the leader has some choice in determining the resources he may use in meeting organizational requirements. As an *administrator,* he will rationally consider the requirements of the job and the possible resources he can apply: the skills, experience, and availability of employees as well as the dislocations and interruptions each particular assignment will cause to the assignment immediately at hand.

As a *leader,* he must also consider the amount of commitment he can expect from various combinations of follower personalities. He may "bend" the formal organization structure by loose interpretation of job descriptions or of standard operating procedures so that a tough job will be assigned to highly committed followers, or to those whom he feels he can influence the most. Sometimes he may even reach all the way out of the organization to enlist aid from some group, possibly volunteer, with high commitment to a particular goal. An administrator may, for example, enlist the aid of a local garden club in planting public areas—perhaps partly to save money and partly to involve others in city affairs—but often because these people will jump to a task that doesn't fit his followers' proclivities.

Leader Innovation and Follower Loyalty. The amount of innovation which the leader exercises is often regulated, in part, by his assessment of the loyalty of his followers. Particularly spiteful employees have been known to watch eagerly for mistakes caused by the boss's innovation, to "save them up," and spill them out before a higher audience following some major setback. Innovation invariably creates risks since, by definition, it implies the use of new and untried methods. These risks will cause the leader who lacks faith in his followers to be more timid in his managerial style, and to be more likely to pick the safe, old way to do the job.

The rare charismatic leader can range far and wide in innovative management without risking the doting affection of his coterie. The realistic leader, who recognizes the limitations of follower loyalty, accepts the possibility that informal, extra-hierarchical channels may someday carry vivid accounts of his failures over his head. This possibility ought not, however, prevent reasonable forays into new territory, nor should its threat sour the relationship between leader and followers with mutual suspicion. Such unhealthy relationships are vicious circles: the surest way to engender disloyalty is to distrust followers; the resultant disloyalty will cause more distrust; and so on.

Rather than be caught in this spiral some leaders are scrupulously candid with subordinates, trusting their integrity while risking betrayal as the price of building follower confidence. A leader may even purposely reveal some of his own otherwise unknown mistakes and shortcomings to followers so as to demonstrate the extent of his confidence in them. Occasionally such tactics backfire, but the risk is minimal, especially if the leader has obtained the respect and confidence of his followers. Follower loyalty is a very real resource, one which only the leader can manufacture, and well worth the effort and risk to obtain it in the benefits that accrue to the organization.

Tactics and the Tough Job. The leader sometimes must forsake all hope of relying on the follower's organizational commitment. Onerous jobs, especially when obscurely related to organizational goals, will frequently cause the leader to drop his motivational tools and resort to the sanctional approach involving threats and penalties. In unusual circumstances, the leader may even attempt to become hated by his followers as a device for spurring them on toward a very difficult objective. This tactic, common in adventure tales and war stories, is not unknown in real life. It is used to draw strength through transference of adrenalized pugnacity from the hated leader to the adversary, or to cause the follower to overlook unpleasant realities of his life "at the front," "on the frozen tundra," or "over the bounding main."

In contrast, the leader with a tough job to assign may strike the tactical pose of the workers' buddy, and a critic of the organization, so as to attempt some retention of his informal group membership. In this role he says: "Sorry, but we *have* to do this foolish job; let's get it over with."

With any of these tactics he spends some leadership currency. As the user of direct sanctions or the object of hatred he reduces followers' potential for voluntary commitment; as an organizational turncoat, siding with the subordinate group, he must weaken his organizationally borrowed authority by calling its ultimate holders "commanders of foolish jobs." The canny leader often avoids either horn of the dilemma by finding an extraorganizational scapegoat: the "foolish job" becomes a requirement of another bureau or of another level of government (always at a higher level, which may partly explain the federal governments' not always deserved reputation for requiring unnecessary red tape).

Tedious work can often be made more exciting through the encouragement and the formalization of competition between individuals or work groups. The competitive activity may be directly related to the work, or it may be extraneous to the organization's productive goals, such as the establishment of sports contests. In either event, the leader's prime motive is to introduce more proximate, less abstract goals to direct his follower's activities toward organized effort, and to increase the individual's identification with his work team or with the organization.

The performance of many followers will improve when the results of their efforts are publicly reflected by the course of a line moving across a chart. But this tactic has its dangers also. For each winning team there must be at least one loser. Since esteem is a *need,* the constant loser will have to seek it outside the organization. It must also be remembered that the strengthening of primary group identification is not certain to produce organizational commitment. The winning lunch-hour ball team members may have great morale but care very little about their work.

Clearing Dysfunctions in the Informal Organization. Organizations frequently contain thoroughly "hardened" informal structures and operating procedures which may resist every effort to change them. Many governmental leaders have been astonished to find that subordinate employees will, on occasion, simply refuse to change their work habits, even upon simple, direct, explicit orders from formal sources to do so. A very real dilemma arises when such an employee is an otherwise valuable member of the organization, and where dismissal for insubordination would mean a net loss to its effectiveness.

The leader, in dealing with such cases, must make his choice of two possible actions: acceptance of the subordinates refusal, or the instigation of formal action against the employee. He must estimate the results of each course, keeping in mind the debilitating effects to his authority of an unchallenged refusal.

If he chooses direct confrontation using formal action he will be well advised to follow certain more or less obvious principles. First, he must know the facts of the case thoroughly. Nothing is more devastating to his case than an overlooked mitigation. Second, he must choose his battleground to the organization's best advantage: should his fight be waged in public view, or in closed executive session, or in legalistic civil service proceedings? The

manner of his original instigation can often control the location of the ensuing discussion. Third, his issues must be as simple as possible, at best represented by direct and objective omissions or commissions. Fourth, his charges should be directed at the employee's *actions,* not at his character.

This last principle is vitally important, especially if the leader desires to derive some positive good from an otherwise negative proceeding. Even if a lawful dismissal could be summarily made by the leader, he may derive valuable information if the confrontation of opposing viewpoints occurs before a third party, a situation not usually difficult to construct. Third party participation is often important. As issues are discussed, the tendency will be to "make a case" for each side, thus revealing basic points of conflict. If scrupulous care is taken to maintain an atmosphere of responsible inquiry, free of invective, invidious personal comparison, and character assassination, confrontation may well lead to an identification of otherwise hidden problems and to the resolution of conflicts. More often than not, such hearings touch on emotional issues, causing communications barriers to tumble, and if no irreparable damage is done to the personal relationship between the leader and his subordinate, their future communicative ability is likely to be enhanced. Much mutual respect can be created between participants in a clean, hard-fought battle.

A more reprehensible tactical device, and one which is more dangerous, is the deliberate manufacture of employee conflict. Sometimes the leader sees the socially-integrated primary group of subordinates as a closed information system, containing data which the leader wants but can't obtain. Instead of valuing the close personal relations he observes in the "cozy" work group, the leader attempts to create conflict by playing one member against another. Members of the subordinate group may find that remarks made to their formal leader in confidence have been transmitted to coworkers, sometimes even in a distorted form, in order to cause conflict. If he is successful in destroying the group as a social entity the leader may receive a "spin-off" of information as it disintegrates, as interpersonal channels are clogged by mutual distrust, and as charges, counter-charges, and rebuttals are made by group members.

Such tactics may result in apparent gains to the organization. If a subordinate primary group is setting norms and establishing procedures which hurt the organization its destruction can be beneficial. Splitting the group can substitute vertical leader-follower influence for the horizontal group pressures which have operated against the organization's interest.

Very easily, however, this tactic can work against the leader's aims. Behind-the-scenes tampering with employees' personal friendships is a morally indefensible activity. Coworkers who are also close personal friends may discover the leader's actions through frank discussion with each other, and may view his efforts with contempt. Or, if coworker antagonisms do develop, informal coordination will necessarily suffer. The leader may find himself with more vertical inputs than he expected and, hence, more coordinative effort. He may also find many more jurisdictional disputes and arguments over resource allocation, as well as lessened commitment for the organization as a whole.

Conclusion

To reiterate the assertation in the introduction to this chapter, leadership is the most important demand placed upon the urban administrator. The most saleable quality posed by a city manager, county executive, or other similar official, is his ability to coordinate, direct, and motivate others.

The poet has written, "For forms of government let fools contest, that which is best administered is best." There is something to this notion. No wise or sophisticated policy, no technique or piece of equipment, no good intention is of value unless it can be "delivered" through the human maze of organization to citizens in the office, on the street, or in their homes.

Leadership, then, is the administrator's primary duty, and ought to be his primary object of study and thought.

6

Making Decisions

Few ideas so engross the student of management as the making of decisions—how they are made, why they are made, and what causes one choice to be made over another. Decision making has been the subject of major research during the past 10 years. There has been endless theorizing about it. Members of a half-dozen academic disciplines have constructed and tested different kinds of decision-making models. Several new hypotheses concerning organizational behavior have been advanced. As a result, there is hope that a major breakthrough in management theory may be about to take place.

Such possibilities are more intriguing to the theoretician than to the practitioner. To begin with, the man on the job is likely to feel they have no particular meaning to him. Whether decision making is, indeed, an art or a science, he is likely to continue to have problems with it for a long time to come. Even if he is himself successful with the decisions he makes, he may still question the relevance of both "model making" and "system building" which the literature tells him are necessary not only to what he is doing, but also to how he is going about it.

The late Ben Fairless, chairman of U.S. Steel, epitomized this viewpoint when he said: "You don't know how you do it; you just do it." The president of International Harvester agreed with him: "It's like asking a pro baseball player to define the swing that has always come natural to him." Another successful executive has said: "I can tell when I make a good decision. I sleep well at night."[1] Such observations may not make much sense to the social scientist, but they do to the man on the firing line.

Yet there *is* an art—and perhaps also a science—to the making of good decisions. In this, as in so many other areas of human life, valid generalizations can be made and techniques derived from them. Those who have tried seriously to understand the decisional process know there is still much to be learned, but they know with equal sureness that they have gained meaningful insights from their inquiries. Results can be seen on both the individual and organizational levels. The purpose of this chapter, accordingly, is to sum up what is known about how individuals and groups make their decisions, to evaluate the effectiveness of these processes, and to explore ways of improving them.

How Decisions Are Made

DECISION MAKING DEFINED

Decision making is the name given to the process by which an individual or a group of individuals chooses among alternatives. This may involve a personal choice—such as the selection of a tie—or an organizational one—such as a decision to pave a street. It may be important (the rezoning of an area, for example), or relatively inconsequential (the choice of a

[1] John McDonald, "How Businessmen Make Decisions," FORTUNE, August, 1955, p. 85.

luncheon entree). But whether it is done well or badly, consciously or instinctively, whether it is an individual or a group decision, and whether the issue is important or trivial, decision making involves some version of the following steps:

Recognition of a Problem. The decision-making process starts when an individual or a group becomes aware, however dimly, of a situation in which it is possible to act one way or another—or to elect inaction. The awareness may be dim indeed; so dim that, if required to talk about it, the decision maker might deny that a decision was in process. *One of the major impediments to sound decision making is the obliviousness of many individuals and groups to the critical relationship between what they are doing, or not doing, and later events.*

In fact, the majority of all decisions, personal and organizational, are repetitive and routine, with the choices assumed ahead of time and elected without thought. Many are so embedded in private habit or group custom that no one thinks of them as decisions at all. There is, of course, a place in life for the automatic decision, but all too often its occurrence means that action is taken and resources are committed without any real evaluation of need, cost, or consequences.

Identification of Factors. This means answering the questions: What matters in this situation? Who wants what? What are the significant material elements in the picture— available resources, technical problems, financial considerations? And, on the human side, who will be affected and how?

Identification of Alternatives. It is one thing to know that a situation involving choice exists, another to know what the choices are. Much of the effectiveness of decision making has to do with how well the decision maker explores the real nature and extent of the possibilities actually and practically open to him.

Weighing and Testing of Alternatives. Once alternatives have been identified, the decision maker looks ahead to consequences. What advantage is there in this course of action as opposed to that? What are the comparative costs in money, physical difficulties, hu-

man opposition? How surely can these be predicted? How do the long-range possibilities relate to the immediate results?

Choice. Out of the intricate, often largely or partly subconscious, measuring of value against value comes choice. A course of action is chosen; the other alternatives are rejected. Even if nothing is done, a choice is made in that certain alternatives are ruled out and others accepted.

Implementation of Choice. Once a selection has been made, decision is realized in action. It is here that the decision maker enters the world of events where the soundness of his choice meets the ultimate test.

This, of course, is by no means the whole story of decision making, either for an individual or for an organization. As they probe more deeply, students of the subject are increasingly aware of how many illogical byways and false signals there may be along the way as a person or a group of people moves from option to decision. They are aware, too, of how different the process can be, depending on whether it is an individual or a group decision.

INDIVIDUAL DECISIONS

Psychology, for all its great advances in recent years, still recognizes vast areas of *terra incognita* in the human personality. Just what happens mentally when an individual decides between alternatives is among the phenomena which cannot yet be described with any precision. Character type affects the process. So do special aspects of the circumstances in which the need for decision arises. So do many other factors, including the time element; the form of the question; skills the decision maker possesses; his lifetime habits, customs, and practices; the views of others; the emotions he feels; and personal needs. The following paragraphs describe some of the effects of these factors.

The Time Element. Ideally, of course, all decisions should be well considered ones, made in the fullness of time after a careful assembling of facts, a full discussion of alternatives, and a shrewd estimation of consequences. Unfortunately, however, the everyday world has a way of frustrating the idealist's dream. All too many individual decisions are made in a context of unreadiness.

Moments of crisis evoke crisis solutions, which is to say quick decisions. Resources are often as limited as time. The decision maker simply does the best he can in the face of the existing strictures. The result may be good—or it may be bad. Some crisis solutions are exemplary ones, not only for the moment of first need but also as guides for future action as well. Many more such decisions, however, continue to shape noncrisis action when they should have been void as soon as the crisis was over.

Akin to the crisis decision is the "off-the-cuff" decision. A question too casually answered may turn out to be a commitment. The decision maker then feels he must follow through. Other people are affected, and what was an off-the-cuff reply becomes, for better or worse, standard operating policy for all months or years to come.

The Form of the Question. The way a question is phrased can determine the response it gets. Its form can direct channels of thinking, restrict choices of alternatives, and establish criteria for measuring its results. This is particularly noticeable in cases where the profession or specialization of the questioner asserts itself in the question. A lawyer, an engineer, and a philosopher describing the same problem would emphasize different aspects of it in the questions they asked. Thus, the answer given—and the decision made—may be molded by the manner in which the issue is posed, and by whom.

Skills and Habits. An individual is the prisoner of his own knowledge, skills, attitudes, and values, and his decisions emerge from that context. New learning and new skills can, of course, be acquired, and new values accepted. It is simpler, however, to generalize from what is already known and believed, and to practice skills already mastered, than to be constantly searching out new and, from the individual point of view, untested solutions. Decision making, like all human actions, tends to become a product of habit.

With age, experience reinforces the tend-ency to rely on old certainties. Two plus two equals four—there is no need for recomputing or retesting the fact. People eat the same breakfasts day after day because they have become accustomed to them. They follow accepted job routines because their effectiveness has been accepted. They use old approaches to new problems because it is convenient to do so.

Custom. Custom is habit on the societal level. Some customs are part of religious heritage. Others come from the nation and still others from the subcultures of which the individual is a part. For most people, customs have the force of law. One does this and doesn't do that because it is what is or is not done. This is the basis of respect for authority and of acceptance of its prescriptions and restrictions—an acceptance necessary to the survival of society.

Group Approval. Most personal decisions are strongly influenced by the opinions of others. Ours, as Riesman has suggested, is a strongly "other-directed" society. A school child's choice of clothing is colored by feelings with respect to the manner in which his peers will view it. The parent who provides the clothing may be moved in his choice by economy, health, beauty, or convenience, but the child responds to these only in terms of his own group relationships. To know what his choices will be, it is necessary to know the nature of his peer relationships. The adult world is, of course, not really very different.

Passion and Prejudice. Individual decisions are often strongly affected by a variety of emotions. People are swayed by love, hate, pity, pride, and anger. These control action. A decision made in the heat of argument will more often reflect the decision maker's feelings about his antagonist than a clear view of the facts.

One of the more important emotional forces affecting the decisional process is prejudice. Prejudice is a short-hand way of identifying something without fresh examination of its characteristics. It *pre*judges the individual person or situation, not by its unique attributes, but according to an already accepted formula covering a general category. It fastens upon one identifiable aspect—race, religion, economic level, or political background, for example—and produces a reaction in terms of that alone. There is no effort to take into account the full range of relevant facts. It contributes little to rational problem solving, but it must be taken into account.

Personal Needs. Personal needs can also direct individual choices. Maslow has suggested that these needs are arranged in a hierarchical fashion, with the more basic needs having precedence over others. At the lowest level are immediate physiological needs. Then come the demands of physical self-protection on a longer range basis. The social needs—approval of one's peers, for instance—are next in order, followed by ego needs—"the need to be identified for one's individual contributions." At the top of the pyramid are needs for self-realization.[2]

People seek to satisfy their needs in a variety of ways, depending on their perception of what it is they really require, and the opportunities open to them. Not infrequently, some ramification of self-interest colors a decision which, on the surface, seems unrelated to personal needs.

ORGANIZATIONAL DECISIONS

On the face of it, organizational decisions should be easier to understand—and also to predict—than individual ones. Most groups have well-established objectives and a discernible organizational structure, with regular functions assigned to recognized parts. Power and responsibility flow through accepted channels. Procedures are developed to routinize and direct the flow of action through accepted channels. Organizational decision making, then, should be a highly visible process.

So it is—on the surface and at the top.

Everyone is familiar with the decisions made at the top of an organization. These are the acts of presidents, governors, generals, mayors, managers, and directors. They are handed down to subordinates in a variety of ways: by regulation, directive, letter, memo-

randum, and word of mouth. Sometimes penalties accompany them to force compliance.

Most such "orders" are obeyed. The extent of compliance varies greatly, however. Sometimes directives are followed to the letter. But sometimes, as those in high positions know only too well, they are not obeyed at all. Most frequently, there is *both* compliance and noncompliance, and in a variety of patterns. This is true for several reasons, some having to do with the manner in which the institution is organized, some with communication and leadership structures, and some with basic conflicts within the organization.

When there is conflict—and those at the top are aware of it—their views may well prevail. More often, they seem not to be aware of what is taking place. While the power of those at the top, man for man, is far greater than that of those at lower levels, the number of the latter and the difficulty of forcing an unpopular policy on them can make a critical difference. Top management saves face by not knowing, or pretending not to know, that there has been noncompliance. (In the Army it is called "being undutiful.") As a result, little or nothing is likely to be done about it.

Noncompliance, however, is not always the result of conflict or disagreement. It flourishes where there are organizational vacuums. In spite of the attention given in recent years to the planning of group structures, there are still, in many organizations, gaps, twilight zones, and even areas that escape supervision completely. Where such exist, there is bound to be uncertainty about function. An employee under such circumstances can be forgiven if he hesitates to act, or, as is more likely, if he decides on his own course of action.

Here the visibility of the organizational system fades. Choices of individuals throughout the organization now become a part of the decision making process. Each may be modest or limited in its nature, concerned primarily with individual tasks, but this does not make them less far-reaching in effect.

As Gore has suggested: "The roots of the decision-making process are deep in the subsoil of an organization. Hidden from common sense observation, they lie far below the forms

[2] Abraham Maslow, MOTIVATION AND PERSONALITY (New York: Harper and Row, 1954), pp. 80–92.

and rituals of formal organization and the crust of rationality."[3]

Decisions at all levels, for whatever purpose, affect policy. They are, in fact, the substance from which policy is made. It makes no difference that the decision is a procedural one, concerned with methods rather than with objectives, for policy involves administration and administration involves policy. Sir Goeffrey Vickers has put it bluntly:

Policy making. . . . depends on all who help to formulate the concrete alternatives between which the policy maker must choose; on all who must help to carry it out; on all whose concurrence is needed *legally or in practice,* to put it into effect; and by no means least, on all those who, by giving or withholding their trust, can nurse or kill its chance of success.[4]

The increasing use of delegation and decentralization in modern organizations has emphasized the distribution of decision making power at subordinate levels. It has come about partly as a reflection of concern for client relations, partly from a belief in the desirability of making the decisions where the problems are. It has many advantages. At the same time, one should not be surprised to find that the dispersion of decision-making authority sometimes means the amendment negation by lower levels of decisions made at the top.

Students of management have belatedly recognized the great power of lower-level decision makers. The clerk at the counter, for example, can commit the department store. The soldiers at the front can make or unmake their senior officers. "The decisions that stick," a former Secrtary of the Air Force has opined, "are those made at the top and those made at the bottom. Sometimes I think there are very few in between."[5]

What is often easiest to perceive in organizational decision making is its failure in implementation. Often this stems from defective communications. As the organization grows larger, internal communication becomes more difficult. As more and more is demanded of the individual by way of quality, quantity, the meeting of time requirements, and the many extraproductional elements of the job, the burden on the communications system increases. In addition to mechanical obstacles, there are these human ones: failure to listen and to comprehend, indifference, lack of responsibility, inflexibility, and prejudice. These can forestall the implementation of a decision no matter how good the mechanical communications system.

There is, however, an even more basic reason why directives from the top are so often revised elsewhere in an organization. Conflicts exist in most organizations between general management and the professional specialist, the broad and the specific, policy making and operations. Much of the time those at operating levels find it difficult if not impossible to do what is asked of them without sacrificing some other objective they hold dear. They also are constantly being importuned to "use your judgment." They do. If they did not—if they tried to do all the contradictory things demanded of them and in the fashion prescribed —the organization would collapse. But, in exercising judgment, they also apply their own sets of values to the functions of the organization.

Thus, decision making in the large organization occurs in a variety of ways and involves large numbers of people. It takes place as the deliberate act of those in approved policy-making positions, but it may also be the result of chance pronouncement or casual choice. It comes about through delegation of authority and function. It may be the product of misunderstanding and error. It is influenced by the "law of the marketplace," by "act of God," by the private predilections of those at operating levels, and by the expression of client attitudes.

Sometimes organizational decisions are part of a well ordered process involving the contemplation of large objectives and the relationship of each step to the whole. Sometimes they are made in bits and pieces—each a separate

[3] William J. Gore, ADMINISTRATIVE DECISION-MAKING: A HEURISTIC MODEL (New York: John Wiley and Sons, 1964), p. 36.

[4] Sir Geoffrey Vickers, THE ART OF JUDGMENT: A STUDY OF POLICY MAKING (New York: Basic Books, 1965), p. 225 (italics added).

[5] Statement of Eugene Zuckert, made to the writer.

decision, logical in itself, yet each committing the organization to a direction it would not choose were the issue faced as a whole. Sometimes those responsible for carrying out the decision are consciously involved in the decision-making process; more often they are not. Sometimes decisions are made, often at lowly levels, without anyone being aware that they are decisions. And sometime decisions are made by default. Those officially responsible stand aside and let fate and the fumbling of their subordinates resolve the question. Speaking of the presidency, Neustadt has said, "Decision is so often indecisive and indecision so frequently conclusive that choice becomes the preferable term."[6]

These are some of the ways organizational decisions are made. Even in the best intentioned organizations, the process is not likely to be an orderly one.

Evaluating the Decision

There are, as the foregoing suggests, "good" decisions and "bad" decisions—and many, many in between. Some produce the results needed and wanted while others handicap and impede those who must live by them. Still others commit their makers to unanticipated and often undesired directions.

This leads to such queries as: What, in fact, is a "good" decision? Can standards for decision making be developed? Can decision making be separated from decision implementation? What can be done to improve both individual and organizational decisions? These are reasonable questions.

The making of decisions can indeed be analyzed and evaluated just as any other administrative action. It is also possible, as management specialists are beginning to discover, to identify the factors involved in the act of decision. Under certain circumstances, they can be given numerical weights and programmed for computers. And the decision-

making process, individual and organizational, can of course be improved.

STANDARDS FOR DECISIONS

Individuals and organizations vary, but there are general standards by which all decisions can be judged. Those discussed below, for example, are as applicable to a lumber mill or an urban police department as they are to the individual executive. Variations due to organizational type may be compensated by the weight given individual items.

A scale similar to that suggested in Figure 6–1 provides a range of choice. A rating of zero suggests total failure; 100, on the other hand, is complete success. Most decisions would fall somewhere in between.

Some idea of the "success" or "failure" of an organizational decision can be had from an evaluation of it once it has been made and tested. It can be viewed in an overall way, or judged on its component elements. The most important of these will be suggested below. An average of the numerical ratings of the components will produce an overall average, assuming that each has an equal weight. Those scoring in the upper percentiles (65 or above) qualify as "better than average." Those scoring in the lower percentiles (40 and below) are not really adequate.

The ratings can be made by a single person or there can be a shared judgment. The value of a rating system, similar to the above, is that it provides an opportunity for discussion and self-analysis—something that most executives should welcome.

There are, of course, a number of caveats to be observed. The decision should be a recognizable one, preferably one in which pros and cons have developed. Also, it should be one in which the decision maker has had authority to act. Raters should bear in mind also that the ultimate test of decision is *what happens* as a consequence of it. This may not be immediately apparent; sometimes months or even years must pass before the results are clear. On the other hand, indicators are often available at an early period. Much of the time the perceptive executive can quickly begin to spot the results of the action taken.

---

[6] Richard E. Neustadt, PRESIDENTIAL POWER: THE POLITICS OF LEADERSHIP (New York: Science Editions, Inc., 1962), p. 56.

Decisions may be judged on a number of standards. Four particularly useful criteria are the following:

1. Furtherance of organizational goals
—Increase in the quantity of production
—Improvement of quality of product
—Enhancement of efficiency of operations
—Profit or other return to decision-makers
—Prestige
—Development of new opportunities
2. Improve relations with clients or publics
3. Cost
—Money
—Technical difficulty

—Time
—Interpersonal problems within the organization
—Opposition from outside the organization
4. Methods used in making the decision

ANALYZING THE STANDARDS

Furtherance of Organizational Objectives. The good decision is made within the context of organizational goals and seeks to advance them. The difficulty, of course, is that many organizations have given little or no attention to the formal analysis of objectives. Many managers assume that the group's objectives are

1. Furtherance of Organizational Goals

0	25	50	75	100
Failure	Poor	Average	Good	Success

2. Improvement of Relations with Clients and/or Publics

0	25	50	75	100
Failure	Poor	Average	Good	Success

3. Cost

0	25	50	75	100
Very low	Low	Average	High	Very High

4. Methods Used in Making the Decision

0	25	50	75	100
Very poor	Poor	Average	Good	Very Good

5. Other

0	25	50	75	100

6. Summary

0	25	50	75	100

FIGURE 6-1. *Suggested system for evaluating decisions (Directions: First, identify the decision to be rated. Then on the basis of available information, rate it according to the four criteria indicated below. A fifth possibility is provided in case additional standards are pertinent. Once the rating has been made, the sixth continuum provides an opportunity for indicating the average of the other four or five. Note: A greater weight on certain elements can be expressed by doubling or tripling the value attached to any one rating element. Further individual criteria can have subsidiary scales for which they serve as the summary: e.g. the organizational goals criterion can have a subordinate scale for each of several different goals.)*

obvious and understood at all levels of the organization. Others hesitate to discuss them because of fear that differences of opinion about them within the organization may disrupt operations. A common failing is for management to accept a partial or too narrowly conceived goal (profit making for a corporation; the carrying out of a city ordinance for a municipal government department) as representing the totality of an organization's proper objectives.

The introduction of "management by objectives" to both business and government in the past ten years has done much to focus attention on the need for clarifying purposes as a first step toward successful decision making. A frequent complaint at middle and lower managerial levels is that it is hard to find out what is really wanted. Unless he knows, the decision maker cannot act with maximum effectiveness.

1. Quantity, Quality, Efficiency, and Time. Paramount among the criteria for good organizational decisions is their effect on the quantity, quality, and time schedule of the product. It is not always a popular test. The increase since World War II in the number of white collar jobs in both industry and government has helped to de-emphasize the importance of measurable productivity. Unions and employee associations tend to mistrust quantitative rating, harking back to abuses of the piecework payment system and overlooking the fact that no profession can evaluate its achievement without reference to quantitative standards. Performance must be measured in hours of work, clients served, cases investigated, and actions taken. As a single standard, of course, this approach is inadequate; combined with others, it is a useful yardstick.

Of equal value are time and productivity standards. Productivity, of course, represents a quantity–quality–time-cost ratio. Its definition and measurement have intrigued at least two generations of students of management. Not being an absolute, it can be applied in only a relative sense. Several norms are appropriate: units of work achieved, numbers of persons involved, time required, and unit cost. While comparisons can often be made with similar

undertakings elsewhere, the most satisfactory gauge of increased efficiency is improvement over previous performance.

2. Profit or Other Return to the Decision Maker. One of the gauges by which the private businessman determines his success or his failure is the profit-and-loss statement. While other factors must be taken into account, no business can continue to operate at a loss over a long period of time. The public administrator has other guidelines. His objective may be service, in which case he will be concerned with the manner in which this is performed by those who work with him. Or he may be involved in regulation—as in a traffic department. He will need to know how what is being done affects the flow of automobiles throughout the city.

There are many indicators by which the executive, whether in private or public business, judges his success. One of these is the acceptance of his efforts by his superiors. The wise use of authority is a potent argument for its continued grant. There is also the evaluation of the operation by other professionals. And, of course, there is always the matter of client acceptance. This is discussed in greater detail below.

3. The Development of New Opportunities. It is important that the organizational decision maker think of the organization's long-range interests as well as its immediate goals. Sometimes the temporarily unprofitable or unpopular move promises ultimate benefits outweighing its momentary disadvantages; sometimes it is the other way round, and the immediately advantageous move is likely to involve prohibitive future costs and penalties. What the decision maker needs is perspective. Such perspective is one of the standards the decision evaluator should use.

Improvement of Relations with Clients or Publics. All organizations have their client systems. For private companies, these are the individuals, groups, or other companies which buy the products or services the company has to sell. For public agencies, they are citizens, reacting either as individuals or as members of appropriate groups.

A mark of an organization's success is its

standing with its clientele. Prestige and good will are not luxuries to be lightly regarded. The private company values its customer relations as an index of market potential. The government agency, existing at the people's pleasure to do what the people want, is no less dependent on a clientele. It performs services and exercises controls. How well it can function depends on legislative support and public acceptance.

Whether in government or industry, the decision maker must be ever alert to the impact of what he does on the public. He must also be aware of the influence outsiders may have on what takes place inside the organization. The interaction of a given group and the society surrounding it is an often neglected element in the analysis of organizational achievement.

Cost. What will the decision cost? Is it worth it? On one side of the decision maker's scale are the advantages of the various courses he may take. On the other side, there is the matter of what it costs.

There is almost always some effort to count costs when decisions are made. Unfortunately, however, costs are usually difficult to measure. Many are indirect and hidden and, more often than not, a realistic accounting of the cost of a decision would be as much concerned with intangibles as with dollars and cents.

Direct costs include such obvious expense items as advertising and production change costs for a business about to launch a new line of merchandise, or the money needed to pay for new equipment, property, and facilities for a municipality preparing some new project. Indirect costs are more subtle. The time spent by employees in learning new methods is an indirect cost. So is time wasted because of outdated methods or lack of challenge. A deteriorating relationship with the public is also an indirect cost.

Contemplating the allotment of limited resources, the administrator must take into consideration not only the cost of making a new decision but the cost of *not* making it. Where "standard practice" means an outmoded or wasteful system, "business as usual" may turn out to be more expensive than an innovation calling for an initially heavy investment. The other side of the coin is hard to see, but it is always there. Just because it cannot be "proven," does not mean that the "what might have happened *if*" should not be taken into account.

Methods Used in Making the Decision. Subordinates as well as superiors have views on how decisions should be made. Often they react favorably (or unfavorably) to what has been decided because of their feelings about the manner in which it was decided. Increasingly, there is pressure in today's organizations for a broader participation in the decision-making process. This means that the wise executive will consider ways by which the views of others can be heard.

This is often all that is necessary. Most persons understand the need for the making of decisions by those who have been given responsibility for them. They realize that, with many differences of opinion, someone must decide. President Truman's desk placard, "The buck stops here," contains a well understood and well accepted idea. But subordinates also want an opportunity to express themselves on matters of interest to them and on which they have information to convey. It is, in fact, to the organization's interest that they be given this opportunity. An evaluation of the decision-making process will enable the executive to find out how well this has been done.

Today's manager safeguards the internal dynamism of his organization by asking himself questions such as these when there are decisions to be made:

1. Is the need for the decision generally understood?

2. Is the decision itself understood?

3. Were the proper persons consulted about it?

4. Do they accept what was decided?

5. Have steps been taken to implement the decision?

6. What new problems is this decision likely to cause?

7. How will they be handled?

Toward Better Decision Making

IMPROVING THE INDIVIDUAL'S DECISIONS

The improvement of organizational decisions begins with the improvement of individual decisions, and the improvement of individual decisions begins with the improvement of one's own. Starting the regenerative process with self, one moves on to a better understanding of others and, ultimately, greater mastery of designated situations. As the comic strip character, Pogo, has observed, "We have met the enemy and they is US!"

Thus, bettering individual decisions involves individual effort to see past the limited vision of prejudice and custom, to inquire beyond what one knows through "regular channels" and "common knowledge." It requires self-motivation above the petty fears, intolerance, and self-interest that lead decision makers to neglect both the real ends they should be pursuing and the added resources available to them through the creativity of others.

Improvement can and should be approached in a systematic and intelligent way. A useful guide is the development of a decisional check list. Such lists, for example, are placed in the cockpits of airplanes to remind the pilot what he must do to prepare for takeoff, landing, or other critical maneuvers. Similar lists have a contribution to make to management as well. The 12 questions below constitute a typical management list, and, accordingly, will be of value to the decision maker at any level:

1. What is the problem?
2. What are the pertinent facts?
3. Who should be involved in the decision?
4. What are the objectives?
5. What are the alternatives?
6. What do they cost?
7. Which course of action best serves these objectives?
8. What does the decision imply for the future?
9. What are the procedures for making it work?
10. How are the results to be tested?

11. What arrangements are there for its modification or change?
12. Is the decision maker prepared to live with the result?

1. What Is the Problem? A misjudgment of the nature of a problem is the surest guarantee that it will not be properly solved. "A good decision," Massie reminds us, "is dependent upon recognition of the right problem. Too often, a decision maker is so intent upon jumping to the right answer that he fails to look first for the right question."[7]

Those concerned with formal logic emphasize the importance of pausing long enough in problem solving to find out, for example, whether the problem is the one it seems to be. What, for example, do others say about it? Why is it a problem? When did it become one?

It is also important to know what kind of problem one is dealing with in terms of the long-range situation. Does it represent a special coincidence of forces unlikely to recur, or is it fundamental—a natural outgrowth of a set of continuing circumstances? Does it, therefore, call for one-time-only action or for the establishment, on the other hand, of rules, principles, and policies to control future occurrences?

2. What Are the Pertinent Facts? It is almost never possible to have *all* the facts. Nevertheless, more can usually be had than most problem solvers get. It is an axiom of administration that "management gets what it wants—not what it says it wants." Those willing to accept incomplete information, prejudiced information, misinformation, and sometimes no information at all, get just that.

An administrator's greatest asset is an alert and questioning mind. Persistent, imaginative, and critical questioning of those who have knowledge of the situation brings answers. Needless to say, the key point is knowing what information to seek, and probing for the essentials rather than inundating oneself with extraneous detail.

3. Who Should Be Involved in the Deci-

[7] Joseph L. Massie, ESSENTIALS OF MANAGEMENT (Englewood Cliffs, New Jersey: Prentice Hall, 1964), p. 35.

sion? Substantive decisions are often made by those who have a stake in their settlement. With each person consulted, a new set of private opinions and individual biases becomes a force in the situation. Professional and functional interests make themselves felt as well. Inescapably, lawyers make legal decisions, economists make economic ones, and budget officers financial ones.

Rather than constituting a reason for excluding people from consultation, functional bias is often a good reason for bringing them into the decisional process. The contrast among specialized points of view often brings to the fore possibilities that might not otherwise have been suggested. This is particularly true in large new undertakings of unknown potential. A good rule to follow is to hear ideas from anyone who will have a major hand in carrying out the decision, even though it may mean going well outside the usual command and policy structure, and even though it exposes the decision maker to the danger of either diluting responsibility or—that old, bugaboo—losing control.

4. What Are the Objectives? "A clear statement of purpose universally understood is the outstanding guarantee of effective administration."[8] This, to Dr. Luther Gulick, was one of the greatest administrative truths to come out of World War II.

To be clear about objectives, one must know not only what is wanted but why. How are they trying to achieve their end? When, and in what order of priority? How well do they want to do it? How much in resources are they prepared to commit?

5. What Are the Alternatives? Most problems offer more than one solution. A housewife planning a dinner menu, for example, has only to glance at the cookbooks on her shelves to be reminded of the number of different things she might do. Her family's tastes, her own culinary abilities, time, the household budget, and food supplies already on hand quickly narrow the range of practical choice. Still, recognition of all her actual alternatives

enables her to make a choice that is likely to be "better" from many angles than if she had not considered them.

The same is true for the executive. The greater his commitment to the idea that there is more than one "right answer" to a given problem, the more likely he is to make an effective choice among them. Inventors stress the need for "investigating the obvious"; successful decision makers are equally aware that they often find their best solutions to problems by re-examining alternatives at first thought not to apply at all.

6. What Do They Cost? No one is ever so well endowed as to escape the need for economical use of his resources. Similarly, no one fully understands the cost factor without taking into account both short and long-range implications of the way he uses his resources. Limited funds may make it seem more desirable to patch a street than to resurface it, but consideration of ultimate costs, both in money and in citizen reaction, may suggest the opposite decision.

This points up the importance of costs which cannot be measured in money terms. If a decision means improper use of personnel—untapped energies and wasted talents in an organization—it is expensive. Such elements as time and goodwill must be listed among other cost factors. The impact on morale of a decision may be hard to assess, but there should be some attempt to weigh it. In Appleby's words, "Who will be mad? How mad? Who will be glad? How glad?"

7. Which Course Best Serves the Purpose? This is the point at which the relative merits of alternatives are finally judged. Hopefully, each alternative will present a clear picture of what it can be expected to do and what it involves by way of risk and cost.

A proper—indeed, an essential—element of the discussion which should take place is the manner in which each decision will serve the purposes of the organization. If it were possible to lay out the dimensions of each in the fashion in which a commodity is weighed, measured, and defined, a comparison could then be made against what is wanted. Sometimes this is possible; more often not. But it is always

---

[8] Luther Gulick, ADMINISTRATIVE REFLECTIONS FROM WORLD WAR II (University, Alabama: University of Alabama Press, 1948), p. 77.

possible, by use of questions, to explore areas that would otherwise have been taken for granted and often overlooked.

The importance of relating alternatives to organizational purposes cannot be over-stressed. Leavitt notes that most people have two goals in a work situation—to do the job and to please the boss. These objectives are seldom completely congruent; they may not, in fact, even overlap. What their pursuit leads to, more often than not, is what Simon has called "satisficing" behavior. "Most human decision making," he points out (with March), "whether individual or organizational, is concerned with the discovery and selection of *satisfactory* alternatives; only in exceptional cases is it concerned with the discovery and selection of optimal alternatives."[9]

Put another way, people are more intent on "getting by" than on doing what is really needed—or even on doing their own best work. This is why it is so important to make the selection among alternatives a positive step in the decision-making process, and also why it is useful to involve in the decision those with knowledge of its elements and a concern for its success. Such structuring may not eliminate "satisficing" behavior or the personally oriented decision, but it helps to limit them.

8. What Does This Decision Mean for the Future? Decisions may be thought of as separate and discrete or as parts of a process, the components of a direction. Regarded as units in a continuum, individual decisions may take on unexpected significance. Thus, one decision rests on another, as steps overlay and build upon what has gone before. From near at hand, each may be distinct. From a greater distance, all can be seen as interrelated, moving clearly, sometimes inexorably, in a given direction.

This is what a series of decisions, each sound enough in itself, did with respect to the Bay of Pigs crisis in 1961. This is also the real story of America's involvement in its third largest war, Vietnam. The same pattern has a way of appearing in city hall as well. The de-

cision maker must understand how, with a cluster of decisions, the whole may, in the end, seem quite different from the sum of its parts. It is thus useful to review past choices as they relate to present prospects and to be eternally sensitive to the emergence of trends which may need redirecting.

9. What are the Procedures for Making It Work? A decision is incomplete until it is put into effect. Twenty-five-mile-an-hour speed zones may be decreed, but unless there is enforcement, they do not really exist. There must be enough highway signs, lights, radar equipment, driver education programs, and policemen to influence those who travel the roads in question. The decision maker needs to make sure there is positive support, both internal and external, for what he wants done; to see to it that there are adequate procedures for carrying out the desired action; and to satisfy himself that those involved understand and will fulfill their assignments. As Huxley suggests, the great end of life is not knowledge but action. A decision is not a decision without implementation.

10. How Are the Results to be Tested? It is important for those who have been a part of the decision-making process to know how its success will be determined. Are there objective tests, and if so what are they? Who will administer them? Or is this primarily a matter of personal judgment? Whatever ways of testing may be appropriate, the results of a decision should be reviewed and analyzed for what can be learned from them and applied in future decision-making situations.

11. What Provisions Are There for Modification or Change? Even fireproof buildings contain "in case of fire" equipment. Decision makers, however skilled, should remind themselves that, in the normal course of human affairs, no decision is so perfect as to be change-proof.

When there is a favorable organizational climate, formal arrangements for modification or appeal may be unnecessary. If a decision is not accomplishing what was intended, it is a simple matter to review it and have it changed. So, at least, runs the theory. The bleached bones of those who have borne bad

---

[9] James G. March and Herbert A. Simon, ORGANIZATIONS (New York: John Wiley and Sons, 1958), pp. 140–41 (italics added).

news upward in the hierarchy bear witness, however, to the fact that it is not always that way in practice. This being the case, decision makers should provide for machinery to review what has been done and consider possibilities of revision or repeal as necessary.

12. Is the Decision Maker Prepared To Live with the Results? Living with other people's decisions is bad enough. Having to live with one's own can be unbearable. Self-doubt, defensiveness at criticism, the absence of scapegoats—all make the decision maker's role an uneasy one. But, as the head of a giant corporation has said, "A good manager makes the right decision 55 percent of the time; a poor manager 43 percent."[10]

The decision maker must be prepared to forgive himself a certain number of mistakes. At the same time, until a bad decision is changed, he should stand firmly by what he has decided. He should support those who have stood with him. Uncertainty and timidity can lead to loss of confidence in self which, in turn, will forfeit the confidence of others. The decision maker should leave no doubt as to what the choice has been. If he has misgivings, he should keep them to himself. Otherwise, he will not have the backing needed to implement his decision and it will disintegrate in futility.

IMPROVING ORGANIZATIONAL DECISIONS

Improving organizational decisions is more than a matter of improving individual decisions. It also requires the development of an organizational system and the creation of a climate in which decision makers can minimize confusion and delay in settling issues as they arise. Despite good people and good organization, decisions will still be only as good as the management processes which deal with them.

Improvement can be approached from two directions: via betterment of the organization as a functioning system, and through more telling use of leadership skills.

Wanted: A More Workable Hierarchy. Divisional lines and authority patterns often impede rather than assist the decision-making

---

10 McDonald, *op. cit.*

process. A network of divisions, sections, and branches in an organization can also be a system of filters and barriers, screening information before it is passed along, inhibiting action, and, in the end, preventing optimal decisions from being made. Some of the structural defects which can cause an organization to work against itself are:

1. Excessive stratification. The more levels, the greater the difficulty of getting anything either up or down.

2. Patterns of departmentalization which emphasize separation and dispersion rather than integration.

3. Powerful control systems whose concern is with conformity rather than productivity, creativity, and related norms.

4. Overcentralization, as against decentralization and delegation.

5. Extremes of specialization and standardization.

6. Insistence upon orderliness at the expense of imaginativeness.

Such overly formal approaches to management not only slow the exchange of information within the organization, but they also serve to prevent appropriate people from getting together to pool their ideas. The organization hardens into a collection of bureaucratic enclaves and duchies, each concentrated on its own parochial interests.

Management specialists have become increasingly aware of the dangers inherent in rigid hierarchy. As a result, the many tiered organization is no longer sacrosanct. Present emphasis is on the advantages of a broad span of control, chief among which is the effect on communications. If, as has been said, the important decisions are made at both top and bottom, this is a significant change. By shortening the distance between the two, the flattened organization gives those at operating levels a greater stake in what they do. It also ensures both of being better informed.

Greater appreciation of the hazards of vertical organization has engendered new interest in shared decision making. The employee, whatever his position on the organizational chart, brings knowledge and skill, pride, and loyalty to the group. The greater his sense of belonging—being part of the inner workings of the organization—the better service he can and will want to give.

Recognition of this "participation need" is, however, only the beginning. The problem is to find ways in which more people can take part in decision making without unduly delaying or decelerating action. The search has been complicated by management's commitment to status and hierarchy and its fear of "losing control."

There are, of course, dangers in too much decision sharing as well as in too little. There are many occasions when action is essential, when delay would be disastrous. Lines of authority should never be so scattered that, when such a moment arises, there is no one to give the fateful order. Furthermore, it is pointless to involve people needlessly in affairs that do not legitimately concern them. In most cases, however, decision making might be more widely shared without running afoul of either of these possibilities.

After all, group decision making has a solid record of acceptance and success in many areas of society. The committee and the conference are routine devices in problem solving. The group is always a greater source of information than the individual. It offers an opportunity for discussing and criticizing the proper course of action. It provides assurance that the judgment has been a considered one. It suggests that those who have agreed to it will give it their support.

It has been argued, notably by Mary Parker Follett, that it is the "Law of the Situation," rather than the contribution of a particular individual, that brings forth the decision. A kind of administrative parallel to the theory behind trial by jury, this line of thought holds that, given a general agreement on objectives and the nature of the problem, plus the relevant facts, most groups—certainly most management groups—will come to roughly the same conclusion.

To the extent that this is true, the broadening and deepening of support for a decision becomes an important function of the participative system of deciding. Thus, the public advisory committee becomes "an invaluable instrument for breaking the issue on the back of the public."[11] Groups like this have proliferated at all levels of government during the 1950's and 1960's. The advisory committee, once the bane of orthodox administration, is suddenly popular with administrators and citizens alike. Boards, panels, and conferences are everywhere. Citizen opinion is solicited on every type of question by poll takers and opinion samplers.

Government administrators have become increasingly conscious of what citizen acceptance, rejection, or apathy can do to the programs they are trying to carry out. Pressures come from every side. Business groups, which once shunned politics, are now urging each other to become more active in this direction. Leagues of women voters, parent-teacher associations, service clubs, and ethnic, religious, professional, and area civic groups testify to ever greater understanding of citizen responsibility and power.

The formal advisory committee is, however, more than a device for taming this power for official ends. Advisory committees are being used today for many purposes: for finding practical solutions to difficult problems, for testing alternatives, for mediating disputes, for assuring that minority views will be heard, for educating individual citizens, for providing "courts" of appeal, and even for undertaking selected administrative tasks. Understandably, they do some of these things better than others. But the views brought to government bodies by members of the public are useful in the decision-making process even when they are of a critical or hostile nature. Forewarned of opposition, the administrator can either alter his policies or strengthen his defenses.

The Use of Programmed Decisions. Among the newer techniques in organizational decision making, perhaps the most significant is the use of the programmed decision. "Decisions are programmed," Simon explains, "to the extent that they are repetitive and routine, to the extent that a definite procedure has been worked out for handling them so that

[11] Sir Arthur Salter, as quoted by Harold Laski, A GRAMMAR OF POLITICS (London: Allen and Unwin, Ltd., 1925), p. 376.

they don't have to be treated *de novo* each time they occur."[12]

The term "program" is, in fact, borrowed from the computer. As Simon goes on to say:

A program is a detailed prescription or strategy that governs the sequence of responses of a system to a complex task environment. Most of the programs that govern organizational response are not as detailed or as precise as computer programs. However, all have the same intent: to permit an adaptive response of the system to the situation.[13]

The availability of equipment and systems has made it possible for organizations, both private and governmental, to consider the application of a variety of new techniques to the solution of old problems. Most modern administrators are familiar with computer applications in such areas as billing, stock inventorying, accounting, scheduling, assembly line balancing, resource allocation, time and attendance records, tax collection, and disbursements. All of them understand in a general way the process by which information is provided and directions given. They are aware of the machine's ability to follow such directions, even those with many ramifications, in a fast, accurate, and generally economical way. This is why the computer recommends itself.

Less well understood, however, is the adaptation of the systems approach to more complicated problem solving and decision making. This is because it is not easy to understand how certain kinds of problems can be expressed in terms that the computer can use. Suffice it to say, major progress is being made in a number of areas originally thought outside the purview of the computer. Once such basics are mastered, it can be focused on the optimal or best solution. Nor is its scope limited by the intelligence of the individual decision maker. Its resources are the resources of the disciplines engaged. (See Chapter 9 for a fuller treatment of the use of computers.)

Operations research has provided a variety of ways of looking at and solving problems. Linear and mathematical programming have applied sophisticated mathematical techniques to wholly new sets of problems. Program Evaluation Review Technique (PERT) is a system for scheduling the complex elements needed for the finished product. These are examples of the range of the new decision making, with the computer the vehicle which makes them possible.

An unfamiliar term turns up now and then in discussions of the process by which complex problems are unraveled—*heuristic*. Borrowed from the vocabulary of formal logic, the word means "aiding in the discovery of truth." In the vocabulary of management, the term is, as one writer puts it, applicable to "any device or procedure used to reduce problem-solving effort—in short, a rule of thumb to solve a particular problem."[14]

Thus the search by those now exploring the field of heuristics is for devices by which a larger percentage of organizational (human) decisions can be systematized and programmed. If they can be found, many elaborate and time-consuming computations will be rendered unnecessary. Heuristic methods also offer hope of dealing with problems of a qualitative nature not readily adaptable to mathematical terms.

Experience with heuristics is still in its infancy, but machines have already learned how to translate language, to play chess, to compose music, to design motors, and to do other things once thought beyond them. What they offer today's administrator is the promise of further applications in the future.

Meanwhile, the computer is available. Available with it are the experience and skills of a new breed of professionals, the systems analysts, who are able to suggest how it can most profitably be used. Where the dimensions of a problem can be ascertained and quantified, where there is large volume and much of the work is repetitive or recurring in character, there is a good chance for a programmed solution. Today's administrator cannot do his job without determining what the prospects are in his operation.

---

[12] Herbert Simon, THE NEW SCIENCE OF MANAGEMENT DECISION (New York: Harper and Row, 1960), pp. 5, 6.
[13] *Ibid.*

[14] Jerome D. Wiest, "Heuristic Programs for Decision Making," HARVARD BUSINESS REVIEW, September–October, 1966, p. 130.

The Role of Leadership in Organizational Decision Making. Computer or no computer, human leadership is still very much in the picture where organizational decision making is concerned. The improvement of such decision making depends largely on how interested key people are in achieving it. A real interest in the kind of decisions that are made and how they are made will express itself in a probing curiosity about all the organization does. People will notice and be affected in desirable ways.

This kind of useful curiosity will seek not so much to pass judgment on matters already decided or to look over someone's shoulder as to find out what is being done, why, and by whom. It will try to find out how old judgments are working and where new ones will be needed. As it is, all too many executives talk about being anchored to their desks as if a visit to a subordinate's office or place of duty were a violation of the rules. As a result, they are often badly informed—prisoners of hearsay.

Sometimes, too, the executive may be the prisoner of what looks like the greatest efficiency. This is one of the dangers in the doctrine of "completed staff work," which does, indeed, provide an orderly way of getting ideas and recommendations before the executive. Unfortunately, its orderliness is the source of its greatest weakness. By emphasizing the single alternative, it often closes out others. By laying out a course of action which requires only the signature of the superior, it encourages the endorsement of an approach which might not have been fully explored.

Those who support the idea of completed staff work (it is a standby of the military) argue persuasively that this is not intended. Nevertheless, it happens. The administrator who uses this technique must learn what the alternatives are and satisfy himself that they have been seriously considered.

Succumbing to the pitfalls of completed staff work is only one manifestation of a failing common among executives—neglect of communications flowing upward. It is admirable for the executive to concentrate on keeping his staff up to date on the full range and meaning of policy; it is also important that each staff member know the exact nature of the executive's expectations concerning his performance. But unless the executive takes care to keep open the channels of information from lower echelons to himself, he is likely not only to miss important information, but also to dull the enthusiasms of his subordinates. A common criticism of low-ranking employees is that they are unwilling to assume responsibility. What may be happening is that no one has noticed when they tried to act with initiative. Uncertainty—not lack of responsibility—therefore envelops and dominates them.

Such a "lack of responsibility" may point to other leadership failures. Some executives, for example, make a pretense of consulting subordinates and colleagues about matters which have already been decided—a course of action expensive in the loss of respect it entails when it is found out, as it is sure to be. It is perfectly proper for the administrator to have begun to formulate his own ideas when consultations begin. But he should be genuinely open to change if evidence develops that another way is better.

At the heart of organizational leadership is the making of decisions about decisions. What shall the leader decide himself? How much margin for decision should stay with his subordinates? A large share of the leader's time should be given to *establishing the bases* of decision making, refining objectives, emphasizing values to be sought, and clarifying roles. Selznick expresses it this way:

Group leadership is far more than the capacity to mobilize personal support; it is more than the maintenance of equilibrium through the routine solution of everyday problems; it is the function of the leader statesman—whether of a nation or a private association—to define the ends of group existence, to design an enterprise distinctively adapted to these ends, and to see that the design becomes a living reality.[15]

The executive decision maker must avoid becoming so infatuated with policy making that he neglects its implementation. Developing procedures, making assignments, and

---

[15] Philip Selznick, LEADERSHIP IN ADMINISTRATION (Evanston, Illinois: Row Peterson, 1957), p. 37.

working out the systems to report what has happened are, in essence, anticlimatic. Many executives are more at home in policy than in administrative areas. Operational responsibilities may be sloughed off as mere details, or too casually delegated to others, with the result that the decision never really comes to life in action. Sorenson made this point strongly in his *Decision Making in the White House.* It is not enough, he argues, that a decision be acceptable: "It must also be workable. It must be enforceable. It must be possible."[16]

The "possibility factor" is always of primary concern to the decision maker as he contemplates the kind of support this or that action is likely to produce. Quality as well as quantity is involved where support is concerned, and mere numbers may be deceptive.

A decision by plebiscite, where the will of the greater number prevails, sounds good and looks good on paper. In practice, it may mean nothing at all. It may even have a negative significance if, for example, it should bring with it a determinedly hostile minority. The administrator, therefore, must concern himself more with the quality of his support and with the intensity of any dissent from it than with a mere count of noses.

Here again, decision making shows itself to be an art, which is to say, a human activity in which the likelihood of success can be increased by the use of sound guidelines and even mechanical aids, but one in which ultimate effectiveness will be determined by the quality of the judgment and the thoughtfulness and skill with which it is made.

Summary

The ability of an organization to achieve its objectives depends in the final analysis on the quality of the decisions made by those who are a part of it. These decisions concern not only the ends the organization seeks, but also the plans for achieving them, and the operations necessary to support them.

Each decision is, of course, an individual matter, and in this sense the individual is the basic element of the organization. If one would understand how organizations behave, he must first learn how individuals behave. Such factors as custom, habits, skills, individual needs, emotions, and the approval of others all have major influence on what is decided. But so also do procedures—how the question is asked, its setting, the time available for consideration of it, and the timing of it.

Organizational decisions are those which commit the group to a particular course of action. They may be made in a structured and logical way, or they may occur in a nonplanned or casual fashion. Because they are made by individuals, they are influenced by all of the factors which influence the individual making them. The organizational leader must understand how and why this occurs.

Both individual and organizational decisions can be improved. Programmed decisions, where facts and values can be ascertained and ascribed, offer one such opportunity. But a more promising one, one which, incidentally, holds possibilities of application in the urban organization, is the development of a more systematic approach to the matter of deciding. By reminding the administrative leader of those factors which must be taken into account, systemization assures that attention be given them. Good decision making depends not only on having good information but also on providing an opportunity for it to be considered by the proper persons in the context of organizational purposes. This is out of reach of no one. In fact, the means of improving both the individual and the group decision are available to all willing to be guided by its requirements.

---

[16] Theodore C. Sorenson, DECISION MAKING IN THE WHITE HOUSE: THE OLIVE BRANCH OR THE ARROWS (New York: Columbia University Press, 1963), p. 26.

Part Three

The Organization

7

Organizing America's Cities

IT IS, OF COURSE, possible to study complex modern organizations from a variety of perspectives and with a wide range of emphases. Entire books have been written on such aspects and dimensions of organization as designing the effective organizational system, human behavior in organizations, relations with organizational clienteles and publics, leadership in organizations, and organizational communication patterns and processes, to name but a few. To consider organizations with any degree of adequacy of treatment in a single chapter is a most formidable task. Choices need to be made as to which elements will be included or emphasized in the coverage, and hence those which are to be omitted or given less attention than perhaps they deserve. Topical treatment that would be broadened and deepened, if space permitted, must be contained to permit consideration of other important dimensions of organization.

This chapter will focus on four key topics:

1. The nature of organizations, with particular emphasis upon individuals in "organizational society."

2. The development of modern organizations. This will emphasize both the changing nature of modern organizations and the philosophic and functional dichotomy which is increasingly manifesting itself in the organizations of modern civilization. One contemporary example of this dichotomy, particularly evident on the urban scene, is the conflict between the "establishment" or "the power structure" and "maximum feasible participation" of clienteles in policy formulation and implementation.

3. The elements of complex, modern organizations and the dynamics of their integration, direction, and control.

4. The organization of the future: Will it be man's servant or his Orwellian master?

The Nature of Organizations

ORGANIZATIONS DEFINED

Certain sociologists, following Talcott Parsons, define organizations as those social units or human groupings deliberately constructed and reconstructed to seek specific goals. Amitai Etzioni,[1] for example, describes organizations as those social units characterized by: (1) divisions of labor, power, and communication responsibilities, divisions which are not random or traditionally patterned, but deliberately planned to enhance the realization of specific goals; (2) the presence of one or more power centers which control the concerted efforts of the organization and direct them toward its goals; these power centers also must review continuously the organization's performance and repattern its structure, where necessary, to increase its efficiency; (3) substitution of personnel, i.e., unsatisfactory persons can be removed and others assigned their tasks; the organization can also recombine its personnel through transfer and promotion.

Included in this definition are corporations, armies, schools, hospitals, churches, and prisons.

---

[1] Amitai Etzioni, MODERN ORGANIZATIONS (Englewood Cliffs, New Jersey: Prentice-Hall, Inc., 1964), p. 3.

Excluded are tribes, classes, ethnic groups, friendship groups, and families. Considering the contemporary union job security provisions of labor contracts and the civil service regulations governing continuance of public employment, it is easy to conclude that, in modern society, it is probably easier to change wives than employees. Further, considering the emergence of leadership in certain primitive tribes[2] and the degree of deliberateness with which certain of them were organized and managed, it would further seem that such restricted definitions do not serve best the need to realize a fuller understanding of the nature and functioning of managed social units.

This chapter therefore uses the broader definitional parameters, provided by Chester Barnard, of an organization as a *"system of consciously coordinated activities or forces of two or more persons."*[3] Such a definition can be applied to all forms of organization, including the family and certain tribes. As with Etzioni, social classes, ethnic groups, and friendship groups are not included herein as organizations.

INDIVIDUALS IN THE ORGANIZATIONS OF MODERN SOCIETY

Contemporary society has been characterized as "the organizational society,"[4] for, as Etzioni has observed, "We are born in organizations, educated by organizations, and most of us spend much of our lives working for organizations. We spend much of our leisure time paying, playing, and praying in organizations. Most of us will die in an organization, and when the time comes for burial, the largest organization of all—the state—must grant official permission."[5]

A Historical View. Organizations are not, however, the creatures of modern civilization; indeed man has functioned in organizations from earliest times. *The Bible,* for example, is rich with illustrations of the process of organizing and of organizational functioning and dysfunctioning.[6]

From his earliest recollection, man has been subjected to substantially continuous influences, both overt and covert, directed toward securing his absolute adherence to the beliefs and values embraced by the social unit of which he is a member, and his complete conformity with the mode of dress and patterns of behavior sanctioned by his social grouping. Furthermore, to ensure realization of an organization's paramount goals of survival and prosperity, each individual, as an organizational member, is expected at all times to contribute his fullest efforts to the accomplishment of these collective goals.

Failure to contribute to the realization of organization goals, inadequate levels of contribution as defined by the organization, or failure of contribution usually results in the designation by the organization of the non, or inadequate, or erring contributor as a deviant, and it can have the consequence of a group response ranging from withdrawal of organizational membership to the taking of his life.

A Functional View. An individual's functioning in organizational activity is greatly complicated both by the fact of the multiplicity of his organizational memberships and by his awareness that as a unique, distinctive human organism, motivated by highly idiosyncratic needs and particularistic drives, he requires periodic isolation from, and independence of, organizational engagement. The multiplicity of his social unit memberships frequently subjects him to competitive influences and, more than occasionally, contradictory organizational pressures for conformity and maximization of organizational contribution.

Man's sense of individuality demands that, on occasion at least, he subordinate the multiple forces working toward his total involve-

---

[2] See, for example, Kenneth E. Read, "Leadership and Consensus in a New Guinea Society," AMERICAN ANTHROPOLOGIST, June, 1959.

[3] Chester I. Barnard, THE FUNCTIONS OF THE EXECUTIVE (Cambridge, Massachusetts: Harvard University Press, 1948), p. 73.

[4] Robert Presthus, THE ORGANIZATIONAL SOCIETY (New York: Alfred A. Knopf, Inc., 1962).

[5] Etzioni, *op. cit.,* p. 1.

---

[6] For example, the 18th chapter of Exodus, verses 13–26, describes an organizational problem confronting Moses, the solution proposed by a consultant, and the process of reorganization from an idiosyncratic into a bureaucratic authority and communication structure.

ment in, commitment to, and concern for those several organizations which claim him, and seek, outside of their social vector fields, to be himself alone. As observed above, to give such expression to his sense of individuality not infrequently places the individual in jeopardy of exclusion from membership, or at even more serious personal disadvantage or danger.

The complex of these multiple organizational claims which almost daily impinge upon an individual have been described by Chester Barnard:

. . . I select at random a man who is chiefly identified by his connection with the organization with which I am also ordinarily identified. He is an engineer whose career and living for many years depended upon that organization. Without special inquiry, I know that he has the following important organization connections also: He is (1) a citizen of the United States, the State of New Jersey, the County of Essex, and the City of Newark—four organizations to which he has many inescapable obligations; he is a member of (2) the Catholic Church; (3) the Knights of Columbus; (4) the American Legion; (5) the Outanaway Golf Club; (6) the Democratic Party; (7) the Princeton Club of Newark; (8) he is a stockholder in three corporations; (9) he is head of his own family (wife and three children) ; (10) he is a member of his father's family; (11) he is a member of his wife's family; (12) to judge from his behavior he belongs to other less formal organizations (but often seems not to be aware of it) which affect what he wears, how he talks, what he eats, what he likes to do, how he thinks about many things; and (13) finally he gives evidence of "belonging" also to himself alone occasionally. Lest it be thought that his "major" connection is predominant, and the others trivial, it may be stated that he devotes to it nominally less than 25 per cent of his approximately 8760 hours per annum; and that actually while he thinks he is working, and despite his intentions, he dreams of fishing, reflects on family matters, and replays a part of the previous evening's bridge, etc. Yet he considers himself a hard worker and is properly so regarded.[7]

Efforts by organizations to influence and direct their participants toward ever more substantial contributions and to guide and control member values and behavior have not been made without difficulty, participant disaffection, member resistance, withdrawal from organizational membership, and, on numerous occasions, direct collective opposition. The history of mankind and of organizations is replete with descriptions of revolutions, rebellions, coups, strikes, work slowdowns, member sabotage of organization efforts, personnel turnover, and other forms of member protest and resistance to such attempts.

Chester Barnard, indeed, has hypothesized that organizations, by their nature, inherently are unstable, and that successful cooperation in or by formal organization is an abnormal, not a normal, condition; that organizational life is characterized by failure to cooperate, failure of cooperation, failure of organization, disorganization, disintegration, destruction of organization, and reorganization. While it is true, Barnard observes, that organizations of all sorts are omnipresent, what is observed are the successful survivors among innumerable failures.[8]

A Societal View. Individuals and social units have become increasingly interdependent as populations have grown and clustered in ever smaller and smaller geographic areas, and as a consequence of industrialization and technological advance with the increased specialization and division of labor which characterize such economic progress and development. Interdependency and minute division of labor in modern society have called forth ever more deliberate, rational, and complex organizations, and even a whole system of second-order organizations fashioned to organize, regulate, and oversee other organizations (e.g., corporate holding companies and conglomerates, the Interstate Commerce Commission, the Securities and Exchange Commission, and municipal boards of health in their licensing and inspection of food processing, handling, and serving) .

An Overview. Modern organizations, therefore, are many times more numerous, substantially larger on average, exceedingly more complex, by general agreement more efficient, and increasingly more pervasive in their scope than earlier organizations. Indeed, recently in the United States, organizations such as law enforcement agencies, government prosecu-

---

[7] Barnard, *op. cit.*, pp. 71–72.

[8] *Ibid.*, p. 5.

tors' offices, and the courts have even concerned themselves with the regulation of marital relations between husband and wife in the "privacy" of the bedrooms of their own homes. (See, for example, the recent decision of the U.S. Supreme Court regarding a Connecticut law prohibiting the use of contraceptive devices,[9] and the also recent criminal prosecution and imprisonment of an Indiana husband found guilty of committing "unnatural" sex acts with his wife in his own home.[10])

Such increases in the scope, complexity, rationality, and pervasiveness of organizations have been accompanied by considerable social and human frustration, unhappiness, and alienation.

A major concern of modern administrative science, therefore, is how to design and manage rational organizations that will serve man effectively and efficiently without becoming his master; that will disaccommodate, frustrate, and alienate him least; and that will provide maximally for his satisfaction, contentment, and happiness.

THE NATURE OF ORGANIZATIONAL OBJECTIVES AND GOALS

Organizations are conceived and function for the purpose of realizing specific or multiple goals, such as the making of profit, providing a service or spectrum of services badly needed by elements of society, or of satisfying individuals' affiliative and play needs through the provision of opportunities for social interaction and transaction. Examples of organizations created to realize these three types of ends would be (1) General Motors Corporation, established to earn profits for its stockholder-owners through the manufacture and sale at a profit of Chevrolet, Pontiac, Oldsmobile, Buick, and Cadillac automobiles, GM trucks, and related automotive accessories; (2) a not-for-profit hospital established to provide medical and health care services to the ill and injured; and (3) a bowling league initiated for the purpose of encouraging and arranging bowling functions and competitive events for individuals

desiring to participate in such recreational and social activities.

Objectives and Goals Defined. While the terms *objective* and *goal* generally are used interchangeably both in management literature and in organizational practice, a distinction between these terms is made by certain students of organization. These students argue that if the terms are indeed synonyms, then organizational communication would be simplified by the use of either one or the other rather than both. The distinction that the advocates of semantic differentiation make is to reserve the term "objective" for the designation of long-range, ideal, realistically unattainable organizational ends, as in the case of the objective of realizing an efficient organization.

In the final analysis, what is meant by "an efficient organization" is a system which functions without inefficiency. It is, of course, self-evident that an organization comprised of humans, possessing different capacities, and reflecting in performance varying degrees of motivation and self-actualization, can never be totally efficient. A brilliantly managed, competently staffed, and highly motivated organization may approach complete efficiency, but its approach to this objective nonetheless will be asymptotic.

In this differentiation of terms, "goal" is used to describe those organizational ends which are shorter-run and realistically attainable, as the goal of realizing a 5 percent increase in sales volume in the fiscal year compared with the prior fiscal period, or the goal of reducing by 5 percent the cost of operating a municipal department of sanitation while maintaining the same level and quality of services.

The Two Goals of Organization. Most organizations function with two sets of goals, although usually they are unaware that they do. The first set is formally expressed and freely communicated, both internally and externally; the second set is not communicated, though it still governs effectively. The former is a desired state of affairs which the organization attempts to realize or believes it is attempting to realize. The latter comprises the

[9] *Griswold* v. *Connecticut,* 381 U.S. 497, 14 L.ed, 2d 510, 85 S.Ct. 1678 (1965).

[10] *Cotner* v. *Henry,* 394 F. 2d 873 (1968).

goals which the organization *is* pursuing or realizing. This distinction between *stated goals* and *real goals* has been illustrated by Etzioni:

The heads of some university departments, for instance, have only very inaccurate information on what happens to most of their "product," the graduates. Thus a department head and his staff might believe that the department is devoted to training future Nobel Prize winners in physics, while in practice it operates mainly to provide the electronics industry with fairly capable applied researchers.[11]

Effectiveness and Efficiency. The principal objectives of organizations are to ensure perpetuity as a system, to function effectively, and, for some, to operate efficiently. In those rare instances when an organization fully realizes its stated effectiveness objective, as in the case of The March of Dimes campaign, the organization usually will redefine and restate its purposes in order to continue to function as an organized system. *Effectiveness,* then, connotes the degree of mission accomplishment; the *efficiency* of an organization is measured by the resource inputs required to produce output: the fewer the inputs needed to obtain a given level of output yield, the greater is the system's productive efficiency.

The Development of Modern Organizations

The earliest concerns of students of organization were primarily with the ethical basis of political authority.[12] Plato and Aristotle, for example, both saw the state as a means to the good life. More recently, organizational development has been affected by three different philosophical approaches to organizational dynamics: the classical or structural approach, the human relations approach, and the attempt to synthesize these two approaches, an effort which can be labeled the analytic-integrationist approach.

THE CLASSICAL OR STRUCTURALIST SCHOOL OF ORGANIZATION

In a sense, Plato could be viewed as the initial advocate of the classical school, holding as he did that the aim of the good life is justice and that the essence of justice is order. In his *Republic,* Plato described the ideal state as one in which justice is realized through each man discharging his proper function, and identified the rational division of labor required in such a state as including rulers, workers, and warriors. Plato saw organization as the embodiment of the rational ideal, and the rational state was held to be essential to the highest form of individual self-realization.

A rational-legal or bureaucratic form of organization evolved in the Roman Republic, but it was not until the publication of the works of the German sociologist Max Weber, especially the posthumous publication in 1921 of his *Wirtschaft und Gesellschaft,* that this philosophy of organization had expression in other than the legal codes of the day.

Scientific Management. The search for more rational, effective, and efficient organizations was given substantial impetus by the seminal work of Frederick Winslow Taylor[13] and the subsequent development of the scientific management movement. Taylor held that the principal object of management should be to secure the maximum prosperity for each employer, coupled with the maximum prosperity of each employee. Antagonism and inefficiency in organizations, he believed, resulted from three causes: first, the erroneous belief of the workers that any increase in output would inevitably result in unemployment; second, the defective systems of management which made it necessary for workers to restrict output ("systematic soldiering") in order to protect their interests; and third, inefficient, rule-of-thumb, effort-wasting methods of work.

The intent of scientific management was to overcome these obstacles through a systematic

---

[11] Etzioni, *op. cit.,* p. 7.

[12] For a more comprehensive historical perspective in the development of a social science of organization, see George B. Strother, "Problems in the Development of a Social Science of Organization," in Harold J. Leavitt, ed., THE SOCIAL SCIENCE OF ORGANIZATIONS: FOUR PERSPECTIVES (Englewood Cliffs, New Jersey: Prentice Hall, 1963), pp. 1–37.

[13] Frederick W. Taylor, THE PRINCIPLES OF SCIENTIFIC MANAGEMENT (New York: Harper and Brothers, 1911), especially pp. 9, 36–37.

study of work to discover the most efficient method of job performance, and a systematic study of management to determine the most efficient methods of controlling workers.

Basic to the Taylor philosophy were four "great underlying principles of management":

1. *The development of a true science of work*—that is, the establishment by scientific investigation of a "large daily task" as the amount to be done by a suitable worker under optimal conditions, for the accomplishment of which the worker would receive a high rate of pay, or failing accomplishment would suffer a loss of income.

2. *The scientific selection and progressive development of workers* to insure that they possessed the requisite physical and intellec-tual qualities to enable them to achieve the designated output, and to enable them to be-come "first-class" men. Taylor believed that it was the responsibility of management to de-velop workers, offering them opportunities for advancement and making it possible for them to do "the highest, most interesting, and most profitable class of work" for which they pos-sessed capability.

3. *The bringing together of the science of work and the scientifically selected and trained men.* Taylor maintained that a "mental revo-lution" in management was required to over-come major resistance to "scientific manage-ment," which he saw coming from management rather than from the workers.

4. *The constant and intimate cooperation of management and workers.* This, Taylor held, was made possible by the fact that both management and men were subject to the same discipline, namely, the scientific study of the work.

Although Taylor's original interests were in the study of interaction between the character-istics of the worker and of the machine, his work became increasingly more limited, and eventually he came to view man as functioning essentially as an appendage to the machine. His students, the embryonic human or indus-trial engineers, concentrated their efforts al-most exclusively on the scientific establishment of standards of work performance and on the development of improved and simplified

methods of work, and contributed little to a general theory of organization.

Division of Labor. In the years following the establishment of the scientific management movement, students of organization, drawing at first rather substantially from Adam Smith's *The Wealth of Nations,* and later more delib-erately from Taylor's *Shop Management* (1903) and his *Principles,* made division of labor a central tenet of classical theory. In 1916, Henri Fayol, a French mining engineer and manager, published his classic *Administra-tion Industrielle et Generale,*[14] in which he suggested that all industrial activities could be divided into six groups:

1. Technical activities, including produc-tion, manufacture, and adaptation.

2. Commercial activities, including buying, selling, and exchange.

3. Financial activities (the search for and optimum use of capital) .

4. Security activities, involving the protec-tion of property and persons.

5. Accounting activities (stocktaking, bal-ance sheet, costs, statistics) .

6. Managerial activities, consisting of fore-casting and planning, organization, command, coordination, and control.

Fayol, then, was the first student of organi-zation to perceive management as a unique, contributing activity in the division of labor, rather than as simply "rulers," the hierarchy, or the providers of capital and their repre-sentatives, the overseers.

Bureaucracy. Max Weber's major contribu-tion of a theory of bureaucracy[15] appears to have been made without reference to the then-forming classical school. Yet it has much in common with classical organization theory. Strother has written:

Weber's theory of bureaucracy . . . resembles classi-cal organization theory in its emphasis both on technical efficiency and on the hierarchical struc-ture of organization. Both theories owe much to

---

[14] Henri Fayol, INDUSTRIAL AND GENERAL ADMINISTRA-TION (London: Sir Isaac Pitman and Sons, Ltd., 1930) , p. 9.

[15] Max Weber, THE THEORY OF SOCIAL AND ECONOMIC ORGANIZATION, Talcott Parsons, ed. and A. M. Hender-son and Talcott Parsons, trans. (New York: Oxford University Press, 1947) .

their observations of industrial organizations and of the problems created therein by specialization of function. Both propose a structural answer to the problem. Classical theory has been traditionally more preoccupied with detail: optimal span, assignment of responsibility and authority, number of levels, grouping of functions, and so on; bureaucratic theory has dealt more with the grand design.

They differ, too, in that Weber's method is essentially inductive whereas the classical organization theorists have used mainly a deductive approach. Even more fundamental is the difference in scope of the two kinds of theory. Weber's theory of bureaucracy is part of a general theory of social and economic organization. The classical organization theorists have been concerned largely with modern industrial organizations. Furthermore, classical theory has consistently had a normative orientation whereas Weber's orientation is positive.[16]

Weber's theory of social and economic organization included a theory of authority structures. He distinguished three typical ways by which authority in organizations is legitimized: *charismatic, traditional,* and *rational-legal* or bureaucratic. The first involved the exercise of power based on the personal authority of the leader. Weber used the Greek *charisma* to mean those qualities of an individual's personality which set him apart from ordinary men and cause him to be seen as supernatural, superhuman, or specifically exceptional. The authority bases in *traditional* organizations were seen as precedent, usage, and custom.

Weber saw the *rational-legal* system of authority operant and dominant in a large majority of the institutions of modern society. By rational he meant that the means are expressly designed to achieve specific goals; by legal he meant that authority is exercised in accordance with a set of rules and procedures governing the office which an individual occupies at a given time. Those organizations in which the basis of authority usage was rational-legal Weber called bureaucracies, and he spelled out in considerable detail fundamental categories, features, and characteristics of the bureaucratic structure:

(1) A continuous organization of official functions bound by rules.

(2) A specified sphere of competence. This involves (a) a sphere of obligations to perform functions which have been marked off as part of a systematic division of labour. (b) The provision of the incumbent with the necessary authority to carry out these functions. (c) That the necessary means of compulsion are clearly defined and their use is subject to definite conditions . . .

(3) The organization of offices follows the principle of hierarchy; that is, each lower office is under the control and supervision of a higher one . . .

(4) The rules which regulate the conduct of an office may be technical rules or norms. In both cases, if their application is to be fully rational, specialized training is necessary. It is thus normally true that only a person who has demonstrated an adequate technical training is qualified to be a member of the administrative staff . . .

(5) In the rational type it is a matter of principle that the members of the administrative staff should be completely separated from ownership of the means of production or administration . . . There exists, furthermore, in principle complete separation of the property belonging to the organization, which is controlled within the spheres of the office, and the personal property of the official . . .

(6) In the rational type case there is also a complete absence of appropriation of his official position by the incumbent. By this Weber meant that organizational positions cannot be monopolized by any incumbent; they need to be free to be allocated and reallocated in accordance with the needs of the organization.

(7) Administrative acts, decisions, and rules are formulated and recorded in writing. . . .[17]

The underlying premise both of the Weberian theory of bureaucracy and of the classical approach to organization is essentially rationality of design. Urwick perhaps best described this predominant emphasis on rationality:

Manifestly [planning the formal structure] is a drawing-office job. It is a designing process. And it may be objected with a great deal of experience to support the contention that organisation is never done that way . . . human organisation. Nine times out of ten it is impossible to start with a clean sheet. The organiser has to make the best possible use of the human material that is already available. And in 89 out of those 90 per cent of cases he has to adjust jobs around to fit the man; he can't change the man to fit the job. He can't sit down in a cold-blooded detached spirit and draw an ideal structure, an optimum distribution

---

[16] Strother, *op. cit.,* pp. 11–12.

[17] Weber, *op. cit.,* pp. 330–332.

of duties and responsibilities and relationships, and then expect the infinite variety of human nature to fit into it . . .

To which the reply is that he can and he should. If he has not got a clean sheet, there is no earthly reason why he should not make the slight effort of imagination required to assume that he has a clean sheet. It is not impossible to forget provisionally the personal facts. . . .[18]

The Importance of Individuals in Classical Theory. The classicists did not deny that organizations can be affected and altered by personalities, but departures from essential rationality made necessary by the presence in organizations of the human element were perceived as "temporary adjustments in order to deal with idiosyncracy of personality." Again Urwick presented a representative view when he observed that the planner:

. . . should never for a moment pretend that these (human) difficulties don't exist. They do exist: they are realities. Nor, when he has drawn up an ideal plan of organisation, it is likely that he will be able to fit in all the existing human material perfectly. There will be small adjustments of the job to the man in all kinds of directions. But those adjustments can be made without harm, provided they are conscious adjustments, deliberate and temporary deviations from the pattern in order to deal with idiosyncracy. There is a world of difference between such modifications and drifting into an unworkable organisation because Green has a fancy for combining bits of two incompatible functions, or White is "empire-building"—a technical term describing smash-and-grab raids on other people's responsibilities—or Black has always looked after the canteen, so when he is promoted to sales manager, he might just as well continue to sell buns internally, though the main product of the business happens to be battleships.

What is suggested is that problems of organisation should be handled *in the right order.* Personal adjustments must be made, insofar as they are necessary. But fewer of them will be necessary and they will present fewer deviations from what is logical and simple, if the organiser first makes a plan, a design—to which he would work if he had the ideal human material. He should expect to be driven from it here and there. But he will be driven from it far less and his machine will work much more smoothly if he *starts* with a plan. If he starts with a motley collection of human oddities and tries to organise to fit them all in, thinking first of their various shapes and sizes and colours,

he may have a patchwork quilt; he will not have an organisation.[19]

The classical school never addressed itself to the question of *why* people in organizations should be expected to undergo a "mental revolution" if rational design were to function or why *esprit de corps* was required for the "principles" to be applied successfully.

THE HUMAN RELATIONS APPROACH

The philosophy of Aristotle provides an historic antecedent to the human relations school of organization theory. Like Plato, Aristotle saw the state primarily as a means to the good life. Unlike his teacher, however, he held that this ideal could not be realized if the happiness of individuals within the society were to be subordinated to the transcendant state. He believed that the form of government needed to be in harmony with the social milieu and the character of the people to be governed. In the absence of the ideal—a single, good and wise ruler—Aristotle favored an organization governed by the people themselves through constitutional processes, a collective sharing of decision making.

Employee Motivation: The Hawthorne Studies. In the modern sense, the human relations movement was born when certain organization theorists, principally Elton Mayo,[20] irritated by doubt about the viability and adequacy of the classical model, undertook experimentation in an effort to learn more about critical factors in the determination of levels of worker productivity in organizations. The famous Hawthorne studies,[21] initiated and directed by Mayo and carried out between 1927 and 1932 at the Hawthorne works of the Western Electric Company, and especially the Bank Wiring Room experiment, presented an opportunity to test many of the assumptions of scientific management and, inferentially, the basics of the classical school.

The Hawthorne studies were undertaken to

---

[18] L. Urwick, THE ELEMENTS OF ADMINISTRATION (New York: Harper and Row, 1943), pp. 36–37.

[19] *Ibid.,* p. 37.

[20] Elton Mayo, THE HUMAN PROBLEMS OF AN INDUSTRIAL CIVILIZATION (London: Macmillan, 1933).

[21] F. J. Roethlisberger and W. J. Dickson, MANAGEMENT AND THE WORKER (Cambridge, Massachusetts: Harvard University Press, 1939).

determine the effect on output of such environmental factors as illumination in the work area, the length of the working day, and the number and length of rest pauses. A group of women who assembled telephone equipment were assigned to work in a special room where their production performance could be carefully observed as the experimenters varied the conditions of work.

With each major alteration in the work environment, there occurred a substantial increase in work output. Even when the experimenters reestablished the original working conditions of poorly illuminated work benches and long work days without rest pauses, output rose still further, exceeding even the levels achieved under the best of the experimental conditions. At this point in the studies, the researchers were forced to the conclusion that production levels were influenced by factors other than those which had been considered.

Further investigation revealed that high morale had developed in the test room and the women were highly motivated to work hard and to produce at high levels. The reasons for the high morale and the high-productivity attitude were discovered to be that the women felt important because they had been singled out to be studied; they had established good interpersonal relationships with each other, and related well with their supervisor primarily because they enjoyed considerable freedom to establish their own production levels and to divide the work among themselves as they elected; and the cordial and pleasant associations which had developed between and among the girls made the work more pleasant.

As a consequence of this discovery, the investigators formulated a new hypothesis which held that motivation to work, worker productivity, and the quality of output were all related to the nature of the social relationships in the work group and between the work group and its supervisor. To test this hypothesis, a new work group, consisting of 14 men, was established. Some of the 14 workers had the task of wiring banks of equipment, others soldered these banks, and two inspectors examined and "passed" the completed assembly. A trained observer also was present in the

test room to note patterns of behavior and the effect on output of emergent social relations.

It was discovered that although the group identified as a total group, two subgroups or cliques developed, comprised of those situated in the front of the room and those located at the back, although some workers did not belong to either clique. The subgroup at the front of the test room thought of themselves as higher in status than the other clique.

Furthermore, two important group norms, or standards governing member behavior in the work group, developed. One group norm held that there was a level of production which was "fair" both to the company, considering what it paid, and to the worker. Members were expected to produce at this group-determined level, neither "rate-busting," that is, producing more, nor "chiseling," producing less. Nonconformity with this norm resulted in the member being viewed as a deviant and in his being subjected to group pressure to comply. Continued nonconformity had the consequence of social ostracism. The effect of this norm was to establish levels of output below the capacity of the workers.

The second important group norm concerned the work relations between the group supervisor and inspectors and the work group. This norm held that those in authority should not act officiously, the group here reflecting its belief that inspectors were no better than the other workers. Attempts by the inspectors to display superiority were met by group social pressure and ostracism.

It was also observed that workers in the test room violated company regulations in a number of matters. Despite the fact that it was forbidden to exchange jobs, the workers often did so to relieve monotony and to engage in social interaction with other members of the group. They also reported their output as being essentially the same each day, whereas their actual production varied widely depending upon fatigue, morale on a particular day, and other circumstances. Extra units produced on a good day were "banked' to be reported on a bad day along with the fewer than usual units actualy produced on that day. The group supervisor and inspectors were aware of this practice but did not interfere, for to have done so would have subjected them to group pressure and possible exclusion from the social group.

Finally, it was learned that individual production rates were a function of position in the work group's social system. The high status clique consistently produced more than the low status subgroup and the highest and lowest individual producers were social isolates belonging to neither group.

The major conclusions of the Hawthorne studies could be summarized as follows:

1. Generally, production levels are set by social norms rather than by the physiological capacities of workers.

2. Social and psychic rewards and sanctions significantly affect the behavior of workers and substantially constrain the effect of economic incentives.

3. Workers frequently act as members of groups rather than as individuals.

4. The studies also disclosed the importance of *group* leadership in the setting and enforcing of group norms, and revealed the important organizational distinction between formal and informal authority.

Publication of the findings of the Hawthorne studies resulted in a largely analytically uncritical repudiation by many theorists of *all* that was embodied in classical theory. The principles of organization promulgated by the structuralists were characterized by Herbert Simon as the "proverbs of administration." He wrote:

A fact about proverbs that greatly enhances their quotability is that they almost always occur in mutually contradictory pairs. "Look before you leap!"—but "He who hesitates is lost" . . .

Most of the propositions that make up the body of administrative theory today share, unfortunately, this defect of proverbs. For almost every principle one can find an equally plausible and acceptable contradictory principle. Although the two principles of the pair will lead to exactly opposite organizational recommendations, there is nothing in the theory to indicate which is the proper one to apply.[22]

New "Principles of Organization." Following the Hawthorne experiments and the subsequent writings of Mayo, Barnard, and also of Kurt Lewin, students of organization increasingly concerned themselves with communication between the hierarchical levels of an organization, with securing the fullest possible participation and involvement in organizational decision making, and with explanations of the reasons why democratic-participative leadership was superior to hierarchical (authoritarian—*sic*.) leadership. The new "principles of organization" became, in essence:

1. Flat, nonhierarchical, colleagial organizations are *inherently* superior to hierarchical (authoritarian—*sic*.) structures.

2. Democratic leadership is more effective than hierarchically imposed "leadership" for the reasons that it is highly communicative, participative, more just, fair, and equitable, and is people-oriented rather than simply task-oriented.

3. The organization that is most satisfying to its members is also the most efficient organization.

But the happy assumptions of the human relations school have not always been supported in subsequent analytic studies. As noted by Strother, the "happy, unproductive worker and the unhappy, productive worker have been discovered; permissive and employee-centered supervisors have not always bossed the most productive groups; and consultation with workers has often created more problems than it has solved."[23]

Such disclosures have resulted relatively recently in a substantial refocusing, re-emphasis and reintegration of theory, although this process of regrouping and reorientation has been somewhat inhibited by the still large group of human relationists who cling tenaciously to the original tenets of their school, a group who Etzioni observes "have learned little and forgotten little since Mayo wrote his first books."[24]

---

[22] Herbert A. Simon, "The Proverbs of Administration," PUBLIC ADMINISTRATION REVIEW, Winter, 1946, p. 53.

[23] Strother, *op. cit.*, p. 14.

[24] Etzioni, *op. cit.*, p. 48.

THE ANALYTIC-INTEGRATIVE APPROACH
TO ORGANIZATION

Contemporary analytic-integrative theory recognizes the legitimacy both of structural and human concerns in organization, emphasis being placed, however, on the processes of interaction between the structure and the organization's participants; on the analysis of organizational conflict; and on the development of more cooperative, accommodating, and symbiotic models. Etzioni notes that organization analysis has broadened its concerns to include:

1. Both formal and informal elements of the organization and their articulation;
2. The scope of informal groups and the relations between such groups inside and outside the organization;
3. Both lower and higher ranks;
4. Both social and material rewards and their effects on each other;
5. The interaction between the organization and its environment;
6. Both work and nonwork organization.[25]

The following discussion of the elements of complex modern organizations is based principally upon the analytic-integrative approach to organization; hence further elaboration on this approach is deferred to it.

The Elements of Complex Modern Organizations

As already noted, organizations can be analyzed in terms of their structural components, their human elements, and the interaction between structural and human ingredients. This section of the chapter will touch upon all three, but it will emphasize the latter. Needless to say, the agencies of urban government in today's world all qualify as "complex modern organizations."

This section of the chapter will review the elements of complex modern organizations by examining the structural elements of organization as viewed by the analytic-integrative approach; systems of interaction within organizations, again principally as viewed by the

analytic-integrative approach; the relationship between leadership or managerial styles and organizational climate; informal organization; and, finally, interactions among organizations themselves.

STRUCTURAL ELEMENTS OF THE
ANALYTIC-INTEGRATIVE APPROACH

Hierarchy. In their criticisms of bureaucratic organization, some human relationists have tended to confuse hierarchical structure and the style of management employed in such organizations. It is, of course, possible for management to be democratic and participative in a large and complex bureaucracy. It is also possible for management to be highly authoritarian in a small and hierarchically flat system.

Simon has noted this distinction between departmentalization and structural hierarchy on the one hand, and the organization's authority on the other, and suggests that *large organizations are almost always structurally hierarchical.* He observes:

Large organizations are almost universally hierarchical in structure. That is to say, they are divided into units which are subdivided into smaller units, which are, in turn, subdivided, and so on. They are also generally hierarchical in imposing on this system of successive partitionings a pyramidal authority structure. However, for the moment, I should like to consider the departmentalization rather than the authority structure.

Hierarchical subdivision is not a characteristic that is peculiar to human organizations. It is common to virtually all complex systems of which we have knowledge.

Complex biological organisms are made up of subsystems—digestive, circulatory, and so on. These subsystems are composed of organs, organs of tissues, tissues of cells. The cell is, in turn, a hierarchically organized unit, with nucleus, cell wall, cytoplasm, and other subparts.

The complex systems of chemistry and physics reveal the same picture of wheels within wheels within wheels. A protein molecule—one of the organismic building blocks—is constructed out of simpler structures, the amino acids. The simplest molecules are composed of atoms, the atoms of so-called elementary particles. Even in cosmological structures, we find the same hierarchical pattern: galaxies, planetary systems, stars, and planets.

The near universality of hierarchy in the composition of complex systems suggests that there is

---

[25] *Ibid.*, p. 49.

something fundamental in this structural principle that goes beyond the peculiarities of human organization. I can suggest at least two reasons why complex systems should generally be hierarchical:

1. *Among possible systems of a given size and complexity, hierarchical systems, composed of subsystems, are the most likely to appear through evolutionary processes. . . .*

2. *Among systems of a given size and complexity, hierarchical systems require much less information transmission among their parts than do other types of systems.* As was pointed out many years ago, as the number of members of an organization grows, the number of *pairs* of members grows with the square (and the number of possible subsets of members even more rapidly). If each member, in order to act effectively, has to know in detail what each other member is doing, the total amount of information that has to be transmitted in the organization will grow at least proportionately with the square of its size. If the organization is divided into units, it may be possible to arrange matters so that an individual needs detailed information only about the behavior of individuals in his own unit, and aggregative summary information about average behavior in other units. If this is so, and if the organization continues to subdivide into suborganizations by cell division as it grows in size, keeping the size of the lowest level subdivisions constant, the total amount of information that has to be transmitted will grow only slightly more than proportionately with size.[26]

In addition to its recognition of the near universality of structural hierarchy, the analytic-integrative approach also acknowledges the existence within organizations of *multiple loci of power,* emanating from the application of three substantially differentiated types of authority: headship, leadership, and functional.

Headship, or formal authority, also called authority of office or position, rank, or scalar or hierarchical authority, is synonymous with Weber's rational-legal authority. It is the authority possessed by the occupant of a particular organizational position or status category and is the product of delegation within the formal structure.

Leadership,[27] also identified as *charismatic*

authority, or authority of personality, is that authority assigned by the governed. It reflects the governed's willingness to follow an individual who may or may not be the formally designated, official head.

Functional authority, or authority of expertise or knowledge, is generally *ad hoc* in its exercise within organizations. When matters to be decided are highly technical in their nature, organizational participants, including hierarchical superiors, tend to defer to the judgment of experts whose understanding of the subject they recognize and accept as superior to their own. The analytic-integrative school is concerned, among other elements, with analyzing the dynamic interplay between and among these multiple power centers in complex, managed systems.

Authority, delegation, responsibility, and accountability. Inasmuch as modern, analytic-integrative theory shares with the classicists the goal of creating rational systems of organization which are effective and efficient, though with the broadened perceptions and modified emphases noted above, it would appear to be appropriate, for the sake of comprehensiveness of treatment herein, to define certain terms used in contemporary organization to describe the functioning of the system of formal authority and hierarchical communication in bureaucratic structures.

Authority, in the formal sense, is the right, by virtue of office or trust, to command compliance and obedience, coupled with the power to enforce such right. Formal authority may be *delegated* to lower-ranking officials in the bureaucracy. Where delegation occurs, that portion of the authority formerly vested in the superior, the delegator, vests subsequently in the subordinate, the delegatee, and should *not,* in good management practice, be exercised by the delegator.

The important distinction between delegation and abdication needs to be emphasized. In delegation, the delegator retains *residual* authority, or the power to recall the authority delegated, while in abdication, the powers of office are assigned to another or others irrevocably.

The act of delegation, in theory at least,

---

[26] Herbert A. Simon, THE NEW SCIENCE OF MANAGEMENT DECISION (New York: Harper and Brothers, 1960), pp. 40–42.

[27] For an excellent and comprehensive treatment of leadership, the leader, and leader behavior, see Cecil A. Gibb, "Leadership," in Gardner Lindzey (ed.), HANDBOOK OF SOCIAL PSYCHOLOGY, Vol. II (Addison-Wesley, 1954).

establishes the parameters of *responsibility*, which is, then, the organizational sector or area in which delegated authority properly may be exercised. If, for example, a mayor or city manager were to appoint a fire chief and delegate to him authority to manage the municipal fire department, that chief's responsibility would be the municipal fire department, not the police department or department of sanitation.

Delegatees, recipients of delegated authority, have the obligation or duty to *account* or answer to the delegator concerning their use of delegated authority in their area of responsibility, and also for performance.

Forms of Organization. Four categories or major types of organization may be identified: the *line*, the *line and staff*, the *functional*, and the *program management* form. Each will be described in turn.

1. The Line Form. The *line*, or military type, is the oldest and simplest organization. It is a pure chain of command system in which each executive or subexecutive is in direct charge of his subordinates and subject, in turn, to the higher command and coordination authority of his immediate superior. Though subexecutives may, from time to time, be called upon to advise superiors, they

do so in their line roles, there being no specifically constituted advisory offices in the line form of organization.

Students of organization have distinguished two distinct subforms of this type of structure. In its *pure* form, the line organization is represented by mere division of personnel into identical groups with no specialization among them. All personnel are arranged according to a definite hierarchy of rank, the duties and the authority of all members of each rank being, for purposes of control, exactly the same. The organizational purpose of such a system is to reduce a large number of participants into controllable groups by simple mathematical division and subdivision.

The second subform of the line type of organization is the *departmental* line, which differs from the pure type only in that each of the divisions or groups performs somewhat differentiated functions. In relatively small, uni-purpose systems, the line structure is frequently the most appropriate and efficient form of organization. Relatively small municipal police and fire departments usually are organized in the line form, which is illustrated in Figure 7–1.

When organizations are functionally or technologically complex and multipurpose,

FIGURE 7-1. *The line form of organization*

the line type is usually an inadequate form of organization, principally as a consequence of the substantially greater knowledge requirements imposed on the chief executive, under these circumstances.

2. The Line and Staff Form. The distinguishing feature of the *line and staff* organization is the presence of officially constituted offices of expertise. To the basic line structure illustrated in Figure 7–1 is added a staff of specialists whose designated role in each instance is purely consultative and advisory, these experts presumably exercising no direct authority over the line. In practice, however, functional authority or authority of expertise frequently, indeed usually, conflicts with authority of rank.

In organizations containing several levels of staff with similar expertise, the tendency is strong for experts at higher levels to relate "functionally" downward to expert counterparts at lower organizational levels, and in so doing to build functional authority bypasses of line authority. When these functional linkages are fully operational, the authority of the responsible and accountable line official may be substantially eroded. If, as he frequently does, the line officer undertakes to maintain or to re-establish his authority of rank, significant interpersonal and communication problems may develop within the organization. The line and staff form of organization is pictured in Figure 7–2.

3. The Functional Form. The *functional* form of organization, like the line and staff type, develops from the need for specialization. Functional systems add the further dimension that the staff expert, instead of remaining outside the lines of authority, is brought into the main body of the organiza-

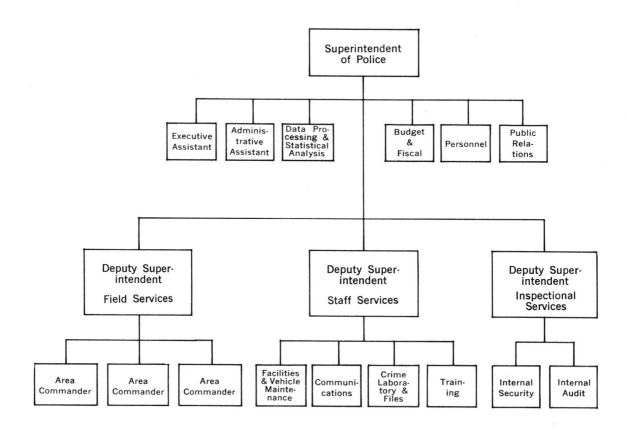

FIGURE 7-2. *The line and staff form of organization*

tion and delegated authority over all phases and operations of the function in which he possesses expertise.

In the functional type, the organization is departmentalized into its major functional activities, such as health, public safety, administrative or support services, building inspection, public works, and so on. Each function is headed by a specialist in that activity cluster. Such functional heads have three distinct responsibilities; each is line head of his functional grouping, staff advisor to the chief executive, and *substantively* responsible for the performance of his function throughout the entire organization.

In the discharge of this latter responsibility, a functional head, unless considerable care is exercised both as to protocol and procedure, may come into conflict with another functional head in whose activity cluster there is performed some work for which the former expert has substantive responsibility.

An example of this would be a sewage disposal plant, organizationally situated in the department of sanitation, which has on its staff a payroll clerk whose functions would be included within the functional responsibility of the head of the department of administration. An important organizational question to be answered in this situation is: who is the payroll clerk's direct superior—the sewage disposal facility manager or the director of the department of administration?

This dilemma is usually resolved by specify-ing clearly and unequivocally that the plant manager is the clerk's direct superior, the director of administration having responsibility for substantive determinations of payroll activity exclusively. Such specification is then implemented through procedures designed to insure that substantive instructions and directions, emanating from the administration function, are transmitted to the clerk through the office of the plant manager, rather than directly. As in the line and staff form, the potential for structurally-based interpersonal and communication difficulties is substantial. The functional form of organization is illustrated in Figure 7–3.

The functional arrangement, which has been the dominant organizational form in industrial corporations and in many larger government agencies during recent years, presently is being subjected to mounting criticism from students of organization and from executives in both the private and public sectors. Its critics feel that this form of structure rapidly is becoming outmoded and increasingly has demonstrated its inadequacies under contemporary conditions of dynamic environmental change. As summarized by one management writer, the criticism centers around nine basic arguments:

1. Functional organizations tend to emphasize the separate functional elements at the expense of the whole organization.

2. Under functional departmentation there is no group that effectively integrates the various func-

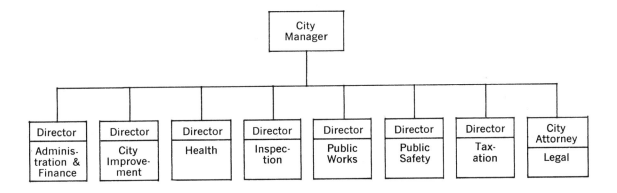

FIGURE 7-3. *The functional form of organization*

tions of an organization and monitors them from the "big picture" standpoint.

3. Functional organizations do not tend to develop "general" managers.

4. Functional organizations emphasize functional relationships based on the vertical organizational hierarchy.

5. Functional organizations tend to fragment other management processes, such as planning and control, which are structured by the formal organizational hierarchy.

6. Functional organizations tend to be closed systems.

7. Functional organizations develop a strong resistance to change.

8. Functional segregation through the formal organization process encourages conflict among the various functions.

9. The emphasis on the various operating functions focuses attention on the internal aspects and relations of the [organization] to the detriment of its external relations.[28]

4. *Program Management Form.* The recent development and selective application to organizations of general systems theory has resulted in the emergence of the *program management* form of organization. General systems theory may be described as an approach to the management process which places emphasis on the organization's totality, seeing it as "an organized or complex whole; as assemblage or combination of things or parts forming a complex or unitary whole."[29] General systems theory views the organization's subsystems as secondary in importance to the primary system, and as mutually interdependent. Hence it insists that a subsystem cannot be altered without such modification affecting other subparts of the whole and therefore the primary system as well.

The program management form, still in its experimental stages of development, establishes each individual project or product as a distinct organizational unit. The essence of program management is the decentralization of functional authority—this form grouping requisite expert resources temporarily around a specific project to be accomplished.

Heading the several functional groupings which collectively make up the program organization is a program manager, whose duty is to develop the single project assigned to him; he is required to plan, organize, coordinate, motivate, lead, and control the functional and multifunctional subunits concerned with various aspects of the total program task to ensure that the assigned program goals are realized. Carlisle observes that:

Because they are involved with only one project and working with groups who have responsibility for only one project, mission-oriented personnel become closely attached to the work being performed. Communication is more efficient and response time in problem solving is cut to a minimum. The whole predominates and functional suboptimization occurs less frequently. Furthermore, resistance to change and the tendency to closed organizations are minimized because the program organization is acknowledged as temporary, to be terminated upon completion of the project.[30]

It is reasonably certain that while the program management form of organization apparently overcomes a number of the difficulties associated with the functional form, experience will demonstrate that this mode of organization subsequently will manifest structural and interactional problems of its own.

Larger, more complex organizations frequently choose to combine basic forms of structure, utilizing for example the line and staff arrangement at the top of the organization and functional groupings in the line operations. The United States Internal Revenue Service, as an illustration, is organized on the line and staff basis at its national office and again at the level of its regional offices, while activities within district offices are arranged functionally.

Unity of Direction. One of the "principles of organization" strongly advocated by the structuralist school was that of unity of direction. This "principle" held that each person in an organization should be directed by only one superior. In the original formulations, the

[28] Howard M. Carlisle, "Are Functional Organizations Becoming Obsolete?" MANAGEMENT REVIEW, January, 1969, pp. 2–9.

[29] Richard A. Johnson, Fremont E. Kast, and James E. Rosenzweig, "Designing Management Systems," in Peter P. Schoderbek (ed.), MANAGEMENT SYSTEMS (New York: John Wiley and Sons, 1967), p. 113.

[30] Carlisle, *op. cit.,* pp. 8–9.

expression appeared as unity of command, inasmuch as the concept and the term came, presumably, from the military. In formal organization (structural) theory, the hierarchy is seen as an authority transmission conduit, a chain of command, through which authority flows downward from a single office or position at the apex of the chain. Each subordinate office had certain authority of "the chief" delegated in turn to it, and could subsequently delegate portions of received authority to still lower-ranking line officials.

The writings of Barnard, Simon, and other proponents of the human relations or administrative behavior school cast considerable doubt upon the viability of this highly formalistic view of organizational functioning. As a consequence, the "principle" increasingly came to be seen as unrealistic, especially so under the conditions of modern organizational life, as systems more and more became populated with specialists and technicians who, though lower in "rank," frequently possessed greater knowledge of technical features of the organizational task than did their "line superiors."

With the growth of technical complexity in organizations demanding increased numbers of experts, functional (expert) superiors were added to the member mix. As this occurred, the formal authority–functional authority dichotomy discussed previously in the sections on the line and staff and functional forms of organization increasingly manifested itself.

A major cause of communication problems and interpersonal difficulties in such contemporary organizations as mental hospitals, universities, health and welfare agencies, research organizations, and many others has been identified as the failure of the system to articulate and managerially delimit these frequently conflicting authorities.

For example, in a mental hospital a common organizational arrangement is the line and staff form with a "chain of command" extending downward from the hospital's superintendent through two presumably equivalent assistant superintendents, responsible respectively for treatment (sometimes clinical or medical)

and for administration. Below the assistant superintendent, clinical, the organizational departmentation is divided into treatment units or wards, headed by unit or ward directors and staffed by therapeutic teams of psychiatrists, clinical psychologists, social workers, nurses, and attendants. The superintendent of the hospital is advised by a specialist staff of department heads for nursing services, psychological services, social services, and others. A principal organizational problem in this complex technological system is: who is the organizational superior of the nurse with duty assignment on the ward—the ward director or the director of nursing services?

The presence of two superiors, one in the chain of command, the other a functional head, almost invariably results in confusion over priority of assignments, sources of appeal, absence of or conflict over responsibility for the subordinates' training, development, performance evaluation, promotion, and a myriad of other difficulties.

As the number of highly trained specialists, planners, computer programmers, and others rises in local government, urban administrators will decide who should manage the experts, their superiors in the line or their functional counterparts at higher organizational levels. The evidence appears to be increasingly indicating that, whatever problems may be associated with the application of the "principle" of unity of direction, even more serious problems appear to arise from fragmentation of authority to manage subordinates.

Span of Control. One of the primary principles of the classical approach to organization was that of the limited span of control of the executive and supervisor. Based upon the observations of Graicunas[31] and Davis,[32] this principle held that an executive whose work was perceived as largely mental, dealing with

---

[31] V. A. Graicunas, "Relationship in Organization," L. Gulick and L. Urwick (eds.), PAPERS ON THE SCIENCE OF ADMINISTRATION (New York: Columbia University, 1947), pp. 183–87.

[32] Ralph C. Davis, THE INFLUENCE OF THE UNIT OF SUPERVISION AND THE SPAN OF THE EXECUTIVE ON THE ECONOMY OF LINE ORGANIZATION STRUCTURE, BUREAU OF RESEARCH, Research Monograph No. 26 (Columbus, Ohio: Ohio State University, 1941).

intangibles and abstractions and more exacting and demanding than physical work, would suffer a decrease in the effectiveness of his managerial direction and control if he were called upon to manage more than 3 to 7 immediate subordinates. In the case of the supervisor whose activities were seen as largely physical and mainly concerned with control of current operations, a similar decline in supervisory effectiveness was felt to occur if the number of workers supervised exceeded the range of 15 to 20.

Davis identified the optimum executive span, in most cases, as not more than 5 immediate subordinates. Graicunas contended that these limitations on managerial effectiveness were the consequence of geometric increases in the number of interpersonal relationships in the unit organization as work-group membership enlarged. He identified and classified three types of such interpersonal relationships, direct single, direct group, and cross relationships, and indicated the mathematical formulae[33] for determining the number of such relations potentially existent in a unit organization.

A number of human relationists denounced these principles of span of control as fables. They argued that these formulations were too mechanistic, control oriented, and without empirical validation; that they failed to take account of the development of primary relationships among the members of the group, relationships which frequently result in a high degree of group control over individual members; and, perhaps most importantly, that the application of such principles was antithetical to the "new" principle of the inherent superiority of the nonhierarchical, participative form of organization.[34]

It was contended that much broader spans of management than those indicated by Graicunas and Davis were possible without loss of managerial effectiveness,[35] and some indeed even suggested that broad spans were desirable in order to prevent the development of authoritarian organizational systems, to facilitate fuller and more effective communication within organizations, and to encourage enlarged participation in the processes of organizational decision making.

More and recent research and further field observations of processes of communication and interpersonal interaction in varied group settings have revealed that the principle was in part viable,[36] as contended by the classicists, and in part a fable, as suggested by the human relationists. The classicists were certainly correct in observing that there are limitations on managerial effectiveness imposed by increases in the number of interpersonal relations as work group size enlarges. The principle of limited span of control implicitly assumed that limited spans would enable managers to *control* operations more effectively, by which was meant higher levels of production through closer management attention and oversight. Numerous studies,[37] however, have disclosed that *sustained* high levels of output, under usual organizational conditions, cannot be controlled even with a limited span, but can only be realized through the exercise of effective leadership which earns the following of the workers and results in their acceptance of the leader's high productivity norm.

---

[33] The number of direct single relationships = n (the number of immediate subordinates); the number of possible direct group relationships = $n\left(\frac{2n}{2}-1\right)$; and the number of possible cross relationships that can occur is given by the formula $n(n-1)$. The total number of such potential relationships is then Σ [n, $n\left(\frac{2n}{2}-1\right)$, $n(n-1)$].

[34] See for example, Waino W. Suojanen, "The Span of Control—Fact or Fable?" ADVANCED MANAGEMENT, November, 1955.

[35] James C. Worthy, "Organizational Structure and Employee Morale," AMERICAN SOCIOLOGICAL REVIEW, April, 1950; C. L. Shartle, "Leadership and Executive Performance," PERSONNEL, March, 1949; and John M. Pfiffner, "The Third Dimension of Organization," *ibid.,* March, 1952.

[36] Berelson and Steiner have observed in relation to group size that ". . . the watershed seems to be around size 5–7. That is about the number of people, apparently, that can be taken into account at one time, as individuals: the council of the Indian village is called the *panchayat*—group of five, and the correct number for a dinner party, according to an English adage (from Disraeli?), is 'more than the graces and fewer than the muses.' "

[37] As summarized by Berelson and Steiner (*ibid.,* p. 374), the findings are: "the more friendly-helpful the boss, . . . the more the productivity (if that is a goal of the organization and the unit) ."

Leadership can be earned and maintained over time only if the managerial span is sufficiently narrow to allow adequate time for the development and expression of meaningful personal interaction with the other members of the task group. No research or field studies have lent support to the classical view that the appropriate supervisory span was in the range 15 to 20 subordinates. Here, the classicists clearly were wrong in their identification of the supervisory role as largely concerned with physical activities and with the control of current operations. The supervisor, like the executive above him, is a manager and is confronted with exactly the same group development and maintenance responsibility.

Leadership of a work group, then, can only be realized if the supervisory span, like that of the executive, is sufficiently limited to enable the supervisor to take into account each work group member as an individual and to relate adequately and meaningfully with each subordinate. If *any* manager's span is too extensive, increased formality in communication and in relationships results and the manager will lose expressive (interpersonal) leadership to informal leaders, having thereafter the capacity only to exercise instrumental direction, or the control of means into the organization and their distribution within it.

The human relationists, in their "critique of the fable," should be faulted for their too ready acceptance of the assumption that broad spans would result in more effective organizations. The development of primary relationships among the members can be obverse to the instrumental goals of the organization. Broad spans of management do not result in high levels of production simply because the system is less hierarchical or the communication flow fuller. Indeed, broader managerial spans, as noted above, make difficult the operation of other than the highly formalistic communication and relationships between organizational levels that the human relations school inveighs so strongly against.

It should be emphasized that narrow managerial spans do not of themselves result in the development of cohesive task or work groups and higher levels of output. A manager

may function as formally and autocratically over 5 to 7 subordinates as over 20, but limited spans do afford the interpersonally competent manager the time to earn and to maintain the leadership which he requires to discharge fully his managerial responsibility, and in addition provide a task group that corresponds in size with natural human interaction groups.

INTERACTIONAL ELEMENTS OF THE
ANALYTIC-INTEGRATIVE APPROACH

As observed previously, the contemporary analytic-integrative approach to organization emphasizes the processes of interaction between the structure and the organization's participants, and between and among various participants in their organizational roles. It is concerned with analysis both of intra and interorganizational conflict and processes of accommodation and seeks the development of more cooperative and symbiotic models and forms of effective and efficient organization.

Components of Organizations. A most useful way to encapsulate major intrasystem elements of the contemporary approach is by consideration of the valuable descriptive model developed by Jacob W. Getzels.[38] Figure 7-4 portrays a modified version of the Getzels' formulation.

An organization is described, in this "benzine ring" model, as a goal-directed behavior system, composed of an *instrumental* component (upper line), the formal, rational-legal, or bureaucratic organization, and an *expressive* component (lower line), the bureaucracy's informal organization or adaptive social system, the aggregate of patterns of interpersonal choice and rejection by the organization's individual members acting socially rather than in their organizational roles.

The former component consists of the *institution* (or bounded system) which presents to its membership a particular kind of organizational climate and projects to those outside the institution a usually somewhat distinctive image. The institution is made up of a set of *positions*, usually rationally designed and hi-

---

[38] J. W. Getzels and E. G. Guba, "Social Behavior and the Administrative Process," THE SCHOOL REVIEW, Winter, 1957, p. 429.

erarchically arranged, associated with each of which are *roles* or sets of expectations, shared by the institution's membership, of the behavior individuals will exhibit when occupying such positions or status categories. This rational-legal system of positions is related, generally hierarchically downward, through an authority system which presumably enables the formal organization to direct occupants of positions toward instrumental or organizational goal accomplishment. Too, the instrumental organization has certain systemic expectations, e.g., that its members will contribute maximum efforts at all times toward the accomplishment of its goals.

The expressive component is made up of the various *individuals* who hold organizational membership, each a unique, distinctive *personality* and motivated by psychogenic *needs* in differing combinations and intensities. These individuals relate socially with each other within the formal organization in various patterns of affection, indifference, and hostility.

When the instrumental component exercises formal authority through its system of hierarchical positions, authority directed to the realization of instrumental goals, the member-

recipients of orders or instructions have the option, as individuals though not as occupants of positions, either of accepting the validity of the order and complying with it or of withholding their consent in whole or in part. In those cases where substantial numbers of participants withhold fully their consent, e.g., by striking, the formal organization usually is unable to enforce its authority and cannot, at least temporarily, realize its instrumental goals.

Problems and Conflicts within Organizations. The areas in which the most significant organizational problems and conflicts usually arise are those encircled by the dashed lines in Figure 7-4.

1. Institutions versus individual: Unfortunately for their members, and frequently for the system as well, a significant number of modern organizations are managed in a cold, aloof, impersonal, and dehumanized manner, and frequently imperiously as well.[39] As a conse-

[39] President John F. Kennedy, after his 1962 dispute with the steel industry, commented: "My father always told me that all businessmen were sons-of-bitches, but I never believed it till now;" to which leaders of unions of government employees, and many of the employees themselves, might add: "And so are all government executives."

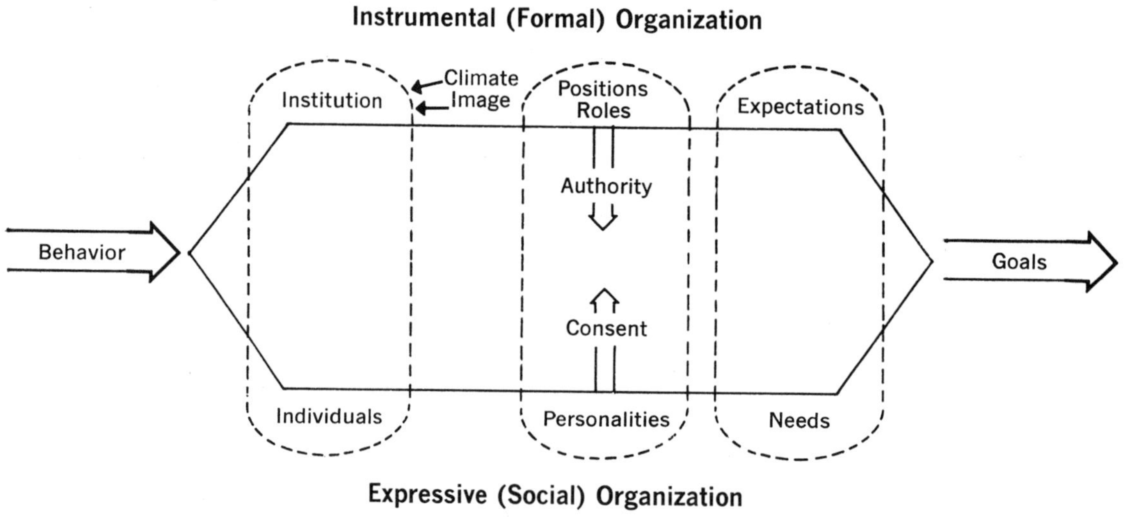

FIGURE 7-4. *A model of contemporary organization*

quence, organizational participants feel unknown or forgotten, unappreciated, even abused, believe they are treated immaturely rather than as the mature individuals they know themselves to be, and find within the organization little opportunity for expression of their individuality.

In many organizations they are told how to dress, where to live, how big their home may be, what persons they may associate with and who are improper companions, what community organizations they are expected to join, and to what community efforts (Boy Scouts, Community Chest, etc.) they are expected to contribute their "off-duty" time. It is not surprising, therefore, that many organizational participants come to think of themselves as mere cogs in a great, all-embracing organizational machine. As Max Ways has written, "The man who says, 'I am a cog' does not thereby become a cog—but he may become an unhappy and 'alienated' man."[40]

2. Role versus personality: In many organizations, little or no attention is paid to the harmonizing of the positional requirements of the system and the personalities of the members of the organization. In cases where substantial mismatches of personality and position occur, either the organization suffers through inadequate or inappropriate performance by the employees or by incurring high costs in employee transfer and turnover.

Further, the employees themselves suffer,

[40] Max Ways, "Tomorrow's Management," FORTUNE, July 1, 1966, p. 85.

coming perhaps to detest their jobs and the organization which appointed them to positions which demand—8 hours a day, 5 days a week, 50 weeks a year—performance expressions which are the antitheses of their personalities. This problem is particularly acute, from the employee point of view, when alternatives to an undesirable position are severely limited or virtually nonexistent, as is the case (1) in specific geographic areas dominated by one organization or industry, (2) in times or areas of economic depression, or (3) for the employee with little or no skill, or who is advanced in years.

3. Systemic expectations versus human needs: A significant number of organizations "demand" performance and "expect" loyalty, yet fail to provide either adequate reward for member contributions to the realization of instrumental goals or sufficient organizational opportunity for satisfaction of member needs. In such cases, the organizations' participants, through the mechanism of the expressive system, will probably restrict output, withhold commitment and loyalty, and seek by collective means to gain a more equitable balance between the burdens which the organization imposes and the rewards—economic, psychic, and social—which it provides to its membership.

Dynamics of Organizational Interaction. In the dynamic sense, then, a "good" organization may be described as one in which the instrumental and expressive components are essentially congruent and in substantial harmony, as portrayed in Figure 7-5.

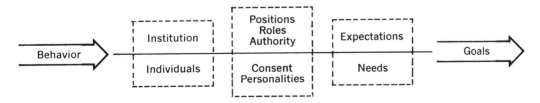

Instrumental (Formal) Organization

Behavior → Institution / Individuals → Positions Roles Authority / Consent Personalities → Expectations / Needs → Goals

Expressive (Social) Organization

FIGURE 7-5. *A model of the ideal organization*

The good, or well-managed, organization is one in which the attitudes and values of the individual members are in substantial accord with the attitudes and values of the institution, and one in which organizational positions are well matched with the personalities of the occupants. It is also an organization which attempts to provide adequate satisfactions for the needs of its members as they contribute their efforts on its behalf; and it is one in which the organizational participants, voluntarily and willingly, undertake to do what it is organizationally necessary that they do.

This is, of course, a most unusual state of affairs. The much more common situation is that pictured in Figure 7–6.

As a consequence both of errors of management commission and omission, the instrumental and expressive components drift or are driven apart until the strains in the three critical areas described above become so severe that they result in a bifurcation or separation of the components of the organization. Following such division, the self-served expressive system usually then formalizes itself, as in the case of a union, and re-presents itself to the instrumental system as a countervailing formal organization with the goals of redressing grievances and of affecting and maintaining a more equitable balance between the instrumentally imposed burdens and the formal organization's provision of rewards and satisfactions.

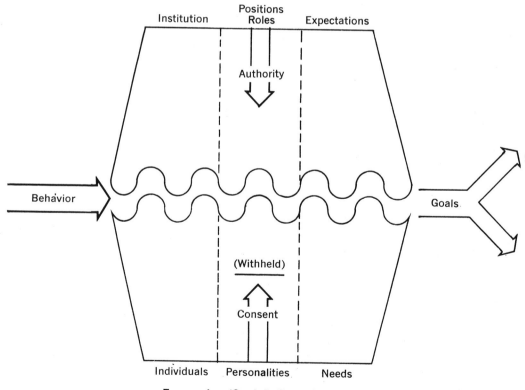

FIGURE 7-6.   *The process of organizational bifurcation*

INTRAORGANIZATIONAL DIMENSIONS

The climate prevailing in an organization is substantially the consequence of the management style favored and practiced by the elite group of managers at the apex of the structural hierarchy. If these managers are autocrats, the system below them will reflect this. If, on the other hand, they are democratic, participative, and share in decision making and in the distribution of the rewards of instrumental accomplishment, the organization will likely become more democratic and participative.

Tradition is, of course, a factor to be reckoned with in organizations. Attitudes and modes of organizational behavior favored by previous administrations carry forward and influence participant attitudes and modes of behavior in subsequent administrations. Still, it is true that a new management group at the apex can significantly alter an organization's climate. One has only to review the administration of the United States Secretary of Defense, Robert McNamara, or of the late Pope John XXIII of the Roman Catholic Church to appreciate that this is so.

Inasmuch as the managerial style of key decision makers determines in a major way the climate of an organization or subparts of it, it would seem appropriate to discuss style and organizational climate simultaneously. Four quite different styles of management or organizational climates may be identified: the bureaucratic, the technocratic, the idiosyncratic, and the democratic-participative.

The Bureaucratic Managerial Style. The bureaucratic manager or climate is rule-oriented, position-focused, and downward directed in communication flow. Military organizations and paramilitary systems, such as police and fire departments, are examples of bureaucratic-climate organizations. Dedicated bureaucratic managers perceive their jobs as requiring loyal, unswerving, unquestioning execution of organizational policy handed to them from above, in the best tradition of Balaklava.[41]

The tendency of the bureaucrat is to avoid

[41] In the *Charge of the Light Brigade,* Tennyson wrote: "Their's not to make reply, / Their's not to reason why,/Their's but to do and die."

the development of personal relationships with subordinates in the belief that personal involvement weakens his "authority." The military view that "officers ought not fraternize with enlisted men" is an illustration of this attitude. Bureaucratic managers may range across the spectrum from the absolute despot on the one extreme to the benign, benevolent, paternalistic, even kindly father-figure on the other. This latter type of bureaucrat frequently believes that he is democratic with his "children" and, indeed, sometimes is seen as such by a number of the organization's participants.

Inasmuch as a bureaucratic organization is a downward-oriented authority and communication system, real (as distinguished from mechanistic) input into the organization in the form of suggestions, ideas, innovations, and danger signals usually is restricted to those few in high office; consequently, reality feedback to the elite from operating strata of the organization is slow at best, occurs with considerable difficulty, and perhaps not at all.

Perceptions of problems the organization confronts (1) in the areas of its interface with clienteles, and (2) as a consequence of operating experience in the implementation of policy directives and administrative issuances from above in the system, are gained by the elite decision group almost exclusively through reports and compilations of statistics. These reports may be incomplete, inaccurate, nonreflective, or even deliberately colored to present lower, often indifferent and noncommitted system participants in the most favorable light. Recognizing their relative isolation from reality, high-level bureaucratic managers frequently avoid risk-taking behavior.

The reasonably efficient bureaucracy is an adequate and sometimes excellent action system. It may do quite well what it knows how to do, but it is almost universally a poor system for analyzing the need for change, for innovating strategies to deal effectively with such change, and for gaining and holding member commitment to the development and expeditious realization of its goals, particularly so under conditions which demand rapid alteration or modification of goals.

The Technocratic Managerial Style. A second managerial style is the technocratic, wherein the manager views himself as the principal expert in his organization or subpart thereof. The technocratic manager largely discounts the importance of hierarchical position, which he associates with "administration," i.e., paper work, preferring rather to define his role as requiring reinterpretation, modification, and improvement of organizational programs and work to fit the changing needs of the technologic situation.

The technocrat performs a management role as the senior in expertise, relating personally with colleagues, but striving to remain dominant through his perceived superior technical knowledge and his ability to give specific directions on jobs where such expertise is required. Research and laboratory directors frequently are technocratic in their managerial application.

Within the larger technical organization, where a number of technologies simultaneously are operational, a "pecking-order" of expertise customarily develops over time, certain types of experts ranking higher in organizational or field status than other types of experts. A prime example of this system of "pecking" is to be found in any reasonably large mental hospital. A very elaborate status hierarchy exists within the mental health field, which is reflected in the hospital. The highest-status expert is, of course, the psychiatrist, board certified in psychiatry and neurology, who is also an analyst.

From this premier expert the status system "pecks" downward through progressively lower status levels of psychiatrists lacking board certification, Ph.D. clinical psychologists, psychologists possessing only master's degree credentials, psychiatric social workers, degree-holding registered nurses, diploma nurses, paramedical specialists such as those in occupational and industrial therapy, until finally the lowest status group—the attendants, aides, or technicians—is reached. They, naturally, in accordance with the status model presented above them, arrange themselves in descending order of experiential expertise or seniority.

When certain higher hierarchical positions in the oganization are occupied by individuals with lower expert status, intriguing functional authority and communications bypasses develop, which significantly alter the designed or intended structural relationships.

The Idiosyncratic Management Style. The idiosyncratic manager views his role as administering organizational rules and regulations flexibly so as to articulate them to specific individuals. In the best sense, he manages by attempting to stimulate, guide, and develop individual subordinates to carry out their responsibilities to the best of their respective abilities. He also, however, may manage by personal manipulation. The idiosyncratic manager is likely to reserve a substantial amount of decision making to himself (see footnote 6), and frequently bypasses subordinates in his efforts to influence the behavior of individuals several echelons below in the hierarchy. Such a manager's need to know in order to be able effectively to motivate, influence, or manipulate individuals may cause him to become preoccupied with personal contact or organizational detail. He usually supposes himself to be adept at the practice of psychology and often believes that control over the organization's affairs and its prosperity are substantially dependent upon his capacity to deal effectively with differing kinds of personalities, or indeed even upon his charisma.

The application of such a style is likely to result in certain problems, especially in the larger organization. First, the idiosyncratic manager tends to make decisions more on the basis of the personal interest he has in the issue or in the personalities involved than on the organizational significance of the matter for decision. Second, since delegation of authority is seldom employed by such a manager, save in those areas which hold little or no personal interest for him, it is more "relegation" than true delegation—queuing-up in decision making generally occurs, subordinates waiting "from morning unto even" for his resolution of matters. Third, in the more manipulative applications of this style, the organizational consequences are likely to be either that the organization will lose its more interpersonally skillful subordinates or will tend to deteriorate in a pathology of executive suite intrigue. Empathic subordinates, themselves astute in the analysis of personalities, are likely to perceive quickly their superior's efforts at manipulating them, however sophisticated these efforts may be, and either will depart the organization or will respond to these efforts in kind.

Of the four managerial styles herein described, the idiosyncratic is the most likely to be the result of personal pathology, based in gross arrogance, substantial personal insecurity, or both, in a compensatory reversal of behavior.

The Democratic-Participative Managerial Style. The fourth style of management or organizational climate is the democratic-participative. Such a manager is group oriented and perceives his managerial role as involving the integration of the work group and its development into an effective team. Toward this end, the democratic-participative manager believes he should maintain an informal, friendly relationship with all employees separately or, in the larger organization, in groups and, besides sharing information with them, should solicit and respect their opinions about the work situation. The democratic-participative manager can become too concerned, even sentimental, about his organization or unit, and since he dislikes conflict and lack of harmony, may, on occasion, tend to sacrifice the organization's instrumental requirements in his efforts to gain or hold member acceptance and cooperation.

Congruence and dynamic equilibrium between an organization's instrumental authority and communication transmission system and the agglomerate of its social system components is most likely to be realized when the organization's managers flexibly employ the various styles described above, carefully articulating the style employed to the nature of the intrasystem managerial or organizational problem confronting them at a particular time, striving the while to avoid the detrimental interpersonal and organizationally dysfunctional

consequences associated with the application of each.

INFORMAL ORGANIZATION

The term "informal organization" refers to those patterns of interpersonal interaction and of social relationships within an organization, and sometimes extending beyond the institution's boundaries into other social units, which influence and affect formal system decisions both in their formulation and in their implementation. These social patterns and relationships also result in the establishment and enforcement of group norms, or rules governing the behavior of persons as members of a total social unit and its various subsystem components.

Such aspects of organization are designated "informal" because the patterns of interaction and the associated groupings of persons are not specified in the bureaucratic schema of hierarchal positions and formally designed, instrumentally focused communication and relationship linkages. The aggregate of such personal associations, social interactions, and the friendship groupings which develop therefrom comprises the organization's expressive or social system, referred to above.

An understanding of the existence and functioning of informal organizations is important for two reasons. Informal or social association usually precedes the establishment of formal organization. Blau, for example, has written:

The decision of the members of a group to formalize their endeavors and relations by setting up a specific organization, say a social and athletic club, is not fortuitous. If a group is small enough for all members to be in direct social contact, and if it had no objectives that require coordination of activities, there is little need for explicit procedures or a formal division of labor. But the larger the group and the more complex the task it seeks to accomplish, the greater are the pressures to become explicitly organized. Once a group of boys who merely used to hang around a drugstore decide to participate in the local baseball league, they must organize a team.[42]

---

[42] Peter M. Blau and Richard W. Scott, FORMAL ORGANIZATIONS (San Francisco: Chandler Publishing Company, 1962), p. 7.

Of much more substantial operational significance to the manager of a public or an enterprise organization is the functioning of informal organization within formal or bureaucratic structure.

Elite Groups. As noted previously, the formal structure is the system of designed, intended, determinate relationships extending downward from the elite group component of the total organization. Small groups of associates who originate bureaucratic organizations and therefore become, temporarily at least, their structural elite, are likely to be relatively homogeneous in background and to embrace relatively similar or at least complementary values, for these elements are interactional requirements both in the establishment and in the continuity of small social groups.[43] It was because of this homogeneity and similarity of values among its members that such groups developed into and functioned as cohesive social units.

The elite group within a long-lived bureaucratic organization is likely to have remained relatively homogeneous and to have continued to embrace substantially common values despite member turnover across time, through the management process of executive selection into such a group and through the effect of the group's established norms on new member attitudes, beliefs, values, and behavior. Replacement members of the elite group not only were probably screened by the remaining members of the original elite as to their backgrounds, attitudes, and values before gaining entry into the group, but also were required, upon their admission, either to adhere to existent, carried-forward group norms or to risk expulsion from group membership. "Different" individuals would probably have been denied entry into the elite; deviant members would have been persuaded into reasonable conformity with prevailing elite norms or expelled from group membership as a consequence of their adherence to nonconformist values.

The Impact of Heterogeneity on Organizations. As, however, organizations grow in size, the total social unit tends to become more heterogeneous, dissimilar, and consequently less viscid as a system. The elite group usually formulates, for the total organization, goals which *it* has determined are necessary and important. Its view relative to these goals may be said to be *cooperative*[44] in the sense that the accomplishment of organizational ends has direct, personal meaning for the individual member of the elite group. He has had a voice in the formulation of these goals; in part, at least, they are a reflection of him as a person; and their realization is likely to provide substantial satisfaction of one or more of his own psychogenic needs.

The view of the nonelite of the system relative to organization goals, however, is essentially *subjective*[45] in that the organization's purpose and goals, as conceived and expressed by the elite group, have directly no meaning for the largest number of the diverse and heterogeneous members of the organization. What is important to the nonelite is the organization's relation to them personally—"what burdens it imposes, what benefits it confers," to quote Barnard.[46] Since the rather wide range of *personal* goals of the varied and diverse elements of the nonelite of the organization and their individual and collective views of the *organization's* goals stated by the system's elite may be at considerable disparity with the view of the elite group relative to organization ends, actual work relationships and organizational functioning can be, and indeed often is, at substantial variance from both the intention and the perception of the structural elite.

Patterns of Informal Organization. Dalton[47] identifies three general classes of cliques or informal organizations: *vertical, horizontal,* and *random.* He further subcategorizes vertical

---

[43] Berelson and Steiner (*op cit.,* p. 327) have observed, ". . . small groups rest on shared values and shared contact . . . The shared values include not only those associated with such social positions as educational status, age, class, or ethnicity, but beyond that they reflect such matters as attitudes, tastes, beliefs, and behavioral norms."

[44] Barnard, *op. cit.,* pp. 86–89.
[45] *Ibid.*
[46] *Ibid.,* p. 88.
[47] Melville Dalton, MEN WHO MANAGE (New York: John Wiley and Sons, Inc., 1959), pp. 57–65.

cliques as being either vertical *symbiotic*[48] or vertical *parasitic;* and horizontal cliques as being either horizontal *aggressive* or horizontal *defensive.*

A vertical clique usually occurs in a single department of an organization and consists of the top officer and some of his subordinates. "It is vertical in the sense that it is an up-and-down alliance between formal unequals," to quote Dalton. The vertical symbiotic clique is one in which the top officer is concerned with aiding and protecting his subordinates. As described by Dalton:

He does this by concealing or minimizing their errors, occasional lapses, etc. He does what favors he can to meet their immediate needs and to solidify their future in the firm. He interprets their behavior favorably to critical members of the department and to his own superiors. He humanizes the painful impersonal situations and the demands he must make.

The subordinates fully advise him of real or rumored threats to his position. They tell him of current work situations, confer on ways of dealing with "troublemakers" outside the clique, and discuss interdepartmental manuevers. When urgency demands action and the chief is unavailable or there is no time for consultation, lower members confer and make moves with the chief's welfare in mind, and in terms of his known attitudes. Thus for all levels involved, there is a satisfying exchange of services. This is the most common and enduring clique in large structures. It is more than "team work" because only a nucleus of departmental personnel is involved. As it sweeps other members along they may follow gratefully, indifferently, or with some hostility. It is most effective when lower members are relatively indifferent about promotion or reasonably patient in waiting.[49]

A vertical parasitic clique, according to Dalton, is one in which "the exchange of services between lower and higher clique members is unequal. The lower ranked person or persons receive more than they give and may greatly damage the higher officer." Such relationships often are based on blood or marriage.

A horizontal clique cuts across departmental lines and includes officials of approxi-

mately the same rank. A horizontal defensive grouping is usually the result of what the members perceive as crises. This type of clique generally remains cohesive for only the limited time necessary to turn back or adjust to a threat. Dalton observes that the horizontal aggressive social unit is distinguished from the defensive clique ". . . chiefly by its goals and the direction of its action." The members of a horizontal aggressive clique are similar in organizational positions to those who constitute the defensive variant; their action, however, ". . . is a cross-departmental drive to effect changes rather than resist them, to redefine responsibility, or even directly shift it."

A random clique is referred to as random "because its members usually cannot be classified in terms of formal rank, duties, or departmental origin, though they associate intimately enough to exchange confidences." The attraction in this case, more than in the other classifications, is one based on friendship and social satisfaction.

Informal Leadership. Of organizational significance also is the fact that persuasive influentials or informal leaders frequently arise within such informal organizations. Through the exercise of their leadership, these influentials, with varying degrees of skill and effectiveness, coalesce small social units, bring confederation between and among such groups, and even fashion from elements of the expressive component of a bureaucratic system deliberate, purposive formal organizations (such as labor union locals) with their own instrumental goals which may be at some variance with, or even diametrically opposed to, those of the original formal organization.[50]

Summary. It should, of course, be noted that the distinction between formal and informal aspects of an organization is purely an analytic one. There is in fact only one functioning organization, but the manner of its

---

[48] The term *symbiotic* is adapted from the biological term *symbiosis* which refers to a mutually beneficial *internal* partnership between two different kinds of organisms.

[49] Dalton, *op. cit.,* pp. 58–59.

[50] For a detailed description of these social processes in one organizational setting, see Kenneth K. Henning, and Gus L. Economos, "Patterns of Natural Leadership: Part I, The Genesis of Informal Organizations in Naval Recruit Companies" (Chicago: Center for Programs in Government Administration, The University of Chicago, 1962) .

functioning and the degree of its effectiveness and efficiency as a system are determined in substantial measure by the nature of the interfaces and interactions between the organization's participants in their formally designated roles, related one to the other in prescribed patterns of instrumentally-focused authority and communication, and the organization's membership, related socially in the work setting in personally determined patterns of friendship choice and rejection, affection, and disaffection.

INTERACTION AMONG ORGANIZATIONS

As was observed at the beginning of this chapter, modern society is a society of organizations. Satisfaction of the socioeconomic needs of the larger social order, and realization of the survival and prosperity ends of the society's organizations themselves, require that such organizations exchange with and relate to certain other organizations both within and outside the society: as suppliers of goods and services needed by other organizations for their functioning, as recipients of such provisions, as monitors or regulators of the productive or organizational activity of other social units, as regulated organizations relating with regulatory bodies and agencies, and in numerous other ways.

Interaction between Organizations and Employee Associations. One especially significant category of interorganizational interface is that involving an organization and the single or several social units representing some number of the organization's members, e.g., the relationship between city government and its employees' labor unions, professional associations, or expert groupings such as the American Medical Association, American Public Works Association, International Association of Chiefs of Police, or the National Association of Social Workers. Inasmuch as labor unions increasingly are becoming more prominent and vigorous in the area of municipal government, and since rapid technological advances surely will result in substantial increases both in the number and percentage of professionals, paraprofessionals, and high-level technicians serving in local

government, relationships with such advocate or representative units probably will become an ever more substantial and, perhaps, troublesome element in the developing role of the urban administrator.

With reference to these latter groups, municipal administrators need to be cognizant of the distinction, in terms of organizational identities, between *cosmopolitan* and *local* experts. As noted by Gouldner,[51] cosmopolitans are those professionals, paraprofessionals, or high-level technicians ". . . low on loyalty to the employing organization, high on commitment to specialized role skills, and likely to use an outer reference group orientation," whereas locals are ". . . high on loyalty to the employing organization, low on commitment to specialized role skills, and likely to use an inner reference group orientation."

These differing organizational identities can have important managerial implications. Cosmopolitans, oriented in terms of their identity outside the specific social units employing them, tend to complicate the managerial task of coalescing the organization and to make interfaces with the various reference groups a much more substantial element of the managerial work load. Too, intrasystem conflict may arise between cosmopolitans and locals in the same field of expertise, thus contributing to the management's human relations problems and concerns. In such conflict situations, cosmopolitans frequently attempt to invoke the assistance of their outside reference groups, which may have the consequence of adding significant organizational interface dimensions to what otherwise would be simply a problem in intrasystem human relations.

Since bureaucratic organizations, as social systems, require loyalty from their organizational memberships, the outer reference group orientation of cosmopolitans may be perceived by an organization's management as threatening to the bureaucracy's survival

---

[51] Alvin W. Gouldner, "Cosmopolitans and Locals: Toward an Analysis of Latent Social Roles—I and II," ADMINISTRATIVE SCIENCE QUARTERLY, December, 1957—March, 1958, p. 290.

and prosperity ends, inclining them as a consequence toward staffing with local, rather than cosmopolitan, experts. But management needs to be aware of the fact that loyalty considerations frequently restrict or limit expertise. Therefore, by opting for the loyalty of its experts, an organization may lose very significantly in the worth of its expertise. As stated by Gouldner, "The need for loyalty sets certain limits within which the need for expertise is pursued and vice versa."[52]

Interaction between Organizations and Clientele Groups. Organizational relationships of an extramural nature also include those with various clienteles, such as customers or citizen recipients of public services and stockholder-owners or taxpayer-voters. Considering the difficulty of reconciling the contradictory interests of such client groups as welfare recipients and taxpayer organizations concerned about rising levels of taxes, it is easier to appreciate the organizational and managerial significance of interfaces with multiple clienteles and the difficulties that they present.

The Process of Organizational Interaction. Unfortunately, interorganizational interaction has not to date been systematically explored by students of organization. In this regard, Etzioni has said, "We know a great deal about interaction among persons, something about interaction among groups, but surprisingly little about interaction among organizations."[53]

What can be said is that at the polar extremes of social philosophy lie two very different views about the extent to which organizational interaction ought to be regulated by the larger society. At one extreme lies the laissez-faire ideology, holding essentially that interorganizational transaction and interaction ought not be regulated by the larger societal system except in those rare instances where grave social damage would result from nonintervention. At the other extreme is the totalitarian view that all organizations within a society exist for the benefit of the whole society and therefore must be regulated by the social order both in their relations with other organizational components of the society and in their internal affairs in order to realize the greatest social good. Between these two extremes lies a broad spectrum of views, representing various admixtures of these divergent philosophies.

Successful interorganizational interface is the consequence of a difficult managerial process. This process is time-consuming, involving usually long, repeating contacts; it also involves negotiations. In this regard, Leonard Sayles has written that:

Trading, compromise, give and take are the order of the day. Many, if not most, of the subjects dealt with have no fixed, objective answer even in a technical environment. Interpolation and judgment mean differences of opinion, and the manager must expect to engage in extended bargaining. Failure to do so would probably place him at a substantial disadvantage, as the man on the other side of the desk may overstate his original position for the sake of bargaining.[54]

It is also the case that a manager cannot use his "authority" in most of these relations, as he is dealing with representatives of organizations quite outside his own.

Occasionally these relationships involve societally superior organizations, as in the case of government or regulatory agencies or the courts; or collectives of individuals which "outrank" an organization's management, as would be the case in an interface between a city administrator and a group representing a majority of voter-constituents in the municipality. Such interface situations obviously require very sophisticated managerial behavior to enable management to realize results favorable to the organization which it represents.

The Organization of the Future

As Max Ways has observed, "The essential task of modern management is to deal with change."[55] In order to function effectively and

---

[52] *Ibid.,* p. 466.
[53] Etzioni, *op. cit.,* p. 110.

[54] Leonard R. Sayles, MANAGERIAL BEHAVIOR (New York: McGraw-Hill, 1964), pp. 130–31.
[55] Ways, *op. cit.,* p. 84.

efficiently in today's dynamic and fluid environment, organizations need to be flexible. Most students of organization would agree that if a system knows exactly what it needs to accomplish and exactly how best to accomplish it, a highly structured organization is probably the most efficient delivery system, if managed with sufficient benevolence and if it has developed sufficient *esprit de corps* to be able to avoid the systemic bifurcation tendency previously noted.

Under conditions of rapid environmental change, however, organizations cannot know exactly what needs to be done or exactly how best to proceed. The urgent requirements confronting modern organizations are, therefore, to order themselves in such a way, and to conduct their organizational affairs in such a manner, that their respective memberships voluntarily will embrace the organization's instrumental purposes and will freely offer their continuing best efforts. Such efforts should both realize a fuller understanding of the nature of the altering milieu and the organizational consequences of such changes, and develop those strategies which are most appropriate for the accomplishment of the organization's goals under conditions of dynamic disequilibrium.

To meet these contemporary requirements, organizations need to replace their old bureaucratic-directive management orientation and structure which, in the words of Warren Bennis, was ". . . capable in coordinating men and power in a stable society of routine tasks [but] cannot cope with contemporary realities,"[56] with a philosophy, an organizational form, and managerial behavior which can meet the urgent demands of modern society.

The publication *Trans-action* has described the changing circumstances confronting contemporary organizational management as follows:

As more and more organizations outgrow rigid bureaucratic forms, new and extraordinary demands will be placed on their leaders. Nineteenth-century images of autocrats and captains of industry have already been broken in the late twentieth century's service-oriented society, with challenging and perhaps disturbing consequences for today's managers. The new organizations will require leaders more skilled in interpersonal relations than substantive knowledge, men who are finely attuned to the real capacities and career ambitions of their employees as much as to the goals and identity of the organization itself.[57]

The older orientation was predicated upon a set of beliefs about human nature and human behavior labeled by the late Douglas McGregor as Theory X, and which assumed that:

1. The average human being has an inherent dislike of work and will avoid it if he can. . . .
2. Because of this human characteristic of dislike of work, most people must be coerced, controlled, directed, threatened with punishment to get them to put forth adequate effort toward the achievement of organizational objectives. . . .
3. The average human being prefers to be directed, wishes to avoid responsibility, has relatively little ambition, wants security above all.[58]

McGregor challenged the validity of these assumptions and proposed instead his Theory Y, which held that:

1. The expenditure of physical and mental effort in work is as natural as play or rest. The average human being does not inherently dislike work. . . .
2. External control and the threat of punishment are not the only means for bringing about effort toward organizational objectives. Man will exercise self-direction and self-control in the service of objectives to which he is committed.
3. Commitment to objectives is a function of the rewards associated with their achievement. . . .
4. The average human being learns, under proper conditions, not only to accept but to seek responsibility. Avoidance of responsibility, lack of ambition, and emphasis on security are generally consequences of experience, not inherent human characteristics.
5. The capacity to exercise a relatively high degree of imagination, ingenuity, and creativity in the solution of organizational problems is widely, not narrowly distributed in the population.
6. Under the conditions of modern industrial

---

[56] Warren G. Bennis, CHANGING ORGANIZATIONS (New York: McGraw Hill, 1966) , p. 189.

[57] Anon., "No More Indians, No More Chiefs," TRANS-ACTION, May, 1969, p. 32.
[58] Douglas McGregor, THE HUMAN SIDE OF ENTERPRISE (New York: McGraw-Hill, 1960), pp. 33–34.

life, the intellectual potentialities of the average human being are only partially utilized.[59]

The assumptions of McGregor's Theory Y regarding human nature and behavior are being augmented and modified as greater insight into human complexity is gained from recent and contemporary empirical research. Students of organization today perceive man as more complex than either the traditional view or the Theory Y model assumed him to be. Edgar Schein has written that "Not only is he more complex within himself, being possessed of many needs and potentials, but he is also likely to differ from his neighbor in the patterns of his own complexity." Schein also has summarized the assumptions which underlie the "complex man" view of human nature, as follows:

a. Man is not only complex, but also highly variable; he has many motives which are arranged in some sort of hierarchy of importance to him, but this hierarchy is subject to change from time to time and situation to situation; furthermore, motives interact and combine into complex motive patterns (for example, since money can facilitate self-actualization, for some people economic strivings are equivalent to self-actualization) .

b. Man is capable of learning new motives through his organizational experience, hence ultimately his pattern of motivation and the psychological contract which he establishes with the organization is the result of a complex interaction between initial needs and organizational experiences.

c. Man's motives in different organizations or different subparts of the same organization may be different; the person who is alienated in the formal organization may find fulfillment of his social and self-actualization needs in the union or in the informal organization; if the job may engage some motives while other parts engage other motives.

d. Man can become productively involved with organizations on the basis of many different kinds of motives; his ultimate satisfaction and the ultimate effectiveness of the organization depends only in part on the nature of his motivation. The nature of the task to be performed, the abilities and experience of the person on the job, and the nature of the other people in the organization all interact to produce a certain pattern of work and feelings.

For example, a highly skilled but poorly motivated worker may be as effective *and satisfied* as a very unskilled but highly motivated worker.

e. Man can respond to many different kinds of managerial strategies, depending on his own motives and abilities and the nature of the task; in other words, there is no one correct managerial strategy that will work for all men at all times.[60]

As a consequence of the demands of contemporary society, the philosophy underlying managerial behavior in certain avant-garde organizations recently has shifted fundamentally. Bennis has observed that the change is reflected most of all in the following three areas:

1. A new concept of *man,* based on increased knowledge of his complex and shifting needs, which replaces the oversimplified, innocent push-button or inert idea of man.
2. A new concept of *power,* based on collaboration and reason, which replaces a model of power based on coercion and fear.
3. A new concept of *organizational values,* based on an humanistic, existential orientation, which replaces the depersonalized, mechanistic value system.[61]

These recent shifts in management philosophy and emergent managerial behavior, discerned by Bennis, result from an increased awareness by modern managements of the complexity, diversity, and richness of the human resources which staff their systems. The history of recent organizational experience clearly reveals that only those managements which are able to recognize the nature, the magnitude, and the rapidity of the changes which are occurring, and which can marshal, by enlightened management practice, the fullest commitment of the varied and complex individuals who make up their organizational memberships, will be able to design and direct the effective, efficient, adaptive, responsive, and anticipatory organizations which the immediate future clearly is calling out.

---

[59] *Ibid.,* pp. 47–48.

[60] Edgar H. Schein, ORGANIZATIONAL PSYCHOLOGY (Englewood Cliffs, New Jersey: Prentice-Hall, 1965) , p. 60.

[61] Bennis, *op. cit.,* p. 188.

Organization in Today's City *

The multivaried and often dramatic nature of problems currently impinging upon the nation's communities has given rise to the widely held view that urban America is "in crisis," a pathologic state increasingly perceived as at or very near the terminal condition. That severe, indeed grave, problems confront numerous cities cannot be seriously disputed. The suggestion, however, that urban America presently is facing an imminent and insoluble crisis of catastrophic dimensions results both from a misunderstanding of the nature of the developing urban milieu and a serious underestimate of our society's capacity, given its rich economic, technologic, and managerial resources, to solve the frustratingly complex montage of problems which are rising in the wake of rapid national urbanization.

Societal capacity, in terms of both national wealth and demonstrated technical and managerial expertise, though a necessary condition for effective urban problem solving, is not by itself sufficient to treat effectively the problems associated with rapid population clustering. American society requires a fuller appreciation of the rapidity with which the process of urbanization is occurring in the United States, the character of such urbanization, and of the human, social, organizational, and political consequences which are emanating from ever denser population clustering. Also needed is a national willingness to modify or in some instances even abandon certain inherited social values[62] and to redesign or replace archaic and anachronistic social and governmental institutions with more modern and appropriate organizational forms.

FROM GOVERNMENT "FOR" THE PEOPLE TO GOVERNMENT "OF" THEM

The proposal, if implemented, to build a substantial number of new cities dispersed across the nation[63] will not effectively treat the urban "problem" if these new cities are simply architecturally updated and technologically sophisticated reproductions of present metropoli. Garbage in these new urban places may automatically be vacuumed away; traffic flow regulated by computer; high-speed monorail trains may quickly convey residents from their homes to the central business and service centers; and grassy malls and recreational facilities may abound, interspersed optimally among the aesthetically pleasing buildings; but unless such cities also are socially engineered to restore interpersonal meaningfulness to urban living, the urban "problem" will not have been solved, but temporarily deflected. Unless there is innovative, appropriate social engineering designed to establish and maintain a "sense of community" in such new cities, they will, at best, temporarily suspend the phenomena of mass society, including alienation from the bureaucratically remote and interpersonally indifferent processes of urban government.

Of substantially greater significance and more immediate concern is the urgent need to re-establish in existing cities a sense of neighborhood—of true "community"—and, relatedly, to develop innovative administrative mechanisms to ensure fully effective communication with these communities and their immediate and effective access to the decision-making and service-delivering centers of urban government. Government in the cities needs once again to become more *of* the people. Too often it is now a bureaucratically remote, frustratingly inaccessible, humanistically sterile delivery system for the indifferent and occasionally hostile provision of necessary public "services" *for* the people who *happen* to reside in a particular jurisdiction.

* *Editor's Note:* The following section was prepared for this chapter on organizations at our request. Mr. Henning was asked to relate the substance of his chapter to the organizational problems of city hall. He has done much more: he has clearly and cogently challenged urban administrators everywhere to meet the humanistic, participative needs of their constituents and to restore human dignity as the pre-eminent organizational value in urban governance.

[62] See, e.g., Philip M. Hauser, "Urban Society: A Blueprint for the City of Tomorrow," in 1970 BRITANNICA YEARBOOK OF SCIENCE AND THE FUTURE (Chicago: Encyclopedia Britannica, Inc., 1969), p. 202.

[63] See, "New Cities: A Look at the Future," *U.S. NEWS & WORLD REPORT*, January 26, 1970, pp. 64–65.

There are, of course, myriad ways to prevent further deterioration of such residual "communities" that still exist, and to develop and nurture a rebirth of a "sense of community" where it does not exist. Urban management can, for example, work to prevent new expressways from bifurcating or otherwise disrupting areas in which some "sense of community" prevails, even though many citizens and some suburban "penetrators" may thereby experience certain diseconomies of time and convenience. Indeed, municipal officials should consciously use new expressway locations, street widening projects, and traffic flow patterns to develop and encourge "community." Urban planners can incorporate community-building features into urban development and renewal projects, and renewal officials can be stayed in their community "search-and-destroy" efforts. Public housing authority managers can be encouraged and trained to function as social leaders of resident groups rather than simply as landlords and rent collectors.

Citizens may again come to feel more *of* their government if city halls earnestly strive to develop rapport and maintain effective communication with *informal* representatives of individual communities. Such communities, furthermore, *must* be permitted to choose and determine the legitimacy of their informal spokesmen if government *of* the people is to be re-established and if communication between neighborhoods and city hall is to be improved. Even in better managed cities, urban administrators—mayors, city managers, department heads alike—frequently favor "cooperative" community representatives over more vigorous or independent advocates, and usually lend support to those who favor "city hall" programs. But what city hall may see as cooperation, a community may perceive as nonadvocacy.

To further facilitate communication between city hall and neighborhoods, urban government must decentralize most of its direct service-rendering functions, those activities likely to generate numerous inquiries, and those which involve a high volume of intercommunication between citizens and their

government. Neighborhood offices of urban government, rendering a broad spectrum of municipal services, for example, could be established in larger cities with the hours of duty taking account of the work hours of the citizens of the neighborhood. It makes absolutely no sense to establish local offices of urban government if these offices are closed by the time the residents of the community have returned to their neighborhoods from work.

Too, salaried community ombudsmen[64] roles might be established to which citizens could complain if they felt aggrieved by their local government. Such ombudsmen would be roughly analogous to the inspector general role in the military, and would require the same degree of authority to stimulate changes, ameliorate situations, and render satisfactory responses to legitimate problems.

EFFICIENCY, PROFESSIONALISM, AND
TECHNOLOGY AS COUNTERVAILING FORCES

At the present time, three significant administrative forces and technologic developments are impinging powerfully on urban government. By their nature, these forces and technologies essentially are impeding efforts to build and maintain a sense of "community" in cities. These are, first, the increasing demand for more rationality, efficiency, and economy in government through the application of "business-like" practices; second, the increasing use, at the local government level, of professionals and other highly trained technical experts, especially in such areas as urban planning and electronic data processing; and, third, the increasing application of management science technologies, such as computers and operations research technics, in conducting the business of urban government.

No thinking professional urban manager possibly could object to the desire for more rationality in the design of government organizations; to efforts directed toward a realization of greater efficiency and economy in

---

[64] See, for example, Stanley V. Anderson, OMBUDSMAN PAPERS: AMERICAN EXPERIENCE AND PROPOSALS (Berkeley: Institute of Governmental Studies, University of California, Berkeley, 1969).

government through the use of better and more modern practices; to upgrading the quality of public personnel and utilizing the most competent professional expertise; or to the application in government of the most advanced technologies of information processing, data handling, and decision making. But urban administrators need to appreciate and compensate for the fact that these forces and technological developments are biased strongly in the direction of *rationality, impersonality,* and *centralization* of decision making, and that uncompensated application can place urban management on a "collision course" with its citizens as they respond emotionally to the increasing anonymity and impersonality of contemporary urban life.

Consolidation of municipal departments, cities, and counties, and processes of annexation, may "improve" the delivery of public services, and indeed may effect significant economies in government, but citizens thereafter may feel less "of" and more remote and alienated from the—not "their"—consolidated government.

Professionals in urban government may render decisions which indeed are in the long-range "best interests" of the people, but such government "for" the people is not likely to increase their sense of being one with their government. In this regard, it would be well to ponder the words of a British expert, economist Barbara Wootton, in commenting on the unwillingness of workers to move from areas of labor surplus to those of labor shortage:

Free choice of employment is, of course, itself, just as much as freedom of consumption, dependent upon the game being played according to the rules. The most important rule here is that people should be willing to move from job to job as the demands of industry require, in response to what we have called the method of inducement. *An inert and sluggish public might have to be kicked around.*[65]

Computers, without doubt, greatly improve and enhance processes of data collection, handling, and storage, but they are also extremely difficult to talk with, to judge from the highly frustrating and alienating experiences that a number of credit card holders have recently had.

Too, a metropolitan area's resources may be allocated optimally through the application of operations research techniques, but not distributed in accordance with citizen wishes and desires.

NEED FOR APPLICATION TO URBAN GOVERNMENT OF THE ANALYTIC-INTEGRATIVE APPROACH

It well may be the case that it is impossible to effect a re-reconciliation of government and the people in a pluralistic, highly urbanized, technologically advanced society, and thereby to prevent the systemic bifurcation previously discussed. William G. Scott, for example, is pessimistic about the possibility. He has written:

Pluralism is not a viable alternative ideology of organization government. . . . The form of organization government which we may expect is an elite aristocracy with power vesting in the technicians. . .[66]

Whether or not one feels a case can be made [for a truly participative system of organizational government] depends on the optimistic or pessimistic state of one's psyche. I am pessimistic for two reasons.

First, I do not believe the organizational citizenship has the will to sacrifice a single quantum of rationality for those values of a truly participative government which conflict with the quest for the one best way. I am not imputing to this citizenship a lack of moral conviction, necessarily. The web of technological determinism has too completely enfolded its beneficiaries. The expectations of organizational citizens are nearly entirely in the technical and material orders. Each element of the citizenship anticipates rational behavior from the other. Taken together they expect efficient organization performance. The technical elite are supposed to accomplish this. For their part, the elite, at once a segment of the citizenship but preeminent among citizens, perceive rationality as their unique role. Where can this chain be broken?

Second, there might be some hope for breaking it if the managerial elite and the . . . humanists endorse the cause of representative government in organizations. But I do not see this leadership

---

[65] Barbara Wootton, FREEDOM UNDER PLANNING (Chapel Hill, North Carolina: The University of North Carolina Press, 1945), pp. 92–93 (italics added).

[66] William G. Scott, "Organization Government: The Prospects for a Truly Participative System," PUBLIC ADMINISTRATION REVIEW, January/February, 1969, p. 47.

coming from the practice or from the intellectuals.

Management supports democracy as long as it remains in the never-never land of "authentic confrontations, meaningful dialogue, interpersonal competence, and loving-kindness." But management is less supportive of organizational forms which enfranchise employees (interest groups) and reenfranchise ownership (decision making) in the legislative process. In a grudging way management may institute judicial procedures as long as they are controlled by the managerial hierarchy using incumbent executives (or "cooperative" citizens) as the judges.[67]

There is, of course, a considerable body of evidence to support such a pessimistic view of the possibility of realizing a truly participative system of organization government. But it is also fervently, though perhaps heroically, to be hoped that enlightened, informal, professional management might be able to *innovate* pluralism *into* contemporary ur-

ban government; that the urban managerial and technical elite might become more socially and humanistically conscious and concerned than at present they generally are; and that, conceivably, it might be possible to fashion urban government that will serve citizens effectively and efficiently without becoming their master; that will disaccommodate, frustrate, and alienate them least; and that will provide maximally for their satisfaction, contentment, and happiness.

The philosophic theme, as the nation confronts the urban challenge of the decades ahead, should be as expressed in the words of Chester Barnard,

. . . To try and fail is at least to learn; to fail to try is to suffer the inestimable loss of what might have been.[68]

---

[67] *Ibid.*, p. 51.

[68] Chester I. Barnard, THE FUNCTIONS OF THE EXECUTIVE (Cambridge, Massachusetts: Harvard University Press, 1948) , Dedication.

8

Administrative Communication

Organizational studies in governmental, industrial, hospital, school and other agencies indicate that communication is one of management's greatest stumbling blocks.[1] When problems arise in any situation where humans interact, the classic cry appears to be: "We have a communication failure here." Consequently, there are probably few subjects that have been discussed more volumnously in recent years. Turn to almost any trade or professional journal and it is a safe bet the previous year's issues will have had at least a half dozen articles dealing with communication. But few go very deeply into the process, and it continues to be high on management's list of problems for further study.

The municipal administrator continually is involved in the communication process. He is faced with the necessity of interpreting citizen needs and council desires and moving these through the program and implementation stages. If he is to exercise his leadership role, he must be able to listen, ask questions, inform, persuade, and bring about effective group participation. Frequently confronted by a questionable departmental organization structure, he finds himself in the position of having to deal with and coordinate the efforts of anywhere from several to as many as 30 departments, each of which tends toward operating as an independent dynasty. He works (like a telephone operator) at a point where many communication lines come together.

Yet, however necessary, communication is a two-edged sword. It is a continuing process, always working, but the messages carried may either improve or lessen understanding. Communication which enhances organizational effectiveness is normally termed "functional" communication; that which impedes successful operations is "dysfunctional" communication.

Dysfunctional communication is probably the root cause of more management problems than any other single factor. It is the product of ineffective psychological and behavioral patterns at both the management level and the level of those who are managed, but can also quite frequently be traced to questions of skill. Why are some administrators more skillful at communication than others? The answer is that some consciously practice and develop communications skills while others have learned the essentials of the process in a very haphazard manner.

Learning about communication normally begins very early in life. Not too long after birth the child begins to establish a communication system with his mother. Each experience puts him farther along in the process. He soon learns to offer a smile for a smile; though he may sometimes giggle at a frown, once he experiences the consequences he learns to respond in the appropriate manner.

He finds such signals are a means for making his feelings and desires known to others. Long before he reaches adulthood he has had many experiences with the complexities of the communication process. While a general understanding forms, it is not complete or

---

[1] Conclusion drawn from numerous organization surveys conducted by the Industrial Relations Center of the University of Chicago.

comprehensive. As a result, dysfunctions in the face-to-face communication of adults are common; difficulties in using the complex communication channels of a large organization are even more frequent.

The Nature of Communication

Communication processes within organizations can be analyzed in abstract form through the use of models. These tools serve a useful purpose in that they highlight features and problems in communication. Such models range, of course, from the very simple to the quite complex.

A BASIC COMMUNICATION MODEL

One basic model of the communication process, developed by Claude E. Shannon at the Bell Telephone Laboratories, appears in schematic form in Figure 8–1.

Originally developed for physicists and mathematicians to illustrate a telephone communication system, it consists essentially of five parts: (1) an information source, (2) a transmitter, (3) a channel, (4) a receiver, and (5) a destination.

The information source could be a person, radio or television studio, stock exchange, or the news room of a press service. Information is selected by the source to be transmitted through the transmitter which could be a microphone, television camera, or a teletypewriter. The transmitter encodes the message into a form suitable for transmission over the channel. In a telephone system this consists of changing sound pressure into a proportional electric current. The channel may be a pair of wires, as in a telephone system, or a coaxial cable, as in a television network. As the message passes along the channel it may have to overcome a noise source—possibly static—and in the process can suffer some distortion. The receiver decodes the message into a form understandable by the destination, which is the person or the thing for which the message is intended.

Five components thus make up a basic model for communication, or at least for the exchange of information. The message is selected through the information source, encoded by the transmitter, sent along the channel, decoded by the receiver, and passed on to its destination. The model is quite adequate to illustrate the transfer of a message.

AN EXPANDED COMMUNICATION MODEL

Communication in the interacting organization, however, is much more complex than Shannon's model is able to illustrate. The latter's elements are mostly mechanical or elec-

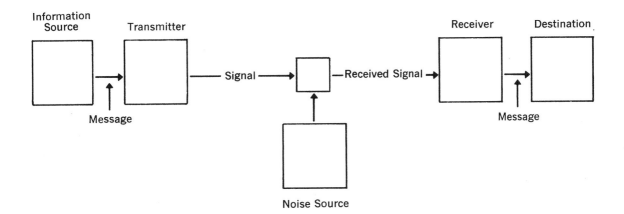

FIGURE 8-1. *Diagram of general communication system*

tronic: subject only to "noise" distortions, they can be expected to transmit and reproduce messages quite accurately. When humans serve as transmitters, channels, and receivers, such faithful reproduction is much less certain.

One way in which human factors can affect the communication process became apparent in studies of employee morale during the 1950's. An initial research hypothesis centered on the notion that effective communication could raise the level of morale among the work force. It soon became evident, however, that the reverse was true: morale levels affect the quality and quantity of communication. In order to give more meaning to Shannon's basic communication model, it is necessary to consider some of these human factors involved in an organization's communication process.

In a fashion similar to that through which a child learns communication skills (described above), the individual also acquires "likes" and "dislikes," a system for evaluating experiences and situations. This evaluating system, illustrated in Figure 8–2, may be termed a "need-motivational framework."

The diagram can be described as follows. Communication starts with an action input to person A. This action input is decoded through the need-value motivational framework of person A, encoded within this framework, and emerges in the form of an action output. This action output passes along the channel where it may meet some interference or distortion and emerges as an action input to person B. Here it is decoded within the need-value motivational framework of person B, encoded within this framework, and emerges as an action output which then passes along the channel, where it may also meet interference or distortion, to person A. The process continues until terminated by either person, or disrupted by a third.

The several key elements involved in the expanded diagram include overt and covert behavioral factors and social climate factors. See Figure 8–2 for a depiction of these terms. Overt behavioral factors, however, are

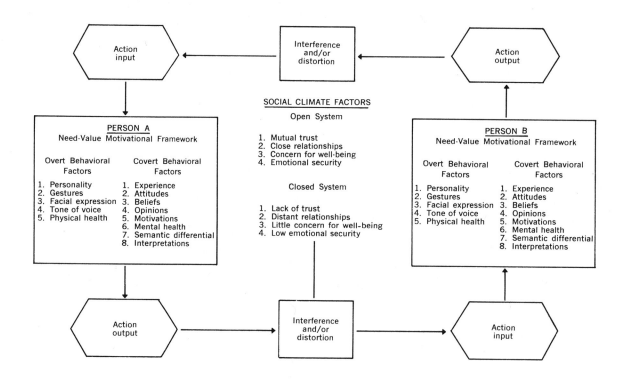

FIGURE 8-2. *Diagram of intra- and interpersonal communication*

influenced by both the covert behavioral factors and the social climate factors. The "ideal" communication combination might consist of favorable covert behavioral factors in each person coupled with an "open system" involving mutual trust, close relationships, concern for well-being, and high emotional security. Under such circumstances it is likely that communication would be open and effective.

Where unfavorable covert behavioral factors are coupled with a "closed system" involving a lack of trust, distant relationships, little concern for well-being, and low emotional security, communication will generally be dysfunctional and very possibly nonexistent.

Frequently an open system will encourage effective communication in spite of unfavorable covert behavioral factors. Likewise, favorable covert behavioral factors may bring about effective communication in spite of a closed system. It is not uncommon to find systems that are neither open nor closed, but somewhere in between, coupled with both favorable and unfavorable behavioral factors. In such instances communication may or may not be effective. In addition, situations, conditions, subject matter, and time may collectively or individually influence one or all of the factors in the communication diagram.

BEHAVIORAL FACTORS

1. Experience. One of the most significant elements influencing covert behavior involves experience. If person A's experience in dealing with person B has been favorable it may have a great deal of influence on the effectiveness of the communication. If it has been unfavorable, the opposite will generally be true. The kind of experience with the social climate, situation, or conditions may also influence communication effectiveness.

2. Attitudes, Opinions, and Beliefs. Significantly involved in communication are attitudes, opinions, and beliefs, listed under covert behavioral factors. These exert a direct influence on the behavior of the communicator and on his decoding processes, thus affecting not only the content of the message, but also the intent attributed to the message.

Where individuals in the communication hold different attitudes, opinions, and beliefs (AOB's), there will be a tendency for each selectively to perceive those parts of the message which reinforce his own attitudes, opinions, and beliefs. By the same process he will tend to reject those AOB's that are not in harmony with his own.

3. Motivations. Motivations may be categorized as (1) self-oriented, (2) receiver oriented, or (3) jointly oriented. Messages falling in the self-oriented category may be sent merely to influence the receiver to accept the kind of information that the transmitter wants him to have. Self-orientation may also lead to the use of false or deceptive messages. When the transmitter assumes it to be rewarding to have the receiver believe that information between them has been equalized, he may send deceptive messages. In competitive situations, or when one wants to avoid blame, messages may be sent deliberately to unequalize information. Since this may take place in receiver oriented messages as well, the category is often termed "individually oriented communication." Jointly oriented messages are useful in promoting teamwork and are more akin to group oriented communication.

4. Semantic Differential. Words or other stimuli serve as signs or symbols in the communication process. If one person has access to more signs or symbols than the other, this may constitute a semantic differential. More frequently, however, semantic differential will exist when signs or symbols mean one thing to one person and another thing to the other person. In speaking of signs and symbols, some sociologists label as "signs" those words or other stimuli that aim at evoking overt behavior, and as "symbols," those that encourage concept formation. In rule or technology oriented situations, signs are best used to communicate, and in individual or group oriented situations, symbols are best used to communicate.

Semantic differentials may exist also in nonlinguistic communication. The most common form, of course, is body motion or gesture. Some gestures used as symbols have more or less agreed upon meanings, such as the meanings involved in a handshake, nod, frown, wink, and many others. Still other gestures must be considered within the context in in which they take place. As they interact, person A and person B encode into signs or symbols some aspect of their own psychological state. As the symbols are decoded by each, they are decoded in such a manner that the interpretations, whatever they mean, are represented in the psychological state of the decoder.

5. Interpretations. As information passes between person A and person B, many interpretations are available to either or both persons. Through each action input and action output, the number of alternative interpretations may be reduced and a level of mutual understanding reached. If the action inputs and action outputs increase the number of interpretations available, there is great danger of the exchange ending in dysfunctional communication. There will be instances, however, during the course of the interplay between A and B, where the number of alternative interpretations may initially be small, rise to a large number, and taper off or abruptly center on one or a few. Effective communication, in short, reduces the number of available interpretations.

Perception also plays a large part in interpretations. In the interplay between person A and person B, each plays a dual role as the perceived and the perceiver. While person A is playing the role of the perceiver, he is also playing the role of the perceived as person B perceives certain qualities or lack of qualities in him. Each has motives and attitudes as well as many other dispositional properties. During the interplay, as they become more aware of each other, each will look for cues about the other. These cues are organized within the person's own need-value motivational framework which, in turn, has a great deal to do with the way in which cues are interpreted.

6. Situation, Person, Self. Effective communication, therefore, depends in many ways on the ability of the communicators to judge people. Perception of others represents a complex set of learned skills that come into play in relation to conditions in the person being judged, conditions in the observer himself, as well as conditions in the situation, and conditions in the social or organizational climate.

During the interplay, each person searches for constancies in the other, and usually will also be aware of discrepancies. If a communicator is confronted with enough discrepancies, he may re-evaluate his impression and come up with a new or modified view of the person. Other factors, of course, may enter into the re-evaluation, and the period of time before this re-evaluation takes place will vary with individuals.

In any interaction, the perceiver will be influenced also by situational cues and these may enter into his judgment. Thus knowledge of the situation, of the person involved, and the communicator himself will influence the degree of effective communication: the more knowledge the communicator has of the situation, the person, himself, and his attunement to the social climate, the better results he will have with the communication process.

EGO PROTECTION AS A BEHAVIORAL FACTOR

One of the most difficult barriers arising out of the need-value motivational framework involves ego protection. Most people have a need for others to see them in a favorable view—the view which they hold of themselves. Psychologists refer to this self-view as the ego and the need as an ego-need. It can be demonstrated in a very simple form by using three circles as in Figure 8–3. In the diagram, circle no. 1 represents the real self; circle no. 2 represents the self as seen by others; and circle no. 3, the self as seen by the self. Circle no. 3 is all important. While representing the person as he sees himself, it also represents the person as he would like to be seen by others. To some degree, for him, this is his real self. When it is threatened, or he imagines it is threatened, he feels an obligation to protect it. This protective mechanism works in many and varied ways; when it comes into play in the communication process, it frequently becomes a barrier to effective communication.

The space where the three circles overlap

represents the area where effective understanding, and consequently effective communication, can occur. As communication takes place, the area of understanding becomes larger, reinforcing and expanding communication. When the ego is threatened, the area of understanding decreases and communication moves into a win-lose situation in which both parties usually end up losing. Ego protection is almost always a win-lose situation. The parties to the communication, sometimes unknowingly, begin to focus on the ego of each other rather than focusing on whatever the real problem was initially.

By subordinating his ego, by adopting a sense of humility, an administrator is able to feel more secure in respect to his own ego and thus is able to react more constructively. In this manner he increases his understanding of the other person and of the problem at hand.

Informal Channels of Communication

Those factors in the need-motivational framework which can distort formal communication "through channels" can also produce informal channels of communication—and distort the information which passes through them as well!

It is doubtful if an organization ever existed that did not have such informal channels of communication, such as "grapevine." The municipal organization is no different in this respect. Because of the widespread interest of citizens and the press in the activities of the municipal organization, there are probably even greater opportunities for a grapevine to flourish here than in organizations of other types.

Grapevines come into existence when normal communication channels fail to provide enough information, are used to misinform, or simply convey information too slowly. Their existence illustrates an important rule: every person wants the information coming to him to "make sense." When it does not, he generally tries to make sense out of it. In this search for meaning, he may invent additional information or place unjustifiable interpretations upon fragmentary data. The whole of his thought—actual information plus personal speculations—is normally passed on to others.

Of course, it is true that sometimes the information an employee receives does really make sense, but not to him. It is also true that sometimes he has only a part of the infor-

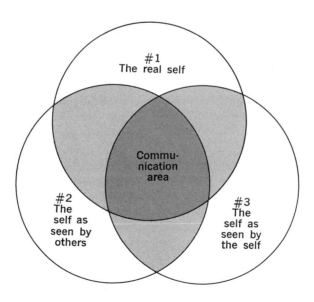

Figure 8-3. *Diagram of ego protection*

mation, and that this portion—out of context —does not make sense. However such grapevine data are generated, the end product is quite similar.

Administrators typically discuss the grapevine solely as a network for rumor and malicious gossip. Grapevines, however, are not necessarily without administrative utility. They can serve a functional purpose through helping to create and reinforce an interest in the workings of the organization.

A healthy grapevine can exist, however, only if employees receive enough information so that the messages they receive make sense to them. If the information being fed into the system *does* seem sufficient, yet an unhealthy grapevine flourishes, the cause may be a blockage at some point in the chain of command: information is being filtered out, and employees are receiving too little. A similar filtering process may also work in reverse, and filter out too much upward communication.

In municipalities where the city council frequently holds executive sessions or informal sessions "off the record," a grapevine will generally flourish. It will be the result of both internal pressures and external pressures from the press and citizens. In such cases, information traveling the grapevine is usually far more harmful than the real facts could be if they were known.

Erroneous reporting by the news media also feeds the grapevine. Any planned change incorrectly reported will travel very rapidly— sometimes constructively, but frequently with undesirable ramifications. Every available resource should be used to see that news of municipal actions and pending actions is correctly interpreted by representatives of the media. An open attitude of leveling with all employees and with all segments of the community, consequently, is the best insurance against a harmful grapevine.

Communication Circuitry

Communication, then, provides the circuitry in the interacting organization by which work groups deal with change and reduce uncertainty about work goals and social interaction. When communication becomes dysfunc-

tional, it increases uncertainty about work goals, hampers social interaction, and prevents the organization from dealing effectively with change.

Since individuals, work groups, and organizations all have a characteristic tendency to move toward a state of equilibrium or stability, the administrator's job becomes extremely difficult in a period of technological change and social upheaval. Faced with adapting a largely authoritative structure to a complex participative structure under a new set of circumstances, the administrator must be able to utilize the communication process to the best interests of all concerned. He must be able to operate effectively with individuals, groups, and other organizations, all within prevailing circumstances.

Communication Skills

Along with developing a reasonable understanding of communication processes, the administrator must also master communication skills himself and at the same time help his subordinates to master them.

The Art of Listening

The ability to listen is perhaps the most basic of communication skills. Listening, however, is not only a skill but also an art and a discipline. As with other skills, it requires control —intellectual, emotional, and behavioral. Hearing is not necessarily listening. It becomes listening only when one pays attention to what is being said and follows it closely. To listen, the administrator must subordinate his own ego and actively encourage the other person to speak either by remaining silent or through the use of judicious questioning.

In listening, the administrator has certain objectives which relate to the communication process. Basically these include five goals:

1. He wants the person to talk freely and frankly.

2. He wants the person to cover matters and problems that are important to both of them.

3. He wants the person to furnish as much information as he can.

4. He wants both the person and himself to get greater insight and understanding of the problem as they talk it out.

5. He wants the person to try to see the causes and reasons for the problem and to figure out what can be done about it.[2]

There is an old Arabian adage that goes, "Listen to what men say, but find out how they feel." The administrator must remember that everyone listens to people through a baffle screen made up of his own attitudes, values, beliefs, and preconceived notions and judgments—illustrated as the need-value motivational framework in Figure 8–2. Thus, in listening to others, the administrator will tend to add something to what is actually said in terms of what he already thinks, feels, and believes. He must try to minimize this. Some listening "Do's" and "Don't's" appear in Figure 8–4.

Reproduced in Figure 8–5 is another table developed by Robert K. Burns of the Industrial Relations Center of the University of Chicago. It sets forth some of the key listening techniques, the purpose of each, and examples of how these can be used.[3]

QUESTIONING TECHNIQUES

Listening, however, is only one of the skills an administrator must develop. In addition, he must be able to ask questions. Asking the right questions in terms of the needs of the individual and the needs of the job is a basic part of development and an important administrative skill. The power of the question is that it requires an answer. If the right question is asked in the right way (in terms of information, experience, reactions, or other data sought) it follows that one will get a useful answer. If the wrong question is asked, even the "right" answer will be of little use.

Frequently the administrator feels that, since his job is to manage, he must tell people what to do, how to do it, and make all the decisions. No better example of dysfunctional communication exists. An administrator's decisions are only as good as his information.

---

[2] Robert K. Burns, THE LISTENING TECHNIQUES (Chicago: Industrial Relations Center, The University of Chicago, 1958), p. 4.

[3] *Ibid.*

DO
1. Show interest.
2. Be understanding of the other person.
3. Express empathy.
4. Single out the problem if there is one.
5. Listen for causes of the problem.
6. Help the person to associate the problem with the cause.
7. Encourage the person to develop the competence and motiviation to solve his own problems.
8. Cultivate the ability to be silent when silence is needed.

DON'T
1. Don't argue.
2. Don't interrupt.
3. Don't pass judgments too quickly or in advance.
4. Don't give advice unless it's requested.
5. Don't jump to conclusions.
6. Don't let the person's sentiments react too directly on your own.

FIGURE 8-4. *Listening do's and don't's*

TYPES OF LISTENING	PURPOSE	EXAMPLES
1. **CLARIFYING**	1. To get at additional facts 2. To help him explore all sides of a problem	1. "Can you clarify this?" 2. "Do you mean this . . .?" 3. "Is this the problem as you see it now?"
2. **RESTATEMENT**	1. To check your meaning and interpretation with his 2. To show you are listening and that you understand what he is saying. 3. To encourage him to analyze other aspects of the matter being considered and to discuss them with you.	1. "As I understand it then your plan is . . ." 2. "This is what you have decided to do and the reasons are . . ."
3. **NEUTRAL**	1. To convey that you are interested and listening. 2. To encourage the person to continue talking.	1. "I see" 2. "Uh-huh" 3. "That's very interesting" 4. "I understand"
4. **REFLECTIVE**	1. To show that you understand how he feels about what he is saying. 2. To help the person to evaluate and temper his own feelings as expressed by someone else.	1. "You feel that . . ." 2. "It was a shocking thing as you saw it." 3. "You felt you didn't get a fair shake."
5. **SUMMARIZING**	1. To bring all the discussion into focus in terms of a summary. 2. To serve as a spring board for further discussion on a new aspect or problem.	1. "These are the key ideas you have expressed . . ." 2. "If I understand how you feel about the situation . ."

FIGURE 8-5. *Listening techniques*

He cannot know as much about certain problems as his subordinates. If he cuts off communication with them he will be without sufficient and adequate information. He will make poor decisions, and he will lose his subordinates' respect and willing cooperation.

Asking. By asking questions, the administrator increases his stock of information and discovers the feelings and sentiments of subordinates; these invariably affect what the administrator will do, what he will say, and how he will act. When he asks the subordinate about his work, the subordinate is able to indicate his needs, interests, problems, and concerns. The administrator is then in a better position to give him information, extend help, pass on advice, or issue orders or instructions.

Telling and ordering leads to dysfunctional communication. It tends to weaken the self-respect, the sense of independence, and the initiative of the subordinate. It increases his dependence upon the administrator and consequently retards the subordinate's own development as a self-directed, fully functioning person. Asking, questioning, and listening tend to stimulate the subordinate, to motivate him, and to encourage him to take initiative and responsibility. The proper use of questioning methods can have an important effect in building a man-boss relationship that is stable, satisfying, and productive. Such a relationship depends upon and supports effective communication.

Positive Attitude. The administrator must, then, have a positive attitude toward the importance of asking rather than telling. Once he has this basic attitude, he must supplement it with the attitude that people are important, and that through communication with them he can draw on their unique experiences, background, and training. In this way, he is helping them to make a personal contribution to the management process. With these attitudes, he must:

1. Understand the different types of questions—their nature, purpose, and use.

2. Understand the direction of questions—how to channel and handle them.

3. Develop skill and proficiency in using questioning techniques in appropriate situations.

Burns identifies seven types of questions, and four directions questions may take. The two lists, which come from Burns' extensive work with management development groups, are reproduced in Figures 8–6 and 8–7, along with the purposes and examples of each.[4]

LEADERSHIP STYLES AND COMMUNICATION

Related to listening and questioning is the administrator's own leadership style. His leadership style will have a great deal of influence on the climate of the organization, which in turn affects the degree of openness of the system and the kinds of responses elicited through listening and questioning techniques. Using the Nelson Leadership Scale, the Industrial Relations Center at the University of Chicago has identified four basic styles of leadership found in governmental and other organizations. These include: (1) rule oriented leadership, (2) technology oriented leadership, (3) individual oriented leadership, and (4) group oriented leadership.[5] Rule and technology oriented leadership tend toward authoritarianism and place human values below the values of the organization, while individual and group oriented leadership tend toward participation and attempt to reconcile human values with the values of the organization. Definitions of the four styles are set forth below.

1. Rule Oriented Leadership. The administrator focusing on this style of leadership relies primarily on the rules and policies of the organization to communicate with and control employees. When a problem arises, he cites provisions in the charter or the employee manual to reinforce communication. His communication is usually one-way—downward—and he tends to operate in an authoritative manner. His relationships with subordinates will generally be rather distant.

2. Technology Oriented Leadership. This

[4] Robert K. Burns, THE QUESTIONING TECHNIQUES (Chicago: Industrial Relations Center, The University of Chicago, 1958), p. 4.

[5] Charles W. Nelson, THE LEADERSHIP INVENTORY ANALYZER (Chicago: Industrial Relations Center, The University of Chicago, rev. ed., 1960) p. 6.

TYPE	PURPOSE	EXAMPLES
1. **FACTUAL**	1. To get information 2. To open discussion	1. All the "W" questions: what, where, why, when, who and how?
2. **EXPLANATORY**	1. To get reasons and explanations 2. To broaden discussion 3. To develop additional information	1. "In what way would this help solve the problem? 2. "What other aspects of this should be considered?" 3. "Just how would this be done?"
3. **JUSTIFYING**	1. To challenge old ideas 2. To develop new ideas 3. To get reasoning and proof	1. "Why do you think so?" 2. "How do you know?" 3. "What evidence do you have?"
4. **LEADING**	1. To introduce a new idea 2. To advance a suggestion of your own or others	1. "Should we consider this —as a possible solution?" 2. "Would this—be a feasible alternative?"
5. **HYPOTHETICAL**	1. To develop new ideas 2. To suggest another, possibly unpopular, opinion 3. To change the course of the discussion	1. "Suppose we did it this way . . . What would happen?" 2. "Another city does this . . . is this feasible here?"
6. **ALTERNATIVE**	1. To make a decision between alternatives 2. To get agreement	1. "Which of these solutions is best, A or B?" 2. "Does this represent our choice in preference to—?"
7. **COORDINATING**	1. To develop consensus 2. To get agreement 3. To take action	1. "Can we conclude that this is the next step?" 2. "Is there general agreement then on this plan?"

FIGURE 8-6. *Questioning techniques by types of questions*

leader is the expert. Most of his leadership and communication will be in terms of the technology and this will play a large part in his decision-making system. His communication will generally have a tendency to be one-way, downward. He, too, will tend to operate in an authoritative manner.

3. Individual Oriented Leadership. In this style of leadership, the administrator focuses on the individual. His relationships with subordinates are generally warm and close. His communication is two-way—both upward and downward. He depends heavily on his friendship with his subordinates in the communication system and makes decisions in terms of how these will affect individuals on his staff. The style's disadvantages are that it encourages currying favor with the boss and sometimes gives rise to petty jealousies.

4. Group Oriented Leadership. The administrator practicing this style of leadership engages in three-way communication—upward, downward, and horizontal. He involves the group in problem solving and setting ob-

TYPE	PURPOSE	EXAMPLES
A. **OVERHEAD:** Directed to group	1. To open discussion 2. To introduce a new phase 3. To give everyone a chance	1. "How shall we begin?" 2. "What should we consider next, anyone?" 3. "What else might be important?"
B. **DIRECT:** Addressed to a specific person	1. To call on a person for special information 2. To involve someone who has not been active	1. "Al, what would be your suggestions?" 2. "Fred, have you had any experience with this?"
C. **RELAY:** Referred back to another person or to the group	1. To help the leader avoid giving his own opinion 2. To get others involved in the discussion 3. To call on someone who knows the answer	1. "Would someone like to comment on Bill's question?" 2. "John, how would you answer Bill's question?"
D. **REVERSE:** Referred back to person who asks question	1. To help the leader avoid giving his own opinion 2. To encourage the questioner to think for himself 3. To bring out opinions	1. "Well, Dick—how about giving us **your** opinion first?" 2. "Bob, tell us first what your own experience has been"

FIGURE 8-7. *Questioning techniques by direction of questions*

jectives, and most of his decisions are based on group consensus. His relationships are generally warm and close and people in his work group generally feel a sense of participation.

It is doubtful that many administrators practice any of these styles of leadership in their pure form. Most, however, tend to focus primarily on one particular style. None of the styles are absolutely right or wrong. The best administrators tend to practice a balanced style of leadership, determining from the situation which style is appropriate and following through on that. Nevertheless, even when practicing a balanced style of leadership, all administrators tend to lean more heavily on one style of leadership than on the other three.

DEALING WITH COMMUNICATION PROBLEMS

To illustrate communication under role and technology oriented leadership and also under individual and group oriented leadership, the following role-play used in training municipal management and supervisory personnel at the Industrial Relations Center of the University of Chicago is cited. The role-play is based on an actual case, and the two ways of handling the situation came out of two different training sessions. The italics after each paragraph refer to the type of communication taking place.

To set the scene, the situation involves a conversation during a coffee break, where two employees (B and C) are razzing a third (A) about the preparation of a periodic report that is generally assigned to A. All three know it will be assigned soon—probably that day. A is saying that he does not like to handle the report and that he hopes the department head won't assign it to him. He feels others in the work group should handle the job from time to time. B and C jokingly imply that A really likes to prepare the report and they wouldn't think of depriving him of this; besides, both of them are busy at more important work. They also imply that A is afraid to tell the department head how he really feels about the particular job. (*Informal communication from the grapevine challenging A's need-value motivational framework.*)

From this point on the role-play develops in a spontaneous manner. The person playing the part of the department head knows nothing of the razzing; he has been out of the room during the first part of the role-play. He knows only that A usually handles the job, that it has to be done within two days, that B and C and others in the work group are tied up on higher priority jobs, and that A is not.

The department head mentions the report and in a nice way tells A to handle it. He is somewhat surprised when A resists the order and tells him that someone else should handle the job. A claims that the job he is on now is rather high priority and he shouldn't leave it. (*Individual oriented communication, with subtle ego protection overtones, resulting in a combination of rule and technology oriented response.*)

Deliberately restraining himself, the boss points out that others are working on higher priority jobs than A's and gives A a direct order to handle the job, adding that he'll look into the matter at some later time. (*Rule oriented communication—ego deflating—with possible individual oriented overtones.*)

When A continues to tell him he doesn't want to take on the job, hints that he might quit, and then flatly refuses, the boss is really exasperated. He forcefully points to the logic of A preparing the report adding that A is the only one he can assign it to today. He'll just have to do it and any misunderstanding can be cleared up later on. (*Combination of technology and rule oriented communication—definite ego deflation.*)

When A refuses again, the boss has just about had it. In no uncertain terms he points out that he is head of the department here, that he has given A a direct order, and that he damn well better carry it out. A's reply is to tell him to carry it out himself. The role-play ends with A quitting, and the department head having to find someone else to prepare the report or do it himself. In addition he has to recruit and train a new man for A's job. (*Rule oriented communication—challenging ego of both communicators and leading to dysfunctional communication.*)

After one use of this role-play, the person

playing the role of A adamantly defended his position and said that "in real life he certainly would quit his job if he had to work for a boss who put him in a position of being ridiculed by his fellow workers." He admitted that he was trying to save face and that he felt "looking into the matter later" didn't give him any out. (*Need-value motivational factors at work.*)

At this point, the person playing the part of the department head entered into the discussion with: "How the hell was I to know you were trying to save face? Nobody told me those guys were razzing you." He added that he had given A a direct order and "when a boss gives a direct order it has to be carried out. If it isn't he loses all his authority." (*Rule oriented communication and leadership, ego, and need-value motivational factors also at work.*)

After this exchange, the two participants, with some help from the group, began to work through the "communication breakdown." But it soon became apparent that in the role-play they really were communicating. It was dysfunctional communication, but communication nonetheless. Through their behavior, each was saying: "I'm more concerned about me than I am about you. I don't know what your problem is, but I know what mine is if I lose out in this struggle." In other words, early in the role-play encounter, each had taken a win-lose position. But when the situation was analyzed, both had lost.

The above role-play has been used with many groups. In another experience, the person playing the boss took a different approach and demonstrated effective communication. The event went very much the same up to the point where A implies that he may quit if he has to prepare the report. At this point the boss calls a halt in the trend of the conversation by telling A that he is much too valuable a man for the boss to let him quit over the assignment of a job. He frankly admits that he didn't know A found the job unpleasant. In a spirit of concern he helps A to talk about the report. (*Individual oriented communication, responding to ego and need-value motivational framework.*)

A tells him that it's a rather boring job, that he's not sure the report is even necessary,

that nobody in the work group likes to handle it, and that he always seems to get stuck with it. As the department head listens, A becomes a bit more relaxed and hints at the razzing he has received from his coworkers. As this comes out, the boss expresses understanding. As the tension subsides in A the boss is able to explain his position. He asks A how he feels the report should be assigned. The role-play ends with A agreeing to draft a recommendation for assigning the job in the future for presentation at the next staff meeting, and to handle the job today to keep the work group from getting into a bind. (*Individual oriented communication with group oriented overtones.*)

In the discussion that followed, A pointed out that he knew he was in a difficult position with his coworkers, that he couldn't let the department head push him around, "But the boss didn't try to push me around. He kept trying to help and I couldn't keep clubbing a man who was trying to help me." (*Responding to need-value motivational framework.*)

The person who played the part of the boss said at first he didn't know what was going on. I could see "something was bugging him and I didn't think I could get him to do the job until I found out." He added that once it was out in the open and they could level with each other, "There didn't seem to be much of a problem in working out a solution." (*Encouraging an open communication climate.*)

This was a prime example of a win-win situation brought about through effective communication. Once it became evident that nobody had to lose in the situation, the participants could work out a satisfactory solution. Once the department head realized that A was threatened by his order, he didn't dissipate his energies by defending his authority and resorting to rule oriented communication. Asserting his authority, as in the first example, could only have widened the communication gap and led to dysfunctional communication.

COMMUNICATION AND MANAGEMENT BY OBJECTIVES

If open systems, which take into consideration individual human needs, promote effective communication, what then can the manager do to bring about such conditions in the organization? One approach involves managing by objectives. Most managers use a variant of the management by objectives technique, though their understanding of it can be quite vague. In some cases objectives may be well thought out and planned—and still fail—and, with others, objectives may involve little more than an attempt to meet every crisis; some may be as general as "just keeping the store open." No matter how vague these objectives are, communication will be necessary if they are to be accomplished.

Two of the most frequent causes of failure in managing by objectives result from unclear definitions of objectives and lack of commitment on the part of those who have to accomplish them. Figure 8–8 provides a means for overcoming these two shortcomings. The headings across the top of the matrix list Knowledge, Skills, Attitudes, Job Performance or Clarifying the Job, and Objectives or Results. Down the left side of the matrix are listed four broad categorizations of the elements involved in management: I. Participants, II. Organization, III. Technology, and IV. Evaluation and Feedback, with subcategories under each. It is possible that this listing could be expanded, but it should suffice for purposes here.

In managing by objectives, the administrator starts from the right side of the matrix and works through the top headings, first by defining the objective or the desired results, next determining the job performance necessary to accomplish the objective, then the attitudes, skills, and knowledge necessary. If he stops here, however, he is programming himself for communication problems, unless the objective is something he can accomplish all by himself. What has happened is that he has set himself up for a tell-and-sell job, or worse yet, a tell-and-force job. There are many variations to these two approaches, but rarely are any of them completely satisfactory.

If the administrator can involve those who will have to accomplish an objective in either the process of setting it or more clearly defining it, his chances of utilizing management by objectives as a motivating force become much greater. When objectives are set elsewhere, say by the city council, he can still utilize this motivating factor by involving subordinates in reaching a clear definition of the objective and determining the kind of job performance that will be necessary to accomplish it.

While there is some overlap in setting and defining objectives and determining job performance, these areas are among the most frequent causes of subordinates' gripes about their relationship with the boss. Typical statements include: "I know what he wants me to do, but I just don't want to do that," or "If I knew what he wanted me to do, I'd do it, but most of the time I just don't know."[6] It's no wonder that administrators are frequently frustrated.

Reading down the left side of the matrix, starting with the participants, and again referring to the objective, the administrator then asks himself, "What kind of a communication job will be needed to get agreement with the participants on the objective?" He may decide he will get better commitment and a higher degree of motivation if he involves them in rethinking the objective—perhaps even better, defining the objective. If the objective is one over which he has little control, he can involve the participants at this point by enlisting them to help define it more clearly.

If neither of these approaches is feasible, he may move on to the next step, job performance, and ask the question: "How can I best communicate with the participants on the kind of performance that will be necessary to accomplish the objective?" Generally, the same alternatives that were open to him in communicating the objective are open to him in dealing with job performance. As he continues to work through Attitudes, Skills, and Knowledge, he asks the same kinds of questions.

Tackling the subcategories under Part I of the matrix, he considers the participants in terms of their motivation, relationships, and

---

[6] Unpublished research on management practices in various metropolitan Chicago suburbs, conducted by the Government Projects Division of the Industrial Relations Center of the University of Chicago.

	Knowledge 5	Skills 4	Attitudes 3	Job performance (clarify the job) 2	Results (objectives) 1
I. Participants					
1. Motivation					
2. Relationships					
3. Individual Needs					
a. physical b. social c. egoistic					
4. Group Needs					
a. physical b. social c. egoistic					
5. Training					
6. Unions					
II. Organization					
1. Structure					
a. formal b. informal					
2. Policies					
3. Leadership Climate					
a. rule oriented b. technology oriented c. individual oriented d. group oriented					
III. Technology					
1. Equipment					
2. Physical conditions					
3. Systems					
IV. Evaluation & Feedback					

FIGURE 8-8. *Predictive communication model*

individual and group needs, all in terms of the objective, job performance necessary, attitudes, skills, and knowledge. He also takes into consideration any training, past, present, and future, in terms of the objective, and attempts to anticipate the reaction of any unions involved, both favorable and unfavorable.

Moving down the left side of the model to Part II, he considers the structure of the organization, both formal and informal, organization policies, and leadership climate. Here he will determine whether the objective, in terms of the participants and their knowledge, skills, and attitudes, will be best communicated and accomplished through one or a combination of the four styles of leadership —rule, technological, individual, or group.

After making this determination, he evaluates the technology of the organization, considering the equipment, physical environment, and the systems of the organization. After reconciling the foregoing factors with the limits of the technological factors, he is ready to set up an evaluation or feedback system for checking on the accomplishment of the objective and to make adjustments in the plan as new data are developed through ongoing work. The framework for this evaluation and feedback system will vary, but will be reasonably evident by the time the administrator gets to this point in the model.

Summary

In the interacting organization, overlapping groups offer the best opportunity to use the communication process effectively. To maximize utility, the organization must provide a supportive, ego-building atmosphere in which persons feel valued and respected—one where openness and mutual trust exist and where ego-deflating and threatening communication is minimized.

In addition to the development of functional skills, attention must be given to the development of interpersonal and group process skills. Members of the organization must possess at least a minimal level of skill in leadership roles and membership roles and a reasonable degree of sensitivity to the reactions of others. This will be enhanced to the degree to which members of the organization know other members of the organization and the work groups and units of which they are part. Members must also receive an accurate flow of information concerning the state of the organization and its present performance. Such a flow of information will facilitate sound decisions and a more objective evaluation of results.

The open organization, where interpersonal skills are encouraged and developed, leads to full, candid communication. Persons tend to pass relevant information to others and tend to be interested in and receptive to relevant information themselves. This is to behave in a supportive, ego-building manner. To show no interest in information from others and to withhold relevant information is to behave in an ego-deflating manner. A full flow of useful and relevant information provides accurate data to guide action, calls attention to problems as they arise, and assures sound decisions based on a maximum amount of available facts.

As persons receive an acurate flow of relevant information, they will develop a feeling of having greater influence upon what happens in the organization and what happens to themselves. This effect will be noticed at all levels within the organization, and will be particularly true in the individual's own unit or department. With a feeling of being able to exercise influence, individuals will tend to respond more favorably and cooperatively to influence exerted upon them. Such a reciprocal influence process will help to weld the organization into a tough, highly effective institution.

Part Four

Managing the
Organization

9

Tools of Modern Management

ORGANIZATIONAL MANAGEMENT has been viewed traditionally as the art and science of "getting work done through people." In recent years, a new concept of organizational management has begun to emerge. This new concept, called "the systems approach," does not replace older organizational concepts, but does direct attention more emphatically to the goals or purposes for which the organization exists.

The Systems Approach to Management

The systems approach has two primary characteristics. First, objectives are stated clearly in measurable performance terms, rather than in terms of manpower levels or rates of expenditure. Objectives are defined in terms of changes which are achieved or prevented in the environment which the organization serves. To take a familiar example, a housing improvement program might include, as one objective, the reduction of occupied dwelling spaces which lack modern sanitation from an existing number of 250 to a future number of 150 within one year. Compare this way of stating objectives with the alternative method of specifying that two sanitation inspectors will make 20 inspections each per month. In the latter case, there is no specific identification of the changes to be brought about in the community, but simply a specification of the activities to be performed by a unit of the organization.

The second principal characteristic of the systems approach is the emphasis on the rela-

tionships within the system. In the example, examination might reveal that many of the dwellings lacking modern sanitation facilities were structurally unsound, failed to conform to the city's fire prevention code, and were beyond economic rehabilitation. These additional factors would lead to a more detailed definition of objectives, such as, for example, rehabilitation of perhaps 50 of the dwelling spaces and the demolition of the remainder.

It would then be necessary to add the objectives of providing adequate housing for the displaced families and of providing for appropriate re-use of the cleared land. Within the organization, attention would be directed to the activities necessary to achieve the objectives. Rather than being concerned simply with the number of inspections to be carried out by sanitation inspectors, plans would be made for the related activities of sanitation inspectors, fire prevention inspectors, structural inspectors, the legal office, the planning office, the utilities and public works departments, and perhaps the public housing and welfare agencies.

As can be seen from even this simple example, the systems approach highlights the need for comprehensive administrative planning so that implications of each set of objectives are related to overall objectives, and to the total pattern of organizational action. The systems approach provides a comprehensive framework within which the administrator can exercise his knowledge of how to manage the organization to achieve community goals.

The purpose of Chapters 9, 10, and 11 is to examine some of the tools, processes, and techniques which municipal officials can use to increase the effectiveness of their organization in achieving community goals.

COMPUTERS AND MANAGEMENT

The recent development and widespread adoption of electronic computers by business and governments has been called the "computer revolution." Chapter 9 will examine the characteristics of computers and related equipment, review ways in which computers are used in municipal governments, investigate the factors which administrators must consider in organizing for computer utilization, explore ways of determining the practicality of computer applications in a particular municipality, and identify the action which must be taken to employ computers effectively.

ADMINISTRATIVE PLANNING

As has been noted, the systems approach to management requires comprehensive administrative planning in order to define and achieve the objectives which have been assigned to the municipal government in the broad context of community goals. Chapter 10, "Administrative Planning," explores the scope of administrative planning and the process through which community goals can be translated into organizational action. The relationships of planning, programming, budgeting, scheduling, and management direction are explored along with typical applications of administrative planning in municipal government. Particular attention is given to the distribution of planning responsibilities and functions within municipal government, and the action which the manager must take to establish and carry out a successful administrative planning program.

ADMINISTRATIVE ANALYSIS

The systems approach to management and the availability of computer capabilities provide the administrator with a significantly expanded potential for continuing analysis of the organization in relation to the community environment. Chapter 11, "Administrative Analysis," reviews both old and new techniques of analysis which can be employed to increase the effectiveness and efficiency of the organization. Included are guidelines for setting objectives and selecting techniques of analysis and a survey of the subject matter of administrative analysis with examples of typical applications in urban government.

Considerable attention is given to the important matter of developing measurement techniques for determining the impact of the organization on the environment and for evaluating the effectiveness and efficiency of operating departments. Chapter 11 concludes with an examination of the action required to organize and staff for modern management, relating tools and techniques to administrative planning and administrative analysis, and identifying sources of outside assistance to the administrator involved in organizational improvement.

Computer Technology

The terms *electronic data processing* (EDP) and *automatic data processing* (ADP) have become commonplace. They are often used interchangably to refer to the processing of data by one or more electronic or electrical machines in such a way as to minimize the need for human action. In a general way, EDP refers to the use of computers and related equipment for the automated handling of paperwork, such as the production of tax bills, checks, and accounting records.

The capability of modern computers for automating paperwork at vastly increased speeds and reduced costs is only one of the important uses of computers. Equally valuable uses include analyzing vast quantities of information, performing complex mathematical calculations, improving the ability of decision-makers to predict and evaluate the consequences of their decisions, and the actual control of operations such as public utilities. It is the capability which computers provide to accomplish objectives never before possible, as well as to reduce significantly the

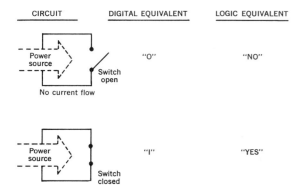

FIGURE 9-1. *Representing digits and logic with electrical circuits.*

cost of previous work, that accounts for their rapidly spreading use.

The first general purpose electronic digital computer, here called simply a "computer," was invented as recently as 1946. In just twenty years, the first experimental computers underwent such rapid improvement that by mid-1966 over 34,000 computers were installed and operating in the United States and 24,000 more computers were on order. By 1966 every state operated at least one computer facility, and the majority of cities over 50,000 population were making use of computers. Many cities under 25,000 population had also begun to utilize them.

DIGITAL DATA CONCEPTS

The ability of computers and related equipment to handle information is based on the simple electrical principal that current either is flowing or is not flowing in a particular electrical circuit at a particular time. Figure 9–1 illustrates how these two basic circuit conditions can be used to represent digits and logic.

The binary number system, using only the digits "0" and "1," was developed for use in computers in place of the decimal system, which requires ten different digits. By combining the digits "0" and "1" (each of which is called one *bit* of information), decimal numbers, alphabetic characters, and special symbols can be represented as shown in Figure 9–2.

Digital computers use thousands of tiny electronic switches and storage elements to receive, store, manipulate, and produce information. By using some of these electronic elements as logic devices, the computer can make decisions such as answering the questions, "is A equal to B?" "is A greater than B?" and, "is A greater than B and less than C or D?"[1]

HARDWARE AND SOFTWARE

Digital data concepts allow electronic machines to handle complex data processing operations, but it is necessary to break jobs down into very minute and precise steps in order to carry out even simple functions. The techniques for preparing work and instructing computers so that they can carry out the work has been given the general term *software*. The term *hardware* is used to refer to the equipment itself. The term software especially applies to all those techniques for instructing computers which are available as standard sets of instructions or *programs* for causing computers to carry out frequently

---

[1] Charles J. Sippl, COMPUTER DICTIONARY AND HANDBOOK (Indianapolis: Harold W. Sams and Company, Inc., 1966), Appendix M, for explanation of how computers handle mathematics and logic by electronic switching.

Binary Code	Decimal Numbers	Alphabetic and Special Symbols
00 0000	0	
00 0001	1	
00 0010	2	
00 0100	4	
00 1000	8	
00 1001	9	
01 0010		/
11 0010		S
11 0011		T

FIGURE 9-2. *One way of coding decimal numbers, alphabetic characters, and special symbols in a "six-bit" binary number system (In the illustrated coding, 11 0010 01 0010 00 1000 00 1001 means S/89 and could be represented by 24 electronic switching, or storage, elements.)*

used operations. Before exploring software and computer programming in more detail, it will be useful to examine the hardware itself.

CHARACTERISTICS OF COMPUTERS AND RELATED EQUIPMENT

General purpose electronic computers are designed to be used in combination with a wide variety of specialized devices. The particular type of computer and the particular items of related equipment with which it is combined are determined by the specific requirements of the work to be performed in each case. While it is not necessary to be concerned with all of the thousands of different types of computers and related equipment, it is important to be familiar with the major characteristics of computers and with the characteristics of related equipment frequently utilized in urban government. In addition to digital computers and directly related input and output devices, punched card data processing equipment, analog computers, communications devices, and certain other data handling devices are commonly required in municipal computer utilization.

Punched Card Equipment. In the 1890's, nearly a half century before the invention of the digital computer, the U.S. Census Bureau invented and began to use punched card data processing equipment. The original use of the punched card equipment was to speed up tabulation of the returns of the census of 1890, and the key concept was the idea of coding, in numerical form, the information obtained. The numerical codes were punched into heavy paper cards. Machines were then used to "read" the holes in the cards and automatically tabulate the returns. This method proved highly successful and with continuing refinements spread widely throughout government and business. Punched card data processing is still used extensively for many kinds of relatively simple, high volume, repetitive operations such as accounting, billing, and inventory control.

The standard punched card has 80 vertical columns, each of which can contain an alphabetic character, a numeric character, or a special symbol such as a minus sign. The pattern of holes punched in each column designates the particular character in that column. For any particular use, the columns are grouped into *fields* that represent one complete piece of information, such as the date. It may be necessary to use several cards to provide sufficient space for a complete record, as might be necessary for the record of a utility customer or a taxpayer. Figure 9–3 shows a punched card containing information arranged in fields.

The creation of punched cards is relatively simple. A machine similar to an electric typewriter, called a *keypunch,* is used to transfer information from forms and other documents onto punched cards. The typing process automatically punches the holes. Where high accuracy is required, the cards either can be visually compared with the original document, or a specialized keypunch machine called a *verifier* can be used by a second operator to type the same information onto the same card. The verifying machine does not actually punch holes, but signals the operator if there is any difference between the second typing operation and the holes which are actually in the card, allowing corrections to be made.

Because the use of punched cards causes them to wear out in time, and also because it is sometimes desirable to transfer part of the information on a punched card to a new card, a special machine called a *reproducing punch* has been developed. The reproducing punch automatically copies all or part of the information on one card to another, typically operating at a rate of up to 165 cards a minute.

After a *deck* or file of punched cards has been created, it is frequently desirable to place the cards in alphabetic or numeric order using, for instance, last name, date, or account number. Machines called *sorters* have been developed which arrange cards in a prescribed order at rates of about 2,000 cards a minute.

When it is necessary to add additional cards to a deck which has already been placed in a desired sequence, a machine called a *collator* is used. An electronic *accounting machine,* or *tabulator,* performs the functions of adding, substracting, summarizing, rearranging, and printing information from the punched cards. The accounting machine can be controlled through a plug-in wiring panel to perform the desired functions. It also can be connected to a reproducing punch to allow transfer of selected information to a new set of punched cards.

By combining manual procedures with the capabilities of these machines, fairly complex work can be accomplished at lower costs than with manual methods, and with increased accuracy and speed.[2] Figure 9–4 shows part of a payroll preparation procedure for 1,500 persons working in a job shop.

Punched card data processing is limited by two major factors. The first is that all machine readable information must be kept on punched cards which require considerable manual handling, are subject to damage and loss, and must be physically manipulated dur-

[2] See E. Wainwright Martin, ELECTRONIC DATA PROCESSING (Homewood, Illinois: Richard D. Irwin, 2nd ed., 1965), Chapters 1 and 2.

ing each stage of processing by relatively slow electromechanical equipment. The second major limitation is the accounting machine itself, which is slow and is restricted to very simple functions like adding, subtracting, and rearranging information.

Punched cards are still a valuable means of converting information into machine readable form, but small digital computers have been developed which are rapidly replacing punched card equipment for actual data processing.

Analog Computers. The analog computer is another type of electronic equipment which is rapidly being replaced in many applications by the digital computer. Principally used by cities for automatic control of water distribution and of the generation and distribution of electricity, the analog computer is designed particularly for one job, and one job only.

A very simple example of such a computer is the thermostat in a home heating system. The thermostat has an electrical element that senses the temperature in the room and

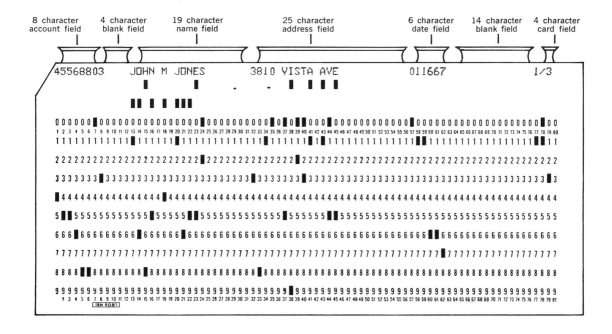

FIGURE 9-3. *80-column punched card with alphabetic and numeric—"alphameric"—data punched in field (Columns may be grouped into fields as desired for a particular use, and several cards may be used to make one record.)*

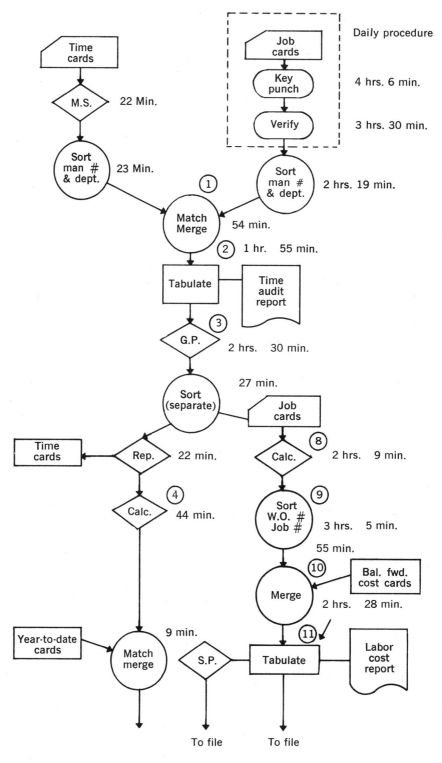

FIGURE 9-4. *Part of a payroll procedure using punched card data processing (Adapted from E. Wainright Martin,* ELECTRONIC DATA PROCESSING, *Richard D. Irwin, 1965, p. 92.)*

converts it to an electrical impulse when a preset level is reached. The electrical impulse is used to turn on the furnace, and after room temperature has been brought within preset limits the thermostat generates another impulse which shuts off the furnace. In a water distribution system, sensing devices continually measure the water pressure at selected points in the distribution network and the analog computer automatically regulates pumps to maintain preset pressures throughout the network.

Today, the tendency is to use digital computers rather than analog computers, sometimes attaching specialized analog units to the digital computer where advantages can be gained through such a combination.

General Purpose Digital Computers. Nearly all computers now being manufactured are general purpose digital computers which, when equipped with the necessary related equipment, can be used to perform an almost unlimited number of tasks. Unlike punched card data processing equipment and analog computers,

these computers do not require rewiring or other physical changes to shift from one job to another. Instead, the computer is given instructions for a particular job in the form of a *program* which can be read by the computer and stored in its internal *memory* for use in performing the job at hand. Digital computers now available range in size from small tabletop devices to groups of equipment filling several large rooms. They range in cost from a few thousand dollars to over seven million dollars, with an equivalent variation in capabilities.

Central Processing Units. Whether large or small, the essential part of any computer is the *central processing unit (CPU)*, which may be thought of as the basic computer. The CPU is entirely an electronic device; it performs no physical or mechanical operations. Figure 9–5 is a diagram showing the relationship of the following five functions performed by the CPU:

1. It receives input information in the form of electrical signals;

2. It electronically stores received informa-

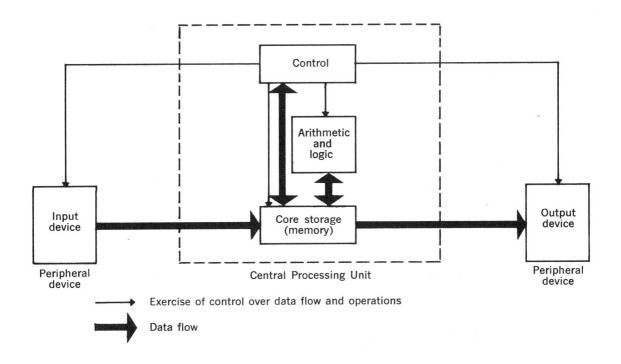

FIGURE 9-5. *Internal functions of a central processing unit.*

tion, information which is being processed, and information ready for transmission to output devices;

3. It performs arithmetic and logic operations on the information it is processing;

4. It electronically controls, in accordance with its program of instructions, the input, storage, processing, and output of information; and

5. It transmits information to external output devices.

In addition to controlling its own internal operations, the CPU also controls related equipment such as card readers, printers, and magnetic tape units. The complexity of the work which can be accomplished by the CPU, and the number of external devices it can control, is largely determined by the size of its internal storage. Each *position* can store one character of information. A CPU with four thousand positions of internal storage would be identified as a 4-k CPU. Because the program instructions being used by the CPU must be retained in internal storage along with information being processed, the size of internal storage is of major importance. The speed with which internal operations are carried out also varies, with the fastest computers capable of over two million simple additions per second.[3]

Input and Output Devices. The devices used to transmit information to the central processing unit are known as *input devices,* and those which are used to convert the results of the CPU's operations into a form useful to humans are known as *output devices.* One of the most common input devices is the *card read/punch* machine. These machines can read the information on standard punched cards and transmit it to the central processing unit at speeds up to more than 1,000 cards a minute. They can also be controlled by the CPU to punch output information into standard punched cards. High speed *line printers* are capable of typing over 1,000 lines of printed information a minute, with each line containing up to 131 characters of

information. Line printers are used to prepare standard forms such as payroll checks, vouchers, and tax bills. Paper tape read/ punch machines are also commonly used as input and output devices.

External Storage Devices. Most computers use magnetic tape as the primary means of storing files of information to be processed, and employ punched cards mainly as a means of keeping the tape files up to date. One 12-inch reel of magnetic tape contains 2,400 feet of tape and can contain as much information as several hundred thousand punched cards. Magnetic tape units under control of the CPU can be used to read or record more than 300,000 characters a second, compared with a rate of about 300 characters a second for typical card reading devices. By connecting several tape units to a CPU, large files of records can be sorted, merged, or processed fully automatically.

Magnetic tape units are known as *serial access* devices because items of information are listed one after another, or serially, on the tape. To find any given item of information, as when posting an entry to an account, it is necessary to read along the length of the tape until the desired item of information is found.

In many cases, the time required to read the tape is a serious limitation on the efficiency of the computer, so that other kinds of devices allowing faster access to individual pieces of information have been developed. A common example is the *disc file,* which magnetically records items of information on sets of discs. These discs are kept spinning at extremely high speed so that the entire contents of the discs pass before magnetic reading and recording elements thousands of times each minute. By using special techniques to predetermine the location of information on the discs, the CPU can position the reading and recording elements so as to gain access to any item of information on the discs in less than a second. Because of this ability to go directly to a specific item of information, magnetic disc files are referred to as *random access* devices. A single disc unit can store several million characters of information, and more than

[3] See Ned Chapin, AN INTRODUCTION TO AUTOMATIC COMPUTERS (Princeton: D. Van Nostrand Company, 2nd ed., 1963), Chapters 2 and 8.

one disc unit may be connected to a single central processing unit. Other random access devices include *magnetic drums* and *data cells.*

Figure 9–6 shows a CPU with magnetic tape units as external storage devices and typical input/output devices attached.

Remote Terminals. The extremely rapid internal operating speeds of computers, compared with the relatively slow speeds of input/output devices and the even slower speed at which human beings operate, make it possible for the CPU to handle many input and output devices at the same time that it is carrying on internal processing operations. By adding special control features and units, dozens or even hundreds of teletype units or special terminal devices can be connected to a single computer. Each of these terminals can be used to put information in, or to get information from, the files maintained by the computer.

Off-Line Devices. Not all devices needed for computer operation are connected directly to the CPU. Data reduction devices, which are used to convert information into machine readable form, are frequently completely separate from the computer. The keypunch machine, for instance, is a common data reduction device. Other devices for converting information into machine readable form include optical scanners which read pages of printed information, magnetic ink readers which read special characters like those commonly printed on bank checks, and paper

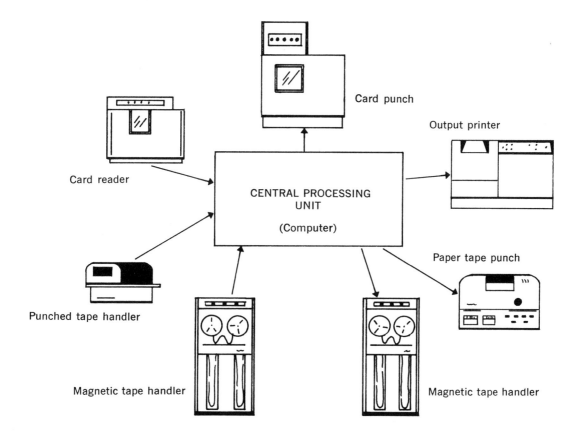

FIGURE 9-6. *Central processing unit with typical input/output devices (Source: John J. Connelly,* AN INTRODUCTION TO ELECTRONIC DIGITAL COMPUTERS, *System Development Corporation, March, 1965, mimeograph, p. 9.)*

tape devices which are used to punch holes in paper tape rather than in cards. Other off-line equipment frequently used in connection with computers includes special equipment for transcribing information recorded on paper tape and punched cards into magnetic tape form.

Communications. It is not necessary for off-line equipment or even on-line input/output devices to be physically located at the same place as the central processing unit. Any of the devices can be connected through telephone lines, teletype lines, and special lines designed for high speed transmission of digital data. There are communications devices designed solely for transmitting information on punched cards, paper tape, and magnetic tape from one location to another.

Modes of Operation. Computers may be used in several distinct patterns or *modes* of operation. *Batch processing* is by far the most common mode of operation, and is one for which even the smallest computers are suited. In batch processing, work is accumulated until there is sufficient volume to justify setting up the computer to perform the particular job. In payroll preparation, for instance, employee earning information is usually accumulated until the "books are closed" for the particular earning period. The computer and related equipment are then used to prepare the payroll, employee checks, withholding statements, and related documents. In batch processing, jobs are scheduled and performed one after another.

Not all jobs can be done effectively by waiting for a batch of work to be accumulated. Some police information—for example, wanted persons information and stolen vehicle information—must be available almost instantly to a police officer inquiring as to whether or not a given individual or vehicle is wanted. Medium and large computers can meet this kind of requirement when operated in a *real-time mode*. By storing the wanted persons and wanted vehicles information on random access files, and providing special equipment and programming, the computer can *interrupt* whatever operations it is performing in order to respond promptly to the

inquiry of the police officer. A computer operating in a real-time mode can be carrying on batch operations in the *background* while remaining on the alert for priority inquiries from remote terminals. Even though the computer interrupts its batch processing each time it responds to an inquiry, the time required for answering inquiries is usually only a small percentage of the total time. The key characteristic of real-time processing is that the computer is used to respond to requests for information, or to process information, while another action is being carried out.

The third mode of operation, which is possible only for the largest computers, is called *multi-processing* or *time-sharing*. When a computer is operating in a time-sharing mode, many different users can be processing entirely different jobs on the same computer with each user having all of the capabilities of the computer and related equipment available for his own use. A computer facility operating in a time-sharing mode can be performing one or more batched processing jobs during the same time period that it is being used for several real-time purposes. The time-sharing mode of operation represents the most advanced development of computer hardware and software, and requires extremely complex software as well as expensive equipment and highly skilled technical specialists.

Time-sharing is, however, of great interest to even small municipalities. Large commercial firms are establishing time-sharing computer facilities which offer customers—including municipalities—the use of the computers and related equipment with charges based on the actual amount of time that a particular customer utilizes. In one commercial time-sharing computer facility now in operation, nearly 400 different customers use the same computer facilities. Each customer is connected to the computer facility by a simple teletype terminal, or more advanced equipment such as a satellite computer, which is used as the input and output device. Some of the customers are located as distant as 2,000 miles from the computer facility. By using such time-sharing facilities, municipalities may have the use of more versatile computers than they could otherwise afford.

Computer Configurations. There are more than 20 major computer manufacturers which produce over 140 different central processing units, most of which are available with a variety of optional features. In addition, there are well over 1,000 different input and output devices and special units. Hence there is an extremely large number of different combinations of computers and related equipment which can be assembled.[4]

Volume, variety, and complexity of work to be performed are the major factors in determining the appropriate computer configuration for a particular organization, but the mode of operation is also a significant consideration. Monthly costs of renting a computer configuration adequate for batch processing begin at about $1,500; for real-time processing, monthly rental costs begin at about $5,000; and for time-sharing, monthly rental costs begin at about $25,000. Personnel, facilities, and supplies generally cost as much and frequently twice as much as the cost of equipment rental. As is discussed in detail later, cities need not pay the cost of establishing computer facilities in order to make use of computers, so that these minimum costs of computer configurations are cited only to illustrate the variation in scale of computer configurations required for the several modes of operation.

DIGITAL COMPUTER PROGRAMMING

The ability of a digital computer to perform a particular job depends partly on the program of instructions provided to it. Once prepared, a computer program can be stored on punched cards, magnetic tape, or in mass storage devices and can be placed into operation in a matter of minutes or split seconds. In effect, the knowledge which the computer uses to perform different tasks is contained in the programs which it uses: it can do only what

its programs direct. Programming is thus of crucial importance in computer utilization.

Elements of Computer Programming. Programming is the process of converting a job performance plan to a set of instructions which can be carried out by the computer.[5] When preparing work for computer processing, a programmer follows a series of steps that necessarily begins with the analysis of the work to be performed, or the problem to be solved. Working closely with those who are responsible for the performance of the work, the programmer obtains a detailed definition of results to be achieved; information available to be used in producing the required results; volume and frequency of work to be performed; accuracy requirements; and other significant factors. The programmer prepares alternative plans for carrying out the required work and evaluates the plans to arrive at the most satisfactory alternative. He then prepares a *flow chart* showing the sequence and relationships of operations required to accomplish the job. The flow chart breaks the work down into components that will be performed by the computer and each item of related equipment, and defines each separate major operation, or *run,* in terms of the input provided, the operation performed, and the resulting outputs. The next step is preparation of a *block diagram* which shows the individual mathematical, logical, and input/output operations which must be performed by the CPU for each operation shown on the flow chart.

Following preparation of the block diagram, the programmer proceeds to write the actual *instructions* for the computer. This process of converting block diagrams into machine instructions is called *coding,* since it involves the use of special sets of characters and symbols which enable the control section of the CPU to carry out specified operations. Figure 9–7 is an example of part of a block diagram and the corresponding instructions writ-

---

[4] See "The Computer Directory and Buyers' Guide," published annually as the June issue of COMPUTERS AND AUTOMATION (Berkeley Enterprises, 815 Washington Street, Newtonville, Massachusetts) for descriptions and prices of computers and a directory of computer services and organizations.

[5] See Robert H. Gregory and Richard L. Van Horn, AUTOMATIC DATA PROCESSING SYSTEMS (Belmont, California: Wadsworth Publishing Company, 2nd ed., 1964), Chapters 8–13 for a thorough general treatment of programming.

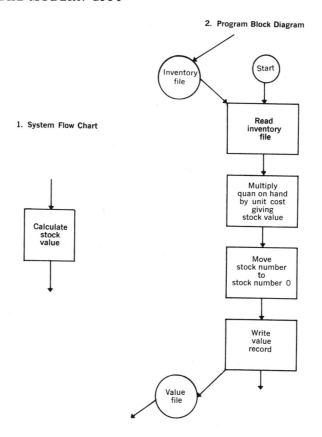

FIGURE 9-7. *Element of inventory control procedure defined at three stages of programming (Source: Adapted from Robert H. Gregory and Richard L. Van Horn,* AUTOMATIC DATA PROCESSING SYSTEMS, *Wadsworth Publishing Co., 2nd ed., 1964, pp. 255, 257.)*

ten in machine code. After the programmer has completed coding the instructions, he proceeds to test the program which he has written, using samples of the data that will be used in carrying out the actual job. It is rare for a computer program to be completely correct when it is first written; the machine testing phase of the programmer's work may involve extensive trouble shooting, often called *debugging,* of the program before it will operate without error.

Programming Languages. It was noted earlier that digital computers operate internally in terms of extremely minute "bits" of information, consisting of the digit 1 or the digit 0. The program instructions for the simple act of reading a card, specifying the particular information which is to be used, and defining the particular storage location of each piece of information, may require hundreds of individual, specific instructions to the computer. Similarly, hundreds of instructions are required to enable the computer to perform the simple act of multiplying one number by another. If it were necessary for a programmer actually to write each one of these detailed instructions for every program, it would be practically impossible to make use of a digital computer. Consequently, computer manufacturers have developed "languages" for use with each of their machines.

These languages may be thought of as a set of words, or terms, each of which has an accompanying program already written. Thus there is a word and an associated program, or *subroutine,* for each of the functions commonly used in computer programming. For example, the manufacturers' languages all contain the word "add" and therefore provide a subroutine for performing addition. In writing a program using the manufacturers' language, the programmer need only write the instruction "add" in order to generate the detailed machine language instructions needed for the computer to carry out addition. After a programmer writes the program in the manufacturer's language, the program is punched into cards and then read into the computer along with an *assembly program.* The assembly program translates the lan-

guage used by the programmer into the detailed machine language program.

Manufacturers' languages are designed to use to maximum advantage the features of each particular computer. As a result, each manufacturer has developed different programming languages, and frequently has a special programming language for each major type of equipment manufactured by the company. Using manufacturers' languages, a program must be rewritten every time it is to be run on a different computer. Because of the desire among users of computers to exchange computer programs and thus to cut costs, and also the desire to avoid having to rewrite all of an organization's computer programs each time a change is made in the kind of equipment used, more generalized programming languages have been developed.

Generalized programming languages, sometimes called *problem oriented languages,* have been agreed upon by all computer manufacturers so that a program written in one of the generalized languages can operate on all but the smallest computers. The two major languages of this variety are COBOL (Common Business Oriented Language) and FORTRAN (Formula Translation Language). COBOL is specifically designed to meet the common needs of business data processing jobs,[6] while FORTRAN is a language intended to be generally useful in scientific applications.

In COBOL, for instance, the programmer can write a statement such as "add interest to tax due" while in FORTRAN a programmer can write "x = a + b/c." After a program in COBOL or FORTRAN is written, it is punched on cards and read into the computer along with a *compiler* program provided by the manufacturer. The compiler translates the COBOL or FORTRAN program into a machine language program. Many specialized "machine free" languages also have been developed. For instance, QUIKTRAN and BASIC are languages developed especially for use at remote terminals linked to time-sharing computer in-

[6] See Sippl, *op. cit.,* Appendices O and P, for a brief description and comparison of COBOL and FORTRAN.

stallations. SIMSCRIPT is another specialized language developed for programming simulation models.

Generalized computer languages such as COBOL and FORTRAN are much less efficient than machine oriented languages supplied by the manufacturer. A COBOL program may take as much as twice as long to run on a given computer as would the same program written in the language provided for that particular machine. But because computers are rapidly becoming faster and less expensive to operate, and programming costs are steadily rising, many computer users have found it desirable to write their programs in COBOL and FORTRAN.

Software. The usefulness of a computer is directly dependent on the speed, flexibility, and convenience of the programming languages and programming aids which are available. These programming aids are generally referred to as *software*. The scope of software is not limited to the machine oriented and generalized programming languages already mentioned, but includes other aids such as special program subroutines which are not a part of a standard language, exchange services for sharing among a group of computer users the programs which each user has already written, and programs developed by the manufacturer for widely used techniques such as PERT (Program Evaluation and Review Technique). For larger computer configurations, software frequently includes *executive systems* which are programs that make it possible for computers to operate in the real-time and time-sharing modes.

Application of Computers in Municipal Government

Computers have been put to use in practically every municipal activity. Because of the wide variation in the types and importance of different functions in each community, and because of the differing priorities from one city to the next, it is unlikely that any city has yet made maximum use of computer potential. Even so, there are cities which are already

making use of computers in hundreds of different applications.[7] This section will review the different ways in which computers are being used in urban government. For convenience in presentation, several categories of uses will be examined. Because of the nature of the equipment and techniques employed, these categories do not conform to the traditional departmentalization of urban government. In fact, the use of computers requires the broader systems approach, which emphasizes the "wholeness" of the organization and its activities, so that as many of the organization's requirements are served as possible. This emphasis on the overall needs and activities of the organization is sometimes called the *integrated systems* or *total systems* approach.

USES IN OPERATING FUNCTIONS

Computers are increasingly being used to improve the effectiveness and efficiency of those operations which provide goods and services directly to the community. In these operating functions, the emphasis is frequently on increasing the convenience to the public, improving the quality of the goods and services, and increasing the speed and efficiency with which they are provided. The monitoring and control of a continuous production flow of materials (or energy) is known as *process control*.

Process Control. The production and distribution of water, electricity, and gas are processes which can be controlled almost entirely automatically through the use of computers and related equipment.[8] In the case of a water distribution system, for instance, pressure and rate of flow meters at key points in the pipe network continuously monitor and transmit to the control unit the status of the system. The control unit continuously com-

---

[7] See Public Automated Systems Service, AUTOMATED DATA PROCESSING IN MUNICIPAL GOVERNMENT (Chicago: Public Administration Service, 1966) for a partial inventory of municipal computer applications.

[8] See Harry H. Fite, THE COMPUTER CHALLENGE TO URBAN PLANNERS AND STATE ADMINISTRATORS (New York: Spartan Books, 1965), Chapters 6–8, for more extensive treatment of process control applications in municipalities.

pares these measurements with its programmed instructions which tell it what the allowable limits are for operation of the system. When pressure or rate of flow exceeds allowable limits, the computer transmits electrical signals to automatic controls on valves and pumps in the distribution system. The effects of regulating the valves and pumps are determined by *feedback*, or modified readings, from the *sensors* in the distribution system. When pressure and rate of flow have been restored to acceptable limits, the computer allows the settings of valves and pumps to remain unchanged until further control is necessary.

The computer can be programmed to determine where leaks or stoppages are located in the distribution network by comparison of pressure and rate of flow at each point in the system. The quality of the water provided also can be monitored by using chemical sensors, allowing the computer to control the treatment of the water, including the operation of filter mechanisms. When situations occur beyond the range programmed for the computer, the computer signals the human operator to take corrective action.

Process control techniques also have been applied to traffic. In traffic control systems, the flow of automobiles on the street network is treated much as is the flow of water or electricity through a system. Special sensors buried in the streets or mounted on traffic signals continually provide information to the computer on the status of traffic throughout the street system. The computer operates traffic signals to provide the maximum practical flow of traffic. Experience in the Toronto metropolitan area suggests that an increase of up to 40 percent in the traffic handling capacity of the existing street system can be obtained without widening streets or construction of expressways.

Direct Support of Operations. Computers are being used to improve the effectiveness of vital public services such as police, health, welfare, and schools. In many cities, police officers can now radio the license number or description of a suspicious automobile to the dispatcher and receive, almost instantaneously from a central computer, information

as to whether or not the vehicle has been stolen or whether the operator is known to have been involved in a crime. In California, a single computer and communications system operated by the state police provides "wanted vehicle" information to all law enforcement agencies within the state. In hospitals, computers are used to assist doctors in making diagnoses of illnesses. Schools use computers in *computer assisted instruction* which allows students to receive information, ask questions, and be continuously tested on subject matter through direct communications with the computer. Libraries have begun to use computers to allow the library user to state his interests and have the computer search through the materials in the library for relevant references. In the welfare field, computers relieve case workers of clerical details by automatically determining the eligibility of applicants and calculating the amounts of grants while clients are being interviewed.[9]

The use of computers and modern communications in direct support of operations tends to reduce red tape and to free operating personnel of routine clerical duties. Services can be provided more quickly, costs can be reduced, and the quality of services can be improved by allowing personnel to spend more of their time in carrying out their primary functions.

Techniques and Equipment Requirements. The use of computers in either process control or direct support of operations requires a real-time mode of operation. The computer must be available continuously to operating personnel and be able to provide the needed information or perform the necessary functions in time to affect the action being taken. This means that computer configurations must be relatively large, with remote terminals and associated communications systems. This does not mean, however, that only large governments can afford to use computers in these applications. While it is impractical for most governments to operate the necessary

---

[9] See John K. Harris, "System Design for Welfare Programs: The Role of EDP," PUBLIC WELFARE, April, 1966, for a good illustration of the use of computers in direct support of operations.

computer facilities exclusively for their own use, a number of states have established state-wide police information systems and welfare systems. City governments can also cooperate with other governments and agencies in a metropolitan area to obtain the benefits of these computer applications without assuming the entire cost of the computer facilities, or they can use commercial time-sharing.

PAPERWORK AND RECORDS AUTOMATION

Most city officials are familiar with the use of EDP and computers in tax billing, accounting, payroll, and similar applications where there is a high volume of routine, repetitive handling of information and there are clearly defined rules and standards.[10] The primary objectives in paperwork automation are to reduce unit costs and to increase the usefulness of information. This is true whether the particular application is the preparation of assessment rolls and tax bills or the production of payroll checks and related documents.

Ideally, the information needed for the organization as a whole is obtained only once and is then stored and processed using the computer to provide the information in all the different forms required for the entire organization. Manual recording, transcription, and manipulation of the information is reduced to an absolute minimum. The need for each department to maintain massive files for essentially the same information is eliminated, since the information is available whenever desired from the central source. When summaries, documents such as vouchers or tax bills, or special reports are needed, the line printer of the computer is used to print the desired information.

Records automation is closely related to paperwork automation. When the computer is used to produce tax bills, it can be easily used to produce, as a by-product, a complete listing of all tax bills issued—arranged alphabetically, arranged by property, and arranged by any districts which are important. The tax roll is then available without further work as a permanent record of the tax bills issued during a given period. Microfilm equipment can also be used in combination with computers to store maps, deeds, and other official documents required by law to be maintained by the city.

Some of the benefits of paperwork and records automation can be achieved through the use of simple punched card equipment, but it is necessary to employ computer configurations with magnetic tape units or other mass storage devices to obtain the full benefits of computer use. Batch processing is usually entirely satisfactory in these applications. Larger computers operating in a real-time mode provide additional advantages, but are rarely justified unless paperwork and records automation is combined with applications in the direct support of operations.

ANALYTICAL AND PLANNING USES

Computers (as the name implies) were principally developed to perform intricate calculations. The use of computers for analytical purposes, including mathematical calculations, is important to cities in engineering, in organizational and environmental analysis and planning, and in analyzing the interaction of the organization with its environment.[11]

Engineering Analysis. Standard computer programs are available for many of the common engineering calculations involved in survey work, highway design, sewer design, cut and fill operations, and bridge and structure design. Computer programs are also available to test the relative advantages of one design over another, including comparisons of strength, cost, and efficiency. By use of standard programs, the engineer is able to eliminate errors in calculation and to reduce the time required to a small fraction of that needed for manual calculation. Since engineering analysis usually does not require large volumes of data as is the case in tax bill-

---

[10] See Office of Records Management, U.S. General Services Administration, SOURCE DATA AUTOMATION, FPMR 11.5 (Washington, D.C.: National Archives and Records Service, 1965) for a good general treatment of paperwork and records automation.

[11] See Tulsa Metropolitan Area Planning Commission, METROPOLITAN DATA CENTER PROJECT (Tulsa: The Commission, 1966), for description of a data system for general community planning.

ing, the computers used do not require high speed line printers and other mass data handling devices. In engineering analyses, the emphasis is on a large internal memory to be able to handle the complex formulas involved.

Organizational Analysis and Planning. While administrative planning and analysis are given extensive treatment in Chapters 10 and 11, it is worth noting at this point that computers can be of considerable value in organizational analysis and planning. The computer can be used to determine the unit cost of services by analyzing budget expenditures by account and activity in comparison with work performed. Work units or levels of activity can be expressed in terms of types and quantities of materials and supplies; personnel numbers and costs, including fringe benefits; facilities; equipment; or other resources. By programming these relationships for the computer, budgets can be prepared which automatically reflect various combinations of program levels, and can be revised automatically to reflect priorities and limitations set by the council and chief administrator. Where computers are used in operating and auxiliary functions, statistical series can be produced as a by-product to allow analyses of seasonal and other fluctuations which will facilitate more effective management of the organization. Trends may also be plotted and projected to aid in policy formulation.

Environmental Analysis and Planning. Computers are used extensively for analysis of the massive quantities of data involved in conducting economic, transportation, population, and land use studies for community planning.[12] Community planners also use computers extensively to test the effects of alternate plans and locations for community facilities such as schools, parks, and industrial centers.

Computers are equally valuable in planning the operating programs of the city through analysis of the community. Studies of the seasonal pattern of crimes, for instance, can

facilitate manpower planning and scheduling in a police department. Analysis of traffic patterns throughout the community may lead to changes in the work of the street department, the traffic department, the police department, and may lead to modification of running routes for fire companies. By analyzing the pattern of population characteristics in comparison with the distribution of services, the administrator may find important needs not being met by existing services. Frequently, the information needed for such analysis can be gained as by-products from the use of computers for operating and auxiliary functions. Where the data are readily available, the analyses themselves may be carried out on a relatively economical basis.

Techniques and Equipment Requirements. Even the smallest computers can be valuable as aids to analysis, especially where there is a need for classifying and summarizing large volumes of data. Where complex mathematical analyses are to be made, extremely large-scale computers may be necessary. Since most analyses are carried out by batch processing, it is usually practical to rent time by the hour at a commercial service bureau or at a university when it is necessary to make use of large-scale computers. Graphic display devices are available for the larger computers which allow automatic preparation of graphs, charts, maps, and other visual displays of the data. Computer programs are available which use the line printer to produce graphs and charts.

MANAGEMENT INFORMATION USES

In the broadest sense, any use of computers in the organization may be expected to produce, as a by-product, information of importance to administrators at all levels. Analytical and planning uses in particular are generally carried out for the specific purpose of helping the chief administrator and his department heads manage the organization.[13]

Computers are also used to aid the administrator in day-to-day decision-making. "Management by exception techniques" al-

[12] See Britton Harris, ed., "Urban Development Models: New Tools for Planning," JOURNAL OF THE AMERICAN INSTITUTE OF PLANNERS, May, 1965.

[13] See M. Valliant Higginson, MANAGING WITH EDP, AMA Research Study 71 (New York: American Management Association, 1965), especially Chapters 4–7.

lows the administrator to state objectives in terms of acceptable rates of accomplishment and to be notified only when the acceptable limits are exceeded. In the finance area, for example, the administrator might approve a weekly or monthly expenditure rate in carrying out budgeted activities. Through computer analysis, accounting records would be examined periodically to determine whether expenditures and obligations were within the prescribed limits, and where the limits had been exceeded a full report would automatically be produced for the administrator's attention. Work performance can be monitored in a similar fashion so that the administrator is alerted only when there is a deviation from approved plans.

These techniques do not require the use of computers; on the other hand, they can be exceptionally effective when computers are employed in the day-to-day work of the organization, making it possible to obtain needed management information with minimum cost and effort.

Municipal Utilization of Computers

ORGANIZATIONAL CONSIDERATIONS

The early utilization of EDP and computers in financial data processing led naturally to the assignment of data processing responsibilities to finance departments. Now that computer utilization has spread to virtually all areas of urban government activity, there is a strong trend toward establishment of separate data processing departments or units reporting directly to the chief administrator and serving all city agencies. At the same time, there are also strong trends toward intergovernmental cooperation in computer utilization and toward making increased use of commercial computer services. For these reasons, it will be worthwhile to examine some of the major considerations in organizing for computer utilization before going on to ways of determining computer applicability and implementation.

Systems and Computers. Any functionally interdependent group of activities can be viewed as a system, whether or not computers are involved. The common practice of referring to accounting systems and personnel systems bears evidence of the familiarity of the concept in municipal government. In these and other systems, required results are specifically defined, standard methods and procedures are developed and used, work is divided into groups of specific activities to be performed by given positions and organizational components, and responsibilities for each part of the work are clearly assigned to workers and supervisors. Nevertheless, a large portion of the knowledge required for the system to operate effectively is possessed by the individuals involved. In addition, most organizational systems have been developed over a long period of time and are continually being modified by the people involved to adjust to changing requirements. For these reasons, there is a tendency for top management to take existing systems for granted until some major difficulty arises, such as the loss of several key people.

When computers are introduced into an organization, major changes are brought about in existing systems. Methods and procedures are changed, the flow of work is directed along different lines, responsibility shifts, and the activities carried on by people filling given positions are altered. From this point of view, the introduction of a computer may be viewed as a major reorganization of existing systems. Unlike people, however, computers are not capable of independent thought and consequently carry out only those activities for which they are specifically programmed: they require detailed and specific instructions for any change in the work they perform and are not capable of automatically varying their performance to work as a member of a team, to adjust to changing requirements, or to "fill in" for a coworker who is suddenly taken ill or who is on vacation.

The important point is to remember that a computer is capable of enormous quantities of work, but always functions only as one part of a system. To take advantage of the capacity of a computer it is necessary to redesign carefully the entire system, including the activities to be performed by each position, the methods and procedures to be used by people as well as the computer, lines of responsibility, the flow of work, and the allocation of materials, supplies, and other resources.

People and Computers. Those who are enthusiastic about the impressive results which can be obtained through intelligent use of computers are sometimes inclined to neglect the crucial importance of people in any "computer-based" system. Computer specialists frequently are unaware of the complexity of the work to be done and may tend to emphasize only those parts of the work which the computer can do well. There is often a tendency to devote considerable effort to the design and programming of the elements of work to be performed by the computer, without sufficient attention to the related change to be made in the responsibilities and activities of the people involved in the job—or to their need for complete understanding of the work to be performed by the computer and their related need for retraining to enable them to perform their changed functions effectively.

Since the introduction of computers is frequently based on the opportunity to reduce costs, there is usually a displacement of positions. Contrary to common belief, there is seldom a net reduction in the current number of positions in the organization, although the need to add additional positions in the future is frequently reduced. Elimination of clerical positions in departments may be offset by creation of keypunch, programmer, and computer operator positions in the data processing unit. These kinds of changes naturally create anxiety on the part of employees who are not sure of what the future will hold for them. Yet these difficulties can be avoided by careful personnel planning and by informing all the individuals to be affected of exactly in what way and at what time they will be affected. Where it will be necessary to eliminate positions, the employees should be given as much advance notice as possible and should be afforded the opportunity to qualify for other positions.

Setting Priorities. Computer utilization should be only one part of an overall management improvement program. The administra-

tor, his department heads, and personnel throughout the organization will find that conversion from manual methods or simple punched card methods to computer systems will require a substantial amount of their time.

Before a decision is made to utilize computers, it should be determined that computer methods actually represent the most favorable way of reducing costs or increasing effectiveness. Sometimes a good work simplification program can achieve the same advantages as computer utilization, but at lower cost and in less time. (Management improvement programs will be discussed at greater length in Chapters 10 and 11.) The administrator, using his staff and department heads, should review the effectiveness and efficiency of the organization as a whole and identify those areas where major improvements are needed. Priorities should be assigned to each problem area. If it appears that computer utilization offers the possibility of achieving high priority improvements, it is then practical to proceed to a feasibility study as discussed in a later section of this chapter.

System Development. After the feasibility or usefulness of a particular computer application has been established, time and resources must be allowed for developing the system. System development includes a detailed definition of the objectives to be achieved, specification of limitations such as cost and time, and the design of a complete computer-based system to meet the objectives within the limitations.

Usually the system development team will include a member of the department to be served who is thoroughly familiar with the work to be done and the present methods of accomplishing the work. A systems analyst, who is familiar with the type of computer to be employed and the ways of designing a system utilizing computer processing, works with the departmental staff person to block out the work flow and determine input and output requirements. The systems analyst also develops manual methods and procedures, form designs and instructions, and procedures manuals for action to be accomplished at each step in the processing of the work. System design is followed by computer programming and testing with sample data. This process may require from several months to more than a year before it is possible to make actual use of the computer.

Responsibility for system development should be clearly assigned to a person directly responsible to the chief administrator, or to the department head where only one department is involved. The same person should have continuing responsibility for regular evaluation of the system after it is in operation, and should be responsible for initiating needed changes as time goes by. Wherever possible, the systems analyst and computer programmer involved should be members of the organization so that when inevitable modifications of the system are required they can be accomplished at minimum cost with minimum disruption of work.

System Operation. Primary responsibility for the continued operation of the computer-based system resides with the chief administrator or supervisor responsible for performance of the function which is being aided through computer utilization. Where the city operates its own computer facility, responsibility for successful system operation is shared by the data processing manager or unit head. Since the data processing unit, like a personnel or finance unit, usually will be serving more than one department, the chief administrator can expect conflicts which arise from the demands of the several departments on the data processing unit. One technique used to minimize such conflicts is the formation of a data processing advisory committee composed of department heads utilizing computer techniques, which meets periodically with the data processing unit head.

DETERMINING COMPUTER APPLICABILITY

The final decision to utilize a computer for a particular application or group of applications generally follows a detailed feasibility study of the potential advantages of computer utilization compared with existing methods and other potential new methods for performing the work. Because the feasibility study requires a substantial investment of time and money, there must be a reasonable expectation that computer techniques are applicable even before the feasibility study is undertaken. While there is no precise formula for determining when a feasibility study should be made, experience has shown that a number of factors have an important bearing on the decision to investigate computer applicability.

Size and Functions of the Municipality. The size of the city in terms of population or number of employees is not conclusive in itself, but it should be evident that the larger the municipality and its government, the greater the chances that computer techniques will be of value. Equally important are the number and types of functions carried out by the city. Voluminous, repetitive clerical work such as that involved in utility billing and accounting may make computer techniques appropriate in even a small city.

Trends in Development of the Municipality. Cities undergoing or expecting rapid population increases are well advised to consider early adoption of computer techniques, even though the present size and functions of the city make computer utilization of marginal value. By beginning a long-range computer utilization program while the community is still small, the problems of converting from manual methods can be minimized and a sound basis can be laid for preparing the organization to implement more advanced computer applications as the volume and complexity of work increase. In stable cities or those declining in population, long-range advantages of computer utilization may be less significant. Even so, the trend toward new and expanded functions for cities and the tendency for residents to expect continual increases in service quality may be more important than projected changes in the size of population alone.

Management Objectives. Computer utilization can be a valuable aid in achieving management objectives. One such objective may be reduction of administrative and clerical costs; another is the ability to handle increasing administrative work loads with a minimum of staff increase and without the need to expand existing facilities. In still other cases the main objective may be to improve the quality and speed of service without substantial increase in cost. Particularly in rapidly growing cities, there may be an urgent need for improving the exchange of information among operating departments, and to make comprehensive information available to all departments and agencies for operational planning and coordination purposes. Where new functions are being assumed, the objective may be to obtain the most effective and efficient operation possible within available resources.

Achievement of management objectives such as these often can be facilitated through computer utilization. When management improvement objectives are poorly defined, or of low priority, it is less likely that computer utilization will prove feasible.

Political Acceptability. In cities where unemployment is severe there may be strong opposition to computer utilization from those, including council members, who associate computers and automation with reductions in the work force. But with the widespread utilization of computers in business and industry, and the extensive advertising and publicity devoted to computers, it is increasingly common for local leaders to associate computer utilization with progressive and efficient management. In some cases, this may lead to political pressure for computer utilization even when there may be no economic justification. The administrator who carefully investigates and evaluates the advantages and disadvantages of computer utilization, and who keeps the governing body fully informed of his studies and findings, greatly increases the likelihood that decisions on computer utilization will be made on a sound basis and that political extremes will be avoided.

Availability of Competent Staff. The ability to use computers effectively depends, first and foremost, on the availability of competent staff to plan, implement, and supervise the operation of computerized systems. If the chief administrator does not have a staff member capable of assuming full responsibility for computer utilization, he must be prepared to assume that responsibility himself. In addition, at least one technically competent analyst-programmer will be needed in even the smallest city, and in most cases several analysts and programmers will be required along with personnel to operate the equipment and to prepare data for processing. Computer manufacturers sometimes foster the illusion that the equipment will do the work without human effort. Yet experience in both government and business has shown that personnel costs involved in computer utilization seldom are less than the rental costs of the equipment itself, and frequently are more than twice as high as the cost of equipment rental. Furthermore, months and sometimes even years of intense staff work are required before the computer can be put to effective use. If the administrator is not prepared to reassign or hire fully competent staff, he is not ready to begin computer utilization.

ALTERNATIVES FOR OBTAINING COMPUTER SERVICES

Computer salesmen frequently attempt to convince prospective customers that the only way to make use of computers is to establish a computer facility in the organization and to rent the equipment on a full-time basis for the exclusive use of the organization. This may be the most profitable arrangement for the computer manufacturer, but it is frequently not the most advantageous course of action for the city. Several alternatives are available to most cities, each of which should be carefully considered before any final decision is reached on computer utilization.

Purchase. When computers were first introduced, improvements were made so rapidly that most equipment was obsolete in two or three years. Under those circumstances, most organizations were well advised not to purchase equipment, but rather to lease the equipment with a month-to-month rental contract which could be canceled in 30 days. (Monthly rental charges are usually calculated so that the cumulative rental cost equals the purchase cost of the computer in about five years.) When it was likely that a computer would be replaced in two or three years, monthly rental was a sound arrangement for most organizations.

Computers and related equipment, however, have now been improved to the point where some organizations can expect to retain the same equipment for as long as ten or fifteen years. Many of the newer computer models, furthermore, allow expansion of capability without replacement of basic equipment or reprogramming. Investments in software and computer programs are frequently a much more significant consideration than any marginal improvements in equipment. Consequently, purchase of computers and related equipment can offer major savings in the long run for those cities which carefully plan a long-range program of computer utilization and are able to afford the relatively high initial purchase cost of the equipment. Some cities now consider the purchase of computer equipment as a capital expenditure payable from the capital budget rather than the operating budget. There is also a growing market in used computers, which offers important possibilities for the purchaser as well as the seller of used computers. All computer manufacturers offer service and maintenance contracts for both new and used computers of their manufacture.

Lease and Lease-Purchase. As has been noted, the most common arrangement for equipping a computer facility is to lease the equipment on a monthly payment basis. Although this is seldom the most economical arrangement in the long run, it is often the easiest way to obtain the equipment because it avoids the high initial cost of purchase. Computer salesmen may prefer the monthly rental arrangement because, in many cities, rental agreements are not subject to competitive bid requirements. This permits the salesman to negotiate for the city's account without having to subject his proposals to a critical comparison with the equipment and services offered by other manufacturers.

Often overlooked by cities is the opportunity to obtain some of the advantages of purchase by entering into a lease-purchase agreement with a manufacturer. Typical provisions of a lease-purchase contract provide for applying all or part of monthly rental costs to the purchase of the equipment at a reduced price after a certain number of years. In effect, a lease-purchase arrangement may allow the city to buy the equipment at perhaps 30 percent of its initial cost after the city has used it for a period of five years.

Intergovernmental Cooperation. Cities, counties, school districts, and other local government agencies can reduce substantially the cost of computer utilization by jointly establishing a computer facility and sharing the cost of equipment and operating personnel. Even for those governmental agencies which might be able to afford their own equipment, such an arrangement can make faster and more flexible equipment available at considerable savings. Joint facilities also can allow twenty-four hour a day use of the equipment, which is an advantage because rental charges are reduced when the equipment is used for more than one working shift. If the equipment is purchased outright, the advantages are even greater since the only added expenses for twenty-four hour operation are equipment operators' salaries, the small cost of electricity, and slightly increased maintenance costs. Where governmental agencies establish a joint facility it is still important for each agency to have at least one qualified analyst-programmer responsible for developing computer applications and keeping them up-to-date and operating smoothly.

Another important form of governmental cooperation for computer utilization is found where a larger governmental agency makes its computer facilities available to other governmental agencies and charges only for the actual services provided. This benefits the larger unit because the greater volume of operation reduces unit costs. In some cases, such as in Dade County, Florida, the larger unit of government may provide complete services, including administrative management, system design, programming, equipment operation, materials, and follow-up work, for a particular function, such as tax billing, charging local jurisdictions only a small percentage fee for the entire effort.

Commercial Service Bureaus. The telephone directory for almost any metropolitan area now lists one or more data processing firms which operate computer facilities solely for the use of customers who cannot afford their own installations or who need to make use of specialized equipment which they do not have.

These service bureaus typically provide a variety of services. The customer may rent individual pieces of equipment by the hour and bring his work to the service bureau where he operates the equipment himself, or, alternately, he may contract with the service bureau for performance of a complete job such as payroll accounting. In the latter case, the service bureau staff will design and program the entire system, provide necessary forms and instructions, collect the needed data periodically or obtain it by mail, perform the processing, and return the checks and related vouchers and withholding documents to the organization. In addition to service bureaus specializing in these kinds of data processing services, in many cities banks and other business concerns now offer similar services because they have found that the staff and equipment required for their own operations are not fully utilized.

Commercial Time-Sharing. The development of large-scale computers capable of operating in the time-sharing mode makes possible even for small organizations the use of computers which were available until recently only to the largest business and governmental organizations. Commercial service bureaus offering time-sharing services are being established in most major metropolitan areas, and several large firms are developing nation-wide time-sharing computer services. By installing a teletypewriter, or other remote input/output device, a customer can obtain access to extremely large and flexible computer configurations by paying a small monthly minimum charge, and then paying by the minute for the time actually used on the computer.

Time-sharing arrangements give the customer full use of the computer and related equipment when needed. He may enter his own computer programs through his terminal, or make use of standard computer programs available to the computer at the time-sharing facility. Time-sharing is especially valuable for real-time applications involving large random access files and for applications involving complex mathematical calculations. The location of the time-sharing computer facility is relatively unimportant, unless it is so far distant that communications charges outweigh the other advantages. In special cases, organizations are using commercial time-sharing facilities located more than 2,000 miles distant.

University Computing Centers. All large colleges and universities now operate at least one major computer center which may be used for administration as well as research and teaching. Many of these computing centers, particularly where the college or university is state supported, will allow cities and other governmental agencies complete use of their staff and facilities. In some cases, system design and programming is available from the computing center while in other cases the customer must make his own arrangements for programming and preparation of data. University computer centers generally charge far less than other organizations for the services provided since they operate completely on a nonprofit basis. Even when the institution does not make its computer facilities generally available, contracts with university organizations or faculty members for research and problem solving will provide access to the computer resources of the institution.

Consultants and Contractors. There are many business firms and nonprofit organizations which offer a wide variety of services to cities utilizing computers. The services range from professional and technical advice in particular problem areas on through complete development and operation of computerized systems. Consultants can be particularly valuable to cities in exploring potential computer applications and planning long-range programs. Consultants can also be of great assistance in designing and implementing complex computer applications. It is always advisable, of course, to check business references carefully and to check with previous customers about the work of the particular firm. Reputable consulting organizations will always discuss a city's particular needs at no cost and, if they feel that they are able to provide useful assistance, they will submit a written proposal outlining the work which they will do and stating the costs and time required.

Combining Alternatives. City administrators experienced in computer utilization frequently find that their city is best served by a combination of the alternatives mentioned. A city of 25,000, for instance, may find it desirable to purchase some items of punched card equipment, such as keypunch machines, and to lease a small computer and related equipment on a monthly basis. At the same time, the city may be cooperating with the county for tax billing and other applications beyond the capacity of its own equipment. The police department may be participating in a police information network operated by the state while the planning department may be using a university computing center or a commercial service bureau to carry out large-scale analyses of land use and transportation plans.

The city also may have engaged a consulting firm to use techniques of computer analysis for evaluating alternate locations for a new civic center, and be using still another firm to assist in preparing a long-range plan for computer utilization as the city grows. A larger city might be employing all these alternatives and, in addition, taking advantage of commercial time-sharing to assist its engineering units in design of highways, buildings, and other work.

The particular combination of alternatives which serves a particular city's needs best will change from time to time; the chief administrator should periodically review his plans and make whatever changes are appropriate.

FEASIBILITY STUDIES FOR COMPUTER UTILIZATION

The large number of possible uses of computers and the wide variety of equipment available through various arrangements necessitate a methodical approach by cities considering the possibility of computer utilization. Governments and businesses faced with similar problems in evaluating the potential benefits of computer utilization have developed a general approach known as the feasibility study.[14] Figure 9–8 shows the major elements in a typical feasibility study.

Purposes of the Feasibility Study. There is no question that computers can be used in almost any municipal function. That is, it is *possible* to make use of computers and related equipment and techniques. The general question to be answered by the feasibility study, however, is "to what extent is it practical for a particular city to employ computers now and over the next few years?"

The feasibility study is concerned with the characteristics and requirements of the particular city and the potential of computer techniques in achieving management's objectives when contrasted with alternative techniques such as work simplification and reorganization. The feasibility study begins with the general assumption that computers may be of value and then proceeds to test that assumption before making detailed studies and plans for computer utilization. The study may be terminated whenever it becomes clear that computer utilization is not practical in the foreseeable future. The conduct of the feasibility study may reveal possibilities for management improvement which are related only indirectly, if at all, to computer utilization. In the city of San Diego, for instance, work simplification techniques were used during the feasibility study to achieve immediate improvements in paperwork processes that resulted in annual work load reductions of over six man-years. A thorough feasibility study will ordinarily require from six months to three years of effort, depending on the size and complexity of the city. As in San Diego, a carefully planned and conducted feasibility study may lead to major improvements in organizational management and functioning quite aside from the primary objective of determining the desirability of computer utilization.

Conducting the Study. The feasibility study is usually conducted in a number of stages,

[14] See Gregory and Van Horn, *op. cit.,* Chapters 16 and 17 for more complete treatment of feasibility studies and equipment procurement and installations.

including a preliminary survey, application studies, a general plan for computer utilization, and preparation of specifications for equipment to be purchased, leased, rented, or otherwise utilized. The most essential single action required to ensure a successful study is the assignment of responsibility for the entire study to a competent staff member who will be able to devote all—or at least a major part—of his time to the work. The person assigned should be thoroughly familiar with the organization and its management objectives, and there should also be a reasonable expectation that he will remain with the city for the entire conduct of the study and, preferably, for at least one year thereafter. It is also valuable to establish a study advisory committee composed of the major department heads in the city since they will be directly involved in the study itself and in any action which results from the study. The chief administrator himself must make it clear that the study has his whole support and he should arrange for frequent review of its progress. Since the study encompasses every activity of the organization,

there is no substitute for the close involvement of the chief administrator himself.

Preliminary Survey. The preliminary survey includes a review of all activities of the city to identify those for which there is a strong likelihood that the application of computer techniques would be of value. Each department head or one of his key assistants should participate fully in the preliminary survey of his department so that his knowledge of the objectives and operations of the department, and of particular problem areas, will be fully utilized. The preliminary survey takes into account reports and documents produced by the units; files maintained for production and reference use; information produced or collected by the units; processing activities of the unit; volume, time requirements, and approximate costs for each of the foregoing; improvements desired by the chief administrator or department head in processing operations; special legal and policy limitations or requirements; and expected increases in work load or changes in operation. A written report covering these topics should be pre-

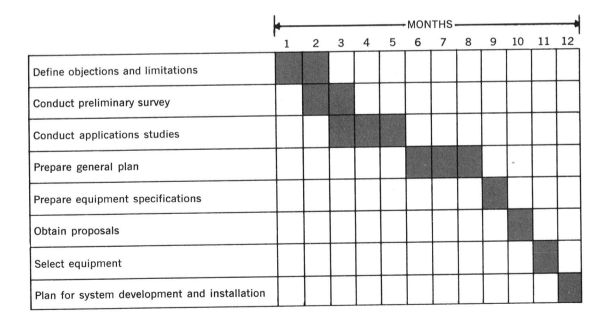

FIGURE 9-8. *The feasibility study process (Actual time may vary considerably.)*

pared for each department and major agency to assist in the overall evaluation of the preliminary survey.

Because a preliminary survey requires the evaluation of complex information, it is frequently desirable to obtain outside assistance in compiling it. Both nonprofit and business consulting firms are able to provide such aid. A valuable source of assistance frequently overlooked is the expertise of experienced personnel in other cities and governmental agencies. Most city administrators are willing to make available, for limited periods, their directors of data processing, systems analysts, and programmers to assist other cities develop their preliminary surveys.

If the preliminary survey reveals a strong likelihood that computer techniques eventually will be employed in the city, it is advisable to consider adding an experienced analyst-programmer to the staff immediately. An alternative is to select a current employee for intensive training in systems analysis and programming (such training can be obtained through commercial data processing schools or university courses). In any case, the study director should be encouraged to visit other cities which are employing computer techniques similar to the applications identified in the preliminary survey and to become thoroughly familiar with the equipment, techniques, and work organization involved.

Applications Studies. Each potential application identified in the preliminary survey requires more intensive analysis by departmental personnel and by an experienced analyst-programmer. The applications study includes a detailed analysis of the way in which work is currently performed and the suggested methods of employing computer techniques. Improvements which could be obtained by simple changes without computer techniques should also be carefully studied. A comparison is then made between the existing methods and the proposed methods involving computer techniques to estimate potential improvements in costs, speed, accuracy, and quality of the proposed innovations.

Application studies include detailed investigation and design of input, files, data handling, work processing, output, interdepartmental work flow, and measures of effectiveness. It is especially important to document thoroughly the application studies because they will form the basis for action to be taken. After every potential application is individually studied, they must all be studied collectively to ensure that relationships have been taken into account and that all practical efficiencies have been achieved. The application studies, individually and collectively, identify the general types of equipment capabilities required, proposed changes in methods and procedures, and changes in staff requirements and relationships.

General Plan. The next step in the study is the preparation of a general plan and schedule covering the succeeding three to five years. The general plan defines responsibilities and action to be taken for each approved application and identifies staff, facilities, equipment, supplies, and other resources required to carry out the proposed program. The plan should be reviewed thoroughly by the chief administrator and, if approved, should be reviewed by the governing body to ensure that future budgetary requirements and organizational changes are generally acceptable.

Equipment Specifications. After the general plan is approved, detailed specifications should be prepared for any equipment which must be leased or purchased. The specifications should, of course, be written so that at least several major equipment manufacturers can submit proposals. To ensure the best possible bids, the application studies and general plan should be made available to prospective bidders. It should also be made clear that bid proposals will be evaluated in terms of the degree to which they meet the overall requirements of the organization, and not on the basis of price alone. Where possible, performance specifications should be used rather than equipment operating characteristics. Finally, manufacturers should be encouraged to submit alternative proposals if they believe that differing combinations of equipment or different methods might be equally acceptable. Figure 9–9 summarizes points which manufacturers should be required to cover in their bid proposals.

1. Degree and extent of automation in the system

2. Equipment composition
   (a) Description: make, model, number, and quantity of each unit
   (b) Form of data handled: numeric or alphanumeric, and fixed word or variable or selected field
   (c) Storage capacity and method: random or serial access
   (d) Adequacy of controls, method of checking, and average length of time between malfunctions
   (e) Operating instructions for each major unit
   (f) Operating supplies needed

3. Operating requirements
   (a) Acceptance of input documents and data
   (b) Time required for each type of equipment to handle each major job and the total time available
   (c) Delay after cut-off before reports are available
   (d) Flow charts of jobs showing recommended techniques
   (e) Examples of detailed coding for applications

4. Delivery of equipment
   (a) Delivery date
   (b) Length of time to check equipment and get it into operating condition
   (c) Penalties for late delivery or complete failure to deliver equipment that is contracted for

5. Installation requirements, including both recommended and extreme conditions for manufacturer's guarantee
   (a) Size, weight, floor space, and height for each unit, including auxiliary equipment
   (b) Electric power — public utility or special equipment—and wiring requirements
   (c) Air conditioning: humidity, temperature, dust and special protection
   (d) Space for files, supplies, maintenance parts, test operations, personnel, and visitors

6. Manufacturer's assistance
   (a) Availability of engineers or technicians for analysis, programming, and installation
   (b) Training courses for customer's programmers and operators
   (c) Availability of manufacturer's or a customer's equipment for use in program debugging
   (d) The manufacturer's software package for programming and assistance available by participating in the equipment users' associations

7. Rental or purchase or combined agreements
   (a) Rental rate, term of contract, renewal, and cancellation clauses
   (b) Number of hours for operating in one, two, or three shifts or on a monthly basis and rate adjustment for excessive down time
   (c) Terms of payment, discount, and financing arrangement
   (d) Guarantees on equipment operations, availability of magnetic tape and special supplies, cost of maintenance parts and supplies
   (e) Terms of any purchase option: initial deposit required, fraction of rental payments credited toward purchase, and option expiration date

8. Maintenance contracts
   (a) Maintenance contract cost, service personnel, scheduled maintenance period, availability of a similar machine during extended down time, and renewal conditions
   (b) Term and rate of initial contract and renewal period
   (c) Provision for replacing parts, testing equipment, and maintenance

9. Design changes
   (a) Replacement of unsatisfactory units
   (b) Arrangements for securing improvements or new models, including trade-in value

10. Expansion and integration
    (a) Additional units that can be added: input, output, storage, processing, and interrogation
    (b) Other equipment that will accept media directly from this equipment
    (c) Equipment available for media conversion

FIGURE 9-9. *Checklist for bid proposals (Source: Robert H. Gregory and Richard L. Van Horn, AUTOMATIC DATA PROCESSING SYSTEMS, Wadsworth Publishing Company, 2nd ed., 1964, pp. 634-36.)*

Relationships with Equipment Manufacturers. Administrators should realize that individual salesmen representing even the most reliable equipment manufacturers may resort to sales methods which are contrary to the interests of the city. These sales methods range from attempts to persuade the city to enter into a negotiated contract without the necessary feasibility study and without consideration of competitive equipment, to use of political pressure to force selection of their equipment. Such attempts should be reported directly to the manufacturer since no responsible firm approves of such techniques. Because all computer manufacturers are rapidly expanding their sales forces to take advantage of the booming computer market, control of individual salesmen is seldom fully effective. Thus it is advisable to keep all computer and related equipment salesmen "at arms length."

With this caution in mind, the city should take full advantage of the information which can be provided by equipment manufacturers concerning both the capabilities of their equipment and the uses which have been made of the equipment in other cities. By obtaining information from several manufacturers throughout the course of the study, the city can avoid receiving a one-sided picture. During the time when equipment manufacturers are preparing their proposals, it is important that the city make available to them any reasonable information that may aid them in preparing a sound proposal.

Evaluating Proposals. All equipment proposals received should, of course, be compared carefully with one another and with the bid specifications to determine which proposal most closely meets the overall needs of the city as expressed in the applications studies and general plan. In some cases, one proposal will clearly be superior to all the others; when this is not the case, two approaches may be useful in determining the best proposal: a consulting firm which specializes in evaluating equipment proposals can be engaged or a panel of data processing experts can be formed to assist in evaluation. If an evaluation panel is formed, members can be drawn from experienced data processing personnel in business corporations located in the city, from data processing personnel from other cities, and from university and college computer centers. The panel should always include the city's study director and major department heads.

Planning for Installation. After any necessary equipment has been selected, the general plan should be amended as required and expanded to include all action required prior to installation of the equipment. This will include preparation of facilities, hiring and training of needed personnel, ordering necessary office equipment and materials, and detailed system design and programming for those applications which will be converted to computer processing as soon as the equipment is installed. Once the equipment has been ordered, manufacturers will provide technical assistance and training of personnel to prepare for computer utilization. Manufacturers also will make available at other locations equipment similar to that ordered which can be used prior to installation for programming and testing of applications. The general plan should allow sufficient time before installation so that the computer can be put to productive use as soon as it is installed.

DEVELOPING AND IMPLEMENTING COMPUTER-BASED SYSTEMS

While the feasibility study usually serves to select equipment for a wide variety of uses, system development focuses on the work necessary to make use of the equipment in one or more applications. Therefore, some of the feasibility study steps must be retraced and amplified in detail.

Whether the city installs its own equipment or uses computers at some other location, the process of developing and implementing the systems remains essentially the same. Figure 9–10 shows the relationship of the major steps in this process. In a given city, several different systems may be under development at one time, some of which may be undertaken by city staff while others may be done by consulting firms. The total time required for development of a given application depends, of course, on the magnitude and complexity of the application. The actual length of time may vary from as little as one month up to several years. A typical payroll application, for instance, could be expected to require three to four months.

Working together, the system analyst (or analyst-programmer) and departmental personnel begin by reviewing and refining the input and output requirements for each particular application as defined during the application study. The requirements should be reviewed by the department head and the chief administrator, who should set specific limits on the time and resources which are allowable for the system development phase. The administrator should also be sure that clear criteria have been set for evaluating overall system performance in meeting input and output requirements.

System Investigation. The next step is a thorough study of the work to be performed in comparison with the detailed capability of the staff, computer, and related equipment. Special attention should be devoted to the relationship of the system under study to other systems and work activities of the organization.

System Design. The art of designing a system that takes fullest advantage of staff abilities, equipment capabilities, and available methods and procedures requires the fullest cooperation and use of knowledge and ingenuity by departmental personnel, the system analyst, the computer programmer, and the equipment operator. The process of system design includes complete flow charting of all work elements, the design of all necessary documents and forms including punched card layouts, the identification of input and output at each step of machine processing, and the writing of instructions for each person to be involved in the system.

Programming. After the system design has been reviewed and approved, the computer program is written and debugged using sample data. During the course of programming, it may be found that greater efficiency can be

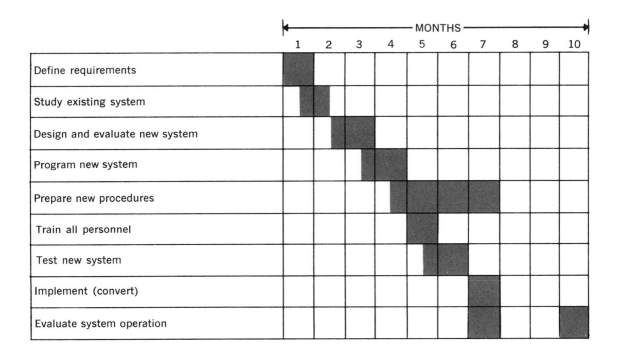

FIGURE 9-10. *The system development process (Actual time may vary considerably.)*

achieved by modifying the system design, perhaps by changing the format and classification of input data, the format of output, or the initial plan for computer processing.

Procedures. When the computer programs have been written and debugged, and any necessary modifications in system design have been made, the design is "frozen" and detailed procedures are written for the work to be accomplished by each person involved in the system. The procedures should be reviewed carefully with each of the persons who will carry out the work to be sure that they are clear and complete. Procedures are written not only for equipment operators, but also for those administrative and operating personnel who are involved in providing input into the system or in using the output.

Testing. Before relying upon the new system, it is important to test all elements of the system thoroughly. In many cases this can be accomplished by "parallel operation" which involves operating the new system side by side with the old system for at least one full cycle of operation. In a typical example, the payroll would be prepared using old methods at the same time it is prepared using computer techniques and the results of the two operations would be compared. Errors in the new system frequently will be revealed during parallel operation and corrective action can be taken until the new system is operating without error. When parallel operation is not practical, technical methods can be employed to aid in detecting errors of operation.

Implementation. The time when full reliance will be placed on the new system, discontinuing the old system, must be chosen carefully. Implementation of the new system should not be scheduled until all needed data files have been converted to the new format, all needed forms and supplies are on hand, and the entire system has been tested thoroughly. Implementation should be scheduled for the beginning of a work cycle, such as the beginning of a fiscal year in the case of accounting applications or the beginning of a pay period for payroll applications. All personnel affected should receive clear instruc-

tions on when the new system is to be implemented and when old methods can be discontinued.

Evaluation. Regular evaluation of each new system should be planned and carried out to be sure that the system continues to meet organizational requirements and continues to conform to the criteria initially established when the requirements were defined. Without regular review, computerized systems may not be modified to keep up with changes in either the work or the organization and undesirable modifications may unintentionally impair the efficiency of the system. In such periodic reviews, it is important to ensure that all forms, procedures, systems flow charts, and computer program documentation is kept up to date so that modifications can be made with a minimum of effort and confusion.

Trends in Computer Technology and Municipal Utilization

INCREASES IN COMPUTER CAPABILITIES

The improvements which have been made in computers and related equipment over the last few years have far exceeded even the most optimistic predictions. Equipment that can produce output in the form of spoken English is already available, and it is likely that the next few years will see the introduction of special devices which enable computers to understand spoken English as well. Available equipment is capable of accepting input in the form of printed documents and, to a limited extent, in the form of hand-written information.

But the most important developments which can be expected over the next decade probably will be those in the area of software. Programming languages which can be learned by untrained personnel with a few hours of instruction are being developed. More and more standard computer programs are being written which can be used with a minimum of adaptation to a particular job. Highly complex computer programs have been developed and are being improved which allow the computer to schedule and control automatically the work it performs, making modes of operation such as time-sharing increasingly useful. Perhaps the greatest limiting factor on the use of computers will continue to be the scarcity of qualified personnel in comparison with the rapidly expanding demand.

In 1953, authorities in the computer field predicted that the cost of performing a given job using computers would be more than 70 percent less in 1973 than it then was. But the actual decrease in costs far exceeded this figure even before 1968. The opportunities for rental of computer time by the hour, service bureaus, the use of time-sharing computer facilities, and the opportunities for joint computer facilities make it possible for a city to carry on a computer utilization program at only a small fraction of the cost that would have been incurred a few years ago when the only practical approach was to establish an internal computer facility to meet all needs.

INTERGOVERNMENTAL COMPUTER-BASED SYSTEMS

The number and variety of statewide and regional computerized systems are increasing rapidly. Law enforcement and police information networks which combine the information resources of dozens or hundreds of individual jurisdictions are a common example of this new pattern of computer utilization. Regional planning organizations also are moving toward unified land use, transportation, economic, and demographic data banks which serve all of the local jurisdictions in the region. The effectiveness of these and similar

[15] See Edward F. R. Hearle and Raymond J. Mason, A DATA PROCESSING SYSTEM FOR STATE AND LOCAL GOVERNMENTS (Englewood Cliffs, New Jersey: Prentice Hall, 1963), for a good presentation of the potentials of intergovernmental cooperation in computer utilization.

multijurisdictional systems depends on standardization of information classifications, codes, and recording practices. In return for agreeing on standardized practices, individual jurisdictions can receive benefits which would be completely unattainable if each jurisdiction proceeded independently.[15] In addition, the expense in intergovernmental systems is shared by all participants, thus significantly reducing costs.

SUMMARY: THE COMPUTER'S IMPACT ON MODERN MANAGEMENT

Present trends, including rapidly increasing computer capability, decreasing cost of computer utilization, and rapid development of time-sharing services, make it reasonable to expect that by 1975 every city large enough to have a professional administrator will be making use of computer techniques. For smaller cities, computer utilization may be generally limited to participation in regional and state computer-based systems and to contracting with larger governmental units for computer processing of tax bills and similar work. For most cities these forms of computer utilization will be only part of an overall program.

It is already clear that the computer has become a major tool of modern management. Just as the introduction of automotive vehicles and telephones had a major impact on governmental organization and functioning in the early part of the century, the computer is now the major technological factor in the current evolution of management. Yet because a computer can perform many tasks which previously could be performed only by people, it is likely that the impact of the computer and related techniques will far exceed that of any previous technological development.

10

Administrative Planning

ADMINISTRATIVE PLANNING is concerned with deciding in advance what the organization will do in the future, who will do it, and how it will be accomplished. Nearly everyone in the city government is continually involved in one form of planning or another. The city council and the chief executive offices may be planning to introduce new programs and to change emphases among existing programs. The finance officer may be planning to meet the city's requirements for the sale of bonds to support the long-range capital improvement program. The director of public works may be planning a snow removal and ice control program in anticipation of winter storms. The supervisor of public health nurses may be planning to conduct a series of clinics on prenatal care. The stock clerk in a warehouse may be planning purchases of materials and supplies for the next month.

Scope of Administrative Planning

In all of these cases, the individuals are carrying on a process which is in many ways similar, even though the particular situations seem to have little in common. All of the people mentioned are making assumptions about what they expect to happen in the future, and are then evaluating or interpreting the expected future in terms of their own responsibilities and their knowledge of what should be done under differing circumstances. Where they see a need for action, they set objectives which are specific results that they believe should be achieved. They then consider the different

ways in which they might be able to bring about the desired results and finally settle on one course of action which they think is practical and will achieve the objective without undesirable side effects. The next step is to decide just how to implement the course of action which they have selected—what will have to be done; who will do it; when it needs to be accomplished; and what material, supplies, money, or other resources will be needed.

Planning is such a common type of activity that it may take longer to describe the process than it does to carry it out. A considerable amount of administrative planning is usually carried on so routinely that it is not even recognized as planning. This is especially true in small organizations and those responsible for activities which do not change perceptibly from year to year. But responsibilities in a typical city government are broad and complex, and both the organization and the community it serves are in a continual state of change. Under these circumstances, a sound program of comprehensive administrative planning is one of the most important responsibilities of the chief administrator.

PLANNING FOR ACHIEVEMENT OF COMMUNITY GOALS

In one sense, the primary reason for the existence of local government is to provide a means through which communities may achieve their goals, whether the goals are to provide education for their children, to protect their lives and property, or to create a pleasant and attractive environment in which to live. Planning to achieve community goals is complicated considerably because the goals are often unclear and because there is frequently conflict over the goals and the ways in which they can or should be achieved. It is generally agreed that the political process is primarily concerned with the clarification of goals and the resolution of conflicts related to goals, but, in order to achieve this, a continuous working partnership between elected and appointed officials is required.

For example, it may be quite generally agreed that the community should provide a good education for all its children. Yet when this abstract goal is translated into operational objectives—such as new facilities, student-teacher ratios, and laboratory equipment—and programmed for implementation in the capital and operating budgets, there may be community opposition to paying the higher taxes required. Also, at this point, it is not unusual for groups in the community to demand that an increase in taxes be used for their own special concerns rather than for the improvement of the schools. The result may be that administrative planning is reinstituted to modify the plan so that the objections revealed through the political process are removed. In most cases, of course, the city council and the chief administrator will know community values well enough to anticipate possible objections and plan accordingly.

PLANNING FOR MANAGEMENT IMPROVEMENT

One of the chief administrator's most important responsibilities is that of ensuring that city government is as effective and efficient as possible. He has primary responsibility for maximizing the achievement of community goals and objectives with the resources appropriated for that purpose. Management improvement planning, sometimes called "organization and methods research" or simply "administrative analysis," is designed to assist in the discharge of this responsibility. By maintaining a constant search for more productive ways of performing the line and staff duties of the operating agencies, the administrator can better evaluate the city's ability to

meet its changing obligations and ensure that it is doing so at the lowest practical cost.

RELATIONSHIP TO "COMMUNITY PLANNING"

The first half of the 20th century saw the parallel development of city planning and the council-manager form of government. In many communities it was thought that planning of the physical aspects of the community, so-called "community planning," could somehow be separated from action to bring about the physical improvement of the community, and also could be separated from governmental programs concerned with the people who lived in the community. By now it is clear that it is impossible to separate city planning from city government.

If a new expressway is placed in a certain location, for instance, it will affect the community and the pattern of governmental services. Where will the people live who are displaced by expressway construction? What will the removal of taxable real estate do to the city revenue structure? How will police protection and fire protection be provided to areas cut off by the new expressway? How will people be affected by the change in access to libraries and parks? Will the children still be able to walk to school or will it be necessary to transport them by bus? What effect will the expressway and interchanges have on residential neighborhoods? What changes in traffic routing and control will be necessary to prevent high volume traffic on residential streets?

Such a list of questions is nearly endless, but even this simple example illustrates the inseparability of city planning and administrative planning. Because of this, there is a trend toward placing all responsibilities for governmental action concerned with community development under the city council and the chief administrator. But whatever the current form of organization, administrative planning must be concerned with coordinating all governmental activities for community benefit.

Elements of Administrative Planning

Planning is sometimes equated with the production of maps, blueprints, and other forms of graphics. Usually, however, these graphic illustrations are only expressions of a design concept showing what something should look like if and when it is built. While such graphic illustrations are sometimes a useful way of giving other people an idea of the designer's objectives, they are only a very small part of any plan. Most plans, in fact, are directed toward objectives which do not lend themselves to graphic illustration. For instance, how would a plan for improving the quality of education, or increasing the effectiveness of crime prevention, be illustrated visually?

Planning is actually concerned with developing programs of action which will bring about desired conditions or events at some specific time in the future. Planning is also concerned with preventing certain situations from occurring in the future, such as preventing fires, crimes, or disease. But, regardless of whether it is directed toward bringing about desirable situations or preventing undesirable situations, planning is always concerned with both objectives and actions to achieve those objectives. Because planning is seldom perfect, it is nearly always necessary to make continuing modifications to planned action, and frequently it is also necessary to modify objectives as time goes by. Therefore, planning should be viewed as a continuous process rather than as an activity that can be done once and forgotten.

Figure 10–1 shows the relationship among the vital elements in the planning process,

each of which will be reviewed briefly before considering applications of administrative planning in municipal government. It must be emphasized that the planning process does not necessarily proceed directly from one step to another, but involves frequent revision of each element in the process and may be terminated at any point if it appears continued planning would not be of value.

DECIDING TO PLAN

In most municipalities, the annual preparation of the capital program and the operating budget necessitates at least a minimum amount of administrative planning. New programs, whether initiated by local, state, or federal governments, also require planning. In these cases, the chief administrator may be concerned primarily with deciding how extensive the planning should be, assigning responsibilities, and controlling the planning process. In most instances, however, he must rely on his experience, knowledge, understanding of the organization and the community, the advice of his principal assistants, and his own judgment to determine when to undertake a specific planning activity.

DESCRIPTION AND PREDICTION

The decision to undertake a particular type of planning necessarily depends on certain initial assumptions about the community and the organization, both in the present and in the future. For planning to be effective, these

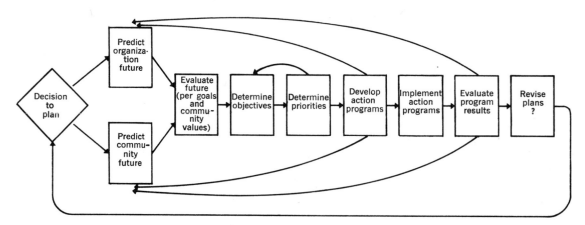

FIGURE 10-1. *The planning process*

assumptions must be spelled out and carefully examined. Considerable effort may be required to identify, describe, and predict those factors which are important to the problem at hand.

In planning a community recreation program, for instance, it is necessary to describe the present facilities, programs, and activities available to the community. These will frequently include not only those provided by the recreation department, but also those provided by the schools and other public agencies as well as those available through private organizations. At the same time, it is necessary to describe the use made of existing opportunities and the public's preferences and values concerning recreational programs in general. This may require substantial study, including surveys of both the users and nonusers of recreational facilities presently available.[1]

In addition to describing the present opportunities provided by city programs in the light of community preferences, it is also necessary to predict changes which are likely to occur in the future. Is the city population increasing or decreasing? Are the characteristics of the population changing so that recreation demands will be different in the future? Where are the people located in relation to recreational opportunities which they may wish to use? Are new recreational resources already being added to meet projected needs of the community?

The answers to these and similar questions will largely determine whether or not planning need be continued. Further, certain predictions must be made about the values and preferences of the community in the future. Will they be more or less interested in community recreation? Will their preferences change toward active sports and programs, or will they place greater emphasis on spectator activities? Is the community likely to place greater value on education as compared with recreation in the future? There is no easy way to answer questions relating to future values of a community, but it is important to make clear the assumptions upon which predictions are based.[2]

DEFINING OBJECTIVES

When situations indicating or requiring action are found to exist in the present or are predicted for the future, the specific responsibility of the city government for bringing about clearly defined results must be determined.[3] If, for instance, it is found that there are presently 100 substandard dwelling units in the city and that the number is likely to increase to 200 within a five-year period if no corrective action is taken, the city may set the objective of taking action to bring all 100 currently substandard units up to standard conditions and to prevent an additional 100 units from becoming substandard by the end of the five-year period. If the city had confined its effort to describing the present situation, it would have defined its objective simply as bringing 100 units up to standard condition. The city might then have overlooked the 100 units which were likely to become substandard in the next few years, and might have ended the five-year period with the same number of substandard units that it had initially.

SETTING PRIORITIES

If a city had unlimited knowledge and unlimited resources, it would have no need to set priorities, for it would be able to begin all needed action at once. In reality, cities are always limited in available knowledge about how to accomplish objectives, and are frequently even more severely limited in the availability of resources. Under these circumstances, priorities must be established for all

---

[1] An excellent method for planning and evaluating service programs is described in Janet S. Reiner, Everett Reiner, and Thomas A. Reiner, "Client Analysis and the Planning of Public Programs," JOURNAL OF THE AMERICAN INSTITUTE OF PLANNERS, November, 1963.

[2] A careful consideration of community values and planning approaches is contained in the following articles: Paul Davidoff and Thomas A. Reiner, "A Choice Theory of Planning," JOURNAL OF THE AMERICAN INSTITUTE OF PLANNERS, May, 1962, pp. 19–27, and John Dakin, "An Evaluation of the 'Choice' Theory of Planning," JOURNAL OF THE AMERICAN INSTITUTE OF PLANNERS, February, 1963, pp. 19–27.

[3] See especially Harry P. Hatry and John F. Cotton, PROGRAM PLANNING FOR STATE, COUNTY, CITY (Washington, D.C.: State Local Finances Project of the George Washington University, January, 1967), pp. 14–22.

planned action so that needs which are considered most urgent can be met while others may be set aside until resources or knowledge become available. The setting of priorities includes the relative emphasis to be devoted to different objectives as well as to the sequence in which objectives will be accomplished. In the example of substandard housing, a higher priority might have been given to eliminating existing substandard housing than to prevention of further housing deterioration.

DEVELOPING ACTION PROGRAMS

There are usually a variety of possible courses of action which may help to achieve objectives within a given set of priorities. Using the example of substandard housing, possible courses of action might include conferences with property owners, legal action to enforce housing codes, acquisition and demolition of the properties, acquisition and rehabilitation of the dwelling units under an urban renewal program, and so on. Each possible action program will have differing chances of success in particular situations, may involve different parts of the city organization and the community, will require differing lengths of time, and may involve different direct and indirect costs.

Careful analysis of the advantages and disadvantages of each of the courses of action and of the various combinations of courses of action should be completed before an action program is developed.[4]

IMPLEMENTING ACTION PROGRAMS

After action programs have been formulated, detailed planning is required to assign specific responsibilities, provide detailed instructions for action to be taken by the various participants, arrange for the availability of facilities, staff, equipment, and materials, ensure control and coordination of the conduct of the action program, and provide for specific means of measuring the degree of success in accomplishing objectives. Individual action programs also must be meshed with the overall activities of the organization, and must be reflected in the capital and operating budgets of the

organization as well as in other comprehensive planning processes.

EVALUATION AND REVISION OF PLANS

The planning process requires a multitude of assumptions about what is likely to happen in the future and about the probable consequences of one activity compared with another. Administrative planning involves not only assumptions about the organization and the community, but also assumptions about regional and national factors such as economic conditions, peace or war, technological development, changes in standards of living, and a host of other uncontrollable factors. Under these circumstances it is a foregone conclusion that nearly every plan will require continual modification as time goes by.[5]

Therefore, the planning process must include specific provisions for periodic evaluation of all aspects of planned action programs. Yet this need not be an overwhelming job, for a well developed plan may need no more than a brief, monthly or quarterly review session by the chief administrator with the principal persons involved. Such evaluation does require that plans include specific measures of performance and effectiveness so that it will be relatively easy to determine whether the program is meeting prescribed objectives.

Comprehensive Administrative Planning

How can the chief administrative officer be sure that there are not important gaps in the administrative planning activities carried on by the departments and agencies of the municipal government? What can he do to improve the quality of administrative planning and ensure that the result is improved performance in achieving community goals? As long as administrative planning is carried on haphazardly, the chief administrator will be able to do none of these things. Yet if he takes action to establish a comprehensive administra-

---

[4] *Ibid.,* pp. 40–44.

[5] Herbert Simon, Donald Smithburg, and Victor Thompson, PUBLIC ADMINISTRATION (New York: Knopf, 1950), see especially Chapter 20, "The Strategy of Planning."

tive planning program, and to review and coordinate that program, he can expect to bring about significant improvements in the overall effectiveness of the city government.

To do this, he must establish a general framework within which program planning and management improvement planning can be brought together into an integrated action program.[6] Nearly all cities have some of the major elements necessary in a comprehensive planning program, but few of them have combined all the elements to gain maximum advantage. A brief discussion of the major elements necessary in an annual comprehensive administrative planning program follows.

FORECASTING

One of the most frequently overlooked elements in comprehensive administrative planning is the vital necessity for regular forecasting of changes in the community, city government, and general environment. Some cities rely on the most recent U.S. census report to gain an idea of the present characteristics of the city, even though the census report may be many years out of date. While this practice is clearly useless in rapidly developing cities, experience shows that even in those cities where the total population is not changing there are usually important shifts taking place in the characteristics and location of the population, and in physical characteristics of the city.

Some cities are satisfied with twenty-year predictions of community development, usually prepared by the planning department as part of the master plan. These long-range forecasts are almost always greatly in error, and almost never give any insight into immediate and near future changes which will affect governmental programs. Still other cities use annual gross estimates of the population, without any attention to changes in various areas of the city and without relating overall population changes to the specific program-

matic concerns of the departments and agencies of the government. Where one or another of these practices is followed, individual departments and agencies are required to make their own estimates of current and future conditions in the city without benefit of the staff or technical resources needed to make accurate estimates. Frequently the result is that each of the various units of the city government is actually planning for a quite different city and with no idea of the expected future conditions on which other units are basing their plans.

What is needed is an annual estimate of current conditions, and a forecast of changes expected in each of the next five years, so that all units of the city government are doing their planning on the same general basis. This annual estimate and forecast should include characteristics of general interest concerning the development of the community, expected changes in the city government, the overall financial picture for the city government, and any significant changes expected in the social and economic environment. While individual parts of the forecast may be prepared by different departments and agencies, it is essential that the individual components of the forecast be consolidated and reviewed so that the forecast represents the best possible basis for planning future action.

Community Development. The forecast of community development should include at least such factors as numbers of people, numbers of school children, numbers and types of new residential and other buildings, and numbers and location of automobiles. Wherever possible, the forecast should include changes in the characteristics of the population, of land use, and of transportation patterns. This information will generally be of greatest use if it is broken down by census tracts so that it may be combined with other statistical and operating records as explained in Chapter 11.

Consideration should be given to making the forecast of community development available to the public for use in planning private schools, churches, and other facilities, public utilities when they are not owned by the city, and business expansions.

Organizational Development. Major changes

---

[6] Adrian M. McDonough and Leonard J. Garrett, MANAGEMENT SYSTEMS (Homewood, Illinois: Richard D. Irwin, 1965), pp. 83–94; and William M. Fox, THE MANAGEMENT PROCESS—AN INTEGRATED FUNCTIONAL APPROACH (Homewood, Illinois: Richard D. Irwin, 1963), Section 1, "Planning for Management."

in city organization expected to occur within the next five years should be included in the forecast to the extent that they are known with reasonable certainty. These changes would include those resulting from mergers, consolidations, annexations, and program modifications. Changes in the locations at which services are offered and substantial changes in staffing, such as those connected with the opening of new capital facilities, are also important. Because this information is primarily of importance to city departments and agencies in planning their future activities, it is usually *not* made available to the general public.

Finances. The forecasts of community and organizational development provide a better basis for financial estimates than do simple projections of past trends, although such historical information should be included in forecasting. The financial forecast for the five-year period should include the forecast of the tax base, estimates of revenues for each tax at the current tax rate, and estimates of governmental expenditures considering the forecasted organizational development. It is important that the financial forecast take into account not only current cost factors on the expenditure side, but also expected increases in the prices of goods, contractual services, and known future costs of the payroll plan and fringe benefits. Like the forecast of organizational development, the financial forecast is generally prepared for internal governmental use rather than for public purposes since many of the assumptions included in the financial forecast will eventually become questions of policy for the city council.

General Environmental Factors. In addition to the specific components described, the five-year forecast should take note of any additional factors which are considered to be important to the particular community. These may include expected changes in state and federal legislation and programs; overall trends in employment and in the general economy of the surrounding region; anticipated trends in regional conditions such as air pollution, traffic, or open space programs; and major changes in programs or services by other governmental agencies serving the com-

munity and by privately operated public utilities. Assistance in preparing this part of the forecast may be obtained from other governmental agencies, from universities and colleges, and from the business community.

POLICY PLANNING

While the five-year forecast provides a solid foundation for comprehensive administrative planning, departments and agencies also require policy guidelines if their efforts are to be productive. In the policy planning process, the chief administrator must work closely with the city council, his staff, and department heads to review and interpret the forecast in terms of needs, objectives, priorities, and overall resource allocation. While the policy planning process seldom follows any set pattern and is actually a continuing process, it is worthwhile to examine the major considerations which should be included in the policy guidelines provided by the chief administrator to city departments and agencies.

Needs. The policy guidelines should highlight the major unmet needs toward which program planning is to be directed. These critical unmet needs may be described in terms of areas of the city which are to receive special consideration; in terms of social problems which require attention, such as an increasing crime rate or dependency on welfare payments; or the needs may be expressed in terms of deficient programs such as inadequate fire protection or substandard library services. Every effort should be made to describe needs in terms of situations to be met, rather than in terms of programs which should be modified, since the latter type of proposed action will be included in program plans themselves.

Objectives. For each of the identified needs, specific objectives should be identified for each of the succeeding five years. For instance, where there is a need to bring 100 dwelling units up to minimum standard conditions, the objective may be stated in terms of bringing 20 dwelling units into conformance in each of the five years.

Priorities. The policy guidelines should also include the assignment of relative priorities to the various objectives for each of the five years. While the definition of objectives for each of the years indicates a general set of priorities for the entire period, it is equally necessary to show the relative emphasis to be placed on the various objectives within each year. In the first year, higher priority may be given to those objectives which can be achieved immediately through operating programs, while in later years the higher priority may be given to those objectives which can be accomplished only at the time new capital facilities become available.

Resource Allocation. In some cases it may be necessary to accomplish all objectives without any overall increase in resources, while in other cases additional funds or other resources may be available as a result of revenue increases or new programs of other governmental units. The policy guidelines should make clear what, if any, additional resources will be available to the city and should indicate major purposes for which additional resources may be made available, as well as those for which no increases are expected.

Care should be taken to explore general program and departmental requirements in the preparation of the financial forecast, but the policy planning process itself should not become a budgeting session. The purpose of policy planning is to review the overall needs of the community and to relate them to a set of guidelines which can be used in preparing program plans.

Because of the need to be as accurate and comprehensive as possible in the preparation of the financial forecast, the resource allocation guidelines must take into account the support needs of the city's auxiliary or staff functions, such as personnel and finance activities, as well as needs of direct service programs.

Statement of Guidelines. It is important to structure the guidelines in terms of community needs and organizational objectives rather than by departmental designations; department heads should address their efforts to ways of meeting the needs, whether or not the needs would ordinarily be thought of as falling within their jurisdiction. For instance, the urban renewal department may be able to provide the facilities needed for recreation, the

welfare department may find ways of reducing unemployment and decreasing juvenile delinquency, and the public works department may make major contributions to eliminating environmental health problems.

PROGRAMMING AND SCHEDULING

The preparation of five-year forecasts and policy guidelines provides the fundamental framework for comprehensive administrative planning. With the forecasts and guidelines, all departments and agencies should be able to make maximum use of their knowledge and skills in developing effective program and management improvement plans. In many cities the related portions of these individual plans are brought annually into a five-year capital improvements program which incorporates all planned physical improvements to be begun within the ensuing five years.[7] In the more advanced cities, five-year plans for all operating programs are also constructed annually.[8] The importance of five-year capital and operating programs, and techniques of effectively preparing such programs, are discussed at considerable length in *Municipal Finance Administration*.[9] This discussion will, therefore, be limited to only a few key considerations in both capital and operating programming.

These comprehensive administrative programs provide the means for applying the highest level of political and professional knowledge in developing workable action strategies for meeting community needs. It is at this point that the relationship among all programs, and among goals and available resources, must be brought into balance. It is also at this point that the implications of current programs and activities for the future be-

[7] George A. Terhune, CAPITAL BUDGETING PRACTICES IN THE UNITED STATES AND CANADA (Chicago: Municipal Finance Officers' Association, 1966).

[8] George A. Terhune, PERFORMANCE AND PROGRAM BUDGETING PRACTICES IN THE UNITED STATES AND CANADA (Chicago: Municipal Finance Officers' Association, 1966).

[9] International City Managers' Asociation. MUNICIPAL FINANCE ADMINISTRATION (Chicago: The Association, 1962), see especially Chapter 13, "Long-Term Financial Planning."

come clear. Plans must be expressed in terms of cost as well as benefits, and the schedule of action must be brought into conformity with the availability of funds and other resources in each of the five years.

The Capital Program. The capital program usually describes plans for the construction of streets, buildings, and other items of capital outlay which have a cost in excess of $10,000 and a useful life of ten years or more. Each of these planned projects is supported by a program of work and resources required to produce the facility, and the timetable that will be followed in acquiring or constructing it.

Frequent planning errors in capital programming include: (1) failure to give adequate attention to the need for staff effort to plan and supervise the construction of the facility; (2) insufficient attention to the relationship among facilities, such as the relationship of buildings to streets and public utilities; (3) failure to allow for increases in the costs of construction and to ensure that sufficient funds will be available to carry forward all capital projects as scheduled; and (4) failure to analyze and plan carefully for operating program requirements and costs associated with the construction and utilization of new facilities. In recent years, municipalities have often neglected to work out methods of carrying forward their capital programs in the event that federal and state funds for particular projects do not become available as anticipated.

The Operating Program. The five-year operating program is more than a simple extension of the annual budget. In fact, just as the annual capital budget represents the first year of the capital program, the annual operating budget should be developed after the preparation of the five-year operating program. The operating program, which is sometimes called the *public services program,* consolidates all program plans of the government into a coordinated set of actions to meet community needs. The operating program must, of course, take into account the effects of the capital program in terms both of the availability of new facilities and of the requirements of the capital program for additional financing, staffing, and services.

Many factors which are relatively fixed in the operating budget are subject to policy changes in the operating program. Substantial changes in the allocation of staff and other resources among programs may require several years of carefully planned recruiting, training, reorganization, and equipment procurement. Other programmed action may require one or more years of detailed study and analysis prior to the beginning of implementation. Just as the capital program provides continuity from year to year in carrying out physical improvements, the operating program permits well organized action to bring about long-term improvement in public services.[10]

BUDGETING AND CONTROLLING

Many cities are required by law to prepare annual operating budgets for adoption by the governing body. Unfortunately, some cities still view budgets as merely financial devices for determining salaries or limiting the amount of supplies or the cost of equipment to be purchased. This approach may have some value in those few cities where graft and corruption in public service is accepted practice. For the vast majority of municipalities, however, the annual budget, combining capital and operating budgets, is an important element in the administrative planning process for the achievement of community goals. Properly used, the operating and capital budgets authorize current action to meet community needs. They assign responsibility to various agencies and departments for accomplishing specific objectives, and allocate the resources necessary for accomplishing those objectives. Finally, the budgets should be accompanied by a performance reporting system which measures and evaluates progress toward meeting these objectives.

THE ANNUAL PLANNING CYCLE

It has been stressed that comprehensive administrative planning is a continuing process

---

[10] *Ibid.*

which involves elected and appointed officials of the government. Figure 10–2 illustrates the annual planning cycle and the relationship among the major components in comprehensive administrative planning. In a typical city, responsibility for accomplishing the various elements in administrative planning may be delegated to staff aides or distributed among the departments and agencies of the government. But it is the responsibility of the chief administrator to ensure that the planning process is effective and coordinated. To a large degree, the quality of administrative planning will determine the success or failure of the city government in meeting the changing needs of the community it serves.

As illustrated in Figure 10–2, city planning, program planning, and management improvement planning are closely related to the comprehensive administrative planning process. Program planning and management improvement planning are given direction through the forecasts and policy guidelines provided in the comprehensive administrative planning process. In turn, program plans and management improvement plans provide the input to the city's capital and operating programs as well as providing the basis for preparation of annual budgets. The comprehensive planning process provides performance objectives which allow evaluation of progress toward planned achievements. The city planning process depends on city programs for implementation of recommendations, including enforcement of zoning and other ordinances as well as the provision of physical improvements and services. Thus there is an inseparable relationship between city planning and program planning. Since Chapter 12 discusses city planning at some length, the remainder of this chapter will be concerned primarily with program planning and management improvement planning.

Program Planning

Constant change is one of the dominant factors in municipal government as in life generally—today. In most urban communities the population is constantly changing in overall numbers, location, density, patterns of living, aspirations, and values by which residents judge governmental programs. The economy of the nation and of most urban areas is constantly changing, both in terms of levels of production and employment and in types of economic activity. State and federal activities are expanding with major impacts on municipal government.

In many geographic areas, the physical environment itself is changing in ways which directly affect municipalities and their programs: air pollution and water pollution are becoming hazards to life, water supplies are becoming exhausted, and careless development increases hazards from floods and forest fires. Under circumstances such as these, municipal programs require constant reevaluation and revision if they are to retain and improve their effectiveness.

Program planning, like administrative planning in general, follows a process of description and prediction of the organization and relevant factors in the environment; definition of objectives; setting of priorities; development of action programs; implementation; and evaluation and subsequent revision of plans. The professional literature in each of the substantive program areas includes considerable discussion of the techniques and considerations important in each area.[11] Therefore, the following discussion will be limited to the major types of program plans and their relationship to comprehensive administrative planning.

FUNCTIONAL PLANS

Functional plans, such as those for health, education, public safety, and recreation represent the most important of the several types of program plans. Recognition of the importance of these functions has led to the formation of municipal departments charged with planning and implementing programs in these

---

[11] See, for instance, MUNICIPAL POLICE ADMINISTRATION, PRINCIPLES AND PRACTICE OF URBAN PLANNING, MUNICIPAL PUBLIC WORKS ADMINISTRATION, MUNICIPAL FIRE ADMINISTRATION, and ADMINISTRATION OF COMMUNITY HEALTH SERVICES, all published by the International City Management Association.

areas. In recent years, increasing emphasis has been placed on other functions which in many cases have not yet been assigned to separate municipal departments; these include such functions as economic development, housing improvement, and reduction or elimination of poverty.

Even where departments have been created to carry out particular types of programs, functional planning invariably cuts across departmental and agency lines.[12] The health function, for instance, is concerned not only with medical programs, but also with water supplies, waste disposal, air pollution, housing standards and controls, commercial and public food handling, the safety of beaches and swimming pools, environmental hazards, and so on.

[12] See Hatry and Cotton, *op. cit.*, pp. 16–19 for one possible general classification structure of governmental objectives and activities.

To take another example, the education function is concerned not only with public schools for grades 1 through 12, but also such community needs as post–high school education, adult education, job training, retraining for those whose job skills are no longer marketable, and education of the handicapped and the retarded who are not able to benefit from standard school programs.

Because of their breadth, functional plans ordinarily emphasize needs, objectives, priorities, and responsibilities for action to achieve particular objectives, with less emphasis on detailed activities.

DEPARTMENTAL PLANS

Within the structure provided by functional program plans, departments and agencies are in a position to accomplish detailed program planning for those components within their

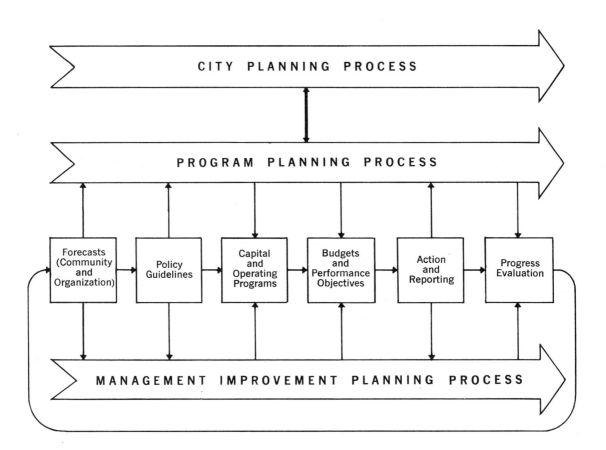

FIGURE 10-2. *The annual planning cycle*

area of responsibility. A police department, for example, may be responsible for certain components of traffic control, for major elements of criminal justice, for aspects of crime prevention, for portions of the civics content of education, for certain types of emergency medical service, and so on. Departmental plans focus on defining detailed operational objectives and development of specific action plans for meeting those objectives with the minimum feasible expenditure of resources.

Departmental plans must be reviewed and evaluated in the light of functional plans, just as functional plans themselves must be considered in terms of the comprehensive administrative plans. This is not to imply rigid procedures, for all of the elements of the planning process affect one another and frequently are carried out, at least partly, by the same individuals. Nor should the planning process be taken to imply voluminous paper work, since many of the decisions made can be incorporated in brief policy statements and standard formats.

PLANS FOR NEIGHBORHOOD IMPROVEMENT

Where there are significant differences in program requirements from neighborhood to neighborhood within a community, it may be desirable to provide comprehensive plans for improvement of a particular area or areas. Such plans include special functional plans for each major program where the needs of the area differ significantly from those of the community as a whole. In the past, communities frequently have prepared area plans for rapidly developing sections of the community or for areas to be annexed. More recently, area plans have been used extensively for parts of the community which are already developed but where there is a need for substantial improvement. Such areas include those which are encompassed in urban renewal programs, neighborhood improvement under the federal demonstration cities program, and community improvement programs not related to particular federal programs. In general, area improvement plans emphasize objectives and priorities which differ from those for the community as a whole and focus

on the specific program action required to meet these unique requirements.

DISASTER AND PREPAREDNESS PLANS

Nearly all communities must be prepared to cope with various types of major community emergencies. Depending on the location and nature of the community, these emergencies may include riots, floods, hurricanes or tornadoes, crashes of aircraft in heavily populated areas, commercial explosions, forest or brush fires in populated areas, loss of water supply, failure of power supply, epidemic diseases, and blizzards. In each of these cases effective planning can reduce death and injury and limit the severity of the emergency. Like functional plans, disaster and preparedness plans frequently cut across departmental lines: unlike functional plans, however, they cannot be scheduled for implementation at a time known in advance and must, therefore, depend on diversion of resources from other activities to accomplish their purposes. Because these types of plans deal with events which are unpredictable as to their details, they must be kept as flexible as possible. In addition, such plans should take into account the possibility of two or more types of emergencies occurring at the same time: for example, plans should anticipate the possibility of major fires occurring during severe storms and accompanied by the loss of electric power and telephone communications.

LONG-RANGE FINANCIAL PLANS

The planning of the financial program should not be confused with the forecasts of municipal finances which are a normal part of the comprehensive administrative planning process. Financial forecasts assume that the municipal revenue policies and tax structure remain the same while analyzing the effect on finances of changes in the community and in governmental programs. In contrast, planning of municipal financial programs requires careful consideration of changes which might be made in city financial policies, including sources of revenue which might be added or deleted, changes in tax rate and structure, initiation or abandonment of service charges, and possible changes in debt management policy.

The planning of the financial program is especially important: financial policies directly affect the citizens of the community and may be a determining factor in their satisfaction with life in the community. Equally important, the financial program indicates to a large degree the variety and quality of services that can be provided by government.

SPECIAL EVENT PLANS

In addition to the types of program plans already considered, most municipalities are involved from time to time in special events which may require formal planning. These types of special events may include centennial celebrations and other community-wide festivities, dedication of major new facilities, visits of public dignitaries, and special commercial events such as circuses, carnivals, and industrial fairs or expositions. Careful planning for such events is required to ensure that they are successful, cause minimum disruption of community affairs, and are properly controlled to minimize hazards to the public and to participants in the event. Municipal resources required for such events obviously will not be available for other programs; this must be taken into account in each of the programs affected.

Management Improvement Planning

Opportunities for improving management exist in every municipal government. The structure of the organization itself is frequently in need of modernization. Budgeting, accounting, and performance reporting systems are frequently inadequate. Training programs, when they exist, seldom meet all the needs of supervisory and operating personnel. New methods, equipment, and technology may be overlooked entirely or may be adapted inappropriately because of lack of careful evaluation and preparation for implementation. Old regulations and procedures may be continued long after they have lost their effectiveness.

Even in organizations where administrative analysis techniques such as those discussed in Chapter 11 are being used, management improvement efforts may be devoted to relatively trivial matters while major needs go unattended. The purpose of management improvement planning is to identify potential areas for management improvement and to ensure that appropriate action is taken to achieve the desired improvements.

To be effective, management improvement must be carried out as part of a continuing planning process, and cannot be pursued haphazardly. Priorities must be established, specific objectives must be set, responsibility must be clearly assigned for each project, adequate resources must be made available for conducting the program, and means of measuring progress toward the objectives must be provided. As with program planning, management improvement planning must be closely coordinated with the overall administrative planning process, and requires regular review by the chief administrator to ensure that individual projects are progressing satisfactorily. These regular review sessions also facilitate reevaluation of priorities within the overall management improvement plan and acceleration of those projects which have increased in importance.

Making Planning Effective

Planning is not an end in itself. It is worthwhile only if the planning process results in improved performance of the organization. Administrative planning cannot be judged in terms of the number or appearance of reports prepared. Instead, the planning process must be evaluated in terms of the action which results from the planning process.

CHECKLIST FOR IMPROVING
ADMINISTRATIVE PLANNING

How can the chief administrator increase the usefulness of administrative planning? The first step is to review existing administrative planning practices in the organization. The administrator may find it helpful to refer to Figure 10–2 and to ask questions such as the following:

1. Is there now an organized administrative planning process that includes all the major elements in the annual planning cycle? If not, is there a valid reason for omitting those elements which are not present?

2. Who is responsible for making annual forecasts of changes in the community and the organization? Are these forecasts accurate? Are they used by department and agency heads in planning their programs? If not, why not? What can be done to improve the quality of forecasts and make them more useful?

3. Does the chief executive provide annual policy guidelines identifying priority objectives for program and management improvement? Are these guidelines followed? Would additional policy guidance allow departments and agencies to focus their efforts more effectively?

4. Are long-range capital programs and operating programs prepared and revised annually? Are they consistent with forecasts and policy guidelines for program emphasis in relation to community needs? Are the capital and operating programs analyzed to ensure that facilities will be available when programs require them, and that staffing will be adequate to operate new facilities?

5. Do the annual capital budget and operating budget incorporate measures of performance and specific objectives for accomplishment? Do the budgets provide adequate means of implementing plans? Is action regularly evaluated and progress compared with planned and budgeted objectives?

6. Is there a regular program planning process? Does it provide for implementation of results of the city planning process? Are functional plans up-to-date for each major function of the government? Are departmental plans adequate? Is area improvement planning effective? Do all units of the organization know what to do and how to do it in the event of a disaster? Do long-range financial plans provide the resources necessary for implementing the capital program and operating pro-

gram? Are special events carried out smoothly, without disrupting other activities of the organization?

7. Is management improvement carried out on a planned basis? Are all major areas of potential management improvement being accomplished in accordance with overall priorities?

If the administrator is not satisfied with the answers to questions such as these, his next step will be to select those elements where immediate improvment is required. In small cities, it may be necessary for him to take the needed action himself. In larger cities, he will likely assign the responsibility for remedial action to his assistants, staff agencies, and department heads. In either case, he should allow for adequate time and resources, for good planning cannot be accomplished on a hit-or-miss basis.

TRAINING FOR ADMINISTRATIVE PLANNING

The success or failure of administrative planning is directly related to the knowledge and skills of personnel carrying on the planning activities. It is not enough to have strong executive direction and clearly defined responsibilities if employees do not have the ability to do the necessary work.

In most organizations, implementation of administrative planning will require extensive orientation and skills training for supervisory and staff personnel at all levels. Each of the persons involved in administrative planning must be thoroughly familiar with the concepts, goals, procedures, responsibilities, and methods of the city's administrative planning process. In addition, many employees will require extensive training in such skills as statistics, report writing, graphic presentation, work planning and scheduling, budgeting, and performance evaluation. Additional training in community analysis and organization analysis may be required, along with basic study of economics, public administration, and subjects such as systems analysis and operations research.

The needed training resources can be obtained through a combination of "in-house" programs, training programs of professional associations, and seminars and courses offered by universities and colleges.[13]

ORGANIZATION FOR ADMINISTRATIVE PLANNING

The topic "Organization for Administrative Analysis and Planning" is considered at some length in Chapter 11, along with means of obtaining assistance from agencies and organizations outside the city government. While particular organizational arrangements will vary with local conditions, it is important to recognize that planning cannot be effective unless there is strong executive leadership, clear assignment of responsibility and authority, and provision of sufficient staff time and other resources to carry out the planning function.

NETWORK TECHNIQUES FOR PLANNING

In recent years a variety of methods have been developed for planning, scheduling, and controlling projects and the implementation of new programs. The most important of these are generally classified as "network techniques," and the more common methods are sometimes referred to as "PERT/CPM."[14] (PERT stands for Program Evaluation and Review Technique and CPM stands for Critical Path Method. Since their original development, both techniques have been modified until there is little difference between the two.)

PERT/CPM identifies the individual activities which must be accomplished to complete a project, which may be anything from writing a report through construction of a complex of buildings. The activities are then shown on a diagram, illustrating the sequence in which activities are scheduled. The length of time required to complete each activity, the manpower and other resources needed for each activity, and the cost of each activity are estimated. Then the network diagram is modified until a desirable combination of time, resources, and cost is found. Responsibilities for

accomplishing each activity are assigned to appropriate managers and supervisors, and the network is used to control the progress of the work. Delays in accomplishment of activities, excessive expenditure rates, or changes in the availability of resources are reported and the network is used to analyze the implications for the project as a whole. As often as necessary (usually monthly), the network is "updated" to reflect current accomplishment, the remainder of the project is replanned as necessary, and the network is revised.

Network techniques have an almost unlimited number of uses in administrative planning.[15] They have been used extensively by governments to plan and schedule a wide variety of activities, including highway right-of-way acquisition, urban renewal projects, capital budgeting, and facility construction. Figure 10–3 illustrates the use of a network technique to plan and control the preparation of a "Demonstration Cities" grant application.

For extremely large, complex projects it is usually desirable to use computers for processing of progress information, calculating the effects of delays, rescheduling completion dates, and calculating the costs of alternative actions to keep the project on schedule. Standard PERT computer programs are available from most computer manufacturers, but usually only for large computers. By far the majority of projects can be handled more economically by manual calculations, including networks with as many as five hundred individual activities.

For administrative planning purposes, it is seldom necessary to construct a network of more than 75 or 80 activities, and in many cases general estimates of time, resources, and costs are used without the detailed calculations which have been developed. In general, only as much detail should be included in the network and accompanying material as is absolutely necessary to allow realistic planning

[13] Charles A. Willis, "City Training Nears Point of No Return," PUBLIC MANAGEMENT, February, 1967, pp. 35–39.

[14] See John Dearden and F. Warren McFarlan, MANAGEMENT INFORMATION SYSTEMS (Homewood, Illinois: Richard D. Irwin, 1966), Chapter 4, "PERT and the Critical Path Method," for a general overview.

[15] For additional examples and a useful discussion of some administrative uses of PERT/CPM, see Mary F. Arnold (ed.), HEALTH PROGRAM IMPLEMENTATION THROUGH PERT (San Francisco: Western Regional Office, American Public Health Association, October, 1966).

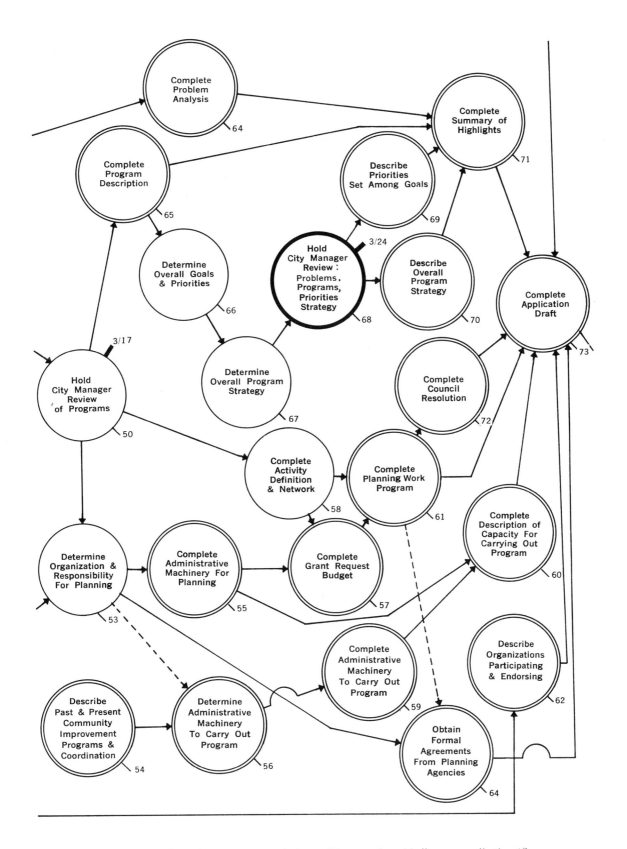

FIGURE 10-3. *Part of an event network for a "demonstration cities" grant application (Source: Alexandria, Virginia, city manager's office.)*

and effective communications among the key management and staff members responsible for the program.

Summary: Importance of Executive Direction

Administrative planning is a vital tool of management. It provides the means for translating community needs and policies of the city council and top administrators into action. It facilitates orderly accomplishment of long-range goals, supplies a framework for co-ordinating the activities of the various units of the city government, and is the foundation of a sound evaluation program. Because administrative planning performs these essential functions, it can be effective only if the chief administrator devotes a major part of his time and effort to it and requires that his department heads give administrative planning a major part of their personal attention.

11

Administrative Analysis

COMPUTERS AND OTHER ADVANCES in technology provide important new capabilities for increasing the effectiveness and efficiency of municipal government. As discussed in Chapter 9, implementation of technological advances also means changing organizational relationships, work flow patterns, and individual responsibilities. Administrative planning to adapt governmental action to changing community needs brings further changes in the organization and workloads as new programs and activities are implemented and existing activities altered.

How can these unending changes be incorporated in the organization without disrupting essential work? And how can the organization keep changing to meet community needs and still achieve the efficiency that can ease the pressure of increasing service demands on scarce resources? Certainly these questions represent major and continuing challenges to the chief administrator, and in that sense have no final answer. But administrative analysis does offer approaches and techniques which can help the chief administrator adapt the organization and its work to changing needs and changing technology, and which can aid in gaining increased efficiency.

This chapter will explore the nature, purposes, and techniques of administrative analysis including work measurement, the uses of statistics, records and their uses, organization for administrative analysis, and resources within and outside the organization which may be used in the analytic process.

The Nature of Administrative Analysis

Administrative analysis is essential to development and implementation of new and improved plans and programs; it is equally essential in adjusting the organization and its activities to the changing requirements of ongoing programs and to making use of advances in the art and science of management. It seeks answers, for instance, to such questions as: What changes in organization will be required by the city council's decision to inaugurate a municipal recreation program? Would the advantages of a central stenographic pool outweigh the disadvantages? Could the welfare department maintain present standards of service with less cost by a change in procedures or organization? What changes in procedure can be made to reduce the "red tape" connected with purchasing? Would a rearrangement of office layout reduce the need for messenger service? What standards can be devised to measure the efficiency of the various departments?

Administrative analysis can be applied to the smallest unit or to the largest: it has application to a one-man operation or to the city organization as a whole. The following examples illustrate the wide variety of uses for administrative analysis.

1. Planning for implementation of new programs and services.

2. Reorganizing existing services and operations for greater efficiency.

3. Establishing the basic organization of the city.

4. Determining specific work assignments.

5. Scheduling the use of equipment and material.

6. Isolating the causes of breakdown in an operation.

7. Establishing records systems for control and reporting.

8. Planning and scheduling line and field operations.

9. Studying and improving office and plant layout.

10. Organizing employee training programs.

11. Accounting for use of resources (men, money, material, time).

12. Establishing workloads, production schedules, workload standards, and a work measurement system.

13. Developing a system of reports for the city council.

14. Evaluating the cost and effectiveness of alternate program approaches.

Even though many types of studies are performed best within individual departments, all administrative analysis is a managerial responsibility of the chief executive, subject to general guidance by the council. It is up to the chief executive to achieve steady progress in implementing the overall analysis program and to ensure the implementation of the government's management improvement plans (see Chapter 10).

PURPOSES OF ADMINISTRATIVE ANALYSIS

Administrative analysis can help the chief administrator increase his government's capacity to achieve community goals. There are four management improvement purposes which may be served by administrative analysis:

1. Clarification of needs and objectives.
2. Increased performance.
3. Improved effectiveness.
4. Increased efficiency.

All of these purposes are closely related to one another and to administrative planning. Until community *needs* have been analyzed, it is impractical to determine organizational *objectives* for action to meet those needs. Increasing the *performance* (or productivity) of an individual, piece of equipment, or facility makes sense only if it contributes toward a greater degree of *effectiveness* in the action taken by the organization to satisfy community needs. *Efficiency*, which is concerned with achieving the lowest practical cost for a given level of effectiveness, requires analysis and selection of standards of effectiveness and performance.

Needs and Objectives. In general, community needs are determined through the political process and are translated into organizational objectives through administrative planning. Before specific action can be initiated, however, it may be necessary to clarify the meaning of needs and objectives in terms of particular organizational capabilities, facilities, methods of operation, and standards.

For example, the need for fire protection in the community may have been widely recognized and objectives may have been set (e.g., reductions in average fire losses to be achieved in a certain period of time). In the process of planning to meet these objectives, administrative analysis may help answer questions such as: Is the personnel department filling fire prevention and fire fighting vacancies promptly with fully qualified men? Is purchasing providing the right equipment when needed? Is technical assistance in records management and statistical analysis being given to the department to aid in planning for changing requirements? Are facilities and equipment adequate and used fully? Are personnel performing in accordance with acceptable standards?

When questions such as these are answered, it becomes possible to translate general objectives into specific objectives for various organizational components and to determine where changes are most urgently needed.[1]

Performance. Administrative analysis frequently deals with performance of individuals, groups (teams and crews), organizational units, equipment, and operations. The chief administrator must know not only how much work is being accomplished, but also whether work performance is on schedule and where

---

[1] For a more complete treatment of translating community needs into organizational action see INTRODUCTION TO SYSTEMS ANALYSIS, MIS Report Number 298, November, 1968, published by the International City Management Association.

and how performance can be increased. Administrative analysis of performance includes developing units of measurement, performance recording and reporting systems, means of increasing productivity, and analysis of variations in performance so that the chief administrator and his department and agency heads may control the work of the organization and take corrective action when deviations from acceptable performance occur.

Effectiveness. The comparison of actual performance with established objectives provides a measure of effectiveness. Because work performance is not necessarily related directly to results, management must always be concerned with the question, "How well is the work performed accomplishing the objectives of the program?" The importance of this question may be seen in the example of a unit responsible for minimum housing code enforcement. A housing inspection may increase its performance (measured in terms of numbers of inspections made) by 100 percent without making any progress at all toward the objective of bringing 50 substandard dwellings per year into conformance with the minimum housing code.

Through comparison of changing community characteristics with objectives and performance, administrative analysis can help to identify requirements for management action, and can provide recommendations for accomplishing needed action.

Efficiency. Analysis of effectiveness alone leaves unanswered one very important question: How *efficient* is the administration? It is the administrator's function to maximize the attainment of governmental objectives by the most efficient employment of the limited resources available to him. From the administrative standpoint, a "good" public library is not one which owns all the books that have ever been published, but one which has used available funds to meet the greatest proportion of community needs for library services.

A high degree of efficiency basically means getting the most effective program possible for the amount of money expended; in other words, achieving the maximum output for a given dollar input. A program can be ef-

fective without being efficient (that is, it produces results, but at too high a cost) ; or in turn, it can be highly efficient but not effective (that is, there was not enough to do a good job, but management did the very best possible with the dollar resources which it had) .

Administrative analysis is often used to gain greater efficiency by simplifying work, eliminating unnecessary activities, and standardizing forms, procedures, equipment, and supplies. But it is essential not to lose sight of overall effectiveness of the organization when seeking greater efficiency.

RESOURCES FOR ADMINISTRATIVE ANALYSIS WITHIN CITY GOVERNMENT

As used in this chapter, the term "administrative analysis" includes activities sometimes performed by managerial aides, research assistants, administrative assistants and analysts, or personnel in operating departments and special agencies. There is no consistent pattern in cities for the distribution or designation of administrative analysis functions. However, a brief review of some of the most common agencies or offices performing such duties will indicate the variety of resources that can be used in the analysis of municipal operations.

Operating Departments. Operating departments employ administrative analysis in seeking to make their services to the public as effective and efficient as possible. In addition, the special skills found in operating departments may be of value to other elements of the organization.

Members of public works departments frequently have highly developed skills in establishing work units, developing performance measures, analyzing standards and specifications for materials and equipment, and scheduling production.

Health department personnel may help design safe and productive working environments for municipal employees in various types of jobs, including analysis of lighting and noise factors, temperature control requirements, and analysis of fatigue reduction in equipment, working positions, and furniture selection. The health department may also help determine physical characteristics and capabilities required for various jobs and develop effective physical examinations to test for required characteristics before and during employment.

As another example, police and fire departments are especially qualified to analyze the requirements for security of facilities and equipment and for the safety of employees. Members of these departments may also be experts in the design and operation of both electronic and manual communications and records systems.

Managerial Aides. Managerial aides may include the budget officer, the finance officer, the purchasing officer, the personnel officer, and the administrative assistant. The duties of each of these positions usually involve responsibility for administrative analysis.

In the process of budget preparation and control, the budget officer is directly concerned with achieving organization-wide effectiveness and efficiency. He frequently assists in clarifying needs and objectives as they relate to the organization, and he may be responsible for devising progress and performance measures and reporting systems. Problems of organization and facilities utilization are often handled by him, and he may be involved in procedures and work flow studies.

The finance officer is usually responsible for cost accounting methods used in the productivity analysis of operations. He also analyzes financial practices throughout the organization.

The purchasing officer analyzes requirements for materials, supplies, and equipment, and he develops standards for these items. He also performs studies to determine efficient inventory systems and procedures.

Among the studies conducted by the personnel officer are those to establish position specifications, to analyze personnel performance, to estimate staffing requirements for new or modified programs, and to assess the adequacy of retirement plans.

The administrative assistant may participate in the types of analyses mentioned above, or he may assist the chief administrator in co-ordinating and directing the analytical activities of the agencies and departments. In addition, he may perform a variety of special studies such as analyses of operations in comparison with other municipalities or analyses of the impact of proposed new ordinances and programs.

Special Agencies. Additional important capabilities for administrative analysis may be located in special agencies such as city planning departments, data processing units, administrative analysis units, and municipal reference libraries.

While city planning departments are concerned primarily with guiding the physical development of the city, they frequently analyze changing community needs and requirements for service and they may play a major role in studies to establish service standards. Members of the staff are often skilled in statistics, demography, and the analysis of spatial relationships among facilities, services, and community activities.

Data processing units often have personnel skilled in systems and procedures techniques, especially in areas such as forms design and control, records systems, clerical work simplification, and information storage and retrieval.

Some cities have established special administrative analysis agencies. The scope and duties of such agencies may include those which would in other cities be found in the organizational units described above, and they may also include special assignments such as annexation studies and coordination of federal and state grant-in-aid projects.

A good municipal reference library can facilitate administrative analysis by providing standard reference books, reports on municipal activities in other cities, general and technical bulletins dealing with municipal problems, and other materials. Municipal reference libraries may regularly circulate bibliographies of reports and materials received, do bibliographical research, and send out inquiries to outside libraries and other information sources.[2]

---

[2] For cities which do not have facilities for a reference library, a bibliographical listing service on public administration materials may be secured from the Joint Reference Library, 1313 East 60th Street, Chicago.

ADMINISTRATIVE ANALYSIS 259

Conduct of Administrative Analysis

METHODOLOGICAL APPROACH

Administrative analysis in cities is a more complex subject than some are willing to admit. Still, with study and experimentation, it is a manageable one. An understanding of what can and cannot be done is essential for effective utilization by management of the right tools at the right time and for the solution of the right kinds of problems. More reliance than ever before is being placed on facts, tested results, and other products of quantitative measurement, and new experiments with measurement tools and techniques are yielding results.

Knowledge of the purposes and processes of municipal government and administration is a prerequisite for the administrative analyst. Knowledge is not sufficient in itself, however. Principles must be applied systematically and intelligently to all administrative problems. The administrative analyst must approach his assignments with a keen awareness of their importance both to the chief administrator and to operating departments.

The study process for administrative analysis generally follows the outline provided below, which is used with minor variations by many cities:

1. Determine objectives of study.
2. Review present situation.
3. Define scope of project.
4. Identify problems to be tackled.
5. List questions to be answered.
6. Select methods of analysis.
7. Plan and schedule study.
8. Collect data and information.
9. Analyze data and information.
10. Consider alternative proposals and their effects.
11. Review conclusions; make recommendations.
12. Review conclusions and recommendations with those involved.
13. Submit report.

Illinois 60637. Other bibliographical listings may be found in the MUNICIPAL YEAR BOOK and most of the periodicals and professional journals concerned with municipal government.

14. Implement approved action.
15. Evaluate results.

The analyst's proposals in all likelihood will form the basis for many administrative policy decisions. This places a great deal of responsibility upon the analyst to make sound recommendations. To carry out his responsibilities to the administrator and operating officials, the analyst should apply several special approaches to his assignments. These are: (1) the scientific method, (2) objectivity, (3) completed staff work, (4) salesmanship, and (5) the "service concept."

The Scientific Method. Applying the scientific method directly to productive operations means "the standardization of data on human behavior and the study and correlation of facts so as to facilitate, coordinate, and simplify work. It means figuring out how to get the most output for the least input."[3]

Objectivity. Objectivity on the part of the analyst goes hand in hand with the use of the scientific method. The lack of objectivity can disrupt the analyst's relationships with operating departments, and once the analyst has lost the confidence of the operating official, he loses much of his value.

Completed Staff Work. "Completed staff work" is the study of a problem and presentation of a solution in such form that all that remains to be done on the part of the division head or the administrator is to indicate his approval or disapproval of the completed action.

This does not mean that the responsible manager can or should be "kept in the dark" about the work of the analyst. He must play a major role in setting the objectives of the study, should review and approve the study plan and methodology, and must periodically review the progress of the study. On the other hand, the analyst should present clear, concise proposals and interim reports so that the manager can simply indicate approval or select alternatives without wasted time.

The procedure for completed staff work may be briefly stated as follows: (1) work out all

[3] Comstock Glaser, ADMINISTRATIVE PROCEDURE (Washington, D.C.: American Council on Public Affairs, 1941), p. 185.

details completely; (2) consult with other staff members; (3) study, write, restudy, rewrite; (4) present a single, coordinated proposed action and do not equivocate; (5) do not present long memoranda or explanations since correct solutions are usually recognizable; and (6) advise the administrator what to do—do not ask him.

Use of Salesmanship. Resistance to change is one of the most fundamental human reactions and one which an analyst is likely to encounter in proposing solutions to administrative problems. This would be a less difficult problem if the analyst possessed the authority to proceed with a recommended change, but usually he does not. The analyst must then sell his recommendations to the department or division head and to the employees who will be affected.

Therefore, the analyst should endeavor to establish a reputation for making only recommendations of real merit. If he is successful in this respect, future recommendations are more likely to meet with attentive hearings. Further, both before and during administrative analysis, he should maintain continuing consultation with those who will be affected by the analysis. Recommendations should be presented to operating personnel and supervisors in meetings where proposals can be discussed, questioned, and examined by those who are responsible for the activities.

The "Service" Concept. An administrative analyst receives many assignments which on the surface may appear to involve a greater or lesser degree of control over departments and divisions. These assignments usually also require an inquiry into some of the operating details of other agencies. Because of these peculiar characteristics of analytical work, it is not unusual to find administrative analysts stepping beyond the scope of their normal functions.

Administrative analysts should not place themselves in a position where they make final decisions that are the responsibility of operating officials. Neither should they place themselves in the position of playing detective and spying on the activities of personnel in other departments and divisions.

The primary function of the analyst is to determine facts, analyze them, discuss these facts and possible alternative solutions with operating personnel, and make recommendations for improvements. Officials in other departments should be made to feel that the administrative analysis unit exists in order to help them solve their problems and improve the efficiency of their departments. Only when this attitude exists in the minds of both the analysts and the operating officials can the administrative analysis unit accomplish the mission for which it was created.

TECHNICAL AIDS FOR ADMINISTRATIVE ANALYSIS

A variety of techniques have been developed for doing the job of administrative analysis. Some are vague and superficial; others are complicated and difficult to use. There are, however, several well-standardized techniques or "tools" in general use by analysts that have proved to be valuable aids in making administrative surveys and work methods studies. These include use of organizational charts, a variety of work simplification charts, space layout charts, and related devices for analyzing and presenting information. Several such devices are discussed below, followed by a brief description of some of the more complex techniques, such as operations research.

Organization Charts. Although organization charts have definite limitations, they are useful both for making organization and administrative studies and as management tools for use in day-to-day operations. A plan of organization becomes clearer and more useful when it is put on paper so that everyone concerned can see and study it in relation to the organization's problems and objectives. An organization chart helps the analyst see working relationships more clearly; aids in defining areas of authority and responsibility; defines formal channels of communication; and shows generally where each operation fits into the organization. Charts are helpful in keeping lines of authority straight and in avoiding confusion in giving or receiving instructions. They also help orient and train new employees.

Three variations of the organization chart

are commonly used by analysts. These are: (1) the simplified chart, (2) the functional chart, and (3) the staffing chart. The simplified chart, illustrated in Figure 11–1, is a skeletal outline of the organization with blocks representing each segment. Each block contains only the name of the department, division, or agency. The primary value of this simplified chart is to show lines of authority and responsibility and the relationship of the various units to each other.

The second type, the functional chart, contains blocks representing each segment of the organization connected with lines showing the flow of authority and responsibility, in much the same manner as the simplified chart described above. In addition, however, each block contains not only the name of the unit, but also a carefully worded statement of the functions or activities assigned to each unit. This type of chart, shown in Figure 11–2, illustrates the manner in which responsibility is placed and work is divided among the various units.

The third type, the staffing chart shown in

Figure 11–3, contains blocks representing each segment of the organization, and these blocks are connected with lines showing the flow of authority and responsibility. In addition, each block contains the name of the unit and a listing of each class of employees that the unit is authorized to employ, together with the number of employees authorized for each job class. The principal benefit of this type of chart is the quick reference it provides to the number and classes of employees assigned to the unit.

Work Simplification Charts. Work simplification has been defined as "a method of attacking procedural problems for the purpose of analyzing the division of labor, the flow of work, and the volume of work."[4] Perhaps work simplification can best be summed up, however, as an organized plan for the application of common sense in finding better and easier ways of doing work. Work simplification may be described as systems and procedures, methods work, or O and M (organization and

---

[4] John M. Pfiffner and S. Owen Lane, A MANUAL FOR ADMINISTRATIVE ANALYSIS (Dubuque, Iowa: William C. Brown, 1951), p. 26.

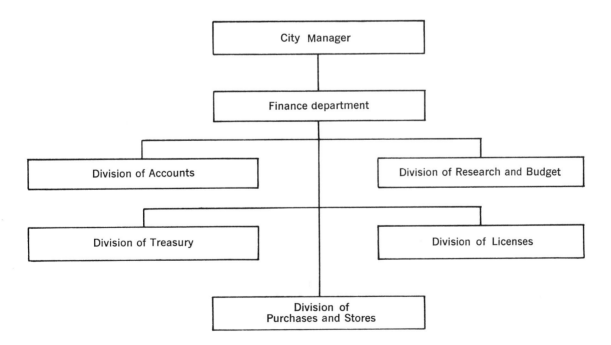

FIGURE 11-1.   *Simplified city finance department organization chart*

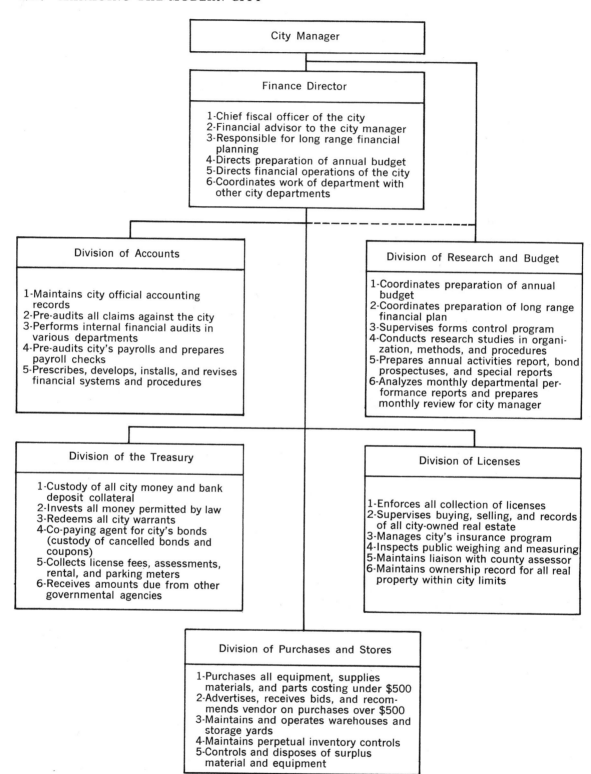

FIGURE 11-2.   *Functional organization chart of a city finance department (Notice the use of an added line to show that the division of research and budget has primary functional responsibility directly to the city manager. Such a line usually would not be shown on the formal, or simplified, chart.)*

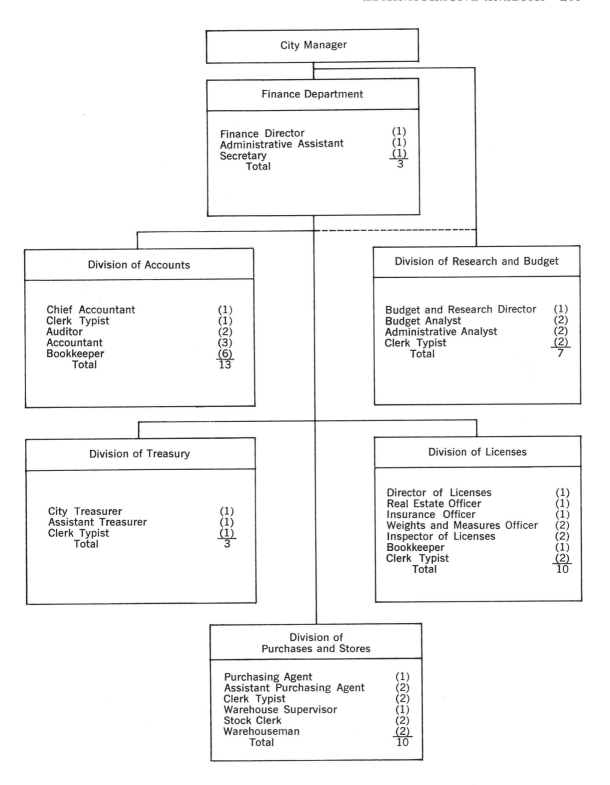

FIGURE 11-3. *Staffing organization chart of a city finance department*

methods). All of these terms, however, have basically the same meaning.

Work simplification can contribute to better management in the following ways: (1) reduce the number and cost of office procedures by eliminating unnecessary operations and by combining or eliminating forms, records, file copies, and so on; (2) utilize personnel more effectively by eliminating unnecessary work; (3) improve services to the public by eliminating or decreasing time-consuming requirements; (4) increase job satisfaction and improve morale by making work easier to perform, clarifying the purpose of the job, and relating the work to other jobs; and (5) bring broader problems of procedure and organization to the attention of department and division heads and the chief administrator.

A considerable variety of formal work simplification tools are at the disposal of the administrative analyst. Their primary purpose is to systematize the gathering of factual data and to facilitate the analysis of work processes. In using these tools, the analyst should remember three principles which apply to any work simplification problem. First, all activities should be productive and contribute to the desired end result. Second, an activity should be arranged in an orderly and logical sequence to provide a smooth flow of work and to establish balanced workloads among the employees performing the activity. Finally, activities should be kept as simple as possible by eliminating unnecessary steps and reducing jobs to their barest essentials.

The conduct of work simplification studies is described in considerable detail in several books and manuals listed in the bibliography. While it is beyond the scope of this chapter to discuss all of the steps in such studies, the principal work simplification tools are discussed briefly in the following sections.

1. Work Distribution Chart. The first step in work simplification is to analyze the work distribution within the office being studied. The work distribution chart is a tool designed to provide this information. It shows (1) all of the activities of the unit, (2) the contribution of each employee to each activity, and (3) how much time the unit and each employee

takes for each activity.

In preparing the work distribution chart, two types of data are needed: (1) an activity list and (2) a tasks list. An activity list is a general inventory of the principal activities of the office being studied. Listing of detailed activities should be avoided. A "miscellaneous" category can be used to group many secondary activities which do not directly contribute to the main objective of the unit. Tasks lists are prepared by each employee in the office to show jobs or duties performed and the estimated number of hours spent on each one. The form used should show the employee's name and position title as well as the unit being studied.

From the above information the work distribution chart is prepared, showing in a consolidated form the activities performed by both the unit and individual employees, and the total time spent on the activity both by the entire unit and by each employee. Examples of a work distribution chart, as well as activity lists, are shown in Figure 11–4.

An analysis of the chart should be made to determine:

1. What activities take the most time?
2. Is there misdirected effort?
3. Are employees' skills being used properly?
4. Are employees doing too many unrelated tasks?
5. Are tasks spread too thinly among employees?
6. Is work divided evenly among employees?

As previously stated, the work distribution chart is only the first step in work simplification. It helps to spot activities which take the most time and indicate areas where other work simplification tools can be used profitably.

2. Work Flow Charts. A work flow chart is used to study the sequence of major operating steps and the organization units involved in the performance of the activity. While it is used to trace procedures between units, the work flow chart is in a sense similar to the work distribution chart since it often will indicate specific areas where further investigation should be made.

The chart shows the various units involved

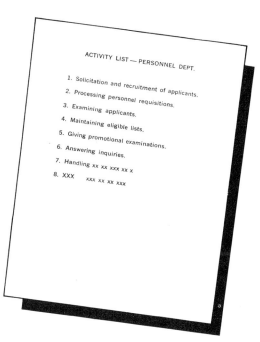

TASK LIST

DIVISION _____
DEPARTMENT Personnel
TITLE Clerk-Typist

Wilma Jackson

Task Number		Hours Per Week
		8
1	Wait on counter	2
2	Check old employee file	1
3	Stamp in Requisitions	3
4	Type	15
5	Operate PBX	10
6	Handle Pxxx xxxxx xx	
	TOTAL HOURS PER WEEK	40

ACTIVITY LIST — PERSONNEL DEPT.

1. Solicitation and recruitment of applicants.
2. Processing personnel requisitions.
3. Examining applicants.
4. Maintaining eligible lists.
5. Giving promotional examinations.
6. Answering inquiries.
7. Handling xx xx xxx xx x
8. XXX   xxx xx xx xxx

WORK DISTRIBUTION CHART

ACTIVITY	TOTAL MAN-HOURS	Wilma Jackson Clerk-Typist	MAN-HOURS	Jack Moody Personnel Assistant	MAN-HOURS	H. Melody Principal Clerk	MAN-HOURS	M. Dickson Clerk-Typist	MAN-HOURS	Daisy Hahn Clerk-Typist	MAN-HOURS	Mrs. Stern (Record Room) Principal Clerk	MAN-HOURS
Solicitation and Recruitment of Applicants	39	Wait on counter / Check old employee file	8 / 2	Write want ads / Wait on counter / Check old employee file	1 / 8 / 2	Write want ads	2	Type want ads / Wait on counter / Check old employee files	1 / 1 / 3	Wait on counter / Check old employee file	7 / 3		
Processing Requisitions	32	Stamp in Requisition	1	Check Requisition / Keep Requisition Register / Maintain Suspense File	2 / 2 / 2	Check requisition / Allocate / Keep Requisition Register / Certification	2 / 10 / 2 / 5	Assist Miss Melody	3	Assist Miss Melody	3		
Examining Applicants	1					Make request for needed examination to provide names for certification	1						
Fingerprinting New Employees	16	Type Fingerprint form	3	Fingerprint new employees / Maintain fingerprint file	10 / 2					Type fingerprint forms	1		
Giving Promotional Examinations	1					Request needed promotional examination	1						
Maintaining Eligible Lists	21					Supervise maintenance of Eligible and Promotional Lists	8	Maintain Eligible and Promotional Lists		Maintain Eligible and Promotional Lists			
Answering Inquiries	32	Operate PBX	15	Answer inquiries	5	Answer phone, letter, and personal inquiries	2	Answer Inquiries	2	Answer Inquiries / Relieve on PBX	6 / 2		
	240		40		40		40		40				

FIGURE 11-4.   *Work distribution charting (Source: Figures 11-4, 11-5, 11-6, 11-7, and 11-8 are from* THE TECHNIQUE OF MUNICIPAL ADMINISTRATION, *International City Managers' Association, 4th ed., 1958, pp. 293, 295, 296, 298, 300, respectively.)*

in an activity and a general description of the sequences involved. Connecting lines drawn between the different units show the flow of work. Each one of the sequences performed by a unit may require detailed study such as those with single-column process charts discussed in the next section. The work flow chart, however, is an excellent starting point since it affords an overall view of the units and sequences involved in a specific activity.

3. Work Process Charts. Work process charts are used by the analyst to study time-consuming activities involving either a single organizational unit or two or more organizational units. Process charting has been defined as "a graphic representation of the sequence of all operations, inspections, delays, and storages occurring during a process and includes information considered desirable for analysis such as distance moved and time required."[5]

This graphic picture is obtained through the use of symbols which describe the various operations in a sequence of work. These operations are generally illustrated as follows:

1. A large circle indicates an operation or action when something is being created, changed, or added.

2. A small circle indicates transportation or movement when something is moved from one place to another.

3. A triangle indicates storage when something remains in one place awaiting action, or is filed.

4. A square indicates inspection when something is checked or verified.

In addition, some process charting systems use the letter "d" to indicate the delays when something is idle or awaiting action. This additional symbol is used to distinguish planned storage or filing from unplanned delays which may occur. As such, the additional symbol may be useful to the analyst in spotting bottlenecks.

Two types of process charts are commonly used depending either upon the complexity of the procedure or the number of organizational units involved.

Single-column process charts, often drawn

on printed forms such as the example shown in Figure 11–5, are used to study the detailed steps in a relatively simple procedure within a single organization unit. The work flow is shown by connecting the appropriate symbol with each step described. The time required for storages and the distances in feet for transportation required are recorded on the form. When each step in the procedure has been recorded, the analyst can add the number of different steps performed, the time required for storage, and the distances in feet.

Multi-column process charts, while used in much the same manner as the single-column chart, are needed when the analyst is studying a complex flow of work often involving more than one organizational unit. An example of a multi-column process chart is shown on the "Chart Selector" in Figure 11–6. The same symbols are used, but notes on what is done at each step, time required, and distances are inserted on the chart next to the symbol.

When the analyst has completed charting a work process, he analyzes each step by asking himself several questions designed to eliminate, combine, simplify, or change the sequence of steps in the process. These questions are: (1) What is done? (2) Why is it done? (3) Where should it be done? (4) When should it be done? (5) Who should do the job? and (6) How well is the job being done?

If changes in the process are indicated after the analysis, the proposed procedure should be charted in the same manner as the existing procedure. This affords a comparative picture of what is proposed.

4. Forms Distribution Chart. The forms distribution chart is another work simplification device. Each form and each copy of a form used in an office requires an employee in the organization to perform a particular task. Forms as such are therefore one of the starting points in many work simplification studies.

A forms distribution chart is useful in studying the flow of copies of a multiple-copy form since it graphically shows the distribution and use of each copy. It is useful where the handling of forms constitutes a large portion of the time required in a process. Often the information shown on the chart will eliminate the

---

[5] Research and Budget Department, Kansas City, Missouri, MUNICIPAL WORK SIMPLIFICATION (Kansas City, Missouri: The Department), unpaged.

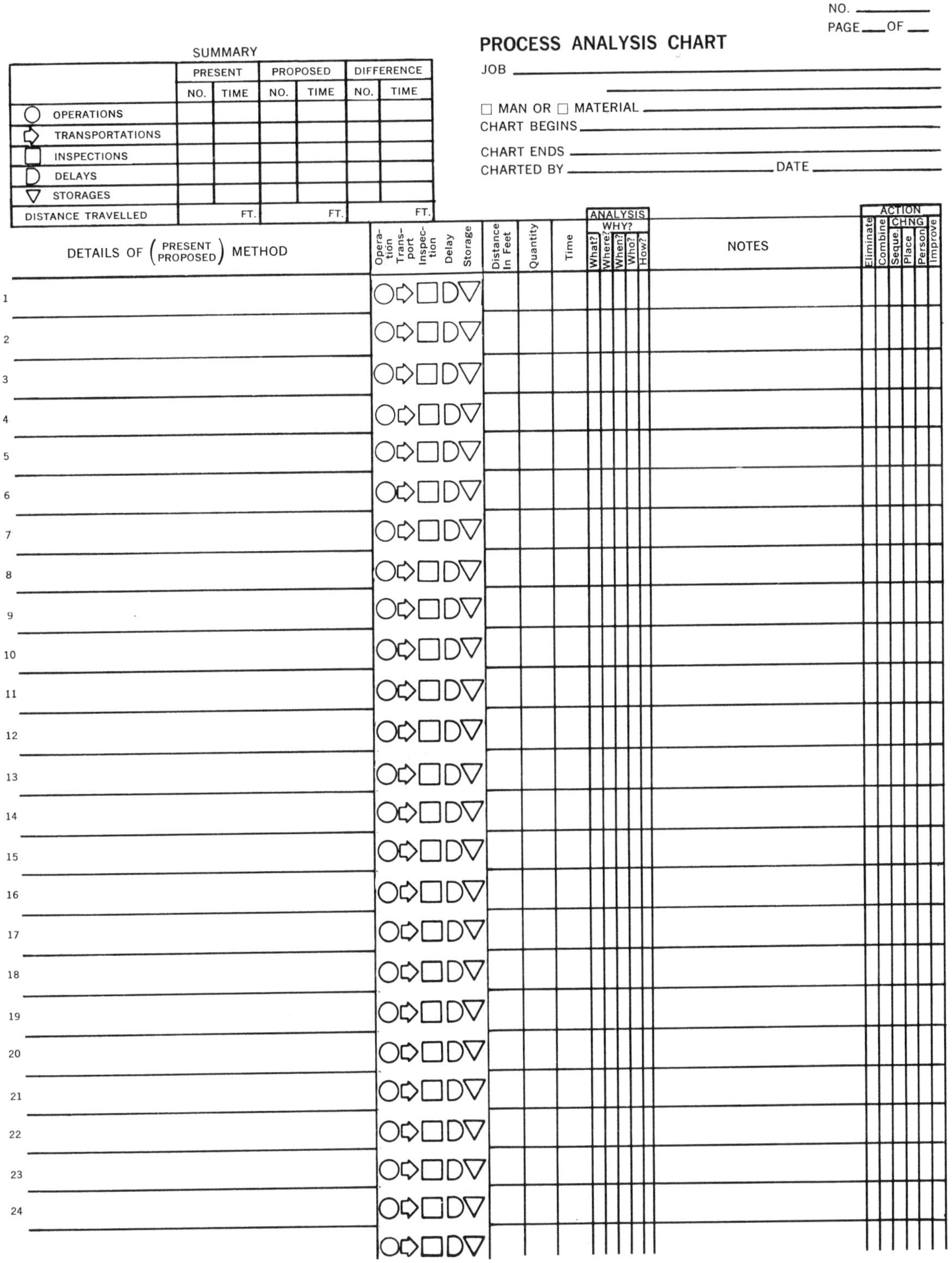

NO. _____
PAGE ___ OF ___

PROCESS ANALYSIS CHART

JOB _____

☐ MAN OR ☐ MATERIAL _____

CHART BEGINS _____

CHART ENDS _____

CHARTED BY _____ DATE _____

SUMMARY	PRESENT		PROPOSED		DIFFERENCE	
	NO.	TIME	NO.	TIME	NO.	TIME
◯ OPERATIONS						
⇨ TRANSPORTATIONS						
☐ INSPECTIONS						
D DELAYS						
▽ STORAGES						
DISTANCE TRAVELLED	FT.		FT.		FT.	

DETAILS OF (PRESENT/PROPOSED) METHOD	Operation Transport Inspection Delay Storage	Distance In Feet	Quantity	Time	ANALYSIS WHY? What? Where? When? Who? How?	NOTES	ACTION Eliminate Combine CHNG Seque. Place Person Improve
1	◯⇨☐D▽						
2	◯⇨☐D▽						
3	◯⇨☐D▽						
4	◯⇨☐D▽						
5	◯⇨☐D▽						
6	◯⇨☐D▽						
7	◯⇨☐D▽						
8	◯⇨☐D▽						
9	◯⇨☐D▽						
10	◯⇨☐D▽						
11	◯⇨☐D▽						
12	◯⇨☐D▽						
13	◯⇨☐D▽						
14	◯⇨☐D▽						
15	◯⇨☐D▽						
16	◯⇨☐D▽						
17	◯⇨☐D▽						
18	◯⇨☐D▽						
19	◯⇨☐D▽						
20	◯⇨☐D▽						
21	◯⇨☐D▽						
22	◯⇨☐D▽						
23	◯⇨☐D▽						
24	◯⇨☐D▽						
	◯⇨☐D▽						

FIGURE 11-5. *Process chart (Source: see caption for Figure 11-4.)*

OBJECTIVE	CHART TO USE	ILLUSTRATION OF CHART				

To study the sequence of major operating steps in an activity and the organization units performing them.

WORK FLOW CHARTS give a general description of the steps in one column; other columns represent organization units. The connecting lines show the flow of work.

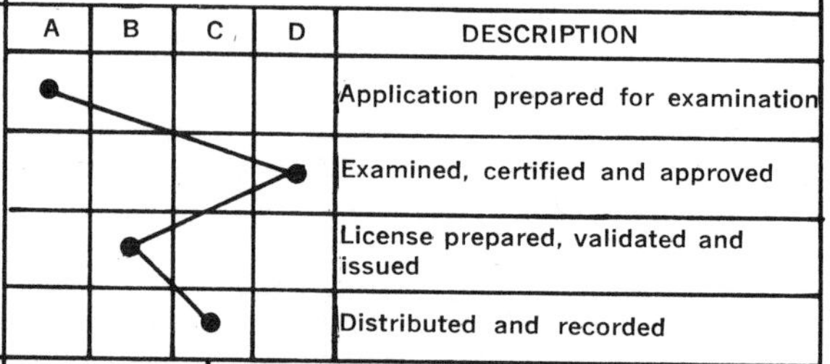

A	B	C	D	DESCRIPTION
●				Application prepared for examination
			●	Examined, certified and approved
	●			License prepared, validated and issued
		●		Distributed and recorded

To analyze the detailed steps in a flow of work that is quite complex or involves several organization units.

MULTI-COLUMN PROCESS CHARTS show steps in greater detail than on a work flow chart—symbols are used to describe steps.

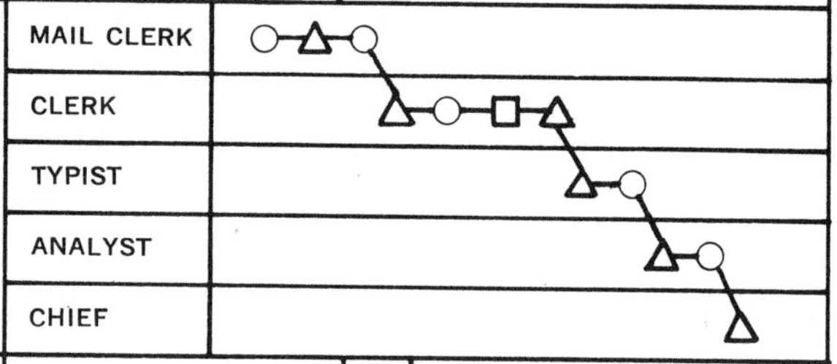

MAIL CLERK ○—△—○

CLERK ○—□—△

TYPIST ○

ANALYST △—○

CHIEF △

To study the detailed steps in a relatively simple procedure such as one within a single organization unit.

SINGLE-COLUMN PROCESS CHARTS are often drawn on printed forms; work flow is shown by connecting the appropriate symbols.

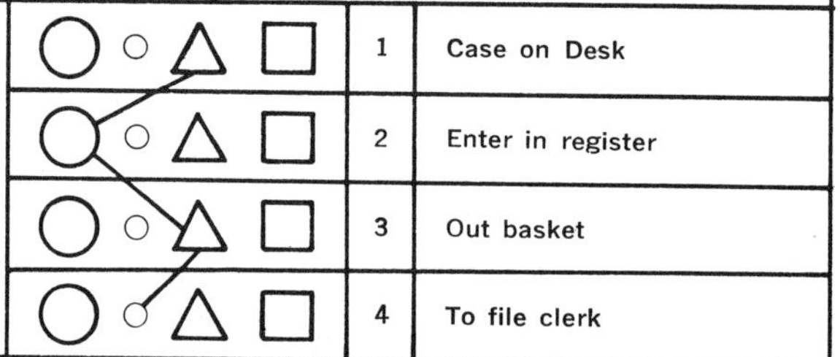

○ ○ △ □	1	Case on Desk
○ ○ △ □	2	Enter in register
○ ○ △ □	3	Out basket
○ ○ △ □	4	To file clerk

To study the flow of copies of a multicopy form.

FORM DISTRIBUTION CHARTS show the number of copies in the first column. The flow of each copy of the form is traced from unit to unit.

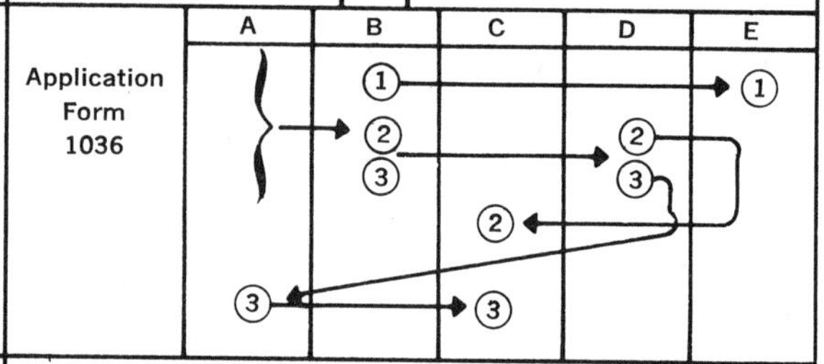

Application Form 1036	A	B	C	D	E
		① ② ③		② ③	①
		③	②		

To improve the layout of the office so that unnecessary steps can be avoided.

LAYOUT FLOW CHARTS involve a diagram of the office made to scale—the flow from desk to desk is shown by arrows.

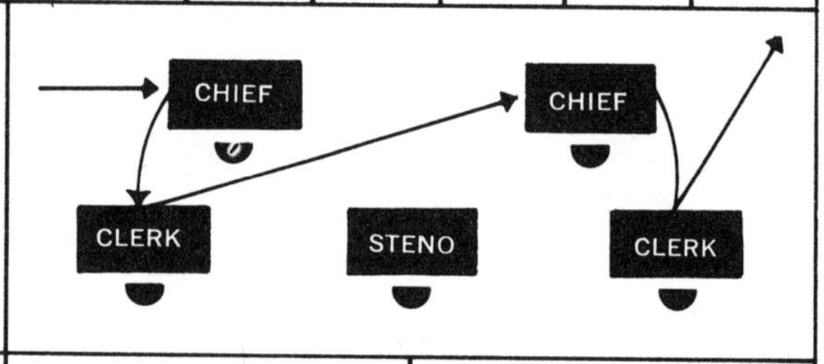

CHIEF   CHIEF
CLERK   STENO   CLERK

To simplify the steps in an operation performed by one employee.

OPERATION CHARTS are of several types; the one shown in the next column is commonly used to study the motions of each hand.

LEFT HAND	RIGHT HAND
1. Move to drawer	1. Move to paper
2. Pick up clip	2. Pick up paper
3. Move clip to paper	3. Idle
4. Attach clip to paper	4. Idle

FIGURE 11-6. *Chart selector (Source: see caption for Figure 11-4.)*

necessity for lengthy, narrative descriptions. As shown on the "Chart Selector" in Figure 11–6, the forms distribution chart shows the number of copies and traces the flow of each copy from unit to unit with notations on the use and disposition of the copies.

The chart will assist in suggesting answers to several questions which have important implications in simplifying work:

1. Is each copy essential?

2. Does any one department or individual receive any unnecessary duplication of copies?

3. Are too many departments maintaining files of the same form when one would be sufficient?

4. Are all departments which need copies receiving them?

5. Are all departments which need clear copies getting original and early copies?

6. Are other forms created from the original form when additional copies would serve the same purpose?

5. Layout Flow Chart. Office layout has important effects on the efficiency of work processes. The layout flow chart is used to study office layout in order that unnecessary steps and time are avoided. It consists of a diagram of the office made to scale with the work flow from desk to desk indicated by arrows. The layout flow chart is intended to show unusually long transportations and back-tracking and is not concerned with what is done with the material. An example of a layout chart is shown in Figure 11–7.

Listed below are some of the questions which the analyst should ask in studying the chart:

1. Do the principal work flows follow straight lines without undue backtracking and crosswise travel?

2. Are persons having most frequent contact near each other?

3. Are files, cabinets, and other records and materials located near employees who need them?

4. Is there surplus furniture which can be moved to provide space for other purposes?

5. Is the best lighted and ventilated space used for work requiring closest attention and concentration?

6. Do the locations of files or other equipment obstruct proper light and ventilation.

7. Does the office arrangement facilitate supervision?

8. Are the employees who use the same equipment grouped together?

6. The Work Count. In many administrative studies the analyst will want to determine the volume of work involved. There are numerous ways to count items and obtain volume data, and the most desirable method will depend on the particular situation as well as the item being counted. In many instances, a representative sampling of the work will adequately serve the purpose of the study and lessen the time and effort involved.

Some of the means of making work counts are: (1) actual count, (2) existing reports, (3) serially numbered forms, (4) weighing, (5) measuring, (6) tally, and (7) recording meters. Typical among things that may be counted are inquiries, checks and vouchers, interviews, posting, letters, phone calls, files pulled, and so forth.

Work counts may be indicated for (1) steps where process charts indicate that work piles up, (2) steps where the flow of work branches off from the main flow, and (3) questionable activities shown on the work distribution chart.

The work count is useful in scheduling work to actual conditions, determining the value of a step, dividing work, spotting bottlenecks, demonstrating personnel needs, and promoting better utilization of personnel. Work counts ordinarily will supplement information the analyst has already obtained through the use of various work simplification tools.

Graphic Presentation. Graphic presentations are quite useful devices in "selling" proposed solutions and in illustrating statistical matter which otherwise might not be clearly understood or might be glossed over in a report if presented in tabular form.

Line or curve graphs are useful in showing peaks and valleys or seasonal trends in various activities. Often a limited number of different types of related statistical data can be shown on the same graph through the use of lines shown in different colors or with different

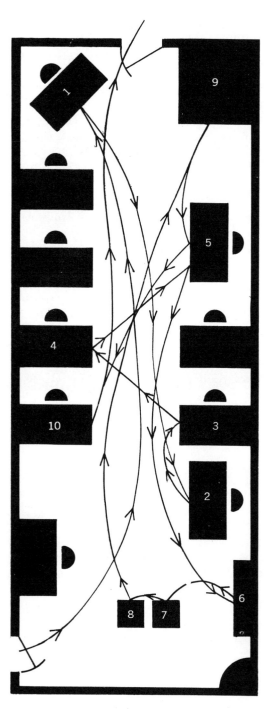

Before study

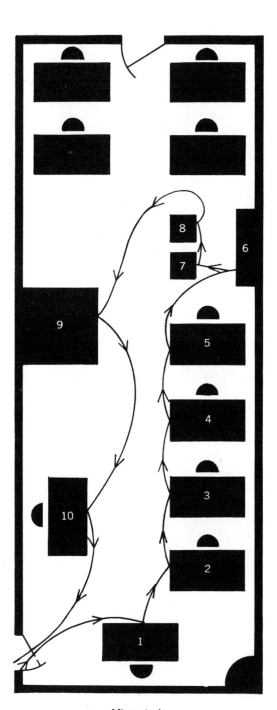

After study

FIGURE 11-7. *Layout chart (Source: see caption for Figure 11-4.)*

symbols if only one color is available for use.

Bar charts are commonly used to compare quantities over a period of time. If a single type of statistical information is being presented, a solid bar will be used for each designated period of time. In some instances, a comparison of parts to the whole over a period of time can be shown on a bar chart by using white, black, and shaded areas on each bar.

Pie charts or area diagrams are the usual method of presenting statistical information in a manner designed to show the relative importance of parts to the whole. Its most common application by cities has been in showing the importance of different revenue sources in financing city government and in showing what activities are financed with the revenue: "where the money comes from" and "where it goes."

Geographic distribution of data can be shown with statistical maps. Such maps may be used to show police and fire manpower requirements in different sections of the city, to determine the adequacy of parks and recreational facilities, or to analyze growth and future growth trends.

Work progress can also be shown quite effectively with the use of charts. This type of chart is known as the *Gantt chart*. Estimated time schedules for the completion of certain projects and tasks can be compared on these charts with the actual progress that is being made. Many variations of these progress charts are available and some are incorporated in patented "control boards" that are for sale. The basic principle involved in all such charts, however, is illustrated in Figure 11–8.

Advanced Analytical Techniques. Since World War II, there has been a rapid development of advanced analytical techniques for solving management problems such as those encountered by the U.S. Department of Defense, other federal agencies, and large business firms. Although these techniques are frequently grouped together under the general title of *management science,* they are often labeled *operations research,* or *systems analysis.* Whichever of these terms is used, the techniques involved all employ rigorous logic, mathematical and statistical approaches, precise definition of objectives and variables in quantified terms, and the calculation of results of possible actions in measurable and comparable terms.

Many management science techniques have potential in municipal problem solving, although the cost of using the techniques may outweigh the advantages in smaller cities.

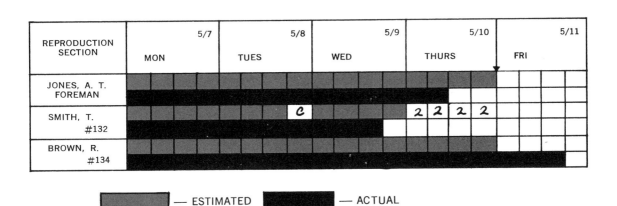

FIGURE 11-8. *Work progress chart (Based on Gantt Man Record Chart. Chart is read as of end of work day on May 10. Foreman was present but failed to get estimated production completed as scheduled for Thursday night, largely because Smith lost two hours in a conference on Tuesday and took Thursday off. Brown has worked four full days and is 6 hours ahead of schedule. Source: see caption for Figure 11-4.)*

IMPROVING ORGANIZATIONAL EFFICIENCY
THROUGH ADMINISTRATIVE ANALYSIS

Increased efficiency, or achieving greater results with limited resources, is one of the most
important objectives of municipal administration. Among the ways in which administrative
analysis may be used to achieve this objective
are organization and administrative studies;
work methods and procedures studies; preparation of procedures manuals; establishment of
work measurement and reporting systems; records management studies; office management
studies; and special studies to provide information needed by executive and legislative officials of the government.

Organization and Administrative Surveys.
Changes in programs, new activities, and the
introduction of new and improved methods
all demand alterations in the organization
structure. An essential corollary of every substantive plan is therefore a study of the necessary changes in organization.

A complete management survey involves a
thorough review and analysis of every segment
of the organization and how well it is being
managed, but opportunities to make such a
survey or to start from scratch and plan a completely new operation are relatively limited.
Most administrators and analysts run into organizational problems in connection with the
reorganization of existing activities, usually involving only one or two units or agencies. Regardless, such a survey can best be performed
by someone who has had some training and
experience in the process of piecing an organization together, and who has sufficient time to
give the problems serious study and analysis.

While it is beyond the scope of this chapter
to delve into the techniques of making an organizational or administrative survey, it may
be helpful to point out some illustrations of
this type of work.

If, for example, the desirability of establishing a central purchasing office is being considered, the chief administrator will want to
know, among other things: (1) how many departmental officials are now engaged in purchasing activities, (2) how much time these
employees are devoting to purchasing, (3) the
total volume of municipal purchases per year,
(4) how many departments are purchasing
identical or similar supplies or equipment, (5)
the amounts and prices of these purchases, (6)
what savings could be expected as a result of
consolidated orders, (7) whether the volume
of purchases is sufficient to require a fulltime
purchasing agent, (8) if not, could purchasing duties be combined with the duties of some
other official so as to permit centralization, and
(9) what items of equipment or supply, if any,
require departmental purchasing.

To find answers to these and related problems requires not only time, but also familiarity with departmental practice and operation. The chief administrator should not have
to spend his own valuable time in making
such a survey, even though the final decision
must be his. Such a problem, however, does
not come within the scope and duties of any
of the traditional departments and agencies. It
is a managerial problem, and its analysis requires specially trained personnel.

A number of organization problems are related to the geographic distribution of work
and personnel. In the smaller cities there may
be no district offices or substations in any of
the departments. In most medium and large
cities, however, consideration should be given
to decentralization of fire and police departments, public health field offices, building inspection substations, conveniently located
street maintenance equipment and supply
yards, and perhaps other district offices and
substations. If this decentralization is to be
based on logic rather than tradition or local
pressure, careful study of the various problems
is needed. In too many cases a geographical
distribution which once may have been logical
has been perpetuated long after the circumstances which justified it have changed. Such
problems are particularly appropriate for study
by an administrative analysis unit.

Work Simplification. Work simplification
studies focus attention on *how* the work is being performed, and seek to simplify or otherwise improve the process so that greater productivity will result. There is a normal tendency in most organizations to add controls,
checks, and reviews as different problems or sit-

uations appear to point out the need for them. There is not the same inclination, however, to review the entire procedure and discard the steps, forms, or processes that have outlived their usefulness. A periodic appraisal of these work methods and procedures is essential if the organization is to continue operating efficiently.

Procedural studies have been prominent in the application of scientific management to private business. Time and motion studies of every operation have been made in some companies in order to find the one best way to do a job and to eliminate unnecessary routines. Although municipal officials may not need to go to the extremes that private industrial engineers have in their study of procedures, the basic approach can be very much the same.

Among the many procedures that need frequent reexamination are those connected with accounting and cost accounting, payroll preparation, issuance of licenses and permits, purchasing, tax collection, and control over municipal stores and supplies. In addition, there are countless minor procedures or established routines in every office. The easy way is to follow the old established patterns and procedures. The better way is to subject all procedures and routines to frequent reexamination by persons trained to appraise the effects of procedures on administrative efficiency.

Records Management. Nearly every activity of a municipal government requires a considerable amount of record keeping. An indication of the growth and significance of record keeping is that today there is one office worker to every eight nonoffice employees, while in 1900 there was only one office worker to every 30 nonclerical workers.

The importance of the custody and retention of records is evident from the serious legal penalties attached to "willfully and unlawfully concealing, removing, mutilating, obliterating, falsifying or destroying" records, to quote from a typical law. Such laws exist because records are the means by which public officials in a democracy render accountings to people. They also protect legal rights of countless citizens. They are important tools of administration and the sources of many kinds of information. They may be termed the "official memory" of an organization.

A unified records management system ensures management that records exist and are used for control of operations, accountability to the public, and protection of legal rights of citizens and the government, without being cluttered by records which have outlived their useful retention periods. Such a system should include a forms control program, a files control program, and a systematic records disposal program.

1. Forms Control. Printed and duplicated forms constitute a high percentage of the records requiring control. The records control program is made easier if control is exercised over the creation of forms. Forms control seeks elimination of unnecessary forms, consolidation of related forms, better design of forms for easier use, and selection of paper and ink of a quality in keeping with the retention period determined under the records control program. Study of forms for these purposes cannot be divorced from appraisal of procedures with which forms are used. Process charts, work distribution charts, work counts, and other techniques are often valuable for the study of procedures for form utilization.

2. Files Control Program. This is a program of improving office filing systems and methods to facilitate the use of office records, organizing the office filing systems to simplify the removal of office records for disposal or transfer to inactive storage, and controlling the flow of records into and out of office files.

3. Records Disposal Program. Not all forms placed in a file must be retained indefinitely. Some can be destroyed after a relatively short period; others must be retained for a longer period either because of use or legal requirements, although they may be placed in an inactive file which occupies comparatively inexpensive storage space; and still a third category of records, such as deeds to property, must be retained virtually forever. The goal of a records disposal program is to inventory all existing records, establish schedules for removal to inactive files, and ultimately to dispose of all records which the organization is not required by law to retain.

Work Measurement Standards and Report-

ing. One of the most essential steps in establishing management control is to devise methods for measuring and evaluating the work of the various departments and agencies. Not only is some means of reporting productivity essential, but standards or other measuring devices are also needed to give meaning to, and serve as the basis for evaluating, the reports. These reports provide the supervisor with information about what his subordinates are doing, how well they are doing their jobs, and what problems they are encountering. If supervisors are to receive the information they need for managerial purposes, the records system must collect sufficient and reliable data and the reporting system must relay this information to the proper officials in the most useable form.

Office Management. The term "office management" is used differently in public and private administration. In private business, office management usually includes such functions as accounting, building maintenance, collection of statistics, general efficiency studies, the organization and operation of stenographic and clerical services, and other related functions. In governmental organization, office management has no very definite or generally recognized meaning.

Regardless of how the term is defined, there are some aspects of office management that have broad administrative significance and require careful study. A few of these problems will be suggested and briefly discussed by way of illustration.

1. Office Design and Layout. Office layout has a vital effect upon efficiency of clerical operations and upon organizational relationships in general. Departments which have frequent interrelations of a routine character should be located in adjoining quarters. For example, the agencies of the treasurer, city clerk, and controller might well be given adjoining offices. Those departments that have frequent contacts with the public should be given locations within city hall or other public buildings that will facilitate these contacts.

Internal office design is even more important. In too many agencies, office arrangements have grown up without any plan or pattern. As a result, many offices are badly crowded while others waste valuable space. Not only must employees be given sufficient areas and adequate fixtures and equipment, but the location of individuals and of office furniture and equipment should be based on two primary factors: (1) convenience to the public, and (2) flow of work.

The first factor should be predominant in departments having a large number of public contacts, and it dictates not only the arrangements for public convenience, but also the assignment of the newest furniture to those coming in closest contact with citizens. The second factor involves the movement of papers and materials through and between departments. Work should flow, as nearly as possible, in an unbroken straight line from desk to desk and from department to department.

2. Selection of Office Machinery and Equipment. The increasing volume and the complexity of municipal business call for modern machinery and equipment in many municipal offices. There are now available many new types of machinery for bookkeeping, accounting, addressing, mailing, record keeping, and other common activities. The need for modernization of office methods by the adoption of new machines is generally recognized, but actual decisions as to what machines are most appropriate and what can be afforded require careful investigation.

Equipment selection studies involve complete analyses of present operating methods as to time, total cost, accuracy, and final form, together with analyses of such questions as what machines are available, what their cost is, what savings in time and expense can be produced by machine methods, and the adaptability of different machines to various uses. Such studies require personnel who are familiar not only with routines and mechanics, but also with the administrative implications of office methods and procedures.

3. Standardization of Office Supplies. Unless careful supervision is exercised, there is a natural tendency for individual municipal offices to use too great a variety of office supplies.

Personal preference and habits become crystalized, with the result that the city is purchasing too many different kinds of paper, typewriter ribbons, carbon paper, and other items of supply. To a certain extent this problem is one which the purchasing agent may solve by consultation with different department officials.

In many cases, however, it is more than a problem of standard specifications. For example, studies may be made to determine the most appropriate and economical duplicating methods for various types of reports. The specific duplicating method used will affect the cost of the materials used. If employees are aware of the results that can be attained with the different methods, they will be more likely to choose the method of reproduction involving costs consistent with the results desired. There will be less likelihood then that the most expensive duplicating method will be used when another method would be sufficient.

Preparation of Manuals. The development of procedure manuals is one of the best available means for accomplishing improvements indicated by administrative analysis. Whether the development of these manuals provides the motivation for procedural studies or is the culmination of a series of studies, they can be important tools in achieving uniform work within a single unit or throughout the organization as a whole.

The major reasons for developing procedure manuals are:

1. To develop and simplify standard working procedures and practices.

2. To coordinate and define policies, functions, and activities of the organization.

3. To train employees in the details of new procedures.

4. To aid in the development and training of new employees.

5. To encourage improvement in operating methods.

A typical procedure manual for an organizational unit will include or make reference to laws, rules, regulations, and directives which affect all units, and it will include descriptions and illustrations of the standard work methods or procedures to be followed. Illustrative materials such as forms used, work flow charts, process charts, and forms distribution charts are helpful in presenting the procedures so that they are both comprehensive and easily understood.

Clarity is the key to a good procedure manual. The manual, to be useful, must be used by the persons concerned. The best procedures, however, will be of little value unless they are written in such a way as to be clear to every employee—not just to the analyst preparing the manual.

The information presented in the manual will be gathered in much the same fashion as material for other administrative studies, and many of the analyst's techniques and tools will be used. After the necessary materials have been gathered and analyzed and preliminary drafts have been prepared and edited, the tentative manual should be submitted to key supervisors to obtain their constructive criticism as to the clarity and usefulness of the information. Supervisors should note and describe any differences between actual procedures and those stated or illustrated in the manual, and add procedures that may have been omitted. In addition, supervisors may be able to clarify the description of new or revised procedures.

Special Assignments and Studies. The chief administrator and council members frequently have special questions concerning various activities which may require a considerable amount of investigation or research to answer. Unless there is someone in the organization to whom these special projects can be assigned, the questions may go unanswered. The administrative analysis unit is especially well equipped to make these studies and submit reports to those who raise the questions.

A somewhat different task that might also be assigned to the administrative analysis staff is the drafting of administrative orders, rules, and regulations. The person drafting the order must be thoroughly acquainted with the administrative organization and with current procedures or practices in the government. He must know what personnel in the organization will be affected and then draft the order so that its meaning will be clearly understood by those for whom it is prepared.

Aside from the need for skilled drafting of orders, it is helpful to have all new orders and regulations cleared through some one office or agency so that they will be correlated with other orders and regulations and with current practice.

Administrative Measurement

Administrative measurement is a way of describing and recording important aspects of the community and of the operations of the government. Even in the smallest community the chief administrator cannot personally observe and remember everything for which he is responsible; nor could he rely entirely on personal experience and memory to provide the information for effective administration.

Administrative measurement, then, is concerned with answering two major questions: What is to be measured to permit effective administration? And, how will the measurements be made in meaningful, standardized terms? When statistics and records are combined with adequate measurement, the chief administrator gains an overall view of the operations of his organization as they change with time. Further, he gains a framework within which administrative analysis can be used to good advantage.

Administrative measurement may be a continuous process, as when it is used in cost accounting or performance reporting. In other cases, administrative measurement is used for a special study such as cost-benefit analysis or a work simplification study. In all cases, the results are for the use of management in bringing about improvements in performance of the organization.

Who does the measurement? Many employees may be involved: time clerks, supervisors, statistical clerks and cost clerks; or even at higher levels, cost accountants, budget staff, personnel staff, the organization and methods specialists, statisticians, the city engineer, the traffic engineer, the head of the police records

bureau, an administrative assistant to the city manager, the research staff, and perhaps others.

TYPES OF ADMINISTRATIVE MEASUREMENT

Among the common types of administrative measurement are the following:

(1) Simple counting and recording (by hand or mechanically);

(2) Cost accounting (by jobs or projects, or for continuous operations);

(3) Cost and performance measurement (of a particular operation, activity, or program, or of the work of a particular employee or group);

(4) Statistical analyses and computations (e.g., correlation of two or more sets of data to measure meaningful relationships);

(5) Measurement of community characteristics (including crimes, fires, and similar occurrences); and

(6) Mapping (and the showing of related data in proper spatial juxtaposition).

Since the purpose of administrative measurement is to assist in decision making, there is need for continuing development and revision of measurement standards and techniques to keep them responsive to management needs. The job of perfecting measurements is not an easy one, and it is never finished, but it is an important part of any management improvement program.

USES OF ADMINISTRATIVE MEASUREMENT

Much of administration rests on intuition and impressions, but these are not satisfactory substitutes for careful, objective analyses of governmental services. The administrator's eyes are not all-seeing, his judgments are subject to error. He needs to make use of every available device for increasing the range of his vision and the soundness of his decisions. The difference between good and bad management, or between good management and mediocre management, is often in the quality of decision making. Measurement's most important contribution is in supplying the basis for better decision making. The administrator will not sharpen his decision making, or in more general terms "will not learn from experience," unless he constantly reappraises objectively.

Applications in the Budget Process. Measurement supports decision making throughout the programming and budget formulation period. Each year the administrator must submit program plans and financial estimates for the ensuing year. Measurement results are embodied in the vast number of decisions that go into budget formulation. This is true whether management is engaged in preparing a capital budget, a current budget on a line-item or lump-sum basis, or a current budget on a performance basis. Measurement becomes increasingly important, however, as the budget moves closer to a program or performance basis.

The availability of such measures as work program data, unit costs, and statistically established standards determines in large part the realism of the budget. Value judgments must be made at every step of budget formulation, but administrative measurement data can improve the quality of these value judgments.

Administrative Control. Another important use of measurement is in exercising administrative control over departments and personnel. Measurement techniques furnish the administrator with an operating audit instead of the traditional accounting audit with all of its limitations.

A system of administrative reports will permit control, not only of the operations of an entire department, but also of individuals within the departments. Departmental reports are ordinarily a composite of reports by individuals, and they should show not only how well the department is functioning as a unit, but also how well each of its employees is working. For example, public works records may identify a truck driver or sweeper operator who is covering too few miles, while the police reports may reveal a police officer who is unable to cover his assigned area.

Regular study of the various administrative reports of measurements, together with comparison with reports of previous periods, is a useful way for the administrator to maintain current knowledge of the operations of departments and to determine when corrective action is needed.

Public Information. The products of measurement often assist the chief administrator in presenting a full and understandable account of his stewardship, both to the council and to the citizens. Work performance data and unit costs make good reporting material, especially when graphically presented and compared with standards of prior years' performance.

Limitations to the Quantitative Approach. The uses of measurement in municipal administration, however, are not clearly understood until one also understands the limitations upon the application of yardsticks, ratios, and unit costs. Not all decisions require quantitative facts as a base. Typical are decisions in the realm of human relations and public relations. Even performance sometimes defies quantification. The millions of gallons of water purified monthly at a water filtration plant can be metered, but the end products of a research worker, a staff member of the city planning department, or of a staff lawyer in the corporation counsel's office cannot accurately be measured. In most municipalities, however, there are important operations where administrative measurement is practical but has not yet been used to full advantage. It is these operations that should be reviewed first.

SOME PROGRAM APPLICATIONS

To illustrate how measurement can be used by the administrator in dealing with problems, four situations where such techniques have been applied successfully will be presented: the development of a police beat layout, the use of cost accounting in administrative control, the use of standards in inspectional activities, and the analysis of the fire problem.

Layout of Police Beats.[6] The desirability of making an effective distribution of police personnel is quite evident. The greatest efficiency cannot be reached except by a distribution of manpower that will result in an equal amount of work for each officer and a distribution of police service over the city during the hours of the day and night in

---

[6] The basic approach described here was worked out by Chief O. W. Wilson, and has been applied, with modifications, in a number of cities: Berkeley, Wichita, San Antonio, Cincinnati, Greensboro (North Carolina), and others. O. W. Wilson, POLICE ADMINISTRATION (New York: McGraw-Hill, 1950), pp. 500–512.

proportion to the needs and to the total force available.

How, then, does the police chief distribute his force equitably? In some cities the patrol force is simply divided into three platoons of equal size, and each platoon works an eight-hour shift. Further, the total area of the city is divided into fixed beats which are patrolled by members of whichever platoon is on duty. Yet conditions vary in each hour of the day, and varying hazards create varying demands for police service. A police hazard may be created by a poorly lighted area; by the residence of a large number of truants and delinquents in an area; by pool halls or "social clubs" and dance halls where gangs may thrive; by valuable stocks of easily moved merchandise in stores or warehouses; and by many other conditions.

Hazards may seem to be too abstract a device to use as a measure of the police service which must be supplied, but for the most part police hazards are definitely measurable in two ways. First, hazards may be measured by the amount of crime which accompanies them, expressed in terms of major offenses, minor offenses, miscellaneous complaints, property loss, and arrests. Second, hazards may be measured by the amount of routine duty time required for adequate protection against them.

Data from police department records then may be used to measure the percentage of complaints, major offenses, arrests, and property loss which fall on each platoon and, likewise, the relative load of routine duty time falling on each platoon. If it is found that one platoon carries 45 percent of the load then that platoon should normally have 45 percent of the available resources of the force, augmented as necessary in special situations.

The next task is to divide the city into beats for each platoon so that each beat will carry about an equal portion of the load. If there are ten patrolmen available for a given platoon, then the city may be divided into ten beats for that platoon so that the work represented by each beat will average about one-tenth of the total.

While a system based on these methods will not be perfect, it will be far in advance of the system of distribution based entirely upon arbitrary rules of thumb. Further progress may be achieved by isolating the above mentioned factors, adding to them many others, and determining the relative value of each as a crime determinant and as a crime deterrent. Then, instead of giving an equal weight to a few of the factors, each factor could be weighted in proportion to its value as a deterrent or determinant of crime.

Work Measurement. Two examples will indicate how work measurement can be applied as a tool for analysis and control of departmental operations and in decision making.

1. Office Operations. The city of San Diego, California, has applied work measurement to clerical operations. The measurement units listed below were established for office activities incident to the administration of city licenses and sales tax. The standard unit man-hours were developed after the entire procedure had been subjected to a thorough methods study, advantageous revisions accomplished, and personnel trained in the new methods. The unit man-hour standards were established by the same trained analyst who had made the methods revisions and trained the employees in their application. The standards were developed, operation by operation, through a combined method of actual, on-the-spot observations for repetitive operations, and estimates based on past experience for the more elusive elements. Where operations were performed on machines of fixed operating speeds, machine time was computed from the known speed of the machine with observed handling time and normal allowances added to complete the standard.

The work units used were:

1. Number of combined business licenses and sales tax permits issued to licensees for the first time.

2. Number of business license renewal applications prepared and mailed.

3. Number of renewal business licenses issued.

4. Number of business license delinquent notices mailed.

5. Number of sales tax returns prepared and mailed.

6. Number of completed sales tax returns processed.

7. Number of sales tax delinquent notices mailed.

8. Number of dog licenses issued.

9. Allowance for the part of the group leader's time actually spent in supervision using the hours worked by employees supervised as the work unit.

10. Allowance for handling telephone or personal requests for information based on the total actual working hours for the group.

Wherever possible, work units were selected which could be accumulated as a by-product of an essential operation. For example, the register on a mailing machine counted the pieces mailed, and a data processing machine (tabulator) furnished a count of business licenses and sales tax permits as a by-product of preparing revenue summaries.

The cost control reports served several purposes. Tabulations of periodic reports furnished excellent supporting data for annual budget requests. The establishment of standards furnished all levels of supervision with yardsticks, and any unfavorable variation in the relationship between actual and standard performance directed attention to unauthorized changes in established methods which might otherwise have remained undetected.[7]

2. Standards in Building and Safety Inspections. In the city of Los Angeles, the building and safety department consisted of several divisions. Some years ago the bureau of budget

[7] Abstracted from Orin K. Cope, "Cost Controls for Office Operations," MUNICIPAL FINANCE, February, 1950, pp. 117–22.

and efficiency, after investigating the nature of the inspectional work in four divisions, and after examination of statistics of prior years and consultation with independent contractors and engineers, set up the standards shown in Table 11–1.

The standards were used to determine the personnel requirements of the department, to prepare and control the department's budget, to adjust personnel requirements during the year, and to increase departmental efficiency. For example, on the basis of past records plus forecasts of building trends, it is possible to estimate the number of permits likely to be issued, and thus to arrive at the number of inspections required. Again, a knowledge of the number of inspections to be made and the mileage per inspection makes it possible to estimate the number of miles to be traveled and the amount to be allowed for travel expenses in the budget. Finally, the standards can be used as a basis for increasing the efficiency of work performed and reducing costs. If, for example, the mileage per inspection increases over a period, the causes are determined and appropriate action taken.[8]

Methods of Measuring the Fire Problem.[9] A final illustration of the use of measurement in administrative research is in determining the nature and extent of the fire problem.

[8] Municipal Finance Officers' Association, GOVERNMENTAL COST ACCOUNTING IN THE LOS ANGELES AREA (Chicago: The Association, 1941), pp. 8–9.

[9] Abstracted from MUNICIPAL FIRE ADMINISTRATION (Chicago: International City Managers' Association, 1956), pp. 6–14. For an alternative approach see Simon, Shepard, and Sharp, FIRE LOSSES AND FIRE RISKS (Berkeley, California: Bureau of Public Administration, 1943).

Table 11–1. STANDARDS FOR INSPECTIONAL WORK

Unit of measurement	Standard for			
	Building division	Electrical division	Plumbing division	Heating & ventilating division
Average no. of inspections required per permit	5.0	2.3	2.6	2.3
Average no. of inspections possible per man-day	25.0	15.0	22.0	22.0
Mileage per inspection	.78	1.5	1.3	1.5
Plans to be checked per man-day	3.8	—	—	—

Necessary data would include information on what there is to burn, what is burning, and where it is burning.

A map of the entire city indicating what areas are built up is helpful in showing what there is to burn. One map can be used to show type of construction for the entire city, while another map can be used to show population density and types of occupancy. Such maps, accompanied by a detailed description of building and use characteristics in each area, can be extremely helpful in assessing needs for fire protection.

The next step in analyzing the fire problem involves the study of the common fire hazards likely to be found in any occupancy: matches; smoking; housekeeping; lockers and cupboards; wiping rags and waste; oily materials; packing materials and combustible fibers; furnaces; grinding wheels; blower systems; air conditioning; construction operations; fumigation; and so on. Study of the various hazards in relation to occupancy in a given city can provide the basis for measuring the relative fire risk in each part of the city.

An analysis then should be made to discover the number of fires and loss for each type of occupancy according to the time of day of the fire as well as specific cause or causes.

Given these kinds of data, measurements can be made of the degree of fire risk in each part of the city, expressed in terms of estimated potential loss of lives and estimated potential dollar loss. Such measures may then be employed in determining the location of fire stations and in the assignment of men and equipment so as to provide the greatest capability in areas of greatest risk.

Summary

The need for administrative measurement is present in nearly every aspect of municipal operations. Perhaps because the need is so pervasive, measurement is frequently taken for granted in applications like accounting, work measurement, and performance reporting. Yet the chief administrator should constantly question measurement practices in the organization. Are the measurements used accurate and meaningful for purposes of managing the or-

ganization? If they are not, he should institute prompt action to obtain more valid measures; poor measurement will not contribute to sound decisions.

Administrative Statistics

Like the use of measurement, the use of statistics has become so commonplace that the administrator may give little thought to the statistics he employs. But just as the value of many types of administrative measurement depends on the statistical methods used to interpret the measurements, the value of many types of administrative analysis depends on the statistical methods employed. Statistics frequently occupies a key position between the "raw data" of measurement and the conclusions upon which management decisions are based.

Statistics, in general, refers to a body of methods for making improved decisions where uncertainty is present and where the important factors can be described and summarized numerically. Does this mean that the use of statistics is limited to objects which can be counted? Not at all. What it means is that the analyst must be able to express numerically what he wishes to study. For instance, citizen attitudes toward the quality of a municipal recreation program could be determined through statistical analysis of a multiple choice questionnaire survey which asked the person to rate each component of the recreation program on a scale allowing answers from 1 (outstanding) to 5 (very poor).

Uses of Statistics

What, then, are the major ways in which statistics can be used in administrative analysis? Most uses of statistics fall within five general categories.

First, statistics is used to estimate totals from limited data, usually referred to as *sampling* or *population estimating*. In the example of a survey of citizen attitudes toward the quality of a recreation program, statistical methods could be used to select a relatively small number of citizens who would be surveyed. The results gained from this sample could then be used to estimate statistically the responses which would have been obtained from all citizens. The *population* could also be all the parcels of real property in the municipality, and a sample could be used to estimate the total increases in tax revenues if all properties were reassessed based on current market values.

A second category of statistical uses involves detecting differences—and the magnitude of differences—in characteristics of a number of people, objects, events, or areas. For instance, statistics could be used to determine whether there was any significant difference in citizen attitudes toward the recreation program among different age groups, or among residents of different parts of the municipality.

Third, statistics is often used to infer relationships among variables. If a high proportion of drivers involved in serious accidents was intoxicated at the time of the accident, it might be inferred that intoxication and accidents were related. Statistics alone, however, cannot demonstrate a cause and effect relationship: what statistics can do is to show that two factors vary together, either strongly or weakly—other methods must then be used to determine whether there is a causal relationship.

A fourth important use of statistics is to determine when variations may be attributable to normal randomness, or *probability*. For example, statistics can be used to estimate the probability that the municipal switchboard will be overloaded with calls in the normal course of events. Or, put the other way, statistics can be used to estimate whether overloading of the switchboard on a certain number of days is just an exceptional occurrence, or is actually evidence that added equipment is needed.

The fifth major category of statistical uses is concerned with changes over time; that is, with identifying the presence and nature of trends and exceptions to trends. Thus statistics may be used to estimate future population based on the series of population changes over a number of years, or to conclude that tax rates are rising. Statistical analysis of changes over time also may be for the purpose of spotting exceptions from a general pattern. For example, monitoring the number of miles of streets cleaned per week may show a sharp decline from normal performance, indicating a need for further investigation to determine the cause for the decline in performance so that remedial action may be taken.

These, then, are the more common ways in which statistics can be of value in administrative analysis. The bibliography for this chapter provides references for those who wish to gain greater ability to use statistics in analysis and decision making.

COMPARATIVE STATISTICS

Simple measurement of the quantity of work performed, or the cost of performing a unit of work, does not in itself answer the question of how well the organization is performing. Evaluation requires standards against which performance and cost can be measured, and managers frequently rely on comparisons with other cities to determine where their own organization is most in need of improvement. Comparative statistics cannot, of course, provide the final standard for evaluating an organization, but it can provide a useful starting point.

Statistical Terms. Many of the available tabulations of urban statistics do not give data for individual cities but are merely summaries for all the cities of a given population group. The correct use of such data involves an understanding of the summarizing devices which have been employed.

In almost all cases, an average is shown. The average of measurements for a group of cities is intended to represent the typical value for those cities. In addition to the familiar arithmetic average (which is affected by the extreme values in the figures), the median is often used. The median is a position average. In a group of items it is that item on each side of which one-half of the total number of cities fall, when the items have been arranged in order of size. Thus the median of 21 cities, with respect to per capita library circulation, is the city with the eleventh largest per capita circulation.

An average, whether it be an arithmetic

mean or median, is in no sense a standard. The "average" number of fire department employees in 1965, in cities over 500,000 population, was 1.49 per 1,000 population. This does not mean that cities of that size *should* have that precise number of employees but merely that the average city *did* have that number. The goal of the administrator is not to provide average service at average cost, but to provide the highest possible level of service within the limitations imposed. Averages of performance measures can indicate only what cities are now accomplishing, not what could be accomplished through intelligent administration.

Of equal importance are measures of dispersion, which show how closely the individual items adhere to the average, or how widely they are distributed around the average. The four simplest measures of dispersion are: (1) the lowest item, (2) the first quartile, (3) the third quartile, (4) the highest item. The lowest and highest items are self-explanatory and indicate the total range covered by the items.

The quartiles are similar to the median. When the items are arranged in order of increasing size, the first quartile is that value below which one-fourth of the items fall. One-half of all the items fall in the range between the first and third quartiles. Thus, in a tabulation of salaries in a given department, the lowest salary might be $3,000; the first quartile $4,000; the median $5,000; the third quartile $6,000; and the highest figure $9,000. In other words, all the employees receive $3,000 or more; one fourth between $3,000–$4,000; a second fourth between $4,000–$5,000; a third fourth between $5,000–$6,000; and the upper fourth between $6,000–$9,000.

Comparison of the statistics of an individual city with the average will indicate only whether it is out of line with usual practices and suggest the need for further analysis of operations. Comparisons with quartiles and range will indicate how far the city departs from the typical and will help to determine whether the deviation is of sufficient magnitude to be significant.

Per Capita Data. One additional measure deserves special consideration. This is the measurement index reduced to a per capita basis. It is often assumed that by reducing statistics to a per capita basis, valid comparisons between cities can be made.

The usefulness of such an index is severely limited by the fact that population is only a very crude measure of problem magnitude. Fire risk, for instance, is related directly to the amount and type of burnable property and only indirectly to population. The per capita fire risk will therefore vary with valuation per capita and with types of property, and per capita fire loss is only a very approximate measure of adequacy of service. Similarly, the street cleaning problem is measured by the length and type of streets, a factor that is only indirectly related to population.

A further limitation on the usefulness of per capita data is that accurate population statistics are available for only a very limited time after each decennial census. A procedure, however, has been developed whereby the United States Bureau of the Census conducts a special, intercensal population count at the request and cost of the local government.[10]

Measures of performance per capita, effort per capita, and cost per capita are even more severely limited in their usefulness. A high per capita cost may indicate (1) that population does not adequately measure problem magnitude—that is, that climatic, structural, economic, social, or other extragovernmental factors affect the problem; (2) that the level of service provided is high; (3) that the activity is being inefficiently administered. Thus, a high expenditure for the fire department may result from a high per capita fire risk, from a successful effort to keep losses at a very low level, or from inefficient administration of the fire department.

However, if care is taken to compare cities which are similar in type and situation, and if allowance is made for unusual conditions, then per capita statistics will be very useful to the administrator in focusing attention on problems and suggesting questions to be answered by further investigation.

---

[10] Further information can be obtained from the Director, Bureau of the Census, Washington, D.C. 20233.

Limitations of Comparative Statistics. Statistics on urban government should not be used without a full recognition of their limitations. The first of these limitations is accuracy. The original data usually must be compiled from questionnaires returned by individual cities. In many cases there is little or no uniformity in the local records systems from which replies to the questionnaire are compiled. Furthermore, questions may be interpreted differently by the persons answering them. In the case of statistics compiled by reliable agencies, every attempt is usually made, however, to increase the accuracy and validity of the statistics by cross-checking data derived from different sources and by following up questionable returns. The probable margin of error can be determined only by a careful analysis of the kind of data involved and the means by which the data were obtained. Refined analysis of the data beyond the limits of their accuracy is an unjustifiable waste of time and energy.

The problem of comparability already has been raised. Operating statistics cannot be compared between cities unless consideration is given to the relative magnitude of the governmental problem, the level of service provided, and the cost. Cities differ in total population; in age, sex, and race distribution; in the pattern of land use and the types and distribution of structures and occupancies; in industries and occupations; in economic and social characteristics; and in physiography and climate. All of these factors will influence the operation of city government and will invalidate any comparisons in which they are not considered by the chief administrator in making a final evaluation.

Another factor in comparability is the variability in organization and functions of city governments. Services which are provided by counties in some states may be provided by cities in other states. This is the case with welfare functions, which are generally administered by cities in New England and by counties elsewhere. The line of demarcation between private and public facilities and services may also shift from one city to another. The visiting nurse service may be administered by the health department in one city and by private charity in another.

Finally, each unit of measurement must be assigned its true significance. A cost index cannot be used to measure results or an index of problem intensity to measure performance. Efficiency can be determined only from a consideration of accomplishments in relation to cost.

Proper Use of Comparative Statistics. With all these limitations on their use, what good are urban statistics, and what justification is there for publishing them? First of all, summary figures for various population groups are valuable as indicating trends in costs, performance, and accomplishments. Second, it is useful to compare the figures for individual cities with the averages for cities of similar size as a starting point for further analysis. If a city is employing many more employees per 1,000 population than the average, it must find valid justification in unusual climatic or other conditions, superior and more extensive services, or conclude that employment is excessive. The latter conclusion should lead the city to search for the fault.

Third, the information for individual cities can be combined with other data which may be at hand. The annual budget of a personnel agency acquires new significance if related to the number of employees. Information regarding individual departments helps to explain aggregate data for the government as a whole. Fourth, with due care, the information for individual cities enables city officials to make comparisons with other cities similarly situated. For example, the official of a wealthy suburb may want to compare salaries with those of other wealthy suburbs. Again, an official of an industrial city of 100,000 population may want to make comparisons with other cities of the industrial type and of similar size.

EVALUATING DEPARTMENTS

In very small communities, it may be possible for the chief administrator to have personal knowledge of the characteristics of every family and business and to know what each municipal employee is doing every day. In such a situation, he is able to revise continually his estimates of the needs of the community, the effectiveness with which the needs are being met by the municipal government, the efficiency with which resources are being used to meet the needs, and the level of output or performance of each of the individuals in the city government. But in the vast majority of municipalities, the chief administrator is forced to augment his limited personal knowledge with statistical information concerning needs, effectiveness, efficiency, and performance if he is to make continuing evaluations of city departments and agencies.

Evaluation of city departments must be accomplished in the context of changing community needs, which provide the basic criteria for determining whether a department is successful in fulfilling its assigned objectives. Assuming that continuing measurement of needs is carried out as discussed in Chapter 10, regular statistical reports of the performance of each department will permit the development of standards and methods for periodic evaluations of the effectiveness and efficiency of each department. These continuing evaluations can assist the executive and his department heads in identifying areas where management improvement is needed, and may lead to intensive administrative analysis.

The statistics required for departmental evaluation vary considerably depending on the characteristics of the particular community and its government. A brief survey of the types of statistics commonly used by municipalities will illustrate their usefulness.[11]

Fire. Three of the criteria in common use can be employed as a means of approximating the general level of fire department effectiveness: the loss per $1,000 valuation probably is the most reliable in comparisons from city to city; the loss per building fire is preferable in comparing results from year to year; and the number of building fires per $1,000 valuation is a check upon fire prevention work. The casualty grading schedule of the American Insur-

ance Association used in rating cities' fire defenses for insurance purposes is a recognized measure of fire department potential performance in terms of physical facilities and equipment. Although the grading schedule gives inadequate emphasis to intangible factors such as training and morale, and is technologically outdated, it can be a useful evaluation device.

Police. Because the work of the police department is so closely related to the social characteristics of the community, there is no entirely satisfactory index which provides a comprehensive measure of police department effectiveness. There are, however, a number of indices in common use which give a general guide for evaluating police departments.

Major crimes (Part I classes of the uniform system)[12] are best measured on the basis of "offenses known to the police per 1,000 persons" and "percentage of cases cleared by arrests." These measures indicate police effectiveness in dealing with known crimes. For crimes against property, useful indices include "percentage of value of stolen property recovered" and "percentage of stolen automobiles recovered."

Some additional insight into the effectiveness of the investigational activities of the police can be gained by the index of "percentage of convictions of persons arrested." In many cases, however, this index is more a measure of the prosecution and the courts than of the police department.

Public Works. Much of the work of the public works department results in a physical product which can be measured directly. Therefore, work measurement, performance reporting, and cost accounting for standard work units have found wide application in public works.

Public Health. Three types of measurement are in general use in public health: (1) mortality (death) and morbidity (illness) rates; (2) cost and time involved in providing health services; and (3) appraisal of the health program, using the evaluation schedule of the American Public Health Association. A very

---

[11] A more detailed discussion and bibliographical references will be found in Clarence E. Ridley and Herbert A. Simon, MEASURING MUNICIPAL ACTIVITIES (Chicago: The International City Managers' Association, 1943).

[12] UNIFORM CRIME REPORTS, issued by the Federal Bureau of Investigation.

thorough evaluation technique, combining all three types of measurement, has been developed through cooperation between the American Public Health Association and municipalities.

Recreation. The recreation department is usually evaluated in terms of the numbers of people who participate in the department's programs or use the facilities provided, and in terms of expressed satisfaction or dissatisfaction by community groups. Evaluation of the recreation program can be aided by use of the appraisal form of the National Recreation Association in conjunction with other measures of effectiveness and efficiency.[13]

Welfare. The tremendous growth of social welfare activities during the past several decades has created an important demand, which is as yet only partly met, for improved methods of evaluating the work of welfare departments.[14] It is often extremely difficult to determine whether changes in the rate of economic dependency in the community are due to the effectiveness of the welfare program or to changes in the general economy and changing population characteristics in the city.

One useful general measure of effectiveness is the backlog of pending cases expressed either in numbers or as a percent of cases processed. Other indices in common use include the ratio of acceptances to applications, the caseload per individual worker, and the number or percentage of inactive cases.

Public Education. The final evaluation of the school system must be in terms of the quality of the education which it provides to the individuals it serves. The most successful attempts at the measurement of educational results have been made through the survey technique, by testing the intellectual and social attainments of the graduates of the schools, and by follow-up of graduates to determine their success in adjustment to life. Less accurate measures which are frequently used include the student-teacher ratio, the

school dropout rate, and the use of standard achievement tests at each grade level.

Public Libraries. As is the case with recreation, the difficulty of measuring the effectiveness of public library programs has led to the general use of relatively simple counts of persons who use the programs. Common measures of library services include per capita circulation and registration statistics. There is almost universal awareness, however, that the number of registered readers and the actual count of volumes loaned do not allow adequate evaluation of public library service.[15] In addition to the use of professional standards for evaluating the variety and quantity of materials, surveys of library users and of the general population can provide useful insight into the degree to which the library programs meet the needs of the community.

Personnel. The departments considered up to this point have been operating agencies whose function it is to provide services directly to the public. The personnel agency, on the other hand, is largely an auxiliary agency concerned with the internal administration of the city government itself and offering few services directly to the public. Its value ultimately must be found in the increased effectiveness and efficiency it brings about in the operating departments.

Taking these factors into account, the personnel agency can be evaluated in terms of: (1) the quality of recruits, as indicated by qualifications and by examination, (2) the rate of turnover of personnel, (3) absenteeism, and (4) safety records in hazardous phases of municipal administration.

Finance. The objectives of finance administration may be characterized as fiscal soundness and facilitation of administration. Fiscal soundness can be evaluated by the city's credit rating, the annual audit, and by the effective-

---

[13] National Recreation Association, SCHEDULE FOR THE APPRAISAL OF COMMUNITY RECREATION (New York: The Association, 1951).

[14] A provocative evaluation of measurement and research needs in public welfare appears in David G. French, AN APPROACH TO MEASURING RESULTS IN SOCIAL WORK (New York: Columbia University Press, 1952).

[15] Over the years the American Library Association has worked on standards. A substantial revision of its principles and standards appears in American Library Association, PUBLIC LIBRARY SERVICE: A GUIDE TO EVALUATION, WITH MINIMUM STANDARDS (Chicago: The Association, 1956). A supplement, with illustrative budgets, is used to translate standard services into changing cost levels. See COST OF PUBLIC LIBRARY SERVICE FOR 1965—A SUPPLEMENT.

ness of its administrative methods. The facilitation of administration is a service activity that, similar to the personnel function, must be evaluated in terms of the information and assistance given to operating departments.

The performance of many specific finance activities can be measured and effectiveness evaluated. For example, the percentage of current collections of taxes due is a common criterion used in evaluation of the effectiveness of revenue collection activities.

Planning. Program planning and facilities planning can be evaluated in terms of results over a relatively short time period, and specific activities such as site planning and administrative processing can be measured in terms of administrative efficiency. To a large extent, however, the work of the planning agency must be evaluated in terms of the contribution of the agency to the action taken by operating agencies in executing plans.

Records for Administrative Analysis

The information needed for continuing administrative analysis can be obtained only if adequate records are maintained. Records, to be adequate, must produce the information needed for administrative purposes, must produce it promptly, and must produce it without an excessive amount of "paper work." Records do not exist for their own sake. They can be justified only insofar as they are necessary and useful for administrative purposes.

MODEL RECORD SYSTEMS

Basic records maintained by cities should conform to established national standards for two reasons. In the first place, a system based upon records which have been developed by agencies of national scope after considerable research and consultation will, if properly adapted, be far superior to a system based on the limited experience of a single city. In the second place, use of nationally accepted records will allow the gradual development of a valuable body of statistical knowledge about American cities, compiled by the individual cities on a somewhat comparable basis. The

Uniform Crime Reports, published by the Federal Bureau of Investigation, are illustrative of what can be done through the voluntary cooperation of local officials.

Model records systems which can be used with slight adaptation by almost all cities are available in a number of fields. In measuring police service, *Uniform Crime Reporting,* published by the International Association of Chiefs of Police and the Federal Bureau of Investigation, and *Police Records,* by O. W. Wilson, published by Public Administration Service, will provide guides which should be closely followed.

For public health departments, a standard work by the Commonwealth Fund contains a chapter on record forms and their construction.[16]

The Committee on Statistics for Public Recreation, a committee of the National Recreation Association, has developed a *Manual on Recording Services of Public Recreation Departments.*

In the welfare field, wide differences in administrative organization in different jurisdictions make standardization difficult. However, some agencies will find useful a little manual entitled, *Substitute Handbook on Statistical Recording and Reporting in Family Service Agencies,* Family Service Association of America, 1956.

Satisfactory uniform standards for records are not yet available in the fields of education, libraries, personnel, and planning.

For the city's financial records, the various publications of the National Committee on Governmental Accounting should be consulted. In several states, accounting manuals have been published which reconcile the recommendations of this Committee with state law.

In addition to data obtained from his own records, the administrator will find statistics from other cities useful to him. *The Municipal Year Book*[17] includes each year a list of

---

[16] See Frances King and Louis L. Feldman, OFFICE MANAGEMENT FOR HEALTH WORKERS, 1949.

[17] Published annually by the International City Management Association.

sources of municipal statistics. This list is a guide to those published compilations of statistics which show comparative data for a number of individual cities. Most of these statistical sources are readily accessible or available at nominal cost.

ORGANIZATION FOR RECORDS SYSTEMS

What staff is needed for operating records and what should be its place in the organization? To what extent should records be departmentalized, and to what extent centralized? What agency or official should be responsible for statistical research? Specific answers cannot be given to all of these questions since they will depend in large measure upon the size and organization of the city, but several considerations must be kept in mind if the records are to reach maximum effectiveness.

Personnel Needs. If records and statistics are to be used effectively, there must be somewhere in the city hall at least one person who has more than an elementary knowledge of statistical methods. The task of designing and utilizing records is more than a clerical job and requires a high level of training and imagination.

In large cities, trained statisticians should be available in the various departments. The police department in a city over 100,000 population can profitably use a full-time statistician as a part of its records division staff. In a somewhat larger city, the health department should have the services of a statistician with special training in vital statistics. Even if cost records are centrally maintained, a cost accountant should be attached to the public works director's office in the larger cities.

Equipment. The analysis, classification, and reclassification of records data is a long and painstaking job, and for all except the simplest analyses may entail considerable clerical expense. Most cities will find that the use of electronic data processing equipment to create, maintain, and analyze records will cut costs and improve results. Chapter 9 discusses the variety of alternatives available to cities for obtaining the advantages of data processing capabilities. Where electronic data processing methods are employed in operations, central statistical files or "databanks" may be maintained as a by-product of other required work.[18]

Statistical Research. As has already been suggested, in many cities the statistical analysis of records data will be part of the work of the statistician attached to the central analysis unit. In these cities the individual departments may wish to make statistical analyses for their own use, and the statistician should be available for advice and consultation in laying out and carrying through such projects.

Census Tracts. Data gathered by the United States Bureau of the Census ordinarily are available for small cities only in the form of summary statistics for the entire city. A few simple items such as total population usually can be obtained for individual enumeration districts, but the boundaries of these districts are changed from time to time so that there may be no comparability from one census to the next.

In larger cities and their adjacent areas the Census Bureau is willing to lay out census tract areas (usually between 3,000 to 6,000 population) and to make available certain population and other data for these individual tracts. Cities are tracted upon request of local officials or other interested agencies who wish to make use of the data. The value of tracting lies not only in the relative permanence of the areas from census to census and in the data made available by the Census Bureau, but in the fact that all other statistical data which are being gathered in the city may be classified on a tract basis. Thus crime records, fires, cases of communicable diseases, and other matters upon which the city is gathering data can be allocated to the same set of census tract areas. In this way, the relationships among different but interdependent phenomena can be detected as a basis for cooperation between city departments dealing with different aspects of the same problem.[19]

---

[18] John K. Parker, "Operating a City Databank," PUBLIC AUTOMATION, June 1965.

[19] See the September, 1970, issue of PUBLIC MANAGEMENT for a thorough review of data potentials and limitations of the 1970 Censuses of Population and Housing.

Even in cities too small to be tracted by the Census Bureau, permanent districts of from 1,000 to 5,000 population should each be laid out by agreement among the various city departments as a basis for the uniform compilation of all city data.

Coordination. It is an obvious point, but sometimes overlooked, that someone must be responsible for the "system" of administrative measurement and records. Cost accountants may keep the cost records and the work performance data, and others may keep additional information. Someone, however, must coordinate and mold the separate segments into a workable system. Equally important, he must be responsible for research and study to improve the system so that administrative problems can be resolved.

Several questions must be asked about each element of the records system: (1) Who will fill out these forms, and (2) who will use the information contained in them? (3) What agency in the city hall has the equipment and trained personnel necessary for managing and maintaining these records? (4) What is the attitude of departmental officials toward the records? If department heads are aware of the usefulness of records procedures and eager to employ them for administrative purposes, a greater measure of departmentalization may be allowed than when the departmental officials are suspicious of records and condemn them as "so much paper work."

Conversely, if a managerial or auxiliary agency is able to produce the desired information promptly enough for the administrative needs of the department, the records usually can be operated centrally with more economy than if they are departmentalized.

The possibilities for cooperation among the various city departments in securing data necessary for administrative purposes have been fully exploited in few cities. For instance, data on the land use pattern in a city have been exceedingly difficult to obtain, and usually have been secured, if at all, only on the basis of costly periodic surveys which are soon out of date.

Land use data are almost indispensable to planning commissioners, to assessment bodies,

to housing authorities, to fire and police departments, to public works departments, in planning city services, and in numerous other aspects of city affairs. Much information on land use and occupancy is constantly flowing into the building inspector's office, the fire department records, and the assessor's office. Yet in few cities have cooperative techniques been developed for maintaining current up-to-date files of land utilization data. Here is a striking example of the possibilities which lie in interdepartmental cooperation for statistical and research purposes.[20]

Organization for Administrative Analysis and Planning

The need for an organized administrative analysis and planning program as an integral part of the municipal operation has been recognized only in very recent years and by a relatively small number of cities. There are at least two factors that will tend to bring about its rapid acceptance in other municipalities. The first is the rapid urbanization of the population, which makes the job of providing essential municipal services larger and more complex, and this in turn calls for the greater application of sound principles of organization and scientific management. The second, although somewhat related to the first, is the recognition by many chief executives that administrative analysis and planning activities can be delegated in much the same manner as finance, personnel, budgeting, city planning, and other staff functions.

ORGANIZATION FOR ANALYSIS AND PLANNING

In general, the most logical location for an administrative analysis and planning unit is in the agency responsible for preparation of the budget. In smaller cities this function may be assigned to the chief executive's adminis-

[20] The larger the city the greater may be the need for coordination. See, for example, the guide, STATISTICAL AND RESEARCH ACTIVITIES OF MUNICIPAL WELFARE, HEALTH AND EDUCATION AGENCIES OF NEW YORK CITY (New York: Welfare and Health Council of New York City, 1955).

trative assistant, who in turn may find the assistance of an administrative trainee to be of considerable help. In larger cities a department or division of administrative management or budget and research should be established.

Regardless of where the administrative analysis and planning unit is located, it must be recognized as essentially a managerial agency. To a certain extent its services have an auxiliary character, i.e., they are technical or specialized services rendered to operating departments by a central agency. For the most part, however, the problems of administrative planning are broader in scope than a single department, and the outlook of the administrative planner must be broader than that of the technician or specialist.

The recommendation that the administrative analysis and planning unit should be placed in the budget office under the general supervision of the budget officer means simply that the budget officer should be the principal administrative planning aide of the administrator, coordinating the studies and recommendations of the analysis and planning staff with the fiscal and operating aspects of programming and budgeting.

Activities normally assigned to the administrative analysis and planning unit include responsibilities for preparing coordinated plans and programs; making organization and administrative surveys; methods and procedures studies; special factual studies and reports for the chief administrator and city council; review of office layout and design, which might also include making recommendations for assignments of office space; central control over the design and printing of office forms; and the development of policies relating to records management and disposal. The chief executive also might request the unit to review departmental work progress reports and prepare a digest of work accomplishments for the information of the city council and the general public.

The administrative analysis and planning unit also may provide guidance and assistance to other departments and agencies in their analysis and planning activities. Its staff might provide a consulting service on techniques, advising and training personnel of other agencies, as well as serving as a clearinghouse for municipal studies, plans, and information.

In its role as a clearinghouse, such an agency can serve as a central source of reference on all analysis and planning information. It would be the business of the central agency to keep track of all the analysis and planning activities of the various departments and agencies of the city. Studies conducted by private agencies in the community would come within the scope of the agency's interests and records. In the files of the central agency would be references to past studies and reports, information available from local agencies and also from outside sources, and schedules of studies under way or being planned for the near future.

The advantages of such a clearinghouse are many. It can help to eliminate duplication and overlapping of study projects. Information collected by one department or agency can be made available to others. Studies conducted by private agencies can be related more easily to each other and to official research. The chief administrator and council are able not only to keep in constant touch with the varied planning and analysis activities, but also to give effective direction and guidance to the study of municipal problems.

Structure of the Administrative Analysis and Planning Unit. There is little point in attempting to prescribe in detail the organization of a central administrative analysis and planning agency, because the size of the city, the organization of other departments and agencies, and other local conditions will require modification for each city. A few general suggestions may be offered, however.

1. The central agency should be within the direct control and supervision of the chief administrator.

2. The central agency should have a single head rather than an administrative board or commission.

3. Liberal use should be made of advisory committees. Although the managerial character of the central agency calls for a single head responsible to the chief administrator, there

are many planning and research problems which require the special involvement of several points of view or fields of knowledge. Thus what is needed is not one more or less permanent group or commission, but *ad hoc* committees appointed for specific purposes as the need arises. When the problem has been taken care of, the committee should cease to exist.

The nature of municipal analysis and planning and the wide variety of subjects requiring study make it impossible to concentrate all such activities in any one special agency. Even if it were possible to assign all such activities to some central body, it would not be desirable to do so for such segregation would further aggravate the already serious problem of promoting unity and continuity between the formulation and the execution of plans and policies. In fact, there is need for more, not less, departmental study and investigation of municipal problems.

Personnel Requirements. The staff assigned to the central administrative and planning unit will vary considerably according to the size of the city. In the smallest cities it may not be feasible to employ any specially trained administrative expert other than the chief administrator. In such cases, the chief administrator may have to do his own administrative analysis and planning, and he may find it necessary to devote considerable time to this.

In cities of moderate size, administrative analysis and planning problems may be assigned to an administrative assistant, to the budget officer, or to some other managerial aide who is qualified to do the work. Considerable use is also being made of administrative interns or trainees assigned either to the chief administrator or the budget officer. In cities of all sizes, outside consultants may be employed for major projects which call for qualifications not possessed by regular personnel.

The complexity and scale of governmental responsibilities in larger cities require a full-time staff with a variety of competences for administrative analysis and planning to be effective. In addition to management analysts, necessary staff competences may include economists, sociologists and social psychologists, statisticians, operations research and management science analysts, systems and procedures analysts, and industrial engineers who specialize in work simplification. In these larger units, adequate technical and administrative support must also be provided, including draftsmen, computer programmers, technical writers for manual preparation, stenographers, and clerical personnel.

Use of Trainees in Administrative Analysis and Planning. A number of cities throughout the country have adopted "management trainee" or "administrative intern" programs in conjunction with their administrative analysis and planning agencies. Under these programs, students graduating from universities with specialized training in municipal management, public administration, and related fields are recruited to serve for periods extending from six months to two years in the capacity of administrative trainee or intern. Ordinarily these trainees are assigned to the agency responsible for administrative analysis and planning.

OTHER RESEARCH AGENCIES

In addition to agencies and employees within the city government, a number of outside agencies can and should be used occasionally in the analytical work of the city.

Other Governmental Agencies. Other governmental units—federal, state, and local—carry on research programs and analytical studies that often have a direct bearing on municipal problems. The recent development of metropolitan and regional planning agencies is particularly notable, for many problems facing municipalities are not confined to the city limits. In some cases, personnel from other governments are available as consultants either on an informal or formal basis. State planning agencies may be able to supply very useful information and advice on local planning problems, while state finance and personnel departments may provide assistance in their fields.

Many federal departments and bureaus collect and publish statistical data from cities on subjects such as population, finance, housing, governmental employment, crime, education, airports, libraries, and public health. Federal agencies publish model ordinances on subjects such as airport zoning, building and housing codes, health and sanitation standards, plumbing and electrical codes, traffic and subdivision regulation, and air and water pollution control.

Private Agencies. Study of governmental problems is by no means confined to the activities of governmental agencies and personnel. A variety of semipublic agencies are also working in this general field.

1. Citizen Research Agencies. In many cities privately sponsored municipal research bureaus are important sources of management research. Some of these bureaus play a militant role in municipal policies, taking positive stands on policy questions, while others are content with obtaining and releasing reliable factual information to citizens. In either case they often study and investigate municipal problems and propose possible solutions. The quality of their research, of course, depends upon the attitude of the sponsoring body and the qualifications of the staff employed.

Taxpayers' associations, chambers of commerce, and other special interest groups also conduct studies of municipal problems in many cities. Although such groups are likely to have biased interest, most of them maintain high standards of accuracy and integrity in their research activities.

2. University Research Bureaus. Many state universities have established municipal or governmental research bureaus which provide services to cities. Although some of the bureaus have staff members who are assigned full time to governmental research, most rely primarily on professors of government and public administration, supplemented by the part-time services of graduate students. The most active university governmental research bureaus have been developed at those universities which have established graduate programs to prepare students for careers in municipal management or public administration.

The services of these bureaus may include in-service training programs, correspondence courses, research on governmental problems of state-wide interest, distribution of information

and research materials on specific governmental problems, and sponsorship of meetings and conferences for governmental officials.

In recent years there has been a definite trend for university departments and faculty members in the fields of education, business, economics, political science, medicine, social work, and engineering to perform special studies and provide consulting assistance to municipalities, even where there is no institute or school of public administration. This growing interest in urban problems makes available a new source of highly talented assistance to those administrators who will take the time to establish relationships with university faculty and staff members.

3. Technical and Professional Associations. Technical and professional associations of municipal officials have become increasingly important as sources of information in a wide variety of fields. These associations span the full range of municipal activities since they have been largely organized and supported by officials engaged in different functions of municipal government—city managers, finance officers, personnel officers, public works officials, and others.[21]

A few of these organizations are equipped to provide limited field consulting services, but most confine themselves to a "clearinghouse" type of operation including collecting and disseminating information and materials in their respective fields.

Technical and professional agencies are particularly helpful in furnishing information regarding plans and procedures adopted by other municipalities. A city official can use these materials as models or guides and adapt them to the needs of his city. Most of these agencies also publish periodic journals and issue special reports which deal with problems of current interest in their fields.[22]

State leagues of municipalities are usually

---

[21] For a listing of national technical and professional associations and their headquarters addresses, see THE MUNICIPAL YEAR BOOK (Washington, D.C.: International City Management Association), published annually.

[22] See David S. Arnold, "Sources of Management Information," PUBLIC MANAGEMENT, August, 1965, pp. 173–77.

especially good sources of information on problems which are having a state-wide impact on cities or which are peculiar to a specific state because of legal requirements.

4. Municipal Consultants. Many private individuals and firms specialize in surveys and consultation on municipal problems, including physical planning, construction and operation, and other special fields. In addition, there are private consulting firms which specialize in general organization, administrative systems and procedures, personnel, finance, records systems, and the like.

5. Others. A number of miscellaneous agencies may occasionally contribute information, advice, or active assistance in the study of municipal problems. Privately owned public utilities in the community are interested in plans for physical expansion and for adjusting their physical plants to the changing needs of the community. The local telephone company may have information relating to the rate and direction of extensions of its services that may be useful to city officials in forecasting future city growth. Manufacturers of business machines and equipment are sometimes prepared to offer limited consulting services on some administrative problems, particularly those involving procedures and the flow of paper work.

Use of Outside Consultants. Mention has already been made of the research services that can be provided by municipal consultants. The use of professional consultants in specialized and technical fields such as city planning, law, engineering, and utilities has for some years been standard practice in many cities. Employment of consultants who specialize in personnel, finance, general administration, and computer utilization is a more recent development. That municipal consultants can make significant contributions in these fields is evidenced by the fact that both large and small cities frequently engage consultants for such projects and studies.

Three basic reasons can be listed for employing outside consultants: (1) the urgency or time required for a project and the regular workload of the city's staff indicate that a study can be accomplished more expeditiously by a consultant; (2) the project under consideration is of such a specialized or technical nature that it is felt that a consultant can do the job better; and (3) the final recommendations will be more readily acceptable on a potentially controversial subject because of an outside consultant's professional reputation and because his recommendations are less likely to be subjected to a charge of bias from persons opposed to the program or activity being studied.

1. Types of Consulting Service. Consulting services fall into two general categories: (1) the survey and report project and (2) the installation project.

The "survey and report" project involves a particular subject or problem of municipal administration. An example of this type of project is the general administrative survey of a city to propose a reorganization of functions and departments. In studies of this type the consultant ordinarily departs after submitting a report and recommendations. If the consultant's recommendations are carried out in such cases, it is done by the city officials themselves—the city council, city administrator, or department heads, depending upon the nature of the study, the recommendations, and the action required.

The installation project differs considerably. Under this type of project the consultant develops administrative improvements in a prescribed area and assists in putting these improvements into effect without being required to go through elaborate reporting procedures. This type of project is perhaps the more practical when the administrator is aware of the problem and possible remedies, but lacks time or staff to make the indicated improvements. In such cases the consultant may be assigned to develop and install a new system of operation in some field such as in personnel administration; revision of accounting, budgeting, or purchasing practices; or the installation of a computer system.

2. Selection of a Consultant. The first step in hiring an outside consultant is to define the general nature, type, and scope of the problem, list the technical resources available locally, and decide what technical services are

desired. On the basis of such general specifications, inquiry can be made of a number of consulting firms and agencies.[23]

Where a consultant expresses interest in the undertaking, he should be required to indicate at least generally how the project would be staffed, scheduled, and otherwise conducted; to provide appropriate references in jurisdictions previously served; and give estimates of the cost of professional services to be rendered.

3. Competitive Bids for Consulting Services. While it is desirable for the city to secure from several consultants statements on the extent and kind of work they would perform, and a cost estimate, the city generally is under no obligation to engage the lowest bidder. Even where competitive bidding is required by law on all contracts, the law usually makes an exception for obtaining professional services.

This exemption from bidding is based primarily on the fact that the quality of the work performed by professional or technical personnel depends very largely upon their training, ability, and integrity.[24] Under these circumstances, competitive bidding is clearly against the public interest and should not be practiced.

4. The Contract or Agreement. Once the consultant has been selected, the city and the consultant should enter into an agreement or contract specifying the type and amount of services to be rendered and their cost and scheduling. This agreement may take the form of an exchange of correspondence between ap-

propriate officials or may be incorporated in a formal contract document.

5. Services Provided by the City. A city employing a consultant normally is expected to provide the consultant with necessary office space, furniture, and equipment; local telephone service; necessary office supplies; and clerical, stenographic, and related facilities as necessary to assure the effective use of technical staff.

It is also advantageous to the city if one or more of its employees can be assigned to assist the consultant. Such an arrangement can do much to expedite progress on a consulting project and minimize the cost of the outside services. It also provides employees with useful training and with valuable knowledge of what was done, why it was done, and what future operational requirements will be.

6. Form of End Product. Since results of consulting services may take several forms, an early decision should be made concerning the type of end product to come out of a survey or installation project, with due regard to the audience to which the end product is to be directed.

7. Cost of Consulting Services. To assure a satisfactory experience in the use of consulting services, the cost of the service should be fixed in the contract or agreement as accurately as possible.

Where the scope of the job and the extent of local participation can be determined accurately, the most satisfactory agreement is for the consultant to fix a maximum beyond which no charges will be made. The consulting firm should then bill against that amount for transportation costs, staff time, and other items devoted to the project.

8. Follow-Up on Consultant's Work. The responsibility for following through on work done by a consultant rests primarily with the city. Most of the follow-through aspects of an undertaking lie beyond the authority of the consultant, and even the best of consulting work can be no more effective than the degree of follow-up exercised by local officials.

In most instances systems must be continuously revised, at least in detail, to conform to changing circumstances. The consultant will

---

[23] Names and addresses of consultants and consulting firms are listed in most magazines and professional journals concerned with municipal government, such as AMERICAN CITY, WESTERN CITY, PUBLIC MANAGEMENT, and many others. Another excellent source is the MUNICIPAL INDEX published by the Buttenheim Publishing Corporation.

[24] This point of view has been quite consistently held by the courts in many states. For example, in McQuillen on MUNICIPAL CORPORATIONS, Vol. 2, 2nd ed. revised, p. 1182, sec. 1292, it is stated with citation of cases: "Provisions as to competitive bidding have been held not to apply to contracts for personal services depending upon the peculiar skill or ability of the individual such as the services of . . . an attorney at law, a superintendent or architect . . . or a consulting and supervising engineer. And generally the requirement does not apply to the employment of a professional man in which case the authorities have a discretion as to his qualifications."

almost always be glad to assist in such follow-up operations and, as his prior work gives him intimate familiarity with the situation, it may be advisable to have him come back occasionally for general review and to assist in working out any new problems that have arisen.

The authority and responsibility for making decisions rest with local officials and not with the consultant. Accordingly, local officials must make decisions on all recommendations, accepting them, rejecting them, modifying them or, in some instances, establishing a specific schedule and procedure for their reconsideration. Also, local officials should make known to the consultant difficulties encountered in the continued operation of systems which the consultant has developed.

Summary

The expanding scope and complexity of municipal responsibilities challenges the chief administrator to achieve even greater organizational responsiveness, effectiveness, and efficiency. And, while "organization" once referred primarily to people working together, today it is more appropriate to think of the organization as a man-machine system employing resources to achieve public purposes.

The impact of the first few generations of computers is already significant in municipal government. These machines—the first to extend man's brainpower as well as his muscle-power—have become important tools of management. But while computers expand the capabilities of municipal government, they intensify the requirement for administrative analysis and planning.

As municipal objectives, programs, and operations increase in complexity, comprehensive administrative planning—for community development, for area improvement, for functions and programs, for revenues, and for disasters and contingencies—emerges as a key management responsibility.

The need for reliable information and sound decisions in the planning process, and the mounting demands placed on scarce resources emphasize the importance of administrative analysis to the executive who is striving to make his organization more responsive, effective, and efficient.

The municipal executive who masters these areas of management, who harnesses the potential of the computer, who makes planning a fundamental part of operations, and who develops and uses the full power of administrative analysis can substantially improve the performance of the municipal organization in serving the community.

Part Five

Administrative
Functions

12

City Planning

Though still an underdeveloped activity in many municipalities, city or urban planning is neither new nor novel. Indeed, in recent years planning has become so firmly accepted as a part of the legitimate role of municipal government that it is, in some communities, as much in danger of becoming a part of the "conventional wisdom" as it is, in others, in danger of being neglected or misunderstood. In Europe and Asia, the planning of cities as a deliberate, intellectual endeavor and a legitimate governmental function can be traced back for at least 5,000 years. Yet only in recent years have techniques and concepts become sufficiently sophisticated to make urban planning a science in the modern usage of that term.

Today urban planning can properly be viewed as an interdisciplinary science, taking its techniques and perspectives from a variety of disciplines. Early contributions came from engineering, architecture, and the law. More recently the disciplines of public administration, political science, economics, geography, and sociology have added new weapons to the planning arsenal and new perspectives on the roles and functions of urban planners.

Increased sophistication, however, has not resulted in increased clarity of purpose. In recent years, city planning has been identified in both lay and even professional circles with an inordinate amount of confusion and frustration. In large part, this is a reflection of the confusion and frustration in the society which planning must serve. American institutions of local government have been undergoing severe strain, awkwardly groping to find solutions to problems the nature and origin of which are frequently not well understood.

This has been a period of rapidly rising municipal costs. The federal-state-municipal relationship has shifted markedly. The migrations of a rural population to cities and of the city population to suburbs are in evidence on every hand. Delinquency and other forms of deviant behavior have been on the increase, with cause and effect less than certain. Urban transportation has been recognized as a major city problem, but solutions are usually beyond the fiscal capacity of cities. Slum renovation and removal projects lag behind the rate of deterioration. In many states, municipalities lack not only the fiscal capacity to cope with these problems, but also the legal structure to do so.

An old American proverb asserts that "if you want to clear the stream, get the hog out of the spring." The problem of the planner is one of how to clear the stream when few observers are able to identify the hog—and the location of the spring is uncertain. But, in many respects, it is this same complexity of problems that has nurtured the planning process and sharpened the tools of analysis. The story of the rise of planning as an intellectual activity is in large measure the story of the rise of modern cities, urban culture, and the associated skills of social science and urban administration. Planning has become sophisticated as has the society it must serve.

The Nature of Planning

From the chief administrator's perspective, planning may appear to be only another dimension in the total process of municipal administration. This is not an inaccurate view. Much of the day-to-day routine of a planning department is administration, and much of the administrative process is planning. The director of planning in municipal government is an administrator of a policy formulating, research, and analysis function.

COMPREHENSIVE PLANNING

A simple definition of urban planning might describe it as "the process of making rational decisions about future actions directed toward the attainment of predetermined community goals."[1] Planning, then, is a continuing program of data collection and analysis, public policy formulation (in the light of available data and forecasts), and the administration (implementation) of the resulting policy. Yet this is incomplete. The search for an adequate definition of urban planning is somewhat similar to the plight of several blind men attempting to describe an elephant, each feeling separate parts of its anatomy. The planning function carried out by the planning consultant, trained in architecture and employed by the community to produce a plan for its civic complex, will be different from that of the economist engaged in an economic base study for the whole community, or of the public administrator concerned with the political-administrative apparatus for plan implementation.

Planning, then, has many perspectives. It is a technical process involving design and engineering. It is a social process involving the enumeration and realization of human goals and the promotion of environmental frameworks more conducive to human life. It is a political process involving the formulation and execution of public policy.

Those who persist in viewing planning as restricted in scope to land use inquiries may be surprised to learn that the function is now much more broadly interpreted. In the research and analysis phases, it also includes economic base studies, recreation inventories, surveys of housing conditions, transportation studies, the examination of a jurisdiction's current and future fiscal capabilities, and other investigations into a host of social, economic, and political conditions. Planners must also concern themselves with the many means of implementing plans, including the consolidation of codes and ordinances, development of interjurisdictional means of cooperation, urban renewal programs, capital investment budgets, the preparation of zoning ordinances and other devices for land use regulation, and the day-to-day administration of policies, ordinances, codes, and other legal and administrative mandates.

From the perspective of the chief administrative officer, the complexity which is comprehensive community planning can be viewed in terms of four broad categories. These are (1) physical development planning; (2) economic development planning; (3) capital improvements and public facilities planning; and (4) planning for the human dimension, for social well-being. Such planning, indeed, merits the prefix "comprehensive," for it touches upon nearly every public aspect of human aspirations.

PHILOSOPHIES OF PLANNING

The goals as well as the techniques of urban planning remain in flux. Early in this century, the spectacular success of Chicago in developing lake shore vistas inspired the "city beautiful" movement: "Make no little plans; they have no magic to stir men's blood and probably themselves will not be realized . . . Let your watchword be order and your beacon beauty." This call to magnificence, said to be the philosophy of the Chicago Plan's author, Daniel Burnham, did indeed capture the imagination of the nation.

There is still much commendable in the Burnham view, despite harsh criticism now leveled against it for placing principal, almost exclusive, emphasis on urban aesthetics. To-

---

[1] OBJECTIVES OF ORGANIZATION AND OPERATION OF COMMUNITY PLANNING PROGRAMS (A report of the Joint Committee of the Philadelphia Regional Chapter, American Institute of Planners, and the Fels Institute of Local and State Government, 1960), p. 2.

day when urban blight is found on every hand and the scale of urbanization seems to magnify all that is ugly and undesirable, an attractive city remains a worthy goal.

Still, the reaction against the city beautiful movement also merits sympathy and support. The "city practical" movement, a product of the depression, stressed a sober, responsible view of urban life and of the role the municipality should play vis-a-vis its citizens. It recognized that a beautiful facade is of little consolation if the community is stagnant or if well-planned boulevards and parks are filled with the delinquent and unemployed.

The success of planning, however, is perhaps not as much dependent upon a philosophical stance as it is upon the practical question of whether those with responsibility for community affairs are dealing effectively with problems as they arise. It is unlikely that a community which fails to deal intelligently and effectively with the problems confronting it today will be able to deal with problems (some of which cannot be foreseen) which will arise in the future. This observation suggests that the functions of planning can be interpreted through, and in part are determined by, their relationships with the broader governmental, administrative, and political processes within which community decision making occurs.

Organization for Planning

Planning is a function of municipal government, but there is no final agreement as to its proper placement in the governmental structure. Much of the confusion is of historical origin, but part is also due to the nature of the planning activity. As government becomes more complex and sophisticated, the importance of the "professional" and his expertise (in planning or other activities) is bound to be more keenly felt, and his role proportionately magnified.

Sensitive issues, however, surround the function of expertise in a democratic government. The placement of policy-making authority in the hands of administrators not directly elected by the people and, hence, not directly responsible to them, may seem contradictory to the traditional assumptions of democratic theory. The democratic ethos senses danger and impropriety when it is assumed that professional public servants are better able to interpret the public interest than are the people or their elected councils. On the other hand, it is also in the nature of things that "professionals" tend to resent political interference with their functions and to feel that the product of expertise is seriously adulterated by political adjustments. Because of planning's reliance upon expertise, and because the role and place of expertise in democratic government is so ambiguous, popular consensus about the place and role of the planning function in local government is still lacking, although professional planners now are well agreed that their place is close to the center of decision making.

ORGANIZATIONAL PLACEMENT OF THE PLANNING AGENCY

Historically, there have been at least three popular concepts of organization for planning: (1) as an independent activity of an autonomous or quasi-autonomous planning commission; (2) as a staff aid (department) under the chief executive; and (3) as a policy-making function of the city council.[2] Planners today generally support the second alternative.

The Autonomous Commission. The autonomous planning commission enjoyed its greatest popularity before World War II, although it remains in scattered use today. It first gained status with its adoption by Alfred Bettman, Edward M. Bassett, and the other authors of the 1928 Standard City Planning Act[3] which became a model for many communities in the 1930's.

The rationale behind this autonomous form was essentially a restatement of the view that planning should not be subjected to political influence. The autonomous citizen's commission was designed to serve as a buffer between the planner and the political process. In some

---

[2] T. J. Kent, Jr., THE URBAN GENERAL PLAN (San Francisco: Chandler Publishing Company, 1964), p. 12.

[3] Prepared by a nine-member committee appointed by then Secretary of Commerce Herbert Hoover.

larger cities, including San Francisco, Cleveland, and Philadelphia, this arrangement proved satisfactory. It was also used with success in many smaller communities.

The precise organization of the planning function under the independent or autonomous planning commission varied from state to state and city to city. However, the general framework usually provided for a commission established by ordinance pursuant to state statute, and for the appointment of the commission membership by the mayor or city council. The size of the commission usually varied from five to nine members, though much larger bodies existed. Terms for commission members were normally prescribed either by state statute or municipal ordinance or charter. Once appointed, commissioners were not legally responsible to elected municipal officers, although political loyalty to the appointing source often remained strong.

As professional staff was acquired, it was usually organized directly under, and made responsible to, the planning commission. Not infrequently the planning staff had few ties with the municipal chief executive, and enjoyed a similar autonomy vis-a-vis the city council. Many believe that this arrangement renders the planning process ineffectual. Planning goals cannot be implemented unless they are fully integrated with the operating programs of other city departments—and, hence, under the direction of the chief executive. Moreover, the task of obtaining council approval seems less difficult when policy recommendations come from the executive.

Substantial arguments in support of the autonomous commission are heard infrequently today. By the 1940's the autonomous planning commission had begun to lose some of its support. The decline of its popularity matched the date of the publication of a book by Robert A. Walker, *The Planning Function in Urban Government*.[4] Walker, in a study of 37 city-planning commissions, found that the independent commission was having little im-

pact on community development. He therefore concluded that the elimination of independent commissions was in order. Within the past few years there have been growing signs that Walker's counsel may generally be taken seriously.

In the early years the citizens' (independent) planning commissions were essential instruments for making planning legitimate and acceptable to the broader community. Distinguished citizens sitting as planning commissioners were able to transfer some of the community's confidence in themselves to a confidence in the planning process. David Craig, a former chairman of the Pittsburgh City Planning Commission, has argued that support for the appointment of planning commissions as part of the official structure should be continued in those local governments which, as yet, have not obtained adequate support for planning. However, in those communities which have achieved public and political acceptance of planning, the abolition of the separate commissions, as official institutions, should be considered seriously, with policy activities transferred to the elected local governing body. "The execution of that transfer depends upon the planning maturity and political circumstances of each community for its feasibility and timing . . ."[5]

The Staff Aid Concept. The view of planning as a staff function, directly responsible to the chief executive, has become popular in recent years. This organizational form finds particular favor in council-manager communities: it is in keeping with modern concepts of administrative theory and it fits particularly well with the rationales supporting the structure of council-manager government. Planning commissions composed of citizens appointed by their respective legislative bodies are frequently maintained in conjunction with this scheme, but their functions are necessarily limited to those of advice and counsel.

This approach was summarized in a 1964 article by Peter H. Nash and Dennis Durden, "A Task Force Approach To Replace Plan-

---

[4] Robert A. Walker, THE PLANNING FUNCTION IN URBAN GOVERNMENT (Chicago: University of Chicago Press, 1941).

[5] David Craig (Pomeroy Memorial Lecture, Seattle, Washington, 1962).

ning Boards." It made the following recommendations: " (1) The professional staff should be placed directly under the control of the chief executive . . . ; (2) The advisory role of the old formal multipurpose planning commission should be deemphasized. . . . ; (3) . . . The old formal commission should be changed to a long-range advisory board. . . ."[6]

Viewed as radical at the time of publication, the Nash-Durden article appears prophetic in retrospect. Jerome L. Kaufman, associate director, research, of the American Society of Planning Officials, has observed that the most significant trend in recent years has been the shift of planning functions toward the chief executive. He adds that:

. . . In a number of cities the shift has been paralleled by a greater integration with the development departments. The most prominent change has been to create a combined planning and development department where planning, for administrative purposes, is married to the urban renewal and sometimes to the court enforcement functions. The theory is to mesh the city's planning function with the city's development functions, thus assuring closer coordination between planning and action. Hopefully, this will lead to a situation where planning controls renewal, rather than the other way around, as has happened in many cities where the urban renewal program has become strong.[7]

Policy-Making Agency of the Council. T. J. Kent, in his book *The Urban General Plan,*[8] depicted the legislative body as the primary client of the planning agency since it is the final policy-making authority for municipal government. Kent argued that the planning agency should be structured into municipal government in a fashion so as to make it responsible directly to the council. He saw it as a staff advisor to council. Kent also wanted the chief executive involved in the planning process, with the planning director serving him in an advisory capacity. This arrangement creates a dualism in the planning director's formal relationships, since he works on the one hand for the council while on the other for the mayor or chief administrator.

The view that a professionally staffed agency ought to be responsible directly to the council is not universally accepted by professional planners. Some planners feel that the liabilities of having to educate and sell plans directly to councilmen are greater than any assets that accrue from the arrangement. This is not a surprising view, considering the fact that some planners even argue the relative merits of council approval for the general plan.

Planning under this form is not an autonomous function. Rather, it is closely integrated with the policy processes of local government. The commission and the planning staff are both subordinate to the council, but both continue to have vital and important roles to play. They assume a responsibility for working on a continuing basis with the members of the council, educating them to the planning needs of the community and persuading the council of the practicability and political salability of the plans proposed.

A planning director under this arrangement will find himself devoting relatively greater portions of his time to communication with members of the council. This communication slows the planning process at times and perhaps halts it altogether on occasion. But it is also more likely to produce a planning product that ultimately will receive the endorsement of the council.

One's view of the planning process will color one's thinking about arrangements. If planning is seen as a technical operation outside the political realm and in need of a cloistered environment, the council–planning agency relationship will likely be rejected. On the other hand, if planning is seen as a part of the policy-making process of municipal government, with its implementation closely tied to the political power structure, a verdict in favor of this scheme is more likely. Kent's approach, however, can be criticized for permitting too great an administrative gap to develop between the planning and general executive agencies. He rejected, in his writings, the important political role of the executive and

[6] Cited in Jerome L. Kaufman, "Local Planning Organization in Transition," MINNESOTA MUNICIPALITIES, October, 1966, p. 334.

[7] *Ibid.,* pp. 334–35.

[8] Kent, *op. cit.*

downgraded the need to coordinate planning activities with other ongoing municipal operations. At least in those communities which use a strong-executive form, the separation of planning from the executive can have political liabilities. Kent himself recognized that this structural arrangement is backed by a minority of the planning profession.

Summary. The choice between a planning department responsible to the municipal chief executive and a planning department responsible primarily to the legislative body will depend upon the "climate" and frame of reference for planning in a given community. Whatever choice is made, perhaps the most relevant observation that can be made about planning is that its quality is more nearly related to, and conditioned by, the competency of the planning director and his staff and the political support given planning by community leaders, than to the organizational form it takes.

In its simplest terms, the function of planning is to furnish to responsible authority—both executive and legislative—information needed as guidelines for making decisions. The planning of a street, a new school, a firehouse, the extension of sewage or water mains, or the construction of a park are comparatively routine decisions made in the day-to-day course of municipal affairs. Each requires an analysis of need; of alternative sites; a justification in terms of the public to be served; a consideration of the expenditure to be made vis-a-vis the capital budget of the municipality; and many other factors. It is the function of the planning agency, however constituted, to see that data for these kinds of guidelines are available to the decision makers.

PLANNING CONSULTANTS AND PART-TIME STAFF

No discussion of the organization for planning would be complete without some attention given to the role of planning consultants. Where autonomous planning commissions function without the assistance of a professional staff (not unusual in villages and townships), most professional, technical planning is done by such consultants. Even in larger municipalities with relatively sophisticated planning personnel, the major planning studies may be conducted by private consultants.

Not infrequently, planning consultants offer their services to communities as "continuous planners" for annual retainers. Where this arrangement is made, the consultant usually agrees to participate regularly in meetings of the planning commission, to advise on planning problems as they arise, and to review subdivision plans, zoning changes, and the like as they are submitted. This arrangement may be fairly satisfactory for the small community without the resources to employ a full-time, resident planner. However, municipalities contemplating the employment of a consultant should be careful to investigate the competence of the individual, as well as the reputation of his firm, before entering into a contract. Similarly, the use of a consultant to do specific studies or to prepare a comprehensive plan should be considered with great care before contracts are negotiated. As useful as the services of consultants may be in the planning process, they are never wholly adequate substitutes for a full-time, professional planning staff.

An interesting compromise between a full-time planning staff and a retained consultant is the "shared" planning director. The shared planning director may be employed by two or more cities, or by a city and county, usually in very close proximity. It is understood by all jurisdictions involved that he will serve them proportionately; he will usually agree to supervise such subordinate clerical and technical personnel as may be required. Obviously the success of such arrangements is dependent upon the permissive nature of appropriate ordinances and statutes, the general climate of intergovernmental cooperation, and upon the temperaments of the personnel involved. While such makeshift arrangements are never ideal, they may be valuable as interim measures.

THE PLANNING DIRECTOR

The planning director's primary function is to supervise and coordinate the various planning activities carried on in the municipality. He is responsible for assigning work units to subordinates and interpreting the planning product to his superiors and to the citizens of the community.

The role of the planning director as supervisor of the professional staff is not affected greatly by the organizational structure in which planning takes place. However, his relationship to the municipal government of which he is a part, and his sources of power and authority, will be greatly influenced by organization.

Perhaps the most typical arrangement in American municipal government calls for the planning director to be appointed by the chief executive, with the remainder of the planning staff selected by the planning director under standards established by the personnel procedures of the city. There is no general agreement as to whether the planning director should himself come under the full protection of civil service. Some who have studied the question believe strongly that the planning director should serve at the discretion of the chief executive, and be subject to removal by him. Those who recommend full civil service status for the planning director usually argue that such an arrangement insures continuity and impartiality in the office, and removes it from the arbitrary and capricious actions of politicians.

Public administration theory generally favors the "cabinet status" concept for the planning director. As a member of the chief executive's staff, he would be responsible to him for all planning matters and for the operation of the planning department, just as the chief executive bears the ultimate responsibility for the overall operation of local government. With such responsibility should go full authority to appoint and to dismiss his principal assistants. However, this view more often than not runs afoul of municipal civil service regulations. Still, it is an arrangement that can usually be made insofar as the planning director's position itself is concerned. Where the planning director is directly responsible to the council, these rules would also seem to apply.

The Cost of Planning

Expenditures for planning vary enormously from community to community, even when calculated on a per capita basis. Some of this variation can be traced to differences in local wealth. In recent years, Palm Springs, California, has had one of the highest per capita income rates in the United States; consequently, its citizens have apparently felt they could afford to spend more than $5 per person per year for professional planning. In contrast, Los Angeles' annual planning expenditures are less than $1.00 per capita. Even this much smaller amount was the highest in the nation for cities over one million population.[9]

In planning, as in many other municipal functions, there are at least some economies of scale. Therefore, per capita expenditures for planning in small communities are normally somewhat greater than the per capita expenditures in large metropolitan centers. Differences are also traceable to variations in the expenditure (and planning) philosophies of local communities.

A salary for a professional planner might be expected to run from $10,000 annually for a young man with limited experience and recently out of his planning education to $20,000 and up annually for a mature and experienced senior planner or planning director. Technical assistance from consultants also varies enormously in cost, but many consulting firms feel that a comprehensive plan for a community can be done for under $1 per capita. The degree to which planning is an ongoing process in the community and the quality of data already collected by resident planners will influence these costs.

The General (Comprehensive) Plan

Communities are products of human design: they are no better or worse than the sequences of public and private decisions that shape them. Whether intentionally or not, communities are inevitably "planned" by the consequences of many such decisions. Planning may be deliberate, leading hopefully to desirable

[9] Dennis O'Harrow, "The Organization of the Local Planning Function" (an unpublished paper prepared for the Industrial Relations Center, University of Chicago, 1963).

ends, or it may be completely inadvertent, with a broad range of possible results. Regardless of method, its impact is substantial and long-lasting.

Deliberate planning usually results in what is termed a "general" or "comprehensive plan," an officially adopted document which attempts to describe and direct many aspects of community development during the foreseeable future.

THE COMPREHENSIVE PLAN TODAY

The planning document rests upon research. Using the data and insight gained by analysis, the various policy judgments of the plan are synthesized under one cover and promulgated as a whole. That document must be designed and written in such a fashion that it can be made available to the public at large and still remain a policy statement useful as a guide to officials of the community.

The subtopics of the comprehensive plan might include the following:

Introduction (an explanation of what the comprehensive plan is)

The City and Its History (how the city came to be what it is)

Costs and Strategy (what the planning cost will be, and where the revenue will come from)

Population (the city's people—stratification)

The Economy (the economic base and forecasts)

General Concepts (criteria for planning)

Plan for Industry (where it will locate, and what kind should be sought)

Plan for Commerce (where it will locate, and what its composition will be)

Recreation and Community Facilities (demand level and proper locations)

Plan for Residence (neighborhood development and maintenance)

Plan for Transportation (streets, highways, and public transit systems) [10]

The plan, once in effect, should be used as a standard by which future proposals are judged.

But it is not a static instrument; it should be flexible enough to adapt to the dynamic elements present in all urban life. This means that the preparation of a formal plan is only a first step in a broader and larger process.

Nonetheless, the importance of the comprehensive plan as a policy document cannot be overemphasized. The plan is a compass for the community. It indicates the course a community has chosen. It is a navigational tool which aids in following the course charted by a community's representatives and people. No two communities need follow the same course, but without a plan it is difficult to know what course, if any, a community is on. It is also difficult, if not impossible, to identify the point at which the community wanders off its intended course. This does not mean that once set the course cannot be altered. Like the ship at sea, when there are impelling signs that suggest a need for change, someone in command —armed with adequate information and authority—may make a decision to alter the course. The plan, then, provides the navigational frame of reference.

Most American cities have not yet developed fully adequate comprehensive plans. Many smaller cities have no comprehensive or general plan at all. Other cities have put together documents called "master plans" or "comprehensive plans," but without the research necessary for sound planning. What seems consequential for communities embarking on comprehensive planning is the recognition that: (1) it cannot be done without adequate "tooling up" studies; and (2) comprehensive planning represents municipal policy making that must be adopted and implemented by those in positions of administrative and political responsibility.

NEW DIRECTIONS IN COMPREHENSIVE PLANNING

The flux which, as noted earlier, characterizes both the ends and techniques of contemporary urban planning has implications for the comprehensive plan. There are, in fact, two traditions of planning now existing side by side. One, stemming from the pre-Depression period, is most concerned with urban aesthetics, land

---

[10] This format is adapted from that used in the Philadelphia Comprehensive Plan, 1960.

use, and "efficiency." It is this tradition, perhaps the more important in terms of actual implementation, which is summarized above.

But the Depression generated new and broader social and economic concerns within the nation at large, and laid the basis for action upon such concerns by the planning profession. Now, in the 1970's, this awareness has finally produced some positive responses. Adding as it does new dimensions to the prefix "comprehensive," such "social" planning merits special attention: two of its many implications are considered here.[11]

First, planners have become increasingly aware that their contribution is not made in a normless vacuum, and that plans are not without a normative impact. Every plan, at least implicitly, is based upon assumptions related to community goals, and every plan will make some of these goals easier, others harder, for their proponents to achieve. That the goals of citizens are frequently in conflict does not mean that the task of determining community objectives is rendered impossible, but instead demands that a more conscious effort be made to spell out normative ends and the normative implications of planning proposals.

"Policies planning" has been one result. Community goals are specified in a document which supplements (or might even replace) the comprehensive plan as outlined above. Goals are determined by formal interaction of the public, its elected and appointed representatives, and the professional planning staff; ultimately, the statement is adopted by the legislative authority. The policies plan itself focusing on ends and the broad means for their achievement . . .

contains reasonably detailed guiding principles but not specific proposals. A policies plan may state the principle that "public housing should be scattered throughout the city on sites that contain no more than 100 units," but the plan would not contain a

map pinpointing a half-dozen possible public sites nor would it recommend that a 100-unit development be constructed next year at the corner of Fourth and Oak.[12]

A second new direction is rooted in the recognition that problems of physical development and social welfare are, in complex ways, intimately related. That the two are somehow correlated is, of course, an old notion. Indeed, the city beautiful movement seemed to assume that an attractive city would perforce become an economically vital, socially harmonious city. Ugliness itself was seen as the root cause of most urban ills.

The contemporary view is not a restatement of this proposition; few planners now would accept that position, at least when made explicit. But few would question that the planner does affect nonphysical aspects of community life. In his involvement in the process of determining the nature, size, and location of health, recreational, educational, and housing facilities, the planner is involved in broad questions of human well-being. Specific planning skills—data collection, research, budgetary advice, administrative coordination—can be brought to bear on an even wider variety of social service activities.

The question, then, is not whether the planner is involved in social welfare problems, but whether or not he should confront them directly. Should a portion of the planner's time, and a portion of a comprehensive plan, be devoted to such things as the measurement of social welfare, surveys of social welfare programs, and studies of the attitudes and concerns of the citizenry? The question involves the definition of the planner's role and of the planning function.

There are at this point many alternative answers. While the direction in which the profession will ultimately move cannot be readily determined, it appears increasingly clear that comprehensive planning will embrace at least some social, as well as environmental, considerations. Even the discussion of social welfare issues has, in itself, broadened the awareness and conscience of the professional planner.

[11] A more complete consideration of these questions can be found in William I. Goodman and Eric C. Freund, eds., PRINCIPLES AND PRACTICE OF URBAN PLANNING (Washington, D.C.: International City Managers' Association, 1968); see especially Chapter 11, "Social Welfare Planning," and Chapter 12, "Defining Development Objectives." This brief section relies heavily upon those presentations.

[12] Ibid., p. 331.

The Research Phase of Planning

Since few planners are gifted with clairvoyance, they must conduct research to establish the reality of the present before they can plan with confidence for the future. The major studies undertaken to provide basic information about the community typically consider: (1) population; (2) economic characteristics; (3) land use; (4) public facilities; (5) general thoroughfare or transportation networks; and (6) other special topics which seem necessary in the light of peculiar local circumstances. The first three studies usually require very sophisticated techniques of data collection and analysis. They are often undertaken by outside consultants.

Both the economic base and land use studies are related to population characteristics. Hence, it is generally useful to undertake all three studies (population, economic base, and land use) simultaneously. The three separate categories of data must be viewed as interrelated, since an analysis of one in all probability will require an understanding of the others; it is hard to say what is cause and what is effect. Are people attracted by economic opportunity, or do economic opportunities gravitate to the locus of people? Is land use a product of the economy, or is the economy a product of land use?

However interrelated the data are, the research techniques employed are quite different, and generally speaking it is unusual, even unlikely, that one person will have the expertise required to conduct the various studies. Demographers have developed highly complex methods for studying the composition and growth of population and projecting changes in scale and stratification. Urban economists and some researchers trained in urban planning and public administration have developed methods for analyzing the economic base of a community and making projections about future growth and change. Land-use studies are undertaken by a variety of tehnicians trained in statistics and in the techniques of mapping and photography.

Other experts are involved in the process. Traffic engineers have developed methods for determining the volume and capacity of traffic and predicting induced traffic increments, given changes in the variables which regulate volume. Sociologists and political scientists have developed methodologies for describing the social-political stratification, the power relationships, and the attitudes of the various urban publics served and affected by the planning process. These skills and abilities are used by the planner in developing the understanding necessary to plan for the community's future and to regulate its present.[13]

POPULATION STUDIES

Two types of population studies are usually employed in the planning process. "Current population studies" describe the existing population of the planning area and shed light on its stratification and composition. "Projections" are used to forecast population levels and, from them, to arrive at future land-use requirements, public facility needs, and the general composition of the society of the city at a projected date.

Population forecasts are generally classified as "crude" or "refined." The crude methods are, as the term would imply, less sophisticated and generally simpler to apply, requiring considerably less time and data. They may also be less reliable; for the problems requiring immediate solution, these shortcut methods represent a way of obtaining a first approximation of population at some future date. Refined forecasts depend upon more exact data and rigorous analysis of the data. Usually a planning department will wish to rely upon outside consultants where more sophisticated forecasting techniques are considered necessary.

Basic definitions of population change are required for estimating either current or future population in the area defined for planning. The following definitions may be useful: (1) *natural increase* is the excess of resident

---

[13] For a more detailed description of the techniques and methods of conducting local planning studies, see William I. Goodman and Eric C. Freund, PRINCIPLES AND PRACTICE OF URBAN PLANNING, *op. cit.* Also see F. Stuart Chapin, URBAN LAND USE PLANNING (New York: Harper and Brothers, 1957), reprinted by University of Illinois Press, 1963.

births over resident deaths; (2) *natural decrease* is the excess of resident deaths over resident births; (3) *migration* is population change other than that accounted for by births and deaths; (4) *in-migration* is population increase from movement into the planning area; (5) *out-migration* is population decrease from people moving out of the planning area; (6) *net-migration* (or net-in, net-out migration) is the actual population gain or loss from movements of people into and out of the defined area.

Estimating Current Population. The decennial enumeration of the population by the United States Bureau of the Census represents a good point from which to start an estimate of current population during noncensus years. The Bureau prepares provisional estimates of the civilian population from time to time by national, regional, and state areas. These are published in a series titled *Current Population Reports,* which may be obtained by subscription or by individual report from the Bureau of the Census. This series also includes estimates of the total population in the United States as of July 1 each year. From the annual estimates of population for each state, a crude estimate for a planning area may be derived by assuming that the ratio of population in the planning area and in the state, reflected by the most recent decennial census, would continue to hold true for the present.

Obviously, the validity of the assumption depends upon unaffected rates of change for both the state and local population. If the ratio is to have value and be reasonably accurate, it must be adjusted to take into account factors which may have affected the rate of population growth at either the state or the local level. New annexations, significant additional residential development, large industrial or commercial expansion, or significant new programs undertaken by industry or the military bring new people and activities into the community. Any accelerated rate of growth can be expected to affect the "normal" rate. Conversely, significant out-migration or the shutdown of industry or military installations will quite probably cause a decrease in the rate of growth.

Estimated population data have great utility but should never be considered precise. Where precise figures are required, the best approach may be a recontract with the Bureau of the Census to conduct a special census. Such censuses are undertaken from time to time by the Bureau at the expense of the municipality requesting the census. The cost is usually modest.

Forecasting Population. All long-range planning depends to a considerable extent upon the success of the population forecast. Inasmuch as planning is concerned with the physical environment of people, significant fluctuations in the population over a period of time can have disastrous affects upon the plan if the changes are unforeseen. Also, decisions regarding the size of the area to be planned will depend upon an understanding of the growth expectations for the community. The Bureau of the Census can be helpful here as well. A range of assumptions regarding the national population growth is published in the series already cited, *Current Population Reports.* The Bureau forecasts the population of the United States and these figures are projected in five-year intervals through and beyond 1980. Making various assumptions about fertility, mortality, and in-migration, the forecasts of population change are made for the nation as a whole. Using these data, it is possible to develop forecasts for smaller areas.

The Bureau of the Census has the major role in defining Standard Metropolitan Statistical Areas. In identifying these areas, the Bureau compiles statistical data on population, housing, industry, and trade, and makes periodic tabulations of data gathered by other federal agencies on employment, payroll, and labor supply. These analyses and projections may be very useful for planning purposes.

ECONOMIC STUDIES

Economists have developed numerous strategies for the economic analysis of urban areas.[14] Economic base studies—the determination of the size and segment of local industry and

<hr>

[14] Homer Hoyt, "The Utility of the Economic Base Method in Calculating Urban Growth," LAND ECONOMICS, February, 1961, pp. 51–58.

commerce devoted to "export" from the city —are perhaps the most commonly used. Excellent techniques have, however, also been developed for gathering data concerning employment, categories of occupations, aggregate income, value added by manufacture, volume of production, and other useful data regarding the economic composition of the community. All of these add to the planner's understanding of the nature of the community for which he is attempting to plan, and provide a basis for estimating current demands on the public sector and for projecting future demands.

As land use is directly related to economic activity, economic forecasting becomes intricately entwined with the land-use forecast. Balanced community development cannot proceed unless suitable sites are or can be made available. Left unregulated, economic forces will be a primary determinant of land use.

A sophisticated understanding of the community's economic profile depends upon data collected on the scene and sound analysis in the light of peculiar local circumstances. But before economic base or other extensive and relatively expensive studies are made, the planner may gain substantial information about his community from analyses of data already collected and published in the various reports of the United States Bureau of the Census. While census data do not cover all aspects of the economy, they do provide a base for examining the major economic functions of the community, namely, production, distribution, and consumption.

The planner should be familiar with sources of data continuously needed for the various judgments he must make. The following reports will be of considerable value:

1. *Census of Manufactures:* an indicator of industrial growth with two groups of data— number of employees and value added by manufacture.

2. *Census of Wholesale Trade:* provides data on employees and sales.

3. *Census of Retail Trade:* scheduled for every five years, provides data on total retail activities (establishments, sales, payroll, personnel, and proprietors).

4. *Retail Trends in Central Districts:* a tabulation of retail sales in the central business districts of a number of major retail centers.

5. *Census of Selected Services:* scheduled every five years, along with other census reports, covers such major categories as hotels, motels, and tourist camps, personal services, miscellaneous business services, automobile repairs, automobile services, miscellaneous repair services, motion pictures, and amusements and recreation services.

6. *The County and City Data Source Book:* a statistical abstract supplement for each county in the United States and for each incorporated city having 25,000 inhabitants or more. Pertinent material contained in this volume includes a map for each state showing county lines, Standard Metropolitan Statistical Areas and cities of 25,000 or more inhabitants. Statistical data about smaller geographic areas are also contained in this publication.

A number of additional economic data publications may also be useful for planning purposes. They include: *County Business Patterns* (published by the U.S. Bureau of the Census); *Survey of Buying Power* (published by Sales Management, Inc., New York City); *Surveys of Current Business* (published by departments of commerce in many states); and the *Standard Industrial Classification Manual* (published by the U.S. Bureau of the Budget).

The Census of Manufactures may be used to study growth trends for industrial production. It is primarily useful for analyzing changes taking place in wholesale distribution and retail sales and services. Each segment of the economy requires public services and facilities as well as land for its various operations. Hence, by projecting the growth of the various economic functions, it is possible to translate these data into urban land-use requirements and demands for public services and facilities.

By projecting future employment, land-use requirements of various sectors of the economy may be estimated. A reasonably intelligent approximation of needed public services and facilities may be made by projecting data on personal income and potential resources available for future taxes and other sources of municipal revenues. Income data are equally useful in estimating family expenditures and translating prospective retail sales into future land-use requirements.

LAND-USE SURVEYS

A land-use survey is conducted for the purpose of providing data on the variety of uses to which land is put in the urban community. In its first stage, it is an *inventory of present land uses*. Subsequently, data are put in tabular form and analyzed so as to provide a statistical analysis of location, area, and density of various uses. The analysis usually provides a summary of the amount of land devoted to specific uses, a tabulation of dominant lot sizes, and an analysis of any major problem associated with land use. Data are arrayed so as to be most useful to the planning staff in determining not only current patterns of land use, but also to serve as a framework for formulating plans of long-range dimension.

The objectives that planners hope to achieve as a consequence of land-use studies include the following:

1. A more natural use of land with respect to terrain features. Industry will normally require flat terrain. Housing sites may be planned to considerable advantage on irregular terrain as well. Some consideration of grade must be taken into account in planning for streets, and, of course, sewage and water will not flow uphill unless pumped.

2. The separation of uses. Unless carefully planned, areas should not be interspersed one with the other. Mixed uses have depreciating affects on each other. Industry does not care to be hemmed in by residential neighborhoods and incompatible commercial uses, while the residential neighborhood can be seriously adulterated by the encroachment of most industrial uses.

3. The proper location of specific uses. The proper place for an elementary school is in the residential area and not in an industrial area; the proper place for high-rise office buildings is usually downtown or at other specifically designated points in the city rather than scattered about pell-mell. Many cities may wish to plan areas for hospital and medical facilities, educational centers, and other compatible uses.

4. Community stability is a prime objective of land-use planning. Blighting influences of whatever variety should be avoided.

5. Density control. It is essential to maintain healthy, airy living areas with sufficient vacant land for health standards and recreational uses.

6. The ability to forecast public facility and utility requirements in a systematic fashion is dependent upon adequate land-use forecasting.

By a variety of studies and procedures, the necesary land-use data are collected, analyzed, and put into proper perspective to furnish information about uses, nonuses, and misuses. The procedures and techniques include:

1. A compilation of data on physiographic features (sometimes) presented in map form with accompanying statistical tabulations.

2. The land-use survey also presented in the form of a land-use map (color coded) with accompanying statistical data.

3. The vacant land survey presented in map form and expressed in statistical tabulations.

4. The structural and environmental quality survey expressed in tabular form and also on occasion presented on a map.

5. Cost-revenue studies of land use. These studies relate to specific economic questions and are generally presented as special reports relying on statistical presentation.

6. Land-value studies—assessments of land value are usually presented in statistical form.

7. Studies of aesthetic features. Such studies are usually qualitative and impressionistic but may be highly valuable for planning purposes.

8. Public attitudinal studies regarding land-use preferences. Such studies are normally presented in separate reports and reflect the preferences of people for land-use patterns.

9. Other studies may be made of central business districts, land-use suitability, and determinations of future land-use requirements by types (industrial, commercial, wholesale, residential, recreational, agricultural, governmental, etc.) .

Of particular utility to municipal administration and closely associated with studies concerned with land use are the surveys of tax assessments, tax levies, and tax delinquency. Assessed value studies may be made solely for the purpose of projecting existing assessments, or they may be made as a part of a general re-evaluation of property. Whatever the objective, such studies are normally presented in the form of a map with accompanying statistical tabulations indicating front foot values by classified categories. Properties assessed by the acre show values per acre by classified categories. Maps may also be prepared to show all special assessments and special taxing districts. Tax-delinquency maps with appropriate supporting statistics may be prepared to show all tax-delinquent lands.[15]

THOROUGHFARE STUDIES

Studies should be made of all modes of transportation (public and private) in the urban area, of findings related to estimated future traffic volumes, and of the pattern, size, location, and capacity of existing and planned facilities. The objectives of these studies are to create a basic understanding from which the planning staff can make intelligent judgments about needed improvements for the present and realistic estimates of future requirements. Expressways, arterial streets, feeder streets, residential streets must be systematically projected from the *status quo* to an inevitable future network. However, such projections are not possible without integrating major thoroughfare planning with simultaneous planning for expanded public transit or, at the very least, a conscious assumption that there will be no expansion of public transit.

The basic aims of a thoroughfare plan are: (1) the establishment of a classification system of streets including the establishment of standards of right-of-way, pavement widths, and other particulars; (2) the location of major elements of the street system (freeways,

arterials, collector streets); (3) the establishment of a policy for controlling access to land adjacent to highways.

There are well-understood principles that should be followed in thoroughfare planning. The purpose of the street system is to provide easy and safe access to all parts of the community as quickly and as efficiently as possible. Streets should be designed to provide the least amount of interference with other activities in the community. The system should also be designed on the premise that the traffic volume will not remain stable. Whatever is determined to be an adequate capacity today will be grossly inadequate in a very short period of time unless alternative thoroughfares or alternative transportation systems (rail transportation or the like) are provided. In planning, scrupulous attention should be given to the maintenance of residential streets for residential purposes; collector streets should have low-level traffic volumes; arterial streets should be planned as through streets capable of handling a greater volume of traffic; and expressways should be so designed that they become expressways in fact rather than the linear parking lots they sometimes become at the rush hour.

This is not an easy order to fill. But it is already apparent that traffic-flow patterns play such dominant roles in urban arrangement and rearrangement that, if intracity transportation is not planned with care, it is unlikely that there can be systematic land-use planning for the community. The automobile, in the past few decades, has become the single most significant determinant of land-use arrangements in the urban area. Either a suitable alternative to the automobile as intracity transportation must be found or cities must be planned so they can accommodate it. Today most American communities fail to do either.

PUBLIC FACILITIES

From the perspective of the planner, no aspect of planning is more important than that concerned with public facilities. Policies affecting land use and projecting future urban development patterns are implemented to a large degree by what the municipality does about the

[15] The limitations of space do not permit an adequate discussion of the various land-use studies in this chapter. A good reference for further reading in depth is F. Stuart Chapin, URBAN LAND USE PLANNING, *op. cit.*

provision for public facilities. Land-use patterns are shaped in an impressive way by the location of trunk sewage lines, the availability of municipal water, the extension of major thoroughfares, the construction of schools, the location of public recreational facilities, and the host of other physical facilities normally provided by the public sector.

Although somewhat more difficult to document, it is quite clear that municipal government may also influence developmental patterns by the way it provides for more intangible services such as police protection, fire prevention, welfare services, public health, and related functions.

In every community there are various public buildings devoted to education, culture, health, charitable, and social activities. Government exercises direct control over the location, size, and aesthetic quality of most of these facilities. This control affords the city a unique opportunity not only to satisfy functional and utilitarian demands but also to serve aesthetic ends. The consequence can be the enhancement of the city and the stimulation of civic pride. Even the construction of public buildings in the city by the state and federal governments can often be coordinated with a municipal plan to provide for a governmental complex that can be of significant advantage as a stabilizing influence.[16] In an era when, by comparison with residential shopping centers, central business districts are frequently in danger of becoming commercial slums, the presence of an attractive civic center or governmental complex downtown can be of decided value as a stabilizing force.

Perhaps nothing has as great an impact on the character and composition of a residential neighborhood as its public school. Though the neighborhood concept is no longer dominant in urban planning generally, it is still of significance as it relates to school-age children. Despite its importance, however, integrating public school planning with municipal planning is an especially vexing chore in many

municipalities because the public school system is not operated by the city, but rather by an independent school district.

The lack of integration of public school facilities with overall city or county plans has frequently caused school location to work at cross purposes with city plans for neighborhoods. It is fairly obvious that schools should be located where there will be a minimum of noise, odor, traffic, and other undesirable aspects of urban life. The planning agency should have available basic data about existing population and anticipated growth in order to propose intelligent sites for schools. The task of making these recommendations to independent school-district authorities often lies largely with the planning agency.

In the larger cities, the public school system may have its own planning agency, but may not have equally good data, or may proceed from different concepts of values. Coordination is the key. But this sort of coordination requires considerable imagination. It may seem advisable to enlist the city manager, mayor, or members of the council in efforts to generate a liaison with school board members or with the school district superintendent. Each community will, in all probability, handle this task of coordination and cooperation somewhat differently. But it is quite clear that, in the interest of the municipality and the school district, such joint action should be thoroughly planned and carried out.

Municipal parking facilities, streets, parks, playgrounds, public office buildings, airports, swimming pools, and animal pounds all are public facilities. They represent tangible municipal land uses. Their importance to the planning process is sometimes minimized. This is unfortunate. Where an urban government is not doing an intelligent job of planning its own facilities, it is unlikely that private entrepreneurs will welcome municipal planning controls on their ventures.

STUDIES OF MUNICIPAL LAND-USE
REGULATION AND CONTROLS

A part of any comprehensive plan should be a study of all existing codes, ordinances, and administrative policies dealing with land-use

16 Donald H. Webster, URBAN PLANNING AND MUNICIPAL PUBLIC POLICY (New York: Harper and Brothers, 1958), pp. 163–65.

control and regulation. Normally such items as zoning ordinances, building codes, fire codes, electrical codes, plumbing codes, subdivision ordinances, and the like should be included in this analysis. All relevant documents should be carefully analyzed to determine their adequacy, and revisions should be undertaken where needed. The zoning and subdivision ordinances themselves are discussed later in this chapter.

SUMMARY

This discussion of the research phase of urban planning has described the kinds of research typically considered basic to the development of a comprehensive plan. These include studies of population, the economic base and economic conditions, transportation, public facilities, and land-use controls. Obviously missing from this summary—as they are typically absent from actual planning studies—are analyses of broad social aspects of human life in the community. Traditionally, the urban planning process has focused upon physical considerations; little or no concern has been shown for the dynamics of human life within the physical environment.

This amounts to a significant oversight. Fortunately, planners are beginning to recognize it as such. The search has now just begun for planning processes, procedures, and technologies which can more directly respond to such human needs.

Implementation of the Plan

In some of the literature of planning, it appears that once the research phase has been accomplished and the comprehensive planning document drawn, the function of the planner is satisfied. Quite the contrary is true. With the completion of the planning document, the work of the planner has, in fact, just begun. It should be clear that little purpose would be served by conducting esoteric studies and drafting an exceptional comprehensive planning document unless there were a profound determination to implement the policy reflected in it. To be successful, planning must

integrate its functions with those of government (including politics) more adequately than has often been the case.

The planner must see his role as one of day-to-day administration of an ongoing policy. The planning process is never finished. A completed plan is a dead plan. Most of what has been discussed thus far in this chapter is little more than an overture to the real drama of planning. The technical, economic, and social research studies associated with the preparation of a comprehensive plan merely identify the status quo and project what seems likely to occur in the future. Intelligent zoning, subdivision regulation, suitable codes and the other instruments of planning enforcement must be policed on a day-to-day basis if the future is to look anything like the planned projection.

KEEPING THE PLAN UP-TO-DATE

Even with adequate enforcement, the planner should be prepared to cope with totally unexpected events. The intelligence function cannot be overemphasized. In a time when change is accelerating and complexity is increasing, it is necessary not only to know what the status quo is like and what it suggests for the future, but also it is equally important to monitor, on a continuing basis, the same categories of data originally gathered in the preparation of the plan. This makes it possible to anticipate significant changes in the community before their full repercussions are felt, or what Frederick Bair has called the ability to sense "the unexpected obvious."[17]

For example, if the planner at the turn of the century had had all of the predictive skills and analytical abilities available to him today, it is still highly improbable that he could have found reliable data to reflect the impact of the automobile on the contemporary American city. It seems fairly obvious, though, that by the 1930's American planners should have been able to anticipate the automobile's coming significance. In fact, planners did not be-

---

[17] Frederick Bair (speech before the Pennsylvania Planning Association, Philadelphia, Pennsylvania, November 18, 1960).

come fully conscious of the impact of the automobile until much later, and made very little effort to plan to accommodate or deter it until the late 1950's.

It may be fairly said of the American city that the only thing that is permanent is change. Technological advances in the future will undoubtedly change urban life styles in far more dramatic ways than can be envisioned today. New developments in lighting and air conditioning have already brought enormous changes in many cities. It is now possible to do away with all windows and still improve lighting, ventilation, temperature control, and possibly even the view! Industrial technology is changing at such a rapid rate that it challenges the planner to improve performance standards or, indeed, devise entirely new concepts.

Even the concept of the family residence is changing rapidly. Already available is the technology of using heat to eliminate waste. A single home appliance that could dispose of sewage, garbage, and trash by a process in which heat converts waste to gas might revolutionize the planning of neighborhoods. Similarly, the new product industries of the future may be quite unlike industries of the past; they may be thoroughly compatible with residential neighborhoods. While much of this is in the nature of speculation, the point should not be lost. The planning process is a dynamic one; it must be dynamic to match the pace of urban change.

PRESERVING THE PLAN'S INTEGRITY

The Challenge of Private Interests. It is all too clear that private forces act upon the urban land-use market to determine location, land uses, and the quality and form of construction in ways that exclude most public reviews and controls. The very nature of the free market places most private decisions beyond the formal framework of public planning. The resulting relationship may be traditional, but to conclude that it is a satisfactory one for the future ignores the fundamental dilemma of the community. It is vitally important that those charged with the responsibility for administering planning

policy do so with a sense of urgency, recognizing that conscientious prosecution of public goals is essential to the orderly process of urban existence. Private rights must be respected, but not at the expense of the public welfare.

The "public interest" which the makers of planning policy aspire to reflect is under constant challenge by the very nature of man's egotism and the basic pluralism of society. Planning provides some well-defined ideals, but there is usually a gap between ideal and practice, and the ideals of planning can be approached through the day-to-day compromises and adjustments made by planning administrators and other municipal policy officials.

Special pleaders are ever ready to offer self-serving arguments for the relaxation of disadvantageous controls. It is naive to assume that municipal officials always resist such pressures. The elaborate systems of influence that may be mobilized to affect public decisions in the municipality have been well documented.[18] It is well for public planners, indeed for all public officials, to recognize without undue cynicism the nature of political power and the impact it has on public policy. Through understanding, the public official may cope more effectively with those elements of power which seek to be self-serving only. At the same time, it is necessary to cultivate support for the planning process if it is to be successful. It is of fundamental importance to recognize that no public policy, including planning, can for long be successful without the support of the "community power structure."

The Planner's Response. Lest the picture leave the planner and the administrator standing naked and helpless before an awesome coalition of private parties, the point should be made that these private parties are often civic minded and sometimes willing to subvert their special interests to the broader good and an enlightened public policy. The planner, through his continuous contact with community elites and their representatives, is in a

---

[18] Clyde J. Wingfield, "Powerful Structure and Decision Making in City Planning," THE PUBLIC ADMINISTRATION REVIEW, June, 1963.

unique position to educate, influence, and thereby affect their behavior.

If the planner is to be successful, he must see his role in the community as something other than an abstract designer. Like wealth or social status, skill and knowledge may be transmuted into influence and power. However, the potential for power and influence is not the equivalent of its exercise.

The best way to exercise the power potential is a subject of continuing debate, but one obvious strategy concerns planning's public-education function. The planner is in a unique position to upgrade his constituents' values in such a manner that decisions made by private parties are more likely to be in accord with public plans. Planners and other municipal administrators have contact with top community elites fairly infrequently. However, they work almost daily with the intermediaries of the elites, e.g., lawyers, brokers, realtors, accountants, and others who represent the economic elites of the community. Thus, planners have a unique opportunity for the education and reorientation of a group of people who have easy access to community decision makers. Through this group, access to top decision makers may be obtained and some re-education to public policy values may be accomplished.

Seminars focusing on urban economic development, public facilities, aesthetics and amenities, social problems, and other key concerns may be effective educational vehicles. Where community elites can be involved in such programs, they may serve a dual purpose. While primarily educational, the process may lead to a mechanism for formal access to the community's centers of power. Further, these relatively informal confrontations with social and economic elites in the community provide an opportunity for planners and municipal administrators to gauge their plans and ideals against those of a powerful and usually more sophisticated constituency, without whose approval few public improvements are likely, and none can be permanent.

Problems of role, scale, education, and organization make the task of remolding the attitudes and values of a broad segment of the community an unlikely and, in all probability, inappropriate function for public administrators. And yet the people make the community. Slums are more than structural problems. They are, in the main, human problems. Urban renewal must be more than structural renewal; it must be human renewal as well. Methods to encourage economic and social escalation, motivate skill development, and promote simple adjustment to urban life are exceedingly hard to find. Nonetheless, public leaders, whether they wish it or not, bear continuing responsibility for the education of private individuals with respect to their obligations of community citizenship.

Summary. The formal devices by which planning implementation occurs are the official map, the zoning ordinance, land-use regulations, the various ordinances providing for capital improvements, and human improvement. The importance of rigorous administration of these devices cannot be overstated. Successful implementation of the plan depends, however, upon a great deal more than formal execution of formal ordinances. As suggested above, implementation involves the normative values which accrue when there is an accurate perception of what the community is and an adequate understanding of what planning proposes to do about it. That is to say, the plan provides a set of principles and systematic steps which if followed lead to ultimate goals, i.e., the good life, the orderly and aesthetic community.

It is possible to obtain a high degree of consensus concerning ultimate goals. Thus, for the most part, the ultimate values and goals of planning are not usually in dispute. But the instrumental values, those techniques associated with the means by which the ends are to be achieved, are frequently the subject of disagreement. Public officials responsible for the planning process may be required from time to time to serve as proconsuls for the interests of the broader community as these interests are reflected in the comprehensive plan. Planning without some conflict is unlikely, but conflict may be minimized by an intelligent and judicious strategy for public acceptance of the planners' goals.

LAND-USE CONTROL PROGRAMS

After the comprehensive plan is completed and the appropriate courses of action decided, the task of implementation is advanced by various practices and legal instruments. These include zoning, subdivision controls, and various codes.

Zoning. Zoning is perhaps the most widely used method of enforcing the land-use requirements of the comprehensive plan. It is a legal and administrative process whereby the community protects itself against indiscriminate land uses. In technique and concept, zoning is a simple division of land into districts having different kinds of use and density regulations. It is thus an instrument for guiding the use of land in the future and protecting existing uses which conform to the overall aims of the comprehensive plan.

There is little new in the concept of zoning as a land-use tool. The Massachusetts Bay Province had restrictions as early as 1692. Though not called zoning at the time the provision for fire districts, building regulations, and housing codes in earlier days sought to accomplish similar ends. The United States Supreme Court resolved the constitutional status of zoning in 1926, in *Euclid* v. *Ambler Realty Company.* In that case the Court held zoning to be a proper use of the police power held by the states and their subdivisions. The Court asserted that there was a reasonable relationship between the regulation of the area, height, and use of buildings and land and the police-power concepts of safety, morals, public convenience, and welfare.[19]

Of course, the question continues to be asked: By what right does government control and regulate private land use? The answer, perhaps, can best be found in the reciprocal equation suggested by Frederick Bair. The public right to control use of private land is equivalent to the private right to create problems affecting the public interest. Bair reasoned that the degree of public interest (hence, the public control desired) is proportional to the density and interdependence of

the population in a given social unit.[20]

Statutory zoning authority is granted to most municipal jurisdictions. The legal rationale relies on the concept of police power and usually limits its purposes to the following: (1) to lessen congestion on public thoroughfares; (2) to secure safety from fire, panic, and other dangers; (3) to promote health and safety; (4) to prevent the overcrowding of land; (5) to avoid undue concentration of population and to facilitate adequate provision of transportation, water, sewage, schools, parks, and other public facilities; (6) to promote the general welfare and morals; (7) to conserve the value of property; and (8) to encourage the most appropriate use of land throughout the jurisdiction.

These ends are accomplished by: (1) regulating height or number of stories and size of buildings; (2) regulating the percentage of a lot that may be occupied by a building: (3) specifying the size of yards, courts, and other open spaces; (4) controlling the density (population) by use in relation to the lot size; (5) regulating location and use of building structures and land for trade, industry, residence, or other purposes; (6) dividing municipalities into districts of such number, shape, and area as may best be suited to carry out the purposes of land-use planning.[21]

A zoning ordinance is drawn in two parts: (1) a map showing the location of the various districts or zones (usually color-coded) and (2) the text of an ordinance setting forth the regulations applied to each zone and the general information and definitions necessary for its understanding and enforcement. The zoning ordinance is a highly legalistic document,

---

[19] *Euclid* v. *Ambler Realty Company,* 272, U.S. 365 (1926).

[20] Perry L. Norton, ed., BAIR FACTS: THE WRITINGS OF FREDERICK H. BAIR, JR. (West Trenton, New Jersey: Chandler-Davis Publishing Company, 1960).

[21] Adapted from the Pennsylvania state statutes. The above language is paraphrased from the Pennsylvania codes. However, it should not be assumed that any one of the above purposes or methods of accomplishment would be sufficient in itself, nor do all apply to a given jurisdiction. Furthermore, this list is not exhaustive; additional purposes are sometimes permitted, such as the use of zoning to control the architectural style of homes for aesthetic purposes or the imposition of minimum house sizes to guard against low cost construction in certain areas.

and must be carefully drawn if it is to have validity before the courts. In some states the courts have ruled that the zoning ordinance is not valid unless it is based on a comprehensive land-use plan. In other communities, zoning may be in effect an acknowledgement of the status quo, with somewhat arbitrary projections of future uses.

As has already been said of the comprehensive plan, the zoning ordinance means little without good administration and enforcement. The permissive granting of variances, special use permits, and a general laxity in the prosecution of regulations produce spotty zoning and can quickly negate the best zoning ordinance.

Organization for Zoning. Effective zoning administration usually depends upon the appointment of a responsible and able administrator. The zoning administrator, by whatever title, should be the municipal officer primarily responsible for the issuance of permits authorized by the zoning ordinance. It is his duty to check all new land uses or changes in land uses to insure compliance with the terms of the ordinance. He should not have the discretion to issue permits which deviate from the intent of the ordinance.

While the zoning administrator ought to have original jurisdiction in administrative decisions affecting the zoning ordinance, there must be some appellate process. The zoning board of adjustment or zoning board of appeals is frequently a legal requirement of state statutes. It is the function of this appellate board to hear and decide appeals brought as the result of disagreements between private parties and administrative officers. Normally the board has discretionary powers in interpreting the zoning ordinance; it may grant requests for special exceptions and authorize variances from the zoning ordinance where appropriate. The composition of the appeals boards varies according to the status of the several states. However constituted, it is vitally important that those who sit in this sensitive position be well-informed about the more sophisticated aspects of zoning and be exceedingly conscientious in their duties.

The zoning commission is coterminous with the planning commission. Its basic function is the preparation of the zoning ordinance for presentation to the council. The zoning ordinance, like other municipal ordinances, must be adopted by the council before it has standing at law. Changes in the zoning ordinance may be made only by the council. In some states the planning (zoning) commission is required to make recommendations regarding changes in the ordinance to the council before council action on petitions for rezoning.[22]

Subdivision Ordinances and Building Codes. Subdivision control, like zoning, serves as a preventive measure guarding against improper lot layout, bad street arrangement, and generally inadequate subdivision preparation. Such ordinances are especially useful in areas experiencing rapid land development. The community, individual home owners, and land developers will all benefit from a well-administered subdivision control program. Well planned subdivisions mean better sites on which to live, lower public-service costs, and sometimes even added profits to developers.

A subdivision ordinance is a necessary condition for the effective administration of the comprehensive plan. The establishment of minimum requirements with which developers and builders must comply has come to be generally accepted. Building codes have also proven their worth. Experience has shown that properly constructed buildings will last longer, be safer, be of greater utility to occupants, and contribute more to aesthetics and the general property values of the community. Such features as building size, set-back requirements, safety factors, street design and quality, sidewalk standards (if any), provision for parks, playgrounds, school sites, and other public facilities should be handled in the subdivision ordinance or in related codes. Various other codes, including plumbing, electrical, and health, also serve to police the quality of new subdivisions.

The specific enforcement instrument will vary from one community to another. Proce-

---

[22] For a brief but useful discussion of zoning administration, see Martin J. Rody and Herbert Smith, ZONING PRIMER (West Trenton, New Jersey: Chandler-Davis Publishing Company, 1960).

dures of the large city are not necessarily valid for the rural place. Nonetheless, all subdivision development should be guided by city or county subdivision ordinances.

While the problems may be different in the rural countryside, they are no less serious. Both the planner and the private citizen should realize that the success of any program of planning can be measured only by its ultimate impact upon the community. In a very short time the rapid growth resulting from industrial expansion, highway construction, and general increase of population can swallow up an enormous amount of vacant land. Much of the rural landscape peripheral to cities will be fully developed within another decade.

Orderly urban development depends upon the intelligent use of this land resource and the adequate provision within it for needed public facilities as well as for private uses. Planning for these uses is of utmost importance, but it is not likely to have the impact intended unless the private citizen is educated to the values and advantages of planning. Both are functions of the planning staff and other responsible administrators.

Conclusion

Planning, in the sense of anticipating the future and programming an accommodation to it, occurs in all human endeavor. What has been described in this chapter is the application of that rational process to local government. The results of uncoordinated, piecemeal, and inadvertent planning are all too apparent in American communities today. Slums, traffic congestion, deteriorating central cities, inadequate parking space, air and water pollution, and a whole host of other nuisances are often the by-products of inadequate planning or the absence of planning altogether.

This chapter has been addressed primarily to physical planning. However, it is clear that comprehensive planning of the community must include other dimensions. Comparable attention should be given to the health, welfare, and happiness of people in the community and to the common need for economic development.

Activities essential to good municipal administration generally are discussed separately in this book and elsewhere because history and circumstances have classified them apart in the minds of most people and in the organization of municipal government. There may be sufficient administrative justification to maintain this separation in practice, but there should not be a separation in the minds of those who plan for the future welfare of the city. Coordination among agencies responsible for different kinds of planning is essential for intelligent local government.

Municipal government must also provide for long-range financial planning, paralleling the comprehensive or general plan, if the public facilities and services segment is to keep pace with other facets of urban growth. A capital budget coordinated and integrated with a comprehensive plan provides the first phase of the financial plan. However, an intelligent and realistic assessment of anticipated revenues from taxation, bonding, and other sources must be projected over a long-term period corresponding to that covered by the comprehensive plan. Otherwise, the municipal government finds itself in the somewhat inconsistent position of attempting to project a plan for the private development of the community without a corresponding instrument for the development of public-sector facilities and services.

Planning is no panacea for municipal ills. Certainly a municipality may have excellent planning and still find itself in serious difficulties. It is not realistic to assume that planning is more than it is. Planning is another administrative procedure by which those who are responsible for guiding the course of the municipality, through time, may better chart its course, and steer accordingly.

13

Personnel Administration

IN THE USUAL CITY GOVERNMENT, personal services consume from 50 to 70 percent of the total operating budget. Moreover, public services are rendered by people, not by machines. The degree of citizen satisfaction with public services depends as heavily on *how* they are performed as on *what* is performed. Clearly, effective utilization and management of personnel is a "must" if the municipality is to provide satisfactory services at reasonable cost.

Personnel administration is "the totality of concern with the human resources of organization," according to one authority.[1] This definition helps to establish one cardinal principle: anyone in management—chief administrator, department head, or foreman—is concerned with the human resources of the agency and therefore is engaged in personnel administration. The existence of a personnel department does not lessen management responsibility for personnel administration; such a department is simply an additional resource to aid in carrying out this responsibility.

Responsibility for Personnel Administration

It follows from the above that personnel administration is one of the prime responsibilities of line managers. The chief executive officer of the city is automatically the chief personnel officer as well. He must take the final

responsibility on every appointment, every promotion, every disciplinary action. He either establishes salary rates or recommends them to the council. He must see to it that the city government is properly organized to handle its personnel problems, and that the role of the central personnel department is clearly spelled out for the guidance of all management officials. He has a personal duty —which cannot be effectively delegated—for the selection of key administrators, and for their orientation and development. He must provide the leadership necessary to maintain a high level of employee morale and loyalty. Others may relieve him of many of the duties of personnel management, but not of his ultimate accountability.

ORGANIZING FOR PERSONNEL ADMINISTRATION

The chief executive has available three alternative plans of organization for personnel administration, depending on the size of the community and the basic laws, ordinances, or charter provisions which govern administrative structure.

The Personnel Department. In any medium or large community, it is preferable that the chief executive establish a personnel department whose head reports directly to him. The personnel department should be staffed with enough technical and clerical employees to meet its responsibilities. These responsibilities vary so widely from community to community that it is not possible to develop a meaningful ratio of personnel employees to total employment. As a simple rule of thumb,

---

[1] O. Glenn Stahl, PUBLIC PERSONNEL ADMINISTRATION (New York: Harper & Row, 1962), p. 15.

however, it can be said that the personnel department budget should not be less than 5 percent of the total city payroll, and that few agencies ever receive as much as 1 percent.[2]

Such a department serves as a staff agency to the chief executive and all operating officials. Its specific role, vis-a-vis line officials, is determined by the executive within the framework of laws. The personnel director is a member of the executive's immediate staff, accepted as part of the team, and in an excellent position to make sure that good personnel practices are followed and that personnel implications are not overlooked in any major policy decision.

The Independent Civil Service Commission. In many cities the chief administrator faces the mandated existence of the independent civil service commission. This may be a requirement of the state constitution, city charter, or state law.

The independent civil service commission is deeply rooted in the past. It began as a reform aimed at the administration. In order to curb administrative corruption, the reformers logically circumscribed administrative powers by giving certain authority to an independent body. Typically, these powers were limited to areas in which corruption had been found. Since appointments were handed out on a patronage basis, the power to make appointments was circumscribed by the requirement of civil service examinations.

The philosophy underlying the independence of civil service from the administration violates the principle of authority commensurate with responsibility, considered essential to good administration. Dependent upon the specific civil service law—they vary widely—the administrator may be cut off from such authority as the selection of key officials. Ohio law, for example, mandates the appointment of a police chief by promotional examination from the ranks, with the number one eligible receiving the appointment regardless of any other consideration.

While such limitation is admittedly wrong in theory, this is no license for the administrator to ignore responsibility. Men, not legal framework, determine the quality of government. It is quite possible to win the cooperation of the independent civil service commission and have it operate much the same as a personnel department under the chief executive. Milwaukee is an excellent example of close cooperation; its civil service department operates as a personnel department with full acceptance by departmental officials. In New Orleans, the civil service commission's executive head participates as a member of the mayor's cabinet. When the administration is honest, the civil service commission's "policing" role becomes unnecessary, and the commission's staff competence can be directed toward positive personnel programs.

The Personnel Function as One Assignment of an Administrative Assistant. In smaller jurisdictions, with few employees, there may be insufficient work to justify a full-time personnel officer. In such cases, this role can be assigned to a qualified administrator with other compatible duties. The chief administrator himself may assume the job. He may have an assistant available. He may combine personnel with other staff functions, such as budgeting. Full-time or part-time, large agency or small, the basic responsibilities are still the same.

LEGAL FRAMEWORK FOR THE
PERSONNEL PROGRAM

Good law does not assure good administration. But a good law can bulwark good administration. This is just as true in personnel management as in any other facet of government.

The principal advantages of good legislation are two. First, it helps provide a continuity of policy and practice beyond the tenure of elected officials. This is especially important in the development of a career service wherein employees are looking ahead to permanent employment with the city. They want and deserve some assurance of their future. Second, the legislation should

---

[2] Detailed information on personnel staffing ratios can be obtained from periodic publications of the Public Personnel Association entitled "Budgets, Staffs and Pay Rates of Public Personnel Agencies."

provide management with the tools to manage. Adequate discretion to make proper decisions and to solve problems is necessary.

Basic personnel legislation may be found in a variety of places—state constitutions, statutes, city charters, or ordinances. Generally state legislation of any sort is less desirable from the viewpoint of the local administrator because it tends to ignore particular local conditions. Large and small communities have to operate under identical law, even though their problems differ. Constitutional or charter provisions are proper, provided they are confined to basic policies and do not get into procedural matters. They are too difficult to change for an area such as personnel management in which techniques are constantly revised.

Probably the best solution is a statutory or charter provision establishing a merit system and assigning responsibility for executing it. This, coupled with a personnel ordinance passed by the council, can provide an organizational framework suitable to the municipality. Stability can thus be provided without a strait jacket. The ordinance can be readily modified to meet conditions.[3]

The most essential element to be included in the basic legal provision is the principle of merit. There is no place in any employment situation for special privilege or discrimination, whether it be based on politics, race, religion, or any other factor.

A second element is provision for rule-making authority. This should be delegated to the chief administrator or the personnel director, possibly subject to the concurrence of the council. All procedural aspects of personnel management can thus be included in these rules, with provision for easy change as circumstances warrant.

Finally, the basic legal document should include a provision for an appeal procedure. Where an independent civil service commission is created, this is normally a commission function. Where there is no commission, a personnel appeals board should be established. Employees are entitled to this assurance of objectivity. This personnel board may also be given authority to review the rules and regulations of the personnel director or chief administrator, even though its power may be limited to making recommendations.

In short, the legal framework should emphasize stability of policy and flexibility of procedure. These are not incompatible.

The Supervisor as Personnel Manager

As previously stated, every supervisor is a personnel manager. He cannot escape taking responsibility for his decisions involving his subordinates. A staff personnel agency may help him in his role as decision maker.

Depending upon the size and policy of the organization, certain personnel actions normally fall more heavily on the supervisor than do others. In this section, performance appraisal, handling of grievances, accident prevention, and motivation are discussed as examples of personnel concerns over which the supervisor has widest discretion. Other matters, such as union negotiation, position classification and pay determination, employee development, and the separation process are more likely to be handled either by the staff personnel agency or by the highest levels of line officialdom. This is not to say that the supervisor is unconcerned. It merely means that, in the latter examples, the typical supervisor is expected to consult more, or earlier, before action is taken.

PERFORMANCE APPRAISAL

It is a truism that everyone in this world constantly rates his fellow men, whether they be his colleagues, his superiors, or his subordinates. Yet, despite this inevitable tendency, formal performance appraisal is one of the least understood personnel techniques. So uncertain are appraisal techniques that some highly respected personnel agencies do not even have a formal evaluation program.

---

[3] A recommended charter provision establishing a personnel system is contained in National Municipal League, MODEL CITY CHARTER (New York: The League, 6th ed., 1964), pp. 26–27. This proposal would limit the personnel board strictly to advisory functions.

Where used, rating systems are ordinarily designed by the staff personnel agency, but for use by line supervision. The system chosen should be compatible with the primary objectives to be achieved. Some systems are primarily designed as an aid to the supervisor in his role as a counselor. Some are intended to aid in administrative decisions—promotions, layoffs, salary increases. All are intended to make sure that the rater does not overlook, and thus fail to act on, pertinent aspects of the employee's performance.

A rating used primarily for counseling will be couched in terms familiar to the type of employee being rated. One such system is the "critical incident" method. In this system, the rater will record, as they occur, good and poor incidents of performance which he considers as indicative of the employee being rated. These will normally be noted at the time of occurrence, and summarized on the rating form. Since these are specific acts of commission or omission, the employee can accept a rating based upon this system because he ordinarily recalls the events. He was late for work, he was AWOL, he missed a radio call, he was the subject of a complimentary letter received by the chief administrator. What he might *not* accept in this system is the conclusion reached by the rater as to whether these events add up to good, mediocre, or poor performance. (Such conclusions, however, are not an essential part of this system.) Nevertheless, it is apparent that this system provides the supervisor with a useful springboard to counseling.

At the opposite end of the rating spectrum, the "forced choice" system is designed to force the rater into spreading out the relative ranking of his employees by confronting him with pairs or groups of statements, and requiring him to select from each group the one or two most descriptive (or least descriptive) of the employee. None may actually fit; he must choose the closest. In the following example,[4] the rater is required to check the one most descriptive and the one least descriptive:

	Most	Least
Doesn't try to pull rank	____	____
Knows his men, their capabilities and limitations	____	____
Low efficiency	____	____
Uses a steady monotone in his voice	____	____

Inasmuch as the checked trait may admittedly not be truly descriptive of the employee, it is obvious that showing it to the employee would only create difficulties. Thus this type of rating lends itself only to those situations where the rating is confidential, for administrative use only.

Perhaps the most common form is the rating scale in which a number of traits are listed, with the rater required to check the degree of his satisfaction on each trait for each employee. Quality and quantity of work, reliability, dependability, and other comparable personal traits are usually provided. Frequently there is also a means of determining a score if the rating is to be used for administrative purposes. This may be an arbitrary number of points for each degree of each trait, or it may be up to the rater to determine subjectively, provided he is not inconsistent with the general run of trait ratings.

This system can be used in counseling employees for it represents the supervisor's true judgment on each trait, not a forced decision; the general nature of the traits, however, furnishes little support to the rater in justifying his markings unless he also keeps a record of incidents or writes descriptive comments on the form.

While all of the above systems have their admitted weaknesses, they do have the advantage of placing some common framework in the hands of all raters; they remind them of things important to the agency. The wise administrator will look for the values of the rating system, not faults. He will rate his subordinates, in part, on how they rate their subordinates. He will examine ratings to see if they point up areas of weakness in the agency; for example, when the rating discloses a personal animosity in a group that can be solved only by transfer or other means of removal. He will look for improvement in

---

[4] George Strauss and Leonard R. Sayles, PERSONNEL: THE HUMAN PROBLEMS OF MANAGEMENT (Englewood Cliffs, New Jersey: Prentice-Hall, 1960) , p. 533.

workers whose weaknesses have been reported to them via the rating system. He will use ratings as one of many means to determine who should be given additional opportunities which might lead to advancement or additional responsibility.

Most important, the administrator will expect his rating system to give employees a feeling they know where they stand with the boss. Every employee wants to know, and is entitled to know, whether his performance is or is not acceptable. Without the pressure of a rating system it is doubtful that many bosses would take the time to tell their workers. Inasmuch as the foreman is going to evaluate his people anyway, he should do it systematically and tell them the results. This is the role of performance appraisal.

MOTIVATION

Motivation is the term applied to the thoughts or feelings that cause a person to act. The administrator's objective is to motivate each employee to act in a manner compatible with the aims of the agency. This is not easy, nor is there a formula readily available to help. The problem varies according to the type of worker. As city government usually employs many types of employees, it is apparent that what works in one department will not necessarily work in another. This discussion will consider some of the important attributes of people which influence their behavior, and which therefore must be taken into account in determining which technique of supervision is likely to be successful in a given situation.

Many studies have established that workers seek more than paychecks from their jobs. Appreciation for work well done, a feeling of participation in decisions that affect them, and job security generally rate above pay in determining job satisfaction.

These findings reflect the importance of the various psychological needs of people. Pay, the ability to advance and therefore to get more pay, and security are necessary to satisfy the *off-the-job* needs of employees—to furnish them with food, clothing, shelter, and

other things which a steady income provides. But there are other needs which can be met on the job. These include the need for a feeling of accomplishment, the need to have pride in one's skill and knowledge, the need for social relationships, the desire to help others and to be helped when needed, the feeling of being accepted by one's associates as well as one's superiors, the knowledge of where one stands with the boss.[5]

Helping each subordinate meet his needs is a proper role of supervision. It was not always so regarded. When living standards were low, the mere possession of a job and its income was enough to satisfy most workers; they needed every cent they could get, just for the bare essentials of life. They expected nothing more. As basic wants became cheaper in relation to salaries, it became easier to meet these needs. Few Americans now have jobs which pay so little that their incomes cover only food, shelter, and clothing. A worker can decide whether he wants to get a job with a paycheck big enough to provide luxuries, or stay with an occupation offering him greater intangible satisfactions but less cash.

Different categories of employees have differing "mixes" of these psychological needs. For example, the unskilled laborer is more likely to find his satisfactions off the job, and therefore be more concerned with his pay and security, than is the typical white collar employee. It is more difficult for the unskilled worker to have a feeling of accomplishment, a pride in his skill—in short, job status. The white collar office worker, on the other hand, is more likely to place great emphasis on his closeness to executives, on the personal relationships that occur on the job, on his pride in a job well done. He went into office work knowing that it frequently paid less money than manual work, but he has an inner need for status.

The professional worker usually differs from both of the above types. He is more likely to emphasize the need for a feeling of

---

[5] For a fuller discussion of the psychological needs of people, see *Ibid.*, Chapters 1 and 5.

professional accomplishment and of recognition by his peers—other professionals in his same field. Opportunity for writing technical articles may well build greater job satisfaction than a material benefit. He may even turn down opportunities to move into management if such a move requires that he give up the practice of his profession. The professional is seldom interested in the security provided by the employer; his competence as a professional gives him a strong sense of security.

The professional as well as the managerial employee is concerned with his role more than his job. He is concerned with how he relates to other people in many types of work-related situations. He wants to be able to exercise the aspects of himself that he values most highly. For example, the executive likes the role of decision maker. If he is denied the opportunity to make decisions—if he is second-guessed by higher echelons—his dissatisfaction may well cause him to quit, even though he is well paid, has security, and enjoys every other facet of his position.[6]

What does this brief discussion of motivation mean to the chief administrator? It is intended first to steer the reader away from the very human tendency to look for simple answers to complex problems: the motivation of people defies a pat answer. There are no "across the board" answers to motivation problems. Next, it is intended to warn against expecting others to react in the same manner as the executive. Others do not necessarily have the same system of values. Since all types of employees do not expect the same satisfactions from their work, supervision must be adjusted accordingly. Finally, this discussion emphasizes that, at least for many people, their roles—how they become involved in their work and human associations—are more significant than their specific responsibilities. The administrator interested in motivating his key officials must look to each official as an individual for his answer.

_____

[6] An elaboration of the role concept vis-a-vis the narrow job concept can be found in Marshall McLuhan, UNDERSTANDING MEDIA (New York: McGraw-Hill, 1964).

HANDLING GRIEVANCES

Whether or not employees are unionized, modern management provides a grievance procedure. Usually a grievance procedure is merely a step-by-step appeal procedure through the echelons of supervision. An employee with a grievance can take his problem first to his foreman, then to the next higher supervisor, and up the hierarchy until he gets what he considers justice, or reaches a terminal point which has been predetermined—the chief administrator, a civil service commission, or, in a few instances, third-party arbitration.

What is a grievance? Normally it is a situation wherein an employee believes supervision has misinterpreted the applicable rule, ordinance, or provision of a union agreement. Many modern managements, however, take the position that an employee has a grievance any time he thinks he has a grievance. They use the grievance procedure to let him get it off his chest. The theory is that a sore point should be cleared up and removed. If the employee feels something is wrong, the grievance procedure brings it to the management's attention where it can either be corrected or explained.

If a union exists, the grievant usually has the assistance of a union steward or officer. This can be advantageous to both the employee and to management. The employee gains an articulate spokesman as well as the confidence that his act of grieving will bring no reprisals. Management also gains. The union agent is conversant with regulations; he may have the employee's confidence more than the supervisor. His explanation to the employee may be better accepted.

Because the immediate supervisor usually has made the decision being questioned, too often he resents the grievance process. His judgment is being questioned. Perhaps in some cases he is being overruled by higher echelons. His pride is involved. Management *must* do a good job of educating first-level supervision if the grievance procedure is to work effectively. This training must point out to supervisors that they are not expected to be infallible; that there can be honest differences of opinions on many management decisions. Their attitude toward the grievance procedure can be immeasurably assisted if they are not arbitrarily overruled, but are first given the opportunity to change their own decisions in order to save face.

When there is third-party arbitration as the terminal step of the grievance procedure, it is particularly important to train foremen in how to present their cases before higher supervision and the arbitrator. The value of documenting exactly what happened prior to the grievance must be stressed; the arbitration proceeding may be months after the incident. The foreman, or immediate supervisor, is the key man in the grievance procedure. He must be made to see the importance of his role.

SAFETY AND ACCIDENT PREVENTION

While it is common to give the staff personnel agency certain responsibilities for safety and accident prevention, no safety program can be truly effective unless line supervisors are given the key role. Nothing can replace the supervisor's responsibility to see that jobs are performed safely.

Only the supervisor, for example, can enforce on a daily basis working rules and practices designed to promote safety. Further, in his training of employees, he can best stress safe work habits and, with his disciplinary authority, assure adherence to these habits and rules.

While the ultimate responsibility for safety belongs to the line supervisor, the personnel agency can be of material help. Job applicants should be properly screened for physical requirements and accident proneness during recruitment interviews, accident investigations should be made, formal safety training programs should be undertaken, safety campaigns should be conducted, and accident records maintained. Finally, the personnel agency should be responsible for handling all claims for workmen's compensation.

The cost of accidents justifies the expenditure of considerable time and effort in safety activities. In addition to the intangible costs in suffering and lost production, the direct premium for compensation will frequently exceed 1 percent of payroll. Cities which have been aware of the costs have developed safety programs—always with the involvement of immediate supervision—which have brought about drastic reductions in these premiums.

Recruitment, Selection, and Appointment

Getting qualified persons into the municipal service requires cooperative action on the part of both the central personnel agency and line management. Both should work on recruitment. Both should cooperate in the development of valid examinations and other screening devices. Both should strive to make municipal careers as appealing as possible.

RECRUITMENT

The first element in any recruitment campaign is to have attractive job opportunities. Therefore, assuming the existence of such job opportunities, the best recruitment begins with "institutional" advertising—the development of a "good public image" of the governmental agency, and of the entire government itself! The more favorable the image of the government, the easier the recruitment. Although several studies have indicated that government enters the recruitment race with private industry under the handicap of low prestige,[7] there is also ample evidence that this situation can be improved. Successful recruitment requires that it be improved.

Institutional advertising is not a task that can be relegated to the personnel agency; it is top management's responsibility, shared by every department, every division, every employee.

Assuming that the public image of the government is reasonably favorable, recruitment for specific occupations becomes a joint effort of line officials and the central personnel

[7] Leonard White, THE PRESTIGE VALUE OF PUBLIC EMPLOYMENT IN CHICAGO: AN EXPERIMENTAL STUDY (Chicago: University of Chicago Press, 1929). For a more up-to-date study, with slightly more encouraging conclusions, see Morris Janowitz and Deil Wright, "Prestige of Public Employment, 1929 and 1954," PUBLIC ADMINISTRATION REVIEW, Winter, 1956, pp. 15–22.

agency. The personnel agency should supervise the advertising for candidates and may be capable of doing all that is necessary for recruiting many types of employees. Frequently, and particularly when specialized training is required, the line agencies themselves can best handle the recruiting effort. In other cases, the sheer weight of numbers is on the side of the operating agency: why not, for example, ask all police officers to talk up the next recruitment examination? *It is not an admission of failure on the part of the central agency to ask for line assistance in recruitment.*

Recruitment can be improved if the central personnel agency makes it easy to apply. Too much red tape discourages good applicants. Many well qualified potential applicants can walk into an industrial personnel department and get a job offer on the first visit. The city government should approach this simplicity as closely as possible. Information should be freely given by phone or mail. Application forms should be available on telephone request. Some cities make them available in libraries, fire stations, and other public buildings located in various neighborhoods and open at other than usual business hours. This extra effort can materially assist recruitment, particularly in a tight labor market.

SELECTION

The three basic ingredients for a good selection program are: (1) knowledge of what skills are really needed to perform the work; (2) candidates who have these abilities; and (3) tests which accurately measure necessary abilities. No test technician and no position classifier can possibly determine what is needed to do the work without getting his information from line management. Therefore it is at this point that line participation in the selection process begins.

In determining what qualities are needed to perform the work, the administrator must first distinguish between those positions immediately requiring a high level of performance based on prior experience, and those where longer periods of training are possible

and perhaps even desirable. For example, if the need is for a journeyman carpenter being paid the full union scale for the work, it is obvious that each applicant should be required to demonstrate his experience in his craft. On the other hand, it is commonly accepted that applicants for police work need have no prior experience. The latter approach is justified wherever future potential rather than immediate performance is paramount. It is particularly justified in positions unique to the public service, for prior experience in such work is obviously impossible.

The administrator should also encourage the test technicians and the civil service commission to maximize competition by the elimination of as many artificial barriers as possible. Too often, unreasonable restrictions are imposed with regard to citizenship, residence, age, and sex. In some instances, particularly citizenship, these restrictions are imposed by law. When they are discretionary with the local agency, every effort should be made to be sure they are reasonable. It is one thing to set a low maximum age limit for the police force, with its physical demands and its long period of training; it is quite another to set a low age limit for stenographers. Likewise, local residence restrictions tend to cut down qualified competition. They *may* be justified in some easy-to-fill occupations, but residence restrictions should be waived when potential applicants are scarce.

Examinations. Books have been written on the subject of tests and measurements.[8] The wise administrator will hire good test technicians and know only enough about the subject to be sure that he and his line officials can fully and effectively participate in the selection process.

Once qualifications are determined for any position, or series of positions, the administrator should leave the preparation of examinations to a test technician. This is a special

---

[8] For detailed treatment of testing, see Dorothy C. Atkins *et al.,* CONSTRUCTION AND ANALYSIS OF ACHIEVEMENT TESTS (Washington: U.S. Civil Service Commission, 1947), and Lee J. Cronbach, ESSENTIALS OF PSYCHOLOGICAL TESTING (New York: Harper and Row, 1960), two of the outstanding works in this field.

field of competence; any moderately large agency will have enough demand for tests so that one or more qualified technicians can be kept busy. Technicians can be retained by smaller agencies on a consulting basis.

The administrator, however, is almost certain to become involved in the selection process by interviewing candidates who have successfully completed the prescribed series of written and performance tests. This initial interview is a key portion of the examination process. Most civil service agencies rate candidates on their interview performance and use this rating as part of the grade which determines their eligibility for possible appointment.

Because of the importance of this interview, and because a second interview is universally used in selecting appointees from lists of eligible candidates, skill in interviewing is a basic requirement for most supervisory positions.

Interviewing Techniques. Good interviewing is more than just sitting down for a little talk with a candidate. Informality is fine if it means that the atmosphere will be relaxed and both interviewer and candidate at ease, but the inexperienced interviewer too often feels that he can tell all about a candidate from a few moments of talk. He couldn't be more wrong. Here are some suggestions for making the most of the interview process:

1. Plan the interview. Decide in advance what should be accomplished, then structure the interview in advance to achieve these goals. A written list of questions which will be put to each candidate should be prepared so there can be a valid comparison and so important items will not be forgotten.

2. Put the candidate at ease. Most job candidates approach an interview with apprehension. It means a lot to them, yet they are completely at the employer's mercy. Some nervousness is almost inevitable. Extreme nervousness, on the other hand, negates the purpose of the interview. Therefore it is desirable to put the candidate at ease, to the extent possible. A courteous greeting; a relaxed, friendly manner; a concentration on

the interview; the elimination of all interference—these are characteristic of a good interview. Questions should be put to the candidate in an informal manner, and reworded if he does not understand.

3. Look for what is important. The candidate may have many personal qualities, good or bad, which have nothing whatsoever to do with job performance. Appearance is a good example. A movie-star profile is important for the job of movie star, but not for most city positions. Likewise, the candidate who uses poor English may properly be downgraded if the position requires ability to speak well, but this requirement should be downgraded if he is applying for a mechanic's position.

The good interviewer will also emphasize those qualities which he can reasonably measure in the interview. An interview will not, for example, reveal the candidate's honesty, integrity, initiative, or willingness to cooperate. The only available index on such traits would be his employment history; if he was honest, reliable, and cooperative at the Jones Co., he is likely to remain the same when he works for the city.

Qualities which can be measured in the interview include appearance, neatness, ability to speak distinctly, ability to organize one's thoughts and to express them understandably, and, in general, one's manner of getting along with people. Some of these may be unimportant to the particular job and should be overlooked. On more important positions, particularly administrative positions, and in positions which constitute excellent training spots for future advancement, these qualities should be thoroughly explored.

4. Check the candidate's statements. He will try to put his best foot forward. Some candidates are better personal salesmen than others. Some tend to exaggerate their experience. The interview is an appropriate time to review their applications, particularly their work history, and get a full picture of exactly what they did in each relevant position. Skillfully done, this type of questioning usually

will bring out the real quality of a candidate's background. Further verification can be done by phone or mail.

5. Record the interview. No one's memory is so infallible that records become unnecessary. This is particularly important if there are a number of candidates to interview: they tend to blur after a short time. Notes should be made as the interview progresses, preferably in an unobtrusive manner. Then, immediately following the termination of an interview and before the start of the next, these notes should be summarized into a meaningful record, complete enough so that it will be intelligible at a later date. Specific happenings and impressions should be recorded: if a particular candidate's appearance was less than desirable, it is more meaningful to note the facts on which this conclusion was based—that is, his hair was not combed, or his fingernails were dirty—than to note simply "poor appearance" in the record.

Usually it is considered desirable to use an interview rating form. This form does not supersede the need for good judgment or good interviewing. It is simply a reminder sheet so that essential traits are not overlooked on any candidate.

6. Answer the candidate's questions. Most candidates have some doubts in their minds about the specific position or about general working conditions in the government. The interview is an excellent opportunity for an exchange of information. However, care must be exercised not to draw improper conclusions based upon a candidate's questions. For example, if a candidate asks about a pension plan, it does not necessarily mean he is looking upon the job as a sinecure until retirement.

The proper and candid answering of questions is a good opportunity to build good will toward the government as a whole. However, this impression should not be built upon exaggerated or misleading statements. If he is employed, he will learn the truth. And if this truth disillusions him, he will be a candidate for early separation.

APPOINTMENT

In a typical merit system, selection for original appointment is made by the appointing authority from an eligible list of persons who qualify on the civil service examination. Certification laws vary. Although a few jurisdictions are required to take the eligible with the highest grade, it is most common to give the appointing authority a choice of the top eligibles, usually three for each vacancy. Selection from among these three, or other legal number, is ordinarily made following a second interview and investigation of background and references.

The interview techniques described in the preceding section apply in substance to this second employment interview. In this session, records and ratings take on only a secondary importance while answering the applicant's questions becomes proportionately more important; no candidate should decide his acceptance or rejection of a specific job offer without full information. To do otherwise invites early turnover.

The key difference between the selection interview and the civil service examination interview lies in their relative purpose. The civil service interview attempts to rate applicants on a comparative basis, in terms of their suitability for a *class* of positions. The selection interview attempts to choose the one of a certified number most suitable for a *specific single position*. To cite an extreme example, it is quite possible for a civil service agency to give a high rating for a clerical classification to a one-legged applicant. But if he is certified for a vacancy within the clerical classification that requires heavy emphasis on filing, his physical handicap would become a significant limitation for the job.

The selection process, then, is intended to account for variations among the eligibles and variations among specific positions within the job classification. Specific duties on previous jobs should be explored. Likes and dislikes of each candidate should be known, so that the person selected is most likely to be satisfied with the nature of the position. Positions requiring extensive public contact deserve special attention since not all applicants have the ability to handle the public.

Normally there are no legal restrictions on which person from a certified list of eligible candidates is chosen. Good practice, however, demands that discriminatory selection factors be ignored. The use of the selection interview to perpetuate a racial imbalance, for example, is a proper subject of criticism. The administrator should review selections made by his department heads to ensure against such bias.

In the final analysis, the success of the selection process is usually in direct proportion to the amount of cooperation between the administration and the testing agency. Cooperative setting of test standards and thorough understanding of position requirements help to produce the kind of eligible lists from which selection is reasonably satisfactory.

PROBATIONARY PERIOD

It is typical in government as well as in industry to make all original appointments subject to a probationary period. This is partly a recognition of the limitations of the science of testing, but it also recognizes that skill to work is not always accompanied by will to work. This is perhaps more significant in government than in industry: the commonly-held belief that civil service employees cannot be fired attracts to public employment a number of candidates who are looking for a soft spot.

There is a wide variety of reasons why the administrator cannot be sure of the propriety of his selection without a trial period, including inadequacy of testing, improper position allocation, inability of the new employee to adjust to his environment, slow learning ability, and intangible personality factors. Therefore the probationary period ordinarily permits the separation of an unsatisfactory new employee within a prescribed time without right of appeal.

Proper procedures are necessary to ensure that the probationary period is effectively used. Most important is the need for good employee orientation. The better supervisor spends a disproportionate amount of his time with new employees. His primary purpose is to help them; rating is necessary, but secondary in importance. The new employee cannot do a good job unless he learns specific requirements, standards of performance, work flow, associates, and all other elements of his new environment.

An important part of orientation is the follow-up. How well is the employee actually performing? What questions does he have? Ready assistance from a supervisor, or at least from a designated and qualified old hand, is important.

This follow-up should also include a conference with the new employee at the midpoint of the probationary period. At this conference the supervisor can share with the employee his evaluation of progress. This permits the employee to correct any unsatisfactory facets of his performance before a final judgment is required. Some agencies consider this conference so important that they require a preliminary written rating at the time.

In spite of all precautions, however, some appointments will be made which turn out to be unsatisfactory. The probationary period is the best time to correct such situations. Many agencies require the submission of a performance report covering the entire probationary period so that there is some written explanation of why a separation is necessary. Then the employee can be let go without right of appeal.

The rating form or other records of less-than-satisfactory performance may be significant from a public standpoint even though not legally required. Various classifications require different lengths of probation. A laboring position, in which a limited number of duties are performed repeatedly, lends itself to early determination. On the other hand, a budget technician goes through his cycle of work on an annual basis; a probationary period less than one year would necessarily omit consideration of his performance during some phase of the cycle. Generally speaking, the probationary period should not be longer than necessary; the employee may retain a feeling of insecurity until it is over and this could interfere with top performance. Furthermore, in some agencies employees do not accumulate benefits until passing probation. Rarely is more than one year justified. At the other extreme, a period of less than two or three months is not likely to give supervision enough time to observe work habits.

Position Classification and Pay Administration

POSITION CLASSIFICATION

Position classification is the basic management tool in the field of personnel administration. In any large or medium sized agency, with a full-time personnel officer, the technical aspects of position classification work are best left to the specialist. This is particularly important in a jurisdiction which attempts, as most do, to establish a common plan throughout all departments. Departmental personnel are likely to lack the necessary objectivity in equating positions under their control with those of other departments.

On the other hand, the policies and actual operation of the position classifiers are of great concern to operating management. Any discussion of personnel management for operating officials must therefore include an analysis of this subject.[9]

Purposes of Position Classification. Classification work was initially undertaken to assure equal pay for equal work. This is still important—a morale problem is inevitable if two employees are doing identical work at different pay ranges—but position classification results are used today for a variety of management purposes. These include:

1. Budgeting. It is commonplace to make budgetary allowances for personal services by listing the number of positions by classification rather than by listing individual positions or employees.

2. Pay Plan. The classification plan is ordinarily used as the basis for the pay plan. Each

classification is assigned a pay rate or range based upon the nature of the duties and responsibilities designated for it.

3. Management Analysis. Information gathered by classification technicians is useful to management analysts in determining the amounts of time spent on various tasks and in evaluating the organizational structure of individual agencies.

All of these uses of the classification plan are of interest to administrators. But, as indicated above, the actual task of classification is best left to the technician.[10]

Position Classification Principles and Policies. The principle underlying classification work is that it should produce equality within the service. Most employees are rankled more by partiality within the service than by any other supervisory weakness.

To maintain the principle of impartiality, the classification plan must be dynamic, not static. It must be subject to change as duties change, as agencies expand or contract, as reorganizations take place, as new equipment, tools, and methods are introduced. The initiation of change is the responsibility of line officials. No classification technician can ferret out every changed position for himself; supervision must report changes.

Although the actual work of maintaining a classification plan is normally done by technicians in the central personnel agency, no line manager can eliminate his responsibility for initiating classification reviews. This responsibility is not limited to reporting changes of duties. Civil service examination results rest heavily on the qualifications written into class specifications; unsatisfactory refer-

---

[9] In-depth treatment of position classification can best be obtained from Public Personnel Association, POSITION CLASSIFICATION IN THE PUBLIC SERVICE (Chicago: The Association, 1941).

[10] As with other technical groups, classifiers have developed a jargon. Four definitions are important to any supervisor or administrator who wants to work effectively with classifiers:

1. Position: a set of duties to be performed by one employee.

2. Classification: a group of similar positions which can be treated alike with regard to pay, qualifications, and recruitment.

3. Position description: a list of duties of an individual position.

4. Class specification: a description of a class of positions indicating its title, definition, typical tasks, and minimum qualifications. It may also include lines of promotion.

rals of eligibles should alert supervisors to the need for classification review. This review may show unrealistic qualifications or improper allocation of a specific position.

Supervision should assist in the classification of positions under their control. Most supervisors do not have enough information to compare their positions with those under other supervisors, but they can compare positions for which they are responsible. Good classification technicians welcome this type of help.

Position Classification Procedures. Position classification is normally a three step process. The first step, once a classification or reclassification has been deemed necessary, is to familiarize affected management and employees with all the purposes, procedures, and consequences of the classification work. The second step is to obtain written descriptions for each position being classified. Information for these descriptions should be obtained from the employee, from his supervisor, and from field inspections of the work.

The third step is the process of arranging these descriptions into classes, both as to type of work and level of difficulty. The level of difficulty is usually determined by comparing each position with certain allocation factors, which typically include the knowledge and skills required, complexity of the work, supervision received, supervision exercised if any, other guidelines and instructions for control of the position, the seriousness of error, and the type of contacts with the public and other employees.

After the positions are grouped into classes, the specification is prepared for each class. The plan is then ready for official installation, along with written rules for its interpretation and maintenance. Usually there is a period of time allowed in which employees may appeal for a different allocation.

PAY ADMINISTRATION

Policies. Inasmuch as a city's payroll is such a dominant proportion of its expenditures, it is customary for the legislative body to exercise substantial control over salary and wage rates. The chief executive properly is involved in making recommendations to the council and in supervising the studies preliminary to recommendations. Where unions are present, the executive will very likely be responsible for conducting negotiations, with the results subject to council approval. Therefore it is important that the executive and council agree on the basic pay policies which will govern their actions. These are some of the most important policy questions to be determined:

1. If unions exist within a jurisdiction, to what extent are they recognized in determining pay rates? Some agencies have merely listened to union representatives, then made a unilateral determination. Others have developed policies of negotiation. Some states require that local officials bargain collectively on pay rates and other working conditions. Certainly collective bargaining introduces an element of unpredictability in wage setting because the essence of bargaining is compromise.

2. What level of wages does the city want to establish? In every community there is a wide range of salaries for comparable work. Some employers—frequently in industries whose payrolls represent proportionately small parts of their production costs—pay very high wages as a matter of policy. Others take a more conservative approach. Some are downright niggardly. They pay only what is necessary to meet labor market conditions for minimally qualified employees. The city, as a public employer, normally tries to avoid both extremes. But just where, in the wide range of possible rates, the city wants to end is a question of policy.

3. What, if any, effect should the city's limited ability to pay have on salary rates? Employees argue that if the city's finances will not support a fair wage, then the city should retrench its programs. To do otherwise would mean, in effect, that the employees are subsidizing city activities through substandard wage rates. Moreover, they argue, the citizens will never realize the city's financial plight unless it is brought home to them via a reduction in services.

On the other hand, some city managements

have argued that the process of setting salaries is not so exact that a truly "fair" wage can be defined, and that it is only proper to take income into account. This is commonplace in industry, particularly when unions point to increased profits as an excuse for higher wages. If this is valid, then it is equally proper to consider income limitations in city government, particularly if the limitation is expected to be temporary.

Obviously both viewpoints have their elements of validity. It is equally obvious that extremes must be avoided. A reasonable policy on this question would be to take financial limitations into account when the limitation is expected to be temporary, but to assure employees that proper efforts will be made to relieve their situation after first giving the voters an opportuniy to provide realistic tax income.

In addition to these three policy questions there are some minor policies which should be established—minor in that they lend themselves to ready agreement in most situations:

1. Equal pay for equal work.

2. Nondiscrimination with regard to sex, race, or union organization. It is easy to agree on this as a matter of policy, but far more difficult to put into practice. Pressure from unions for "inequity" adjustments for classifications they represent makes it difficult to be fair to the unorganized. In occupations filled predominantly by women in private industry, it is commonplace to find lower wage rates included in a wage survey simply because of the industrial practice of paying women less. For example, stenographers ordinarily get less than clerks for the same level of responsibility. This fact can distort a city's wage survey and inject into it an unwanted discriminatory element.

3. Incentive pay systems. Generally, the absence of production standards in government makes it difficult to install incentive plans. They have been most successful in industries which can measure productivity with reasonable exactitude.

4. Treatment of noncash benefits. A policy must be established as to whether fringe benefits should be considered in addition to pay or as part of the total compensation package. With fringe costs running 25 percent of payroll or higher, this is becoming less and less of a question; they must be included.

Administration. Some portions of pay administration should be handled in the central personnel agency. Others are a direct responsibility of line officials. Successful pay administration requires cooperation between the personnel agency and the line.[11]

Generally, in the interest of efficiency, the task of making pay studies and keeping other relevant statistics is centralized in the personnel agency. This type of information is necessary if rates are to be kept up to date and particularly if rates are negotiated with unions. In negotiating situations, the central personnel agency ordinarily will have a big role—up to and including the role of chief negotiator. Even if the legislative branch retains close control over negotiations, the personnel agency ordinarily will provide the council with the necessary staff work.

The line's role in pay administration ordinarily starts after the pay plan is adopted. Most pay plans provide within-grade increments for meritorious service. Thus line officials have the responsibility of defining and recognizing meritorious service and recommending increments for employees who meet the standards. Some plans also provide recognition for the outstanding employee in the form of earlier-than-standard increments or double increments. Line officials are charged with the responsibility of making the necessary recommendations in such cases although, because of the special nature of this type of recognition, it is not unusual for the line's recommendation to be reviewed carefully by the staff personnel agency or by top management.

In the course of administration, as new methods, equipment, and organization are installed, the line official has the same responsibility with regard to pay as he has with posi-

---

[11] For detailed discussion of pay problems, see Kenneth O. Warner and J. J. Donovan, eds., PRACTICAL GUIDELINES TO PUBLIC PAY ADMINISTRATION (Chicago: Public Personnel Association; vol. 1 published in 1963, vol. 2 in 1965).

tion classification. Changes in job content and responsibility that affect a position may also affect its pay. The reallocation of a position to an existing classification may automatically take care of the pay problem, but if a new classification is made necessary, then the line supervisor has the obligation to recommend its inclusion in the pay plan at an appropriate level.

Other supervisory experiences may also be related to pay policies. Recruitment difficulties for a particular type of work, for example, may be caused essentially by inadequate pay. Unusual retention difficulties should also be brought to the attention of the pay administrators by the line official. Without this constant cooperative feeding of information, the pay administrator—usually the personnel director—must operate in a vacuum and the results will be less than adequate.

Supervisors should be cautious about jumping to the conclusion that pay is inadequate whenever there is a trouble spot in their agencies. Without minimizing the importance of adequate pay in the minds of workers, it should be kept in mind that other facets of a job can lead to dissatisfaction. These can include such diverse elements as job monotony, lack of job security, dissatisfaction with agency objectives, or poor relationships with other employees and with supervisors. The preemptory conclusion that more pay solves any problem can be costly and fruitless.

Relations with Organized Employees

Many local officials are experiencing for the first time the need for competence in dealing with employee organizations. The American Federation of State, County, and Municipal Employees (AFL–CIO) is reputed to be the fastest growing union in the entire federation. Many other unions have accepted as members employees from local government. In addition, police and fire employees have organized into the Fraternal Order of Police and the International Association of Fire Fighters, with representation in most major cities and in many smaller and medium-sized communities.[12]

During the initial phases of public employee organization, the unions accepted the role of petitioner. Efforts toward bilateral bargaining were sporadic. However, President John Kennedy's Executive Order No. 10988, signed in 1962, gave public employee unionism a big boost through its recognition of unions in the federal service. In addition, the normal growth of the unions gave them the added strength needed to petition legislative bodies for the legal status necessary to remove many objections concerning the propriety of public employee unions. By 1966, some 15 states, led by Wisconsin, had enacted statutes requiring recognition of unions by local officials and providing for bilateral agreements, third-party arbitration, and exclusive recognition of majority unions.

REASONS FOR UNIONISM

Management officials should understand why employees, public or private, join unions. It is true, of course, that some employees join simply because the union promises to improve their economic status. Dissatisfaction with pay or benefits makes the task of the union organizer easier. The management which holds down workers is asking for unionization.

But economic gain is far from the only reason for unionism. For many employees the union is a social club. In fact, the earliest unions were nothing more than social. The members felt comfortable associating with other persons of the same social and economic background. They were called "brotherhoods" for this reason and the name persists with a number of unions, particularly in the railroad industry. Even today, for some employees, the monthly union meeting is an occasion for meeting with friends, just as is the executive's country club or dinner group.

Some of the early unions used their strength to further social causes. In the old days, causes such as land reform, changes in debtor laws, and currency reform were espoused by labor

---

[12] Experience of various jurisdictions is reported in Kenneth O. Warner, ed., MANAGEMENT RELATIONS WITH ORGANIZED PUBLIC EMPLOYEES (Chicago: Public Personnel Association, 1963).

organizations. Now public employee unions frequently engage in political activity which would be forbidden to individual members by little Hatch acts. Private as well as public employee unions are in the vanguard of forces advocating a wide variety of legislation having no particular relevance to the workingman as such —public housing, federal antipoverty programs, and others.

Finally, many workers join unions for what may be termed psychological reasons. Their sense of security is greatly enhanced. This may be less important in governments with a merit system than in private industry, but nevertheless it is a factor. Many aspects of the employment relationship are not covered by typical civil service legislation; the union is considered the buffer against arbitrary supervision, unreasonable work assignments, and other matters normally not within the purview of a civil service commission. Another important psychological reason for joining is the leadership experience: the sense of recognition gained from being elected to an office. This feeling is particularly strong among those whose work gives them little intrinsic satisfaction. Many a steward or officer enjoys his role of representing the union before prominent officials.

Probably the most important psychological reason for unionism is the elimination of paternalism. Only through union membership can an employee feel he is equal to men of other economic and organizational levels. He is no longer the small boy getting his weekly allowance from his dad; he participates in decisions with members of management and—where bilateral agreements are required—his signature on an agreement is just as meaningful as that of the chief executive.

Management, then, should understand these various reasons for joining unions. It is not necessarily a question of employee dissatisfaction. Loyalty to the supervisor or to the organization is not often involved. As each employee is complex, so too his reasons for joining unions may be manifold.

AREAS OF UNION ACTIVITY

Except in those states whose legislatures have defined union-management relations by statute,

the typical public official, faced with the accomplished fact that his employees have formed a union, has few, if any, guidelines. What, under these circumstances, are considered to be proper areas of union concern? Consensus establishes five such areas.

1. Negotiation of Proper Areas of Union Activity. One of the most important functions of the chief executive is to determine, in the absence of any statute, just wherein he will deal with the union. One way of making this determination is by agreement with the union itself. This has the important advantage of being acceptable to the union and it also provides a basis for restricting union activities which interfere with work production. It is a good opportunity, for example, to win agreement against conducting union business on city time and to regulate the time spent by stewards investigating grievances.

2. Negotiation of Pay and Benefits. This is the most important single interest of most union members and is a legitimate concern of employees. Depending upon the policy of the city and the proportion of union members, discussion of pay and benefits may be limited only to management's listening to union leaders prior to formulating recommendations or it may be a complete out-and-out bargaining session resulting in signed agreement. In either event, the administrator who is sensitive to good employee relations will make every effort to provide some level of union involvement. The sense of participation in decision making is important to the union committee, whether or not the union represents a majority of the affected employees.

3. Negotiations on Working Conditions. This area of relationship is similar to the preceding. It is mentioned as a separate item because it is in this area that the administrator can seriously err in limiting his right to manage. This is important. It is perfectly proper to discuss the length of the work week or the most equitable means of allocating vacation periods of overtime. It is quite another matter to discuss what equipment will be used on a job or whether overtime shall be optional or mandatory.

4. Grievance Procedures. Normally the union participates in the establishment of grievance procedures. This is only proper. Employees are obviously concerned with the means established for airing grievances. They want an orderly procedure. They also want someone to represent them in the process because many employees are not sufficiently articulate to do it for themselves. Most important, they want a management attitude toward grievances that permits fair settlement. Too often supervisors resent the use of grievance procedures and consider them a reflection on their ability to supervise. This may sometimes be true, but more often it is simply a question of good faith, differences in the interpretation of a given rule or regulation, or in the application of a given set of facts to a rule.

5. Communications. Management frequently overlooks the opportunity to improve communications through the use of union channels. Many management statements to employees are considered suspect; they are, after all, self-serving. Union discussion and corroboration may frequently help negate any suspicious attitudes which might exist. For example, management's appeal to employees for support on a bond issue or extra tax levy may well be better understood if union leadership confirms the need.

Upward communication can likewise be enhanced. When pay increases are pending, for example, it is usually desirable to know at least whether the employees prefer cash, or a benefit increase, or a combinaion. Unions can crystallize sentiment. Care must be exercised in such situations, however, that the union actually does represent majority sentiment. Sometimes the union committee may be swayed by the bias of a minority. A close working relationship with the union and extended negotiation sessions normally provide enough information on union operation to prevent error in this regard.

Unions will, if allowed, enter into any field. Management must make sure that its right to manage is not inhibited. It is ordinarily considered unnecessary and undesirable to negotiate budget requests, staffing patterns, or methods of promoting employees. In private industry such matters would not even be discussed. As a public officer, an administrator must walk a tight line between the union as a negotiating group and the union as a segment of the general public. Inasmuch as any group can comment on municipal affairs, the union can be given an opportunity to express itself; but *nothing should ever be included in any agreement that bears on such key aspects of governmental operation.*

NEGOTIATION

Negotiating Rules. The chief administrator who must arrive at an agreement with a union on wages, fringe benefits, and working conditions has a number of decisions to make and plenty of work to do. Key aspects of the negotiating process include:

1. A good negotiator, or negotiating committee, should be selected. Ordinarily the personnel director, because of his knowledge of community employment practices, should be a part of the negotiating team. Whether he is chief spokesman would depend on his personal qualifications as compared with other members of the administration. Whenever possible, the chief executive himself should *not* be at the bargaining table. In the rough and tumble of negotiations, a statement, admission, or agreement by a bargainer can be bad, but not irrevocable; even the union committee has to take its actions back to the membership for ratification. The top administrator, however, has no one to correct his errors; they become final.

2. The management negotiators should know the union team well. This again is one of the advantages that the personnel director should bring to the group. He presumably has been dealing with the union throughout the year and knows their leaders well—their strong and weak points, their idiosyncrasies, the things they want most. This information can prove invaluable when negotiations start in earnest.

3. Inasmuch as the process of negotiation is a high form of the art of communication, it follows that negotiators be good communicators. Here the presence of the municipal attorney, whose profession stresses bargaining and communication skills, can make a valuable addition to the negotiating team.

4. The importance of advance preparation cannot be overstressed. Surveys of local wage

conditions for comparable work should be completed. Such surveys give a good picture of what changes, if any, are necessary in the salary and benefit structure. Surveys of other cities may be relevant, depending upon the pay policies already adopted. Line management should be asked to report on conditions they believe should be introduced into negotiations. This is a common oversight; too often management negotiates solely on the basis of union proposals. When line management can accurately do so, it is also desirable to obtain reports on the "shop talk" that indicates what the union employees are really going to emphasize in the bargaining sessions. Usually the union will ask for a large number of items, but some are not much more than window dressing.

5. The negotiating team should establish good liaison with the chief executive and report to him often enough to get instructions. In addition, there should be good lines of communication with the various line department officials so that a bargain is not struck which would make more difficult the work of any agency. Finally, through the executive there should be a means of communication with the council leadership so that chances of approval for agreements are enhanced.

6. It is usually not wise to make final agreements as negotiations proceed. Tentative agreements are, of course, necessary to progress. But if these agreements on minor issues are finalized, then it is quite possible that, upon reaching an important impasse, bargaining leverage has been given away.

7. Avoid "mutual-agreement" clauses in union agreements. This term refers to agreements under which actions such as layoffs and work changes will not be taken unless there is mutual agreement at the time as to how they will be done. This gives the union a veto power over decisions before they can be made, as compared to the right to file a grievance after they have been made. Mutual agreement clauses frequently tie management's hands.

8. Handling the press is as difficult as it is important. Public business is news, and some newspapers emphasize the right of the public to know even to the point of wanting to sit in on negotiating sessions. Other papers are inter-ested only in the results. As in other press relations situations, nothing can replace a basic confidence built up over the years between the administration and the press. If this confidence exists, it is possible to have off-the-record press meetings after each bargaining session to interpret what went on and thus avoid publication of any tactical step which might mislead the public or adversely affect negotiations. It is generally poor policy to attempt to influence negotiations through the press. Seldom will sophisticated union leadership be swayed by publicity releases.

9. Most sentiment favors comparatively short bargaining sessions rather than marathons, unless there is considerable momentum built up to resolve an impasse. Generally speaking, shorter sessions, at least in the initial stages, give both parties the opportunity to determine the course of bargaining and to report back to their respective principals—the chief administrator and the union executive board. Shorter and more frequent meetings also permit adjustments of position, where advisable, and, if tempers happen to rise, provide a necessary cooling-off period.

10. It is generally considered desirable to avoid rigidity in bargaining. It is quite possible to determine, paternalistically, what the best possible conditions of employment should be, but to announce these conditions in a bargaining session and then sit back can only antagonize the union committee. The process requires that management start with a position lower than its final offer, just as the union starts with a position higher than it hopes to get. The "haggling" process has become traditional in industrial unionism and public employee union members do not want to be considered different from their private counterparts. The "take-it-or-leave-it" strategy violates one of the important reasons why employees form unions—the right to participate in decision making. If management enters negotiations with a set package and does not change, it is difficult for the employees to feel they participated in a process which led to decisions.

11. Don't attack union security. The law of self-preservation requires the union to fight such an attack. Attempts to eliminate dues

deductions to reduce the union's right to representation, or to limit unreasonably the bargaining unit will be interpreted as an attempt to get rid of the union itself. This is a principal cause of strikes.

12. Finally, negotiators should not give in on any point that they cannot honestly believe to be acceptable. Negotiation does not mean concession. There must be some way to resolve every disagreement, and it is better to use these procedures than to conclude an improper agreement. Ultimately, of course, the city council can, by ordinance, unilaterally set the pay and working conditions of its employees, and its decisions are final. It is preferable, however, to use some other means of resolving a negotiating impasse.

Resolving Impasses in Negotiations. Even in the most cooperative of labor climates, negotiations cannot always end in agreement. Reasonable men can differ. In industry such differences frequently lead to strikes. In government the strike is generally illegal and always out of place. The essential nature of most public services precludes interruption. Many union officials who operate in the public sector admit the wisdom of antistrike legislation, but believe there should be a balancing factor—impasse machinery to take the place of the strike. Without such machinery, strikes of governmental employees have and will continue to occur, even in the face of antistrike pronouncements and statutes.

Compulsory arbitration of contracts, wherein a third party listens to both sides and renders a binding opinion, is generally considered unsatisfactory. It is opposed by the AFSCME, among others. Experience at the municipal level in Canada indicates too often that both sides, anticipating the possibility of going to compulsory arbitration, will not bargain in good faith, but instead use the bargaining sessions to prepare positions to present to the arbitrator.

Several states have enacted laws requiring the appointment of a fact-finding board with authority to make recommendations for resolving impasses. Such a board hears both sides and renders a conclusion which is not binding.

Latitude is still permitted for further bargaining. Nevertheless, the power of public opinion can be brought to bear. A well-documented report from a neutral board is bound to have substantial weight, especially in a political environment. States which have enacted such provisions into law have also prohibited strikes: Wisconsin, Michigan, and Connecticut are examples.

The municipal employees union has one weapon in its arsenal that is most important, though least discussed. This is the right to petition directly to the board of directors—the city council. Private unions lack this ability. In government, it cannot be withheld unless union members' citizenship is to be removed. The ability of union leadership to sit down with the political leadership over the heads of administration is a powerful tool in negotiating situations. Often such meetings are private. In some instances, the avenue is smoothed further by the presence in the council of one or more union officials. With the council controlling the finances and therefore the wage rates, the importance of this right cannot be overemphasized.

OPERATING OFFICIALS AND UNIONS: WORKING RELATIONSHIPS

As indicated above, the task of negotiating on what is usually an annual basis is relegated to the personnel director, chief administrators, or perhaps a committee of top line officials. Other line supervisors are more concerned with the day-by-day aspects of union relations. This aspect is just as important as the negotiations.

The recommended policy is to remember constantly that workers are employees first and union members second. They should be treated as employees whether or not they are union members. Most supervisors try to treat their employees fairly; any supervisor who works toward such a goal need have no fear, whether or not his subordinates join unions.

Supervisors must understand the government's policy with regard to unions if they are expected to follow and implement it. It is management's obligation to disseminate its policy, in writing, and to be sure that it is understood. It is also management's obligation to be sure that all supervisors be given a thorough explanation of all rules and regulations, whether or not such rules and regulations have been determined by union agreement. Too often the first-line supervisor feels, with reason, that the business agent of the union knows the rules better than he. Thus he may accept a business agent's interpretation without checking, only to find, too late, that the business agent was wrong. With proper training, the knowledgeable supervisor can easily avoid such an error.

Once they understand the union agreement, supervisors should be encouraged to report its inadequacies. The next bargaining session may lead to correction, but only if the negotiators know what is wrong and why.

Supervisors should have confidence that management will back them up just as firmly in dealing with a union situation as it would in a nonunion situation. This is particularly important in handling grievances.

Most business agents are cooperative. This makes their task easier. They cannot cooperate until management at all levels returns the cooperation. The business agent who is kept in the dark by management will in turn make life more difficult for management. If, for example, management develops a firm disciplinary policy in a particular area—for example, control of garnishments—the union business agent should be the first to know of its promulgation, even though, as a disciplinary policy, his approval is not required. In this way he can answer the questions inevitably put to him by members. By saving him the embarrassment of ignorance, he is far more likely to give fair answers to his members, and thus keep down resentment, than if he were kept in the dark.

SOME UNRESOLVED PROBLEMS

Although unions go back to the early nineteenth century in private industry, their legal recognition and present-day strength did not come until the 1930's with the passage of federal legislation guaranteeing their rights. Public employee unionism is even more recent. Thus there has been too little time to resolve all of the problems involved in union–management relations. A brief review of some of these problems may help to convey a better understanding of these relations.

Unionism vs. Sovereignty. Private industry and unions have been made equal at the bargaining table by a higher authority: government. But what happens when one of the parties to the bargain is the very body which can declare or withhold such equal status? If the government has a right to confer equality, does it not then have the right to take it away? It is in this area that the basic status of unions in the public service differs from the private sector. This difference does not affect day-by-day union relations, but it does affect the impasse-resolving machinery which can be established.

Police and Unions. When legislation prescribing union relations is passed by states, it is commonplace to exempt police agencies from coverage. This area of union relations requires more philosophical thought. Many police have joined unions; others have joined the Fraternal Order of Police, which in some jurisdictions carries on the same functions of representation that is typical of trade unionism. A strike by police would be unthinkable; even the American Federation of State, County, and Municipal Employees, which accepts police locals into its memberships, has a constitutional prohibition against their striking. How differently should they be treated? As employees, they deserve to be treated as well as any other group. As a union, they have been circumscribed by special legislation. Sooner or later this question will require resolution.

Supervisors in Unions. Public employee unions frequently accept supervisors as members, sometimes in the same bargaining unit with subordinates. The International Association of Fire Fighters, for example, has always included all ranks, including chief. In private industry, however, unions which wish to include supervisors in the bargaining unit cannot avail themselves of National Labor Relations Board machinery. Supervisors consider themselves part of management and are legally so considered. In the early stages of public employee unionism, this was no problem. However, with the growth of third-party arbitration of grievances, the supervisor is the person who may be required to present management's case to the neutral. Can a supervisor testify, in effect, against his own union? At best his role is tenuous. On the other hand, government has not always handled its pay relationships in such a way as to assure supervisors they do not need a union. In the long range, it may develop that the interests of the union and of the employer will merge sufficiently so that the problem vanishes. Until that time, however, there will be a problem whenever the union accepts supervisors and their subordinates into the same organization.

How Many Unions? In private industry, federal law prohibits any organization from claiming representation rights unless it has an actual majority in the bargaining unit. Inasmuch as public unions grew rapidly without the benefits of legal regulation, there are many situations in which two unions claim membership among the same type of employees. Yet government, more so than industry, attempts to provide the same benefits across the board. For example, it is commonplace for a city to have only one retirement plan covering all employees, regardless of who represents them. How can the employer deal with several organizations in bargaining, yet arrive at the same conclusion with each? The answer seems to be in unions of unions—a concerted action by all unions in a city. Few have reached this stage yet.

Pluralistic Management. The problem of representation has two sides. Unions can legitimately complain, in many cases, that they do not know with whom to deal. In city manager cities, the city manager can be, or delegate someone to be, the administration spokesman. But even then there may be certain boards and commissions with administrative authority outside the manager's jurisdiction. Health, recreation, and parks are frequently excluded from the manager's supervision. The willingness of such independent agencies to go along with the policy of the manager varies. Good union relations requires the closest of cooperation among appointing authorities.

Employee Development

Training is fundamental to administration. Not only is every administrator a trainer of his subordinates, but some think this may be his most significant role. He must inculcate his subordinates with his attitudes of management. This is done, not merely by signing and distributing an administrative regulation, but more importantly by his actions, in his consultations with his subordinates, and during his staff meetings. The top administrator, however, cannot effectively do all of the employee development necessary. A planned program is essential. This section describes such a program.

TRAINING DEFINED

The Committee on Training of the Public Personnel Association defines training as "the process of aiding employees to gain effectiveness in their present or future work through the development of appropriate habits of thought and action, skill, knowledge, and attitudes."[13] This definition emphasizes that training is a process; it is never an action which is completed on a certain day. The definition also emphasizes that improvement is the employee's responsibility—it can't be done to him or for him—but that management has the responsibility for aiding him in this development. Finally, the definition relates training to the work. Only through such a limitation can public expenditures for training be justified.

Training, as thus defined, can be differentiated from fundamental education which is the totality of human mental development. But no clear, sharp line can be drawn between the two terms. Many city positions require a good understanding of philosophical concepts; imbuing employees with these concepts is closer to the usual education process than it is to training an employee in a manual skill.

OBJECTIVES OF TRAINING

No training program should be undertaken unless a need exists. Nevertheless, there are some basic training objectives which are so

---

[13] Public Personnel Association, EMPLOYEE TRAINING IN THE PUBLIC SERVICE (Chicago: The Association, 1941), p. 2.

commonplace in municipal organizations that the need for them is nearly universal. These typical objectives include the following:

1. To provide an employee with specific skills which he either does not have or which he should improve. This is the "how-to" type of training.

2. To provide an employee with information he needs in order to perform his job or to learn a higher job to which he aspires.

3. To make employee attitudes more consistent with operating policies. For example, if the city is an equal opportunity employer, this policy should not be subverted by lower-level supervisors who may not share management's attitudes toward minorities.

4. To provide employees with an understanding of the objectives and programs of the entire city organization and with outside agencies whose activities touch upon those of the city. Presumably this type of training facilitates interdepartmental cooperation.

5. To retrain employees when management changes job content or method. This is particularly important in areas subject to automation.

6. To train employees for promotion.

ESTABLISHING A TRAINING PROGRAM

If an administrator wants to establish a training program, or sees the need to systematize an existing hit-or-miss type of training activity, he needs to do three things almost simultaneously: establish a training policy, make a study of training needs, and develop an organization for training.

Training Policy. A training policy is fundamental. It should: (1) assign responsibility for training, (2) indicate the scope of the training program and the means of financing it, (3) provide acceptable means of recognizing satisfactory completion of training, and, most importantly, (4) define the respective training responsibilities of the central training agency and line officials. Typically this division of function makes the central agency responsible for all interdepartmental programs, all programs utilizing noncity resources, and all studies of training needs. Line supervision is generally made responsible for on-the-job training and, in some instances, for off-the-job

training which is properly confined to the employees of one department. Police and fire training are good examples of the latter.

Training Organization. One person, known as Director of Training or some comparable title, should be responsible for the daily management of training activities. This officer may be the personnel director, an administrative assistant, or, in small municipalities, the chief administrator himself. When he is someone other than the chief administrator or his assistant, he is usually assigned to the personnel department to facilitate cooperation with that agency. Some municipalities, however, prefer a separate department devoted only to the training function.

This size of the training staff will depend upon the size of the municipality and, more particularly, on the size of the training problem. If, for example, the municipality has excellent supervision with a high degree of on-the-job training, a proportionately smaller central agency will suffice. If, on the other hand, the supervision does little training, the central agency will have a bigger gap to fill. Finally, the amount of community resources which can be tapped for training purposes will also affect the size of the staff needed.

Training Studies. A study of training needs should precede any actual training program and should be repeated at periodic intervals to keep ongoing programs in line with changing needs. Such a study requires an analysis of each facet of the entire organization as well as a survey of the adequacy of present training activities. The study should investigate possible training needs in areas of real or potential weakness in the organization, such as agencies with a high or potentially high rate of personnel turnover, agencies where big unit costs might indicate inefficiency, agencies with poor morale, or agencies where work methods will be or recently have been changed by new equipment or procedures. The study should be conducted by the central training unit; line officials usually lack the objectivity necessary for such a survey. Interdepartmental committees, which bring many viewpoints into consideration, also can be useful in conducting such a study.

METHODS OF TRAINING

The term "training program" too often implies a classroom situation or similar group activity. This is regrettable: effective training can take many forms in many situations. Learning by doing, for example, is the oldest form of training. It is the task of the training director to select the training method most suited to each training need. This section outlines some of the kinds of training devices which might be considered for different situations.

On-the-Job Training. The importance of on-the-job training cannot be overestimated for any position. Its utility is most obvious with manual work, but employees in other types of positions can learn equally well on the job. Learning by doing is retained longer than any other kind of learning. What is important is for supervision to recognize the role of on-the-job training and to undertake such training deliberately through patterns of work assignment, methods of explaining work procedures and processes, and the judicious use of inspection and evaluation activities.

Employees doing mental work may also profit from on-the-job training. Initially, a new employee can be assigned to work with an experienced employee and then be given assignments on his own, with frequent checking on his progress by his supervisor. The journeyman metal worker may be given advanced assignments with encouragement to ask for help when he feels he needs it. He may also be assigned to a committee working on new procedures or asked to take over a higher-rated employee's duties during the latter's absence. All of these devices are facets of on-the-job training with the supervisor acting as coach.

Off-the-Job Training. The justification for taking employees away from the work area for training lies in the assumption that something is to be taught which cannot be taught on the job. Training for promotion, training in supervisory methods, or training in the execution of new programs frequently require off-the-job training. A number of methods can be used for such training. The most common are:

1. Lecture. This is generally the poorest

method of instruction, even though the most common. It is bad enough in the college classroom. It is even worse for adult employees. Most employees, especially supervisors, are action oriented. They want to participate. They are unused to classroom discipline. It is difficult for them to sit and listen, even to a good lecture. Inasmuch as psychologists have long established that human beings remember less of what they hear than of what they see or do, the lecture should be supplemented with other methods whenever possible.

2. Conference. Organized group discussion is a valuable way to train articulate employees, such as supervisors. They are encouraged to participate and they can bring to the group practical examples from their daily activity. The conference method requires a skilled leader, one who is able to involve all members of the group and to subordinate his own participation. In this way, the conclusions or solutions to problems ultimately reached have the stamp of approval of the peer group. The conference method is inexpensive, flexible, practical. Generally speaking, it is well accepted by employees.

3. Case Study. For employees who are studying broad problems, such as middle managers, the case method has many values. It requires participation, does not lend itself to dogmatic solutions imposed by the group leader, and requires the type of analytic thinking necessary in solving management problems. Unfortunately, not many cases have been published involving a governmental environment, but the typical public official will have little difficulty in adapting the principles of a business case to his governmental background, if the group leader is reasonably skilled.

4. Demonstration. There are situations in which a study group, off the job, can profit from the demonstration method of instruction. For example, if new equipment is being obtained, it may well be more efficient to show its operation to all potential operators at one time than to wait for the occasion when each employee actually is assigned its operation. This may be particularly important if a manufacturer's representative is dispatched to assist in training for a few days. Whenever possible,

demonstration should be accompanied by actual practice by each participant, under supervision of the instructor, just as is done in on-the-job instruction.

5. Role-playing. In training programs concentrated on modification of employee attitudes, role playing has been found to be effective. In this type of training, each participant enacts the role of some job-related situation. No script is provided, but the characters are identified and a conflict established. Each participant reacts as he feels he would in a real situation. A variation of role playing, "sensitivity training," has won wide acceptance among psychologists and others concerned with innermost attitudes. Neither sensitivity training nor role playing should be handled by amateurs; it is best to obtain the services of a qualified leader from a university if contemplating such training.

Off-the-Premises Training. In any middle or large-sized community, there are numerous resources at the disposal of employers for many types of training. Use of these resources is generally more economical than establishing a program especially for city employees. In addition, such programs are ordinarily run by professionals and, therefore, may be of higher quality than can be provided by city personnel. Assuming that the subject matter is appropriate to the needs of the city government, the following resources should be considered:

1. Local colleges and universities, especially those with evening colleges or extension institutes.

2. Technical institutes at the post–high school level, especially for skilled trades and technical types of work.

3. High schools which offer adult night school programs. Many will set up special courses on the employer's premises if there are adequate facilities and sufficient students.

4. Special institutes sponsored by business organizations in specialized subjects. For example, in some cities the American Management Society sponsors evening classes in foremanship; the Society for the Advancement of Management may have an institute in industrial relations.

5. State departments of vocational education

often have staff competent in conference methods and frequently in other business-oriented subjects.

6. Professional organizations of public officials. Training institutes are held periodically by many such organizations. While travel expenses and tuition fees may be expensive on a per-student basis, the cost of training one or two persons is far less than would be the case if the city attempted to provide equivalent training on its own.

It is becoming customary to provide some financial aid to employees enrolling in advanced training programs. Tuition reimbursement programs typically share tuition costs equally, on the assumption that employees and employer both benefit by job related training. Release time is also frequently allowed when duty hours conflict with training opportunities.

MANAGEMENT DEVELOPMENT

This discussion of employee training applies in general to all echelons of personnel. In recent years considerable attention has been paid to management development as an especially important facet of training, deserving of particular emphasis. Ordinarily, management development is differentiated from other types of training primarily by its attempt to go beyond training in present or future duties into education of the entire person. Fully and successfully done—a rare condition indeed—management development could be likened to a college education, broad enough to cover all facets of life and long enough to influence behavior. Only the military services approach this complete concept of management development. Civilian government, however, can at least help its employees improve their management potential through organized programs.

The growth of government, particularly at a time of labor market shortages, makes it essential to capitalize on every scrap of potential management talent. Local government's problem is compounded, in most medium-sized cities, by the fact that the department and division heads who carry substantial administrative responsibility must also have strong technical skills in their chosen fields; local government departments are frequently not large enough to require the "pure" administrator over a strong technical staff. Therefore, the top officials, except the chief administrator, are likely to have progressed through the ranks by virtue of their technical background and, upon arrival at the top, need all the help they can get in the art of management.

The problem is that these technicians-turned-administrators are specialists. They are likely to suffer from the myopia of specialization. They are likely to look only within their specialties for answers to all problems. Given, for example, an overcrowded city hall, the architect thinks of a new building as a solution. The comptroller wants to reduce the size of the work force to fit the space. The methods analyst wants to move certain offices to other locations. Management development should attempt to help the specialist see beyond his bailiwick, to develop a broad outlook.

In addition to developing breadth of view, management development should have three fundamental objectives: (1) to help the official become more sensitive to human relations; (2) to help him understand himself better; and (3) to equip him with such skills as interviewing techniques and conference leadership that will help him handle specific situations. The development program can then be built around a combination of on and off-the-job training coordinated by the chief administrator himself.

On the job, the trainee can be given insights into human relations by exposure to the proper variety of assignments, by coaching, by working with committees in sensitive areas, and by understudying senior executives. Classroom training can supplement this by teaching specific management skills and by exposing each trainee to the attitudes of his peers. Ordinarily, classes in such basic principles as industrial psychology and organization theory are likely to be more productive than how-to-do-it courses such as public budgeting or the organization structure of the city.

No management development program can accomplish its purposes without the participation of the chief administrator. Management development is a process, never an accomplished fact. It is daily, unrelenting, present in every assignment. The administrator must provide the climate which encourages officials to develop themselves or the process does not start. When the climate is right, classroom work can effectively supplement rounded on-the-job experiences. Without the climate, classroom experience is effectively negated.

EVALUATION OF TRAINING PROGRAMS

Unfortunately, no one has yet produced a measuring stick suitable for evaluating employee training programs. Training often deals with intangibles which defy objective evaluation. Yet training costs money and the administrator owes it to the council to justify training appropriations by results.

Trainees can be the source of evaluations, but not by asking for their opinion of the training program. Rather it is preferable to find out if they have introduced any new ideas into their areas of work responsibility or to determine if supervisors have noticed any changes in trainee work behavior or patterns. Occasionally, too, the training subject lends itself to an estimate of results through statistics. For example, a safety program which is followed by a reduction in time-lost accidents can be credited with at least a portion of the savings, even though other variables involved in accident experience cannot be considered as having been absolutely constant.

In some jurisdictions which have competitive promotional examinations, the analysis of test results may indicate the values of a training program. For example, in one midwestern city, an analysis of a fire lieutenant's promotional examination before a training program on rules and regulations showed a disappointing lack of understanding; the next examination, given after training, showed a great improvement.

These examples are admittedly inadequate; they only confirm the previously stated fact that measurement devices are lacking. Nevertheless, the basic principles of employee training and development have grown over such a long period and over such a wide range of positions and organizations that the administrator cannot dwell too long on the desirability of objective proof. He must also ask whether he can afford *not* to train.

Discipline

The maintenance of discipline is one of the most important tasks of the administrator. Standards of conduct and work output must be established, communicated, and enforced. With a great majority of employees, there is no problem: they want to conform to any reasonable standard established by management. The disciplinary problem arises only among a minority. However, effective handling of this minority is essential if standards are to be maintained.

SETTING STANDARDS OF PERSONAL CONDUCT

The administrator, in contemplating the establishment or revision of rules regarding personal conduct of employees, should aim for what the majority of employees will agree are reasonable regulations. Rules which are not reasonable will not be obeyed by employees or enforced by supervisors. Refusal to permit reasonable work breaks, for example, will not prevent such breaks; rather, breaks will be unregulated because of the absence of an acceptable standard.

Rules which are set forth in writing should be clear so that the typical employee can understand them. Immediate supervision has the responsibility of clarifying new rules to be sure they are understood.

Some facets of personal conduct are so obvious that they do not need to be included in rules. Everyone knows horseplay on the job is wrong, for example, and will expect punishment if caught. The "love God, mother, and country" type of rule merely clutters the manual and means the employees will not read it.

Generally, it is sufficient merely to indicate that the city expects employees to conduct themselves in such a way as not to bring discredit upon the service. This permits a different standard of conduct for different categories of employees. Policemen and firemen, for example, generally are expected to observe a higher standard of conduct than laborers.

SETTING STANDARDS OF PERFORMANCE

Not many municipal operations are amenable to hard and fast standards of performance. To require a building inspector, for example, to inspect a certain number of structures each day would be unreasonable and unwise, inasmuch as he might be properly busy on only one large job. Policemen, of course, should never be required to meet an arrest quota.

Because so many jobs do not lend themselves to exact standards, it is difficult to discipline employees for poor performance. But it is not impossible. Some kinds of work permit measurement: a meter reader, for example, can be given an exact quota of meters to read because his work is repetitive. Other employees can be compared with the average for their units. A police officer who averages few arrests in a district where other men have large numbers should at least be questioned, and probably disciplined. Larger cities will have more groups of employees doing similar work which can be compared than will smaller cities.

Qualitative standards are even more difficult. It is doubtful if many cities have any operations which lend themselves to objective, qualitative standards. However, quality can be judged by supervision and disciplinary action can be taken and upheld on the basis of recorded examples of poor performance.

DISCIPLINARY ACTION PROCEDURES

In any large group, sooner or later some employee will fail. Management should have, *and consistently follow,* a set procedure to cope with the failures.

Only in the most serious cases, such as theft, threat of bodily harm, or commission of a felony should immediate dismissal for a first offense be considered. Corrective discipline should normally precede such a serious penalty. In order to be consistent with the concept of correction, however, the employee must recognize the disciplinary action as fair. This requires fair procedures based on the following requirements:

1. Thorough investigation, so that the exact nature of the violation is known.

2. Prompt action, so that the employee can readily associate the penalty, if any, with the action.

3. A hearing, so that the employee can present his side of the case. It is also desirable to permit union representation at this hearing.

An administrative hearing is desirable even if there is legal provision for appeal to a civil service commission.

4. Formal notification of the nature of the complaint should be given to the employee before the hearing, so that he and his representative can be prepared and, if necessary, have witnesses.

5. The hearing and initial recommendation should be made by a responsible supervisor, but below the level of the appointing authority. This prevents final decisions from being made in the heat of the moment.

PENALTIES FOR INFRACTIONS

The punishment should always fit the crime if it is to be accepted as fair, not only by the employee involved but by his associates. On the other hand, it is generally not considered advisable to have "price lists" showing the penalty to be assessed for each infraction. There are too many mitigating circumstances to permit such arbitrary action. A judge in a courtroom is given considerable leeway in assessing punishment; the administrator needs no less.

Corrective Discipline. The oral reprimand is considered the lightest punishment. It also is extremely effective if the supervisor uses the face-to-face contact provided by the oral reprimand for constructive educational purposes. Generally it is advisable to make a note of each oral reprimand in case later infractions require further disciplinary action.

The written reprimand is intended to impress upon the employee that his pattern of conduct could lead to further difficulty if not corrected. In addition to making the action a matter of official record, it permits the agency to send a copy to the employee's union representative, if any, so that the union is alerted to a potential problem.

In more serious cases, or after reprimands have failed, it may be necessary to suspend an employee from duty for a short period. Generally there is little excuse for a long suspension. The point is made just as well by a few days off as by a longer period. The greater loss of income is more likely to hurt the employee's family and may be offset by his becoming eligible for welfare payments. Also, work production in his unit may suffer because he probably cannot

be replaced while on suspension. The latter problem so bothers the city of Cincinnati that it rarely suspends employees, but instead suspends their vacations as a disciplinary measure.

Demotion to a lower job, at lower pay, is a possible disciplinary action of considerable severity. It is seldom used in most jurisdictions; it is too permanent an action to be effective as a corrective measure. It is most appropriate when an employee, having been promoted through the ranks, proves himself incompetent to perform the level of duties required as a result of promotion.

The gradation of penalty beginning with the oral reprimand and going through suspension recognizes different levels of severity of offense. It also permits greater penalties for repeated offenses by the same employee. Generally, repeated offenses, even though minor, are treated with increasing severity.

Dismissal. Corrective discipline is desirable and, if carefully administered, is usually effective in deterring improper behavior, but complete success is beyond expectation. When failures occur, dismissal, or "economic capital punishment," is necessary to protect standards of conduct and performance. Dismissal, more than lesser disciplinary action, is closely regulated by statute and common law, so that each administrator must be guided by his legal advisor. The suggestions in the following paragraphs must be interpreted in the light of what is legal in any given jurisdiction.

Most civil service laws attempt to protect employees from arbitrary separation and from separation for political, racial, or religious reasons. This objective is accomplished by requiring that dismissals be made only for just cause and only for violation of one or more statutory reasons for separation. Such reasons as incompetency, inefficiency, neglect of duty, immoral conduct, insubordination, drunkeness, and failure of good behavior are typical of many civil service laws.

The law usually requires the appointing authority to place the employee on his fair defense by requiring written specifications supporting the statutory charges. Upon dismissal, the employee under civil service, and in some cases employees of jurisdictions without civil service, may appeal to the commission or to a hearing board. Typically the hearing is conducted in a manner similar to civil court procedures in which testimony and evidence are offered supporting the charges, with the employee-appellant given the opportunity to cross-examine witnesses and to provide testimony on his own behalf. The decision of the commission or hearing board may be binding or, under some laws, may be only advisory. In some jurisdictions the decisions of the commission may be appealable to court.

The heart of any dismissal action is case preparation. This starts with good records. If, as is usually the case, the problem stems from an accumulation of personal delinquencies, good records will permit their documentation. A series of several lesser disciplinary actions will establish that the employee has been warned and that management has tried to correct these delinquencies. Proper recording of delinquencies on performance reports will further substantiate the sufficiency of warnings. Thus, when some precipitating incident occurs and supervision decides corrective measures have been proved ineffective, the case for dismissal is sound.

Because of the legal restrictions protecting the employee, the administrator should rely heavily on the city attorney for procedural advice. Charges and specifications should be reviewed by the attorney, together with substantiating evidence and testimony, so that he can advise on the soundness of the action.

On the other hand, the legal procedural requirements should not be presumed to be so rigorous that infractions are tolerated when separation is warranted. Civil service employees can be fired; it happens every day. No administrator, having followed the law and having recorded the events leading to the decision, need fear appeal proceedings.

Separation from Service

Management should pay attention to all forms of separation, even though some are voluntary acts by employees. Analysis of turnover is a means of ascertaining weak spots in supervision, pay, or working conditions. Such analysis is generally obtained by means of exit interviews, a step in the termination process where the departing employee talks with a member of supervision. Usually the employee can be more frank in this situation than if he expected to remain and thus he can materially assist management in its evaluation of the organization.

TURNOVER RATE

Individual separations from a large agency are separately insignificant, but collectively, as noted, they can be very important. The turnover rate, the measure used to summarize the number of separations, is computed in various ways. Ordinarily it is simply the total number of separations divided by the average number of employees: thus 10 separations from a service of 200 employees in a one year period would produce a turnover rate of 5 percent. Some agencies prefer to use accessions (new hires) instead of separations on the theory that they are concerned only with positions for which persons must be sought.

Regardless of the exact method used, it is important to watch for *changes* in turnover rate and to determine the cause of such changes. Changes in a particular municipality's turnover rate are more significant that comparisons between the turnover rate for different municipalities, although both are important.

CAUSES OF SEPARATION

In addition to dismissals, the following forms of separation are also included when computing turnover.

Resignation. This is the voluntary act of separation taken by an employee, usually one in good standing. These constitute the majority of separations in most agencies. Some resignations are inevitable, but, as indicated above, it is important to watch for sudden increases in resignations. It is also important, when possible, to learn the real reason for resignation inasmuch as it might provide a clue to a correctible unsatisfactory condition. This is usually done by means of the exit interview. In place of the exit interview, some agencies have been successful with a follow-up mail inquiry, inviting the former employee's comments concerning working conditions. When this is done several months after resignation, it is felt that the respondent may be more objective and more honest in his appraisal of the organization. Regardless of the way the information is obtained, there is no point in getting it unless the agency is willing to do something about unsatisfactory conditions that may be uncovered.

Retirement. Some provision for retirement is standard in almost every employment. Federal social security covers almost all private employees and is a part of many public retirement packages. Some local governments have their own independent plans or are covered by statewide plans. Usually, police and fire employees have different systems from nonuniformed city employees.

While most jurisdictions have solved the problem of providing for retirement, they have not always done as well in planning for retirements. This problem has two aspects. One, from the standpoint of the employer, is the problem of planning for replacement. Inasmuch as the ages of employees are on record, it should be fairly easy to learn how many retirements will occur in a reasonable time period, and to plan for orderly succession. There is little excuse for being caught without trained replacements. The other problem involves the soon-to-retire employee. Preretirement counselling is a growing fringe benefit, intended to prepare the potential retiree for the traumatic change soon to come in his life. The Tennessee Valley Authority has been a leader in preretirement counselling, holding a series of meetings at which medical, legal, and other authorities discuss their specialties with prospective retirees. Any reasonably large city can duplicate its effort.

Lay Off. A lay off is a separation caused by lack of work or funds. It can be temporary, permanent, or seasonal. Lay off should not be used as a disciplinary device: if an employee is to be disciplined temporarily, he should be suspended. The difference is more than semantics in many jurisdictions; a lay off is rarely appealable, inasmuch as it implies no wrongdoing, but a suspension may be appealable to a civil service commission.

Normally the appointing authority is the sole judge of the sufficiency of work or funds, and can therefore determine which classifications are to be reduced by how many positions. When this decision is made, it is usually necessary to determine which employees of a large number in the classification will be laid off. Trade unionism philosophy requires lay off of the employees with the least seniority. Many administrators feel the interests of the service require retention of the best employees, regardless of length of service. Some agencies have a compromise formula, including both seniority and performance ratings. Which of these alternatives provide the fewest disadvantages can be argued.

The administrator can frequently render the argument moot by adequate foresight. Lay offs can frequently be avoided if they are anticipated in advance and plans are made to hold equivalent vacancies in other departments. One municipally operated public utility, for example, reduced its complement in one division by 16 percent on one day without lay off by such devices as reserving jobs in other divisions, getting employees to postpone retirements until plant automation was complete, and even getting them to accept pay for vacations so that the division could operate with bare minimum personnel until the plant conversion was complete. This type of management action provides more effective security for employees than any law and helps maintain employee morale at high levels.

Conclusion

Personnel administration is a major portion of the work of every administrator and supervisor. Unfortunately it cannot be routinized, as can many other tasks. Each employee is different. Each employee must therefore be considered as an individual and treated differently from all others. The knowledge of each employee's reactions to supervision's actions is essential if these actions are to be successful. Supervision is an art, not a science, but the principles emphasized in this chapter will generally apply in the management of people.

14

Financial Administration

THE FINANCIAL FOCUS of the city administrator has shifted dramatically in past decades. The traditional discussion of financial administration has focused primarily on the procedural and control methods with which the administrator could most efficiently and honestly conduct the internal fiscal affairs of the city administration. It has dealt with accounting, purchasing, auditing, treasury management, and related activities. Today most cities have developed highly sophisticated patterns of control, usually executed by extremely competent professionals, in each of these fields. While the administrator need express no less interest in these matters now, today he can confidently turn his attention to other pressing problems. Rare is the community which has totally rejected the obvious progress in internal fiscal management.

Now the administrator's financial horizon extends beyond internal management to the financial leadership demands created by his attempts to provide a meaningful public contribution to the quality of urban life. While his performance expectations are high—the "proper" balancing of public services to assure a desirable environment for urban social interaction—his ability to meet these expectations is often severely circumscribed.

The Urban Setting of Financial Decisions

As the United States increasingly evolves into an urban society, concern has focused on the quality of life that can be experienced in an urban setting. Local governments have traditionally borne responsibility for the public services which would create an adequate environment for social interaction.

THE URBAN ENVIRONMENT AND PUBLIC SERVICES

An "adequate environment" is a relative term, reflecting varying standards and expectations from community to community and from era to era. In an earlier period the public service role of local government was largely limited to protective services such as police and fire; transportation services such as street construction, lighting, and maintenance; and a number of safety and regulatory activities. The adequate environment essentially consisted of assurance that the individual could lead his private urban life under conditions of safety and ease of circulation. As standards of living have risen over the decades, greater expectations of what constitutes an adequate environment have also developed. The community's responsibility has now extended to areas of health, welfare, housing, education and culture, park and recreational facilities, transportation, and safety.

Thus, the public service demands imposed upon a city may include health centers, sewerage and other waste disposal systems, welfare agencies, public housing and urban renewal programs, museums, theatres, auditoriums, zoological and botanical gardens, art and music centers, libraries, parks and open spaces, playgrounds, arenas, golf courses, tennis courts, stadiums, mass transportation, and parking facilities, airports, and highways. Obviously this is neither an exhaustive listing of possible public facilities and programs, nor will those listed be found in all communities. Size, geographic location, wealth, and public demands will affect the range of public services, but this listing does demonstrate that wealth is a major variable determining the ability of any city government to satisfy the public service demands placed upon it.

Intergovernmental Considerations. In recent decades a crucial question has been posed: should disparities in wealth among cities be the major (sole) determinant of the presence or absence of some commonly accepted standards of public service? Implicit in the question is the recognition of the high population mobility among Americans. Families and individuals regularly move within a city, from city to adjacent suburb or vice versa, between cities in a state, and from state to state. Population mobility has added support to the concept of the national citizen and his right to expect certain basic services. The problem of providing public services at the community level is no longer viewed as an isolated charge upon a local municipal government, but rather it has been translated into a joint responsibility among the national, state, and local governments.

This means that the city administrator's decisions cannot be made in isolation or in ignorance of external influences. The administrator necessarily will meet his responsibilities only by continuing interaction with representatives of other levels of government. The intergovernmental relationship frequently takes the form of federal or state inducements to communities through financial assistance in general or specified areas.

Metropolitan Complexity. Another factor complicating financial administration is the multigovernment phenomenon in metropolitan areas. Apart from the permanent moves between communities made each year by an individual or family, there are the daily boundary crossings creating the "metropolitan citizen." It is not at all unusual, at least in the major metropolitan areas, for an individual to live in one municipality and be employed in another, while perhaps traveling through one or more other communities daily. There are also frequent examples of people living in one community and shopping or seeking recreational opportunities in still others. An individual thus experiences overlapping memberships among the separate units of government in a metropolitan area.

This fact of metropolitan life is important to the administrator because, in consequence, public decisions made by one community can impinge rather heavily upon the lives of those living or working in others. It is quite apparent that, because problems do spill over from one community to the other, solutions do require coordination. Mutual needs may call for intense, cooperative interaction between and among community leaders.

THE URBAN ENVIRONMENT AND THE COMMUNITY

The demands and expectations placed upon any local government, in the context of population mobility, higher standards, and multigovernments, have many implications for local decision makers, and especially for the chief administrator, who has emerged as the focal point of most local political systems.

Is Local Government Able To Meet Expectations? While the tangible public contribution to community well-being appears as the most visible answer to this question, the evidence is rather convincing that the "public only" approach cannot adequately create the desired living environment. It is both desirable and necessary that a public-private-semi-public meeting of efforts develops within a community. The government must establish a favorable climate which will encourage private contributions to the community. This suggests the need for leadership to instill a public sense of responsibility, and it also requires imaginative innovations in financial administration. Of prime importance here may be meaningful, yet equitable, inducements to encourage property owners to maintain and improve their properties. There must also be inducements to encourage potential investors and developers to provide the types of facilities and services that add quality to the community, but whose provision may be beyond the scope and competence of the local government.

Is the Economic Base of the Community Adequate? The relative ease or difficulty a community has in meeting the demands and expectations of its members depends in part upon the willingness of its leaders to meet the demands, yet in greater part it depends upon the community's resources to support the demands. Because all cities depend upon the property tax, and because the yield of the tax depends upon the gross wealth of the city, the nature and extent of that wealth becomes important.

Cities differ in their economic structure. This is true for generally autonomous cities, but it is especially true among incorporated units within a metropolitan area. On the one hand there are "bedroom suburbs" where most property would be categorized as residential. These residential suburbs can differ in terms of the economic status of their members. Incomes and values of dwellings can be more than twice as great in one community as in another. Further, age distributions can vary, with those having low median ages requiring greater outlays for education services.

On the other hand, some incorporated units may be considered industrial enclaves, with a heavy concentration of manufacturing property and relatively few people, while yet others may be categorized as mercantile centers or as having a disproportionate amount of their land in public or other nontaxable uses. Finally, some units may be typed as balanced communities, reflecting a mixture of economic uses.

The sum of the units with varied economic and social characteristics comprises a single metropolitan social and economic community, but individual units remain distinct politically. Each community's particular characteristics determine its taxable resources and thus have a major impact upon that community's relative and comparative ability to satisfy the public well-being of its citizens. The administrator thus is forced to understand the basic characteristics of his political unit and to act according to the freedom or constraints those characteristics impose upon him.

Is the Government's Decision-making Structure Adequate? The city administrator must develop a structure which will provide for communications and contacts with officials of federal and state agencies, of other surrounding local governments, and of private organizations. He needs an information clearing house in order to be apprised of the service and project intentions of other governments and of private developers and investors. Very often the best utilization of financial resources can be that which stimulates a planned program of public-private contributions.

Most assuredly the various units of government within a metropolitan area should maintain close communications links in jointly programming street improvements; establishing land-use controls; and planning for such area-wide services and facilities as airports, zoos, museums, and stadiums. Establishing communications networks on a continuing basis will reduce the likelihood that public projects of the above type will have to be handled by any community on a crisis basis. Just as the federal government has conceived the idea of the "metro desk" to maintain contact with and develop coordination among the various federal activities in urban areas, so too does the city find it relevant to establish a "state and federal desk." Some cities have done this by developing the position of city coordinator and making the incumbent responsible for maintaining interagency and intergovernmental communication channels.

The administration must also structure the decision process to program for the future, to anticipate the needs of the community, and provide for them. Implicit here is the requirement of long-range planning of services and facilities (see Chapters 3, 10, and 12) and the search for adequate resources to meet those needs. The challenge, then, is to develop a structure to cope with the present and reach for the future.

How Adequate Are Existing Revenue Sources? This question is crucial if the city is to meet its expectations. When considering local governments, an important distinction must be made between the municipality and other units of local government, such as school districts. Although it is not incorrect to speak of a national increase in state fiscal aid to localities, a more accurate appraisal reveals that more than 50 percent of state payments are for education, with municipalities receiving only about 15 percent of the total.[1] The major thrust of intergovernmental revenues has not yet focused on the municipality as it has upon school districts and counties.

Among the existing sources of revenue available to municipalities are the following:

1. Property Tax. The property tax is the major locally derived tax under the control of local officials, and the municipality has necessarily relied on it as the single most important revenue source. Because of the presence of other government claimants (e.g., counties, school districts, other special districts), the legal or constitutional limitations on assessment levels or tax rates, and many of the theoretical and practical political objections to this tax, municipal officials have not felt as free to utilize this revenue source as might be expected.

2. Intergovernmental Revenues. The trend in both federal and state legislation has been for those governments to serve as the taxing bodies and to distribute the proceeds to lesser governments in the form of direct grants, loans, or shared taxes.

At the federal level, total expenditures for aid to state and local governments were expected to exceed 20 percent of all domestic cash payments to the public and to constitute about one-sixth of total state and local revenues in 1968.[2] States, too, increasingly find that a greater portion of their total spending assumes the form of intergovernmental expenditures to local governments. Over 40 percent of total expenditures by seven states take the form of intergovernmental payments while local governments in over half the states receive more than 30 percent of their total reve-

nues in the form of intergovernmental payments from the states.[3]

Yet there is a great deal of variation from state to state in the importance of state grants and aids. While New York and Wisconsin spend over 50 percent of their budgets in underwriting payments to local governments, New Hampshire and South Dakota spend less than 10 percent in this manner. Over 50 percent of the total revenues of local governments in Delaware and North Carolina come from state payments, but New Hampshire communities receive less than 10 percent of their revenues from the state.[4] The less the availability of revenue from the state, the greater is the necessity to search elsewhere or to rely on the property tax.

States also differ in terms of the flexibility or restrictions placed on the use of funds. Some may provide funds for specific purposes (e.g., earmarked funds such as education funds for local school districts), while others may return some of the proceeds of a given tax (e.g., the state income tax) to local communities as a shared tax. The method and formula used affects the discretion available in the use of the funds by the municipality. General purpose aids and grants permit the retention of alternative choices within the local community while earmarked funds are committed to a particular use regardless of whether that use reflects the need priorities established by the community.

The fiscal interdependence among levels of government is thus very strong and appears to be accelerating rather than diminishing. Consequently, it is increasingly urgent that the city administrator keep abreast of programs and aids which appear advantageous to participating municipalities.

3. Other Revenues. While property taxes and intergovernmental revenues loom as the most prominent sources of revenue to the city, many others exist. These include revenues from municipal public utilities, sales taxes, income taxes, licenses, charges for services, and special assessments. Many of these are in-

[1] U.S. Bureau of the Census, CHART BOOK ON GOVERNMENTAL FINANCES AND EMPLOYMENT: 1966 (Washington, D.C.: The Bureau, 1966), p. 8.

[2] U.S. Bureau of the Budget, BUDGET OF THE UNITED STATES, FISCAL YEAR 1968, SPECIAL ANALYSIS (Washington, D.C.: The Bureau, 1968), p. 148.

[3] U.S. Bureau of the Census, op. cit., p. 11.

[4] Ibid.

tended to reflect a relationship to a particular service performed (*e.g.,* assessment) or special privilege granted (*e.g.,* license).

The authority to levy all taxes must come from permissive state legislation. In earlier periods this permission could be thwarted by a rurally dominated state legislature. Reapportionment has reduced the rural influence, but the accretion in power has tended to the suburban portions of urban areas and not to the central cities. State legislatures, while more sympathetic to urban problems, may not necessarily be sympathetic toward city interests. This situation may create difficulties for those municipalities contemplating a change in their taxing powers, such as seeking the adoptions of a sales or income tax as a revenue alternative. Needless to say, many other considerations must also be entertained before embarking on this type of program.

4. Conclusion. Because the potential range of major revenue sources is quite wide, and because the implications attached or implicit in each are so far reaching, the administrator cannot merely select those that appeal to him and that seemingly lend themselves to precise and predictable calculations. Rather, when he finds himself in a situation of continued revenue shortages and crises, he must scan the range of revenue possibilities available to him, assessing their favorable and unfavorable implications, and attempt to "get the most" out of each source within the constraints imposed.

At the same time, he must search for alternatives to existing sources. Meeting the revenue problem each year is as much a sociopolitical process of interaction with other levels and units of government, as well as with varied interests within the community, as it is a matter of intellectual analysis.

Summary. The underlying theme thus far has been the uncertainty implicit in the financially related actions of the administrator as he interacts with representatives of other levels and units of government as well as with citizens and interests within his city. These interactions are necessary to search for revenue alternatives wherever they may be, and he must coordinate expenditure programs with other affected governments.

The Budget

As the uncertainties in obtaining revenues are recognized and acknowledged, this question remains: can the decisions concerning public services and facilities, which affect the quality of urban life and create a better environment for social interaction, be made in a systematic manner which assures rationality, dependability, and predictability? The budgetary process is the means which has been developed to achieve these goals.

CONCEPTS AND DEFINITIONS

An understanding of the process of budgetary decision making necessarily requires preliminary discussion of some of the basic characteristics and notions of budgeting. Quite simply stated, there exists general agreement that the "budget" is a document, perhaps varying in size, style, and content from city to city, but nonetheless containing some type of identifiable schedule of spending and revenues. There is also agreement that the content of the document represents decisions. Agreement does not exist, however, on matters such as the nature of those decisions. The decisions represented by the budget document have different meanings and different implications for different users, readers, and interested observers of the phenomena.

Economic Document. To some the budget is considered as a plan which reflects the allocation of scarce resources among alternative uses, comprehensively balancing public needs against available resources. The expectation is that a decision maker impartially weighs the various alternative expenditures on their merits and arrives at the proper "mix" which best determines relative spending levels to maximize community goals.

Political Document. Aaron Wildavsky has viewed budgeting as being at the heart of the political process.[5] In this context, the budget records, in monetary terms, the preferences of participants concerning "who gets what a government has to give," or "who gets to spend

[5] Aaron Wildavsky, THE POLITICS OF THE BUDGETARY PROCESS (Boston: Little, Brown Co., 1964).

what a government has to spend." Such a determination is political because there is usually conflict over whose preferences will prevail in this determination. Conflict can and does occur because there is no single decision maker, but rather a multiplicity of participants operating at a number of decision points. Each participant has a goal he seeks to achieve which may or may not be compatible with the goals of the others. He therefore makes calculations concerning the funds he feels will meet his goals within the established constraints and develops strategies designed to preserve the figure on which he settled.

Organization Decision-making Document. Finally, budgeting can be viewed as a decision process in which interest focuses on the way participants attempt to reduce complexities to manageable proportions. Questions center on who the participants are; how goals are attended, especially when in conflict; what types of information are relevant for participants; what the sources and channels of information flow are; and on what basis choices are made. Strategy is involved in this notion of the budget as it is in the political concept. Here, however, strategy is deployed to assist the individual decision maker to cope with a complex problem.

Summary. It should be clear that the "budget" can mean different things to different people at different times. This chapter will combine and emphasize the strategic types described above (*i.e.,* the political and the organizational decision-making documents).

TYPES OF BUDGETS

Municipalities often have two different budgets, *operating* and *capital*. This suggests that what is included in each can logically be differentiated. The capital budget may accommodate the notion of the budget as a political document, whereas the operating budget may be more appropriately considered as an economic document. The capital budget may reflect common aspects of organizational decision making better than the operating budget.

Operating Budget. The operating budget is commonly called the annual budget. The term "annual" suggests its repetitive characteristic. Each year participants expect the departments to submit budget estimates to the chief administrator or mayor, covering services, activities, and items that have been included the previous year and for new activities that may have been authorized by ordinance during the preceding year. The size of the estimates may differ from the previous year (though they need not), but there is little doubt that a department will be included in the budget. Normally, uncertainty only concerns the question: how much will this year's figures differ from the previous year?

Thus, the operating budget can be characterized as repetitive, with decisions pertaining to one year related to, and conditioned by, similar decisions made in previous years.

Capital Budget. Numerous municipalities have extracted certain types of decisions from the operating or annual budget and have compiled a separate budget called the "capital budget." This budget, which should also be prepared or revised annually, contains a comprehensive list of capital improvements needed by the community during the succeeding five or six-year period; the assignment of priorities to these needs; a timetable for meeting them; and provisions for financing them.

Specifically, the capital budget includes items that: (1) are unique and unlikely to be repetitive; (2) are likely to be tangible and clearly and readily identifiable (*e.g.,* a construction project); (3) are more accommodating to comparative choice making; (4) are of such major financial magnitude as to require special types of financing; (5) often require formal approval by other than the regular participants in the budget process; and (6) have major consequences for the future.

Some rather obvious consequences and implications result from the distinctions between the two budget types. A capital budget item, stripped of any claim to legitimacy by precedent, is more susceptible to rejection than an operating budget item. The perceived consequences, favorable and unfavorable, of a decision on a capital item exceed those attached to operating budgets. A capital budget item, such as highway construction, a new building, or urban renewal, impinges heavily on the formal decision makers as well as those in the community. Capital items can affect community values or conflict over these values; they can directly and precisely affect the environment of all or a segment of the community. Because they are so visible and can be perceived as a one-time, "either-or" type of decision rather than as part of an on-going pattern, and because gains and losses are more easily calculated, proponents and opposition form and seek to influence decisions.

Some of the essential distinguishing features of the two budget types are categorized in Figure 14–1.

Program, Line-item, and Performance Budgets. In recent years budgets have been distinguished as either *line-item, program,* or *performance* -types. While the basic distinctions between operating and capital budgets can be traced to timing, uniqueness, special fiscal arrangements, and enlarged participation, the basic distinction between the line-item and program budget is the focus of information presented to decision makers. Contemporary distinctions refer to the line-item budget as

Considerations	Operating Budget	Capital Budget
Legitimacy	Based on precedent. Extension of previous commitment. Legitimacy established.	Usually presented as a one time type of decision issue. Legitimacy at issue.
Conflict	Incremental, involving only marginal adjustments. Survival or acceptance not at stake.	Fundamental, clear alternative. Either/or form encourages precise support and opposition.
Consequences	Predictable and subject to adaptation.	Perceived as irreversible gain-loss.
Size of organization for decision making	Primarily the formal participants in the process.	1. Consequences of decision encourage participation by those outside formal centers, those who have a stake in the outcome. 2. Financial magnitude of decision often requires participation by those outside formal centers.

FIGURE 14-1. *Distinguishing characteristics between budget types*

input oriented (the particular expenditure mix required to perform a service) with a program budget being output oriented (the function performed). Proponents suggest that program budgeting permits more meaningful decisions because the consequences of a choice are evident.

While the presentation of information along these two lines affects the frame of reference of the decision makers, additional consequences may ensue. A line-item budget ordinance, incorporating all the details of expenditure—such as personnel allowances, supply costs, and equipment itemization—confronts the administrator with reduced freedom and flexibility in carrying out his activities. Receiving an appropriation in broader program terms affords the administrator the opportunity to select and alter his input mix as he deems most efficient in achieving program expectations.

The performance budget is an extreme form of the program budget. It relies solely on work units and unit costs as the basis for budgeting and for evaluating service levels. Because it requires a well developed system of management records and cost accounting, it is rarely utilized fully.

Capital Budgeting

The capital budget is but one of a number of improvements in budgeting that have been proposed and implemented by municipalities in the past four decades, yet it is unique in terms of its implied scope, expectations, and participants.

JUSTIFICATION FOR SEPARATE BUDGET

The Past. Capital budgeting had high pragmatic currency in the post World War II period as cities, beleaguered by the need to rehabilitate decaying physical facilities necessarily left unattended during the depression and war years, had to discover some orderly way of meeting the demands for capital improvements. The types of expenditure involved also posed problems. They were expensive, often requiring bond issues subject

to voter approval. They also took time and negotiations to complete, and, when completed, often created increases in operating expenses, which in turn were very often either unanticipated or miscalculated. Intermixing these items (*e.g.,* fire stations, libraries, sewer and street rehabilitation, health and recreational centers) in the same budget with routine expenditures (*e.g.,* office supplies, salaries) was viewed as an inadequate method of identifying or solving critical problems.

The sheer volume and diversity of capital projects was sufficient justification to distinguish capital from operating budget items for separate consideration. Further justification was apparent when the construction and subsequent operating costs were calculated and added to the more stable, though increasing, established costs—the existing operating budget base. The financial burden these projects would place on the community's controllable and principal revenue, the property tax, would be overwhelming. Home owners, too, had their personal "catching up" confronting them.

The capital budget was perceived as an informational and decision-making device to: (1) stabilize the volume of capital improvements at some relatively uniform level, and (2) coordinate the capital costs and their financing, usually bonding, with the attendant debt service demands on the operating budget. The goal here was to approach reasonable, overall stability, thereby avoiding major fluctuations in annual decisions on the property tax rate. Thus the capital budget appeared as a possible partial solution to urgent financial planning problems.

The Future. There exists a further rationale for capital budgeting based upon longer-range perspectives. Capital budgeting is viewed as the implementation tool of long-range, comprehensive physical planning. While much community growth depends upon nongovernmental decisions (*e.g.,* general population growth, the development of new industry, and increases in private resources and aspirations), local government itself inevitably becomes involved because public improvements must necessarily precede, accompany, or follow private development. Thus, not only is it necessary to rehabilitate the old, but also to provide the new—streets, schools, libraries, parks, and community centers. Capital budgeting, by plotting the timing and location of public improvements, can provide the link between private developments and the comprehensive physical plan of the city.

CAPITAL BUDGETING AND PLANNING

The logical, sequential relationship between planning and action in capital improvements starts with the preparation of the comprehensive city plan, embracing both the plan for physical development and the plan for changes in the nature and levels of public services. This comprehensive plan envisions the community through a period of up to 20 years in the future. The next step is the capital improvement program, or capital budget, which has a shorter time horizon. Cities have ranged from five to eight years in the length of time over which explicit capital improvements are projected, identified, and scheduled. This program sets forth a year-by-year list of projects and facilities to implement the plan. Finally, reducing the time horizon still further, the third step, contained in either the capital or operating budget, is the specific provision made for the first year of the improvement program.

The participants in the decision process thus make firm commitments for the next year in this third step and tentative commitments for the remaining years of the improvement program. The remaining five or six years constitute a forecast of needs and are not legally binding. Annual review of the capital improvement program in light of changes in plan, forecasts, and conditions could alter the scheduled improvements. These changes are then reflected in the new, succeeding year's capital budget.

Thus, the annual budget year is linked to the capital improvement program which, in turn, is linked to long-range planning. It is a continuous process, just as is the operating budget, but the horizon extends beyond a single year.

ITEMS IN THE CAPITAL BUDGET

The capital budget necessarily includes projects beyond those resulting from the realization of long-range physical planning of new areas of the city and the replacement of worn-out facilities. It also includes projects linked to changing values in the community which could not be anticipated or reflected, at least in terms of timing, in a professionally developed plan. Still others are linked to decisions of other governments: counties, school districts, special districts, and national and state agencies.

Thus, a capital budget can be categorized not only according to activity (*e.g.,* recreation, public works), but also according to participants' influence in the outcome. The above distinctions lend themselves to a suggested division of labor which reflects the advantages of specialization and which can tend to reduce the organizational conflict that appears inherent in a capital budget system under present circumstances.

Category I: Urgent Major Rehabilitation and Replacement Projects. Greater reliance upon department officials' judgments would be expected in this area, with planners speaking less authoritatively. The judgment of the planning agency in these instances would primarily concern the location of a facility, which would require the agency's knowledge of changing neighborhood patterns.

Category II: Community Facilities for New Areas. The capital improvements in new areas would be in the neighborhood type, reflecting the application of community-wide service level standards to the newly developed areas. To the extent that the comprehensive plan has been developed to include new neighborhood plans, reliance upon the planners' judgments would be expected, based upon their analysis of data. Whereas planners assume an advisory role in Category I, deferring to departmental officials, the reverse would occur here.

Category III: Community Wide Projects. Community-wide in nature, these are improvements which can be differentiated from neighborhood facilities such as fire stations, street improvements, and schools, and which will usually reflect the need to reconcile conflicting values before embarking on their construction. This category would include projects that may be unique to a particular community rather than common to all communities. Auditoriums, arenas, boat marinas, and community-wide park and recreation facilities are examples of this type of project. Because these projects require substantial political discussion preceding decision making, the elective participants assume greatest influence and their judgments will receive the greatest weight.

Category IV: Projects Induced By or Dependent upon Other Governments. Many capital improvements in recent years have had their priorities established by decisions reaching beyond the jurisdiction of the formal participants in the municipality's budget process. For example, the availability of state or federal financial assistance has influenced local decision makers to initiate projects that might have been deferred or ignored in the absence of funds. Viewed from a different perspective, the availability of funds has also alerted local decision makers to latent needs.

This category may be called pragmatic opportunism, and relative influence among participants depends upon the awareness, imagination, and strategies of the participants involved. The construction of a new municipal golf course might be more likely to result from an opportune, yet judicious, proposal to include it in an application for federal funds under an urban open spaces program than it would from the weighing of facilities and needs by a recreation director. It is the presence of such alternative sources of financing, which often appear on the fiscal horizon unexpectedly, and the absence of completed comprehensive plans that explain the disruptive or unstable character of capital improvement programs. From the community's strategic perspective, instability in scheduling may be a lesser cost than having to forego such an improvement. It may also be said that opportunities to take advantage of unexpected sources of revenue are often dependent upon the existence of plans to confirm the feasibility of a project. There is, thus, a high interdependence between planning and the disruption of the sequential timing of plans.

FINANCING THE CAPITAL BUDGET

The capital budget, in total or by projects, is financed through appropriations or from the proceeds of bond issues. The actual financing method for each project should be determined by the long-term revenue program—a program independently developed but coordinated with the comprehensive plan. These determinations should be described in the capital improvements program and in the appropriate budgets.

Finally, the capital budget is linked to the operating budget through the appropriations and debt service charges incurred in paying the costs of the projects themselves, and also by the costs of operating the projects once construction has been completed.

PROCEDURE IN CAPITAL BUDGETING

The structural and procedural arrangements for capital budgeting generally differ from community to community, depending upon size, past experience, current practices in the operating budget, and even state statutes. It is possible to differentiate between the sets of participants in the capital and operating budget processes by the inclusion of the planning agency and advisory commission in the former and their general exclusion from the latter. In most cases, the structure for capital budgeting would be: (1) the structure for the operating budget, plus (2) the planning agency, assuming it was not involved in the operating budget beyond perusing its own particular budget.

From this, given the general trend in American communities, the chief executive is in all likelihood the focal point in capital budgeting, whether he be the mayor, the manager, or the principal administrator. The normal practice would include the following:

1. Department heads prepare capital requests for the coming year and for the subsequent improvement program period.

2. Requests are forwarded to the planning commission and its staff for recommendation.

The planning commission may supplement the department requests.

3. The planning agency submits its recommendations to the executive who in turn can alter the items included and the priorities accorded them.

4. The executive presents the capital budget and improvement program, along with a suggested revenue program, to the city council for its approval.

This arrangement does afford the opportunity for numerous informed judgments derived from diverse perspectives to come to bear on these decision problems. An obvious consequence of this multiple participation is the increased likelihood of alterations and amendments to the recommended program—whether they emanate from the planning commission or the chief executive. Planners, feeling relatively free from external pressures, may make recommendations based solely upon their predictions of the future. Department officials, intimately knowledgeable of their own needs for urgent replacement items and extremely sensitive to the needs and demands of existing and potential clientele, are prone to include items and projects not anticipated by the planners. Timing adjustments to proposed projects, as well as the insertion of projects hitherto ignored or rejected, may be forthcoming from both the chief executive and council. The elective participants can be expected to be more interested in the immediate inclusion or exclusion of projects than would be the appointive officials, especially the planning staff.

Given these dispositions and tendencies, most communities engaged in capital budgeting and improvement programs experience frequent shifting, postponement, or acceleration of projects as a decision situation nears. Postponements are caused by inability to reach agreement, error in forecasting, inability to obtain voter approval, inability to issue bonds, inability to control development in predicted direction and magnitude, and failure to obtain acceptance or cooperation from other governments in their construction of projects upon which the municipality's projects were conditioned.

Acceleration could be due to ease in reaching agreement among participants, error in forecasting (development and population growth occurring sooner than anticipated), actions on the part of other governments forcing the municipality to alter priorities (e.g., state highway construction requiring local sewer and street programs, or a new school creating the need for related municipal improvements), or the unanticipated availability of new sources of revenue resulting from state or federal legislation.

CAPITAL BUDGETING IN PERSPECTIVE

The experience of most municipalities reveals that the expectations of capital budgeting have not been realized, in part because the premises upon which they were based did not reflect the capacities of individuals to meet them, and in part because the environment in which the budget was to be relevant is one resistant to control, certainty, and predictability. While the reality of capital budgeting does appear to be less than the total answer in solving all problems in budgeting, it need not follow that the concept and practice must be rejected out of hand. To the contrary, leaders in local government should recognize capital budgeting for what it is, adjust expectations accordingly, and exploit the favorable consequences that can accrue through its use.

Perhaps the single most obvious consequence of establishing distinct capital and operating budgets is the encouragement given to planning at all levels. Not only the planners, but all participants in the process tend to become acutely aware of the status of existing facilities as well as the requirements for future facilities. The motivation required to engage in such exercises is provided by the budget forms and timetable. Department officials have a much more difficult time explaining and justifying requests not previously included in the projected capital improvement program, while requests based upon adequate and accurate planning are likely to receive more favorable attention.

In the absence of a comprehensive plan, communities should take an eclectic approach to capital budgeting, taking advantage of the special skills and insights that all contributors can make. Because communities differ in terms of the sophistication of planning staffs and the contributions forthcoming from them, it should be expected that the weights placed upon the informed judgments of planners will correspondingly differ. Relative weights in the process will be a product of mutual adjustment among participants over time.

In all likelihood, capital programming and budgeting will continue to involve a multiplicity of participants mutually adjusting to each other, deferring to one set of participants under certain circumstances, and to another under different conditions. The need for the specialized knowledge of all is critical and apparent.

From the discussion of the capital budget experience, it is clear that there are no automatic, neat linkages flowing from the comprehensive plan, to the capital improvement program, to the capital budget, and finally to the operating budget. The operating budget has not become a simple exercise involving the calculation of the first year and subsequent costs of capital programs. Rather it is an extremely important and difficult responsibility, requiring all the knowledge and attention that the administrator and all other participants can bring to it.

The Operating Budget

The administrator involved in making budget decisions is simultaneously coping with a complex managerial choice problem: affecting the public influence on the social and economic life of the community; rewarding and depriving, relatively speaking, those structurally inferior to him; satisfying or thwarting his own goals; contributing to or obstructing the access of groups in the political system; and enhancing or reducing legislative influence over the executive. Because these decisions are so important for so many reasons, and because there are so many frames of reference, each equally valid and relevant, that can be used to describe the mechanism of the budgetary process, this section will focus on the dynamics

of the processes used to make budgetary decisions rather than the structural framework in which the decisions are made.

BUDGETING AS A SERIES OF DECISIONS

Budgetary literature has often emphasized "the budget decision" with all preceding activity primarily serving a preparatory function to that single decision. Opinions differ on precisely where that decision is made; to some it is the administrator's budget submitted to the council, while to others it is the council's actions on the budget. Whether the writer is oriented to the executive or legislative view seems to influence the selection of the decision point. The two orientations can, of course, be traced to the concept of the executive budget for the former, and to normative democratic theory for the latter. In either case, a sense of separateness or distinctiveness between the legislature and the executive prevails. Rather the perspective dominated by either the administrative or legislative point of view has often been the implicit premise behind assessments critical of existing patterns. From these complementary but separate perspectives have flowed countless prescriptions toward budgetary reform, generally seeking improved rationality in decision making by altering structural arrangements (the need for better coordination) and by increasing and changing the types of information available to the administrator or council (the need to consider all relevant information or the need to understand the consequences of all decisions).

It may be more useful for the administrator to reject the single decision-maker notion in favor of the analytical concept of a *multiplicity of decision makers* at many decision centers or points. Necessarily, then, there is not one "budget decision," but rather a series of decisions in sequence during a given period of time (the annual budget cycle), with the final decision during period A (*i.e.* council's decision) serving as the premise of the first decision in the sequence of period B (*i.e.* by the smallest unit in a department). By recognizing the multidecision sequential aspects of the budget process, the administrator can perhaps more accurately assess his role and his relationship to others in the process. Further, he can evaluate the effectiveness of certain strategies in meeting his own role expectations and in coping with the complexities of his relationships with others.

ORGANIZATION FOR BUDGETING

The Organizational Pattern. Discarding the single decision maker premise prompts the question: Who are the participants in budgeting and how are they sequentially involved in the process? A graphic answer to this question is provided in Figure 14–2.

Instead of the traditional notion of a hierarchy culminating in the position of the administrator, and with the holder of that position assumedly making *the* budget decision, Figure 14–2 suggests an analytical organization for budget making consisting of several decision points or centers where determinations of a particular budget level are formulated, accepted, or altered. A horizontal relationship of reasonable equality is inferred, at least in part, as far as goals are attended, information received and evaluated, alternatives considered, and choices made. A condition of mutual dependence and influence also exists in that participants at each point do make decisions which are influenced by previous decisions and which influence future decisions.

The more traditional, structural-sequential view of decision making has produced an impression of a formal inferior-superior relationship, however, rather than one of equality or near equality. This impression gains increased credence since the participant at one point can frequently alter the decisions of the participant(s) at the preceding point. While the formal structure can suggest these sequentially superior positions, it is doubtful that absolute superiority can effectively be exercised. There recur examples in government at all levels where the executive laments that he "has no control over X's budget." Thus the formal structural pattern may not at all reflect reality in the behavior pattern it suggests.

Size of Organization. The size of the budgeting organization (i.e. the number of decision points and participants) will vary from city to city, depending upon the size, complexity, and form of government. In Figure 14–2, the organization for the street cleaning budget, for example, would include: (1) the head of the street cleaning unit, (2) the head of the street maintenance division, (3) the head of the public works department, (4) the chief

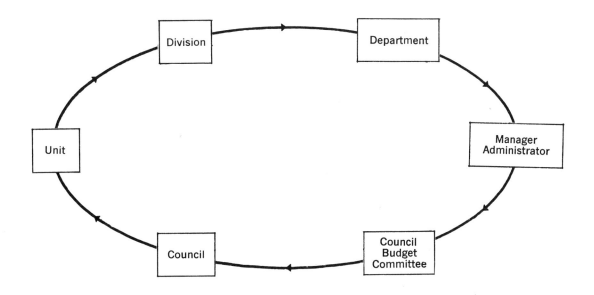

FIGURE 14-2. *Organization for decision making*

administrator, (5) the budget committee of the council, and (6) the city council.

The number of participants at each point will also vary. At the unit level it is quite likely that only the unit chief is involved in budget formulation, though he may informally seek information and advice from others. At the division and department levels, an assistant or deputy might have substantial responsibility for budget work, leaving the department head to set general operating guidelines and to assume an intensive role only when the deputy seeks approval of his recommendations and in later deliberations with the chief administrator. Many department heads, of course, insist on greater involvement.

Again, at the chief executive point, differences exist in the number of participants. In a very small community, the chief administrator alone may process all information and arrive at his decisions. On the other hand, the administrator in a larger city may have a constellation of subcenters to assist him in producing a budget. Some of these may focus almost exclusively and continuously throughout the year on budget matters, such as a budget department or bureau. Others, such as a data processing center, may be involved on an *ad hoc* basis, though with some degree of regularity, while having other nonbudget responsibilities.

Increasingly, too, financial relationships with state, federal, and other local governments will inject intergovernmental coordinators, liaison, and information personnel into the budget operations of executive offices at the municipal level. With capital budgets becoming so intimately linked to the decisions of other governments, this type of assistance becomes as crucial as that of planning and budget staff. Figure 14-3 suggests likely participants assisting the chief administrator in the budget process.

Budget committees of city councils are not uncommon, but only in the very large cities would special committee staff assistance be available on a full-time basis. More likely the same staff assisting the executive is expected to respond to budget committee demands for information and analysis.

In some cities, where both size of budget and council are small, the full council may sit informally as a budget committee, and then the same group in a formal situation will ratify its informal decisions. The information service provided by administration personnel to a budget committee would also be available to the council when the budget is considered.

Thus, while a number of decision centers can be identified, only one, that of the chief administrator, normally commands extensive assistance in arriving at budget decisions. This, of course, should not be surprising, for, as described earlier, the most common type of budget is the concept of the executive budget, where greatest expectations are placed on the chief executive.

Perspective of Chief Administrator toward the Budget Organization. The expectations placed upon the administrator by the executive budget—that he should submit a budget to the council implicitly reflecting his preferences—conditions him to view the other participants in the budget process from two perspectives which may be categorized under "internal processes" and "external processes."

1. Internal Processes. The administrator, in his relationships with others on the "executive side" during the formulation of the budget, attempts to ensure that his preferences in the distribution of resources among competing claims will prevail. His preferences, may be based on his personal values about the proper role of government, on his current organizational goals, or simply on pragmatic, opportunistic responses to available funds. To his advantage in these relationships are: (1) his sequentially superior position, (2) his staff suborganization, (3) such constraints as upper limits on spending which he can impose on others.

Counteracting these advantages are certain strategic advantages the subordinate participants possess, such as: (1) familiarity and specialized competence in the particular areas in focus, affording technical superiority on questions relating to program needs and merits; (2) the initiating role of the units and departments, with the advantages accruing to the agenda setter; and (3) the incremental nature of the process which severely reduces the administrator's latitude, real and perceived, to enforce his preferences through radical departures from the patterns of the past.

2. External Processes.   Once the administrator gains internal agreement on budget levels, he then becomes involved in decision processes with his external environment, attempting to gain acceptance of his budget package by others, including the budget committee, council, and interested and affected groups. Because goals, frames of reference, channels of information, role expectations, and competence may differ, no administrator can assume total, unqualified acceptance of his preferences and proposals. Thus he necessarily resorts to numerous calculations and strategies designed to assure acceptance for his proposals.

The administrator can draw on a number of advantages in his dealings with the council.

Since he presents the budget, he sets the agenda for future discussions: the council must react to his proposals. He has advantages of information and professional competence over the council. He can exercise constraints, principally the tactic of presenting a balanced budget, which reduce the range of discretion available to the council. Finally, the incremental nature of decision making works to the administrator's advantage in external processes just as it works against him during internal processes.

THE PROCESS OF BUDGETING

Discarding the single decision, single decision-maker view of the budget process not only recognizes the complexity of budget decisions, but also the sheer burden of those decisions. A division of labor is necessary; numerous participants are involved; decisions must be made for and about the future which, in turn, is not

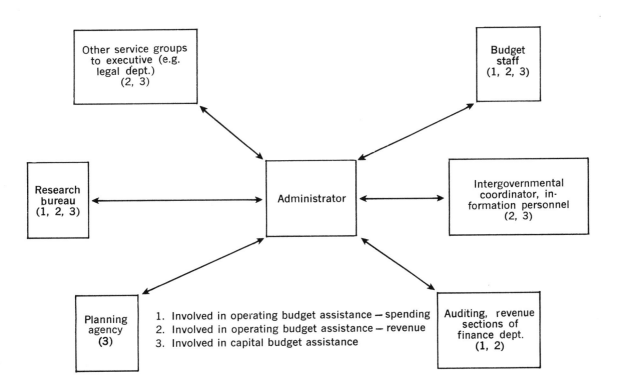

FIGURE 14-3. *Administrator's suborganization for budgeting (Although the figure suggests the direct interaction between the administrator and each subunit, it should also be recognized that the subunits engage in informal interaction with each other.)*

wholly predictable. Uncertainty is injected by variations in timing, weather, political change (new council or chief administrator) at the local level; new administrations and legislatures at the state and national levels and in other local governments; and economic, demographic, and technological change. Thus the usual assumption that the preparation of the operating budget can be reduced to a rather simple computational exercise, a means-end analysis resulting in the authorization of a one-year portion of a long-range plan and capital improvement program, must be discarded as false. This caution is not an indictment of planning and capital budgeting; it is intended solely to dispel any notion that budgeting is a simple problem that can be handled mechanically.

The Multiple Goals of Multiple Decision Makers. The notion that budgeting is a simple computational exercise implies general agreement within the organization on goals. Yet, the existence of a number of participants in the budget process renders such agreement highly unlikely if not impossible. The police department may want higher salaries; the public works department may want new equipment; the park department may want to institute a new recreational program; the council may want to reduce the tax rate. If these goals are not compatible, and it is likely that they are not, then conflict may occur. The organization's problem is to reduce the conflict. The individual participant's (subunit's) problem is to have his (its) goals achieved.

Very probably the only goal that is likely to be shared by all participants is acceptance or acknowledgment that a budget must be passed annually. Within that broad agreement, there is ample opportunity for conflict over what precisely should be in the budget. There are, of course, other broad generalizations that may carry inferences of goal sharing, as, for example, "making our city a better place to live," but the difficulty in translating such vague statements into operational terms acceptable to all is overwhelming.

Determinants of Goal Conflict. The presence of goal conflict among participants can be attributed to a number of factors. Participants represent different units and segments of the city government, and each unit or segment has its own program purposes and goals to satisfy. Furthermore, between and even within units, participants will differ in personal backgrounds, in personal goals and ambitions, and in the values that guide and motivate them. Finally, participants may have been recruited into the system differently (*e.g.* through merit appointment, patronage selection, or election). Such differences can affect the expectations and perspectives of the participants as they confront budget problems.

Certain constraints imposed upon the organization become the goals for some, barriers to goal achievement for others. Constraints such as the need for a balanced budget, the limitations of revenue, and the availability of certain resources (*e.g.* special state or federal funds) are among the most common constraints. In many cases, even when participants are motivationally disposed to share the department's goals, they may be forced to identify with one or another constraint as a goal.

It is sufficient to stress that conflict over goals can and does exist and can be attributed to differences in perspectives of the individual members and also to imposed governing rules which tend to advance or thwart goal achievement independent of member preferences.

Conflict Resolution. Confronted with such goal conflict, and given the need to make decisions, interest focuses on the manner in which the budget organization resolves the conflicts and reaches the decisions. A remarkable affinity has been found to exist between the manner in which government organizations resolve budget conflicts and that found in business firms.[6] This process is actually marked, or obscured, by: (1) a semblance of conflict resolution, (2) the division of responsibility for resolving budget problems, and (3) the sequential nature of the decision-making process, and thus of the attention given to budget goals.

---

[6] Richard M. Cyert, and James B. March, A BEHAVIORAL THEORY OF THE FIRM (Englewood Cliffs, New Jersey: Prentice-Hall, 1963), pp. 117–18.

1. Semblance of Conflict Resolution. Because a budget ordinance is passed annually, it is easy to assume that differences over goals have been satisfied and agreement reached. More likely, disagreement over substantive goals persists, but the participants have come to live with such conflict. A conservationist council member, for example, may continue to oppose programs and budget levels of the traffic engineering division, yet not force his irreconcilable differences into open conflict. The nature of the budget process permits a participant to avoid viewing any decision in either-or terms of finality, and the procedural rules assure that goal conflict need not be resolved on a face-to-face basis.

2. Dividing the Budget Problem. Budgeting decision centers are generally so arranged that participants do not usually have to deal in the open with conflicting goals. For example, a department head may be urged to consider the balanced budget requirement in formulating his estimates, but he can certainly rationalize not doing so on grounds of lacking necessary information, the absence of explicit responsibility, and his responsibility to provide for an adequate service level. His portion of the budget problem is to estimate the funds necessary to provide services. It is the responsibility of the chief administrator and the council to balance the budget. In thus dividing up the problem or burden, it is possible to avoid conflict while at the same time reducing the complexity of the budget to more manageable terms for each participant.

Dividing up the budget problem permits specialization. Departmental participants can bring their professional competence and experience to bear in developing expenditure estimates while chief administrators, with staff assistance, provide financial overview by reconciling estimates with revenue projections. The council contributes its special knowledge about constituency preferences. Specialization thus assures a "better" decision by bringing more information to bear on the budget than could be achieved through reliance on a single participant or decision center.

3. Sequential Attention to Goals. Each participant or decision center is also able, at

least formally, to make decisions pursuant to his (its) own goals in relative isolation. "Budgeting as a series of decisions" means just that. The unit chief making a decision on a budget estimate need not make explicit compromises with the department head, chief administrator, or council during a budgetary conference; his decision can be made before any consultations are held. He undoubtedly will calculate taking many variables into consideration that will tend to constrain and suppress his goal aspirations, yet he has the opportunity to accept or reject the results of his calculations. This explains, in part, the vast range in budget request changes over the previous year by departments and units. The participant may ultimately regret the consequences of miscalculation, but the process itself affords him the opportunity to pursue his goal in arriving at a decision, and to make that decision in substantial isolation.

Following sequentially, the department head need not formally place his goal and his unit's goals into open conflict. He has the opportunity to adjust unit requests to "fit" his own preferences. The chief administrator can subsequently do likewise. Through sequential adjustments, each made in relative isolation, the conflict of inconsistent goals can be ignored.

The stress and emphasis placed on the separate, isolated decision does not imply, of course, that the decision maker acts in ignorance of the environment about him, or that he does not have any contact with the other participants, formally or informally, during the process. Indeed, the major task for each decision maker is to assess the environment accurately. How well he does so may largely determine whether his or another's preference will prevail. Such contact, furthermore, is both formally inevitable and formally prescribed.

Depending upon the size of the community and the tradition of procedural formality, structured hearings on budget estimates may or may not be held. An administrator at any level may require his subordinates to defend or justify their decisions to him. This can assume the form of cordial information exchanges or of adversary-oriented inquiries. Personality traits and situational strategies determine the atmosphere of such exchanges.

In communities having the executive budget, the chief administrator can be expected to have structured contacts with his department representatives, utilizing either formal hearings or informal discussions. Additionally, the administrator will have contacts with those outside the formal decision centers. Interested individuals and groups may make their wishes known. The budget committee of the council will, in all likelihood, hold hearings on the budget. Finally, when the full council meets to consider the budget, a public hearing is in order, usually as a statutory requirement. Here the citizen and representatives of organized groups have the opportunity to make formal contact with other participants regarding the budget, and the full council can use this as an opportunity to question either its budget committee or the executive.

THE PROCESS OF MAKING INDIVIDUAL BUDGET DECISIONS

The budget decision situation poses a complex problem for each participant. He must identify his range of alternatives; he must search for information to assist in selecting the best alternative; he must determine when information and its sources no longer serve his needs; and he must make a choice.

Budget organizations at all levels of government have developed information patterns and procedural and decision rules that serve to assist the participant in coping with his problem.

The Format of the Decision. At each deci-sion point, the process can be viewed as portrayed in Figure 14–4 with the participant defining his situation from the information he receives. The unit chief will likely use the following information initially: (1) the budget figure granted in the previous year's budget ordinance; (2) the expenditure figure for the current year, estimating the final total as accurately as possible; (3) the budget letter or other form of communication from the executive which serves as a general guideline of "what will go" in the coming year; and (4) the budget form itself, whether program or line-item in orientation.

Participants at each subsequent point will utilize the same four sets of information in defining their decision situation, but in addition they can more firmly define their boundaries because the previous participant has established a new figure, the estimate for the coming year. Thus, the department head and all other participants including the council have the added advantage of knowing both the base and the expectation of the previous decision maker. Most participants will define their situation by confining their range of decision to the area between last year's figure and the estimate presented by the previous participant.

The Decision Inputs. Most recent studies of the budget process confirm that the basic determinant in defining the situation is last year's figure. This appears to be a firm "given." Most participants expect to request or grant an amount at least equal to the final figure arrived at the previous year. Very seldom is the entire budget subject to rejection or modification, rather the decision focus con-

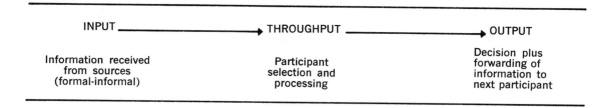

FIGURE 14-4. *The decision process*

centrates on variations (increases or decreases) from the base (previous year's figure). This practice is defended on numerous grounds, of which the two primary are that it reduces the complexities and enormities of the problem, and avoids unnecessary repetitiveness over matters that have stood the test of collective agreement over time.[7]

Reliance on the current year's expenditure figure as well as the budget figure is basically a test of the relevance of the budget figure. The general communication from the executive establishes the broad limits and direction within which the unit chief should calculate. Is the executive setting general expectation levels or has he been precise? If the latter, the unit will need to know whether his activity can expect generally sympathetic or unsympathetic responses at later points.

Finally, budget forms contribute to the definition of the situation because the decisions ultimately made refer to the information included in the forms. The information may be in program or activity terms or presented as objects of expenditure accounts—or both. If both types are included, then the one selected depends upon its relevancy to the user. Thus, a participant may have as his frame of reference a previous year's budget figure of $100,000 comprised of four programs or activities of, say, $25,000 each, or as ten separate objects of expenditure (*e.g.*, salaries, supplies, rent, etc.) also totaling $100,000. Additionally, when both types of information are available, a program frame of reference may exist for one participant at point A, while an object of expenditure frame of reference assumes greater relevancy for another member at point B or C. To the extent that participants do vary in their frames of reference, difficulties in communication may develop.

Frames of Reference. In any budget or-

ganization it is likely that the appointive (administrative or executive) members will have a program or activity frame of reference while the elective members (mayor and council) will rely on the more detailed objects of expenditures format. This can be explained in large measure by differences in background, familiarity, and intimacy with unit or department activities. The language of the administrator tends to be activity-oriented unless otherwise constrained. One study of municipal budget decision making, however, found that administrators would also develop an object of expenditure reference if the budget forms included only that type.[8]

Because participants do vary in terms of the information they find relevant in establishing a meaningful frame of reference, and in assisting them to define their problem situations, there are conflicting values served by any attempt to change the character of the information presented for decision making. On the one hand, a single type of information (*e.g.*, program or activity) should establish similar frames of reference for all participants and reduce possible communications problems.

On the other hand, any change would come at the expense of the participants asked or required to alter their frames of reference and to establish a new definition of their budgeting decisions. Utilizing the program or activity illustration, for example, council members may feel they have lost control of the situation by being forced to deal with unfamiliar information in coping with a complex decision problem. It is primarily for this reason that efforts to impose or encourage information change upon others, especially elective members, should be entertained with caution, and with consideration of the needs and past learning of those elective members. The costs of adapting to new information may indeed be great, and resistance on the part of the elective members should therefore not be surprising.[9]

[7] The one study explicitly testing the reaction when the boundary guide of last year's figure was unavailable concluded that participants were generally unable to reach satisfactory (to them) decisions and that the time and the uncertainty involved was substantial. See Aaron Wildavsky and Arthur Hammond, "Comprehensive Versus Incremental Budgeting in the Department of Agriculture," ADMINISTRATIVE SCIENCE QUARTERLY, December, 1965, pp. 321–46.

[8] John P. Crecine, "A Computer Simulation Model of Municipal Resource Allocation." Paper read at the 1966 Midwest Conference of Political Scientists, Chicago, Illinois, April 28, 1966, pp. 15–19.

[9] At the national government level, Congressional members in the budget process refused to permit the

The Utilization of Information in Budgeting. Early literature of organizational and individual decision making urged that participants engage in an exhaustive search of all relevant information before selecting a particular alternative or policy. This prescription has fallen into considerable disrepute in recent decades as studies have highlighted the limited capacities of, and time available to, an individual to acquire, process, and evaluate all information relevant to a complex problem. Even though the development of the computer has offset the capacity problem to some extent, such a prescription may nonetheless be rejected as uneconomical and unnecessary.

Role of Information in Simplifying Complex Problems. Organizations and individuals do not regularly engage in exhaustive searches, then, and numerous recent studies have identified how and where the search for information does occur. Studies, especially by Cyert and March[10] and Lindblom,[11] have produced strikingly similar conclusions:

1. That decision makers consider only changes from the status quo and not all possible alternatives—and they consider only the amount of the change. This is the concept of incrementalism, or marginal adjustments, or limited comparisons.

2. Search is simple rather than complex and it occurs in the general area of present policy or the existing situation.

3. Through learning, participants come to rely on information similar to that used in the past.

Whether this pattern persists depends upon

the general satisfaction with results from it. Should a decision maker become dissatisfied, he would be motivated to seek new channels and sources of information. Satisfaction most often can be measured by favorable or unfavorable feedback from his decisions. These findings are extremely useful in understanding participant behavior relative to information in the budget process.

1. Consider Only Changes from the Status Quo. As already stated, the most important item of information influencing the choice of a budget level is the previous year's figure. That figure serves to reduce the information search by eliminating the need to consider amounts less than that figure. Last year's figure constitutes an accumulation of decisions and agreements. Rather than question earlier collective judgments, participants focus on the prospective change from those judgments. This decision-making practice has been subjected to criticism on grounds that it places too high a reliance on the general soundness of the earlier cumulative decisions, and that it removes from review programs that conceivably could be eliminated.

It need not follow that because every participant fails to subject the entire figure to scrutiny, no one does. The most highly visible participants, department heads, administrators, mayors, and council, as a result of alternative demands, may necessarily rely exclusively on the marginal adjustment method. Yet the initiating point (*e.g.*, the unit), those most intimately involved and responsible for developing and executing programs, may indeed subject entire programs and their total costs to intense analysis. Programs may fight for their survival at the initiating level, rather than at the later review stages. While there have not been systematic studies focusing precisely on this question, there do exist, from community to community, instances of deletions of programs, activities, and structural units from time to time.

2. Reliance on Familiar, Formally Received Information. Participants, in attempting to cope with their aspects of the budget problem, have come to depend on certain sources, channels, and types of information to serve as guides

exclusive use and reliance on program or activity information in the federal budget by assisting in the passage of an amendment to the 1950 Budget and Accounting Act which permitted the inclusion of new information (program), but insisted on retention of the old (objects of expenditure). For them, it was a matter of preventing the disruption of their frame of reference. For an analysis of this incident, see James E. Jernberg, "Program Budgeting: The Influence, Effects, and Implications of Reform," (unpublished Ph.D. dissertation, Department of Political Science, University of Wisconsin), pp. 7–10.

[10] Cyert and March, *op. cit.,* pp. 120–25.
[11] Charles E. Lindblom, "The Science of Muddling Through," PUBLIC ADMINISTRATION REVIEW, Spring, 1959, pp. 70–88; also THE INTELLIGENCE OF DEMOCRACY (Glencoe: The Free Press, 1965).

in arriving at decisions. This is essentially a learning process where a participant might sample a wide range of information types. After a trial-and-error period, he may reject some as not making a sufficient contribution to the solution of his choice problem, select others, and continue to rely upon them as long as he is satisfied with his decisions.

Because there is a wide range of information available and possibly relevant; because participants come into the budget organization with varying backgrounds, experience, aspirations, expectations, and available time; and because different participants enter the process with different frames of reference, there is no guarantee that all participants will find the same types of information useful and satisfactory. A major phenomenon of budgeting is the disparity in the types of information upon which participants rely and insist. For example, decision makers who rely on a program-oriented frame of reference, such as many unit superintendents and department heads, will find performance data most useful, while budget committees and city councils, relying on their typical objects of expenditure frame of reference, will prefer information presented in traditional line-item fashion.

3. Reliance upon Informally Obtained Information. At each decision center, participants receive information on a regular basis from the previous center. This includes the budget request presented on budget forms plus whatever supporting information the previous center supplied to justify its decision and seek acceptance of it.

If making a budget decision were a simple matter using some procedural formula, total reliance on the information generated at previous points would be adequate. Such is not the case, however, and resorting to incremental analysis only partially reduces the complexity. A participant is still faced with the question of deciding whether agency A should receive all or part of the requested increment. Decision makers, unable to make that determination with formula precision, have developed decision rules-of-thumb, and the information necessary to make these choices is not always provided through the regular budget materials.

Thus participants may seek additional information as well as information already available and flowing to them for other reasons and from other sources. Each participant must select whatever information is reliable and meaningful to him.

4. Confidence. When complete assurance about the validity of any budget request is absent, budget decision makers seek to discover the amount of trust or confidence they can place in it. Behavior and information are the ingredients upon which this trust or confidence is based and serve to ease the uncertainty attendant to any choice that is made. Unable to process all extra information, participants sample information to test whether it will adequately serve to measure confidence. Sampling will differ from member to member depending upon his sources and channels and upon his ability to comprehend, process, and evaluate the information. The information must make sense and bear relevance to the problem before him as he perceives it.

For example, in addition to "squaring" a department's request with his own general policy guideline letter, the chief executive may also draw upon his general experience with the department, the reputation of the director, developments in the community throughout the year, and messages received from interested individuals and groups insofar as they impinged upon the department. In other words, he will have a communications net providing him with favorable or adverse feedback on the agency throughout the year. Drawing upon this feedback, the executive may also hold a hearing on the department's budget request. This is another source of information. While there are no prescribed boundaries of inquiry at a hearing, the executive's continuous contact with the environment as it relates to the department would probably lead him to confine his inquiry primarily to budgetary matters.

Budget committees of the council are usually less predictable in terms of the information sources they utilize. Councilmen, many of whom serve on other than a full-time basis, are less likely to have intimate knowledge of the budget and budgetary language and more likely to have divergent communications networks. It is more likely that their budgetary decisions will rest on information not necessarily bearing a primarily budget orientation, but rather on information directly connected with their own spheres.

Thus, for example, a council committee member, say a machine operator in an industrial firm, who always focuses his budget committee inquiry or program inspections on the equipment request should not be scorned because he ignores the major questions of the request. Not knowing with any certainty whether the requested amount or some figure above or below is proper, this member relies on the area in which he is knowledgable. By asking questions on equipment, he knows that he can accurately assess and evaluate the department head's answer. If he is satisfied with the responses to the specialized questions he asks, he will place greater reliance on the validity of the total request.

5. Conclusion. According to decision-making theory, participants will rely upon and utilize the same types of information as long as they prove satisfactory to them. Satisfaction to a unit or department would mean getting most of the funds requested, while for the executive or council it might mean averting adverse feedback, or assuring control and influence over the department. Information thus is regularly subjected to the test of relevancy and may be modified or rejected over time. Change, however, is something derived from motivation and is not imposed upon an individual.

The Strategic Aspects of the Use of Information. If council members are more likely to grant a budget request in its entirety when they are satisfied by the information they receive regarding it, then executives—including chief administrators, department heads, unit chiefs, and staff members—easily recognize that their goals will be achieved more readily if they anticipate and serve the information needs of the legislators. The following are two major considerations that affect the success of such executives in doing so.

1. The Executive as Information Producer. Because of the budget procedures established, the executive prepares the final budget document, including the departmental estimates. To the extent that the budget document, as well as any supporting information the department may present, constitutes all or a major part of the information for the council, the executive should have little trouble or anxiety in answering questions about it.

Furthermore, a budget document in program terms should provide added ease to the executive in that this is *his* usual frame of reference. Statements from budget officials and executives at various levels tend to support the conclusion that, apart from the questions of whether program budgets constitute better or more meaningful budgets, they do ease the burden of confrontation and interaction with budget committees. Officials find it less difficult to be convincing when justifying programs and activities than when justifying line-item amounts for objects of expenditures. In the former, discussion usually focuses on such familiar topics as what the department has accomplished and intends to pursue, whereas the latter forces the executive to justify stipulated dollar amounts for specific items and he may not be able to provide the precise response.

Budgets in program terms thus not only provide a more understandable measure of communication to the nonparticipant (citizen), but they also serve the executive's strategic advantage.[12] At least one study revealed how one agency official, during budget hearings, consciously attempted to divert legislative attention away from agency programs, and indeed away from the budget itself, and into discussions of agency regulatory work. The strategy was to emphasize successful prosecution of notorious cases as a means of building confidence in the agency so that its budget request would be approved without scrutiny.[13]

Thus, the executive has greater influence over the budgetary environment as long as he

---

[12] That a program budget provides a more understandable measure of communication and intent is a premise offered by advocates of the practice. This is not a universally accepted premise by all participants in the budget process at all levels, for it depends upon the participant's frame of reference.

[13] James E. Jernberg, "Confidence and Committee Decision-making" (unpublished manuscript), p. 18.

can, as producer, control the information utilized by others in arriving at their decisions.

2. Executive Preparation and Anticipation. Information produced by the executive, however, does not constitute the entire range of information used by legislators in coping with budget decisions. Yet a successful encounter with the budget committee or council depends upon satisfactory responses to all inquiries, regardless of source. The executive may have little formal or informal influence or control over the information upon which councilmen base crucial questions, so he must develop methods to overcome this deficiency. Essentially, the executive must be prepared to answer any question, regardless of source or precise relationship to the budget he prepared.

This seemingly impossible task can be reduced to more manageable proportions due to certain facts of budget life and through some preparation and anticipation strategies. For example, there usually exists a rather stable decision structure in the relationships between executives and budget committees. Department heads, chief executives (though greater uncertainty prevails here), and legislative committee members frequently occupy their positions for an extended period of time. Participants tend to rely on existing patterns of information and inquiry as long as they prove satisfactory. These patterns are reinforced annually. Recognizing and relying on this, the alert executive can usually reduce the total number of information sources that must be checked prior to interaction. Prescriptions or advice could take the following form:

1. What are the recurring themes of inquiry pursued in previous years?

2. What are the backgrounds and experiences of legislative members? This could provide the basis for their questions and interest.

3. What programs have been undertaken or are scheduled in areas of special interest to individual members?

4. What statements have been uttered by the members relative to the department throughout the year?

Other strategies could be suggested, but these suffice to emphasize that successfully protecting one's budget request requires more than "knowing your budget." It is crucial, of course, for the executive to answer any question relating to the budget requests—but that is to be expected. Final approval rests on a social process of interaction wherein the executive must convince the legislative members that he is in total command of his situation and that they can confidently grant the amount requested even though thy know they "are playing it on faith."

CONCLUSION:
THE NATURE OF BUDGET CHOICES

In making budget choices, decision makers, especially those nearer the end of the sequence (*i.e.* chief executive, committee, and council) have often been urged to evaluate comparatively all alternatives, weighing the request against itself and all other potential expenditure levels, weighing one program against another and all other programs. In fact, however, they do not do this. This type of evaluation taxes human performance beyond capacity and may very well prove irrelevant.

Decision makers have reduced the problem for themselves by limiting the alternatives to be considered, or by being constrained by various decision rules which also limit the alternatives. When there is room for discretion, the choice pattern has usually been observed as sequential rather than comparative. It appears as if a budget item, whether identified as object of expenditure, program, or as a department aggregate, stands or falls on its own merits and not at all explicitly in relationship to others. Considered generally in isolation, then, the comparative nature of budgetary choice is usually limited to the range offered by the two figures: (1) last year's appropriation, and (2) this year's request. The issue is usually how well the department has justified the request. If the review participants have been satisfied by the justification and attendant department behavior, the request will likely be granted, all other things being equal.

Other factors do enter, however. Beyond the first decision point, succeeding participants also have the benefit of a third figure, the recommendation from the preceding decision center. Where there is symmetry between a request and a recommendation, subsequent participants may feel reluctant to alter the figure, unless of course they have new or additional information that has bearing on the amount. Where a difference exists between the requested and the recommended figure, subsequent decision centers are alerted to this absence of agreement, and yet another adjustment could be forthcoming.

Such freedom to manipulate budget totals depends upon the "slack" in the budget, usually defined as a projected excess of revenues over expenditures. Where this does exist, executives can reconcile differences between department heads and units; legislative members can reconcile differences between the department and the executives or insert their own preferences urged upon them by nonparticipants. For many (most) municipalities in recent years, the situation in the operating budget has not been one of slack, but rather an excess of estimated expenditures over revenues. It is in this situation, the necessity of reducing requests, that the strategic aspects of behavior and information in support of requests come to the fore. Those who prepared and performed well (and this includes accurately calculating the amount to seek) are more apt to be spared budget cuts. Others will fare less successfully.

Where an executive submits a balanced operating budget to the legislative group, this slack also disappears for the participants at that point. The imposed constraints of the balanced budget and limited revenues may severely reduce council freedom to engage in any precise choice making, for the upward adjustment of any figure will require a corresponding reduction of another and there is reluctance to engage in such comparative choice making.

Thus while this account of decision making in budget work does not seem to compare with the pattern prescribed for administrators over the years, it does more accurately reflect how human beings in the budget process attempt to cope with budget complexity. Recognizing that the operating budget is a repetitive activity, usually involving marginal adjustments to prior decisions by a rather stable set of participants who have "learned" the process, adminis-

trators have found that the decision pattern seldom embraces dramatic choices resulting from comprehensive analysis and evaluations, but rather satisfactory responses resulting from procedures by which each participant copes with his aspect of the problem.

PPBS—The New Horizon

INTELLECTUAL FRAMEWORK

The fragmented, incremental, political compromise process of budget decision making described above has received considerable criticism for about 20 years for its lack of conformity to the tenets of economic rationality which are necessarily and implicitly required in making choices concerning the allocation of scarce resources. Economic rationality requires decisions that reflect means-end analysis, explicitly defining goals and selecting the one alternative (among many) that will maximize the attainment of that goal. Such an exercise requires the consideration of all relevant information (alternatives) both in terms of contributions to goal achievement and in terms of consequences. Basic here is the prior establishment of goals, which implies a goal maker—a single central decision maker.

Against these standards, decision making in the budget process has indeed been vulnerable to criticism. The question has always been whether a political process, perhaps achieving political rationality, can or should be critiqued in terms of economic rationality. A case can be made that the decisions represented in the budget are both economic and political decisions. In this context, the question becomes: do the claims of economic or political rationality have higher priority? The attempt to transplant the notions of economic rationality and their implications to the political system (or any organization) has been criticized both as being beyond the capabilities of humans[14] and as inferior to the existing process in stable, democratic, pluralistic political systems.[15]

---

[14] See, for example, James G. March and Herbert A. Simon, ORGANIZATIONS (New York: John Wiley and Sons, 1966), esp. Chapter 6.
[15] Lindblom, *op. cit.*, passim.

It is against this admittedly brief and over-simplified background and context that the newest proposal for budgetary reform should be considered—PPBS (Planning-Programming-Budgeting System) . The developers and advocates of PPBS have initially been the economists, and their focus has primarily been the federal government. However, the interest in PPBS has spread among political scientists and public administrators, and state and local governments have increasingly been viewed as potentially meaningful targets for reform. Thus, a brief discussion of the scope of PPBS and its implications for local budgeting should assist the administrator in assessing its overall relevance for his community.[16] In some respects, though not all, the reader may detect a similarity between the features and expectations of PPBS and of capital budgeting. This is especially true in terms of planning and time horizons.

PROCEDURE FOR PPBS

The PPBS system is an effort to link planning (determining agency goals or purposes) and budgeting (assigning financial resources) through programs. Procedurally, a department would first ask of itself: "What are our objectives?" and "What goals are we pursuing?" Once objectives are accepted, programs of action to achieve the objectives must be identified and implemented. They then must be analyzed in terms of the extent to which they are achieving the objective and with what effectiveness.

A number of tools have been developed to cope with the last phase and which can all be included within the concept of systems analysis. Fundamentally this means that decision makers are to analyze programs in a systematic way. Operationally this has meant questioning existing programs by considering alternatives. If, on the basis of analysis—often termed cost-benefit or cost-effectiveness—an alternative is

deemed preferable to the existing program, the latter would be discarded and the new adopted. Such a decision would be based on extended period costs and benefits, not merely the first or single-year costs. Implicit here is a forward programming perspective coupled with a continuous re-evaluation of objectives, programs, and budgetary amounts as circumstances change.

The purpose is to subject the budget process to hard questions and intensive, systematic analysis which should produce the most appropriate program mix to achieve community goals.

CONSEQUENCES OF PPBS

As an intellectual exercise, the logic of PPBS appears attractive. Students of the budget process, both advocates and skeptics of the primacy of economic rationality, have recently raised a number of questions about the implications inherent in the assumptions of the concept. These questions have been raised within a federal government frame of reference, but local administrators should be aware of and consider them if contemplating a similar system for their own community.

Centralizing Tendency. Proponents and skeptics alike admit the likelihood that PPBS will tend to increase the centralization of budgetary responsibility and effort in the organization. PPBS calls for goal definition and policy choice responsibilities to be centrally determined. Decisions are to flow down rather than up as in the present process. Advocates of PPBS, who recognize the possibility or even the logical likelihood of increased centralization, nonetheless support it because centralization is usually associated with better coordination. One of the basic arguments against imposed centralized policy is that it tends to diminish and discourage innovation and the development of new possible alternatives. The value bias of the central authority may also suppress other ideas.

Because the major choices are made at the highest central level, followed by a downward flow of decisions, the perceived prime beneficiaries of PPBS are the President at the federal level and managers or administrators at the

---

[16] One brief caution is in order. Any comments on PPBS (program budgeting) at the time of this writing must be speculative, for although implementation toward PPBS has begun throughout the federal government, and while urgings and enthusiasm among its devotees remain forceful and high, its implementation is just beginning in a few local governments.

local level. As a strategy, an administrator may wish to pursue PPBS because its inherent logic tends to give him greater influence and authority. Since greater executive influence comes at the expense of decreased department head and unit chief influence, it should come as no surprise that attempts to implement such a system may meet with internal opposition.

Cross Structural Programs. The establishment of a PPBS system necessarily entails modifications cutting across existing structural arrangements in the organization, and logically it could also mean the disruption of existing channels of communication for decision making between administrative agencies and the council. While the impact of such adjustments may not be as severe at the local level as it has sometimes been at the national level, its potential behooves the local administrator to understand this implicit aspect of PPBS in attempting to assess the relevancy of the reform of his community. It may be that a political cost-benefit study is a necessary first step.

Radical Departures. PPBS implies greater flexibility and manipulation in pursuing objectives. A particular program package judged acceptable for one year may be rejected after analysis in the following year or years. Continuous analysis and evaluation would insist on this option. In fact, it is the answer to the criticism of the existing incremental system, where the base is accepted as a given with only small variations from that base considered each year.

There is thus a high degree of uncertainty implicit in PPBS and this causes cumulative uncertainty among all members of the political system over the outputs of that system. One of the features of the existing process is the stability it provides for the system.

Weight of Cost-Benefit Analysis. One of the bases of conflict between devotees and skeptics of PPBS has to do with the role of analysis. Many skeptics charge that the economist insists that the product of his cost-benefit analysis be the sole or primary basis for any budget or program decision. Skeptics wish to stress that cost-benefit analysis provides but *one* argument for or against a particular decision. They further stress that this analysis should not be ignored or rejected, but rather added as part of the data available to the decision maker in arriving at his choice. They insist that not only are economic cost-benefit studies relevant to a decision, but so also are political costs and benefits.

Economists, on the other hand, express concern that political decision makers rely solely on political considerations and reject or ignore economic arguments. In more recent essays, some economists have come to view cost-benefit analyses as serving a more modest role—of assisting and providing a more sound base for intuitive judgment.

Conclusion. A necessary conclusion is that no universally agreeable decision criterion has yet been devised to take budget decision making out of the context of the political process and place it into some solely mechanistic calculation process. The major advantage claimed for PPBS is that it overcomes the irrationality alleged against the present system. In the process, it also serves to alter the balance of influence within the system it seeks to improve.

Administrators at the community level would be well advised to explore the literature of PPBS to determine its appropriateness for their own community. Neither advocacy nor rejection is the proper position to assume at this very early stage of its development. What is necessary is that PPBS be placed in the full context in which it is to operate—as an information and analysis base providing economic arguments pertaining to political decision situations, and with rather certain forseeable consequences accruing to the system as a result of its adoption.

Administering the Budget

In the historical development of budgeting, the central concern of the administrator has been to adhere as closely as possible to legislative intent (*i.e.* to spend only as the appropriations indicate) and to assure that spending did not exceed the financial limitations in the appropriation, however detailed or general. The primary impetus to, and the basic orientation of, systematic budgeting has been control.[17] The administrator's responsibility has been focused on how the funds, the purpose of which was determined elsewhere (presumably by the council), were spent. This emphasis has resulted in a number of techniques and structural arrangements designed to manage and control spending. Properly applied, these tools have been overwhelmingly successful.

Administering the budget assumes two principal responsibilities: (1) managing the spending of funds, and (2) managing the receipt of revenues.

SPENDING FUNDS

In attempting to assure adherence to legislative intent and limitations, a number of devices have been developed and adopted as management practices by municipalities.

Budget-Appropriations Language. It was the emphasis on control which led to the line-item or object-of-expenditure budget. The argument was that the more detailed the budget, the less freedom would be allowed to the departments and the greater would be the control by the council. Structurally this led to the development of accounting departments and systems of account based upon the detailed entries in the budget. Budgeting literally became an accounting activity, and administrators claimed that, while rigid adherence to the specifics of objects of expenditure did indeed result in budgetary control, this was not meaningful control either by the administrator over the departments, or by the council over the executive. Through the detailed objects of expenditure accounts, neither the council nor the executive could directly control the scope or direction of what the departments were in fact engaged in—their programs or activities.

To meet their management responsibilities, administrators have sought, and generally received, authority to transfer funds from among the more detailed inputs and, in some cities, to

[17] See Allen Schick, "The Road to PPB: The Stages of Budget Reform," PUBLIC ADMINISTRATION REVIEW, December, 1966, pp. 243–58, for an excellent categorization and analysis of changing trends in the orientation toward budgeting during this century.

exclude the line-item detail from the budget altogether. Today cities vary according to the extent of detail in their budget and appropriations acts. The greater the detail, the less the discretion for the administrator.

These revelations resulted in recommendations to change the form of budgets and appropriations, emphasizing total costs for each activity or program and identifying only the aggregate amounts of the various inputs that comprise each of them. The inputs (the specific objects of expenditure—*e.g.,* personnel, office supplies) are still itemized, but only for accounting purposes and not as the basis upon which budget decisions are to be made.

Two results are expected: (1) The council will control expenditures by enacting an appropriation for a specific municipal activity (an output) that reflects its collegiate judgment on the upper limit that can be spent, and (2) the chief executive will then manage. He will be directly concerned with administering the identified activity as efficiently and effectively as possible, giving only sporadic or indirect concern to the amount expended in each of the precise input account categories established for the activity.

While the common urge is to think of the information base of the accounts system as relevant only for budget administration, this is not the case. Today's accounts form the basis of tomorrow's estimates, and the nature of their arrangement does make a difference. The framework of the accounts structures the budgetary information base which, in turn, helps structure the frames of reference upon which budgetary participants predicate their decisions.

Allotment Systems. A second major control problem has been the tendency for departments to exhaust their funds prior to the end of the fiscal year. As a consequence, either personnel were necessarily released from their jobs and activities reduced to a standstill or the department requested a deficiency appropriation from the council. The former is abhorred on humanitarian and performance grounds, the latter is difficult because of the usual fiscal constraints within which a city must operate.

To overcome this malady, administrators

established allotment systems, restricting at the start of each year the rate of spending for a department or activity during each month or quarter of the year, using the experience of the past, the character of the activity, and plans for the forthcoming year as a guide. Thus the administrator was assured that a department would (could) not exceed its appropriation prior to the end of the fiscal year. The allotment system has brought balance and order to the spending process, especially when combined with a regular system of internal preaudits and financial reports of spending.

Effective Procurement. The budget and appropriations ordinances give the administrator and department heads authority to spend. At the local government level, spending usually takes the form of payments for goods and services needed to carry out programs. Responsibility for the human aspect of services has been placed in personnel departments while purchasing or procurement departments have been created to acquire and distribute impersonal goods and services for utilization.

The development of the central purchasing department and many of the practices adopted by these departments (*e.g.,* sealed bids) are linked to the growth of local governments and the desire to assure economy and honesty in procuring goods and services. Supporters of the concept of centralized purchasing claim savings of up to 15 percent through lower overhead, discounts for quantity purchases, standardization of items, and expert negotiators. Additionally, centralized purchasing tends to fix responsibility, thus reducing the opportunities for inappropriate arrangements between sellers and decentralized departmental purchasers.

Countercharges made by department representatives assert that centralized purchasing results in delays, reduces the opportunities for local sellers to supply their government, and creates communications breakdowns between supplier and ultimate user. In any event, central purchasing (with variations thereof) appears professionally crucial as the dollar volume of government grows.

The effective management of procurement activities demands that the administrator and his purchasing agent re-evaluate existing practices that presumably met past needs and alert themselves to the trends in procurement practices designed to meet present and future needs. Perhaps the major prevailing practice under scrutiny is that of sealed competitive bids. While some earlier criticisms remain (*e.g.,* the practice is too rigid), a contemporary charge has been leveled that bids are not competitive. There is some evidence of price fixing among suppliers and also instances of identical biddings with suppliers arranging a rotation plan of contract awards. In light of this, many urge disbanding the sealed bid practice in favor of assigning the purchasing agent responsibility to negotiate bids competitively.

Other developments worthy of attention are programs of quality control (scientific inspection), quantity control (inventories), and value analysis (an evaluative role in which the purchasing department advises the seller and the departments of desirable changes in the products or its use). The degree to which a local government can embark on the management innovations cited above depends upon many variables, including size of city, volume of purchases, and resources.

Suffice it to say that the current need for greater effectiveness in procurement is no less than it has been. While this need persists and the complexity of purchasing increases, the techniques employed must be sufficiently capable to cope with these complexities.

RECEIVING REVENUES

There are, needless to say, a number of challenging complexities inherent in the management of the revenue side of the municipal balance sheet, but two of these are central: property assessment practices and treasury management.

Property Assessments. Because local governments continue to rely heavily upon the property tax as a source of revenue, administrators must focus considerable attention and energy on property assessment procedures for at least three reasons: (1) efficiency: to maximize the tax dollars produced by the proper application of the property tax laws; (2) competency: to assure that qualified personnel will handle this sensitive area of activity; and (3) equity: to guarantee fair and equitable treatment for all taxpayers.

Among the trends in this general area are the development of electronic data processing for property assessment records; the inter-municipality, county-municipality, or state-county-municipality arrangements for the conduct of assessments and reassessments; and the upgrading of qualification requirements for the jobs of assessment officials, reflecting an increased professionalization in this crucial field.

These developments have efficiency either as their prime objective or as a principal by-product, but they are also intended to meet the equity consideration. Indeed, the reputation—even the legitimacy—of local government depends upon the degree of equity prevalent in the system. Achieving equity requires, on the part of the assessment official, technical competence on the one hand and extreme sensitivity to physical and social changes in the community on the other hand. Together, these requirements must be joined by the ability of the assessing official to communicate effectively with the concerned taxpayer.

Treasury Management. Just as the funds spent on most activities (*e.g.,* snow removal, street cleaning, recreation programs) vary considerably from month to month, so also is there an irregular flow of cash receipts into the city's treasury. Property tax receipts, for example, may be received by the city only once or twice during the year while grants-in-aid and shared taxes may be received at yet other times during the year. This irregularity in the flow of cash into and out of the city's treasury creates two problems: (1) the city must assure the availability of funds to meet financial obligations as they occur, and (2) the city should also make the best possible use of funds on hand, protecting such funds against possible loss, and earning additional interest on them whenever possible. Advanced management practice has met these problems by combining the use of the allotment system with short-term investment opportunities for idle funds.

The allotment system permits the administrator to calculate in advance the likely monthly spending levels for the city; in fact, it may be possible to develop a reasonably balanced monthly or quarterly spending pattern for the total city government. With the knowledge of fund needs for each period, the administrator can calculate the difference between expected revenues receipts and spending requirements. Any surplus funds can then be invested in short-term government securities which will yield additional revenue in the form of earned interest. Proper management and planning can thus be extremely profitable to the city by keeping idle funds at work.

STRUCTURE FOR CONTROL

Local governments have responded to the call for budgetary and revenue control by creating accounting or auditing departments, treasury departments, and, because the spending of funds usually involves payment for salaries and purchase of goods and services, centralized payroll and purchasing departments.

Cities vary in the extent to which these services and financial units are structurally linked. Some have developed highly integrated finance departments, including budget staff, purchasing, accounting, assessing, and treasury units, while others have maintained interaction among these units through somewhat more informal arrangements.

DEVELOPMENTS IN ADMINISTERING THE BUDGET

Because almost all local governments have developed accounting systems and some form of centralized purchasing, and have met other requisites of sound financial administration in varying degrees of sophistication and complexity, this discussion could close on the complacent note that financial administrative reform programs and proposals have been accepted and adopted. Granting this, it is nonetheless imperative to recognize two basic, major developments that can help administrators execute their traditional financial responsibilities and that can serve to link the traditional role of administering the budget to the more recently recognized role of the decision-making participant in the budget process.

Data Processing. Fundamental to the many related areas of administering the budget is the presence and use of data in enormous and ever-increasing amounts. Accounting, payroll, purchasing, and tax assessment and collection systems individually involve a high volume of quantifiable data. The maintenance and utilization of these records, both for control and future decision-making purposes, have required cities to move from manual fiscal operations to mechanical and electronic data processing devices.

Whether any particular city should move into the use of computers for its own fiscal management operations depends upon a number of variables discussed at length in Chapter 9. Individual cities must determine the relevance and applicability of this tool for themselves. It may be that the scale of operations is not of sufficient size and complexity to warrant the use of computers, especially on a purchase basis. It may be, however, that certain financial activities do warrant the use of the computer (*e.g.*, payroll), but that others do not. A city may also wish to explore the opportunities of contracting these operations to private data processing firms. The latter alternative must be considered in the context of legal limitations (*e.g.*, privacy of information), general coordinative control losses that may occur, and the relationship between costs and benefits.

While no authoritative proposals can nor need be made here relative to computer use, the administrator should recognize its potential contributions as well as its problems and complications for financial administration.

Program Evaluation. The traditional emphasis in budget administration has been the ascertainment of the legality of spending: are expenditures made within the established categories (whatever the categories may be) and have expenditures exceeded the upper limit of the category? While these control aspects are necessary, in recent years there has been a sharp recognition of the relationship between budget administration, the accompanying data, and budget decisions for the succeeding year. The budget process is repetitive: one year's information serves as the base for next year's estimates and the subsequent acceptance, rejection, or modification of those estimates. Thus, budget and financial administration data are not produced for legal and archival purposes only, but as part of the information base for future decisions.

Administrators need to evaluate actual costs against estimated outputs, asking such questions as: "Are we doing what we intended to do with the estimated resources? Could we do more with the same resources, or could we do the same with fewer resources?" Analysis of existing programs and their input mixes are necessary, and some cities have begun to explore the use of such recently developed tools of analysis as PERT and linear programming. These techniques are discussed in Chapter 11. Again, individual cities should refer to their own budget and program evaluations to determine which, if any, of the discussed analytic tools may be applicable and feasible for them.

Conclusion

Financial administration has been confronted traditionally with a dual challenge: to control, on the one hand, the utilization of the resources entrusted to the government by the public and to maximize, on the other hand, the public services provided with those resources. Time, research, experiment, and experience have largely provided administrators with the tools and techniques needed to ensure effective control procedures. With this challenge largely conquered, or conquerable, and with the increased demands for municipal services constantly straining tight budgets still further, the urgency of maximizing the service output of urban governments becomes increasingly apparent and compelling. To some extent, this means still better control procedures. Much more important, however, it means that budget decisions are becoming increasingly crucial and that, therefore, the process of budget decision making must be constantly refined and improved.

Thus attention and concern in financial administration has swung from the prior focus on accounting and auditing to a new concentration on the information utilized in budget decision making, the contexts in which decisions are discussed and finalized, the effectiveness with which they can be implemented, and the meaningfulness with which they can be evaluated. These are the new, challenging, and all-important vistas of finance administration.

15

Public Relations

PUBLIC RELATIONS in the United States can be traced back at least to the American Revolution when men like Samuel Adams and Thomas Paine wrote pamphlets and made speeches to enlist public support for the cause of independence. The origin of modern public relations often is credited to Ivy Lee who worked in the early part of this century to improve the image of the Pennsylvania Railroad and the anthracite coal industry.

Public relations has variously been regarded as obnoxious and deceitful publicity generated by press agents, as manipulation of the public mentality by devious strategists, as blatant propaganda issued by totalitarian governments, and as the hard sell, the soft sell, and the no sell. Public relations has been identified with and mistaken for journalism, advertising, press agentry, human relations, political campaigns, and public opinion polling. While it has been influenced heavily by all of these elements, public relations has over the years evolved enough to attain an identity of its own.

The Nature of Public Relations

PUBLIC RELATIONS: DEFINED

Public relations has been defined in many ways, often to emphasize publicity, information, and public attitudes. One of the more widely used definitions is: P (for Performance) plus R (for Reporting) equals PR (for Public Relations). This definition is a dangerous oversimplification because it neglects dynamic elements of opinions and attitudes, communications systems, and the administrative process.

Public relations is both concept and process. As concept, public relations means informing, influencing, and measuring:

—informing people through news releases, speeches, radio broadcasts, and many other means;

—influencing people by presenting information and arguments to support one or more points of view; and

—measuring opinions and attitudes to evaluate program results and the impact of public policies.

As process, public relations is a key element of administration. It consists of communicating ideas—informing others, learning from others, being sensitive to how people feel, measuring how people feel—and using information thus gained as a basis for proposing new programs and modifying or abandoning existing programs.

The administrative process is generally viewed—both as a theoretical model and in operational terms—as a continuing and overlapping series of steps in the formulation, acceptance, and implementation of decisions. Consent to decisions by those affected is indispensable for effective performance. Consent depends on understanding and acceptance.[1]

It is this framework—this need for understanding and acceptance on the part of all who are affected by governmental policies and programs—that calls for public relations. This view is discussed in more detail in a subsequent

---

[1] Desmond L. Anderson, ed., MUNICIPAL PUBLIC RELATIONS (Chicago: International City Managers' Association, 1966), p. 18. Much of this chapter draws on this book.

section of this chapter on "Public Relations and the Administrative Process."

Distinctions between Business and Government. Public relations in the modern sense of the term had its origin in the early part of this century when the business community sought to gain better public understanding and acceptance for corporation policies.

The government entered the public relations fields much more slowly and hesitantly because of strong opposition from several quarters, especially the field of journalism. Public relations as a function of government first came to general public attention when the federal government undertook a number of controversial programs during the thirties. Certain federal agencies, even at the risk of offending the press and other elements, felt that they had to defend themselves by publicity and other efforts. Today public relations, at least in the sense of reporting to the public, is much more widely accepted as a regular and necessary operation of government.

While there are many similarities between business and government in public relations practices, certain important distinctions should be kept in mind.

In business, public relations sometimes is indistinguishable from advertising; it is geared toward increasing sales, reaching new clients, facilitating consumer acceptance of product changes, and seeking company prestige and good will. Particularly important is the emphasis given to advertising and marketing.

Governments, on the other hand, approach public relations from a different perspective. They are concerned with better service to the people, ascertaining citizen needs and desires, seeking public support, evaluating the effectiveness of programs, and reacting to community problems promptly and decisively. Often these objectives are not met and sometimes cannot be met, but public relations still is an important part of the effort.

From a public relations point of view, perhaps the most crucial distinction is that of public scrutiny. Since the governmental jurisdiction is a public body, it must conduct its affairs in public, consider as best it can the ramifications of the public interest, make information available to the public, and provide a public accounting of its operations.

Public Relations and Publicity. The worst misconception about public relations is that it consists of nothing but publicity. Public relations is of little long-term value when considered only in terms of publicity because this approach neglects the more fundamental aspects of communications, public opinion, attitudes, and the like.

What, then, is publicity as distinguished from public relations? Publicity, one of several tools of public relations, consists of the systematic efforts of a person, a group of persons, or an organization to gain attention for itself, its ideas, and its programs by disseminating information. The news release, widely used by organizations all over the country, is one of the best known ways of seeking publicity. It is quite likely, for example, that a citizens' planning group, upon approving a master plan report, will issue one or more news releases for newspaper reporters, radio and television announcers, and others who might publicly report the action.

A few of the larger cities in the United States operate information offices that regularly issue several news releases a day. The subjects will cover almost everything the city or county government does—a proposal to amend the zoning ordinance to permit construction of apartment buildings, city council adoption of an amendment to the building code to permit the use of plastic pipe, due dates for real and personal property taxes, a proposal for construction of a branch library, the announcement of the dedication of a new municipal playground, appointment of new members to the city planning commission, the position of the city government relative to a tax proposal being considered by the state legislature.

Particular stress is placed on the news release because it provides the fastest and easiest way of getting information to a large number of people—assuming of course that the releases are used by the newspapers and other media. Newspapers, magazines, and radio and television stations receive hundreds of news releases from all kinds of public and private organizations, and they can only use a small portion of the material they receive. City and county governments, however, have a built-in advantage in that almost all of their activities are newsworthy. Therefore, their news releases have an excellent chance of being used.

Publicity of course can be generated by other means. A city can buy radio or television time (although this is rarely done by governmental agencies) ; regular press conferences can be scheduled by a mayor or city manager; special press conferences can be called to announce important events; key city officials can be sent out to address women's clubs, service clubs, labor unions, and other groups about city programs; posters for a referendum on a bond issue can be displayed in public places; paid advertising can be secured in local newspapers; spot commercials can be purchased for radio and television; and parades and rallies can be scheduled.

Publicity is a method. It is value free—that is, it has no morality of its own. On an ethical scale, it can range from the high-minded fund drive for the community chest to cheap attempts to gain newspaper space for movie starlets.

Public Relations and Public Opinion. Public opinion is an amorphous concept made up of views, beliefs, convictions, and attitudes of people. On specific issues, where the public is relatively well-informed, public opinion can be measured rather precisely through well-established polling techniques. Where the subject is complicated, many people will not hold an opinion, feeling that they do not know enough about it.

Public opinion is conditioned by the social setting of a community. It also is enforced by cultural standards, ethnic backgrounds, religious views, educational levels, and a wide variety of other socioeconomic and cultural variables.

How do public opinion and public relations interact? The relationship is close and continuing, but the concepts are not the same. The efficacy of public relations often is predicated on the ability to influence public opinion. Thus, public relations programs often are conditioned on what public opinion is, or what governmental administrators think it is. While public relations continually tries to tune in on public opinion, it is also true that public opinion is constantly being modified by public relations and other external influences.

Public opinion is not new; it goes all the way through human history. The study of public opinion on a systematic basis is a relatively recent phenomenon, however.

Contrary to popular notions and even to the ideas of some practitioners in the field, the study of public opinion did not spring full-panoplied from the brow of George Gallup in the 1930's. Political theorists had always given consideration to the problems of public opinion, even though they did not always call them by that term. A series of writings by political theorists of the 19th and early 20th century began to give the field its modern definition. . . .[2]

Public opinion identification is an interdisciplinary task drawing on sociology, psychology, social psychology, anthropology, and political science. Its importance to city councilmen, state legislators, mayors, county board members, and urban government administrators is self-evident. The more that is known about what the public, and the many publics that make up the public, *really* thinks, the better the governmental job that can be done. Because of the importance of this subject, it will be explored in more detail in a subsequent section of this chapter.

Public Relations and Communication. In its simplest form, communication is the transmission of messages—orally, in writing, or by pictures and symbols. Communication theory draws on sociology, political science, anthropology, and psychology. Communication practice uses statistics, writing and editing, fine and applied arts, signs and symbols, motion pictures, speeches, rumor, gossip, and other oral and visual means.

Theoretical analysis of the communication process emerges in some form whenever social scientists seek to describe society and social change. The crucial pervasiveness of communication activities, evident in the functioning of the simplest and most primitive social organizations, is particularly ap-

[2] Bernard Berelson and Morris Janowitz, eds., READER IN PUBLIC OPINION AND COMMUNICATION (New York: Free Press, 2nd ed., 1966) , pp. 5–6.

parent in industrialized, urbanized and secularized societies.[3]

Communication is such a broad term that it affects almost every aspect of human endeavor. Viewed this way the term is so broad as to be almost useless as a concept in public relations. For purposes of this chapter it will be narrowed to encompass (1) the two-way flow of information through the administrative processes of government, and (2) the reporting of information to the public through annual reports, newsletters, and other media.

Among students of communication, primary attention has been given to mass media, newspaper readership surveys, content analysis of radio and television programs, the influence of mass media on public opinion, the cultural influence of mass media on a mass society, and the problems of communicating with specialized groups. A great deal of attention is paid to such aggregate phenomena as large-circulation magazines, newspapers, radio and television, motion pictures, and advertising.

It is helpful for local government administrators to have some understanding of communication in this sense—especially the pervasiveness of the mass media and the influence they exert on a mass society. Within the confines of his own community, however, the administrator is more directly concerned with other aspects of communication, including: (1) administrative communication from management to worker and worker to management; (2) reporting to the public, both formally and informally; and (3) receiving information from the public, both formally and informally, through various kinds of feedback.

Of these three, perhaps the most important, and certainly the least understood, is feedback. The astute administrator knows that communication means more than broadcasting messages. It also means receiving messages from all elements of the community. This is no simple task. Some groups, particularly poor people with low educational attainment, are extremely hard to reach. They have little indigenous leadership. They are not sufficiently verbal, either in speech or in writing, to make their needs and desires known. They do not know how to gain access to centers of influence, and they live in a culture that distrusts organized institutions of any kind. Yet the administrator who talks only to like-minded persons at service club luncheons is not in touch with many significant elements of opinion.

The racial disturbances that flared up in the mid-sixties in cities both large and small have shown the breakdown of communications between the influence centers—or power structure—of these communities and their disadvantaged groups. A number of methods, including public opinion research, can be used to establish better lines of communication with these silent groups in the community.[4]

Public Relations and the Administrative Process. The preceding paragraphs have attempted to show public relations as both concept and process by distinguishing public relations from publicity, public opinion, and communication. For better understanding, public relations should be considered as ". . . fundamental to and nonseparable from the administrative process"[5] because it facilitates decision-making and effective performance. Therefore it follows that public relations is a management responsibility that cannot be delegated. It is only when the administrator realizes that public relations is an inseparable part of his job that administrative performance can be truly effective. Earlier chapters of this book have pointed out repeatedly that the administrator cannot separate politics and administration. He can only judge policies, proposals, and programs in terms of both political and administrative overtones and plan his actions accordingly. The city manager especially has an integrative community role which is generally accepted and will not be described further.[6]

---

[3] *Ibid.,* p. 145.

[4] See Earl de Berge and Conrad Joyner, "Opinion Research Comes to Tucson" and "Opinion Polls or . . . How To Ask Right Questions of Right People at the Right Time," PUBLIC MANAGEMENT, October and November, 1966, pp. 290–92, 322–27.

[5] Anderson, *op. cit.,* p. 34. This section is adapted from pp. 19–20, 29–36.

[6] For a clear and concise statement of this role, see Clarence E. Ridley, THE ROLE OF THE CITY MANAGER IN POLICY FORMULATION (Chicago: International City Managers' Association, 1958).

When the job of the urban administrator is viewed in total perspective—political, environmental, social, and cultural—the indispensable nature of public relations becomes clear. It is not so well recognized, however, that public relations is built into the entire organization. While theoretically everything in the administrative process has public relations implications, some operations obviously have more significance than others. Three are particularly relevant for administrators:

1. Determining Attitudes. Few public administrators would make major decisions without considering public attitudes. On many public questions, attitudes—as best they can be measured—are of greater importance than objective considerations of economy and efficiency. An interesting example is the public subsidy granted by a local government for construction of a football/baseball stadium. Such a facility is almost impossible to justify on economic grounds, even when the benefit of the doubt is given to peripheral economic activities such as hotel, restaurant, and taxicab business. Nevertheless, a stadium is for most people a point of deep civic pride, an asset that gives their city major league status.

Public relations is built into the decision-making process through the collection and evaluation of data to identify public opinion, the evaluation of policy activities in community as well as organizational terms, and modification of alternatives to accommodate them to the organizational environment.

2. Facilitating Communication. It is a management truism that employees are more likely to support administrative actions if they have been consulted in the formulation of policies and if they are given an opportunity to present their views either individually or through employee organizations. Public relations in this context means facilitating the flow of communications between management and the worker. As the educational levels of employees rise, this kind of communication becomes increasingly important because people must be convinced that contemplated actions are the right ones to take.

3. Influencing Attitudes. Any city or county government program, no matter how worthy, is likely to fail if it is not acceptable to significant publics within the organizational environment. This means that "program advocacy—influencing, molding, and altering value systems within the environment—becomes critical to the successful governmental administrator."[7]

4. Management Responsibility. Good public relations is the result of management support; thus good public relations begins at the top and is a direct line responsibility.

The city manager has an inescapable obligation for public relations, an obligation that is just as compelling as his responsibilities for sound public finance, effective personnel systems, and other areas of management. He must instigate training for employees in all areas of public relations. . . . It is the city manager's job to deal with the press on a knowledgeable basis. . . . It is the city manager's job, using all means available to him, to fashion improvement in the image of the city. He sets the pace for the entire municipality. . . .[8]

Many public relations tasks and activities can be and are delegated to staff assistants and others in the organization. In larger jurisdictions, public relations specialists, often former newspapermen, handle specific assignments such as writing news releases, arranging press conferences, preparing radio and television scripts, arranging meetings, organizing a speaker's bureau, and meeting with community groups. In medium-sized cities, the chief administrator, department heads, and assistants often handle a great deal of this work, especially meeting with community groups and with individual citizens. In the small city, the chief administrator himself is likely to perform most of this work, sometimes with the help of an administrative assistant.

No matter how tasks are organized, however, the administrator must never lose sight of the fact that public relations is fundamental to, and nonseparable from, the administrative process and that it is a responsibility which cannot be delegated.

GOVERNMENTAL PARTICIPANTS IN THE
PUBLIC RELATIONS PROCESS

It is a truism that everyone is involved in public relations—the garbage collector, the police-

[7] Anderson, *op. cit.,* p. 20.
[8] *Ibid.,* p. 33.

man, the counter clerk at city hall, the building inspector, the recreation director, the chief administrator, the mayor, the city councilman. For better understanding, however, it is helpful to consider participation in the public relations process from the political and administrative perspectives of elected officials, the chief administrator, and city employees.

City Council. The city council's importance in the public relations process cannot be overestimated. It is the council that primarily sets the tone for the local government and provides the essential political, legislative, and psychological backing for the chief administrator and rank-and-file employees. The city council is at a crucial point—some would say *the* crucial point—in the cross currents of influence and opinion. It is the city councilman who receives much of the abuse from individual citizens and collective pressures from a spectrum of community groups.

One example will illustrate the pressures that councilmen may encounter. Many suburban communities have been subjected to enormous population pressures from the overflow of central cities. Real estate promoters and retail merchants would like to see apartment buildings put up to provide more business. If this is not possible they would like to see row housing or single-family units built on small lots. Opposing them are the more affluent citizens who generally work elsewhere and want to keep the community open spaces just as they are. The city council is right in the center of this kind of community turmoil which must be opened to full public view at city council meetings.

In assessing the position of the city council it helps to consider the substantial change in local government as it has evolved over the past half century. In the 19th century and well into the first part of the 20th century, municipal government was considered the stronghold for corruption, Jacksonian political partisanship, and mediocre performance. Councilmen of that time generally were elected from wards, even in smaller cities. Each councilman tended to serve in a dual capacity as legislative representative and dispenser of city government services. Often he was assisted by precinct captains who provided a rather effective, decentralized com-

munication network for the city government.

Several major trends in the United States have changed this kind of city government. The professionalization of public welfare in the thirties eliminated the precinct captain's job of providing a bucket of coal and a basket of food for poor families. The increasing complexity of automobile traffic planning and regulation eliminated the city councilman's job of issuing driveway permits, deciding on the location of traffic lights, authorizing stop signs, and deciding which streets should have angle and parallel parking. Thus the professionalization of local government services of all kinds has reduced the handyman chores councilmen used to perform.

The civic reform movement, often dated to the organization of the National Municipal League in 1894, has had a profound effect on city and county government. Corrupt elections are almost gone; the caliber of mayors and councilmen is higher; the number of elective offices has been sharply reduced. In earlier times, in a volatile political context, city councilmen were the focal point of political parties, but partisan political leaders have been replaced by men who are more concerned with issues and their public image.

Citizens now demand more local government services, rendered more effectively and more professionally. This is not surprising considering the rising educational and income levels of the population as a whole.

The city councilman, formerly a patronage dispenser and a personal service provider, has evolved into a "reactor." He is continually tuned to public opinion and attitudes so that he can handle his legislative work more intelligently. The councilman must spend a substantial amount of his time in formal and informal hearings on many subjects, especially major zoning problems, public works proposals, revitalization of the central business district, and racial conflicts and other manifestations of social pathology.

1. Educating Councilmen. The new city councilman's education usually begins shortly after he has been sworn into office and is enjoying the congratulations and expressions of best wishes from friends and family. The first time

an issue of any consequence comes before the council, he quickly discovers in a very practical way the meaning of the term "publics." He will be shocked to find that one of the deacons in his church thinks that the councilman's views on off-street parking in the central business district are idiotic. He will be overwhelmed by the mothers' club that wants a branch library for their neighborhood *right now*. He will be totally unprepared for the cold, hard outlook of the labor union organizer who states emphatically that there is no difference whatsoever between private and public employment with respect to collective bargaining.

Above all he will be appalled at the failure of the public to absorb information on city government policies, programs, and specific activities. Urban renewal projects, branch libraries, school buildings, expressways, and other projects involving acquisition of land can be announced months, even years, in advance, but the city councilman can almost bet that the demonstrations, the mothers' marches, and other noisy forms of protest will not come until actual land acquisition has started.

During these and other times of stress the city councilman learns that it is one thing to adopt a policy or approve a program and quite another to gauge public acceptance.

2. The Public Interest. The conscientious, thoughtful, and empathic councilman soon gains a healthy respect for the complexity of public opinion and attitudes. He then is ready to embark on the never-to-be-finished search for the public interest.[9]

The public interest is one of the most cherished abstractions of American government. Every interest group speaks and acts in the public interest. After all who is going to come out and say he is *against* the public interest? As is so often the case with dialectics, the difficulty comes in definition. Perhaps some clarification can be gained by defining the public interest in several ways.

Probably the most widely held concept of

the public interest is that of consensus—the position that where there is sufficient community support it represents either a majority or a substantial minority with majority acquiescence. If a particular value is accepted by a great majority of the people, it becomes an accepted value and almost completely noncontroversial. In this sense the public interest is easy to find, but of little help in resolving most community problems. The public interest is less clearly ascertainable when a value is held by a significant minority and the rest of the community either doesn't know or doesn't care.

The public interest can be defined, especially by people of high educational attainment, as "superior wisdom." Sometimes the optimum or best solution to a problem does not have general acceptance, and it takes a long period of education and persuasion before a policy can be adopted.

An interesting example of superior wisdom on the international level is provided by the rise of fascism in Europe during the twenties and thirties. Informed observers were pointing out the threat to the United States from the growth of totalitarianism in Italy and Germany, but a majority of the public did not believe it. The public held to the safety they felt was provided by two oceans until the outbreak of war in Europe in 1939 and subsequent developments overturned isolationism and prepared the United States for war.

The major danger of defining public interest by superior wisdom is in determining who the wise men are. In addition, there is no guarantee that superior wisdom will remain superior in the light of subsequent events.

Public interest is sometimes defined as that which is morally correct. It is held that the moral response will be made if people think clearly and act rationally. Abstractions such as life, liberty, equality, and justice fit in well with this definition of the public interest, but it is extremely difficult to make this concept operational.

From the individual's perspective, the public interest may be defined as that which coincides with his own values. This is a treacherous view of the public interest because, if strongly and consistently held, it leads to the doctri-

---

[9] Administrators, both elected and appointed, are also deeply concerned with the public interest, but the emphasis here is on the city councilman because the council must take ultimate responsibility through formal adoption of policy by majority vote.

naire, authoritarian outlook of the person who seeks to impose his values, and his alone, on others.

Fortunately, the city councilman will find that he is not as a practical matter seeking the public interest as if it were clear, unified, and ascertainable. Rather he is seeking an adjustment of a melange of interests competing for the time and attention of elected officials. Thus the astute councilman seeks to balance or synthesize a range of interests on any major question. Local government as it operates in the United States ordinarily gives everyone a chance to be heard, either directly or through spokesmen. The councilman should conceive his greatest responsibility as that of adopting, modifying, or abandoning a policy so as to compromise and harmonize competing and complementary interests.

The Chief Administrator. The chief administrator, although intimately involved with the council in policy formulation, faces a different range of public relations problems. He is more likely to be the point of contact for the public on administrative matters ranging from significant professional and technical decisions to the minor irritations of tax bills sent to the wrong address.

Another difference is that the chief administrator often has more opportunity to draw on a wide range of public relations tools: opinion and attitude surveys, legal advice, professional association memberships and other information resources, professional advice from city department heads, employee training programs, and annual reports, newsletters, bulletin boards, and other means of communication.

He usually is more involved than councilmen in attendance at professional meetings, conferences and workshops with officials from other local governments, shirt-sleeve sessions with executives of health and welfare councils, consultation with state and federal government officials, and confrontations with leaders of labor unions, civil rights groups, and property owners' associations.

Still another difference is that the chief administrator can give continuing attention to programs through systematic research, analysis, and evaluation of results.

The different public relations resources of councilmen and chief administrators thus tend to complement each other. The councilman tends to react and evaluate more impressionistically and intuitively; the chief administrator tends to draw more on reports, professional opinions, and direct observation.

City Employees. Almost all city employees come in contact with the members of the public in their work, and many of these contacts are made daily. City hall employees meet with people who have problems on zoning applications, building permits, dog licenses, subdivision plats, and special assessments. Outside the city hall employees deal with citizens through the provision of police, fire, garbage collection, building inspection, street maintenance, and other services. These person-to-person relationships have an enormous effect on the quality of the city government's public relations.

The citizen who, seeking a building permit, is treated brusquely and shunted from office to office will remember his treatment for a long time. He will make it a point to tell his friends about it. It does not take very many incidents of this kind to undo the hard work of annual reports, tax leaflets, newsletters, radio programs, speaking engagements, and other efforts to improve the impressions the city government makes on people.

The more progressive cities recognize the pervasiveness of employee contacts and have adopted formal and informal training programs to teach a few basic methods and to instill in employees the city's expectations that courtesy and good manners are expected of all employees at all times. Thus attention is given not only to face-to-face meetings, but also to composing friendly and concise letters, answering the telephone promptly, providing accurate information, observing good telephone manners, and treating every complaint and request for information as an item of business that must be completed with dispatch.

Everyone has observed the crucial difference that employee attitudes and behavior can make in their opinion of businesses. Electric, telephone, gas, and other public utilities place great emphasis on their employees' behavior as a crucial part of good public relations. Hotels, restaurants, and other businesses where service is a crucial element give painstaking attention to every conceivable detail of service to the public. In the city hall such attention to detail should extend beyond employee behavior to other visible elements of city government such as keeping delivery trucks, police cars, and street sweepers clean and freshly painted; keeping park and playground equipment in good repair; providing good maintenance for buildings and grounds; providing uniforms, where appropriate, for city employees and requiring that they be maintained in good condition; and keeping offices neat and orderly.

Above all, the city council and the chief administrator should work to instill a sense of pride and achievement. This cannot be done by exhortations and pep talks. It depends on performance, mutual respect, well-defined objectives, and dignified treatment of employees. It takes legislative and administrative backing to provide the setting and to encourage an attitude of service on the part of employees. Where councilmen, the mayor, and the chief administrator are proud of their city, this feeling will spread. Where employees are treated as individuals, with dignity and respect, they will be more likely to treat citizens the same way.

Public Participants in the Public Relations Process

A good understanding of public opinion and the way it interacts with many publics in the community provides the urban administrator with an opportunity to work both idealistically and realistically. To do so he must appreciate the role of public opinion in the formulation and implementation of policy. The administrator should conceive of the community as a social system, continually interacting through many publics in the submission and modification of opinion.

The Multitudinous Publics. The administrator who thinks this way will not make the common error of assuming that "the public" is a monolith that exists outside city hall, waiting to be catered to. Instead he thinks in terms of publics—that is, groups of individuals held together by common interests and objectives.

Publics are not as highly structured as clubs, lodges, and associations. Publics lack any formal institutionalization although they are groups with sufficient cohesiveness to be identified in the flow of influence and opinion.

Some examples of publics with common interests include such racial groups as Negroes and orientals; such age groups as children and senior citizens; such religious groups as protestants and Catholics; such income groups as the poor, lower middle, upper middle, and high; and such occupational groups as retailers, policemen, and doctors.

1. Nature of the Publics. Publics can be identified by the flow of influence and opinion, particularly as it affects the formulation of public policy. Publics also can be identified in a structural sense by distinguishing between opinion-makers and opinion-holders. The opinion-holders, in turn, can be subdivided between the attentive public and the inattentive public. Figure 15–1 illustrates this concept.

That portion of the public in the center, the opinion-makers, might be variously designated as "the intellectuals," "the influentials," "the power structure," and "the elite." The opinion-makers usually include, but are not limited to, governors, senators, and Congressmen who can command a national audience; local political leaders of similar influence within their own areas; newspaper editors and columnists; university teachers and administrators; corporation executives; and, perhaps to an extent not sufficiently appreciated, the well-educated and well-informed people who exert an influence on their family, friends, and acquaintances.

The opinion-holders, on the other hand, usually are those who make up the great majority of the public. One easy way to distinguish between the two groups is by their access, or lack of access, to communication channels.

These relationships are never static. Some persons obviously are influential in some areas and not in others. In today's complex society, nobody can be expert in very many areas. Therefore, opinion-makers and opinion-holders are in constant state of flux.

It may be helpful to use an analogy of concentric circles [see Figure 15–1] to show how members of the internal elements are constantly shifting their

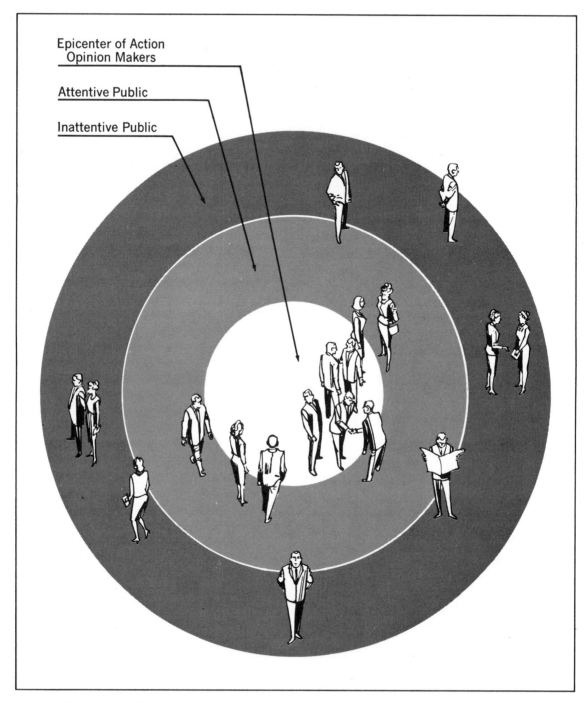

Epicenter of Action
Opinion Makers

Attentive Public

Inattentive Public

FIGURE 15-1. *Gradations of a public: opinion-makers, attentive public, inattentive public (Source: Figures 15-1, 15-2, 15-3, and 15-4 are from* MUNICIPAL PUBLIC RELATIONS, *International City Managers' Association, 1966, pp. 73, 150, 168, and 195 respectively.)*

roles. If the circles in Figure [15–1] are visualized as being in constant spirals, it would indicate that a public is in an incessant state of motion, juggling its position of influence in relation to other rival publics and constantly varying in magnitude of influence and number of members.

The outer limits of the concentric circles represent the inattentive opinion-holders. They have neither the opportunity nor strong inclination to become involved in the opinion-making process. Their accessibility to circuits of communication is limited. . . .

The attentive opinion-holders are found toward the middle of the pattern of influence in a public. They are persons who are inclined to participate but lack accessibility or opportunity. . . .

Located at the epicenter . . . are the opinion-makers. . . . They are the persons who strongly *influence,* as well as *articulate* and *represent,* the opinion of a public. They are engaged in the critical functions of opinion-circulation, opinion-formation, and opinion-submitting.[10]

2. Mobilizing the Publics. Public relations often seeks to mobilize specific publics on specific issues. Sometimes termed "manipulation" or "brain-washing," it is an essential function of public relations that has had to overcome its own bad image. Nevertheless government cannot function unless publics are informed and aware on specific issues. This complex area, involving both sociological theory and practice, will not be elaborated on further except to outline three fundamentals for mobilizing the publics in support of specific issues.

The first requirement is to know what the publics are in terms of their membership, interests, and beliefs. Research techniques have been developed in public opinion measurement that help in answering such questions.

Second, the publics when identified need to be linked with more institutionalized groupings such as lodges, clubs, and associations. One way of doing this is to look for the influentials in both the publics and the more formal associations and find the linkages between them.

After the publics and their more formal associations have been reasonably well identified, it is necessary to channel opinion to them through personal communication, newsletters,

and other organizational media, and through newspapers and other mass media.

3. Evaluating the Feedback. In the whole process of dealing with publics, and through them with more formalized groups and associations, it is necessary to get as much reaction and evaluation—or feedback—as possible. If the whole area of public opinion is considered as fluid and circular, like an air conditioning system that recirculates the water it uses, then it is evident that the process is not complete without the return of the water—or the feedback. It is the feedback that helps to evaluate programs, services, and activities, and to modify them accordingly.

Feedback can be both informal and formal. Informally it can consist of such indicators as letters to the editor, phone calls and letters to the city hall, rumors and gossip, the employee grapevine, and the shifts in attitudes as perceived by the chief administrator. More formal expressions of feedback are often quite unpleasant—the protest march, the petition demanding a new branch library, the stinging letter of resignation from a disgruntled employee, and the demonstrations and other forms of organized petition.

One of the most difficult aspects of feedback is to ascertain opinions and attitudes while they are latent (not dormant) and before they are galvanized into protest. Attitude surveys and other methods of public opinion research can be helpful.

Another way for the chief administrator and city councilmen to get more feedback informally is to widen their range of associations. The administrator who talks only to his social equals at service club luncheons and to his professional counterparts at association meetings can lose touch with significant elements of the community. The councilman who sees people, individually and collectively, only on the "right" side of the tracks may be in for quite a shock when he has his first encounter with a civil rights leader.

Obviously, no administrator or councilman can be all things to all people, but he can make a systematic effort to become acquainted with all of the major publics in his community, both informally and through the

[10] Garth Jones, "The Multitudinous Publics," in Anderson, *op. cit.,* pp. 72–73.

linkages provided by clubs, associations, and other formalized groups.

Community Groups and Associations. When people get sufficiently interested, absorbed, irritated, or agitated, they will look around for formal groups and associations to join so they can channel their feelings. Thus community groups and associations provide an essential institutionalized setting for the expression of influence and opinion.

The United States has a long history of being a nation of joiners, and nowhere is this seen more dramatically than on the local scale with organizations for every conceivable purpose. Some, like Rotary, Lions, Kiwanis, and other service clubs, have national and international linkages with a dedication to service. Others like the local medical society have a professional outlook. Still others are interested in jobs and employment (labor unions), promoting educational objectives (the PTA's), and protecting environmental amenities (neighborhood property owners' associations).

This proliferation of formal clubs, associations, and groups provides the chief administrator and other city officials with an excellent opportunity to keep in touch with many (but not all) elements of the community. Often overlooked in the profusion of formal groups is the large number of people who are non-joiners. It is well known that many people in the United States do not vote in elections; it is not as well known that many people also either cannot or will not participate in churches, lodges, neighborhood associations, Girl Scouts, Boy Scouts, and other voluntary associations. Despite this shortcoming, formal groups and associations provide one of the most reliable means of ascertaining opinions and attitudes.

Formal groups and associations have more of a role to play in the city than merely initiating or reacting to policy proposals affecting their interests. Groups and associations can be mobilized in support of specific programs. These groups collectively provide most of the leadership that a community is likely to have, and these human resources should be used by the city government whenever possible.

To draw on this leadership potential in a systematic way, an inventory of community groups should be made. A good start on this will have been made in most cities by the health and welfare council or the council of social agencies. This list of voluntary organizations can be expanded to include veterans groups, unions, church groups, and other organizations. This inventory can show officers, approximate number of members, major interests, and name and phone number of the principal officer or paid executive.

With this information in hand, it is possible to identify probable groups in opposition to, or in support of, specific programs. The influence of support groups can be mobilized through news releases, speaking engagements, and other informational methods.

It is well to point out the dangers in overt community action—as necessary as it often is. Organizing support groups means that groups in opposition will express their position in no uncertain terms. Many of the issues that involve support and opposition groups are highly controversial, and city officials must be prepared for the crossfire that will ensue. In addition, the community leaders who have been mobilized for support must be prepared to take a certain amount of punishment. Some examples will help make this more specific.

The local dental society may propose fluoridation of the water supply. It can be predicted with certainty that a group will form (if one is not already in existence) to denounce the proposal as socialistic, communistic, and an infringement on personal hygiene.

A local civil rights group will initiate action for an open occupancy ordinance. Immediately the battle lines will be drawn. In opposition will be the local real estate board, neighborhood property owners' associations, and perhaps a few mothers' clubs. On the other side is likely to be the local ministerial association and various civil rights groups.

When an urban renewal project is being proposed for a residential area contiguous to the central business district, the downtown merchants and the local real estate board think the idea is fine. The people residing in the area are convinced that the whole plan is nothing more or less than "Negro removal." Again the battle lines are drawn.

THE POLITICAL ROLE OF MUNICIPAL PUBLIC RELATIONS

At this point the question can well be raised as to how public relations is related to local public controversy. The city's public relations role is both ethical and operational.

It has ethical obligations to work with all of these groups—both for and against—openly and with full disclosure of the facts.

It has an operational role in preparing information and disseminating it through appropriate news media. The city is obligated to furnish full information, promptly and objectively. The way information is handled may have a decisive effect on development and resolution of the controversy.

The objective is to hammer out the differences, reach some degree of consensus, and undertake the program to the extent possible. The city government has the role of mediator, using public relations as an essential part of this mediation process. It is here that public relations can play its most constructive and beneficial role in welding community elements together, in informing the uninformed, and in helping to iron out the sharpest points of difference.

When viewed this way public relations goes considerably beyond newsletters, reports, radio and television programs, and other informational media. It means working with people in both informal and institutionalized settings to develop a better sense of community.

The fields of social group work and community organization have been concerned with developing a greater sense of community identity. This concern has been given national attention through the Economic Opportunity Act of 1964 which provides for "maximum feasible participation" by the poor in developing Community Action Programs that directly affect their own interests. Perhaps the most important consequence of this law will be the official recognition accorded to the importance of developing community groups and associations in areas that lack a voice in community affairs.

Urban Government and News Media

Democratic government essentially is government by consent, but this consent is not easily obtained unless information reaches the people and government officials are informed on public opinions and attitudes. The news media, especially the press, consider informing the public one of their most important roles. Since governmental actions often make news, it is prudent for the governmental administrator to understand what news means and the nature of the media.

NATURE OF NEWS

News generally is defined as the reporting of an event by words, sound, or pictures with timely information of general public interest gathered by trained reporters. Many newsmen would expand this definition, however, to include coverage of the major developments (as well as events) that affect communities and individual lives. Complete, meaningful coverage of antipoverty programs, urban renewal, compensatory education, land use policies, and other manifestations of urbanism are not possible by limiting coverage to specific events. For example, the newspaper that reports only the race riot is reporting only an event. The newspaper that has reported the underlying community conditions leading to the riot, before the riot occurred, is practicing broader and more contemporary journalism.

Irrespective of kinds of coverage, "Timeliness, accuracy, and reader interest are the essential qualities of news."[11] In this definiton are grounds for considerable conflict between reporters and city administrators. Although newsmen and city officials respect each other's jobs and responsiblities, they do have different roles.

City officials, especially department heads

---

[11] Robert F. Wilcox, "Roles of Reporters and Mass Media," in Anderson, *op. cit.*, p. 142.

and the chief administrator, are concerned with the delivery of service programs within legal and financial constraints in the most effective manner possible. The press considers itself as the guardian of the public interest and as the public representative to provide continuing surveillance of city affairs.

Even with mutual understanding of these differing roles, the chief administrator must resign himself to a certain amount of disagreement. The newspaper reporter considers it part of his professional obligation to stimulate, question, criticize, and even attack. For this reason complete harmony with the press is an impossible goal.

Major points of irritation and conflict that can develop in handling news include withholding information, delay in releasing information, favoring one newspaper over another in release of information, favoring newspapers over local radio and television stations in release of news, refusing to grant interviews to reporters except by appointment, and attempting to prevent reporters from talking to anyone except specifically designated city officials and employees.

Of all of the possible points of conflict, the most explosive is that dealing with what is loosely called "the public's right to know." Government secrecy is resented, especially closed meetings of the city council, council committees, the school board, the zoning board of adjustment, and other governmental bodies.

The press will always claim in abstract terms that it needs to know everything. In practice, however, the press will generally agree that certain kinds of news either should not be published or should be delayed in publication. Frank discussion of the problem between news managers or publishers and governmental officials can generally produce agreement on the nature of such limitations. For example, restricted status will generally be accorded such matters as hiring a city employee; dismissal, demotion, ·promotion, or other actions affecting a city employee; matters which, if discussed in public, could affect a person's reputation; matters which, if discussed in public, could benefit a private party (such as city land acquisition) ; and welfare matters where federal grant requirements prohibit publicity.[12]

Press relations for the chief administrator can be best summarized by setting forth a few guidelines:

Make sure that information given to reporters is accurate and complete.

Practice a genuine open door policy for reporters. Be available for interviews that will help them meet their deadlines.

Encourage reporters to talk to the mayor, city councilmen, department heads, and city employees. Never attempt to block their access to any city official or employee.

Learn to live with the skepticism that is built into the reporters' professional background. Always handle news breaks among competing media as impartially and objectively as possible.

Take time to orient reporters to city hall operations.

Don't hesitate to tell a reporter if a newspaper story is inaccurate or unfair.

Encourage the city council and council committees to hold closed meetings only where the nature of business really requires it.

Work with the newspaper editor to set forth ground rules for restricted news coverage, especially those matters that must be considered in closed sessions of the city council or council committees.

NATURE OF THE MEDIA

Local newspapers are by far the most important news medium with which public officials will deal. Occasionally, especially in larger cities, radio and television coverage will be provided. Because of the differences in degree of coverage, however, primary attention will be given to newspapers in the paragraphs that follow.[13]

---

[12] For a dispassionate review of the legal ground rules, see Peter MacDougall, "Open Meeting Statutes; The Press Fights for the Right To Know," PUBLIC MANAGEMENT, February, 1963, pp. 33–37.

[13] The importance of newspapers, in the judgment of city managers serving cities over 100,000 population, is shown in the PUBLIC MANAGEMENT article (March, 1968, pp. 57–61) by Robert Paul Boynton and Deil S. Wright, "Is Anybody Up There Listening?" Their survey clearly showed that newspapers are much more

Newspapers. To work well with reporters, it is essential to have some understanding of the internal organization of a newspaper. On small papers two or three reporters may provide all news coverage. On larger papers some degree of specialization is possible with reporters for police news, city hall news, sports page, society news, and the financial page. Still larger papers can specialize further with reporters for such topics as women's fashions, automobile design and marketing trends, travel and resort news, and book reviews.

Most city and county government officials will deal with a general assignment or city hall reporter. This reporter is responsible to the city editor who supervises all local news coverage. On larger papers the city editor, in turn, reports to the managing editor or editor-in-chief, who is responsible for all elements of the newspaper on a day-to-day basis. The managing editor or editor-in-chief reports to the publisher who is the newspaper's chief executive. The publisher generally is responsible for both sides of the enterprise—that is, the news and editorial side and the advertising and business side.

All daily newspapers, large and small, have reporters who are assigned to cover local government news on a routine basis. On small papers the local government assignment usually goes to a young reporter who also handles general assignments. The advantage of a regular assignment for the local government beat is that the reporter gets to know the chief administrator, department heads, and other persons well, and this usually works to the advantage of all concerned. The reporter becomes knowledgeable on the ins and outs of city government problems and issues, and city administrators gain an appreciation of the nature of news with respect to deadlines, news coverage, and production problems.

Figure 15–2 illustrates the major steps in a news story. The news is gathered by the reporter and typed out by the reporter himself or phoned in from a press room in a government building. The story goes to the copy desk where the process of editing, cutting, and sometimes rewriting takes place. The story then is set in type, the paper is printed and distributed, and the story is available for the interested citizen who wants to read it— all of this in a matter of a few hours.

It is not possible here to provide a detailed explanation of all aspects of newspaper work —that would be another book in itself. It may help, however, to summarize the characteristics of newspapers that have the greatest bearing on the work of local government administrators:

1. The pressure of time is built into almost all aspects of news coverage and reporting. Recognition of the reporter's problem of daily deadlines will provide better understanding for both parties.

2. Any conscientious reporter strives for accuracy in gathering and reporting the news —not only spelling names correctly but also providing the correct analysis and interpretation. Recognize, however, that there are constraints in the form of time and work load. Ignore the minor inaccuracies; bring the major errors to the attention of the reporter, not the city editor.

3. Respect the reporter's judgment on news value. He knows what will be of general interest to most readers. Newspapers must compete with radio, television, movies, sports events, and many other leisure-time activities for people's time.

4. Be patient with the tendency toward sensationalism in some news stories. Since the story that is unread is of little value to anybody, the reporter must use his judgment on how to make the story interesting.

5. Controversy makes news. The mayor, chief administrator, and department heads should resign themselves to this fact.

6. Many cities today are served by only one local newspaper. It is practical wisdom to recognize this in dealing with the publisher or editor. This does not mean subservience or servility; it does mean making every effort to establish good working relationships.

Every newspaper today is locked in by cost elements over which the publisher has little

---

influential on municipal issues and policies than radio and television. The authors suggest that ". . . the press is an integral, operative part of the community decisional process."

control except by cutting standards, services, or news coverage. Wage scales have risen sharply in recent years, not only for typesetters and pressmen but also for advertising salesmen, reporters, editors, and other employees. Other cost elements, especially newsprint, have increased sharply. For many papers circulation and advertising have not increased proportionately. For these and other reasons it is not always possible for the local paper to provide the depth of coverage that the chief administrator thinks is necessary for adequate reporting of city hall news.

Radio and Television. News for radio and television presentation must be gathered in a different manner and reported in a different framework from newspaper coverage. Radio news coverage is very brief. A typical 15-minute newscast may include 3 minutes of commercials and station breaks, or 20 percent of the time; weather and sports for 4 minutes, or 27 percent of the time; national and international news for 5 minutes, or 33 percent; and local news for 3 minutes, or 20 percent. Of the 3 minutes for local news, perhaps 70 or 80 seconds will be available for reporting on developments at city hall. Radio therefore limits itself to fast-breaking and very recent stories. Analysis and interpretation are rare.

Television, because it relies on pictorial presentation, has greater flexibility and variety than radio. It is ideal for showing the front elevation of a proposed city hall; it also is ideal for showing minority group riots. Like

FIGURE 15-2. *The flow of news (Source: see caption for Figure 15-1.)*

radio, television can allow very little time for local government news, usually only one minute or less in a typical 15-minute newscast.

Although radio and television have severe limitations in presenting information in depth, they have advantages over newspapers in other areas. Both can make excellent use of tape-recorded interviews conducted on the spot when the news occurs. Both can provide more human interest in certain circumstances. One hears the person talking on radio and one sees and hears him on television. The mayor himself can appear on television to describe city government proposals that are under consideration by the city council.

Both radio and television lend themselves to panel and interview shows. Although the audience tends to be small for these programs, information can be conveyed forcefully to opinion-makers in the community.

Magazines. Large cities like New York, Philadelphia, Chicago, Detroit, San Francisco, Phoenix, Miami, and Atlanta, are getting increasing coverage in such national magazines as *Harpers, Life, Look,* and *Fortune.* For magazines like *Life* and *Look,* it is a reflection of a long-term upgrading of editorial content. For magazines like *Harpers,* it reflects an increasing public interest in urban affairs in an increasingly urbanized society. Sometimes the coverage is limited to one subject—architecture in Chicago, urban renewal in New Haven, race relations in Detroit, antipoverty programs in New York. Sometimes a city is profiled with respect to its governmental, social, religious, economic, or cultural institutions.

Such national magazine coverage is not available for most cities, but excellent local coverage may be available through feature stories in the Sunday magazine section of a local or metropolitan newspaper. Magazine-type coverage can be provided by feature stories on local historical observances, dedication of buildings, and other events. Such stories provide human interest by interviews, direct quotes, and liberal use of photos.

Aiding News Agencies

It takes the efforts of both reporters and local officials to provide good local government news coverage. The reporter cannot do it alone; he has neither the time nor the resources.

The chief administrator, department head, or other public official can help the reporter in several ways. A copy of the agenda should be made available to the reporter in advance of the city council meeting. If a particularly controversial or dramatic question may come up unannounced at a meeting, a tip to newsmen is a great help.

Reporters should be given advance information on the annual budget, the comprehensive plan, and reports of special study groups, consultants, and citizens committees. For the annual budget and other reports that must not be made public before being presented to council, the reporter must be told that he is being given the material only for background so that he can prepare a better story for the day the report is submitted to the council. The reporter also needs the release date and time so he can schedule his work to meet the deadline for his paper.

Advance information of this kind gives the reporter time to study the document and do a

---

Special characteristics
of the news media

Radio	Brief treatment
	Spot news
	Frequent newscasts
	Speed—speed—speed
Television	Dramatic, flexible treatment
	Live interviews
	Human interest
	Selective coverage
Newspapers	Comprehensive coverage
	Treatment in depth
	Large news-gathering staff
	Special interest in public affairs

Figure 15-3. *Special characteristics of the news media (Source: see caption for Figure 15-1.)*

better job of analyzing and interpreting the information. It cuts down the number of factual errors and lessens the area of potential controversy in matters of interpretation and analysis.

Reporters also prefer to have one person identified as spokesman for the city council, planning board, or other official groups. Normally this should be the mayor or chairman of the council or other group involved.

It is particularly helpful if public officials get well acquainted with reporters assigned to the city hall beat and take the time to coach these men and women in the intricacies of local government operations. Help of this kind is always appreciated.

Finally, officials should make it a point to direct reporters to proper sources of information when they want to follow-up for more detailed information.

In summation, the major ways to help the newsman are:

1. Get to know the reporter.
2. Brief him in advance.
3. Provide him with documents pertinent to the story.
4. Direct him to the proper sources.

CITY HALL PRESS RELATIONS

"Press relations" refers to the methods used to bring reporters and government officials together in gathering and disseminating news. Good press relations provides a common framework for the reporter and the public official and facilitates the transfer of information.

The Press Relations Job. For an important story, the press relations job involves most if not all of the following:

Notifying newsmen of the impending story and when it will break; arranging an interview or press conference if the news stems from an individual; arranging for records to be available, if these are pertinent; developing background materials, such as statistical data or lists of names; furnishing or arranging for pictures and answering questions in person or on the phone.[14]

The chief administrator in the smaller city and, increasingly, the public information officer in the medium-sized and large city are usually responsible for press relations. The public information officer serves as a middleman in the transfer of news. His principal duties are:

First, to advise the official or agency on press relations policies; second, to represent the official or agency in the dissemination of news; and third, to serve the press and public by giving the fastest and fullest possible news coverage.[15]

The public information officer almost always is a former newsman. His experience helps him spot news taking place in the city and provide fast and competent help for reporters. He will do his best work if the local government has a clear-cut public information policy that allocates responsibilities. Such a policy, desirably, should:

1. Make the city clerk, or similar official of a county or other local government, responsible for helping newsmen obtain routine information from records under his control.

2. Define as specifically as possible the latitude that subordinate employees have in releasing information. They should know those kinds of inquiries to handle directly and those kinds to refer to higher authority.

3. Help all employees, through in-service training and other means, develop an awareness of the importance of good press relations.

4. Encourage department heads and other administrators to maintain an open door policy toward the press. Insist on full and frank disclosure of information whenever possible. Insist that administrators be available to reporters, regardless of appointments and schedules, so that reporters can meet deadlines.

5. Require a few informal training sessions for department heads and other key officials to explain the public information policies of the city and to describe newspaper practices with respect to quotations, manipulation of news, deadlines, use of photographs and news releases, and the advantages and limitations of the press conference.[16]

---

14 Wilcox, *op. cit.*, p. 161.

15 *Ibid.*

16 These points are based largely on James C. MacDonald, PRESS RELATIONS FOR LOCAL OFFICIALS (Ann Arbor: Institute of Public Administration, University of Michigan, 1956), p. 12.

Two of the most important tools in press relations are the news release and the press conference. Both are widely used and often misunderstood.

News Release. If handled properly, the news release is a useful way of providing clear and concise information for reporters to use not only for the basic story but also for background and for leads to further information. Releases are perhaps most useful in providing advance announcement of a public ceremony, the text or abstract of a speech, a fact sheet about a change in collection methods for the city income tax, a biography of a person appointed to the planning commission or other public body, or summarized information on a detailed report that has been prepared by a committee or consultant. Sometimes the news story can be written entirely from the release. More often the reporter will prefer to follow-up for further information. For this reason the release always should carry the name, address, and phone number of the source to be contacted if further information is desired. Photos to accompany the release are sometimes helpful.

Press Conference. Properly planned and conducted, the press conference is a time saver for the busy city official. He sees all the reporters at one time and avoids the charge of favoritism if all media are invited to be present. He is better prepared for the questions that will follow because he has planned the press conference in advance and tried to anticipate the questions that will be asked. A few ground rules for press conferences will help both city officials and newsmen:

1. Press conferences should be used sparingly to make it worth the extra time needed for newsmen to attend. The press conference should not be a substitute for the news release or a phone call.

2. Arrangements should be made with careful attention to tape recorders, lighting, electrical connections for radio and television equipment, sufficient seating, and other details.

3. A statement should be prepared and distributed to all attending.

4. Off-the-record statements should be used sparingly; it is much better to avoid them entirely.

5. The news source, often the mayor or chief administrator, should be brief and concise, particularly in reading a prepared statement.

6. Have the appropriate department head, administrative assistant, or other person there to backstop on information. No one expects a person being interviewed to carry all of the answers in his head.

7. Anticipate the interests of the newsmen and the questions that will be asked.

8. Do not ask for written questions to be submitted in advance.

9. Be courteous and informative in answering all questions, even those that are patently offensive.

10. Recognize all questions, provided they are asked by legitimate newsmen.

Municipal Reporting

Every governmental jurisdiction needs to report to the public, both periodically and on special occasions, to account for its activities, and to enlist support for current and future programs. Such reporting usually takes the form of printed materials such as annual reports, tax leaflets, city hall newsletters, and budget summaries. These printed materials range anywhere from dingy, stencil-duplicated newsletters to multicolor reports that have been designed, written, and produced by professionals in the communications field.

Equally important, but not nearly so extensively used, are other forms of reporting, including charts, line drawings, and photographs for permanent and portable exhibits, posters and flip charts to augment talks before clubs and civic organizations, and slide films and motion pictures.

Of these kinds of reporting, perhaps the most important, certainly the most widely used, is the annual municipal report.

THE ANNUAL REPORT

The annual municipal report historically has been a public accounting of the stewardship of municipal officials. For legal and historic reasons this purpose is important. In recent years, however, the annual report has been recognized also as a useful way of increasing the reader's knowledge about his city government in terms of issues and programs as well as revenues and expenditures.

Hundreds of cities issue general annual reports, and, unfortunately, most of them are misdirected or, rather, undirected. In many communities it is next to impossible to prepare an annual report that will be of interest to a majority of the citizens. Recognizing this limitation is practical wisdom in developing a well-rounded program for municipal reporting. The city or county does need an annual report, preferably two or three with differing levels of detail and different kinds of information to reach different segments of the community. The format is not as important as good writing, suitable appearance, and a clear conception of the intended audience.

A city could prepare at least three annual reports.

General Annual Report. This should be a brief report emphasizing a theme or message. "Working with Citizens," "Urban Renewal," and "Transportation in 1970" are examples. It should be a unified story for one year with a brief statement of purpose (a letter of transmittal is seldom read) ; a unified review of selected activities in relation to specific goals of the city government; and, at the back, essential legal and identifying information, including names of city officials and financial data.

The statement of purpose should be as clear and unified as possible. It then serves as a standard against which every element of the report is measured.

Disciplined measurement will help to remove the extraneous and to focus the report. It will help prevent drifting into areas away from the declared purpose.[17]

In addition to unity and clarity the report should be candid in reviewing what happened,

why it happened, what went wrong, and the extent to which objectives have been met.

Few cities report in this way, but foundations, corporations, churches, and colleges and universities increasingly do. They have learned that candor gains respect.

The annual report should be relatively brief, irrespective of size of city, and should be widely distributed, perhaps by mailing with utility bills. The text should be conversational in tone, but not condescending or childish. The photographic situations should be well selected and shot by a qualified commercial photographer, not by an obliging city employee. Careful attention should be given to design and production for an attractive and readable booklet, although not necessarily an expensive document.

The Economic Report. The second might be termed the "economic report." It need not be the same as the annual report of the department of finance, but would be intended to supplement that report. The economic report should give considerable attention to local government revenue, expenditure, and debt, but it also should cover the financial situation for the county, the school district, and other overlapping governments; the local employment situation; industrial development and other factors affecting the economic base; and the financial status of the central business district. This report should be intended for members of the taxpayer's association and the chamber of commerce, real estate agents, bankers, and others with a general interest in the financial community.

Cities and counties with well-qualified finance directors can prepare these reports themselves; otherwise it may be possible to draw on the services of the economics and business departments of local colleges and universities.

The Social Report. The third might be known informally as the "social report," but its official name probably would be something like *Annual Report of the People of the City of* ————. It would describe the "people programs" of the community, such as education (even though schools usually are not a part of the city government), recreation, housing and

---

17 Ned. L. Wall, MUNICIPAL REPORTING TO THE PUBLIC (Chicago: International City Managers' Association, 1963) , p. 10.

urban renewal as they affect the relocation of families, the community action program and other antipoverty efforts, the community relations work of the police department, and the efforts of churches and the many privately funded welfare agencies.

It would be directed to ministers and church groups, community workers, welfare agency executives, county and school district officials, law enforcement officials, and others who have a direct concern in these areas. This kind of a report would need outside help from welfare agency executives and others in writing, editing, and final preparation.

This three-way effort recognizes that *the general annual municipal report is a thing of the past*, that it cannot carry the entire burden of an accounting to the people, and that it needs help from supplemental reports prepared for specific elements of the community. This three-way division for handling reporting is suggestive only. Any imaginative administrator can draw up a reporting framework geared to the socioeconomic structure of his community.

SPECIAL REPORTS

The term "special reports" covers a wide range of leaflets, folders, brochures, and newsletters that are either (1) aimed at a specific, limited audience, or (2) are limited to a specific subject. An example of the former is a folder describing traffic safety rules for children walking to school—obviously directed at families with children of school age. An example of the latter is a folder that welcomes citizens to city council meetings, provides a seating chart, and explains the rules on council procedures.

Special reports have been issued on every conceivable subject affecting cities and counties. They are especially useful in providing advance notice on such things as a change in the refuse collection schedule; an increase in the sewer charge; a change in the schedule for utility billings; an announcement of summer recreation programs, complete with schedules and locations; or an explanation of a bond issue that is up for referendum.

One type of special report, the city hall newsletter, is used by many cities and coun-

ties and worth separate attention. Newsletters come in various shapes and sizes. They tend to concentrate on immediate, personal problems, are generally reproduced by stencil duplicating or other inexpensive method, and are issued rather frequently—weekly, monthly, or quarterly. They can be used to cover almost any subject of concern to the city government and are particularly good for explaining and documenting budgetary or financial matters, regulatory programs, and public works projects. Newsletters can also be used to chart such information as current trends in building permits issued, crimes reported to the police, library books issued, and attendance at city and county playgrounds.

Distribution varies widely, ranging from those inserted with utility bills thereby reaching many citizens to those sent to a selected mailing list.

An often overlooked function of the newsletter is to provide a means of discussing matters of a broad local interest ". . . which might resemble propaganda if issued as a single white paper but which, if published routinely as part of a continuing program of municipal public information, is generally more acceptable to the reading public."[18]

Subjects that might be discussed include proposals for new tax measures, housing codes, an open occupancy ordinance, capital improvement programs, proposed bond issues, and other controversial matters. Obviously such information must be in accordance with the thinking of the city council, both expressed and implicit.

City hall newsletters are intended to supplement other forms of reporting. They are not intended to compete with the local press or with radio and television coverage. They are especially useful in those suburban communities where local newspaper coverage is inadequate or totally lacking.

SPECIAL EVENTS

This is another major form of municipal reporting and includes centennials and other

---

[18] Robert M. Christofferson, "Municipal Reports and Events," in Anderson, *op. cit.,* p. 182.

civic celebrations, open houses, city tours, and other planned programs that attempt to bring city government closer to the people. Probably the most popular special events are the open house at the city hall, public library, or other facility; the "city government day" where high school students are elected to the city council; and town meetings to explain city programs and answer questions, on a city-wide basis in smaller communities, on a neighborhood basis in larger communities.

PERSONAL REPORTING

Reporting orally and in person has many advantages over printed reports, film strips, and other forms because it helps reduce the abstraction of the city. The citizen can see the mayor, city councilman, chief administrator, director of public works, planning director, or recreation supervisor. It provides a personal touch by showing the key people who make up the city government organization.

Oral reporting enables the speaker to adapt his presentation to the needs and desires of the specific audience involved, be it the League of Women Voters, the garden club, the chamber of commerce, the ministerial association, or a group of teenagers. Finally, reporting in person provides an immediate and personal opportunity for feedback. A speech or informal talk can be followed by questions and answers to clarify points and to bring real differences out into the open. This kind of give and take is extremely effective with certain audiences.

Direct confrontation often is the principal benefit accruing from speeches, presentations, and forums. It provides a safety valve for persons who are not sufficiently verbal to write letters and who do not have enough self-confidence to go to the city hall and pound on the chief administrator's desk. Oral re-

FIGURE 15-4. *Visual aids are almost indispensable for certain kinds of explanations* (*Source: see caption for Figure 15-1.*)

porting will become increasingly important in the years ahead as city government expands in areas of urban renewal, antipoverty efforts, police-community relations, and other "people" programs.

REACHING THE HARD-TO-REACH

A common mistake on the part of city officials is to assume that newspaper coverage, because it is extensive, informative, and sometimes influential, will reach all segments of the community. This is a dangerous assumption for the lower social and economic classes. These groups, which usually include the restless racial minorities, rely much more on radio and television. This is an understandable consequence of low educational and literacy levels.[19]

Radio and television are better than newspapers for reaching certain groups; even better are personal efforts by city councilmen, the chief administrator, and other city officials to make sure that they are in touch with all major segments of the community. It is not enough, for example, to talk only before service clubs, PTA's, the local chamber of commerce, and other groups that tend to be upper-middle income in nature. Officials must also seek out organized minority groups, labor unions, boys' clubs, settlement houses, and specialized professional and occupational groups. Chief administrators and other city officials should get to know their communities as well as possible—to know about their socioeconomic intangibles as well as their physical assets, to learn about their socially and culturally disadvantaged groups. Few if any requests for speakers will come to city hall from the "other" side of town. City officials must seek out representatives of these groups so that they can be better known and communication can be maintained.

The importance of this kind of communication has been illustrated dramatically in recent summers by the minority group riots in many cities in the United States. Officials in some cities have made little effort to reach the minority groups. In other cities, however, extensive efforts have been made to keep in

touch with minority group representatives, but these efforts failed because minority group representatives themselves were out of touch with their people.

This kind of advice is easy to set down on paper but difficult to implement. City officials do not have the time to spend all of their working hours getting acquainted with the community. But they *must* learn about the community first-hand; often this can be done quite effectively over a period of time in afterhours time. In addition, it is wise to inculcate in department heads, supervisors, and other city employees the concern of the chief administrator and department heads that city government be kept close to the people through impartial provision of municipal services and continuing effort to keep in touch with disparate elements in the community.[20]

Organization for Public Relations

From the preceding portions of this chapter it is evident that public relations pervades the activities of all city departments and agencies and of almost all employees. Despite its importance it does not require a large professional staff, a large budget, or a complicated organizational structure. What public relations does require is clear management objectives and a definition of functions.

CLARIFYING MANAGEMENT OBJECTIVES

Throughout this book emphasis has been placed on the importance of formulating community objectives and developing city government programs to further those objectives. These objectives are as helpful for public relations as they are for any other aspect of urban government and administration. With objectives clearly understood, the public relations officer and the chief administrator can do a far better job of working with all department heads and other administrators in a continuing, consistent public relations program. They then will be better able to de-

[19] Boynton and Wright, *op. cit.*

[20] See the section on "Programming for Human Needs" in Chapter 3 of this book for a description of some of the imaginative approaches being used in some cities to reach the hard-to-reach.

velop and maintain a high-level concern for the larger role of city government in urban society, to understand that publicity and information, though indispensable, are not the only elements in their public relations program, and to gain a better appreciation of communications in a broad sense.

The 1967 *Municipal Year Book* reported finding four primary public relations objectives in questionnaire returns from approximately 800 city officials in cities over 10,000 population:

1. To serve the public via information, responding to requests, and disposing of complaints.

2. To publicize city activities and programs.

3. To create good will for the city and the community.

4. To persuade the public to support city programs.[21]

Information, publicity, good will, and persuasion are the traditional concerns of public relations. They are not a well-rounded program because they fall short of the integrative role of public relations in determining and influencing attitudes, facilitating informal as well as formal communication, mobilizing publics, reaching community groups and associations, and evaluating information.

DEFINITION OF FUNCTIONS AND GOALS

A clear definition of the public relation function is needed to provide an orderly framework for the public relation officer and others.

The 1967 *Municipal Year Book* showed that press relations was the number one portion of city public relations efforts. The principal public relations activities, listed in rank order, as reported by approximately 800 city officials in cities over 10,000 included:

1. Press relations (press releases, press conferences, TV and radio broadcasts).

2. Publications (annual reports, newsletters, internal publications).

3. Services (complaint bureau, speakers' bureau, open houses, tours, displays, audiovisual aids).

4. Public relations training for city employees (formal instruction in dealing with the public, informal meetings between administrators and employees to discuss public relations techniques).

5. Formal cooperative programs with schools and governing boards.[22]

Ideally the public relations program should encompass all of the major subjects discussed earlier in this chapter, but the emphasis from one city to another quite properly will vary. Resort cities are likely to give primary attention to publicity and promotion of tourism. Some cities will put major effort into promotion of industrial development. Cities with volatile minority groups will almost be forced to give primary attention to attitudes and opinions of groups and subgroups. The community of higher income and educational levels is likely to give extra effort to informative printed reports. Most cities will devote a substantial amount of effort to fostering good working relationships with newsmen.

CENTRALIZATION VS. DECENTRALIZATION

An earlier review of public relations organization indicated five approaches to organization: (1) the "one-man show" with the program as the responsibility of one man, usually the chief administrator; (2) the "do-it-yourself" approach, which is an extension of the one-man show because the chief administrator has the assistance of a particularly well-qualified assistant to help him; (3) decentralization to departments; (4) use of the public relations consultant; and (5) the full-time staff professional.[23] In essence, these five approaches boil down to the question of centralization or decentralization.

The 1967 *Municipal Year Book* survey showed that 38 percent of the reporting cities centralized public relations activties, 48 percent decentralized, and 14 percent had a combination of the two. In addition to actual practice, the survey asked city officials to report the "right" or "ideal" organization for public relations. In ideal terms, centralized organization jumped from 38 to 58 percent; decentral-

---

[21] Marion C. Tureck, "Municipal Public Relations in 1966," in THE MUNICIPAL YEAR BOOK, 1967 (Chicago: International City Managers' Association, 1967), p. 242.

[22] *Ibid.*, p. 251.

[23] Robert M. Christofferson, "Organizing for Public Relations," in Anderson, *op. cit.*, pp. 217–18.

ized fell from 48 to 24 percent; and combination increased from 14 to 18 percent.[24]

The question of centralization or decentralization cannot be answered categorically. It depends on city government objectives, the scope of the public relations program, budget, staff, and other factors. More important than organizational structure is centralized responsibility for public relations with the chief administrator. He not only must be convinced of the importance of public relations, but must help the city council develop public relations policy and must inculcate department heads with the importance of the public relations program. The chief administrator should instigate public relations training for employees, be in the forefront in the development of good press relations, and constantly seek to improve the public's image of the city or county government.

The Public Relations Officer and the Future

"It is claimed that the corporate public relations manager of the future must be a trained behavioral scientist."[25] This assertion indicates that the public relations task of the future, in government service as in private industry, may require a man with background not only in journalism but also in sociology, statistics, organization theory, and other applications of the behavioral sciences.

As the 1967 *Municipal Year Book* survey shows, the full-time public relations officer is likely to have come from a background of journalism and to be operating a program that is narrowly defined. The inexorable processes of social change, described in the first two chapters of this book, will force changes in the entire concept of municipal public relations.

In the future the public relations function will probably be more clearly defined and made specifically responsible to the chief administrator—perhaps through a municipal division on operational effectiveness.

Merging existing administrative analysis and public relations sections, the new staff unit would be manned by assistants trained in the social and behavioral disciplines, including organizational theorists, administrative analysts, and those having social survey, statistical, and journalistic skills. Concerned primarily with applied organizational and behavioral research, including community analysis to ascertain attitudes and reactions, the resources of the new unit would enhance the totality of management decisions and actions. In addition to the publicity function, which would be retained by the new unit, the services available through this research approach obviously have public relations significance, although by no means limited thereto.

For planning and evaluation purposes, an operations analyst would probe opinions, attitudes, and reactions of those concerned with organizational goals, policies, and procedures. The proposed operational effectiveness division would identify current public issues and problems, derive data, and analyze and propose alternative policy and procedural recommendations regarding the environment under which governmental units operate, the degree and extent of program achievement, and the effectiveness of existing organizational arrangements.[26]

This proposal may be extreme when compared with current practice, but it certainly cannot be considered extreme in light of anticipated future changes. With this concept of organization, the public relations officer will need to be a communications generalist. If he comes from outside the field of public administration, as is likely to be the case, he will have to familiarize himself with local government and acquire essential background in public administration and urban affairs. He will need to be broad-gauged in background, wide ranging in interests, and well educated. He will be one of the best trained, most versatile, and important persons on the administrative team.

This is not utopian. Cities and counties are carrying on far more public relations activities than they did a decade ago, and the standards of all professions, public relations included, are rising. In an era increasingly conditioned by communications, it is only a question of time, and not a great deal of time at that, until local governments adapt their definition of public relations to a broader concept.

---

[24] Tureck, *op. cit.*, pp. 243–44, 255–56.
[25] Kenneth Henry, "Perspective on Public Relations," HARVARD BUSINESS REVIEW, July–August, 1967, p. 14.

---

[26] Anderson, *op. cit.*, pp. 35–36.

16

Legal Services and Regulatory Procedures

Pʀᴇᴠɪᴏᴜs ᴄʜᴀᴘᴛᴇʀs ᴏf ᴛʜɪs ʙᴏᴏᴋ have analyzed the role of the chief administrator in organizing and directing the personnel and resources of a city to accomplish its governmental goals in the most efficient manner. In large degree the principles and concepts already covered are applicable to the management of any corporate organization of considerable size and breadth of activity, public or private. In managing a municipality, however, the chief administrator must keep constantly in mind two additional principles: first, a municipal corporation is an entity of limited legal authority whose activities are closely circumscribed by state statutes and common law principles; and, second, in carrying out its responsibilities a municipality exercises the sovereign power of the state to control the conduct of its citizens. The municipal administrator, and indeed all elected and appointed municipal officials, must therefore be as familiar as possible with the extent and limitations of their corporate powers and with the extent to which regulatory activity can be pursued.

Equally important as general familiarity with the law is the judicious use of the advice and counsel of the city attorney and his staff in resolving legal and administrative questions. Just as no good corporate executive will bind his company to a course of action without legal advice, no competent municipal administrator will embark on a new regulatory or service program without first reviewing it with the city attorney.

The purpose of this chapter is to analyze the role of the typical municipal attorney as it relates to the administration of city affairs. Particular emphasis will be placed on the myriad of services, both formal and informal, the attorney can perform for the council and the administration to ensure that governmental decisions will be both in the public interest and within the legal authority of the municipal corporation.

General Considerations

Tʜᴇ Lᴇɢᴀʟ Fʀᴀᴍᴇᴡᴏʀᴋ ᴏf
Mᴜɴɪᴄɪᴘᴀʟ Gᴏᴠᴇʀɴᴍᴇɴᴛ

The constitution and statutes of the individual states provide the basis of the existence of all municipal corporations and establish the framework of rules within which they function. As a political subdivision of the state, the city is under the absolute control of the legislature. The city receives its grant of powers from the state by general or special laws, and sometimes by the adoption of a charter pursuant to constitutional or statutory provisions. As a legal entity, the city's powers and freedom of action are further limited by both state and federal constitutions.

The basic legal document outlining the city's powers is either a charter or an act of the legislature. These documents are usually quite accessible and, in varying degrees, reasonably intelligible to the nonlawyer. While no administrator should proceed on his own interpretation of the charter or statute, all should study it carefully. All too often administrative procedures or legislative steps are taken which violate the city's basic law. If a new procedure is sound and desirable, an inhibiting charter provision should be changed, not ignored, for the eventual result without change could have severe legal ramifications for the city.

In the history of American law, a restrictive principle concerning the legal authority of municipal corporations was developed early. Known as "Dillon's Rule," this principle stated, in effect, that municipal corporations had only those powers specifically granted them by statute and those necessarily implied from the granted power. (The rule was classically applied in *Trenton* v. *New Jersey*, 262 U.S. 182, 1923.) This narrow view of municipal powers still persists in some states, but most progressive courts have taken the view that municipal corporations, particularly those with "general welfare" or "all powers" grants in their fundamental statutes or charters, have a broad range of implied powers in matters of governmental concern and uphold municipal action without a specific legislative grant of authority. Dillon's Rule is, however, universally applied to quasi-municipal corporations such as school districts, counties, and townships. The view of the courts toward municipal powers is of critical importance to the city, and the chief administrator should be generally aware of his own state court's position on this matter.

VARIETY OF MUNICIPAL STRUCTURE

The student and practitioner of municipal administration should be prepared to encounter a wide variety of forms of municipal government. While there is an unquestionable trend toward centralization of administrative responsibility in city government, enough variety exists in internal structure to make the formulation of general rules about the relationship of the legal department to the chief administrator impossible. The best that can be offered are general principles that the administrator can use in working within the legal framework of his own city government.

SOME BASIC FACTS ABOUT THE MUNICIPAL ATTORNEY

Any intelligent discussion of the role of the municipal attorney in city affairs must be premised upon some of the facts outlined below.

Part-Time Attorneys. First, the vast majority of municipal attorneys are part-time officials. Recent studies in Oregon and Minnesota, for example, show that only the two or three largest cities in those states have full-time legal staffs. It is probably safe to say that only a very few cities in the country under 50,000 population have full-time legal staffs. This fact, combined with the variations in the manner of selecting attorneys discussed below, modifies to a considerable degree the relationship between the administrator and the attorney.

It must be emphasized, however, that the legal services performed by the attorney are basically the same whether he serves in a part or full-time capacity, and whether the municipality he serves is large or small.

The Attorney As a Professional. The attorney, a member of an ancient profession with a rigid ethical code, commonly views the municipal corporation, or more specifically the council, as his client. Because of this, and because he is not, generally speaking, trained as an administrator, he will often display a degree of aloofness about administrative principles applicable to other departments of the city.

On the other hand, the legal profession is characterized by precision of thought and expression and by analytical skill, qualities that can be put to good use by the skillful administrator who is able to involve the attorney in the city's administration.

The "Certainty of the Law." The proper function of the attorney is the interpretation of statutes, ordinances, administrative rules, and court decisions. A state law, clear on its face, may have been given an altogether contrary interpretation by an applicable court decision, or even held invalid while still appearing in official statutory compilations. City ordinances are laws, too, and their meaning and application may be quite different from what a quick reading reveals. Finally, even courts change their minds, and what was doctrine may have become dead letter. The attorney's job is to know the difference.

Method of Selection. As will be discussed further below, there is little uniformity about the way the city attorney is selected. If he is elected, his relationship with other departments will be governed solely by charter or statutory provisions which the administrator cannot change. Even when appointed, he is often appointed by the council and feels little direct responsibility to the administrator.

LEGAL SERVICES AS LINE OR STAFF FUNCTIONS

While labeling particular functions "line" or "staff" becomes less valid as the size of an organization increases, a brief analysis of legal services in these terms is helpful in understanding the actual and potential relations of the attorney to other administrative departments.

The officer who enforces regulatory ordinances by prosecution of violators, by licensing, or by inspectional services is performing a line function just as is the fireman in extinguishing fires, or the health nurse in examining children. Some of these enforcement activites are assigned to the attorney or law department, particularly ordinance prosecutions. Others are assigned to building inspection units; the police, fire, and health departments; and other city departments.

When the attorney assists the council or chief administrator in drafting a new ordinance, or advises them on the scope of a state statute, he is performing a managerial or staff function. Similarly, in preparing a contract for the purchasing department, the attorney is performing an auxiliary staff function.

Because of the breadth of the attorney's competence and responsibility, some functions he performs are mixed line-staff while still others defy categorization. A letter to a recalcitrant utility customer on behalf of the public works department has both line and staff aspects, while an appearance before the Supreme Court on a zoning ordinance cannot

easily be labeled as either a line or staff activity.

Legal services, then, like personnel and finance services, have important line and staff aspects which require the chief administrator to have rather close and more frequent contacts with such services than with many of the technical aspects of the work of other departments.

GENERAL OUTLINE OF CHAPTER

The remainder of the chapter will review the services provided by the attorney to the city and its administration. This will take the form of an analysis of: (1) the work of the attorney or law department, including civil and criminal litigation and advisory functions; (2) the organization of the law department; and (3) the preparation and enforcement of regulatory ordinances.

The Work of the Attorney and Its Implications for Administrators

Practically all the legal tasks performed in a municipality, with the exception of some aspects of the regulatory function to be discussed later, are usually brought together in a law department under the direction of the municipal attorney. This is a logical and desirable arrangement, since legal tasks require the supervision of a legally trained administrator, and only the very largest cities can afford attorneys who could supervise these functions in units separate from the law department. The exact duties and responsibilities of the law department will usually be set forth in the municipality's administrative code, if it has one, or in its charter or enabling act, but the general scope of these duties is much the same in almost all municipalities.

THE ATTORNEY'S FUNCTIONS: AN OVERVIEW

The scope of the services provided by the law department (and a good outline of the functions of such a department as well) can be obtained from an inspection of the following provisions relating to the law department in the Model Administrative Code prepared by the National Institute of Municipal Law Officers:

Section 1–308. Department of Law

(A) The Department of Law shall consist of the City Attorney who shall enforce all laws and act to protect the interests of the city and who shall:

(1) *Advise Council.* Advise the Council or its committees or any City officer, when thereto requested, upon all legal questions arising in the conduct of the City business.

(2) *Prepare Ordinances.* Prepare or revise ordinances when so requested by the Council or any committee thereof.

(3) *Give Opinions.* Give his opinion upon any legal matter or question submitted to him by the Council, or any of its committees, or by any City officer.

(4) *Attend Council Meetings.* Attend all Council meetings in their entirety for the purpose of giving the Council any legal advice requested by its members.

(5) *Prepare Legal Instruments.* Prepare for execution all contracts and instruments to which the City is a party and shall approve, as to form, all bonds required to be submitted to the City.

(6) *Prosecute Offenders and Defend Officials.* Prepare, when authorized by the Council, all charges and complaints against and shall appear in the appropriate Court in the prosecution of, every person charged with the violation of a City ordinance or of any regulation adopted under authority of the Charter, or with the commission of a misdemeanor as declared by the Charter or by virtue of its authority. In any prosecution for violation of any regulation adopted by any Board or Commission created under authority of the Charter, the City Attorney shall act under the directions of such Board or Commission, subject to such paramount control as is given to the Council by the Charter.

(7) *Settlement of Claims.* Have the power to adjust, settle, compromise or submit to arbitration, any action, causes of action, accounts, debts, claims, demands, disputes and matters of favor of or against the City or in which the City is concerned as debtor or creditor, now existing or which may hereafter arise, not involving or requiring payment to exceed .... and with the permission of the Administrator may do likewise in matters not involving or requiring payment to exceed ...., provided the money to settle claims generally has been appropriated and is available therefor.

(8) *Make Reports.*

(a) Immediate report of decision. Immediately report the outcome of any litigation in which the City has an interest to the Administrator and Council.

(b) Annual report of pending litigation. Make an annual report, to the Administrator and Council, as of the ...... day of ...., of all pending litigation in which the City has an interest and the condition thereof.

(9) *Control Legal Services Incidental to Council Action.* Have charge of all legal services auxiliary to Council action in connection with the appropriating of property to public use and in the levying of assessments.

(10) *Workmen's Compensation.* Prepare and approve all workmen's compensation payrolls and shall investigate all cases in which workmen's compensation is involved and be responsible for the filing of all documents and papers required by the Workmen's Compensation Act of the State.

(11) *Keep Records.*

(a) Suits. Keep a complete record of all suits in which the city had or has an interest, giving the names of the parties, the Court where brought, the nature of the action, the disposition of the case, or its condition if pending, and the briefs of counsel.

(b) *Opinions and Titles.* Keep a complete record of all written opinions furnished by him and of all certificates or abstracts of titles furnished by him to the City, or any department or official thereof.

(12) *Deliver Records to Successor.* Deliver all records, documents and property of every description in his possession, belonging to his office or to the City, to his successor in office, who shall give him duplicate receipts therefor, one of which he shall file with the City Auditor.[1]

When one adds to this statement of formal duties the informal activities of counseling department heads and elected officials, instructing officers and employees in the elements of public law, examining intergovernmental activities, and answering inquiries from the public in general, it is readily seen that the role of the attorney in city administration is indeed critical.

ADVISORY FUNCTIONS

Under statutes and charters, the attorney is the legal advisor to the municipality. As such, one of his most important functions, if not the most important, is that of serving as advisor to the council, the administrator, to

---

[1] NIMLO Model Administrative Code, NIMLO Model Ordinance Service, National Institute of Municipal Law Officers, Washington, D.C.

boards and commissions, and, indirectly, to the citizens of the municipality. In performing this function, he often is required to be present at council meetings and at the meetings of boards and commissions to render immediate assistance. Even when not required to do so by charter or statute, councils and other bodies will request the attorney's presence at meetings. This advisory function is exercised in both formal and informal ways, and, when properly utilized, permeates the entire governmental structure.

Attorneys by training and experience acquire skills that can be utilized by the administrator in a variety of ways. The lawyer's skill as a negotiator in settling claims against the city can assist in labor negotiations or interjurisdictional disputes. The lawyer's abilities in writing are useful in important correspondence and in completing critical reports and applications. The legal mind, in spite of its reputation for hair-splitting, is trained to analyze problems and to separate critical issues from irrelevant ones. Finally, experienced trial attorneys have devoted their careers to rapidly acquiring extensive knowledge about widely varied subjects. This skill gives the administrator who has a good rapport with his attorney an "instant expert" who may master not only the legal aspects of a subject, but often its technical aspects as well.

A good administrator will utilize the advisory nature of the attorney in yet another way. Experienced administrators know that they cannot always see a legal problem in a set of facts and, therefore, as a matter of routine, "touch base" with the attorney on all substantial matters. Private attorneys earn a large portion of their incomes and most of their esteem and respect from preventing legal difficulties, not correcting them after they have grown to major proportions. Municipal attorneys are no different. Too often skilled administrators feel they have mastered all aspects of a situation, including the legal ones. This can have disastrous results.

Formal Opinions. The city attorney is usually given the responsibility of submitting formal written opinions on legal problems to the city council, the chief administrator, and other city officers. A request for a written opinion asks the attorney to formulate, with all the resources at his command, a recommendation which, in his professional judgment, constitutes the soundest course of action for the city and upon which the city may act with reliance. Formal opinions should always be requested concerning proposed courses of action about which serious legal questions can be anticipated. A city will be on much firmer legal ground when challenged if it can assert that it proceeded on the advice of counsel.

Formal opinions should be requested only on matters of grave importance. Indeed, the attorney will render a formal opinion only in such cases since most matters can be handled satisfactorily by informal advice, and he is usually reluctant, and properly so, to devote the research effort involved in a formal opinion unless it is fully warranted by the circumstances.

Written opinions of the attorney do not, of course, have the force of law. A well-reasoned and researched opinion does, however, affect the body of municipal law since it will become known in the fraternity of city attorneys and will influence courts when brought to their attention. The administrator and his key department heads should maintain an indexed file of these opinions as a working reference.

Briefing Staff and Council on Legal Developments. An important advisory function of the attorney is keeping the administrator and the council fully informed on important new developments in the law. Since municipal corporations draw all of their powers from the state legislature, new laws and bills before that body should be reviewed by the attorney and their implication brought to the attention of interested officials. No session of the Congress in recent years has adjourned without enacting some far-reaching piece of urban legislation and no large city can afford to be uninformed about available federal financial assistance.

State and federal court decisions and administrative rulings often have a direct impact upon local government. The implication of a state court's clear intention to abandon a traditional concept, such as governmental immunity from tort liability for example, should be clearly and forcefully brought to the city's attention. The application of a reapportionment decision on council structure or FCC rulings on CATV are similar examples.

Individual attorneys and administrators should work out their own system of briefing officials on legal developments. Some city attorneys maintain a legislative bulletin service; others use regularly scheduled briefing sessions.

Counseling with Boards and Commissions. The attorney's relationship with independent boards and commissions is far from clear in most cities. Under some charters he is their legal advisor; in others, such entities are authorized to have their own legal staff. Whatever relation exists, the administrator should insure that a constant flow of information on the activities of boards and commissions is obtained from the attorney (to the extent that the attorney is free to do this.)

Relations with the Public. While it is not the duty of the city attorney to advise members of the general public of their legal rights or about the legality of municipal action, it must be recognized that a significant portion of his effort is expended in this field. In some cities, one of the most frequent sources of contact between the public and city government is the attorney's office. The public relations aspect of the office should not be overlooked.

A startling example of the frequency of such contacts appears in records kept by the Kansas City Law Department. In 1953, the department received more incoming calls than any other city department—1,200 incoming calls per week, or about 60,000 per year, supplemented by 40,000 outgoing calls for a total of about 100,000 annual calls.[2]

CIVIL ACTIONS

The city as a municipal corporation may sue or be sued; consequently, it is involved in court actions that run the gamut of civil lawsuits. While the city council, as the governing body of the municipal corporation, has the

authority to make the basic policy decision about bringing or defending civil actions, it will, of course, rely heavily on the attorney's advice in such matters.

The satisfactory handling of civil actions requires that adequate lines of communication exist between the city attorney's office and other city departments. When an action is brought against a city, the legal notice will usually be served on the chief administrator but whoever receives such a notice should immediately transmit it to the attorney.

Civil actions against the city include actions on contracts to which the city is a party, tort actions ("tort" is a generic term used to describe almost every kind of civil wrong other than breach of contract), miscellaneous actions arising out of statutory duties and responsibilities, and actions in defense of city officers and employees. A steadily growing field of civil litigation involves the defense of the city's land use regulations against challenges to their validity.

Tort Liability. A tort may be defined as a wrongful invasion of the legally protected rights of others, other than a breach of contract, for which the law will afford a remedy in the form of money damages. The most common type of tort action is based upon negligence, an unintentional breach of some duty or care owed by the defendant to the plaintiff.

The law of torts with respect to the acts of a private corporation or person is relatively well established, but the legal principles governing the tort liability of municipal corporations, notoriously vague and inconsistent in the past, have, since 1957, been undergoing rapid change. For fully a century before then, no rule was more firmly established than that a municipal corporation was immune from torts committed by its officers and employees when performing "governmental" functions, but was liable for torts committed in the course of performing "proprietary" functions. The classification of functions as governmental or proprietary varied from state to state (and still does where the doctrine of immunity persists) and no satisfactory rationale has ever been advanced for the distinctions developed by the courts.

---

[2] Reported in *City Attorneys and Their Salaries,* National Institute of Municipal Law Officers, Report No. 146, 1960, pp. 9–10.

While a large number of states still retain the immunity principle, the trend is clearly toward the imposition of liability in this field. The courts of several leading states, including California, Illinois, Michigan, Minnesota, Florida, and New York have abandoned the doctrine as it applies to municipal corporations, and other states are rapidly following their example. In some states the void left by these decisions is filled by a statutory scheme governing the extent of and procedure surrounding municipal liability.

Even where immunity is the rule, many states by statute permit cities to circumvent it by authorizing the purchase of public liability insurance, permitting or requiring the defense of police and fire personnel in tort cases, and permitting the indemnification of officers and employees in such actions. It must be noted that no matter what the status of immunity of the municipal employer, the officer or employee who is himself responsible for the tort is still often personally liable. The city may feel a moral obligation to indemnify officers and employees when no willful wrong was involved and authority to indemnify permits this to be done even when the city may not be legally liable.

Finally, in those states where courts still recognize municipal immunity, that immunity is being restricted rather than expanded. The doctrine is almost entirely court-made, and although courts are reluctant to overturn long-standing precedent, they do not hesitate to impose liability in situations where no precedent exists.

Because of this trend toward increasing municipal responsibility in tort, and because of the vast exposure to liability of a large municipality, the number and magnitude of tort claims against cities have risen dramatically in recent years as has the magnitude of settlements and judgments awarded to successful plaintiffs. In many city law departments the defense of these actions has become the largest single activity of the department, and the payment of claims and insurance premiums a significant portion of governmental expense.

The implications of municipal tort liability and its expansion for the chief administrator are many, but the most important are: (1) the administrator must establish a pattern of coordination and cooperation of all departments with the attorney; (2) he must systematically impress upon all employees the importance of safety as it applies to all municipal operations; (3) he must develop an efficient system of record keeping and reporting of all accidents; and (4) the chief administrator must continually review the adequacy of the municipality's insurance program, either through self-insurance funds in the largest cities or by commercial insurance in the typical city.

The successful defense of tort claims depends primarily upon two things: the diligence of the city attorney, and the availability of evidence for use in preparing and trying the case. The attorney must have the full cooperation of other department heads in terms of access to records, availability of municipal employees as witnesses, and proper funding for an adequate program of defending tort claims.

A well-conceived and carried-out safety program will have two beneficial effects in holding down tort claims. Employees who are concerned about and trained to observe their own safety will be more likely to have the same attitude about the safety of the public, for it is negligent, unsafe conduct by officers and employees that is the basis of many tort claims against cities. In addition, safety-minded personnel will tend to be more alert to unsafe conditions to which the public as well as themselves are exposed. The administrator also should impress upon his personnel that because of the broad exposure of municipalities to tort actions, careless or negligent conduct is not only unsafe, but very expensive.

An adequate record keeping and reporting system with emphasis on promptness and accuracy is vital to proper defense of tort claims. It is particularly important that early information be obtained concerning accidents that may lead to claims so that a full investigation may be made by the law department while the evidence is still fresh. Since the trial of tort claims often follows the accident or happening by months and even years, the information must be accurate and recorded in such a way that it can be properly presented in the future.

Finally, the administrator must be sure that the risks of the city in the field of public liability are adequately covered by insurance at the lowest possible premium cost. In this area the administrator, the attorney, the finance director, and the representatives of the insurance industry must work together, integrating safety programs, reporting and recording systems and interdepartmental cooperation into a balanced program to reduce the expense of tort claims against the city. It should be noted here that some cities, particularly the very large ones, self-insure by either advance funding or annual appropriations. The importance of safety and reporting is the same, however, whatever system of insurance is used.

Not all tort claims go to trial. Some are patently nuisance claims. Others involve such clear liability on the part of the city that an out-of-court settlement is advantageous. In still other cases, questionable liability combined with high potential damages dictate a settlement. The administration of claims varies from city to city, but in all cases it is the attorney whose judgment is important in deciding whether to reject the claim or settle. Safety, reporting, and cooperation play just as important a role in settlements as in litigation, for the most fully informed judgment by the attorney in this area can mean great monetary savings to the city. As an example, in Minneapolis, Minnesota, in 1962, there were 234 damage claims filed against the city in amounts totalling $1,509,808.61. The total amount paid on those claims after review and settlement was $14,709.70. In the same year, 76 claims went to trial asking $1,171,230 resulting in judgments against the city of $27,702.[3]

Workmen's Compensation. Closely related to tort claims against the city are claims by employees for compensation for injuries suffered in the course of their employment. The liability of the city in workmen's compensation cases is almost universally regulated by statute and is, generally speaking, the same as that imposed by the state on all employers. That is, it is a liability of the employer in fixed amounts quite apart from negligence or wrong-doing on his part.

The pattern of protection for the municipality in the workmen's compensation field is precisely the same as in the case of tort claims. A proper practice of personnel safety and prompt reporting of injuries will not only save lives, but reduce claims against the city resulting in considerable savings. Again, using the Minneapolis experience in 1962, there were 1,007 workmen's compensation claims filed resulting in payments of $148,156.42.[4]

Contract Liability. Generally speaking, a municipal corporation is bound to the faithful performance of its contractual obligations in the same manner as a private person or corporation. Municipal contracting power, however, is circumscribed by a number of procedural and legal limitations not found in the private sector. The doctrines of public purpose and *ultra viries* contracts, for example, determine the power of a municipality to contract at all, and limitations on expenditures and bidding procedures have a direct bearing on the validity of the contract. These limitations are many and complex, and the administrator should defer to the expertise of the attorney in their application.

What the administrator can and should do about contract liability, however, is to have all contractual obligations of the city, large and small, reviewed in some manner by the law department. It is, of course, impossible to consult the attorney on every individual agreement the city makes. But the attorney can review procedures for routine purchases, for example, and assist in standardizing all contracting procedures for the city. Major and unusual undertakings by the city should, of course, be reviewed by the attorney.

The administrator should be aware also that the primary service of the attorney in the contract field is in the nature of preventive medicine. The actual and potential contractual obligations of a city are staggering, and in many large cities municipal government is the largest single purchaser of goods and services as well as the largest employer. In good

---

[3] Report of the City Attorney's Office, 1962, Minneapolis, Minnesota, p. 3.

[4] *Ibid.,* p. 4.

business—private or public—as in good health, it is far more pleasant and less painful to detect and correct a defect in its early stages than to undergo the trauma of major surgery.

Litigation Involving Land Use Regulations. Accompanying the phenomenal urbanization of recent years has been a parallel explosion in the volume of litigation involving municipal regulation of land use through zoning ordinances, land subdivision regulations, and official street maps. In fast growing suburban cities particularly, a large portion of the effort of the city attorney's office is devoted to defending various attacks on regulations of this type. Although zoning and similar ordinances often carry the same criminal sanctions as other regulatory ordinances, they are seldom enforced by criminal prosecution, but rather violations are prevented by civil actions for injunction. Similarly, aggrieved property owners and their counsel, noting the readiness with which courts review council action in the zoning and planning field, seek redress not by amendment of the ordinance but by challenging its validity, usually on constitutional grounds. Municipalities have not been notably successful in defending such actions in recent years.

The success of the city's planning program thus hinges directly on the ability of its land-use controls to withstand legal attack, and their vulnerability to attack is in turn directly related to the administration's care in building a record of deliberative, well-documented, and reasoned action on its part and on the part of the legislative body. The attorney can be of invaluable assistance at every step of the process. He must, of course, have full cooperation from the administrative staff when land-use matters are tried before a court.

Miscellaneous Civil Actions. There are a number of other civil actions and appearances which the law department will be called upon to defend or initiate. Some of these are: mandamus actions to compel official action; personal defense of individual city officers; eminent domain proceedings to take land for public use; utility rate litigation before courts and administrative agencies; and antitrust litigation for damages.

PROSECUTION OF ORDINANCE VIOLATIONS

The activities of the city attorney relative to criminal or quasi-criminal cases are confined mainly to the prosecution of violations of city regulatory ordinances. He may be required by statute to prosecute minor violations of state laws, but felonies and other major offenses are commonly handled by a county or state attorney. The only obligation resting upon the city attorney in such cases is to see that the complete cooperation of his investigative staff is given to the prosecution.

Ordinarily the police, fire, health, or other inspection departments will report violations of city ordinances, and whenever the ordinance is one designed to be enforced by fine or imprisonment an investigation of the facts should be started immediately. Often the attorney will rely on the investigation made by other city officers, but in some instances his own staff will make the investigation.

The decision to prosecute or dismiss criminal complaints is left generally to the discretion of the attorney. Here, as in the case of the settlement of lawsuits, he has the burden of determining when it would be to the city's financial or other advantage to press the matter by court action. Criminal prosecution to secure compliance with regulatory ordinances is looked upon by most administrators and attorneys, and properly so, as the last resort after persuasion, consultation, or summary enforcement methods such as violations bureaus have failed. Even if prosecution is all that remains, the attorney may recommend dismissing the charge because of the high cost of prosecution, small possibility of conviction, or other good reason.

Successful prosecutions depend upon complete, well-presented testimony and evidence, and upon extreme care in observing the constitutional restrictions surrounding the rights of those accused of crimes. (The right to counsel and confession rules, undergoing development by the courts, have not yet been applied to all misdemeanors, but they do apply to certain misdemeanors of a serious nature.) The chief administrator, particularly where the city charter makes him the chief law enforcement officer, and the attorney have a joint responsibility to ensure that all municipal officers are fully trained in giving testimony in court and in properly informing accused persons of their rights. Many municipalities have established training programs of this sort or utilized the in-service training facilities of colleges, universities, and related organizations.

PREPARATION OF LEGAL DOCUMENTS

An endless array of legal papers must be prepared by the attorney. Among these are contracts, leases, deeds, bills of sale, easements, franchises, forms, notices, releases, invitations for bids, and ballots. This kind of work is the lawyer's stock in trade and the municipal attorney regularizes the preparation of these documents to the extent that it appears quite routine. In fact, some routine matters can be covered by general instructions from the attorney and left to responsible department heads and their deputies.

Extreme caution should be exercised, however, to prevent other than the most routine preparation of papers from being performed by anyone but the attorney. Defects of procedure in legal transactions involving public bodies have far more serious consequences than similar defects where private parties are involved.

As suggested earlier, the attorney's special skill in written expression can be utilized by the administrator in many ways. The attorney's help in the preparation of administrative manuals, departmental rules, and important correspondence should be obtained whenever possible.

LEGISLATIVE DRAFTING

Municipal officials will often find it necessary to seek changes in the municipality's charter or in state legislation affecting the municipality. The municipality's own legislative code is constantly in need of revision and amendments. In these tasks, the attorney has a central role.

Charters or Statutory Changes. When the municipality's charter or basic incorporation act is found inadequate in some respect, the attorney should be asked to draft proposed amendments. The procedural requirements for approving amendments vary from state to state, but the technique of draftsmanship is basically the same everywhere. Since legislative drafting is a fairly recondite skill, the attorney may employ special counsel to assist him. When presenting drafts of proposed amendments to the council, the attorney should be asked to furnish an explanatory memorandum, detailing the precise effect of the draft and the degree to which it meets the council's wishes.

In many instances, a new grant of statutory authority needed by one local government is needed by all municipalities in the state. Whenever a municipality decides to seek new legislation, it should consult with its state municipal league about possibilities for assistance. The leagues can be extremely helpful in all phases of the legislative process, from drafting to actually lobbying the bill through the legislature. Even when the bill is not one of statewide concern, the expertise of the league's legislative representative can be invaluable.

Preparation of Ordinances and Resolutions. A common function of the attorney is the preparation of ordinances and resolutions. It is not necessary at this point to distinguish between these two forms of enactment. The distinction will usually depend upon the city charter or statutory procedure specified in state law.

Many ordinances are routine in form—for example, a budget ordinance, authorization for the payment of bills, and formalities in connection with actions of the council. These do not constitute a difficult problem. They should be prepared by the attorney in advance of council meetings and referred to the official to whom the particular matter has been delegated.

The preparation of regulatory ordinances, on the other hand, is not a simple matter. These are laws of local application, bearing the same binding effect as state law, and they must be prepared with great care. A defective ordinance is unenforceable and thus worthless.

Once the decision is made that a new regulatory ordinance is needed, a memorandum outlining its objectives should be prepared and given to the attorney. The attorney should then prepare a draft of the ordinance and review it with the officials who will enforce it. If the draft is found workable, it should be presented to the council with an explanatory memorandum.

There are several important rules to follow in this apparently simple process:

1. *Always* have requests for new ordinances in narrative form; do not present the attorney with an amateur draft since he will always rework it and may in the process mistake the intent of the request.

2. *Always* ask the attorney to provide an explanatory memorandum with his draft. This will help avoid arguments about the precise meaning of the draft.

3. *Never* attempt to draft an ordinance by committee. The attorney will appreciate suggestions on the mechanics of the ordinance, but preparing the language is strictly a one-man job.

4. *Try to ensure* that the council does not attempt to amend the proposed ordinance without consulting the attorney. Legislative bodies often feel compelled to improve on grammar and style. In addition to dismaying the attorney, this practice can invalidate the ordinance.

Codification of Ordinances. Reference has often been made in the preceding paragraphs to the city's "legislative code," or "ordinance code." An ordinance code is a systematic integration of all municipal ordinances into a single book, organized by subject matter, tied together by a common numbering system, and thoroughly indexed. A municipal code is essentially similar in form to the statutory codes of federal and state laws. Responsibility for integrating new ordinances immediately into the code and repeals of existing ones should be assigned to the attorney.

The advantages of codifying city ordinances are many and obvious. Citizens can be expected to obey regulations only if they have some means of learning what these regulations are. The same principle applies to those charged with enforcement. Further, since many ordinance codes contain the city charter or enabling act and administrative as well as regulatory ordinances, they serve as a basic document for all key elected and appointed officials, as well as for interested citizens and groups.

In spite of the obvious value of ordinance codes, a large number of cities still attempts to operate with nothing more than agglomerations of resolutions and ordinances. Such agglomerations usually contain laws of which some are mere anachronisms, some are plainly invalid, and others have been long since repealed. No city can operate efficiently under such circumstances. While the initial codification of ordinances is an expensive task, especially when outside experts are utilized, as is often the case, the investment in money and effort pays handsome dividends in effective municipal government.

HEARINGS AND INVESTIGATIONS

The city attorney serves the city in advisory and representative capacities in a vast number of hearings, investigations, and formal appearances before administrative agencies and other quasi-judicial bodies.

Within the city structure there are many activities, judicial or semi-judicial in nature, which require the services of legal counsel. Examples are zoning boards of adjustment and appeal, civil service commission hearings on discipline or suspension matters, council committee work on licensing, and investigations of various kinds. The attorney must—and in fact is the only person in city government fully qualified to—ensure that legal requirements of procedural and substantive due process are fully met. This is particularly important since failure to meet rigorously such requirements might negate the entire work of these boards and commissions.

Outside the city structure, the attorney is the legal representative of the city in appearances before state and federal regulatory agencies. In this connection the attorney should be sure the city is notified of proposed rule making by state agencies and that the implication of proposed rules are explained to the city council and administration. If rules adverse to the city's interest are being proposed, the attorney should be authorized to make an appearance before the rule-making body and present the city's viewpoint.

Appearances on legal matters on behalf of the city are often made by the chief administrator, the mayor, or the council president. The advisory role of the attorney here is obvious. Regardless of who makes the appearance, however, close coordination should be maintained with the attorney so that the most effective presentation may be made.

INTERGOVERNMENTAL ACTIVITIES

Observations about the growing interdependence of various levels of government in the federal system are rapidly becoming commonplace. The concept of intergovernmental cooperation grows in importance each year as both a practical necessity in dealing with the phenomenon of urbanization and as a meaningful approach to the solution of regional and interjurisdictional problems. Here again, the problem of coordinated effort by governmental units is much more formidable than similar activity in the private sector, and again the attorney can play a key role.

Relations with Other Local Governments. The attorney's advice should be sought whenever legal questions or problems arise during the course of formal contacts between the city and other units of local government. Further, in addition to his legal expertise, the attorney is often the only official fully aware of the exact boundaries and powers of all of the various local governments, including special districts, with jurisdiction in or near the city. Thus his advice on questions involving the city's relations with its local government neighbors can be indispensable.

In particular, there are two specific instances in which legal advice should be a prerequisite to action by the city. First, the attorney should be at the center of the negotiating and contracting that precedes joint undertakings by the city with other units of local government. Further, the attorney should keep the city advised of its responsibilities in executing such joint agreements and in discharging those functions, such as law enforcement, for

which it shares responsibility with the county or other unit of local government. Second, the attorney is uniquely qualified to assist the city in coping with the problem of fringe-area development, in formulating a proper policy toward the extension of city services beyond city boundaries, and in expanding city boundaries by annexation.

City-State Relations. Many of the functions of the attorney in the area of city-state relations have already been mentioned and need no further elaboration. But one point deserves special emphasis. Cities are completely dependent on the state for the two inputs they must have to do their governmental job— legal authority and sources of revenue. The attorney is responsible for informing the city administration and council about a deficiency in the one and assisting the city in influencing an equitable state policy toward the other. Both aspects require a familiarity with the state legislative process, and increasing emphasis is being placed by cities on their attorneys as legislative representatives.

City-Federal Relations. There are few aspects of municipal government that have not been affected to some degree by the intense activity of the federal government in recent years. The city attorney's office, geared as it usually is to keeping track of state legislative developments, is uniquely suited to performing the same function for federal activity. Because eligibility criteria for participating in federal programs are matters of federal law and agency regulation, the attorney's services are indispensable, not only in deciding whether to utilize a particular aid program, but also in preparing the application and subsequently in administering the program.

MISCELLANEOUS FUNCTIONS AND DUTIES

There are a number of related activities that are the proper work of the attorney. These include participation in state and national organizations, participation in in-service training programs for municipal personnel, and advice in executing a number of financial procedures.

Participation in State and National Organizations. The enlightened city attorney finds active participation in his state organization of municipal attorneys (usually affiliated with the state association of municipalities) and in national clearing houses of municipal information, such as the National Institute of Municipal Law Officers, a necessity in order to keep abreast of developments. The publications, conferences, schools, research services, and scores of other advantages which only united group action can provide, enable the city attorney and his staff to maintain a grasp of the rapidly growing field of municipal law.

Training Functions. A knowledge of fundamentals of public law is of immense value to every department head or other city official holding a position of responsibility. Training of this sort is valuable at all levels, from councilman to typist, and a necessity in the case of inspection personnel and law enforcement officers. Obviously, the attorney should be a key element in any legal training program.

The purpose of such training is not, of course, to make attorneys out of city officials. In this area, as in many others, a little learning is a potentially dangerous thing. Legal first aid is often as necessary as medical first aid, however, and preventive measures can often save the doctor's—or the attorney's—call. The officer or employee who understands the legal requirements that surround the operation of city government and who appreciates the legal implications of his actions will be more likely to recognize legal problems and appreciate the need for legal assistance before a serious legal entanglement arises.

Personnel training takes on special significance in the regulatory field. Police personnel must have regular training in such matters as the laws of arrest, searches and seizures, and the rights of the accused in general. The attorney should be responsible for this training. Inspection personnel, too, need periodic training in the rules of evidence, the meaning and practical requirements of the concept of due process of law, and the statutory and ordinance framework of the programs they enforce. In-service training programs on these subjects conducted by the attorney or other qualified personnel are highly desirable.

Fiscal Procedures. The levying of taxes, administration of city accounts, issuance of bonds, and other fiscal procedures are so governed by a multitude of state laws that careful attention to their legal aspects is necessary.

Cities usually finance their capital acquisitions by selling bonds. Since the procedure for such sales is usually, if not always, specified by statute, the validity, and hence the marketability, of the bonds depends upon these procedures being followed exactly. The function of the attorney here is obvious, and his judgment and care are commonly substantiated by independent expert counsel whose opinion of validity is an integral part of the bond issue. Private bond attorneys frequently are retained for continuing assistance in all phases of bond proceedings, particularly those bond issues of any magnitude.

The proceedings for the imposition of special assessments against benefitted property to finance public improvements must also be conducted with continuous counsel from the city attorney.

Budgeting, funding, financial reporting, and fund management are all functions of the finance department governed by more or less rigid statutory, charter, or ordinance provisions. The attorney can assist the finance officer in conforming to them.

CONCLUSION

This section has examined the broad range of services provided by the attorney and his all-inclusive concern with every aspect of municipal government. It has been emphasized that the administrator can make valuable use of the attorney's combination of talents and skills. The need for close coordination between the attorney and administrator has been demonstrated. All that remains is to state a few basic rules that administrators should bear in mind when dealing with their attorneys:

1. Establish a regularized liaison with the attorney in the form of staff meetings, interchange of memos, and related devices.

2. Keep the attorney informed of proposed regulatory programs, controversial matters on council agendas, and the status of on-going projects requiring his periodic review.

3. Channel all legal inquiries through the chief administrator or responsible deputy. A single response to common problems can satisfy everyone's curiosity, and prevent duplication of effort by the attorney.

4. Rely on the attorney's judgment and never second-guess him. Sound legal advice is the cheapest insurance the city can buy.

A half-serious but effective presentation of these points appears in Figure 16–1.

Organization and Administration of the Law Department

The city attorney, whether employed full or part-time, is a department head in his own right and, for that reason, a certain proportion of his time is taken up with matters which are not legal, but executive or administrative in nature. The size of a city law department varies, from that of the small municipality where the attorney *is* the department to the mammoth legal departments of the great metropolitan cities. The larger the legal staff, the more the chief legal officer tends to become an administrator rather than a lawyer. But even the one-man staff has need of administrative skill since he must very often deal with other officials in his capacity as department head.

The Law Department in the Administrative Structure

Most students of public administration would agree that, ideally, the law department should be coequal with other city departments, with the department head—the city attorney— appointed by the chief administrator and responsible directly to him. This ideal is far from reality, however, and this fact has important implications for the administrator. Attainment of the ideal is impaired largely by two factors: the process through which attorneys are usually selected, and the special nature of the attorney's role as legal advisor to the council as well as to the chief administrator.

Method of Selection. There is little uniformity among municipalities in the method

1. If you are holding regular conferences with your attorney, stop doing so at once. This will keep him from finding out what you have in mind that would require legal guidance.

2. Call him at least once each day on minor problems and always time the calls so that they are in mid-morning or mid-afternoon, never the first thing in the morning or the last thing in the afternoon.

3. When you call him never accept the statement from his secretary that he is in conference, insist in breaking in on him at any time, especially if your question involves a very minor item.

4. Stop following up on projects which he is working on, let him drift along without any information as to changes in plans on these projects.

5. Stop informing him of any proposals you may have which involve legal pitfalls, such as firing an employee with veterans' preference.

6. Proclaim new ideas or plans of action publicly before you check with your attorney on their legality.

7. Start campaigns of enforcement of minor laws or ordinances without warning. This should help to bring the wrath of the tax-payers down upon the attorney demanding legal interpretation of the law.

8. Leave your attorney in the dark, especially in regard to legal points coming up at council meetings. This can be accomplished very simply by not sending him copies of the council agenda before the meeting.

9. Throw him a lot of routine clerical work to do, such as drafting standard resolutions and contracts.

10. Avoid channeling legal inquiries from staff members across your desk. Have your employee go directly to the attorney and he can sort them out.

11. Destroy written decisions which you receive from your attorney. In that way you can make your attorney go back and resurrect his own files when parallel cases arise on which he has already rendered a decision.

12. Consult other legal sources to embarrass him. This may be accomplished quite nicely by getting written opinions from the League of Minnesota Municipalities office and memorizing case histories before you pop the question on your attorney and thereby impress everyone with your excellent legal knowledge on minor points, while your attorney stalls for time.

13. After your attorney has rendered a decision show your dissatisfaction by stating that you still want an Attorney General's opinion in writing.

14. Always make your attorney give his legal opinions at public meetings, thereby putting him on the spot in case troubles arise later.

15. Answer legal questions yourself at city council meetings. This always makes for an interestingly embarrassing situation for your attorney who does not want to publicly point out your ignorance or make it appear that you do not know what you are talking about by his giving the correct information which differs from what you have already said.

Figure 16-1. *How to drive your attorney insane (By Clayton LeFevere, City Attorney, Richfield, Minnesota. Reprinted with permission from* Minnesota Municipalities, *June, 1963, p. 190.)*

of selecting the attorney except for the general rule that popular election is uncommon. As of 1966, the attorney was elected in only 22 cities of over 50,000 population and in only five of the 186 council-manager cities of similar size. Where the attorney is elected, he is, for practical purposes, outside the normal lines of responsibility; the administrator must then rely completely on cooperation or administrative code provisions for coordinated effort with the law department.

Appointment of the attorney is made either by the council, the mayor (in strong-mayor cities), the manager, or some combination of these officials.[5] He is probably less often appointed solely by the chief administrative officers than are most other city department heads. When appointment review or approval by the council is combined with the attorney's lawyer-client view of his relationship to the elected council, it will be seen that most law departments have a dual responsibility to the chief administrator and to the legislative body. Since this is the result of statutory or charter provisions there is little the administrator can do to change it. His important task is to help remove any impediment to efficient government it may create.[6]

Attorney-Administrator Relationship. The discussion of "The Work of the Attorney and Its Implications for Administrators" earlier in this chapter pointed up the need for constant contact and cooperation between the municipal administrator and his legal counsel —the municipal attorney. Interaction between the two was recommended in virtually all matters of consequence that come before the administrator, covering a spectrum of problem situations ranging from law enforcement, labor negotiations, legislative lobbying, and jurisdictional problems between governments to routine contracting, police training, and the preparation of administrative manuals. Thus the relationship between administrator and attorney is a crucial determinant of the city government's operational effectiveness.

Formally, this relationship can and should be described in the city's administrative code. There the obligations of each official to the other can be delineated, their respective prerogatives outlined, and the key points of interaction between them prescribed. Such a formalization, carrying as it does the endorsement of the legislative body, can do much to supply the crystallization of responsibilities and lines of authority so essential to efficient administration. Informally, however, the relationship must be predicated upon mutual trust and respect for one another, personally and professionally.

The Needs of the Law Department. The administrator who fully understands the function of the law department and the foundation of technical expertise upon which it rests will be in a good position to view realistically the financial needs of the department. Competent attorneys command substantial compensation; an adequate law library and its maintenance is expensive; adequate facilities in terms of space and equipment are essential; continuing formal legal education of the staff is imperative. A meaningful allocation of the municipality's financial resources must view costs for legal services in a realistic manner.

INTERNAL ORGANIZATION

While the attorney will probably be working either within a traditional organizational pattern or making innovations to suit his own concepts of internal efficiency, the trained ad-

---

[5] A 1957 study by the city manager of Rome, New York, of council-manager cities above 25,000 population revealed the following pattern of city attorney appointments:

Method of Selection	No. of Cities
Elected	11
Council appointed	96
Council appointed with mgr.'s recommendation	4
Manager appointed	51
Manager appointed with council approval	13
Other (usually involving mayor and council)	9
	184 (84% response)

Source: Robert H. McManus, "How Should the City Attorney be Selected?" PUBLIC MANAGEMENT, January, 1957, p. 4.

[6] An enlightening study of the viewpoints of attorneys and managers themselves to these varying relationships is contained in Allen Grimes, "The Job of City Managers and City Attorneys," PUBLIC MANAGEMENT, January, 1959, pp. 38–42.

ministrator should stand ready to assist him with organizational or administrative problems.

In all but the largest cities, the law department usually employs a relatively small staff. In most cities under 100,000 population the organization of the law department will simply mean a common sense division of work among the city attorney and his two or three assistants. In larger cities the division of work within the department is often formalized in separate divisions or bureaus, each with its own division head. Figure 16–2 depicts a typical organizational layout of a very large city.

In moderate sized cities the department is often divided into a civil and criminal division with the managerial and auxiliary functions subassigned within each division.

In yet smaller cities the attorney and his assistant will perform the auxiliary functions of advice, drafting, attendance at council meetings, and legislative review while employing special counsel to handle such specialized matters as the issuance of bonds, all civil and criminal litigation, special appearances and the like. Under this arrangement, however, the city attorney still retains full responsibility for all legal matters. In this respect legal services are provided to the municipality in much the same way that they are to moderate sized private corporations.

Frequently small municipalities employ an attorney who is a member of a private law firm. In fact, then, the firm is retained to perform the function of a law department for the city.

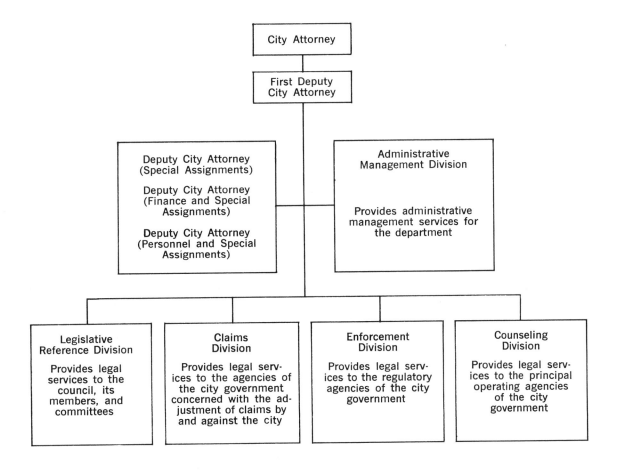

FIGURE 16-2. *The law department in the administrative structure*

These variations in internal structure should not normally be of more than routine concern to the administrator. His basic responsibility is to ensure that work assigned to the department is performed promptly and efficiently and that the department has a clear understanding of its responsibilities.

EMPLOYING OUTSIDE COUNSEL

Municipalities often retain special private counsel to assist the attorney where specialized legal expertise is required. Trial work, in particular, is a legal specialty, as is labor relations work, bond and fiscal counseling, and work with state and federal regulatory agencies.

On the other hand, the law of municipal corporations and public officers is a highly technical field in itself, a field with which the average lawyer has little or no contact. The municipal attorney should, therefore, retain final authority for the conduct of the matter whenever outside counsel is retained.

Administration of Regulatory Programs

This final section of the chapter is devoted to the special problems surounding the establishment and enforcement of municipal regulatory programs. A large degree of the city's operating effort is involved in either direct regulation of persons or things by local laws called ordinances, enacted to protect the public health, safety, or general welfare, or by indirect regulation through ordinances and rules designed to expedite the performance of some operating function. The city shares in the enforcement of state and some federal regulatory programs as well.

Regulatory programs, viewed in their proper perspective, are simply one of the services that local government provides to its citizens. The attorney's role in the regulatory process is twofold: first, an auxiliary role in drafting legislation and advising as to legality of procedures; and second, enforcement through appropriate civil and criminal remedies.

THE REGULATORY COMPLEX

Although local government regulations impinge most directly and most often on the individual citizen, all levels of government in the federal system regulate society in varying degrees. Thus, added to and complicating the network of regulatory ordinances imposed by city governments are similar networks of laws and regulations established by the federal and state governments. Sometimes these other governments enforce their regulations themselves, but often the municipality finds itself performing this task in their stead. Many aspects of traffic regulation and liquor control, for example, fall in this category. In other cases, federal regulations preclude state or local activity, as in the case of interstate gas rates or the regulation of aircraft procedures. Also, local regulatory activities may themselves be circumscribed by rules of a state or federal regulatory agency. While it is the attorney's responsibility to be aware of this complex interrelation, the municipal administrative officer should have a general familiarity with it as well.

THE LOCAL LAW-MAKING PROCESS

Cities regulate persons and property within their jurisdiction by means of local laws passed by the elected council and known, usually, as ordinances. Every regulatory program has its origin in an ordinance passed by the council at the request of the city administration, the public, or at the council's own instance. Occasionally, in particularly complex matters, departments may establish and enforce additional rules needed to carry out the ordinance, but, unlike state and federal agencies, this is not the common pattern of municipal regulation.

Determining Need. When considering a new regulatory ordinance or evaluating an existing one, the city should proceed with caution and act only in cases of demonstrated necessity. An ordinance that either does not reflect the conscience of the community or infringes on personal liberty without commensurate gains in a fuller freedom for the municipality as a whole will soon be amended, repealed, or, worse still, simply ignored. A regulatory scheme that does not take account of practical realities cannot be enforced and will have to be abandoned. To a large degree, the factors just mentioned are policy considerations for the elected council, but it, in turn, will rely heavily on the recommendation of its administrative staff in making its judgments.

Determining Legality and Feasibility. The attorney should be consulted early in the lawmaking process to ascertain whether the subject and mode of regulation is one about which the city can legally legislate. There is a growing tendency on the part of many state legislatures to preempt matters of statewide concern for state regulation. In addition, there are often important state limitations on municipal regulatory powers, particularly in the occupational licensing field. Finally, the attorney will check the presence of safeguards to ensure that constitutional guarantees of procedural due process of law are recognized.

Administering the Program. Where only the criminal sanctions of fine or imprisonment are to be invoked, as in ordinances regulating traffic, nuisances, or misdemeanors, the ordinance is administered simply by prosecution. In the case of other regulatory programs, however, the administrative machinery may become quite elaborate. A system of licenses, permits, and inspections is often required, with its attendant problems of accounting, record keeping, and personnel training.

Licenses and Permits. The most positive method of regulating conduct is to include licensing and permit requirements in the ordinance. The licensing procedure enables the city to impose qualifications and conditions on the licensed activity. The use of permits enables the city to ensure in advance that individual acts within a given area of licensed or other regulated activity will conform to the details of the regulation.

License and Permit Fees. Some cities are authorized to impose license and permit fees primarily as a means of raising revenue, but in most cities the legal rule is that cities may impose fees only in an amount sufficient to cover the cost of enforcing the regulation. This rule is sound from a legal as well as a public policy point of view, and when departures are made from it, they should be in the direction of lower rather than higher fees. A substantial license fee can increase the enforce-

ment problem as well as the public relations problem of obtaining proper public attitudes toward the regulation.

Responsibility for Inspection and Reporting. If the subject of regulation is closely related to the work of an existing department, responsibility for the needed inspection and reporting should be assigned to that department. It is usually impractical to rely on the police department for anything other than routine checking for current licenses and permits in conjunction with normal patrols.

Procedural Due Process. The constitutional protections that circumscribe all governmental action are nothing more than traditional concepts of fair play and aversion to arbitrary action. When constitutional questions are involved the attorney will undoubtedly have provided in the regulatory ordinance for notice, hearing, and related matters. Often these requirements are embodied in state laws governing local licensing activity. Any sound regulatory program will embody similar features, even if not required by law.

SECURING COMPLIANCE

Municipal regulatory programs cannot rely on the threat of punishment to ensure compliance. In dealing with citizens as with employees, the objective is accomplishment of goals, not punishment for infractions. When regulations are imposed on citizens, it is because the local legislative body has found that some important consideration of public health, safety, or welfare requires the regulation. If the regulation is grounded on such considerations, the voluntary compliance of most citizens can be obtained by explaining the reason for the regulation with sufficient force and persuasion. Education and other methods of securing voluntary compliance go hand in hand with the more severe enforcement procedures in any well-conceived regulatory scheme.

Accessibility of Regulations: Codification. The value of ordinance codification has already been discussed. Citizens can be expected to obey regulations only if they know what they are. A readable, well-indexed, carefully numbered ordinance code is indispensible in a sound regulatory program. Many cities prepare special editions of the more commonly used sections of the code—building code, zoning ordinance, plumbing code, licensing ordinances—for use by the public. Printed lists of current license fees, permit fees, and special charges of various sorts are often prepared and made available to the public.

Publicity for New Regulations. Mere publication of an ordinance as required by statute or charter is rarely adequate to inform the public. It is essential that every new regulation and amendment be brought directly to the attention of the persons regulated. Where licenses are required, the applicant will be fully informed when he is granted his license, but publicity will be needed to let him know that a license is required. Often a trade or labor association has worked with the city in developing regulations for their own activity, but even here it will be valuable to let the public at large know the purpose of the program. In other cases, newspaper publicity will help, and direct mailing lists can be obtained that will reach most of the persons affected. If the regulation is at all technical it should be explained in simple terms. When the purpose of the regulation is not apparent on its face—and it seldom is to persons for whom it means inconvenience—publication of the regulation should be accompanied by appropriate explanatory material whenever possible.

Assistance in Compliance. The city administration must extend every effort to make compliance with regulatory programs as painless as possible. Reduction of paper work, centralized license issuance, and personal assistance in interpreting ordinance language and standards can often transform grudging submission into willing and enlightened compliance.

Summary Disposition of Offenses. Citizens resent having a major issue made of a minor infraction, and are usually quite willing to pay a small fine or consent to a warning to avoid involved legal proceedings. Many cities have experimented successfully with ordinance violation bureaus—often known as "tag" ordinances—where the violator is simply issued a tag (or it is left on the premises) calling attention to the violation together with instruc-

tions for handling the matter by mail or by a brief appearance before an appropriate official.

SPECIAL REGULATORY CONCERNS

Some municipal regulations are unique in that they are not designed to regulate conduct or promote safety so much as to accomplish some governmental goal.

Land-Use Regulation. Zoning ordinances, subdivision regulations, and official street maps are devices used by municipalities to implement developmental planning goals by regulating the use of land. Routine enforcement is usually accomplished by a related program of issuing building permits only for the use allowed by the ordinance. In this field, however, interests are often so substantial that enforcement is often accomplished by litigation in which basic issues about the validity of the ordinance are raised.

Utility Regulations. Almost all cities are engaged in the business of supplying some kind of utility service such as water, sewage disposal, or electricity. The ordinances governing the use of these services are more in the nature of business rules than laws, but are, nonetheless, an exercise of sovereign power. When utility services are provided by privately owned utilities, cities in some states may develop a host of regulatory ordinances surrounding the use of streets, rates that may be charged, and standards of service. Enforcement here is a matter of ensuring compliance with the contractual obligations of the franchised utility. Generally, however, such regulation is exercised by the state government.

Consolidated Inspections. Whenever possible, inspection services should be coordinated or consolidated. This can be accomplished by systematic cooperation among the field forces of the city agencies involved to avoid conflicts and duplication of effort, or by actual consolidation of all such services in one department. The latter is more an ideal than a reality, usually, because of departmental pride within the city government and because of objections from labor and business associations. It has been achieved in varying degrees, however, in some smaller cities. Bloomington, Minnesota, for example, combines all inspectional services under a chief inspector who is a department head responsible directly to the city manager.

Organization for Regulatory Administration.[7] There is no single organizational structure that can be recommended for municipal regulatory functions. Such structures must be individually tailored for each municipality. The key to successful regulation is thorough inspection, record keeping, and reporting, and any organizational structure that achieves these goals is a good one.

An overriding consideration, however, is the direct impingement of the inspectional aspects of regulatory programs on the citizens of the municipality. The image of the city is, to a large degree, created by the police officers and inspection personnel who contact the public every hour of the day.

The Role of the Administrator as Chief Law Enforcement Officer. In council-manager and strong-mayor cities (and often in other cities as well), the chief administrative officer is typically designated by law or charter as the chief law enforcement officer. The implications of this responsibility often are not appreciated by the general public (and occasionally overlooked by police department heads), but the successful administrator never loses sight of that fact. As such, his role is that of a chief executive whose function it is to see that all the laws of the city are diligently and fairly enforced and to recommend the enactment of new rules where needed.

This role of the administrator as chief law enforcement officer places two major responsibilities on him. First, he must fashion regulatory programs that his subordinates will pursue with vigor, enthusiasm, and confidence in their propriety. Second, he must ensure that the programs are understandable to the public, acceptable to the legislative body, and enforceable by both voluntary compliance and the imposition of civil and criminal remedies where necessary. There are also important correlative responsibilities, the most important of which are training of personnel in enforce-

ment techniques and publicizing the regulations to facilitate maximum compliance.

ROLE OF THE ATTORNEY IN REGULATORY ADMINISTRATION

In addition to his continuing function of advising, counseling, and drafting ordinances, the attorney has two major additional responsibilities in regulatory administration. First, he must prosecute ordinance violators or invoke the appropriate legal remedies to ensure compliance, and, second, he must help train regulatory personnel in the legal aspects of inspections and in the gathering and presentation of evidence.

When all other attempts at securing compliance with regulatory programs are exhausted, the city must prosecute violators in court. While municipal ordinances partake of the nature of criminal statutes by imposing fine and imprisonment as sanctions, for the most part they are civil in nature and the usual rules of trial by jury and proof of guilt beyond a reasonable doubt do not apply. (There are important exceptions to this rule in each state.)

A successful prosecution depends upon: (1) sound discretion in bringing the action, (2) accurate inspection and reporting by inspection personnel, and (3) well documented, accurate testimony at trial. An action brought without adequate factual background will, even in apparently clear cases, be dismissed and the effectiveness of the program will suffer.

The attorney will rely exclusively on the reports and inspection data of department personnel in proving his case. Systematic and thorough reporting of violations, corrective action, notices, and conferences are therefore absolutely essential. The attorney will also rely on departmental personnel for the presentation of evidence at trial. They should, therefore, be completely familiar with the department's record systems, and trained in stating the data about a violation in an accurate, concise manner.

The following report form (Figure 16-3) was developed by the city of Bloomington. Minnesota, Inspection Department, for use under a state law authorizing municipalities

---

[7] For more complete coverage of this subject, see the International City Managers' Association, MUNICIPAL PUBLIC WORKS ADMINISTRATION (Chicago: The Association, 1957), Chapter 15.

Building Inspector's Report

Site Address .... Date ....

What Inspected ....

Principal Uses ....

Use Zone .... Fire Zone ....

Legal Description ....

Owner .... Address .... Phone ....

Agent .... Address .... Phone ....

Occupants .... Address .... Phone ....

.... Address .... Phone ....

Heirs .... Address .... Phone ....

Guardian .... Address .... Phone ....

Lien-holders .... Address .... Phone ....

.... Address .... Phone ....

Attach additional list of all of above, if necessary.

Construction of Building ....

.... No. of Stories ....

Type of Heating Plant ....

Condition of Heating Plant ....

Other Mechanical Equipment ....

Condition of Mechanical Equipment ....

Electric Lighting & Wiring ....

Condition of Above ....

Kind of Roof ....

Condition of Roof ....

Condition of Basement ....

Condition of Windows ....

Adequate Light and Air Provided ....

Condition of Sills ....

Condition of Chimneys ....

Attic; How Used ....

Condition of Foundation Wall ....

Condition of Bearing Walls ....

Condition of Non-Bearing Walls ....

Condition of Exterior Walls ....

Condition of Plumbing ....

Condition of Other Sanitary Facilities ....

Condition of Cooking Equipment ....

Municipal Water .... Well .... Municipal Sewer ....

Condition of Interior, Lath and Plaster, etc. ....

Type and Condition of Fire Protection Equipment or Facilities ....

....

....

Dimension of Building ....

Setbacks, Front .... Rear .... Sides ....

Distance from Other Buildings ....

Remarks in General, List All Defects Found at Time of Inspection ....

....

....

List Separately All Permits Issued for Building ....

....

Conclusions: ....

Is Building a Fire Hazard .... Why ....

Is Building a Hazard to Public Safety .... Why ....

....

....

Is Building a Hazard to Public Health .... Why ....

Recommendations: Condemnation ....

 Repair .... List All Repairs Required ....

 Photos Taken .... Attach to Report

 Names of Persons accompanying you on inspection ....

.... Signature ....

.... Title

Administrative Review by .... Date ....

Attorney Review .... Date ....

Attorney Action .... Date ....

Council Hearing .... Date ....

Council Action .... Date ....

Building Posted .... Date ....

Order Served .... Date ....

Time for Compliance ....

How Served ....

Court Action Taken ....

Filed with Clerk of Court .... Date ....

Filed with Register of Deeds .... Date ....

FIGURE 16-3. *Form for use under hazardous building law (Prepared by Bloomington [Minnesota] Department of License and Inspection.)*

to raze dangerous buildings. (Many cities have ordinances of the same type.) It is a good example of the kind of reporting that will assist the attorney in a successful court action.

Coordination with Administrative Agencies. There must be a close working relationship between the city attorney and chief administrator if regulatory programs are to be successful. In turn both must be sensitive to the attitudes of the elected council. This rapport between administrator and attorney is essential to a consistent policy of enforcement as well as to building mutual confidence in each other's work.

That the same enforcement policy should be followed by the attorney and the regulatory department is an elementary principle, but one that is not likely to be followed unless the chief administrator brings about a liaison between the two. If the prosecution is less diligent than the regulatory unit, the morale of the unit may drop sharply when it finds that complaints it initiates are routinely dropped by the law department. On the other hand, a crusading prosecutor may find his cases being dismissed for lack of evidence. Any indication of uneven enforcement policy should immediately be investigated by the administrator since a breakdown of communication or confidence has occurred or is imminent.

Both the attorney and the agency responsible for the administration of a regulatory program should be closely involved in all steps of the law-making process. If the attorney is convinced that the program is soundly conceived and will be administered by competent personnel, he surely will be a more enthusiastic member of the enforcement team. Similarly, if departmental personnel are confident they will be backed up by the law department, high morale will be much easier to maintain.

Constant crossfeed of technical information between various inspectional units and the law department is also essential. Attorneys who specialize in certain types of regulation—health, buildings, zoning—often master much of the technical wisdom of those fields. Conversely, there are often experts in the regulatory units who develop a high degree of competence in the law surrounding their specialty

and can keep the attorney alerted to relevant new legal developments.

Summary

This chapter has examined the work of the law department and its impact on city administration. Emphasis has been primarily on the services that the attorney offers and how the administrator can best obtain and utilize these services, rather than on the substance of the law itself. Typical law department organization has been discussed briefly as has the role of the law department in the administration of regulatory programs.

Five general principles run through the chapter and underlie a successful attorney-administrator relationship.

1. Municipal corporations are legal entities of limited powers subject to supervision by state government and close scrutiny by the taxpaying public. The need for legal counsel on corporate affairs is, therefore, correspondingly greater in cities than in private business.

2. A competent, adequately financed law department is a sound investment for the city and pays dividends in the prevention of costly mistakes, the reduction in the volume of tort and other claims against the city, and successful accomplishment of the city's regulatory programs.

3. Because of his highly professional background and his attorney-client relationship with the elected council, the attorney has a degree of independence not found in other city departments. Hence, the administrator must make special efforts to achieve rapport and a high level of coordination with him and with the law department.

4. The administrator should take advantage of the broad range of skills—writing, speaking, analysis, bargaining—that the attorney brings with him to city government. These skills can be used to advantage in many nonlegal fields.

5. An effective municipal regulatory program must involve the law department in all phases of the law making and enforcement process.

17

Intergovernmental Relations

INTERGOVERNMENTAL RELATIONS comprises one of the newest and certainly the most difficult set of issues confronting the urban administrator. As the urban crisis seethes in a great many of the nation's cities, countless problems and associated programs, with their pressures and counter pressures, have focused upon urban political leaders and professional managers. Most of the problems and most of the programs designed to meet them involve not just one unit, or one layer of government, but many units and usually all governmental levels—federal, state and local—and in the densely populated areas of the country a fourth level: the metropolitan region.[1]

At no point in the structure of the American federal system of government are problems of intergovernmental relations so marked, varied, and difficult as in the large metropolitan areas, where the activities of all four of these levels of government function in close proximity. Within such areas, federal, state, county, and municipal agencies, often supplemented by a small host of special purpose units of local government, must carry on their functions in close juxtaposition, subject to an extremely complicated framework of federal, state, and local laws and administrative regulations. Indeed, the crucial governmental and political question of contemporary times is whether the American federal system can survive the crisis that eddies and boils in the cities, or if only a highly centralized and unitary system will be

equal to the tasks. Thus, the issues are grave, and the stakes are huge as the urban administrator strives to make federalism work and to respond effectively to the frustrations and aspirations of the people of his city.

The purpose of this chapter is to examine the intergovernmental scene today, including the variety of problems, programs, and agencies therein, to assess the various organizational and administrative approaches useful in dealing with other units and levels of government, and finally to appraise the present and future prospects of metropolitan government in the United States, an issue lying at the root of much of the urban crisis, but one that continues to defy rational treatment because of the incredible social, political, fiscal, and administrative dilemmas involved.

The Intergovernmental Scene Today

The American system, because it is "federal," is necessarily fragmented and divided. Powers are split among three levels of government: national, state, and local. This fact in itself, at least at present when governmental levels are functionally intertwined, makes intergovernmental matters a necessary concern of the local official.

Yet this three-faceted image is increasingly inadequate, for the "local" level is no longer unitary but is itself complex and divided. Many of the administrator's "intergovernmental" concerns, then, are really "interlocal."

As the decade of the seventies begins, the

---

[1] Throughout this chapter, generous use has been made of reports and other materials published by the Advisory Commission on Intergovernmental Relations.

intergovernmental picture in urban America is characterized by several trends, some of which are contradictory and none of which give comfort to those seeking logical and neat administrative patterns of municipal governance. The number of local government units is increasing; the disparities among these units is growing; programs and projects designed to mitigate the disparities between the haves and the have nots are proliferating, resulting in confusion and duplication of effort; and the overall direction of urban growth and development is caught in cross currents moving back and forth between regional centralization and neighborhood decentralization. To make the best of this situation and, in some way, somehow, to arrange for the delivery of governmental services to his clientele in an equitable and efficient manner is the tremendous challenge facing today's urban administrator.

MULTIPLYING LOCAL GOVERNMENT UNITS IN METROPOLITAN AREAS

One very common feature of urban government in the United States is the existence of many local governments in a single metropolitan area; the average is 91 governments per SMSA, and 48 governments per metropolitan county. The average for metropolitan counties is 12 school districts, 12 municipalities, seven townships, and 16 special districts in addition to the county government itself. These averages, of course, conceal wide variations, especially in the Midwest and Far West, where numerous metropolitan counties have more than 100 local governments each. In the 10 metropolitan areas with the most numerous local governments (ranging from 269 in the Denver area to 1,113 in the Chicago area) the number per county runs from 35 to 186.

The fact that the overwhelming majority of these local governments are relatively small in population and geographic size is another common feature. For example, about half of the nearly 5,000 municipalities in SMSA's have less than a single square mile of land area, and only one in five is as large as four square miles. Two-thirds of them have fewer than 5,000 residents; one-third fewer than 1,000.

A third common feature is multiple layer-ing—the geographic overlapping of separate local governments. Most residents of metropolitan areas are served by a minimum of four separate units—a county, a municipality, and a school district, plus one or more special districts. The average central city has more than four overlying local governments, and in parts of some metropolitan areas the number of layers is much greater. As a rule the boundaries of various local government units are not coterminous; less than one-fifth of the school districts and only one-eighth of the special districts in SMSA's coincide geographically with a municipality, township, or county.

In two parts of the country—New England especially and to a lesser degree the South—metropolitan areas have much less diffused and layered patterns than elsewhere. In New England, local government units per SMSA average only 29 in number, compared with the nationwide average of 91; most local government services are provided through townships and sizable municipalities. The South relies more on counties and there are no townships at all; here the number of local governments averages 40 per SMSA. Two strong trends have emerged in metropolitan governmental structure in recent years: The number of school districts has dropped sharply, and the number of special districts has skyrocketed.

As the term implies, most special districts are like school districts—concerned with only a single function, such as fire protection, water supply, or public housing. On the other hand, they are geographically like municipalities in that they do not blanket the entire state. Usually they are born one by one for particular local areas by local action under a state general law. Many of them can impose taxes and nearly all of them can impose service charges, incur debt, and receive grants from other governments.

Counties do not overlap other counties; nor do municipalities overlap other municipalities. But, with their single-function nature, special districts can and very often do overlie special districts and other local governments in bewildering variety. They account for much of the complex layering of local governments found in many metropolitan areas—sometimes adding as many as another half dozen tiers to the usual four layers of more traditional kinds of governments.

In 1967, special districts in SMSA's numbered 7,049—15 percent more than in 1962—and constituted over one-third of all local governments in metropolitan areas. While the nation's metropolitan areas have less than one-fourth of all the school districts and multipurpose governments (counties, municipalities, and townships), they have one-third of all the special districts.

Nationwide, the number of special districts has nearly doubled in the past 15 years, with much of the change taking place in SMSA's. A small portion of the proliferation can be traced to the need—arising from the sprawling nature of the large modern metropolis—for public agencies equipped to handle specific public services for areas larger than a single county. Of the 7,049 special districts in SMSA's, 527 are multicounty districts that deal with "large-area" functions such as air pollution, airports, and mass transportation.

Yet, there are far more compelling reasons for the alarming proliferation of special districts. One of these, very clearly, is the refusal of many states to relax or remove their restrictive tax and debt limits on traditional types of local governments. The creation of special districts has been one way—sometimes the only politically feasible way—for local areas to get around such limits. Significantly, the number of special districts is greatest in the states that have tight tax and debt limits.

A further strong reason for the mushrooming of special districts is the limited role county governments are permitted to play in providing urban services. In most parts of the nation, counties traditionally have been viewed as agents of the state for the performance of services needed everywhere, and with most of their support drawn from uniform countywide taxes. Consequently, most counties lack the authority and capacity to supply the additional services demanded by residents of the urbanizing parts of their territory. Thus, when service needs expand beyond municipal boundaries, and given the rigid annexation laws in many states, the special district often is the only legal—perhaps the only constitutional—way of meeting these needs.

Still another reason is the common practice of states to specify in detail the organizational structure and the elective offices of traditional types of local governments. For counties in particular, this typically results in a highly diffused internal pattern. In 1967 the average county government in a metropolitan area had 31 elective officials, including nine members of the governing board and 22 additional officials (Figure 17–1). This diffusion of policy-making responsibility, along with other factors has lessened the feasibility of using the county instead of the district in meeting growing urban service needs.

An alternative of course is municipal annexation—once the traditional way for local government to adapt to urban growth. It is still an important tool in some parts of the country. However, the laws of many states sharply limit the feasibility of annexation.

The nature of recent urban fringe settlement, often involving shoestring or leapfrog patterns of development, frequently does not lend itself to annexation. Much nearby territory is so thinly developed at the outset that it clearly is not fully urban but truly suburban, with emphasis on "sub." The metropolitan fringe needs more varied and intensive public services than the sparsely settled rural areas, but less than the range and level normally provided by a municipal government.

Yet annexation tends to be a matter of all or nothing. The annexed area receives all the city's services but it also must bear a full share of the cost of running the city. To many suburbanites the price is too high, especially since they may still benefit from many of the city's services—such as police and fire protection, traffic regulation, and street maintenance and lighting, as well as municipal parks, beaches, and museums—when they go to the city to work, shop, or visit. The trade-off is even less attractive if the county provides some of these services, at a lower level, perhaps, but also at a lower cost. Moreover, if the city, as is usually the case, has a higher proportion of relatively poor "high cost" residents than the outlying territory with the resulting extra drain on the tax base, the trade-off will have almost no appeal. These are among the strong forces impelling newly urbanized areas to choose the piecemeal special district approach rather than annexation to the metropolitan area's central city.

The resulting complex layered pattern of suburban government described in the foregoing pages is rarely stable. As thinly settled parts of the metropolitan fringe become more fully developed, their early minimum needs for urban-type services, perhaps involving only fire protection, expand to also include water supply, sewerage, and often other additional services. The upshot is a crazy quilt pattern of small, disjointed, uncoordinated, and unresponsive special purpose local governments.

GROWING METROPOLITAN DISPARITIES: ECONOMIC, SOCIAL, AND FISCAL

Increasing political fragmentation of metropolitan areas discussed above, both causes and results from an increasing gap between public service needs and public finance resources of the respective neighboring local governmental units. This gap causes those people able to move to flee the declining unit and form a new unit where better services can be provided with lower taxes. This migration causes a further splintering of the tax base, which results in even greater disparities, which causes even more frantic migration. . . . This is the seemingly hopeless treadmill on which many of the nation's metropolitan areas are racing.

The Early "Balanced City." Prior to the great post–World War II exodus of the middle and upper income families to suburbia, our system for governing urban America appeared to conform to Aristotle's view of the "most perfect" way to shield the community from the perils of political extremism.

In every city the people are divided into three sorts: the very rich, the very poor and those who are between them. . . . The most perfect political community must be amongst those who are in the middle rank, and those states are best instituted

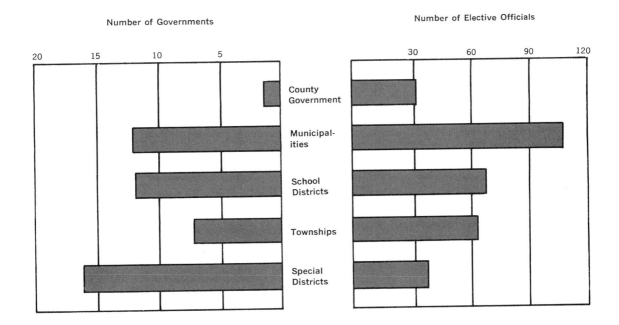

FIGURE 17-1. *Average number of local governments and elective officials per county in Standard Metropolitan Statistical Areas, 1967 (Averages exclude New England states where SMSA's are based on cities and towns rather than counties.)*

wherein these are a large and more respectable part, if possible, than both the other; or, if that cannot be, at least than either of them separate; so that being thrown into the balance it may prevent either scale from preponderating.[2]

Within the city's boundary were found the relatively few rich, the preponderate middle class, and the poor who often lived on "the other side of the tracks." The great cities of America, however, were more than social "melting pots." They were also balanced economically in the sense that they encompassed, within their boundaries, virtually all of the urban area's residential, commercial, and industrial development.

Because they possessed social and economic unity, municipalities were also generally characterized by fiscal balance. The municipality's "deficit" areas—the low-income residential areas—were offset by the "surplus" areas—the high tax producing districts associated with the central business area, the industrial section, and the high income residential neighborhoods.

By far the most important social function performed by the great "balanced" municipalities was political in the Aristotelian sense—that of keeping the public peace by moderating the competing demands of the various classes that comprise the urban body politic.

The Rise of the Lopsided Communities. In many of our metropolitan areas the twin forces of urban expansion and social segregation have combined to burst the shell of the old "balanced" community and in the process have profoundly altered the social and political character of the urban municipality. Whereas the old municipality was socially and economically balanced, the new municipalities are "lopsided," i.e., the wealthy estate and industrial enclaves and the upper, middle, and lower income bedroom communities. While the sprawling and subdivided metropolitan area still has a central or "core" city, typically it is becoming smaller, poorer, and blacker when compared to the burgeoning economy of white suburbia.

---

[2] Aristotle, POLITICS, Book IV, Chapter XI, pp. 126–27. Madison advanced essentially the same thesis in THE FEDERAL PAPERS, Number 10.

The political leadership of the old "balanced" municipality was under constant pressure to blur and moderate the conflicting demands of the urban rich, poor, and middle class. In contrast, the leaders of the new "lopsided" municipalities are virtually forced by their narrow-gauged constituencies to sharpen and reinforce the divisive elements within uptight urban society.

This political transformation becomes even more ominous because the highly decentralized system of government historically has relied almost entirely on the cohesive powers of the municipality to hold together the highly segregated components of urban population. Moreover, the nation has leaned heavily on the local tax base in general and the property tax in particular for financing its domestic needs. It is ironic that the political balkanization of urban areas occurs in the face of a growing need for social cohesion in an increasingly interdependent society.

The tendency for metropolitan areas to split politically along their income and racial seams is most apparent in the Northeast and Midwest, and least noticeable in the Southwest. More and more rare in the Northeast quadrant of the United States is the large city that still encompasses within its boundaries most of the residential areas occupied by the white middle class, let alone those of the wealthy. In striking contrast stand Houston, San Antonio, and Phoenix. Their vigorous annexation policies may be prompted by the spectacle of the older Eastern cities slowly being choked to death by the "white noose" of suburban municipalities.

Darkening Fiscal and Economic Outlook for Central Cities. A few successful annexations, however, cannot mask the grim fiscal prospects for most of the nation's great cities. The findings of recent studies of the Advisory Commission on Intergovernmental Relations clearly substantiate the widespread belief that most major cities are now in a desperate situation:

1. Regardless of the level of the analysis, national totals, or individual area, there is a growing concentration of the "high cost" citizen in the central city. There is every reason to believe this trend will continue. The concen-

tration of high cost citizens in the central city is dramatically underscored by public welfare statistics. For example, 27 percent of Maryland's population is located in Baltimore, yet 71 percent of Maryland's AFDC case load is to be found in that city. By the same token, Boston, with 14 percent of Massachusetts' population, accounts for 38 percent of that state's AFDC case load.

2. The paradox of the poverty in the midst of plenty emerges most strikingly in the central cities of the large metropolitan areas—and especially in the older central cities of the industrial Northeast and Midwest. The decline in absolute poverty and increase in absolute affluence is overshadowed by the economic disparities between the large central cities and their suburbs.

3. The large central cities are in the throes of a deepening fiscal crisis. On the one hand, they are confronted with the need to satisfy rapidly growing expenditure requirements triggered by the rising number of "high cost" citizens. On the other hand, their tax resources are growing at a decreasing rate (and in some cases actually declining), a reflection of the exodus of middle and high income families and business firms from the central city to the suburbs.

4. A clear disparity in tax burden is evident between the central-city and outside-central-city areas. Local taxes in the central cities of the 37 largest SMSA's in 1966–67 were 6.1 percent of the personal income of their residents; outside the central cities they equaled only 4.3 percent of income. Higher central city taxes are reinforcing the other factors that are pushing upper income families and business firms out of the central city into suburbia.

5. The central cities increased their relative tax effort during a period when their property tax base either showed a deceleration in the rate of growth, or an absolute decline. The observed changes reflected either increases in property tax rates, introduction of local non-property taxes (especially in the case of municipal governments), or, most generally, a combination of the two. The central city tax development contrasts sharply with trends on the outside where high income and a continua-

tion of the growth of the property tax base mitigated tax pressures.

6. On the educational or "developmental" front, the central cities are falling farther behind their suburban neighbors with each passing year. In 1957 the per pupil expenditures in the 37 metropolitan areas favored the central city slightly—$312 to $303 for the suburban jurisdictions. By 1965, the suburban jurisdictions had forged far ahead—$574 to $449 for the central cities. The gap was still widening at the start of the seventies. This growing disparity between the central city and suburban school districts takes on a more ominous character in light of the fact that the central city school districts must carry a disproportionately heavy share of the educational burden—the task of educating an increasing number of "high cost" underprivileged children. Children who need education the most are receiving the least!

7. To make matters worse, state aid to school districts actually aggravates this situation by favoring the rural and suburban districts.

8. On the municipal service or custodial front, the presence of "high cost" citizens, greater population density, and the need to service commuters force central cities to spend far more than most of their suburban neighbors for police and fire protection and sanitation services. The 37 largest cities had a non-educational (municipal) outlay of $230 per capita in 1967—nearly $100 greater than their suburban counterparts.

9. Of growing significance are the fiscal disparities among rich and poor suburban communities in many of the metropolitan areas—disparities that often are even more dramatic than those observed between central cities and suburbia in general. Many of the older suburban communities are taking on the physical, social, and economic characteristics of the central city. This type of community is especially vulnerable to fiscal distress because it lacks the diversified tax base that has enabled the central city to absorb some of the impact of extraordinary expenditure demands.

It is true, indeed, that America's great urban areas contain both most of the country's wealth and most of its social and economic problems. The 233 Standard Metropolitan Statistical Areas in the United States account for:

65 percent of the population;
At least three-quarters of federal personal income tax collections;
70 percent of taxable assessed valuation;
80 percent of bank checking accounts.

But also they account for:

Most of the nation's poverty;
Most of the nation's crime and delinquency;
Most of the nation's current dissatisfaction, disarray, and civil disorder.

One set of jurisdictions (usually the central city) has the problems and the other set of jurisdictions (usually the suburbs) has the resources. But it is impossible in most areas, due to state laws and political boundaries, to apply areawide resources to areawide problems.

The Advisory Commission on Intergovernmental Relations followed these frightening findings with the following call to action:

Regardless of actions taken by the public sector to control riots, regardless of actions taken by the private sector to protect or increase economic investment and opportunity and regardless of efforts by private and public enterprise together in combating poverty and disease among low income residents of central cities or depressed suburban areas, state, local and federal legislative action is necessary and urgent to bring fiscal needs and resources of our urban governments into better balance.[3]

Cracks in Suburbia's Picture Window. Comparing the fiscal behavior of the central city with the entire suburban area, however, tends both to obscure and to distort the disparity story because it lumps together diverse suburban jurisdictions. Anyone familiar with the fiscal landscape of suburbia is keenly aware of the fact that it does not present a uniform picture of affluence. On the contrary, suburbia fairly bristles with contrasts between rich, poor, and middle income jurisdictions.

In most metropolitan areas, the range be-

tween the most affluent and impoverished suburban jurisdiction is considerably greater than that between central city and suburbia in general. For example, elementary school districts in Cook County, Illinois, showed a range of about 30 to one in their property tax base per pupil in 1964 and various studies have reported ranges of 10 to one or more in the per capita tax base of municipalities within various metropolitan areas.

Because they lack a diversified tax base, most of the lower to middle income residential suburbs can also expect a steady deterioration in their fiscal prospects.

There is evidence which indicates that, as the suburban expansion grows, it is increasingly the lower middle class white collar worker and the blue collar worker who are fleeing the central city for suburbia, giving increasing rise to the demand for suburban development which caters to the economic capabilities of these groups. The composite of these trends seems to indicate that the newly developed suburban community of the future will be developed with tax bases which fail to provide adequate fiscal capacity for the support of municipal and educational services.

Much of the migration and consequent political and fiscal splintering now taking place in metropolitan America has social rather than fiscal or economic roots, and much of the social chasm that has developed over the last two decades is attributable to the controversies surrounding school segregation and integration. As higher income whites have left the center city the academic achievement of the city schools has declined commensurate with the increase of culturally disadvantaged pupils. Declines in achievement and increases in violence are today's bleak hallmarks of urban education.

PROLIFERATING GOVERNMENTAL PROGRAMS AIMED AT URBAN POPULATION

In 1960 federal grants-in-aid to state and local governments totaled about $6 billion, of which $5 billion was for highways and welfare. The decade of the sixties saw the burgeoning of the "urban crisis" and an unbelievable multiplication of federal, state, and local programs to

---

[3] Advisory Commission on Intergovernmental Relations, FISCAL BALANCE IN THE AMERICAN FEDERAL SYSTEM, Vol. 2 (Washington, D.C.: Government Printing Office, 1967), p. 7.

meet domestic problems and needs. By 1970 the number of federal programs had reached 430 with a total of $28 billion of grants included in President Nixon's budget for fiscal year 1971.

State aid to local governments has also expanded tremendously during the past two decades, growing from $3.3 billion in 1948 to $19 billion in 1967. These figures include federal funds going to local government *via* the state. In 1967 this was $4 billion, so a *net* of $15 billion was moving to local units from strictly state sources. This was a 75 percent increase over 1962, and it is likely that the 1970 *net total* will approximate $20 billion. Nearly three-fourths of current state aid goes for education and welfare. State aid for pollution abatement, mass transit, housing, and urban renewal is now rising quite rapidly but does not presently exceed $2 billion.

CONFLICTING PRESSURES FOR NEW URBAN ORGANIZATION

As population has overrun political boundaries in metropolitan areas, as service functions have become more technical and costly, and as the auto has made the metropolitan population more and more mobile, it has become increasingly apparent to many city administrators that interlocal cooperation must occur on a fairly broad scale if costs are to be kept under control. With respect to physical facilities especially, it has become evident that planning can no longer be carried on in isolation or on a unit-by-unit basis but must take into account what one's neighboring jurisdictions are doing and thinking. The regionalization of utility and mass transit functions is no longer the exception; it is becoming increasingly frequent in many metropolitan areas. This regionalization usually is accomplished through special purpose districts, but sometimes by city-county consolidation.

However, strong forces—social and political —are at work in the opposite direction:

As our cities have grown larger, and as governmental services have become increasingly professional and specialized, the psychological distance from the neighborhood to city hall has grown from blocks, to miles, to light-years. With decreasing

communication and sense of identification by the low-income resident with his government have come first apathy, then disaffection and now—insurrection.[4]

The problems of coping with urban life may be unmanageable for the migrant from a cotton farm, or Appalachia, or Puerto Rico, or for one who is native to a ghetto. He may need employment, or health services, or shoes for the children, or all of these and more. These and other services may well be available to him if he only knew where. Even if he is aware that a social service agency will help him or that there is some government office he can go to, he may not know which one to seek out. Or he may be told that he lives in the wrong area, or he doesn't meet the qualifications for help, or the agency he calls doesn't offer that service, and he gives up. These roadblocks, particularly to one who is unaccustomed to complicated urban life, may be overwhelming.

Thus, there is significant sentiment for the development of new forms of organization within the large cities that would somehow mitigate the barriers of distance, size, complexity, and impersonality that now stand tall before disadvantaged neighborhoods and their inarticulate, frustrated, and increasingly angry residents. These possibilities will be examined later in this chapter.

COORDINATION AMONG PROGRAMS, JURISDICTIONS, AND LEVELS OF GOVERNMENT

Surely an appraisal of the *totality* of the intergovernmental landscape makes obvious that urban governance will become impossible in the years ahead unless the most vigorous kind of action is taken by federal, state, and local governments alike to make the system administratively manageable. The vast proliferation of federal programs must be reduced drastically through grant consolidation; state governments need to modernize their own institutions and must take painful but necessary steps to civilize the jungle of local government boundaries in metropolitan areas, and, in the urban centers, political, civic, and professional

---

[4] National Commission on Urban Problems, BUILDING THE AMERICAN CITY (Washington, D.C.: Government Printing Office, 1968).

managerial leadership of the highest order must be brought to bear in coping with the hundreds of daily decisions that involve not only one's own jurisdiction but the interests of one's neighbors as well.

Intergovernmental Agencies

LOCAL AGENCIES

The role of the major intergovernmental agencies at the local level has already been described in earlier chapters of this book. They include: (1) special purpose metropolitan districts (e.g., Southern California Metropolitan Water District); (2) multipurpose metropolitan districts and authorities (e.g., Seattle metropolitan municipal corporation which is authorized to undertake multiple functions but only the sewage function has been undertaken to date); (3) metropolitan planning agencies, which in a number of areas are being replaced by (4) regional councils of governments.

STATE AGENCIES

Departments of Urban (or Local) Affairs. An indication of state government disinterest in the substance of urban and local government problems at the beginning of the decade just ended was the fact that, in 1960, only two states (New York and Alaska) were providing within their organizational structure for continuing attention and assistance to local governments regarding emerging urban problems.

However, during the sixties, at the behest of the Council of State Governments and the Advisory Commission on Intergovernmental Relations, and from growing initiative within the states themselves, half the states moved to establish an agency concerned principally with urban problems. Such state urban affairs agencies not only offer a central clearing house and a point of contact for local governments and their officials, they also provide research, coordination, and technical assistance. A few of these agencies have important planning responsibilities and administer urban renewal, redevelopment, housing, or urban poverty programs. In addition, they may influence local government structure through their research and advice on

annexation, charters, and fiscal arrangements, although as yet few of them have played a really significant role in stimulating basic restructuring. In the long run, however, through their broad knowledge of existing conditions and problems, their familiarity with applicable state laws, and their contacts with officialdom at both local and state levels, they may serve as catalysts for basis structural change.

Figures 17–2 and 17–3 summarize the activities of these offices and provide basic information concerning their organization in each state.

State and Local Boundary Adjustment Commissions. At various points in earlier portions of this book the problem of local government "fragmentation" in metropolitan areas

Function	No. of States Assigning Function to Office of Local Affairs
Advisory, coordinating, & technical assistance	
Fiscal advice	14
Municipal management	16
Engineering & public works	10
Legislative aspects of intrastate governmental relations	10
Research, statistics, & information collection	24
Personnel training	12
Assist in coordinating state activities affecting localities	23
Recommend programs & legislation	21
Interlocal cooperation	20
Boundary and fringe problems	6
Financial assistance	9
Supervise local finances	7
Planning functions	
Statewide planning	9
Local planning assistance	17
Coordination with regional planning	21
Coordination with statewide planning	15
Program responsibility	
Urban renewal & redevelopment	8
Poverty	11
Housing	10
Area redevelopment	10
Total number of states with offices	24

FIGURE 17-2. *Functions of state offices of local affairs, 1969 (Adapted from* ELEVENTH ANNUAL REPORT, *Advisory Commission on Intergovernmental Relations, January, 1970.)*

has been assessed with emphasis upon the inescapable role of the state in "civilizing the jungle" of local government. (A typical case of overincorporation of municipalities is shown in Figure 17–4.)

The principal administrative vehicle developed for the task of "civilization" has been the state boundary commission, with California and two or three other states choosing a local counterpart—the local agency formation commission—for the task of controlling new incorporations, annexations, and special district formation, and the even more difficult task of encouraging and promoting consolidation of fractionated local governmental units, particularly special districts.

As a minimum, boundary commissions should endeavor to assure that proposals for new incorporation or district formation are scrutinized closely from the standpoint of

their long-range and intergovernmental effects. Had there been effective review of this kind in the past, many of the crazy quilt governmental arrangements that clutter the urban scene today could have been avoided. In addition to this minimum review function, both the Committee for Economic Development (CED) and the Advisory Commission on Intergovernmental Relations (ACIR) have urged states to enact legislation designed to "phase out" units of local government not meeting state statutory standards of fiscal, structural, and political viability. This in effect would apply to units of general local government, the approach so successful over the years in achieving consolidation of school districts.[5]

Interstate Compact Agencies. More than a

[5] Committee for Economic Development, MODERNIZING LOCAL GOVERNMENT (New York: The Committee, 1966).

State	Name of Agency	Administrative Location	Year Established
Alaska	Local Affairs Agency	Office of Governor	1959
California	Intergovernmental Council on Urban Growth	Office of Governor	1963
Colorado	Division of Local Government	Executive department	1966
Connecticut	Department of Community Affairs	Independent department	1967
Florida	Department of Community Affairs	Independent department	1969
Iowa	Division of Municipal Affairs	Office of Governor	1969
Illinois	Office of Local Government	Office of Governor	1966
Massachusetts	Department of Community Affairs	Independent department	1968
Minnesota	Office of Local and Urban Affairs	State planning agency	1967
Missouri	Department of Community Affairs	Independent department	1967
Montana	Department of Planning and Economic Development	Independent department	1967
Nebraska	Division of State and Urban Affairs	Department of Economic Development	1967
New Jersey	Department of Community Affairs	Independent department	1966
New York	Office of Local Government	Within executive department	1959
North Carolina	Department of Local Affairs	Independent department	1969
Ohio	Department of Urban Affairs	Independent department	1967
Oregon	Social and Government Relations Division	Executive department	1969
Pennsylvania	Department of Community Affairs	Independent department	1966
Rhode Island	Department of Community Affairs	Within executive branch	1968
Tennessee	Office for Local Government	Office of Comptroller of Treasury	1963
Tennessee	Office of Urban Affairs	Office of Governor	1967
Vermont	Office of Local Affairs	Office of Governor	1967
Virginia	Division of State Planning & Community Affairs	Office of Governor	1968
Washington	Planning and Community Affairs Agency	Office of Governor	1967
Wisconsin	Department of Local Affairs and Development	Independent department	1967

FIGURE 17-3. *Information concerning state offices of local affairs, 1969 (Adapted from* ELEVENTH ANNUAL REPORT, *Advisory Commission on Intergovernmental Relations, January, 1970.)*

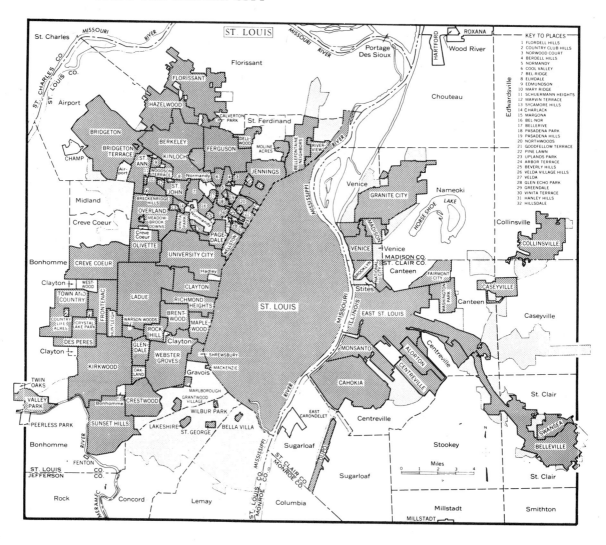

FIGURE 17-4. *The St. Louis urbanized areas as of 1960—one example of the "governmentally crowded" modern metropolis (An urbanized area with more than 100 municipalities [dark-shaded part] plus adjoining unicorporated territory [lighter-shaded] with at least 1,000 persons per square mile. The heart of a seven-county Standard Metropolitan Statistical Area, as defined in 1967, served by 474 local governments—232 in Missouri and 242 in Illinois.*

	Land area	1960 population
St. Louis City.............................	61	750,026
Urbanized area.............................	323	1,667,693
SMSA.............................	4,119	2,104,669

Source: URBAN AMERICAN AND THE FEDERAL SYSTEM, *Advisory Commission on Intergovernmental Relations, October, 1969.)*

quarter of the nation's population resides in interstate metropolitan areas. The problems cited with respect to the difficulty of matching political jurisdiction and responsibility with the needs, requirements, and financial resources for governmental services are compounded in the case of the interstate metropolitan areas. In these areas additional sets of state constitutional provisions, statutory requirements, and state administrative regulation and control are involved. To achieve simplification and restructuring of governmental services in these areas requires not only that the local governments of a particular state obtain a meeting of the minds and successfully fight for permissive legislation or friendly administrative action at the state capital. In addition, the local governments of the other state or states concerned must join in the combined local effort and pursue parallel paths and endeavor to obtain parallel success at their respective state capitals. If one group succeeds and the other fails, the obvious temptation of "going it alone" presents itself to the successful group.

Although the interstate compact device has been used with success in many areas of state government responsibility, its use in solving or ameliorating metropolitan area problems has been relatively limited. The most notable example of activity in this field is that of the Port of New York Authority, established by interstate compact in 1921. The Authority, created under a compact between New York and New Jersey, has carried on extensive operations in the New York metropolitan area (although opinion differs as to the wisdom or effectiveness of some of the Port Authority's operations with respect to the mass transportation problem in the metropolitan area). Except for a limited early use in the Kansas City region, compacts have been employed in only a few other major interstate metropolitan districts, such as with the creation in 1949 of the Bi-State Development Agency for the St. Louis area and the Pennsylvania–New Jersey establishment of the Philadelphia Port Authority and a broadened Delaware Bridge Commission in 1951. Establishment in the late 1960's of the Washington Metropolitan

Transit Authority by compact among the District of Columbia, Maryland, and Virginia marked the first use of an interstate agency to construct a mass transit system "from scratch."

It is very likely that due to the establishment of regional councils of governments or other metropolitan-wide bodies for purposes of grant review, planning and program coordination will result in increasing use of the interstate compact device to meet urban needs.

NATIONAL AGENCIES

Vice President's Office of Intergovernmental Relations.   In the very early days of his administration, President Nixon moved to consolidate functions of operational troubleshooting and political liaison with state and local governments that under the preceding administration had been split between the Director of Emergency Planning (liaison with state officials) and the Vice President (liaison with city and county officials). President Nixon, in Executive Order 11455 of February 14, 1969, assigned these functions to a new Office of Intergovernmental Relations under Vice President Agnew. The following functions were assigned to the new office:

(a) serve as the clearinghouse for the prompt handling and solution of federal-state-local problems brought to the attention of the President or Vice President by executive and legislative officers of state and local governments;

(b) identify and report to the Vice President on recurring intergovernmental problems of a federal interdepartmental and interprogram nature;

(c) explore and report to the Vice President on ways and means of strengthening the headquarters and interagency relationships of federal field offices as they relate to intergovernmental activities;

(d) maintain continuing liaison with intergovernmental units in federal departments and agencies and with the staff of the Council for Urban Affairs, and provide the staff of the Council with information and assistance regarding issues arising in federal-state-local relations; and

(e) review procedures utilized by federal executive agencies for affording state and local officials an opportunity to confer and comment on federal assistance programs and other intergovernmental issues, and propose methods of strengthening such procedures.

Intergovernmental Relations Subcommittees of the Congress. In the field of federal-state-local relations, responsibility in the United States Congress for consideration of legislation, exercise of legislative oversight over executive branch activities, and the conduct of inquiries and investigations is vested in the Government Operations Committees in the Senate and House. Each of these committees has an Intergovernmental Relations Subcommittee. The present Senate subcommittee was established in 1961; the House subcommittee was established in 1949.

The two subcommittees have devoted considerable effort to hearing proposed legislation dealing with federal-state-local relations and have each published valuable surveys and reports. The Intergovernmental Cooperation Act of 1968 was a legislative product of the Senate subcommittee. Legislative jurisdiction of the two subcommittees and their parent committees depends upon whether a proposed measure is not only primarily intergovernmental in its applicaton but also is governmentwide in character—that is, applying alike to all federal grant programs regardless of function.

Advisory Commission on Intergovernmental Relations. In response to numerous urgings, including the recommendations made by the First Hoover Commission and by the Kestnbaum Commission, the U.S. Congress, in 1959, created the Advisory Commission on Intergovernmental Relations as a permanent, bipartisan body of 26 members to give continuing study to the relationships among local, state, and national levels of government. The enabling legislation, as subsequently amended in 1966, now provides that the Commission will:

1. Bring together representatives of the federal, state, and local governments for consideration of common problems;

2. Provide a forum for discussion of the administration of federal grant programs;

3. Give critical attention to the conditions and controls involved in the administration of federal grant programs;

4. Make available technical assistance to the executive and legislative branches of the federal government in the review of proposed legislation to determine its overall effect on the federal system;

5. Encourage discussion and study at an early stage of emerging public problems that are likely to require intergovernmental cooperation;

6. Recommend, within the framework of the Constitution, the most desirable allocation of governmental functions, responsibilities, and revenues among the several levels of government; and

7. Recommend methods of coordinating and simplifying tax laws and administrative practices to achieve a more orderly and less competitive fiscal relationship between the levels of government and to reduce the burden of compliance for taxpayers.

The composition of the Commission is specified by the Act: three private citizens appointed by the President; three members of the U.S. Senate; three members of the U.S. House of Representatives; three officers of the executive branch of the national government; four governors; three state legislators; four mayors; and three county officials. The President designates the chairman and vice chairman of the Commission.

Of the 26 members of the Commission, nine represent the national government (six from the legislative, and three from the executive branch), 14 represent state and local government, and three the public at large. Consequently, although created by the Congress, the Commission from a practical point of view is not a federal agency in the usual sense of the word. Rather, it is a national body responsive to all three levels of government and to their executive and legislative branches.

Members of the Commission serve for a term of two years from the date of appointment and are eligible for reappointment. However, except for the three public members, any member ceasing to hold the official position from which appointed to the Commission ceases simultaneously to be a member of the Commission.

The Commission meets at the call of the chairman. To date it has met an average of four or five times a year.

The staff of the Commission is headed by an executive director, appointed by and serving at the pleasure of the Commission. The staff work of the Commission is organized into three major areas— (1) taxation and finance, (2) governmental structure and functions, and (3) program implementation.

Four organizations maintain particularly close ties with the Commission, both legally and substantively. These are the Council of State Governments, including the Governors' Conference; the National League of Cities; the National Association of Counties; and the United States Conference of Mayors. These organizations are charged under the Act with participating in the appointment of members of the Commission. Furthermore, the membership of these organizations is closely concerned with the work of the Commission, both in terms of bringing problems to the attention of the Commission and in acting upon the Commission's recommendations to state and local governments.

In selecting items for its work program, the Commission is guided by: (1) The relative importance and urgency of the problem; (2) its manageability from the standpoint of financial and staff resources available to the Commission; and (3) the extent to which the Commission can make a fruitful contribution toward solution of the problem.

A considerable share of the resources of the Commission are devoted to the promotion of legislative or administrative action to carry out the recommendations which it makes to the legislative and executive branches of the various levels of government. Specifically, when the Commission makes recommendations for legislative changes at the national level, it develops draft bills and amendments for consideration by the Congress. Congressional members of the Commission introduce these bills and amendments which are referred to appropriate committees in the normal course and considered along with other legislation before the Congress. The Commission transmits its recommendations for administrative changes at the national level to the President, his Executive Office, or heads of individual departments and agencies, as appropriate.

Legislative recommendations to the states are translated into draft bill form and appear in the Commission's *State Legislative Program,* which is published and distributed to governors, legislators, and other officials of the several states. The Commission makes every effort to encourage favorable consideration by the state legislative bodies. Recommendations for executive action by the states are channeled to the governors and other pertinent state executive officers.

Recommendations to local governments are channeled both directly and through the National League of Cities, the National Association of Counties, the U.S. Conference of Mayors, and other appropriate organizations.

The Commission explains and seeks formal support for its recommendations from the various organizations with which it cooperates. The Commission also works with the Council of State Governments, state leagues of municipalities, state associations of counties, citizen groups, business, professional and labor organizations, taxpayer leagues, bureaus of governmental research, and other public and private interest groups in behalf of legislation proposed, particularly at the state and local level.

Since its establishment the Commission has issued more than 30 policy reports and more than a score of other reports of an informational or technical character. The policy reports contain a total of 281 recommendations: 131 to the federal government and 150 to the states.

The Commission is financed from a variety of sources. Its fiscal year 1970 budget totals about $780,000, of which approximately $100,000 is nonfederal (foundation grants and voluntary contributions from state and local governments and miscellaneous nonprofit organizations). Over the 10-year period its professional staff has averaged 10 to 12 in number.

NATIONAL ORGANIZATIONS OF STATE
AND LOCAL GOVERNMENTS

Six organizations of state and local governments play a very important role in intergovernmental relations, especially regarding urban problems. They are: National Association of Counties; National League of Cities; U.S. Conference of Mayors; International City Management Association; National Governors' Conference; and the Council of State Governments. The executive directors of these organizations form a closely knit group that constitutes a board of directors for an intergovernmental policy center, a common staff group that acts in behalf of all in collecting and exchanging information of mutual value.

The six organizations listed exercise a great deal of influence with the federal executive agencies as regulations for the administration of grant in aid programs are formulated or revised. Except for ICMA (which has more of a professional and technical orientation) they likewise engage in extensive lobbying activity on Capitol Hill in the enactment or modification of federal aid programs or in the consideration of other legislation affecting the interests of state and local governments (e.g., tax bills dealing with exemption status of state and municipal bond interest).

The local government organizations listed represent units of *general* local government as does the National Association of Townships. Additionally, there are a score or more functionally oriented organizations in Washington, Chicago, and New York such as the American Public Welfare Association; National Institute of Municipal Law Officers; American Institute of Planners; American Society of Planning Officials; National Association of Housing and Redevelopment Officials; American Public Works Association; and American Water Works Association. These organizations likewise represent the interests of their respective clienteles in the framing and administration of federal programs.

LABOR, BUSINESS, AND CIVIC ORGANIZATIONS

Of increasing importance in intergovernmental relations affecting urban affairs are numerous nonprofit organizations and agencies. The Chamber of Commerce of the United States, in collaboration with state and city chambers, conducts a vigorous educational program addressed to the modernization of state and local government; the AFL-CIO has long been active at the national level in support of greater federal involvement in domestic affairs, especially through grant-in-aid programs; the National Urban Coalition

brings together city officials, civic, business, labor, and minority group leadership in behalf of higher domestic priorities for treatment of urban ills; the National Municipal League, the Committee for Economic Development, and the National League of Women Voters have long been active in encouraging state and local government modernization. Except for CED and the Municipal League, these organizations are headquartered in Washington. The Citizens Conference on State Legislatures, headquartered in Kansas City, spearheads a national movement for modernization and increased responsiveness of state legislatures, especially in their attention to urban problems.

The very powerful role of Ford, Carnegie, and some other private foundations in the field of intergovernmental relations should also be mentioned. Although somewhat interested in this field in the fifties and early sixties, this interest doubled and redoubled following the city riots of more recent years.

From the variety and power of the agencies mentioned in this section, one must conclude that intergovernmental relations has not only become a widespread and permeating concern of specialized agencies of local, state, and federal governments but also is of increasing interest to executives and legislators at all levels of government and to a huge array of quasigovernmental and nonprofit agencies and organizations. These groups together constitute a tremendous reservoir of information and possible technical or financial assistance to the beleaguered urban administrator endeavoring to operate in the incredibly complex maze of multitudinous programs and governmental jurisdictions.

Intergovernmental Programs

GRANT-IN-AID PROGRAMS

Federal. As mentioned earlier, federal grants-in-aid to state and local governments now total over $25 billion, scattered through 400-plus programs. Indeed, if one is meticulous in including subcategories of programs a count of several hundred more can be reached. Many of the newer grant programs contain characteristics rather disturbing to the urban administrator, although he always welcomes—and usually seeks—the financial help provided by the particular grant.

First, practically all of the new grant programs initiated in the sixties were functionally oriented, with power, money, and decisions flowing from program administrators in Washington to program specialists in regional offices to functional department heads in state and local governments—leaving Cabinet officers, governors, county commissioners, and mayors less and less informed as to what was actually taking place and making effective horizontal policy control and coordination increasingly difficult at all levels of government.

A majority of the new programs were in the form of "project" grants—an approach under which a state or local agency desirous of receiving federal assistance prepares an application, submits it to the nearest federal regional office, and hopes for the best. In contrast, under a "formula grant" approach, allotments of funds are made to governmental jurisdictions to cover a designated fiscal period for a designated purpose, with selections of individual projects left to the recipient governments, in the light of their own respective priorities.

Demonstrated mainly in the Economic Opportunity Act but present in other programs as well was a growth in "private federalism" —an increasing tendency to make federal assistance available to nongovernmental organizations. This seeming antipathy toward the state or local "establishment" was most marked in the human resources programs. Also, the Economic Opportunity Act heralded a new concept of local government— maximum feasible participation of the poor— in the framing and administration of service programs directed primarily to low income people. Even though grant funds were also made available to governmental bodies, requirements for advisory committees were designed to dilute somewhat the decision-making responsibilities of elected officials.

Finally, the new grant programs being directed to urban problems channeled funds directly to local governments without significant involvement of the governor or the state legislature. This has come to be known as "direct federalism." Twenty-three of the 38 grant programs that completely bypass the states were enacted after 1960. While "direct federalism" is deplored by governors and other state officials, most mayors and county commissioners and their professional administrative staffs usually prefer dealing directly with the federal funding agency rather than going through the state government.

One disadvantage—from an equity standpoint—of direct federal-local project grants is the necessity to date of extending the same fiscal matching requirements to rich and poor local governments alike. No adequate body of data exists currently upon which a system of differential matching can be based and even after such measures are developed, considerable time and effort will be required to gain sufficient political acquiescence to permit their use.

State Grants-in-Aid. As indicated earlier, state aid to local government is large—in fact nearly as large as federal—but its political impact is not so noticeable to most urban administrators because three-fourths of it is for welfare and education. However, state aid in many states today represents the "wave of the future" in terms of meeting some of the worst fiscal disparities among local governments within metropolitan areas. Increased pressure—both political and judicial—is being placed upon state governments to reverse policies and aid formulas that have the effect of providing affluent suburbs with more dollars of aid per capita than lower income core cities, despite the fact that for many aided services such as education and law enforcement a larger *number of dollars* per capita to poor areas is necessary to assure *equality* of treatment and opportunity for recipients of the service.

Also, states are finding it necessary, in order to wield substantial policy influence with regard to federal urban programs, to "buy into" these programs through an infusion of state funds—often picking up half of the nonfederal share. This kind of state involvement provides the urban administrator with additional program dollars but at the price of having a "third partner" in the particular program enterprise.

One of the most promising avenues of state financial relief to hard pressed urban areas is state assumption of substantially all financial responsibility for elementary and secondary education. This step is being considered seriously in Michigan, California, Maryland, and some other states; if taken it would relieve the local property tax of much of the school load and release it for use in meeting other pressing urban problems.

TECHNICAL ASSISTANCE

Technical assistance from one unit of government to another usually but not always flows from a higher governmental level to a lower or from a larger unit to a smaller unit. Thus, agencies of the federal government sometimes extend technical assistance to counterpart agencies of state or local governments, especially in connection with federal grant programs; state agencies provide a wide variety of technical assistance to local governments, particularly smaller units; and central cities, in metropolitan areas provide technical assistance to their smaller neighbors.

In these cases the assistance rendered may be with or without reimbursement. Title III of the Intergovernmental Cooperation Act of 1968 authorizes federal departments and agencies to provide technical assistance and services to state and local governments on a reimbursable basis (though not interfering with or limiting the provision of nonreimbursable assistance under existing or future specific statutory authorizations). Under this title, for example, training courses conducted by federal agencies for federal personnel may be opened up to state or local personnel, statistical tabulations may be furnished at cost, and a wide range of other federal services and facilities made available for state and local use.

Quite a sizable proportion of technical assistance provided by states to localities is partially supported by federal funds. Planning assistance by state planning agencies is supported by grants from the Department of Housing and Urban Development under Section 701 of the Housing Act. State technical assistance in the establishment and conduct of local poverty programs is supported by federal funds under the Economic Opportunity Act. However, a number of state technical assistance programs have been in existence for a long while which are not dependent in any substantial degree upon federal funding—these include assistance to local school districts by the state education agency; assistance to local road or street authorities by the state highway agency; and specialized assistance to local law enforcement agencies by the state police or highway patrol.

Interlocal technical assistance is often rendered pursuant to intergovernmental agreements described in an earlier chapter.

Intergovernmental Management

Intergovernmental management is the coordination of highly complex relationships to improve the capability of government to deliver services in a responsive and effective manner. This statement, of course, is a truism, but what is not often consciously realized is that intergovernmental management has existed as long as the nation; what is different today is its scope, intensity, and the fact that it is carried on at two levels: political and program. Few local governments have organized themselves to operate effectively within the management arena of intergovernmental relations.

THE POLITICAL LEVEL

Intergovernmental management is political because in its simplest form it is involved with the ebb and flow of power from one level of government to another (whether it be neighborhood unit to the city, or city to the region, etc.) to solve problems and at the same time balance competing value systems that exist within society. It is based on political questions of who controls what, for what.

An administrator should develop, therefore, an accepted set of policies that guide his city's intergovernmental relations. These policies must relate to the issues of power distribution: (1) regionalism, (2) the neighborhood, (3) the state's role, (4) federal control, and (5) the influence of the functional bureaucracy.

Regionalism. The issues outlined in the first section of this chapter have resulted in various proposals for restructuring—or at least formalizing—relationships. Local government officials will increasingly face questions of what is and what is not of regional concern. It is incumbent upon the city to define these concerns in order that it can more effectively participate intergovernmentally. An example will illustrate.

Housing is one fundamental urban problem. Is it intergovernmental? If so, to what extent—just in planning or in execution as well? If a balanced supply of housing is to be provided (i.e., low, medium, and high price) will it be necessary to have an area housing program? This question becomes even more complex when such factors as social aims of integration or mixing the poor and the affluent are considered. These are cutting-edge issues. A local government that has not thought about its policy may well find itself ignored when important housing decisions are made. Its own local housing policy can hardly be made in a vacuum—what is done by its neighbors will affect it.

As important will be decisions on how regional relations will be constructed. There are no easy answers, but up until recently the predominant answer, as indicated earlier in this chapter, has been the special district. But there are other viable alternatives discussed such as councils of governments. Cities need policies to determine such organizational arrangements.

The issue of regionalism involves, in many areas, more than metropolitan areas. For instance, the Virginia Metropolitan Areas Study Commission was created by the General Assembly to examine the state's urban issues. Its report stressed a direct relation between the state's urban and rural problems. The outcome was that in 1968 the Virginia legisla-

lature authorized local governments to organize planning district commissions which could later be converted into service district commissions. The legislation required the state Division of State Planning and Community Affairs to map the state into logical districts for areawide planning. Other states, such as Minnesota, Texas, and to some extent California, have taken similar action. The mapping of states into planning areas will become more predominant—largely because of a relatively new 1969 Bureau of the Budget regulation requiring that many federal grants be reviewed by state and "regional" clearinghouses as designated by the state.

The Neighborhood. The larger cities are facing demands for neighborhood control. This reverse pressure has largely grown out of a requirement in the Economic Opportunity Act (mentioned earlier) calling for "maximum feasible participation of the poor" in the formulation and conduct of local community action programs financed by the Office of Economic Opportunity. This requirement became one of the most controversial aspects of the "war on poverty" program because it was exercised with vigor by militant representatives of low income and minority groups and because it was resisted with equal vigor. This concept was carried forward into the model cities program, described elsewhere in this book. Despite the debate over participation and its problems, it is clear that participation is here to stay.

Some type of neighborhood organization, occasionally government-sponsored, is an increasingly common participant in programming services. The proposed charter for Los Angeles, California, would create neighborhood organizations, an elected neighborhood board, and an appointed "neighborman." The provision allows a community formally to establish itself as a neighborhood by election. Essentially enabling legislation, the proposed charter would authorize formation of neighborhood organizations according to specified criteria. Thus neighborhood organizations would be *available* for all parts of the city but would not necessarily be *created* in all parts of the city. The neighborhood board would act as an adviser to the city on all local matters and appoint the neighborman. The neighborman would be a full-time, salaried employee who serves as the principal liaison between the neighborhood and the city. The city would cover expenses of such an organization.

It might be argued that the strongest form of neighborhood organization is the small metropolitan incorporated city. In many ways such cities are neighborhoods within a larger community (not necessarily the whole metropolitan area). Of course such cities have powers of control, whereas the proposed Los Angeles neighborhood board is only advisory.

However, experience shows that neighborhood boards can, in effect, rule; San Mateo County has such an organization that was studied by the Los Angeles charter commission. The commission reported that the county board consistently has approved the neighborhood council's recommendations.

Neighborhood organizations, on a small scale, epitomize the question local officials must face—the distribution of power. While formal authority need not be delegated to such organizations, they do have a legitimate role to play in community affairs. The public official who dismisses the views of such groups invites serious problems. Neighborhood groups increasingly are viewed as legitimate vehicles by neighborhood residents for the expression of their opinion and for the exercise of their influence. Public officials need not be bound by such opinions or influence, but failure to give them serious consideration is to invite serious political difficulty.

The State's Role. One of the fundamental intergovernmental issues of the late 1960's and the 1970's is the state's role in solving urban problems. Cities and states have not generally cooperated. States have restricted the ability of cities to respond by rigidly controlling local government powers; in response, cities have fought for home rule, in some cases expanding their power. But effective state-local cooperation has been the exception, partly because states have not had what might be termed an urban policy.

In 1962 the U.S. Supreme Court ruled (in *Baker* v. *Carr*) that state legislatures must be apportioned so that representation was equal—i.e., one man, one vote. This changed the make up of state legislatures, and governors and legislators suddenly "discovered" the urban problem and the city. A number of states established state departments of community affairs and a few states (notably New York) developed specific grant-in-aid programs to supplement some of the federal programs.

As urbanism spread, state-local relations then became a major policy issue of the Republican party. States were to be strengthened. Federal aid programs (at least new ones) were not to bypass the state government but were at least to involve states in an advisory capacity. In many cases aid was to go through the state governments to the cities. And thus one of the most basic issues of our political system developed, where the large city mayor found himself in opposition to state governments concerning national policy. This condition may be temporary as state governments become more responsive to local governments and, just as important, as cities and states find that they must combine forces to obtain significant federal aid.

Closely related to the above issue is the fact that many local governments—especially those under 100,000 population—tend to look to the state, not the federal government, for assistance. This has put them in opposition to the larger cities of the state.

Take the above two conditions, and add the trend toward development of regional planning areas by the state, and intergovernmental management then becomes increasingly a matter of power distribution. The state's role will be prominent; cities would be advised to have well thought-out policies as they relate to the state and its growing urban involvement.

Federal Power. The federal government is involved with all levels of government; any thought that the federal influence over local government will not continue to grow fails to recognize that many so-called urban problems are not the problems of the city per se, but *national* problems of an urban society. This means that national policies will be developed that affect the delivery of services by the local government. The real issue is not the extent of federal involvement and direction, but how such involvement can provide for maximum innovation in carrying out federal policies.

From a local view, two issues need strong local policies. The first is revenue sharing. It will not supplant the categorical grant, but it will provide funds both to the states and to local governments that are "free," thus increasing local government's ability to innovate. However, many people are against revenue sharing because it does increase the effective power of local government. Local officials who ignore this basic issue, on the theory that they will not directly decide it, fail to understand their basic role in intergovernmental relations—the management of services within the ebb and flow of power from one level of government to another.

Another important issue is coordination among existing grant-in-aid programs. As indicated earlier, a number of extremely difficult problems have been created for the urban administrator through the proliferation of aid programs, each with functional lines running from city agencies to federal bureaus. Accompanying this tendency has been increasing difficulty in harnessing related programs when the federal funds derive from separate appropriations.

In recent years proposals have been advanced to authorize federal departments and agencies to pool funds from separate appropriations in order to fund an integrated undertaking proposed in a single application by a state or local government. In essence this legislation shifts the burden of surmounting a myriad of administrative and accounting obstacles from the applicant to the federal government. While this type of funding simplication is necessary, an additional and more basic step is needed—to consolidate many of the overly categorized grants into a smaller number of larger grants, thereby rendering the federal grant-in-aid system more usable by the local administrator and more governable by the Congress and the President.

Curbing the Functional Bureaucracy.

This is an issue that cuts across all levels of government, and may have in the end a profound effect on whether we can develop effective intergovernmental relations. Currently under way at all levels of government is growing recognition of the need to move away from functional and special-purpose governmental institutions toward stronger general-purpose government and toward greater reliance upon politically responsible executives and legislators.

This theme is characterized by recommendations for revenue sharing and grant consolidation at the federal level; shortening the ballot and strengthening the planning and budgeting processes at the state level; and curbing and consolidating special purpose districts and authorities at the local level. It also is marked by proposals for reorganization authority for the governor; for local planning staffs responsible directly to political governing bodies instead of independent commissions; and for channeling state aid funds in such a way as not to prop or perpetuate small special-purpose units of government.

Finally, the overall theme of stronger legislative bodies also is part of this confrontation with the functional administrators. The call for periodic Congressional review of grants-in-aid and increased capability of state legislatures in legislative overview and state planning, while directed primarily to other objectives, should help ensure that the role of functional specialists is discharged within a government-wide and agencywide context. Moreover, for states to develop their own course of action on urban problems, highly important, complex, and controversial legislation must be enacted and continually amended.

Yet relatively few legislatures are equipped constitutionally or administratively to do this, although progress in the past few years has been considerable. Proposals for change (from CED, Chamber of Commerce, ACIR, Citizens Conference on State Regulations) call for annual sessions, year-round professional staffing, and adequate compensation. Strong legislatures are an absolute prerequisite for strong state government and an effective curbing of program specialists.

All of these steps and more are necessary if the tasks of political leadership and public administration are to be kept manageable. Otherwise each functional category with its hordes of professionals at all governmental levels becomes, in effect, a government unto itself—a vertical, functional autocracy.

THE PROGRAM LEVEL

The political level of intergovernmental management is basically one of developing broad policies and attempting to implement them. The program level involves specific functional problems—i.e., providing a service. The program level involves the functional bureaucracy, hopefully under careful political and managerial supervision. It can involve all levels of government, but frequently involves relationships between local levels of governments such as the city and the county. There are a number of specific devices used to make local cooperation effective, four of which deserve brief mention.

1. The most popular is the contract. Two or more governments agree that one government will provide service to another under certain conditions set forth in a contract. Los Angeles County is famous for offering many services to cities on a contractual basis.

2. Reallocation of functions—particularly between the city and county—is another device. In essence, units of government will accept responsibility for one function for both units, while the other may well accept responsibility for another.

3. Cooperative hiring is still another method of cooperation. Two cities or a city and county will hire, for example, one health director. Although the individual may work for both units, obviously over a period of time the administration of the service involved is coordinated between the governments involved.

4. Informal cooperation involves committees, administrative agreements, and personal contracts. These techniques are classified as informal because legal authority and often formal legislative authority are not needed. For instance, a group of purchasing agents can form a committee to arrange for joint purchasing of common supplies. Agreements can often be worked out between administrative personnel; for instance, planning personnel may agree to review each other's subdivision plots that are on the periphery of each jurisdiction. Personal contacts, the most intangible of all methods, are important. If city officials know county officials, council of governments personnel, etc., cooperation is fostered.

ORGANIZING FOR INTERGOVERNMENTAL MANAGEMENT

Since intergovernmental management is political, it is the prime responsibility of the chief elected official and the chief appointed executive. This means that the functional bureaucracy should not act without first being sure that it is in harmony with the top political and managerial leadership. Program management decisions should be made in relationship to basic political policies.

Second, clear-cut responsibility for intergovernmental relations should be delineated. Generally the mayor will be the spokesman and the major policy leader. The chief appointed executive should have major responsibility for developing alternative strategies and for assuring that the objectives of these policies are met. It could be argued that the mayor is like the President of the United States in regard to his foreign policy responsibilities and the chief appointed executive is like the President's chief foreign policy advisor.

Third, it may be necessary to provide staff to ensure that the government can respond in an intergovernmental manner. Many cities and counties have employed federal aid coordinators as staff arms of the mayor or chief appointed executive. Their responsibilities are to know the federal bureaucracy as it relates to processing grants and to keep the local bureaucracy coordinated and in harmony. This type of staff person is highly valuable in a city that has a number of federal grants. As the complexity of intergovernmental relations grows, it may well be desirable to have a "secretary of state" who is concerned with the whole gamut of intergovernmental relations.

Since the cutting edge of intergovernmental relations involves political questions of who controls what for what, it is highly desirable for *each* local government to work as effectively as possible in the policy influencing area within the broader *community* of local governments. This means active participation in state leagues of municipalities and such organizations as the National League of Cities, U.S. Conference of Mayors, the National Association of Counties, and the International City Management Association. It further means participation in councils of governments and regional planning agencies. Local government must assume the responsibility of a much more active role in shaping all levels of governmental policy affecting each other. Finally, the functional bureaucracy of a city should be encouraged to better represent its local government's view to its state and national organizations.

In short, intergovernmental management must be organized so that major policy questions affecting a local government can be answered, and processes and staff must be related in order that the chief political official and the chief appointed executive can exercise effective leadership in the intergovernmental management area.

Conclusion

Opening sections of this book were necessarily concerned with the question, "What is the city?" That question is no longer simpleminded or easily answered. The city as a corporate entity now has little to do with the city socially and geographically. Recognition that the city in law and the city in fact are quite distinct has led many—experienced urban administrators among them—to call for the reorganization and consolidation of governmental units in urbanized areas. The basic concerns of the urban administrator are not only intergovernmental but transgovernmental since the forces which shape his community may lie in the region, nation, state-

house, or capitol. Yet wholesale reform seems a distant goal; the urban executive might therefore be reminded that management can mean to make do, for "satisficing" will be his central aim for the coming years.

Management in the modern city is thus far more complex than was management in yesterday's city. The modern city is increasingly only a part of a broader, ambiguous social framework. Social dynamism must be taken as a "given" in the new environment; community goals and even values are not and cannot be expected to be stable. Change, brought willy-nilly by events in the social, economic, and political environment, is the only equilibrium that the modern city can expect.

Those who seek to manage the city in this milieu must face two sets of dilemmas. One set stems from the governmental structure within which the modern city must be managed; the other is posed by the complexities and challenges of management to which this book has been addressed. Given the dimensions of their importance, each dilemma qualifies for a concluding comment.

THE BASIC DILEMMA OF URBAN GOVERNMENT STRUCTURE

At the very heart of the "urban crisis" is the fragmentation of local government structure and tax bases in metropolitan areas with the attendant and increasing fiscal, social, and economic disparities between "have" and "have not" units. The dimensions of this problem have been detailed earlier in this book, principally in Chapter 3 and in the earlier pages of this chapter. Today there is growing and urgent interest in exploring ways and means whereby this basic problem may be mitigated.

For a long while, metropolitan reorganization has been pronounced a dead issue by political commentators and quite a number of political scientists. Up until fairly recently these obituaries have been justified. Within recent years, however, there has been a resurgence of interest in metropolitan government and especially in city-county consolidation. Since 1962, 12 consolidation proposals have been submitted to local voters. Five were approved; seven others were rejected. Additionally, the Indianapolis–Marion County merger was mandated by the Indiana legislature. In a dozen or more additional metropolitan areas, city-county consolidation is under active consideration. Table 17–1 shows population and income characteristics of city-county consolidation proposals during the period 1962–1969.

Why this resurgence of interest in metropolitan government? One reason may be the growing complexity and frustration of governing badly fragmented areas. Another reason, unfortunately, is race. As suburbanites see the large inner city trending toward a Negro voting majority, and as business inter-

ests in the central city see growing economic decline, new forces for city-county consolidation are brought into being. Conversely, inner city blacks who have been suffering serious disadvantages—taxwise—in relation to affluent suburbs are not so sure that a merger with the lush tax bases just over the line is worth the price of diffused political power that would result. This is not to say that all or most of the recent consolidations were racially motivated.

What is the answer to this newest, further complication in the metropolitan picture? Obviously, consolidation should not be damned out of hand because one of the results may be diffusion of black political power. Neither should the new motivations

Table 17–1.

POPULATION AND INCOME CHARACTERISTICS OF AREAS INVOLVED IN CITY-COUNTY CONSOLIDATION, 1962–1969

Units involved	Population (1960)	% increase or decrease (1950–1960)	% nonwhite population (1960)	% 65 years of age and over (1960)	Median income (1960)	% under $3,000 annually (1960)	% over $10,000 annually (1960)
Successful Consolidations							
1. Nashville—	170,874	− 2.0	37.8	10.3	$3,816	37.9	5.7
Davidson County, Tenn.	399,743	24.2	19.1	7.9	5,332	23.5	13.1
2. South Norfolk—	22,035	111.2	26.3	5.8	4,914	25.4	6.4
Norfolk County, Va.	51,612	−48.7	26.2	4.4	5,599	20.0	13.5
3. Virginia Beach—	8,091	50.1	6.6	6.5	5,378	22.3	15.7
Princess Anne Co., Va.	77,127	80.1	16.6	3.4	5,517	22.2	15.4
4. Jacksonville—	455,411	− 1.7	41.1	9.1	4,433	30.9	9.1
Duval County, Fla.	697,567	49.8	23.2	6.2	5,340	22.4	12.4
5. Indianapolis—	476,258	11.5	20.6	6.5	6,106	15.6	16.2
Marion County, Indiana	697,567	26.4	14.3	8.5	6,609	12.8	20.2
6. Carson City—	5,163	67.5	4.5	8.3	7,003	10.9	24.9
Ormsby County, Nevada	8,063	93.3	15.7	6.6	6,983	11.9	23.8
Unsuccessful Consolidations							
1. Columbus—	116,779	46.7	26.7	5.6	4,267	31.0	8.6
Muscogee County, Ga.	158,623	34.4	23.9	4.7	4,492	27.7	8.3
2. Memphis—	497,524	25.6	37.0	7.8	4,915	27.0	11.2
Shelby County, Tenn.	627,019	30.0	36.3	7.3	4,903	27.5	11.1
3. St. Louis—	750,026	−12.5	28.6	14.8	5,355	21.7	10.8
St. Louis County, Mo.	703,532	73.1	2.7	7.0	7,527	7.2	26.7
4. Chattanooga—	130,009	− 0.8	33.2	9.2	4,438	31.5	9.5
Hamilton County, Tenn.	237,905	14.2	19.9	7.8	5,047	25.6	11.5
5. Tampa—	274,970	120.5	16.8	10.7	4,667	28.2	10.0
Hillsborough Co., Fla.	397,788	59.2	14.0	9.8	4,616	28.4	9.1
6. Athens—	31,355	11.3	29.1	7.7	4,467	29.6	9.4
Clarke County, Ga.	45,363	24.1	25.4	7.0	4,443	31.7	11.3
7. Brunswick—	21,703	20.9	41.1	6.9	4,250	33.7	8.2
Glynn County, Ga.	41,954	44.4	27.8	5.9	4,793	27.9	9.2

for reorganization be welcomed or exploited. Responsible leadership from all races and ethnic and economic groups must strive for an accommodation of fiscal and political interests which will produce a managerially and economically viable arrangement that is also politically equitable. One possible basis for such an accommodation might be the "two-tier" approach recommended by the Committee for Economic Development.[6] Under this structure, most of the existing units of government would be retained for the performance of strictly local functions while some of the more costly and complicated functions would be shifted to the county or other areawide government.

This examination of the intergovernmental scene should make it obvious that the urban administrator faces serious challenges from nearly every quarter. The dilemma of governmental reorganization, with fiscal, political, and racial cross-currents running ever more strongly, may prove to be the most difficult challenge of all for the administrator as well as for the elected political leadership; indeed, it may be the most crucial in the long run for all of urban America.

THE DILEMMAS OF MANAGEMENT

The impact of societal forces, the instability of community goals and values, the magnitude of the decisions which must be made, the need to provide human as well as housekeeping services, the growing activism of groups in the political process, the trend toward unionization among municipal employees, all of these circumstances place new demands upon the urban administrator and make his role more complex. The modern city can no longer be permitted to shape its own destiny only through reaction to social and economic forces; the consequences of ill-advised reaction have become too costly. Riots, tensions, traffic congestion, environmental pollution, housing deterioration, ju-

venile delinquency, neighborhood unrest, official insensitivity to human problems, poverty —these and similar products of social forces, compounded by poor governmental programming, must be obliterated if the modern city is to be a hospitable place for human habitation. In other words, governmental programming in the city must be more carefully and thoughtfully designed so that it can redress these problems and prevent similar ones from arising.

Such programming will demand decisions, good decisions made systematically after careful consideration of all important aspects of a problem. But decision making is not simply a matter of the administrator making up his mind. Organizational decisions are more complex; they involve inputs from many organizational subunits and are predicated upon a careful consideration of alternatives and their probable consequences.

Planning is also necessary to effective programming. The process of systematic foresight which has been applied for years to matters of land use has become a clear requirement in almost every phase of municipal operations. Today's sewer line installations shape tomorrow's development; today's recreation programs affect tomorrow's delinquency. Failure to anticipate the future consequences of today's actions threatens a wanton waste of scarce resources, adverse consequences from unexpected developments, and a distasteful if not unhealthy environment.

Planning and programming must both be based upon a masterful use of developing information technology: electronic data storage and analysis systems, combined with continuing collection and monitoring of basic social, economic, and demographic data, must be viewed as basic components in the attack on complex social problems.

Finally, the urban administrator must lead. Decisions and plans are not self-executing; conflicts do not necessarily resolve themselves in satisfactory ways. The administrator's influence is only as great as the confidence and enthusiasm he can create in others. Sophisticated leadership too is built on the develop-

---

[6] For a detailed description of the "two-tier" concept of metropolitan government, see Committee for Economic Development, RESHAPING GOVERNMENT IN METROPOLITAN AREAS (New York: The Committee, 1970).

ment and implementation of multifaceted strategies for alleviating existing problems, preventing unanticipated problems, and, most importantly, achieving identified community goals and objectives.

The existence of these challenges is clear; the strategies for meeting them are not. Unlike the urban administrator of the past who could increase municipal efficiency by applying specified procedures in such fields as budgeting, personnel management, and purchasing, the urban administrator of today must meet his challenges without precise manuals and their guidelines. Therein lies the fundamental dilemma of, and requisite of success for, *managing the modern city.*

Selected Bibliography

Part One: The City

1. The Developing City

2. The City: Forces of Change

3. The City and Change: Programming for Control

ADRIAN, CHARLES R. *Governing Urban America.* (New York: McGraw-Hill, 3rd ed., 1968) .

THE ADVISORY COMMISSION ON INTERGOVERNMENTAL RELATIONS. *Metropolitan America: Challenge to Federalism.* (Washington, D.C.: The Commission, 1966.)

———. *Metropolitan Social and Economic Disparities: Implications for Intergovernmental Relations in Central Cities and Suburbs.* (Washington, D.C.: The Commission, 1965.)

———. *Performance of Urban Functions: Local and Areawide.* (Washington, D.C.: The Commission, 1963.)

———. *Urban and Rural America: Policies for Future Growth.* (Washington, D.C.: The Commission, 1968.)

———. *Urban America and the Federal System.* (Washington, D.C.: The Commission, 1969.)

BERRY, BRIAN J. L., and JACK MELTZER. *Goals for Urban America.* (Englewood Cliffs, New Jersey: Prentice-Hall, 1967.)

BLOOMBERG, WARNER, JR., and HENRY J. SCHMANDT. *Power, Poverty, and Urban Policy*, Vol. 2, Urban Affairs Annual Reviews. (Beverly Hills, California: Sage Publications, 1968.)

BOLLENS, JOHN C., and HENRY J. SCHMANDT. *The Metropolis: Its People, Politics, and Economic Life.* (New York: Harper and Row, 2nd ed., 1969.)

CHURCHILL, HENRY S. *The City Is the People.* (Cornwall, New York: Cornwall Press, 1945.)

THE EDITORS OF FORTUNE. *The Exploding Metropolis.* (Garden City, New York: Doubleday Anchor Books, 1957.)

EWALD, WILLIAM R., JR. *Environment and Change.* (Bloomington, Indiana: Indiana University Press, 1968.)

———. *Environment and Policy.* (Bloomington, Indiana: Indiana University Press, 1968.)

GOODALL, LEONARD E. *The American Metropolis.* (Columbus, Ohio: Charles E. Merrill Publishing Company, 1968.)

GORDON, MITCHELL. *Sick Cities.* (New York: The Macmillan Company, 1963.)

GREER, SCOTT, ET AL. *The New Urbanization.* (New York: St. Martin's Press, 1968.)

HARRINGTON, MICHAEL. *The Other America.* (Baltimore: Penguin Books, 1963.)

HAUSER, PHILIP M., and LEO F. SCHNORE. *The Study of Urbanization.* (New York: John Wiley and Sons, 1967.)

LOWE, JEANNE R. *Cities in a Race with Time.* (New York: Random House, 1967.)

MARTIN, ROSCOE C. *The Cities and the Federal System.* (New York: Atherton Press, 1965.)

———. *Grass Roots.* (New York: Harper and Row, 2nd ed., 1964.)

NATIONAL ADVISORY COMMISSION ON CIVIL DISORDERS. *Report.* (New York: Bantam Books, 1968.)

SCHNORE, LEO F., and HENRY FAGIN. *Urban Research and Policy Planning*, Vol. I, Urban Affairs Annual Reviews. (Beverly Hills, California: Sage Publications, 1967.)

WILLBERN, YORK. *The Withering Away of the City.* (University, Alabama: University of Alabama Press, 1964.)

WINGO, LOWDEN, JR. *Cities and Space: The Future Uses of Urban Land.* (Baltimore: The Johns Hopkins Press, 1963.)

Part Two: The City Administrator

4. The Environment and Role of the Administrator

5. Leadership Styles and Strategies

6. Making Decisions

ABBOT, FRANK C. "The Cambridge City Manager," in Harold Stein (ed.), *Public Administration and Policy Development: A Case Book.* (New York: Harcourt, Brace, 1952.) Pp. 573–620.

ADRIAN, CHARLES R. "A Study of Three Communities," *Public Administration Review*, 18 (Summer, 1968) , pp. 208–13.

ALBERS, HENRY H. *Principles of Organization and Management.* (New York: John Wiley and Sons, 1961.)

APPLEWHITE, PHILIP B. *Organizational Behavior.* (Englewood Cliffs, New Jersey: Prentice-Hall, 1965.)

ARGYRIS, CHRIS. *Personality and Organization.* (New York: American Management Association, 1966.)

BASSETT, GLENN A. *Management Styles in Transition.* (New York: Harper and Row, 1967.)

BLUM, MILTON L., and JAMES C. NAYLOR. *Industrial Psychology: Its Theoretical and Social Foundations.* (New York: Harper and Row, 1968.)

BOLLENS, JOHN C. *Appointed Executive Local Government: The California Experience.* (Los Angeles: Haynes Foundation, 1952.)

BOSWORTH, KARL A. "The Manager Is a Politican," *Public Administration Review*, 18 (Summer, 1958), pp. 216–22.

BOYD, BRADFORD B. *Management-Minded Supervision*. (New York: McGraw-Hill, 1968.)

BROWN, RAY E. *Judgement in Administration*. (New York: McGraw-Hill, 1968.)

BUECHNER, JOHN C. *Differences in Role Perceptions in Colorado Council-Manager Cities*. (Boulder: University of Colorado, Bureau of Governmental Research and Service, 1965.)

CARRELL, JEPTHA J. "The City Manager and His Council: Sources of Conflicts," *Public Administration Review*, 22 (December, 1962), pp. 203–208.

———. "The Role of the City Manager: A Survey Report," *Public Management*, 44 (April, 1962), pp. 74–78.

———. *The Role of the City Manager: Views of Councilmen and Managers*. (Kansas City, Missouri: Community Studies Incorporated, 1962.)

COOPER, JOSEPH D. *The Art of Decision-Making*. (Garden City, New York: Doubleday, 1961.)

DRUCKER, PETER F. *The Effective Executive*. (New York: Harper and Row, 1966.)

FLIPPO, EDWIN B. *Management: A Behavioral Approach*. (Boston: Allyn and Bacon, 1966.)

HARRELL, C. A., and WEIFORD, DOUGLAS G. "The City Manager and the Policy Process," *Public Administration Review*, 19 (Spring, 1959), pp. 101–107.

KAMMERER, GLADYS M. "Role Diversity of City Managers," *Administrative Science Quarterly*, 8 (March, 1964), pp. 421–42.

KAMMERER, GLADYS M., CHARLES FARRIS, JOHN M. DeGROVE, and ALFRED B. CLUBOK. *City Managers in Politics: An Analysis of Manager Tenure and Termination*. (Gainsville: University of Florida, 1962.)

KATZ, DANIEL, and ROBERT L. KAHN. *The Social Psychology of Organizations*. (New York: John Wiley and Sons, 1966.)

KNUDSON, HARRY R., JR. *Human Elements of Administration*. (New York: Holt, Rinehart and Winston, 1963.)

KWEDER, B. JAMES. *The Role of the Manager, Mayor, and Councilman in Policy Making: A Study of Twenty-one North Carolina Cities*. (Chapel Hill: University of North Carolina, Institute of Government, 1965.)

LOCKARD, DUANE. "The City Manager, Administrative Theory and Political Power," *Political Science Quarterly*, 77 (June, 1962), pp. 224–36.

MILLER, DAVID W., and MARTIN K. STARR. *The Structure of Human Decision*. (Englewood Cliffs, New Jersey: Prentice-Hall, 1967.)

MILLS, WARNER E., JR., and HARRY Q. DAVIS. *Small City Government*. (New York: Random House, 1962.)

MOSHER, FREDERICK C., ET AL. *City Manager*

Government in Seven Cities. (Chicago: Public Administration Service, 1940.)

NEWMAN, WILLIAM H., CHARLES E. SUMMER, and KIRBY E. WARREN. *The Process of Management: Concepts, Behavior and Practice*. (Englewood Cliffs, New Jersey: Prentice-Hall, 1967.)

PFIFFNER, JOHN M., and FRANK P. SHERWOOD. *Administrative Organization*. (Englewood Cliffs, New Jersey: Prentice-Hall, 1960.)

RIDLEY, CLARENCE E. *The Role of the City Manager in Policy Formulation*. (Chicago: International City Managers' Association, 1958.)

SELZNICK, PHILIP. *Leadership in Administration: A Sociological Interpretation*. (Evanston: Row, Peterson, 1957.)

SHERMAN, HARVEY. *It All Depends*. (University: University of Alabama Press, 1966.)

SHERWOOD, FRANK P. *A City Manager Tries To Fire His Police Chief*, Inter-University Case Program No. 76. (University: University of Alabama Press, 1963.)

SIMON, HERBERT. *Administrative Behavior*. (New York: The Macmillan Company, 2nd ed. 1961.)

SORENSEN, THEODORE E. *Decision Making in the White House: The Olive Branch and the Arrow*. (New York: Columbia University Press, 1963.)

STENE, EDWIN O. *The City Manager: Professional Training and Tenure*. (Lawrence: University of Kansas Governmental Research Center, 1966.)

STONE, HAROLD A., DON K. PRICE, and KATHRYN H. STONE. *City Manager Government in the United States*. (Chicago: Public Administration Service, 1940.)

TEAD, ORDWAY. *The Art of Leadership*. (New York: McGraw-Hill, 1935.)

WILSON, JAMES. "Manager Under Fire," in Richard T. Frost, ed., *Cases in State and Local Government*. (Englewood Cliffs, New Jersey: Prentice-Hall, 1961.)

WILSON, JAMES, and ROBERT W. CROW. *Managers in Maine*. (Brunswick, Maine: Bureau for Research in Municipal Government, Bowdoin College, 1962.)

Part Three: The Organization

7. Organizing America's Cities

8. Administrative Communication

ALBERS, HENRY HERMAN. *Organized Executive Action: Decision Making, Communication and Leadership*. (New York: John Wiley and Sons, 1961.)

AMERICAN MANAGEMENT ASSOCIATION. *Effective Communication on the Job*. (New York: The Association, 1963.)

ARGYRIS, CHRIS. *Integrating the Individual and the Organization*. (New York: John Wiley and Sons, 1964.)

————. *Organization and Innovation.* (Homewood, Illinois: Richard D. Irwin, 1965.)

BARNARD, CHESTER I. *The Functions of the Executive.* (Cambridge, Massachusetts: Harvard University Press, 1948.)

BATTEN, J. D., and J. V. McMAHON. "Communications Which Communicate," *Personnel Journal* (July–August, 1966), pp. 424–26.

BENNIS, WARREN G. *Changing Organizations.* (New York: McGraw-Hill, 1966.)

BLAU, PETER M., and RICHARD W. SCOTT. *Formal Organizations.* (San Francisco: Chandler Publishing Co., 1964.)

BORMAN, ERNEST G., ET AL. *Interpersonal Communication in the Modern Organization.* (Englewood Cliffs, New Jersey: Prentice-Hall, 1969.)

CHEERY, COLIN. *On Human Communication.* (Cambridge, Massachusetts: The M.I.T. Press, 1966.)

"Communication in Behavior and Behavioral Science." *American Behavioral Scientist,* 10 (April, 1967), entire issue.

DALE, ERNEST. *Management: Theory and Practice.* (New York: McGraw-Hill, 1965.)

DALTON, MELVILLE. *Men Who Manage.* (New York: John Wiley and Sons, 1959.)

DORSEY, JOHN T., JR. "A Communication Model for Administration," *Administrative Science Quarterly* (December, 1957), pp. 307–24.

ETZIONI, AMITAI. *Modern Organizations.* (Englewood Cliffs, New Jersey: Prentice-Hall, 1964.)

GELLERMAN, SAUL W. *The Management of Human Relations.* (New York: Holt, Rinehart and Winston, 1966.)

GOULDNER, ALVIN W. "Cosmopoliticians and Locals: Toward an Analysis of Latent Social Roles —I and II," *Administrative Science Quarterly,* 2 (December, 1957), pp. 281–306. 1 (March, 1958), pp. 444–80.

HALL, EDWARD T. *The Silent Language.* (Greenwich, Connecticut: Fawcett Publications, 1959.)

LEAVITT, HAROLD J. *Managerial Psychology: An Introduction to Individuals, Pairs and Groups in Organization.* (Chicago: University of Chicago Press, 2nd ed., 1964.)

LIKERT, RENSIS. *The Human Organization: Its Management and Values.* (New York: McGraw-Hill, 1967.)

————. *New Patterns of Management.* (New York: McGraw-Hill, 1961.)

McGREGOR, DOUGLAS. *The Human Side of Enterprise.* (New York: McGraw-Hill, 1969.)

PRESTHUS, ROBERT. *The Organization Society.* (New York: Alfred A. Knopf, 1962.)

REDFIELD, CHARLES E. *Communication in Management.* (Chicago: The University of Chicago Press, 1958.)

SAYLES, LEONARD R. *Managerial Behavior.* (New York: McGraw-Hill, 1964.)

SAYLES, LEONARD R., and GEORGE STRAUSS. *Human Behavior in Organizations.* (Englewood Cliffs, New Jersey: Prentice-Hall, 1966.)

SCHOLZ, WILLIAM. *Communications in the Business Organization.* (Englewood Cliffs, New Jersey: Prentice-Hall, 1962.)

SCHEIN, EDGAR H. *Organizational Psychology.* (Englewood Cliffs, New Jersey: Prentice-Hall, 1965.)

SHANNON, CLAUDE E., and WARREN WEAVER. *The Mathematical Theory of Communication.* (Champaign: University of Illinois Press, 1949.)

SIMON, HERBERT A. *The New Science of Management Decision.* (New York: Harper and Row, 1960.)

SYBOLD, GENEVA. *Employee Communication: Policy and Tools.* (New York: National Industrial Conference Board, 1966.)

Part Four: Managing the Organization

9. Tools of Modern Management

10. Administrative Planning

11. Administrative Analysis

AEKOFF, RUSSELL L., and PATRICK RIVETT. *A Manager's Guide to Operations Research.* (New York: John Wiley and Sons, 1963.)

AMERICAN SOCIETY OF PLANNING OFFICIALS. *Threshold of Planning Information System.* (Chicago: The Society, 1967.)

ARCHIBALD, RUSSELL D., and RICHARD L. VILLORIA. *Network-Based Management Systems.* (New York: John Wiley and Sons, 1967.)

LeBRETON, P. P., and D. A. HENNING. *Planning Theory.* (Englewood Cliffs, New Jersey: Prentice-Hall, 1961.)

GREGORY, ROBERT H., and RICHARD L. VanHORN. *Automatic Data Processing Systems.* (Belmont, California: Wadsworth Publishing Company, 2nd ed., 1964.)

HARE, VanCOURT, JR. *Systems Analysis: A Diagnostic Approach.* (New York: Harcourt Brace, 1967.)

HATRY, HARRY P., and JOHN F. COTTON. *Program Planning for State, County, City.* (Washington, D.C.: State-Local Finances Project of George Washington University, 1967.)

HEARLE, EDWARD F. R., and RAYMOND J. MASON. *A Data Processing System for State and Local Governments.* (Englewood Cliffs, New Jersey: Prentice-Hall, 1963.)

HEIKOFF, JOSEPH M. *Planning and Budgeting in Municipal Management.* (Chicago: The International City Managers' Association, 1965.)

HIGGINSON, VALLIANT M. *Managing with EDP,* AMA Research Study 71. (New York: American Management Association, 1965.)

THE INTERNATIONAL CITY MANAGERS' ASSOCIATION. *Performance Reports for the Chief Administrator.* (Chicago: The Association, 1963.)

————. *Program Development and Administration.* (Chicago: The Association, 1965.)

LAZZARO, VICTOR, ed. *Systems and Procedures: A Handbook for Business and Industry.* (Englewood Cliffs, New Jersey: Prentice-Hall, 1959.)

LEHRER, ROBERT N. *Work Simplification.* (Englewood Cliffs, New Jersey: Prentice-Hall, 1957.)

LINDBLUM, CHARLES E. "The Science of Muddling Through," *Public Administration Review* (Spring, 1959), pp. 70–88.

MANAGEMENT INFORMATION SERVICE. *Developing a City-Sponsored Municipal Research Program,* Report No. 247. (Chicago: The International City Managers' Association, 1964.)

————, Report No. 225. *How To Conduct an Organization and Methods Study.* (Chicago, The International City Managers' Association, 1962.)

McKEAN, ROLAND N. *Efficiency in Government Through System Analysis.* (New York: John Wiley and Sons, 1958.)

OFFICE OF RECORDS MANAGEMENT, U.S. GENERAL SERVICES ADMINISTRATION. *Source Data Automation,* FPMR 11.5. (Washington, D.C.: National Archives and Records Service, 1965.)

OPTNER, STANFORD L. *System Analysis for Business Management.* (Englewood Cliffs, New Jersey: Prentice-Hall, 1960.)

PFIFFNER, JOHN M., and OWEN S. LANE. *A Manual for Administrative Analysis.* (Dubuque, Iowa: William C. Brown Co., 1951.)

PUBLIC AUTOMATION SYSTEMS SERVICE. *Automated Data Processing in Municipal Government.* (Chicago: Public Administration Service, 1966.)

REINER, JANET S., EVERETT REIMER, and THOMAS A. REINER. "Client Analysis and the Planning of Public Programs," *Journal of the American Institute of Planners* (November, 1963), pp. 270–82.

RONAYNE, MAURICE F. "Operations Research Can Help Public Administrators in Decision-Making," *International Review of Administrative Services,* 3 (1963), pp. 227–34.

SIMON, HERBERT A. *The New Science of Management Decision.* (New York: Harper and Brothers, 1960.)

SIPPL, CHARLES J. *Computer Dictionary and Handbook.* (Indianapolis: Howard D. Sams and Company, 1966.)

SISSON, ROGER L. and RICHARD G. CANNING. *A Manager's Guide to Computer Processing.* (New York: John Wiley and Sons, 1967.)

Part Five: Administrative Functions

12. City Planning

ALONSO, WILLIAM. *Location and Land Use: Toward a General Theory of Land Rent.* (Cambridge, Massachusetts: Harvard University Press, 1964.)

ALTSCHULER, ALAN. *The City Planning Process: A Political Analysis.* (Ithaca: Cornell University Press, 1965.)

AMERICAN SOCIETY OF PLANNING OFFICIALS. *Planning.* (Chicago: American Society of Planning Officials, annual.)

CHAPIN, F. STUART, JR. *Urban Land Use Planning.* (Urbana: University of Illinois Press, 2nd ed., 1965.)

GOODMAN, WILLIAM I., and ERIC C. FREUND, eds. *Principles and Practice of Urban Planning.* (Washington, D.C.: International City Managers' Association, 1968.)

GOTTMANN, JEAN. *Megalopolis: The Urbanized Northeastern Seaboard of the United States.* (New York: The Twentieth Century Fund, 1961.)

HOOVER, EDGAR, and RAYMOND VERNON. *Anatomy of a Metropolis.* (Cambridge, Massachusetts: Harvard University Press, 1959.)

KENT, T. J., JR. *The Urban General Plan.* (San Francisco: Chandler Publishing Company, 1964.)

MURPHY, RAYMOND E. *The American City: An Urban Geography.* (New York: McGraw-Hill, 1966.)

REPS, JOHN W. *The Making of Urban America: A History of City Planning in the United States.* (Princeton: Princeton University Press, 1965.)

WALKER, ROBERT A. *The Planning Function in Urban Government.* (Chicago: University of Chicago Press, 2nd ed., 1950.)

13. Personnel Administration

BEACH, DALE S. *Personnel: The Management of People.* (New York: Macmillan, 1965.)

INTERNATIONAL CITY MANAGERS' ASSOCIATION. *Municipal Personnel Administration* (Chicago: The Association, 6th ed., 1960.)

LOPEZ, FELIX M. *Personnel Interviewing: Theory and Practice.* (New York: McGraw-Hill, 1965.)

McGREGOR, DOUGLAS. *The Human Side of Enterprise.* (New York: McGraw-Hill, 1960.)

MUNICIPAL MANPOWER COMMISSION. *Governmental Manpower for Tomorrow's Cities.* (New York: McGraw-Hill, 1962.)

NIGRO, FELIX. *Public Personnel Administration.* (New York: Holt, Rhinehart and Winston, 1959.)

PIGORS, PAUL, and CHARLES A. MEYERS. *Personnel Administration: A Point of View and a Method.* (New York: McGraw-Hill, 4th ed., 1961.)

PUBLIC PERSONNEL ASSOCIATION. *Position Classification in the Public Service.* (Chicago: The Association, 1941, reprinted 1965.)

SCOTT, WALTER D., ROBERT C. CLOTHIER, and WILLIAM R. SPRIEGEL. *Personnel Management.* (New York: McGraw-Hill, 6th ed., 1961.)

STAHL, O. GLENN. *Public Personnel Administration.* (New York: Harper and Row, 5th ed., 1962.)

STRAUSS, GEORGE, and LEONARD R. SAYLES. *Personnel: The Human Problems of Management.* (Englewood Cliffs, New Jersey: Prentice-Hall, 1960.)

WARNER, KENNETH O. *Developments in Employee Relations*. (Chicago: Public Personnel Association, 1965.)

———, ed. *Management Relations with Organized Public Employees*. (Chicago: Public Personnel Association, 1963.)

WARNER, KENNETH O., and J. J. DONOVAN, eds. *Public Pay Administration*, Vols 1 and 2. (Chicago: Public Personnel Association, 1963 and 1965.)

14. Financial Administration

ADVISORY COMMISSION ON INTERGOVERNMENTAL RELATIONS. All Commission published reports since January, 1961, are relevant for administrators concerned with financial administration.

BURKHEAD, JESSE. *Government Budgeting*. (New York: John Wiley and Sons, 1956.)

ECKSTEIN, OTTO. *Public Finance*. (Englewood Cliffs, New Jersey: Prentice-Hall, 1964.)

GROVES, HAROLD M. *Financing Government*. (New York: Holt, Rhinehart and Winston, 1964.)

LINDBLUM, CHARLES E. "Decision Making in Taxation and Expenditures," in *Public Finance: Needs, Sources, and Utilization*. (Princeton: Princeton University Press, 1961), pp. 295–329.

———. *The Intelligence of Democracy*. (New York: The Free Press, 1965.)

NOVICK, DAVID, ed. *Program Budgeting*. (Cambridge, Massachusetts: Harvard University Press, 1965.)

SCHICK, ALLEN, AARON WILDAVSKY, ET AL. "Planning–Programming–Budgeting Symposium," *Public Administration Review* (December, 1966), pp. 243–58.

U.S. BUREAU OF THE CENSUS. Recurrent reports on governmental finances and employment. (Washington: Government Printing Office.)

WILDAVSKY, AARON B. *The Politics of the Budgetary Process*. (Boston: Little, Brown and Company, 1964.)

15. Public Relations

ANDERSON, DESMOND L., ed. *Municipal Public Relations*. (Chicago: International City Managers' Association, 1966.)

ARONFREED, EVA. "Public Relations as a Function of Local Government in the United States," in International Union of Local Authorities, *Local Government in the United States of America*. (The Hague: Martinus Nijhoff, for the Union, 1961.) pp. 71–90.

BACKSTROM, CHARLES H., and GERALD D. HURSH. *Survey Research*. (Evanston: Northwestern University Press, 1963.)

BERELSON, BERNARD, and MORRIS JANOWITZ, eds. *Reader in Public Opinion and Communication*. (New York: Free Press, rev. ed., 1966.)

BURTON, PAUL. *Corporate Public Relations*. (New York: Reinhold Publishing Corporation, 1966.)

CROSBY, ALEXANDER L. *Pamphlets—How To Write and Print Them*. (New York: National Public Relations Council for Health and Welfare Services.)

CUTLIP, SCOTT M. *A Public Relations Bibliography*. (Madison, Wisconsin: University of Wisconsin Press, 2nd ed., 1965.)

HOLCOMB, RICHARD L. *The Police and the Public*. (Springfield, Illinois: Charles C Thomas, 6th printing, 1964.)

MACDONALD, JAMES C. *Press Relations for Local Officials*. (Ann Arbor: Institute of Public Administration, University of Michigan, 1950.)

ROSENAU, JAMES N. *Public Opinion and Foreign Policy*. (New York: Random House, 1961.)

WALL, NED L. *Municipal Reporting to the Public*. (Chicago: International City Managers' Association, 1963.)

16. Legal Services and Regulatory Procedures

McQuillin's The Law of Municipal Corporations. 20 vols. (Chicago: Callaghan and Company, 3rd ed., 1949–51.)

RHYNE, CHARLES S. *Municipal Law*. (Washington, D.C.: National Institute of Municipal Law Officers, 1957.)

———. *Codification of Municipal Ordinances*. (Washington, D.C.: National Institute of Law Officers, 1961.)

SENATE FACT-FINDING COMMITTEE ON JUDICIARY. *Governmental Fact Liability*. (Sacramento: California Legislature, 1963.)

NATIONAL INSTITUTE OF MUNICIPAL LAW OFFICERS. *NIMLO Model Ordinance Service*. (Washington, D.C.: The Institute.)

NATIONAL SAFETY COUNCIL. *A Program Guide to Public Employee Safety*. (Chicago: The Council, 1966.)

17. Intergovernmental Relations

ADVISORY COMMISSION ON INTERGOVERNMENTAL RELATIONS. *Fiscal Balance in the American Federal System*. (Washington: The Commission, 1967.)

———. *A Handbook for Inter-Local Agreements and Contracts*. (Washington, D.C.: The Commission, 1967.)

———. *Metropolitan America: Challenge to Federalism*. (Washington, D.C.: The Commission, 1967.)

———. *Metropolitan Social and Economic Disparities: Implications for Intergovernmental Relations in Central Cities and Suburbs*. (Washington, D.C.: The Commission, 1965.)

———. *Urban American and The Federal System*. (Washington, D.C.: The Commission, 1969.)

ANDERSON, WILLIAM. *Intergovernmental Relations in Review*. (Minneapolis: University of Minnesota Press, 1960.)

BREAK, GEORGE. *Intergovernmental Fiscal Relations in the U.S.* (Washington, D.C.: The Brookings Institution, 1966.)

CAMPBELL, ALAN K., ed. *The States and the Urban Crisis.* (Englewood Cliffs, New Jersey: Prentice-Hall, 1970.)

CLEAVELAND, FREDERIC, ET AL. *Congress and Urban Problems.* (Washington, D.C.: The Brookings Institution, 1969.)

GOLDWIN, ROBERT A., ed. *A Nation of Cities.* (Chicago: Rand McNally, 1968.)

GRAVES, W. BROOKE. *American Intergovernmental Relations.* (New York: Charles Scribner's Sons, 1964.)

———. *Intergovernmental Relations in the United States: A Selected Bibliography.* (Washington, D.C.: House Committee on Government Operations, 1956.)

GREENE, LEE S., ET AL. *The States and the Metropolis.* (University: University of Alabama Press, 1968.)

GULICK, LUTHER. *The Metropolitan Problem and American Ideas.* (New York: Alfred A. Knopf, 1962.)

HAUPTMANN, JERZY, ed. *The County and Intergovernmental Relations.* (Parkville, Missouri: Governmental Research Bureau, Park College, 1968.)

MARTIN, ROSCOE. *The Cities and the Federal System.* (New York: Atherton Press, 1965.)

MAXWELL, JAMES A. *Financing State and Local Governments.* (Washington, D.C.: The Brookings Institution, rev. ed., 1969.)

OFFICE OF ECONOMIC OPPORTUNITY. *Catalog of Federal Domestic Assistance.* (Washington, D.C.: U.S. Government Printing Office, 1969.)

SANFORD, TERRY. *Storm Over the States.* (New York: McGraw-Hill, 1967.)

YLVISAKER, PAUL W. "The Growing Role of State Government in Local Affairs," *State Government* (Summer, 1968).

The Vice President's Handbook for Local Officials—A Guide to Federal Assistance for Local Governments. (Washington, D.C.: U.S. Government Printing Office, 1967.)

List of Contributors

Persons who have contributed to this book are listed below with the editor first and the authors following in alphabetical order. A brief review of experience, training, and major points of interest in each person's background is presented. Since most of the contributors have authored books, monographs, reports, and articles, information of this kind has not been included.

JAMES M. BANOVETZ, Editor (Chapter 1, Chapter 2, Chapter 3, Chapter 5), is an Associate Professor of Political Science and Director of the Center for Governmental Studies at Northern Illinois University. He has also served as the director of the Graduate Program in Urban Studies and of the Center for Research in Urban Government at Loyola University, Chicago, and as a staff member of the League of Minnesota Municipalities. A member of the editorial board of the *Public Administration Review*, he also serves on the Illinois Commission on Urban Area Government. He played active roles in establishing the Council of Governments of Cook County and the DuKane Valley Council of Governments and has served as a consultant to federal, state, and local government agencies. He holds a B.A. from the University of Minnesota, Duluth, and the M.A.P.A. and Ph.D. degrees from the University of Minnesota, Minneapolis.

DAVID S. ARNOLD (Chapter 15) is Assistant Director, Publications, the International City Management Association. He has been with ICMA since 1949 with a variety of responsibilities in research, editing, writing, and publications production. From 1943 to 1949 he was on the field staff of Public Administration Service. He has been president of the Chicago Chapter, American Society for Public Administration, and currently is serving on the executive committee for the project on classification of cities jointly sponsored by ICMA and Resources for the Future. He holds a bachelor's degree from Lafayette College and a master's in public administration from the Maxwell Graduate School, Syracuse University.

DAVID R. BEAM (Chapter 5) is a Research Analyst and Program Supervisor with the Center for Governmental Studies at Northern Illinois University. He has also held positions on the faculty of Waubonsee Community College and on the administrative staff of the village of Glenview, Illinois. Currently working on a doctorate in political science at Northern Illinois University, he holds an M.A. from that institution and a B.A. from Lawrence College.

WILLIAM E. BESUDEN (Chapter 17) is Assistant Director of the International City Management Association. He previously served as the manager of Hudson, Michigan, as the assistant manager of Ottumwa, Iowa, and as a personnel officer for the city of Cincinnati, Ohio. His M.G.A. degree is from the Fels Institute of Local and State Government at the University of Pennsylvania and his B.A. is from Ohio Wesleyan University.

DAVID S. BROWN (Chapter 6) is Professor of Management in the Department of Public Administration of the School of Government and Business Administration at George Washington University. He has also served as deputy chief of the University of Southern California Party in Public Administration in Pakistan and as a visiting lecturer at the Management Centre of the Royal College of Science and Technology, Glasgow, Scotland. He has held a variety of positions in the federal government, including assignments with the Department of Agriculture, the Civil Aeronautics Administration, the Economic Cooperation Administration, and the Mutual Security Program. A consultant to both industry and government, he has also worked with the New York State Department of Education and as chairman of the board of directors of Leadership Resources, Inc. A native of Maine, he received his A.B. from the University of Maine and his Ph.D. from Syracuse University.

WILLIAM G. COLMAN (Chapter 17) recently completed 10 years as Executive Director of the Advisory Commission on Intergovernmental Relations and currently serves as a governmental affairs consultant to the National Urban Coalition and other organizations. He has served as an executive assistant to the Director of the National Science Foundation. A career public servant, he has also worked for the Office of Defense Mobilization, the Economic Cooperation Administration, and the Oregon Civil Service Commission. His education includes the B.A. and M.A. degrees from the University of Missouri and advanced graduate study at the University of Chicago.

W. DONALD HEISEL (Chapter 13) is Director of the Institute of Governmental Research, University of Cincinnati. Previously, he was personnel director for the city of Cincinnati for 13 years. He graduated from DePauw University and holds a master's degree in public administration from the University of Cincinnati, where he has been teaching in recent years in the public administration program.

KENNETH K. HENNING (Chapter 7) is Urban Affairs and Organization Science Associate, Institute of Government and the Georgia Center for Continuing Education, University of Georgia. From 1962 through 1969 he was Associate Director, Deputy Director, and Acting Director of the Center for Advanced Study in Organization Science, University of Wisconsin. Earlier in his professional career, he served as Associate Director, Center for Programs in Government Administration, University of Chicago, and as Chairman of the Department of Management, DePauw University. He serves as a consultant with numerous federal, state, and local government agencies as well as with professional associations and business corporations. He holds the bachelor's degree from DePaul University, Chicago, and the M.G.A. degree from the University of Chicago.

ROBERT E. HOLLANDER (Chapter 5), another veteran city manager is a staff member of the Center for Governmental Studies at Northern Illinois University. Prior to joining the University's staff, he served as the manager of Palatine, Illinois, and Savanna, Illinois. He has also held the positions of public works director and water superintendent in municipal government. He has served on the Ethics Committee of the Illinois City Managers' Association and as secretary-treasurer of the Northwest Municipal Conference in Illinois. Currently a candidate for an M.A. degree in political science and public administration, he holds a B.A. degree from Shimer College. (Editor's Note: Mr. Hollander was appointed City Manager of Punta Gorda, Florida, after this book went to press.)

JAMES E. JERNBERG (Chapter 14) is an Associate Professor of Political Science and Director of Graduate Studies in the School of Public Affairs at the University of Minnesota. He received his B.A. and M.A.P.A. from the University of Minnesota and Ph.D. from the University of Wisconsin. He has also taught at the University of Wisconsin and at the University of North Carolina. Earlier he served for over two years as a budgetary and planning official for the city of Madison, Wisconsin. In addition, he has served as a consultant to local governments in Wisconsin and Minnesota.

DAVID J. KENNEDY (Chapter 16) is an Assistant Senate Counsel to the Minnesota State Senate. Earlier he served as director of the Office of Local and Urban Affairs of the state of Minnesota and as the staff attorney of the League of Minnesota Municipalities. A member of several Minnesota state-wide governmental advisory groups and a lecturer in municipal law and administration, he received his A.B. from the University of Notre Dame and his LL.B. from the University of Minnesota.

JOHN K. PARKER (Chapter 9, Chapter 10, Chapter 11) is Vice President of Parklow Associates, Inc., Rockville, Maryland, management consultants to government, business, and institutions. He has been a faculty member of the Fels Institute of Local and State Government of the University of Pennsylvania, and established and managed the Systems Division of the Institute's Government Studies Center. He has consulted extensively with governments at all levels, and served as an assistant city manager in Alexandria, Virginia. He has lectured and published widely in the fields of public management, computer systems, advanced information systems, PPBS, and related subjects. He holds a B.A. from George Washington University and an M.A. from the Wharton School of Finance and Commerce of the University of Pennsylvania.

STANLEY P. POWERS (Chapter 8) is the Director of the Government Projects Division of the Industrial Relations Center, University of Chicago. He previously was on the staff of the International City Management Association and served as the editor of *Public Management* and the *Municipal Year Book*. He has also been a newspaper editor and publisher in Barberton and McComb, Ohio, and news editor of the Rutherford Publishing Company in Rutherfordton, North Carolina. He received a B.A. in journalism and public relations from Kent State University, an M.A. in journalism and communications from the University of Florida, and an M.P.A. degree from Roosevelt University.

DAVID M. WELBORN (Chapter 4) is Associate Professor of Political Science and Director of the Institute of Public Affairs at the University of Kansas. Immediately before joining the Kansas faculty, he spent a year as Intergovernmental Relations Advisor in the Federal Water Pollution Control Administration under the auspices of the American Society for Public Administration's Public Policy Fellowship program. Prior to that time, he taught at Indiana University, Texas Technological College, and Northern Illinois University. He also participated in the American Political Science Association's Congressional Fellowship Program. He received both the B.A. and Ph.D. degrees from the University of Texas.

CLYDE J. WINGFIELD (Chapter 12) is McElvaney Professor of Political Science at Southern Methodist University. He has also served on the faculties of Texas Technological College, Pennsylvania State University, Northern Illinois University, and was Executive Vice-President of the University of Texas at El Paso. He has served as a consultant to government agencies at the local, state, and national levels as well as to universities. The first person to hold the Eugene McElvaney Chair at SMU, he is currently directing graduate study in public administration and urban studies.

CHARLES A. ZUZAK (Chapter 5) is an Assistant Professor of Political Science associated with the Bureau of Public Administration at the University of Tennessee. Currently he is working in the Office of the Mayor, Metropolitan Government of Nashville–Davidson County, where he is assisting in the implementation of a planning–programming–budgeting system. Formerly a member of the faculty of Loyola University, Chicago, he received his M.A. degree from the University of Notre Dame and his Ph.D. from the University of Maryland.

Index

MUNICIPAL MANAGEMENT SERIES
Managing the Modern City

TEXT TYPE:
Linotype Baskerville

COMPOSITION, PRINTING, AND BINDING:
Kingsport Press, Inc., Kingsport, Tennessee

PAPER:
Glatfelter Offset

PRODUCTION:
David S. Arnold and Betty L. Lawton